Handbook of
Emotional &
Behavioural
Difficulties

About the Book

The behaviour of children in primary/elementary and secondary/high schools has been a consistent source of interest and controversy since the 19th century. Some commentators suggest that the phenomenon has a far more impressive historical pedigree.

As education systems in First World democracies struggle to meet changing social, economic and educational conditions, one group of children has increasingly become the focus of attention. These children are either unable or unwilling to conform to the requirements of formal schooling. As a result they are identified as having Emotional and/or Behavioural Difficulties (EBDs) of one level of severity or another. Contemporary debate increasingly links causation with intervention to form a holistic approach to problem prevention or remediation.

This handbook provides a systematic and comprehensive overview of a series of often related themes which underpin theoretical and philosophical approaches to pupils perceived as having EBDs and their realization in both policy and provision.

The structure of book divides these themes into three core sections. These allow the reader to consider children or young people with EBDs from a number of perspectives and levels. They are viewed in relation to society in general, then in terms of individual education systems and the policies and provision they adopt, as well as in terms of the meaning of these problematic behaviours to the individual 'actors' on whom they impact most profoundly. Each theme or topic is organized to highlight:

- the key principles or characteristics,
- examples of their impact on current practices, and
- issues arising for debate.

Assembled here are contributions from significant authors in the field of EBD. Although contributions are principally from the UK and the US, particular emphasis is given to the international and comparative focus of these writers who have been identified because of their capacity to develop broader transcultural insights.

The development of a comparative approach to special and inclusive education has now been well charted. It therefore remains puzzling that the field of EBD, probably one of the most significant areas of special education in terms of pupil numbers, has largely escaped such international comparison.

This book has been written to enable individual chapters to be useful resources for students, academics and practitioners.

This book is to be returned on or before the
last date stamped below. Overdue charges
will be incurred by the late return of books.

UNiVERSiTY COLLEGE
CHESTER

Handbook of
Emotional &
Behavioural
Difficulties

Edited by
Peter Clough, Philip Garner,
John T. Pardeck & Francis K. O. Yuen

SAGE Publications
London • Thousand Oaks • New Delhi

First published 2005

SAGE Publications Ltd
1 Oliver's Yard
55 City Road
London EC1Y 1SP

SAGE Publications Inc.
2455 Teller Road
Thousand Oaks, California 91320

SAGE Publications India Pvt Ltd
B-42, Panchsheel Enclave
Post Box 4109
New Delhi 110 017

British Library Cataloguing in Publication data

A catalogue record for this book is available
from the British Library

ISBN 0 7619 4066 9

Library of Congress Control Number: 2004090349

Typeset by C&M Digitals (P) Ltd., Chennai, India
Printed in Great Britain by The Cromwell Press Ltd, Trowbridge, Wiltshire

Contents

Contributors

Bob Algozzine (PhD, Penn State University) is a professor in the Department of Educational Leadership and Co-Director of the Behavior and Reading Improvement Center at the University of North Carolina at Charlotte, USA. His current research interests include behavior instruction in the total school, positive unified behavior support, and effective teaching.

Kate Algozzine (MS, University of Florida) is a Behavior Research Coordinator for the Behavior and Reading Improvement Center at the University of North Carolina at Charlotte, USA. Her current research interests include school-wide behavior instruction, improving social skills, and teaching children at risk of continuing failure in school.

Christopher Blake, PhD, is Vice President for Academic Affairs and formerly is Professor of Education and Chair of the Education Department at Mount Saint Mary's University, Emmitsburg, Maryland, USA. His research interests are in the ethnography of teachers' experiences of the reform agenda, and the marginalization of professional discourse in American education.

Tony Bowers, PhD, is Senior Lecturer in Psychology and Special Educational Needs, University of Cambridge, England. He has extensive experience of teaching young people who are hard to educate and has published widely in this area.

Marcelo Castro, PhD, is a research associate at the University of Miami, and focuses on assessment of children and adolescents. His research interests include academic, personal-social, and behavioral outcomes for students at risk for emotional and behavioral disorders.

Tony Charlton, a psychologist, is Professor of Behaviour Studies at the University of Gloucestershire, England. His foremost research interests are located within the broad area of youngsters' emotional and behavioural difficulties. Allied interests include television effects upon young viewers, and mobile phone usage and abusage by pre-adolescents.

Peter Clough is Professor of Education at the Queen's University of Belfast, Northern Ireland. As well as previously teaching and researching at the University of Sheffield, England, he has worked in mainstream and Special schools, including those for students with EBD.

Ted Cole works at the University of Birmingham, England. He has undertaken government-funded research on children experiencing EBD, and has a range of published outputs in this field, including *Effective Schooling for Pupils with Emotional and Behavioural Difficulties* (1998).

Paul Cooper is Director of the Centre for Innovation in Raising Educational Achievement, School of Education, University of Leicester, England. His interests include social, emotional and behavioural difficulties in education, AD/HD, preventing school exclusion and effective teaching and learning in schools. He was co-winner of the *Times Educational Supplement*/NASEN Academic Book Award, 2001.

Shirley Culver is Program Manager at the Mental Health Resource Center, San Diego. She has published numerous articles and conference papers on mental health service delivery for adolescents.

John Dwyfor Davies is a professor in the Faculty of Education at the University of the West of England, Bristol. He has published extensively on matters relating to inclusion, exclusion and problem behaviour and has undertaken research in these areas for the UK government.

Emily S. Fisher, MA, is an advanced graduate student in the Counseling/Clinical/School Psychology Program at the University of California, Santa Barbara, USA. Her research focuses on the change process, especially related to teachers and schools, and the role of the psychologist in facilitating individual and system-wide changes.

Steven R. Forness is Professor and Chief of Educational Psychology at the UCLA Mental Retardation Research Center, Los Angeles, USA. His many publications include a foreword to *Education Deform: Bright People Sometimes Say Stupid Things About Education* (2002) by James M. Kauffman.

Michael J. Furlong is Professor and Program Leader of the Counseling/Clinical/ School Psychology Program at the University of California, Santa Barbara, USA. He also directs the Center for School-Based Youth Development and is an associate editor of *Psychology in the*

Schools and *The California School Psychologist.* He has edited two forthcoming books, *Appraisal and Prediction of School Violence: Methods, Issues, and Contexts* and *Issues in School Violence Research.*

Philip Garner works at the Nottingham Trent University, England, where he is Professor of Special Education. He has worked in teacher education and written extensively on aspects of SEN. He has worked in mainstream and special schools (for children experiencing EBD) for 17 years. He is currently Director of the Teacher Training Agency's Professional Resource Network for Behaviour (www.behaviour4learning.ac.uk).

Barry Groom is Senior Lecturer at University College Northampton, England. He has a specialist interest in children/young people experiencing EBD, and has undertaken comparative research activity in this area.

Dennis Guiney is Specialist Senior Educational Psychologist (Behaviour Management) at the Service for Adolescents and Families in Enfield, Middlesex, England.

Paul Hamill is Head of the Department of Educational Support and Guidance at the University of Strathclyde, Scotland. His major interests include pupil exclusion and the education of children with EBD and other learning difficulties.

Richard Hough is affiliated to the University of New Mexico, Child and Adolescent Services Research Center, University of California, San Diego, and San Diego State University, USA and is Principal Investigator of the Patterns of Care research project on which his contribution to this book is based. His key research interests are racial/ethnic disparities in mental health services delivery to youth and health services research in general.

Michael Hurlburt is a research scientist and IRB Chair at Children's Hospital, San Diego, USA. His interests are in children's behavioral problems – including measurement of care processes, predictors of treatment outcome, and methods for improving services – and in mental health services for abused and neglected children.

James M. Kauffman has been a teacher of emotionally disturbed children and has published widely about special education issues. He is Professor Emeritus of Education at the University of Virginia, USA, where he has been a faculty member since 1970.

Kenneth A. Kavale, PhD, is a professor in the School of Education at Regent University, Virginia Beach, USA. He has an extensive record of teaching, research and publication in the field of special education and EBD.

Katina Lambros is a research scientist at the Child and Adolescent Services Research Center in San Diego, USA. Her research interests include barriers to the translation of evidence-based interventions into schools for youth with disruptive behavior and the impact of school organizational climate/culture on intervention adoption.

John A. Landsverk, PhD, is Director of the NIMH funded Child and Adolescent Services Research Center (CASRC) and Professor in the School of Social Work, San Diego State University. He has a doctorate in sociology and has extensive research experience in the areas of child maltreatment, mental health and mental health service utilization, as well as in the implementation and evaluation of innovative early interventions for families at risk for child abuse and neglect. He has also served on and chaired the NIMH Services Initial Review Group.

Ann Lewis is Professor of Special Education and Educational Psychology at the University of Birmingham, England where she is Head of Division for Inclusion, Special Education and Educational Psychology. Her publications include *Special Teaching for Special Children? A Pedagogy for Inclusion* (with Brahm Norwich, Open University Press), *Children's Understanding of Disability* (Routledge, 1995, 1999) and *Primary Special Needs and the National Curriculum* (Routledge, 1991, 1995). Her current research focuses on methodological issues in interviewing children and young people with learning difficulties.

Timothy J. Lewis is Chair and Associate Professor in Special Education at the University of Missouri-Columbia. His specialty areas include students with Emotional/Behavioral Disorders and students at-risk. His current work focuses on social skill instruction, functional assessment, and proactive school-wide discipline systems.

Kristen McCabe, PhD, has research interests in improving access to and effectiveness of mental health treatments for ethnic minority youth. She is Research Scientist, Child and Adolescent Services Research Center; Assistant Professor, University of San Diego; Adjunct Assistant Professor, University of California, San Diego, USA.

Helen McGrath, PhD, lectures in the Faculty of Education at Deakin University, Australia and has a private practice as a counselling psychologist.

She is also a consultant to schools and runs professional development sessions. She is the author of many books, including *Difficult Personalities, Friends, BOUNCE BACK!* and *Friendly Kids Friendly Classrooms*.

Marjorie Montague, PhD, is a professor at the University of Miami, specializes in learning disabilities, emotional/behavior disorders, and attention deficit hyperactivity disorder and has over 50 publications in these related areas. Her primary research area is mathematical learning disabilities.

Gale M. Morrison is Professor of Education and Counseling/Clinical/ School Psychology at the University of California, Santa Barbara. Her research specialties include the areas of school discipline practices, developmental trajectories of students who are disciplined at school, and schools as a context for antisocial student behavior.

Mark P. Mostert, PhD, is a professor at Regent University, Virginia Beach, USA. He has authored books on managing classroom behaviour and on inter-professional collaborations in schools. His research interests include intervention effectiveness and the use of a history of special education.

Lori Newcomer, PhD, is Research Assistant Professor of Special Education at the University of Missouri, USA, where she works to establish and train school teams in systemic function based support and conducts research that focuses on ways to bring about positive, durable and scientifically validated change.

Tom Nicholson is a professor in the School of Education at the University of Auckland, New Zealand. He has researched and published in a number of areas, including developmental psychology; learning issues; language and literacy; children's real and imaginary friends

Tim O'Brien, PhD, lectures in Psychology and Human Development at the Institute of Education, University of London, England. He has authored books and articles on special education, children's behaviour and inclusion.

Paul O'Mahony, PhD, is Head of the School of Occupational Therapy and Senior Lecturer in Psychology at Trinity College Dublin, Ireland. He was formerly a forensic and research psychologist with the Irish Department of Justice. He is the author of *Crime and Punishment in Ireland* (1993), *Criminal Chaos* (1996), *Mountjoy Prisoners: A sociological and criminological profile* (1997), *Prison Policy in Ireland* (2000); and editor of *Criminal Justice in Ireland* (2002).

Charlie Panting is a researcher in the Centre for Behaviour Studies at the University of Gloucestershire, England. She has worked on various projects whilst working in the Centre, including youngsters' mobile phone usage, television effects, globalization and bullying in schools. She is also a lecturer for the Open University and is studying for her PhD at Warwick University.

John T. Pardeck, PhD, LCSW, is Professor of Social Work at Southwest Missouri State University, USA. He has numerous publications in the area of disability. He is the Editor of the *Journal of Social Work in Disability and Rehabilitation*.

Bill Rogers, PhD, FACE, is an independent education consultant and an associate professor at Griffith University, Australia. He has an international reputation in teacher training and professional development in the management of children whose behaviour is problematic.

Richard Rose is Professor in the Centre for Special Needs Education and Research (CeSNER) at University College, Northampton, England. He has a national reputation in the field of SEN and inclusion and is the author of several books on these and related topics.

Egide Royer is Professor of Special Education at the Faculty of Education at University Laval, Quebec, Canada. He is currently doing research and teaching on the topic of behavioural problems in schools. He is specifically working on teachers' pre- and in-service training regarding intervention in the classroom to prevent behavioural problems and support school success of these students.

Carl R. Smith, PhD, is an associate professor in the Department of Curriculum and Instruction at Iowa State University, USA. He is also Co-Director of the Iowa Behavioral Alliance. His primary research and writing interests focus on assessment, programming, and policy issues impacting persons with significant social, emotional and behavioural needs.

Gary Thomas is a professor of education at the University of Leeds, England. His recent books include *Deconstructing Special Education and Constructing Inclusion* (OUP, with A. Loxley) and *Evidence-based Practice in Education* (OUP, with Richard Pring).

John Visser is a senior lecturer at the University of Birmingham, England. He has worked closely with Professor Harry Daniels and

Dr Ted Cole in the SEBD research team. He has been active in national and international NGOs and is also widely known for his work with teachers and education authorities.

Margret Winzer is a professor at the University of Lethbridge in Alberta, Canada where she teaches in the areas of special education and early childhood education. Her writing and research covers many facets of special education and includes texts on introduction to special education, the history of special education, early childhood special education, multicultural special education, and comparative studies in special education.

May Yeh is an assistant professor in the SDSU/UCSD Joint Doctoral Program in Clinical Psychology, San Diego State University. She is an Investigator with the Child and Adolescent Services Research Center and Assistant Adjunct Professor of Psychiatry at the University of California, San Diego.

Francis K.O. Yuen, DSW, ACSW, is a professor for the Division of Social Work at California State University, Sacramento His practice and research interests are in the areas of family health social work practice, children and families, disability, human diversity, refugees and immigrants, grant writing, and program evaluation.

Acknowledgements

We would like to thank individual contributors for their diligence and honesty in providing a set of chapters that, in their collective variety, provide an indication of the breadth and complexity of emotional and behavioural disorders (EBD) within education. Grateful thanks are also due to a number of publishers who allowed authors to use extracts or amendments of work published elsewhere. Chapter 24, page 385, reprinted by permission of PFD on behalf of Adrian Mitchell. The team at Sage Publications has been supportive and patient, and as editors we have found the help they have offered to be vital in our not losing our original belief that this *Handbook* should draw from as wide a community of educators as possible.

Finally, we would like to extend our gratitude to the many thousands of children and young people who have been the subject of all of our accumulated knowledge in EBD. It goes without saying that most such individuals will be unlikely to access this book; nevertheless, theirs is a huge, if unwitting, contribution to extending both our own knowledge and the effectiveness of service provision in education systems worldwide.

Part One

CONTEXT AND TERMINOLOGIES

Themes and Dimensions of EBD:
A Conceptual Overview

PETER CLOUGH, PHILIP GARNER,
JOHN T. PARDECK AND FRANCIS YUEN

Throughout most of the professional lives of those contributing to this book it is doubtful whether there has been any time during which the issue of 'emotional and behavioural difficulties' (EBD) did not assume signal importance within their national education systems. It is equally doubtful whether few educational professionals, irrespective of ideological persuasion, location, training and current status, remain untroubled by the very term EBD, and the policies and practices that follow from such 'categorization'. In some ways the term itself is a metaphor which aptly summarizes all of those doubts, prejudices, frustrations, inconsistencies and paradoxes that prevail within the wider field of provision known as special education, or in its broader application as 'special educational needs' (SEN) – a term itself which is under great scrutiny at present, representing as it does a potentially fixed and deficit view of human endeavour. Cronis and Ellis (2000) have amplified the special education parallel by reference to those five key issues facing professional educators in the coming decades: inclusion, the research/practice interface, a supply of appropriately trained personnel, individual rights and litigation and scientific advances. In each of these generic areas EBD is substantially highlighted as the student grouping or categorization likely to cause most soul-searching and debate. The reader of this volume will find that these themes, along with other more specific matters addressed by individual contributors, appear with regularity in the chapters we have selected.

In introducing a volume which attempts to offer a set of differential cultural, social and professional viewpoints of what has always been a controversial and in many ways indeterminate grouping (CECB, 1987; Bower, 1982; McCall and Farrell, 1993), we are all too aware of some substantial pitfalls. Not least of these is that we might appear to be advocating a scarcely modified version of a position which validates, without condition or interrogation, the casual allocation of the term 'EBD' to student-behaviours which challenge (DfE, 1994). A potent interpretation of this ideology is that it is used to deflect discussion from seemingly intractable structural issues – resources, traditions, the exercise of professional power – not to mention the underpinning features within society and its institutions (including schools) which contribute (or not) to individual and system resiliency (Nettles et al., 2000). Again, this has been a feature of the EBD (and special education) debate across widely differing cultures and educational systems (see, for example, DES, 1989; Pink, 1982).

Our rationale in developing this book has to be precisely argued – especially so given the audiences, educational contexts and cultures within which it will be read. Moreover, there has always been, within the literature, a significant emphasis on EBD or related matters (Gullotta et al., 1998; Kauffman, 1993; Quay, 1994; Scotti et al., 1999) dealing in depth with the contexts, interventions and outcomes for school students ascertained as such. Often such volumes offer a highly polarized consideration of the field, in terms of its key strands. What we attempt to do, in this *Handbook*, is to provide a collection of chapters which delineate the differential performances that might comprise the term 'EBD', the breadth of professional activity that these prompt and sustain, and the tension, discrepancies and possibilities that emanate from them. In all these we scrutinize EBD primarily in its educational contexts, whilst recognizing that such considerations, in the manner of Bronfenbrenner (1979), have to be dealt with by reference to those systems, protocols and practices which constitute a broader macrosystem.

In assembling these chapters our thinking has been informed by a preoccupation with educational justice and empowerment. Thus, we believe that, of all school-age populations, that defined as 'EBD' – however artificially the term is constructed – has been the most marginalized in terms of street-level empowerment. These are school students who are serially 'done-to' by professionals or critiqued at some distance by career-researchers and theoreticians. What we have sought to do, then, is to encourage individual contributors to bring together theory and practice in their chapters. The reflexivity of these is, we believe, crucial in defining a position beyond that of dispassionate bystander. Each of us has, at some time, been directly involved with the young people who constitute this book's focus. Each of us retains at least some level of affiliation with these students, their teachers, parents/carers and other involved professionals. So what the reader will denote is something of an attempt to balance, both within and between, chapters with a view to defining a principled stance in which practice and theory are immutable. The underpinning commitment is to the empowerment of these school students, either directly or via the professionals and others who work with them.

A further principle which needs to be recognized in this preamble is that the nature of EBD as a field is such that, whether in practical or theoretical terms, it is in essence inter- and intra-disciplinary. For editors of a volume such as this an acknowledgement of this is essential – but it is both an opportunity and a threat. Inter-professional interventions have been viewed by many as a defining characteristic of EBD provision. In part this is because the term itself is interpreted differentially according to one's orientations and beliefs. But irrespective of an individual's allegiance to a perceived causal factor and to a resulting (most) effective intervention, there remains amongst many practitioners and theoreticians a general sense that these exist as possible 'answers' to complex questions. That biological, social and psychological factors combine at every juncture in the aetiology of EBD and lends an interrogatory stance to the mind-set of many of the professionals involved in the field. Whilst highly specific positions – based on a range of evidences – are taken they are seldom exclusive, more frequently interdisciplinary. Our contributors have emerged from a variety of professional backgrounds, and the chapters in this *Handbook* seek to confirm the nature and efficacy of this working tradition – whilst retaining an essential focus on education.

A further preliminary is that, in recognizing the inherent complexity of the term 'EBD', and its preoccupation with a quest for integrated professional strategies, we must equally acknowledge that the spatial distribution of 'cases' of EBD is by no means uniform. In global terms, therefore, it is difficult to escape from the reality that EBD in its general sense has been the creation of essentially post-industrialized nation states. Though the impacts of political violence or re-structuring, of poverty and physical duress, and of cultural globalization can be variously implicated in the rising numbers of school students who are viewed as demonstrating 'challenging' or 'at-risk' behaviour in emerging nations in the developing world, this book largely focuses upon what have been referred to as 'mature' education systems (Daniels and Garner, 1999). It goes without saying that substantial attention to EBD (and its associated descriptors) has been emerging on an international level exemplified by an ever-increasing international literature; the cases of Cyprus (Angelides, 2000), Japan (Letendre and Shimizu, 1999), Finland (Jahnukainen, 2001), South Korea (Park, 1994) Greece (Gavrilidou et al., 1993) and Russia (Kolominskii and Zhiznevskii, 1992) are indicative of the global extent of this. It is not, however, the purpose of this *Handbook* fully to articulate a comparative stance, such is the extent of the discontinuities and paradoxes inherent in this complex field. A task of this nature would become even more problematic in the light of ample evidence that even amongst those countries which fit the crude descriptor of 'post-industrial', there are notable differences and discrepancies at almost every juncture of policy and provision in EBD. What we are seeking to achieve, rather, is some exemplification of broad principles in which readers may, in turn, find resonances within their own educational traditions. As Ainscow (1998) has remarked, '… progress in the field will be more likely if the task is reformulated in order to pay attention to the uniqueness of contexts and encounters.'

Finally, by way of a positioning statement for this volume, we should emphasize that the focus of these chapters is principally upon education-related matters arising from recognition and intervention in EBD. The focus, then, is mainly directed towards schools within compulsory educational provision in a range of national settings. This is not to deny the importance of its (many) other parameters and manifestations, more to make this work even approaching a project that is 'do-able' within the restraints of a handbook of this size.

An amplification of the broad context against which EBD might be considered is further revealing of our own standpoint as co-editors of this international collection of papers. Whilst any mapping of such a diverse and complex territory will be, at best, partial, we offer, in the succeeding section of this opening chapter, four broad headings around which such a context might be considered. And even though even these are suggestive of tensions and omissions, they allow the reader to glimpse some of the conceptual and organizational difficulties, and a subtext of tension, in compiling a set of chapters on such a broad, disparate yet ultimately fascinating aspect of education. What will be readily apparent from these initial observations, and from their further examination in the constituent chapters of this volume, is that interpretations of EBD, its causes, impacts and interventions, are dramatically susceptible to professional stakehold-ings, personal beliefs and societal expediency. Each of these variously come to influence the outcomes for all those involved. Again, in the constituent chapters in this *Handbook*, readers are invited to draw personal, institutional and country-specific inferences from the issues they incorporate.

As far as this introductory chapter is concerned then, we have chosen briefly to highlight just four of the issues which confront policy-makers and practitioners whose substantial preoccupation is with children and young people experiencing EBD. As with the substantive content of the *Handbook*, we use these themes as indicators of the contentious nature of much of this territory, and feel secure that readers will identify with them in terms of their own context and professional operations.

I TERMINOLOGY

It is the way of the world that its dominant political and socio-economic system(s) will exert an overriding influence on the policy and structure of educational provision irrespective of national orientation. At the outset, then, recognition needs to be given to the manner in which EBD is used as a quasi-official term in many countries. It is frequently adopted as an informal descriptor of student behaviour, and its level of use in this respect is often unquestioned by practitioners and policy-makers alike. And yet the term has no statutory basis in several countries – England provides a good example of this terminological paradox, as Thomas, elsewhere in this book, points out. In the United States, the last 10 years marked a continuation of a debate on the term and a struggle to arrive at a common understanding (Kavale et al., 1996).

It is notoriously difficult to arrive at a consensus of what particular behaviours delineate EBD (and the children and youth who wear the label), and how these appear often to be interchangeable with other (apparently) synonymous descriptors. Thus, it is commonplace to hear reference made to school students who are 'disruptive', 'at risk', 'disaffected', 'excluded', 'alienated', 'challenging', 'exceptional', 'troublesome' and so forth. Such are the vagaries of 'descriptive categories of need' in many countries that these terms are routinely used in the context of a single child or young person. That they infer a quasi-scientific legitimacy seems to reinforce, rather than discourage, their usage. Moreover, to be seen to be taking action on matters of educational attainment, under-performance and anti-social behaviour has come to be regarded as a prerequisite function of twenty-first century governments such appears to be the relationship between these and the wellbeing of the nation state. Commitment to those who are 'different' on account of their social or educational performances is brokered by establishing their 'needs' as part of, but apart from, mainstream society. Recognition that such needs are mainly met via resources (financial, human, environmental, emotional and so on) requires that each grouping of the needy is defined for operational purposes. As several of our own contributors suggest, this process is complex, highly contentious and liable to differential interpretation over time, in location and cultural context. One product of all of this is that the 'professional vocabulary' of EBD, notwithstanding its friability in the face of interrogation, becomes seen as a statutory part of the process, further defining these individuals as different.

2 HISTORY AND INCIDENCE

In the seventh edition of a popular reader on the US education system and its interrelationships with social processes, Levine and Havighurst noted that 'One of the most serious problems confronting many schools in concentrated poverty neighborhoods is the tendency for violence in the community to affect teaching and learning conditions in the schools. Violent and other anti-social behavior of one sort or another is more prevalent there than in most other neighborhoods' (1989: 281). They refer to this as a 'growing problem', although it is worth also noting that the theme has been a consistent one, making its appearance in each of the earlier editions of that volume, stretching back to 1957.

The extent of the growth in EBD categorization is worrying, but it should not be viewed as either remarkable or a new phenomenon. In England the 1916 conference of the National Special Schools Union was notable for a survey of juvenile crime given by Spurley Hey, then the Director of Education for Manchester. He professed to '... undeniable evidence of an increase in juvenile offences' (Hey, 1917). Ninety-two per cent of all cases were committed by boys, regarded by Hey as '... dull children, varying in mental capacity from slight subnormality to actual mental deficiency' (1917: 20). Moreover, Hey was able to show their concentration in disadvantaged parts of the city. Further, there was widespread recognition at the time of the overlap and interdependent relationship between these behaviours and problems presented by children in schools in these locations.

More contemporaneous data are revealing of the deeply embedded nature of 'emotional and behavioural difficulties' within and beyond systems of schooling. Thus, in 2001, the US Department of Education reported that approximately 470,000 young people were in receipt of special education or other services under the category of 'emotional disturbance' (US Department of Education, 2001). These numbers are showing year-on-year increases, with the 2001 figure representing an increase of 2 per cent from the previous year, and 20 per cent on the figure obtaining in 1991.

It is difficult to even estimate either the level or rates of increase in EBD. This in part is a product of the dilemma in defining precisely what behaviours constitute the label. Moreover, most statistics on incidence fail to account for a proportion of school populations which, whilst not being ascertained as experiencing EBD, nevertheless may present several or many of the performance indicators used to proscribe the term. These, then, are issues that offer a rich source for critique and commentary and are matters which contributors to this volume will refer to with some regularity.

3 LOCATION AND PROVISION

Behaviour is a matter of experience. 'Bad' or 'challenging' behaviours are defined by the parameters of the environments and conditions in which they take place. So, what boundaries, parameters and baselines of behaviour are set? How are such boundaries drawn? This volume, as we have stated, explores the nature of EBD from an educational context. This is not to say that the behaviours associated with the quasi-official educational term 'EBD' are not manifest in other social settings. Indeed, there are compelling overlaps and relationships at virtually every turn.

It is a straightforward task to present vignettes to illustrate these. In one break-time at a junior school in the centre of a dishevelled housing estate towards the east end of a northern English city, the head teacher is about to 'deal' with six children (aged between 8 and 10). They wait – accompanied – outside her room. Their playground behaviour was deemed 'inappropriate' for the third time that week. There has been swearing (now routinely part of the language heard in the school), a fight, theft of break-time snack money from the pocket of another pupil, spitting at a teacher on duty, and a teacher who reprimanded a pupil for hitting another was told by that 9-year-old to 'chill and naff-the-shit-off'. This is routine. In fact, the head teacher is relieved that nothing unexpected has occurred and that the break-time for these children has passed without major event.

Two miles away, two pupils (both 9 years old) wait – unaccompanied – in shame and silent fear outside the staffroom. During break-time there was an argument over a test question. One pupil called the other a 'cheating bastard'. Such language is never heard in the school. The teacher on duty is genuinely shocked and the boys find themselves outside the office – being there is almost penalty enough.

The point here is that 'challenging' behaviour or 'bad' behaviour is a matter of definition, and such definitions are drawn by virtue of the environments in which those behaviours take place. As Angelides suggests:

> ... the role which schools and teachers play in the development of behaviour problems is major and substantial. This perspective gives rise to the interest in

schools as units, and teachers and pupils are members of those units, and not as individuals with separate unique characteristics. They are, of course, unique individuals but, at the same time, they operate as integral parts of the same institution, under the same culture, so their behaviour must be studied in relation to the specific organisational context. (2000: 57)

For the first school, 'behaviour' is a constant issue – always there, always a matter of degree and always a matter of individuals. The second school, however, has 'enjoyed' a positive discipline policy for seven years or so. Break-times which result in pupils waiting in penance for reprimand outside the head teachers' office are rare (and hence such experiences are 'shameful' when they occur). This school has 'turned around' its behavioural expectations of its pupils, sees behaviour and discipline as an issue of shared culture.

The code in this school includes words like respect, responsibility, courtesy. And the pupils have, in their various lessons, PSHE – Personal, Social and Health Education, for instance, learned not only to recite the rhetoric of 'respect' or 'responsibility' or 'courtesy' or 'restraint' or 'self-control', but they have also begun to understand those words (in childlike versions of such definitions) and to live out those values as they understand them. These pupils can talk (in their 8-, 9-, 10-year-old ways) about what they mean by 'respect' for each other (not copying); for the school (not smashing the windows in the evening); for staff (not being abusive, getting on with the work they give you). They can talk about being responsible for their classroom (not spitting gum on the floor, putting equipment away); for their school (picking up rubbish); for their own work (doing homework when it is set and giving it in on time). 'Restraint' is a big one – how do we teach 'restraint'? The point here? Bad behaviours are defined in the contexts of other bad behaviours.

Whatever the merits of respective arguments regarding causation in cases of EBD, there is little doubt that schools in different spatial settings, with distinctly individual organizational features, do differ dramatically in the levels of 'problematic', EBD-type behaviour they experience. This is pivotal to the contested nature of the 'category', and is also germane to the debate surrounding the very use of such a contentious term. In fact, the accomplishments of Hargreaves et al. (1975) and Bronfenbrenner (1979) still seem to be essential to our attempt to come to some measure of understanding of what 'is' emotional and/or behavioural difficulty. Hargreaves et al. highlighted the perennially useful notion of 'behaviour in context', in which he argues that social actions are viewed as variously problematic or non-problematic according to person, place and timing. Those involved in professional work in this area will attest to the importance of these factors, whilst being equally convinced that they reveal a fundamental weakness in utilizing EBD within a categorical approach to policy and provision.

Meanwhile, in locating discussion of 'behaviour' within an environmental setting, defined as an ecosystem, Bronfenbrenner (1979) allowed us to glimpse the complex map of factors that impact on individuals within their immediate and extended environments. Both writers highlight the pervading dilemma in EBD: it inhabits the territory of loose terminology whilst offering tantalizing glimpses of the risk and resilience ecology for EBD – why is it that some children and youth succumb to EBD-type behaviours and not others?

This is a commonplace *motif* for EBD, and runs across national and cultural boundaries. In England, for example, comparison of schools in similar social and economic catchments, with similar profile in student roll and performance, suggests a degree of variability in the success of schools in managing children who present challenges on account of their behaviours. Such discrepancies, it is suggested, are useful in highlighting the complex nature of EBD and can be seen as being played out across a diverse educational and cultural canvas.

4 POLITICIZATION AND PROFESSIONALIZATION

It is certainly the case that children and young people who are ascertained as experiencing 'emotional and/or behavioural difficulties' carry with them a burden that others identified as 'learning disabled' do not. We do not allocate 'blame' to those who have Down's syndrome or cerebral palsy, and yet make major assumptions about those experiencing EBD. A scarcely disguised assumption, for example, is that these school students are manipulative, capable of controlling their actions and unwilling to comply with the work orientation of school.

This in part has fuelled periodic upturns of moral panic, in which established education systems (usually in first world post-industrial settings) are viewed as being under threat of melt-down, in the face of violence and other anti-social behaviour displayed by an increasing number of school students. Like much of what prevails relating to EBD, such a perception is largely a fiction, fuelled in part by non-educational imperatives; the quest for social order, economic stability and advancement, and the compliance of marginalized groups. We have been experiencing one such era, characterized in response terms by so-called 'zero-tolerance' approaches within education (and, as an interesting parallel, the penal systems) of many countries (Skiba, 2000).

Those involved professionally in education, working either directly or at a distance from EBD children and youth, are variously implicated in all of this. The linkage between stereotyping and the knowledge systems of (particularly) post-industrialized nations, mediated by professionals, allows for the isolation, then exclusion of individual groups of children or young people. Coulby and Jones summarize this process thus:

> A head teacher desires that a troublesome, underperforming child be removed from mainstream school; an obliging psychologist discovers that the child has a low 'IQ'; the child is sent to a segregated school for slow learners (various euphemistic designations). As part of this process the child is discovered to need specialist teaching away from the excitements of mainstream school. The provision that the system intends to impose is legitimated as what the child needs. The fact that the children and young people subjected to these processes are almost exclusively working class … and disproportionately black … is hidden in the ameliorative, pseudo-scientific processes which conceal themselves in the discourse of meeting individual needs. (2001: 66)

The implication, then, is that those who are professionally involved in work with pupils experiencing EBD are involved, whether directly or tangentially, in their continued exclusion. This process is achieved, in most cases benignly, by the application of statutory or quasi-official procedures designed to induce 'better behaviour' and compliance. And yet, as with those serving custodial sentences where remediation is not a core element of provision, the continued professional allegiance to reactive discipline and to the machineries of control is likely to result in further disadvantage in the manner classically described by such writers as Hunt (1961) and Halsey (1972). Moreover, as is acknowledged by at least one of our contributors, this exclusionary process can also have a negative impact on teachers and other educational workers themselves by setting them apart from others working with populations who are viewed as more normative.

The global movement towards inclusive practices in education has been one of the defining features of legislation by governments during the last 15 years, and has come to preoccupy the thoughts of policy-makers and practitioners. International perspectives on this (Booth and Ainscow, 1998; Armstrong et al., 2000; Daniels and Garner, 1999), whilst illustrating its diverse contexts, practices and outcomes, have never really confronted the dilemma that the broad range of 'challenging behaviours' (including EBD) presents in moving towards a more inclusive system of educating. Indeed, there is justification in the argument that it is this group of school attendees who are most frequently cited whenever the efficacy of educational exclusion is being scrutinized (Feilor and Gibson, 1999). Moreover, the same period has seen an even sharper reorientation in education: in many countries, schools are viewed as small enterprises, subject to the wishes of 'consumers' and the dominant laws of the market-place.

THE STRUCTURE OF THIS *HANDBOOK*: METAPHORS IN THE MAKING

We have assembled a *Handbook* that, by its structure and content, foci and directions, and its omissions, discrepancies and paradoxes, stands as a metaphor for the field of 'emotional and behavioural difficulties' itself. As editors we at first struggled to secure a set of chapters which responded to a very specific frame of general reference, even before addressing the specificities of individual issues. As our plans developed, however, we came to recognize that any attempt to force a template or script on our contributors was in stark contrast to the multi-variate, multi-level performances, interpretations and interventions that characterize EBD.

Readers will note, therefore, that whilst our themes are diverse and eclectic, they reveal the particular standpoints and agency of their progenitors, such is the complexity of EBD – even if its consideration is restricted solely to issues arising in educational contexts – that there will inevitably be readers who feel that our selection has been *ad hoc*, our coverage partial. In contrast, we would claim that the spread of chapters, and the individual issues and motifs addressed by their authors, represents an accessible, broad coverage account of EBD as it is experienced by children and young people, by teachers and other education-related professionals, and by those whose experiences and contexts allow for a more detached, academic gaze. Each of these orientations is valid in its own right, and is in keeping with the current policy approach to interventions based upon systemic theory.

We also acknowledge that some will find our decision to allow for considerable variation in style and length to infer that what is presented here is an haphazard assemblage of research and polemic. Nevertheless, we hope that readers will find such interfaces challenging because, we believe, they reveal something more of the true nature of the field. This *Handbook* is an attempt to celebrate that diversity, and to maximize the benefits of the *frisson* secured by differences in personal belief or professional standpoint. This collection of chapters, therefore, seeks out a varied audience and an incrementally different engagement with their respective content. In doing so we seek to recognize further the complexities of EBD, both in terms of how it is experienced and how it is provided for.

We have encouraged each of our contributing authors to provide something beyond an indicative set of references in support of their work. Chapter references will therefore further reveal, in their breadth and extent, something of the true nature of EBD. There is now, in many countries, a significant body of literature regarding EBD issues. The nature of this material is as diverse as the topics it addresses. In that sense, therefore, references are more than simply a useful coda to the substance of individual chapters.

This is a *Handbook* that seeks to offer an international perspective on aspects of EBD. In keeping with the diversity of educational policy and practices that this implies, we have tried to further recognize cultural differences by retaining the nuances of language and terminology, as well as the stylistic distinctiveness, in the various chapters of this book. For instance, our contributors variously use the terms 'children', 'pupils', 'students' or 'young people' to describe those individuals and groups who are the focus of this book – although we recognize that these terms may mean very different things to different audiences. Similarly, we have allowed language to further define and provide context to individual contributions – an obvious example is in the dual use of 'behaviour' and 'behavior'. Whilst some may find this an irritant, it is our belief that standardization in this respect does little to assist our conceptual understanding.

In terms of structure, this *Handbook* follows what is an acknowledged practice in special education pedagogy. Indeed, it must be argued that such an approach is germane to how teachers more generally choose to operate in order to provide an appropriate set of learning experiences in their classroom. The first section provides a context, the second a survey of significant causal factors; the third focuses on intervention. The final section points to some of the dilemmas which remain in the field of EBD, and indicates potential for their resolution. Each of these constituent sections of the book are outlined in greater detail.

The first section of this *Handbook* addresses issues of global and historical context. Constituent chapters hereabouts are especially useful as a means of informing the reader of the approach that we have adopted in our attempt at delineating the characteristics of EBD mapped across a range of educational settings. Margret Winzer maps the social and cultural contexts of EBD, showing how these impact on definition and provision in diverse locations. Moreover, her chapter introduces the notion of educational (and social) inclusion – an issue of dramatic impact whenever EBD is being considered. Ted Cole's chapter deals with the history of EBD provision, using a sharply-focused lens to point-up the manner in which versions of what constitutes 'EBD' change over time and according to the professional capital and traditional protocols existing in a given location.

One of the most pervasive issues over time in EBD is the question of terminology. Indeed, as editors of this volume we have had to deal with the widespread recognition that EBD itself is an artificial 'category', in that it is socially constructed – therefore lending itself to manipulation or even abuse. So the next chapters tackle this pivotal issue. Gary Thomas begins the process by suggesting that lack of specificity has, for many systems, simply provided a convenient means by which those children and young people who are viewed as 'troublesome' could be dealt with. Yet this arbitrary approach has ultimately damaged the educational chances of many of those it was directed towards. Kenneth Kavale and his colleagues reinforce this expression of concern. In their chapter the paradoxes and discontinuities experienced in the US system of categorization are explored, and serve as an indicative overview of the terminological struggles experienced across many cultures and systems. Finally, in this opening section, Tony Bowers surveys the extent to which the emotional status of children and young people in schools is often marginalized. Understandably, teachers often seek to attend to obvious, acting-out performances, as they present a more immediate challenge. This frequently leaves the 'E' in 'EBD' to be perceived as a matter of peripheral importance.

The *Handbook* now turns to the underlying causes of EBD, the focus of its' second section. Again, what is offered is an opportunity to glimpse the complexities hereabouts, and to examine the linkages and overlaps between individual causal factors. But a consideration of these is crucial because an understanding of the role that they play in individual cases is securely linked to successful intervention. The opening chapter, by Paul Cooper, provides an opportunity to consider the nature of this relationship, as it can be applied to the biological bases of problematic behaviour. Recognition of the potential for development in this area is important, but also problematic, in the light of concerns about the apparently deterministic thinking which could follow in professional settings. So Michael Furlong and his colleagues, in the next chapter, offer a useful foil. They cover that territory which has been growing in recognition over the last 30 years – that the way that schools are organized and function do impact, in various ways, on the behaviour of its youngsters. Tim O'Brien and Dennis Guiney extend the consideration of this aspect of causation by examining the way in which education is 'delivered' in contemporary cultural and social systems. In doing so they challenge the notion that 'solutions' based on a top-down, bureaucratically inclusive approach are an appropriate response to those whose behaviour is deemed to be challenging.

The section pursues this theme by next tackling the link between academic performance and behaviour. Here, Tom Nicholson recognizes that these two issues have traditionally been viewed as inseparable in the causal hierarchy. But he goes on to argue that this relationship is not pervasive and axiomatic; the key to change, he maintains, is in professional attention to both social learning and the more formal, taught curriculum. This theme is further articulated by Paul O'Mahoney, in a survey of the relationship between juvenile delinquency and EBD. Here, according to O'Mahoney, academic failure in school is a crucial factor and is implicated as a cause of the criminal career of many young people. Considerable exposure, in the last half century, has been given to the impact of the televisual media on children's behaviour. Tony Charlton and Charlie Panting provide a summary of recent debates in this area, and suggest that the 'context' within which children and young people view television is a mediating factor which has largely been overlooked. Finally, the problematic issue of the over-representation of certain racial or cultural groupings in the 'category' EBD is considered by Kristen McCabe and her team. This is a matter which is currently exercising the minds of governments and educational policy-makers on virtually a global scale: McCabe et al.'s research study is indicative both of the difficulties of researching this theme and of the potential sensibilities that can emerge from it.

At this point the content of the *Handbook* shifts towards a more prospective mode. Part Three therefore concerns itself with an indicative set of educational interventions for those who experience EBD. Again, the vast range of individual strategies currently being operationalized in schools and other educational settings can only be hinted at. But the chapters comprising this section provide opportunities for the reader to gauge the extent to which causation and intervention must be viewed as integral components of effective provision. John Visser's opening chapter for this section draws on both his personal recollections of a career working, in various professional roles and either directly or indirectly, on issues relating to EBD. In much of this a defining theme is the individual orientation and actions of the teacher. Bill Rogers continues the theme by exploring some of the strategies which can be used in moving towards more effective resolution of what, to many, may seem intractable difficulties in the classroom.

There is, in both these chapters, a recognition that individual teachers function as just one part of a broader, organic system. The next two contributions to the *Handbook*, by Timothy Lewis and Lori Newcomer and by Bob and Kate Algozzine, consider ways in which a systemic causal interpretation of behaviour helps to promote a response which is rooted in the school as a whole. Such actions have, of course, become widespread in school systems in culturally distinct settings, an indication of their promise in offering realistic and sustainable interventions. Much, too, has been written regarding the need to include the viewpoints and wishes of those who experience EBD. Indeed, it could be argued that advocacy issues are increasingly coming to be a defining feature of twenty-first century provision for EBD children and youth. Carl Smith and John Dwyfor Davies explore this, drawing on distinct and quite different cultural and educational traditions as they do so, whilst Barry Groom and Richard Rose offer a transnational analysis.

The third section closes with two chapters which provide glimpses of approaches to individual and school-based intervention with those experiencing EBD. In the first of these Helen McGrath illustrates the value of social skills training in this area, noting that such approaches offer potential for more long-term gains with regard to student behaviour. Paul Hamill examines the same issue in the context of a specific school-wide approach aimed at retaining EBD pupils in the mainstream.

The final section of this *Handbook* addresses a number of dilemmas and tensions which have been salient features of the EBD landscape for as long as we can remember. Like what has gone before in this book, we do not claim to provide an exhaustive mapping of these issues. Rather, we have identified some themes which have been highlighted consistently by earlier contributions to the *Handbook*. These, it would appear, remain as vital issues for consideration by all of those – teachers, advocates, policymakers, researchers and scholars – who are professionally involved in the field of EBD. Egide Royer's chapter provides a salutary reminder of a need to close the gap between theory and practice in EBD. Too often, it would seem, opportunities further to develop services for children and young people in this area are being prejudiced by a failure to make linkages between these two equally vital aspects of endeavour. The pitfalls present in researching EBD populations are considered by Ann Lewis, whose chapter provides a framework (or a timely reminder …) to anyone researching or enquiring into this field. Next, the section turns to consider one aspect of EBD – that of 'attention deficit/hyperactivity disorder' – which is indicative of the tensions in respect of categorization, ascertainment and ultimately provision in one area of EBD. Thus, whilst Marjorie Montague and Marcelo Castro focus on ADHD, it could be argued that many other sub-groupings within the general term 'EBD' could be critiqued in the same way.

The final two chapters concern those issues of practice and perspective which sharpen the lens through which we ought to be viewing society's responses to EBD. In the first instance, Christopher Blake asks whether we do enough to ensure that new teachers are equipped with the skills, and the intellectual underpinnings, to meet the challenge of students experiencing EBD. James Kauffman, on the other hand, directs his interrogation to professionals across all sections of educational provision, in asking whether rigid systems and practices and beliefs and conventions do little other than preserve a status quo, which is characterized by missed opportunity or studied indifference. Those involved in work in the field of EBD, he infers, need to adopt a more proactive mind-set in order not to replicate what have, for many experiencing EBD, been largely unrewarding or exclusionary policies and practice.

In conclusion, we hope that readers will be left with a sense of incompleteness and partiality as a result of this *Handbook*'s constituent chapters. As we have indicated, our intention in scoping the field of 'emotional and behavioural difficulties' has been underscored by a belief that there will be more that is omitted than included; for every position taken on definition, causality or intervention there will be many others. Numerous caveats have to be noted, irrespective of the fact that we have attempted to restrict our coverage to that which is located predominantly within educational contexts. And even in doing so we are aware that what we provide in this volume are a series of starting points for the continued scrutiny of an aspect of education which is defined in, and articulated by, cultures and settings on a global dimension.

REFERENCES

Ainscow, M. (1998) 'Would it work in theory?: arguments for practitioner research and theorising in the special needs field', in C. Clark, A. Dyson and A. Milward (eds), *Theorising Special Education*. London: Routledge.

Angelides, P. (2000) 'A new technique for dealing with behaviour difficulties in Cyprus: the analysis of critical incidents', *European Journal of Special Needs Education*, 15 (1): 55–68.

Armstrong, F., Armstrong, D. and Barton, L. (2000) *Inclusive Education: Policy, Contexts and Comparative Perspectives*. London: David Fulton.

Booth, T. and Ainscow, M. (eds) (1998) *From Them to Us: An International Study of Inclusion in Education*. London: Routledge.

Bower, E. (1982) 'Defining emotional disturbance: public policy and research', *Psychology in the Schools*, 19: 55–60.

Bronfenbrenner, U. (1979) *The Ecology of Human Development*. Cambridge: Harvard University Press.

Coulby, D. and Jones, C. (2001) *Education and Warfare in Europe*. Aldershot: Ashgate.

Council for Children with Behavioral Disorders (CECB) (1987) *Position paper on identification of students with behavioral disorders*. Reston, VA: CCBD.

Cronis, T. and Ellis, D. (2000) 'Issues facing special educators in the new millennium', *Education*, 120 (4): 639–48.

Daniels, H. and Garner, P. (eds) (1999) *World Yearbook of Education: Inclusive Education*. London: Kogan Page.

Department for Education (DfE) (1994) *Pupils with Problems*. London: DfE.

Department of Education and Science (DES) (1989) *Discipline in Schools: Report of the Committee of Enquiry Chaired by Lord Elton*. London: HMSO.

Feilor, A. and Gibson, H. (1999) 'Threats to the inclusive movement', *British Journal of Special Education*, 26 (3): 147–52.

Gavrilidou, M., Mesquita, P. and Mason, E. (1993) 'Greek teachers' judgements about the nature and severity of classroom problems', *School Psychology International*, 14: 169–80.

Gullotta, T., Adams, G. and Montemayor, R. (eds) (1998) *Delinquent Violent Youth*. New York: Sage.

Halsey, A. (1972) *Educational Priority, Vol. 1. EPA Problems and Policies*. London: HMSO.

Hargreaves, D., Hester, S. and Mellor, F. (1975) *Deviance in Classrooms*. London: Routledge and Kegan Paul.

Hey, S. (1917) 'Juvenile crime'. Paper to the 1916 Conference of the National Special Schools Union, London.

Hunt, J. (1961) *Intelligence and Experience*. New York: Ronald Press.

Jahnukainen, M. (2001) 'Experiencing special education: former students of classes for the emotionally and behaviourally disordered talk about their schooling', *Emotional and Behavioural Difficulties*, 6 (3): 150–66.

Kauffman, J. (1993) *Characteristics of Behavior Disorders of Children and Youth* (5th edn). Columbus, OH: Merrill.

Kavale, K., Forness, S. and Duncan, B. (1996) 'Defining emotional and behavioral disorders: divergence and convergence', in T. Scruggs and M. Mastropieri (eds), *Advances in Learning and Behavioral Difficulties*. Greenwich, CT: JAI.

Kolominskii, I. and Zhiznevskii, B. (1992) 'A sociopsychological analysis of conflicts among children during play', *Journal of Russian and East European Psychology*, 30: 74–86.

Letendre, G. and Shimizu, H. (1999) 'Towards a healing society: perspectives from Japanese special education', in H. Daniels and P. Garner (eds), *World Yearbook of Education: Inclusive Education*. London: Kogan Page.

Levine, D.U. and Havighurst, R.J. (1989) *Society and Education* (7th edn). Boston: Allyn and Bacon.

McCall, L. and Farrell, P. (1993) 'Methods used by educational psychologists to assess children with emotional and behavioral difficulty', *Educational Psychology in Practice*, 9 (3): 164–70.

Nettles, M., Mucherah, W. and Jones, D. (2000) 'Understanding resilience: the role of social resources', *Journal of Education for Students Placed at Risk*, 5 (1 and 2): 47–60.

Park, Y-K. (1994) 'The effects of free token response cost procedures in modifying disruptive behaviours of mentally handicapped children', *International Journal of Special Education*, 9 (2): 170–91.

Pink, W. (1982) 'Academic failure, student social conflict, and delinquent behavior', *Urban Review*, 14: 141–80.

Quay, H. (1994) *Disruptive Behavior Disorders in Childhood*. New York: Plenum Press.

Scotti, J. and Meyer, L. (1999) *Behavioral Intervention*. Baltimore: Paul Brookes.

Skiba, R. (2000) 'School discipline at a crossroads: from zero tolerance to early response', *Exceptional Children*, 32 (Spring): 200–16.

US Department of Education (2001) *Twenty-third Annual Report to Congress on the Implementation of the Individuals with Disabilities Education Act*. Washington, DC: Author.

2

International Comparisons in EBD: Critical Issues

MARGRET WINZER

The dominant orientation to defining and meeting the needs of children and youth with emotional and behavioural disorders (EBD) has always been a paradox. While the common theme is the demonstration of mal-adaptive behaviours that seriously impair an individual's ability to work, live and function successfully in society, this plays out in such multiple variations that a large array of supports, services, treatment regimes and interventions are necessary.

Complex problems pervade the entire field of EBD. Contemporary difficulties have not emerged from a vacuum; rather, throughout the late-nineteenth and all of the twentieth century, a steady stream of psychological, educational, social and legal changes and events left a store-house of unresolved issues and lasting puzzles facing policy-makers and practitioners in many countries or cultural settings. Few critical issues in the field have been resolved in the past hundred years or so. Kauffman points out that 'current issues and trends seem only to be a recycling of those that have been with us for well over a century' (2001: 96).

Joined to long-standing dilemmas, many issues have acquired a new urgency in the light of current school reform movements. For example, inclusive schooling for students with exceptionalities may have been planted firmly on the educational map, yet, for the EBD population, ambiguity characterizes policy and practice for, and the educational place-ment of, students with EBD. It thus remains one of the most controversial issues in special education within individual nation states or cultures.

Equally compelling are international perspectives and parallels in the field of EBD. While Western societies grapple with the challenges of such students in schools and wider society, other nations hold different views. Not only are there variations in prevalence figures, (re)conceptualizations of EBD as a disability requiring educational intervention, treatment regimes and school programmes, but also in some cultures the very concepts of emotional and behavioural disorder have quite different meanings – or may not have any meaning at all.

Democratizing educational opportunities and delivering a curriculum to all children in the most optimal learning environment is becoming a uni-versal thrust. While a growing list of nations embrace the philosophy of inclusive education, much is unknown about the cultures, characteristics and practices of settings where inclusion is (or is not) occurring. The practice appears in various guises, and nations tailor the philosophy and processes to unique political and educational realities which lead ultimately to the formulation of varied policies, legislation, other administrative arrange-ments and practices, and the way in which teachers and parents conceptual-ize the reform agenda (Winzer et al., 2003).

The scope of this *Handbook* is extensive, addressing a matrix of issues ranging from the historical development of the field of EBD, through causal factors and individual aetiology, to current school-wide interven-tion practices. This short chapter is designed to address only two facets. First, because the role of culture is critical in structuring human behaviour and delineating misbehaviour, the chapter examines the issue of cultural concepts of EBD. The second closely-related theme focuses on the phi-losophy and realization of inclusive education in varied cultural climates as it applies to this student grouping.

A caveat is in order here. Comparative study in special education is not an active domain of study; complex conceptual, methodological and prag-matic problems stand in the way of rigorous and systematic research. Although many scattered single case studies exist, differences in concep-tual and practical domains are often explained without analysis of the social and political contexts. Data on the entire enterprise of special education tends to be sporadic; that on EBD arguably even more diffuse. For example, in a comparative study of special education in 26 countries (Mazurek and Winzer, 1994), references to EBD from non-Western nations were, in general, oblique or absent. But it would be brave to suggest that behaviours descriptive of the term 'EBD' were not an emerging feature of at least some of these emergent nation states.

EBD IN CULTURAL CONTEXT

The complexities that plague the contemporary field of EBD are quite different from that of other disabilities. Unlike measurable and overt conditions such as deafness and visual impairment, disordered behavioural functioning is not an immutable entity that can be detached from the observer. Rather, it is a subjective reality that is constructed on the basis of a judgement as to what is tolerable, appropriate and desirable.

Intimately linked to the subjective nature of EBD are cultural constructs. While disordered and maladaptive behaviour has always been a trait displayed by a portion of people in every society and, typically, deviant behaviour is something perceived to threaten the stability, security or values of a society, an emotional or behavioural disorder is not a thing that exists outside of a social context. A determination of maladaptive, disordered or deviant behaviour is mediated by cultural lenses and embedded in local discourses as relayed in the terms used to describe the condition. As the constraints of an observer's culture and ideological perspective define views and beliefs on causation, on disability and on its impact on an individual and society, the level at which deviancy is recognized varies; what is deviant and maladaptive and what constitutes infractions of the rules are recognized differently. And as there are varying reactions to certain behaviours, behaviour that may be acceptable in one culture is not necessarily so in another.

While each society articulates a framework for responsible, socially acceptable actions and behaviour, universal properties extending beyond cultural constraints of a country may be more appropriate for severe and overt disorders. Criminality, for example, generally has universal applicability. In all societies, offences against property or other persons are likely to be the object of law enforcement. As well, serious and pervasive disorders such as infantile autism and childhood psychoses may be recognized rapidly. Less concordance exists in ideas about mild disorders. Although the range of factors that give rise to these maladaptive behaviours – the sundry personal, familial, social, community and educational factors – may match across cultures, the ultimate conceptions, manifestations, terminology and interventions differ. Parents' conceptions are critical. The importance of parent–child interaction in mediating children's development in different cultures has been widely documented. Suffice to say that parents hold different conceptions of childhood, and different beliefs about child rearing and management and about the place of the child in family and society. All of these tie intimately to cultural and social mores and the interpretation of individual differences and lead ultimately to child development outcomes. For example, in some cultures, parental beliefs about how best to prescribe and regulate child behaviour joined to nuclear and extended family networks may deter the emergence of deviant patterns of child behaviour. If it does appear, some parents may reject treatment as unwarranted interference in the family's domain or some insolent defiance of divine will.

Cultural constraints on the expression of disorder may be seen in Asian countries. Asian cultures frequently show a high level of parental control which aims at disciplining children and making them obedient to adults. For example, Cheong (1996) reports on studies from the Philippines and Thailand showing that direct aggression is frowned upon and rarely manifested. Disability and poor behaviour may bring shame to the entire family or may be seen as a punishment for the sins of ancestors or parents.

The terminology, definitions and educational concepts surrounding EBD are only just beginning to emerge in some countries. For example, Nigeria has 'just a few, poorly defined categories of exceptionality' (Abang, 1994: 79) that do not include EBD. Dukmak (1994) points out that there is no specific labelling in Gaza and the West Bank for those with conduct and emotional disorders. Donald and Metcalfe (1992) spoke of the almost total lack of special educational facilities in African education generally for students with mild disabilities, including those with emotional or behavioural problems.

In the emergent democracies in the central and eastern parts of Europe, 40 years of Marxist-Leninist educational ideas left a residue of concepts which focused on a defectology that stressed the causes, aspects and substance of impairments and their impact on an individual. The tendency of the Communist regime was to deny or minimize any embarrassing or unresolved social problems. Gargiulo and Cerna reported that 'while students who exhibit social/emotional difficulties are served in a variety of educational environments, neither the Czech nor Slovak Ministries of Education report any data pertaining to this population' (1992: 64). In Russia in 1994, Lubovsky and Martsinovskaja reported the absence of 'any kinds of special pedagogical measures or educational structures for emotionally disturbed children and children with behaviour problems' (1994: 261). Changes occurred in the late-1990s, partly because minors became the most criminally active part of the Russian population and may be categorized as among the new category of 'social orphans' (Pervova, 1999).

In addition to ill-defined categories, the standards for identifying children with special needs in many countries are inconsistent between developed and undeveloped or rural and urban sectors. In the former, sophisticated identification and services are often available; the latter frequently lack even minimal services. For example, in large and diverse countries such as Brazil and South Africa, identification and services are distinctly different among regions, states and even institutions (see Mazurek and Winzer, 1994).

Language glosses specificity so that terminology differs. For example, Israel uses the term 'mentally disturbed children'; Iran, Brazil and Indonesia 'emotionally disturbed'; Poland and the Czech Republic 'socially maladjusted'; Greece 'maladjusted'; 'social or emotional disorder' in Scandinavia; 'severely maladjusted' in the Netherlands; 'defective behaviour' in Slovakia. In some Muslim countries (for example, Malaysia and Pakistan) persons with serious emotional disturbance are grouped with those labelled as mentally retarded.

THE QUEST FOR INCLUSIVE SCHOOLING

In many countries around the world, the appropriateness of special education as a separate system, as well as the classification and placement of some students in this system for the majority of their educational experiences, is under attack. In opposition to a separate and dual system of special education, the philosophies and concepts of inclusive schooling for students with special needs have piqued the interest of educators, legislators and parents.

The movement toward integration and desegregation developed in Western educational systems in the 1960s and 1970s as part of a wider process of liberalization and an emphasis on equity characteristic of the decades following World War II. Dating from about 1975, worldwide commitments to the education of individuals with disabilities took root. A series of statements from international bodies then helped to create a climate that placed political pressure on agencies and governments to accede to the notion of special needs as a human rights issue. For example, the United Nations Convention on the Rights of the Child (UN, 1989) recognized that all children are citizens-in-becoming and therefore have fundamental rights that must be available to them; that is, provision, protection and participation rights. The United Nations followed with the 1993 Standard Rules for the Equalization of Opportunities for Persons with Disabilities. The 1994 Salamanca meeting on special needs attracted 300 participants representing 92 governments and 25 international organizations.

The ensuing document, the *Salamanca Statement and Framework for Action on Special Needs Education*, (UNESCO, 1994), stressed the value of education in the general school system and prompted the abandonment of special schools and special classes in favour of more inclusive practices (see also Smith-Davis, 2002).

As a means of stimulating educational change, the various UN declarations and proclamations on human rights, together with the Salamanca Statement, have been extremely powerful. Combined with the widespread demand to establish individual rights as a centrepiece in policy-making, they placed inclusive education for students with special needs firmly on the social change agenda. Indeed, as a growing number of stakeholders around the world begin to accept and enact the premises, inclusive schooling has become a 'global agenda' (see Pijl et al., 1997).

In many countries, the rate of inclusion has increased consistently and substantially in the past decade. Yet, despite the broad sweeps provided by policy statements of international organizations, the tireless presentation of the political language of inclusive schooling and a well-accepted conceptual and philosophical base, the meanings of inclusive schooling for children and youth with disabilities are not uniformly absorbed. While cultural specificity may be dimmed by the gloss of international findings and mandates, a tension exists between the local nature of the issues and international policy perspectives.

Today, many nations have legislation and policy that guarantee students a free and appropriate education, and many have departments dedicated to providing special services. However, liberal thinking has more influence on policy thinking than policy implementation, and educational reform initiatives may be only tacit. Indeed, the gap between rhetoric and reality is often enormous.

Profound differences are seen in educational systems in the experiences of schools and students, in conceptions of the mission of schools, and even in ideas about the meaning and value of learning. To examine the dissonance in the specific realm of EBD, the typology developed by Mazurek and Winzer (1994) in their comparative studies of special education may prove helpful. Founded on each nation's approach to and progress toward integration, the typology delineated integrated education as limited, emerging, segregated, viable and fully committed.

In countries where integration is limited, overwhelming barriers to progress include factors such as momentous political transformations, civil war, profound ruptures in family and social relationships resulting from war, refugees, crushing external debt payments, the flight of capital, exponential population growth, poor sanitation, malnutrition and inadequate health care (see Csapo, 1993). To this list of constraining and severely limited social and economic resources can be added precarious public education systems where the primary necessity lies in resolving the overwhelming need for universal elementary education. When intervention targets are prioritized for persons with special needs, it is the overt and traditional disabilities that are served first. EBD, if acknowledged as a problem at all, is unlikely to warrant specialized attention.

In nations with an emerging system, broad social issues similarly impact on the narrower concerns of the school. After the normative categories, others fall by the wayside (Csapo, 1993). Not only will the lack of an existing structure render innovation somewhat fruitless, but differences in beliefs about the role of schools and the socialization of children may mean that milder forms of EBD are ignored by the educational system. If acknowledged, responses likely mirror traditional modes – non-admittance, corporal punishment, suspension or expulsion.

Many nations with segregated special education recognize EBD as a disability to be served within a complex of special schools. In Germany, as an example, more than 97 per cent of all students with disabilities, including those with EBD, are in separate special schools (Cloerkes, 1997). Schools for children and youth with EBD developed in Russia in the late-1990s but, despite the educational reforms that encompass differentiation and democratization, Russia still operates primarily at the level of separation (Pervova, 1999). Japan has three types of special schools for those blind, deaf and otherwise disabled, such as with physical disabilities or mental retardation. A small number of students labelled as emotionally disturbed are in segregated classrooms (Sugai and Takuma, 1990).

Even in nations well attuned or deeply committed to inclusive schooling, students who are ascertained as EBD are often cited as exemplars of the times when inclusion is not appropriate. Research has consistently demonstrated that students with EBD are rated as the least accepted and the most negatively stereotyped of all exceptionalities: such students are often the last group considered when inclusive options are available (Eber et al., 1997). Indeed, inclusion for students with EBD is 'fraught with peril' (Lago-Delello, 1998: 479). For example, in the United States, as compared to the total of all students with disabilities, almost four times as many students with behavioural disorders are educated in segregated settings and only half as many in general classrooms (Cheney and Muscott, 1996).

DISCUSSION

This chapter has focused explicitly on two fundamental tensions in the broad area of EBD – cultural constraints in identifying, defining and classifying EBD, and the elusive nature of inclusive education in varied contexts.

Western special education embraces certain concepts of the child and human development, certain theories about learning and beliefs about the individual rights of children (Mazurek and Winzer, 1994). In other cultures, the fixity of basic assumptions about child development, disability, maladaptive behaviour and schooling is different. Widely-differing systems of beliefs deny EBD as an objective condition; rather, the operative set of criteria or dimensions is defined by the cultural context.

Not only are cultural constraints in identifying and labelling EBD paramount, but also the West is not a thorough and empirical source of information on EBD. Confusion abounds in definitions of EBD, in classification systems, in intervention and the science of teaching students with EBD is unrefined. As the constructs have questionable validity, even in their original Western contexts, translation to other cultural contexts is treacherous. Behaviour must be understood within indigenous belief systems. As cultural expectations and concepts of deviance differ, reducing the fissionable nature of EBD is not possible. Many of the underlying assumptions about EBD formulated by Western researchers are not applicable in a global dimension. This being said, major issues and problems in the field such as definitions, classification of disorders, early identification, assessment and treatment regimes must be reconceptualized taking account of both mono- and multi-cultural parameters.

Similar cautions apply to the implementation of inclusive schooling. While the language of inclusion is advocated by international bodies, inclusionary concepts are not self-explanatory but rather subject to multiple interpretations. In international contexts, models must evolve to represent a multisystemic approach toward improving the outcomes of students with special needs, including those with EBD.

Reform cannot be independent of time, place and culture. For inclusive education to become a reality, the implicit conventions of highly diverse societies must be recognized and solutions must be contextually driven and reflect realistic strategies. Theoretical frameworks and research paradigms in the field of contemporary special education illuminate a range of possibilities for students with special needs, and as a social and educational principle, inclusion can be advocated unequivocally. Nevertheless, even granting the increased acculturation to Western modes of thinking about schooling and the wholesale exportation of educational knowledge, realization of the ideal must be sensitive to fundamental realities of the prevailing culture and the capacity of school systems to change and restructure to accommodate all students with special needs, including those who may be characterized as emotionally and behaviourally disordered.

REFERENCES

Abang, T. (1994) 'Nigeria', in K. Mazurek and M. Winzer (eds) *Comparative Studies in Special Education*. Washington, DC: Gallaudet University Press. pp. 71–87.

Cheney, D. and Muscott, H.S. (1996) 'Preventing school failure for students with emotional and behavioral disorders through responsible inclusion', *Preventing School Failure*, 40: 109–116.

Cheong, A. (1996) 'The psychology of child and adolescent development in southeast Asian countries', *World Psychology*, 2: 41–69.

Cloerkes, G. (1997) *Soziologe der Bihenderten*. Heidelberg: Heidelberg University.

Csapo, M. (1993) 'Special education in crisis', *International Journal of Special Education*, 8: 201–208.

Donald D. and Metcalfe, M. (1992) *Final Special Education Report*. Johannesburg: National Education Policy Investigation.

Dukmak, S. (1994) 'West Bank and Gaza Strip', in K. Mazurek and M. Winzer (eds), *Comparative Studies in Special Education*. Washington, DC: Gallaudet University Press. pp. 44–63.

Eber, L., Nelson, C.M., and Miles, P. (1997) 'School-based wraparound for students with emotional and behavioural challenges', *Exceptional Children*, 63: 539–55.

Gargiulo, R.M. and Cerna, M. (1992) 'Special education in Czechoslovakia: characteristics and issues', *International Journal of Special Education*, 7: 6–70.

Kauffman, J.M. (2001) *Characteristics of Emotional and Behavioral Disorders of Children and Youth* (7th edn). Englewood Cliffs, NJ: Merrill, Prentice-Hall.

Lago-Delello, E. (1998) 'Classroom dynamics and the development of serious emotional disturbance', *Exceptional Children*, 64: 479–92.

Lubovsky, V.I. and Martsinovskaja, F.N. (1994) 'Russia' in K. Mazurek and M. Winzer (eds) *Comparative Studies in Special Education*. Washington, DC: Gallaudet University Press. pp. 260–95.

Mazurek, K. and Winzer, M. (1994) *Comparative Studies in Special Education*. Washington, DC: Gallaudet University Press.

Pervova, I. (1999) 'The system of special education in Russia', *The Journal of International Needs Education*, 2: 23–9.

Pijl, S.J., Meijer, C.J. and Hegarty, S. (eds) (1997) *Inclusive Education: A Global Agenda*. London: Routledge.

Smith-Davis, J. (2002) 'World initiatives in inclusive education', *Teaching Exceptional Children*, 64: 77.

Sugai, K. and Takuma, J. (1990) 'The current state of computer assisted instruction for the handicapped children in Japan', *International Journal of Special Education*, 5: 132–44.

UNESCO (1994) *Salamanca Statement and Framework for Action on Special Needs Education*. New York: UNESCO.

United Nations (1989) *United Nations Convention on the Rights of the Child*, G. A. Res 44/25, Annex 44, U.N. GAOR Supp. (No. 49) at 167, U.N. Doc A/44/49.

Winzer, M., Altieri, E., Jacobs, T. and Mellor, E. (2003) 'Reform in special education: case studies from Australia, Canada and the United States', *Journal of the Russian Academy for the Humanization of Education*.

3

Emotional and Behavioural Difficulties: An Historical Perspective

TED COLE

'History,' wrote Lord Acton in 1906, 'must be our deliverer not only from the undue influence of other times but from the undue influence of our own' (Carr, 1961: 44). Certainly studying past provision for children now said to have emotional and behavioural difficulties (EBD) helps understanding of the present and should lessen the repetition of earlier mistakes (Kauffman, 2001). It might induce pessimism as 'new' initiatives are seen as re-workings of approaches found in the past to be incomplete answers (Cole, 1989); that known 'good practice' is being ignored (Skiba and Peterson, 2000); or highlight that ideology (such as faith in 'full inclusion') can blind professionals to uncomfortable historical evidence. More encouragingly, programmes that first proved disappointing can meet with success in the altered circumstances of a later generation. Also, there are factors associated with effective practice, seen on both sides of the Atlantic, that endure through time. This chapter will highlight themes from history associated with effective work but also chronic obstacles to good practice. The chapter is written from an English standpoint, but is cross-referenced to American history.

PROBLEMS OF DEFINITION
AND PLACEMENT

In the United States and in the United Kingdom, it has been debated over generations who the children with EBD were and where they should be placed (Kauffman, 2001; Cole et al., 1998). In the nineteenth and early twentieth centuries such children and young people were sometimes confused with 'mental defectives' or 'moral imbeciles' or minor delinquents (Cole, 1989). In the twentieth century, an umbrella term came into usage: 'maladjustment'. In England, this descriptor was in official use by 1930. A legally enshrined category of 'maladjusted children' was instigated by the 1944 Education Act and was to last until the abolition of categories of special educational needs by the 1981 Education Act. The post-1944 Act regulations defined the maladjusted as:

> ... pupils who show evidence of emotional instability or psychological disturbance and require special education treatment in order to effect their personal, social or educational readjustment. (Min. of Ed., 1953, Part 3, 9g)

In 1955, the Underwood Report acknowledged confusion, finding it necessary to stress that maladjustment should not be equated with bad behaviour, delinquency, oddness or educational subnormality (Min. of Ed, 1955). It wished to classify the maladjusted as having nervous, habit, behaviour, organic or psychotic disorders or educational and vocational difficulties to allow for careful matching of provision to children's need. But this was rarely to be achieved and most schools for the maladjusted had generally to respond to a diverse and ill-defined clientele. Laslett described 'maladjustment' as 'a kind of catch-all for children showing a wide range of behaviour and learning difficulties' (1983: 6). Many children labelled 'maladjusted' in the 1960s and 1970s could have been described as 'socially deprived', 'disruptive', 'disaffected' or 'mentally ill'. The choice of descriptor tended to relate to the profession of the person responsible for the child.

Uncertainties over the identification of children with EBD have often been accompanied by haphazard placement procedures on both sides of the Atlantic. A senior English government Medical Officer noted in 1974 that 'only force of circumstance' dictated whether a child went to a school for the maladjusted or residential institutions for offenders or those 'at risk' run by social services or the home office (DES, 1974). From the 1970s, children with EBD could also be placed in special units designed primarily for the so-called 'disruptive'. In fact, dating back to the pioneer work of the Royal Philanthropic Society in the 1790s (Cole, 1989), the precursors of EBD would seem to have been taken under the wing of any one of four government departments – welfare, juvenile justice, education or health. Whether the 'problem child' was 'cared for', 'punished', 'educated' or 'treated' was often a matter of chance, depending upon which individuals in which agency first took up the case. A child's placement often depended on where the vacancies were when the child was perceived by particular professionals to have reached crisis point *or* when funding became available (Grimshaw with Berridge, 1994; Cole and Visser, 1999).

The uncertainties of assessment and placement in England mirrored the situation in the United States. Kauffman (2001), in particular, attacked the official but difficult-to-achieve separating out of the 'socially maladjusted' from the 'severe emotional disturbance' (SED) federal category. He also claimed that identification (and sometimes deliberate 'non-identification') linked to availability of resources and perhaps to fears of litigation. Even when standardised instruments of assessment were used, they resulted in contrasting proportions of the population being identified as needing specialist EBD services (Kauffman, 2001).

DEBATES AND THEMES: c. 1850–1950

Some timeless themes emerge from British historical sources for the century preceding 1950. Kauffman (2001) suggests similar issues emerging during this century in the United States:

- *Nurture or nature?* Some pioneers saw the role of poverty and family influences in behaviour causation, counteracting the influence of believers in the effects of inherited defective genes or medical causes (Cole, 1989; Eddy and Gribskov, 1998; Kauffman, 2001).
- *'Rescue' or community care?* Should children be 'rescued' from their families by residential placement, or should staff work with the parents while children attended day units/schools (for example, American nineteenth-century 'houses of refuge'; English industrial schools; English and New England 'truant schools/classes', c.1870–c.1900; or the Leicester day school for 'nervous or difficult' children in the 1930s; or American mentoring schemes for 'delinquency prone' youth in 1930s/1940s – see Eddy and Gribskov, 1998)?
- *'Discipline'/group conformity or individualized child-centred approaches?* Too many reformatory and industrial schools succumbed to punitive institutionalism, which did little to address individual needs (Cole, 1989). Yet by 1925 in England, following practice in the United States, Homer Lane and A.S. Neill had created democratic, liberal regimes. Individual educational planning, pupils' marking their own

work, peer tutoring and play had been stressed at the 1930s Leicester day school for maladjusted children (Bridgeland, 1971). Eddy and Gribskov (1998) describe similar debates in America, issuing in a range of contrasting provision.

- *The danger of 'contamination'.* It was understood that the placing of disturbed and sometimes delinquent youth together in institutions could lead to worse behaviours, as B.K. Pierce realised in 1869:

  > The [juvenile] penitentiary cannot but be a fruitful source of pauperism, a nursery of new vices and crimes, a college for the perfection of adepts in guilt. (Eddy and Gribskov, 1998: 15)

- *How much resource should be spent?* Lack of money often detracted from the quality of education and care provided (Cole, 1989; Hyland, 1993; Kauffman, 2001).
- *Education, social work or therapy?* The value of education as therapy was seen in some early schools for the maladjusted:

  > The school itself was a therapeutic situation and I would guess that about three-quarters of the children received no other form of therapy. (Headteacher of Oxford day maladjusted school, founded 1939, in Bridgeland, 1971: 298)

This approach contrasted with the growth and application of psychiatry, psychology and social work (Cole, 1989; Eddy and Gribskov, 1998).

PROVIDING FOR 'THE MALADJUSTED': 1950–75

The English Education Act of 1944, reflecting continuing American interest in more scientific identification and classification, required local education authorities (LEAs) to ascertain and to make suitable provision for all children in need of 'special educational treatment' including children who should be placed in the new category of 'maladjustment'. The government encouraged, although did not always realize, practice that was social and educational. Where possible, maladjusted children were to be helped within their local community, by transfer to different mainstream schools, by the use of foster homes or by living in small hostels and attending local day schools (Min. of Ed., 1946). In practice, most development was residential, with most new schools opening in large disused country mansions. However, in 1950 'tutorial classes', the precursors of the small off-site special units of the 1970s and Pupil Referral Units of the 1990s, were started in London. 'Maladjusted' children attended these small centres for a part of the week and their teachers had time allowed for working with the children's families (Cole, 1989). In this era, a wide range of provision, mirroring that made in America (Kauffman, 2001), came into existence.

In 1950, the Underwood Committee, appointed by the English government, began a major and influential enquiry (Min. of Ed., 1955) into all aspects of provision for maladjusted children (see Cole, 1989; Cole et al., 1998). It reflected the theoretical debates of its age, recording 'a considerable difference of opinion about the value of psychodynamic approaches, espoused in a few high-profile pioneer schools and many CGCs (Child Guidance Centres). This Report saw maladjustment not as "a medical term diagnosing a medical condition"... It is a term describing an individual's relation at a particular time to the people and circumstances which make up his environment' (1955: paras 88 and 89, p. 22). Foreshadowing later research (for example, Wilson and Evans, 1980; Cooper, 1993), it saw the centrality of relationship formation: maladjusted children were 'insecure and unhappy, and ... fail in their personal relationships. Receiving is difficult for them as well as giving, and they appear unable to respond to simple measures of love, comfort and reassurance' (1955: 22).

In relation to teaching and care approaches, the Report wanted staff to have a grasp of mainstream education and care approaches before training to work specifically with the maladjusted, through undertaking courses in the emotional development of children. The Committee was influenced by evidence that indicated the value of what was later called 'normality therapy' (Wilson and Evans, 1980):

> Much more can be done for a child who is maladjusted by a teacher who is warm-hearted and loving than by one who approaches maladjustment through the abnormal and broods over him as a problem child. (Min. of Ed., 1955: para. 513)

It had written of the classroom experience:

> The simple fact of receiving individual attention in a small class in an informal non-competitive atmosphere often enables a boy or girl to make progress and this can help in solving a child's emotional problems. (Min. of Ed., 1955: para. 281)

However, it recognized the need for approaches that contrasted with the mainstream school experience: toleration of some 'acting out' in class was necessary as the maladjusted 'were not readily capable of improvement by ordinary discipline' (1955: 22) and, reflecting some psychodynamic pioneers' view, the Committee saw the need to wait until some disturbed children were 'ready' to tackle conventional education. The value of play was also stressed.

On curriculum, Underwood expressed views which could have come from Victorian times or the English Labour government circa 2000: some children who were 'bright but not bookish' found that as the work became more abstract and formal it did not suit them: 'They cannot cope with the variety of subjects and with the many changes of teacher' (1955: para. 133, p. 32). This advice was backed by Wilson and Evans' (1980) research, but did not find favour with English government inspectors pushing the new National Curriculum in the 1990s (see below). Of interest to later doubters of full or even partial school inclusion (see Kauffman, 2001), it wrote about the siting of provision:

> It has often been found better to have the premises of a class quite separate from a school, since school may have unhappy associations for many maladjusted children. (Min. of Ed. 1955:)

'Off-mainstream-site' provision also allowed an alternative regime where perhaps necessary 'acting out' could be tolerated (1955: para. 218, p. 55).

Wanting a proactive and preventative approach involving inter-agency working, the Underwood Report strongly recommended a nationwide schools psychological service or as a second choice, a national system of CGCs. Here is seen trust in aspects of the medical model, but within a social and educational context: the medical professionals must involve themselves in family work and have 'roots in the school' (1955: para.161). It advocated more day schools to obviate the need for so many residential placements.

The Report highlighted timeless tensions over what constituted effectiveness between staff from and within different professions. How should maladjustment be addressed? In England and in the United States, some workers with the maladjusted, espousing a neo-Freudian and psychodynamic viewpoint, saw it as a 'within child' mental health issue to be tackled by psychiatry, psychotherapy and counselling, with formal education of far less importance. A variant of this view was the concept of 'milieu therapy' (Bettelheim, 1950; Redl and Wineman, 1952; Trieschman et al., 1969) or 'environmental therapy' (Franklin, 1945). These advocated the careful structuring of the residential milieu, providing good quality primary care and some formal counselling by qualified staff. Also important was the creative use of the daily events of staff and children living together to allow natural, unforced, informal counselling, described by Redl and Wineman as the 'life-space interview' (LSI). The LSI and a psychodynamic emphasis was stressed in a few special schools or residential treatment centres, which at times preferred to describe themselves as 'therapeutic communities'. Therapeutic communities offered a contrasting alternative to the mainstream schools. Sometimes their forms of organization were very different. Their style, usually distrusted by government inspectors, was characterized by flattened management hierarchies with informal relationships between staff and pupils, democratic community meetings and a non-punitive and permissive regime.

These contrasted with more orthodox special schools run, according to the Underwood Report as 'benevolent dictatorships'. Many senior staff in this era saw most maladjusted pupils as basically normal children, reacting in sometimes extreme or unsocial ways to abnormal childhood experiences. A teacher-dominated life-style in an environment which contrasted in size and location but not dramatically in curriculum or 'discipline' terms from the mainstream was thought sufficient (Min. of Ed., 1955; see also Bridgeland, 1971). This viewpoint was shared by a later Senior Medical Officer at the Department of Education and Science: 'Unfortunately after fifty years of child guidance services there is little firm, recorded data about their role and value' (1974: 12).

Government requirements in Circular 2/75 (DES, 1975), which altered assessment procedures, took some power away from school medical officers, passing them to school psychologists. Laslett (1983) saw this as a sign of the growing ascendancy of a more 'educational model'. His earlier book (Laslett, 1977) had also reflected the growing recognition of the value of the educational curriculum, although in his view this was an aid to meeting the special schools' primary purpose: the addressing of pupils' personal and social development.

PROVISION FOR YOUNG OFFENDERS AND OTHER CHILDREN 'AT RISK'

The punitive, over-regimented regimes of some 'old-fashioned' approved schools for offenders and other 'at risk' youth probably deserved David Wills' (1971) criticism. However, Millham et al. (1975) and Hyland (1993) record better practice that would seem to have passed into later schools for children with EBD. Millham et al. (1975) described the clientele of the approved schools as unstable, anxious boys with low self-image who were guilty only of petty crime 'ineptly performed and of little more than nuisance value', and apparently little different from many of the pupils attending provision for so-called maladjusted children. Millham et al.'s extended participant observation gave rise to their preference for constant-activity training schools which stressed education, vocational training and sport. They noted that:

> Boys differ markedly from adults in the sorts of regimes that they enjoy ... Some flourish on cross-country runs, maths projects and endless showers, and institutions that provide these should not be viewed as less caring than those which discuss problems at length over cocoa and slices of dripping toast. (1975: 84)

In effective schools of this sort the staff were clearly in control, 'impinged on the boy world' fragmented deviant sub-cultures (see Polsky,

1967) and, thought Millham et al. (1975), had lasting beneficial effects on some young people's behaviour (see also Hyland, 1993).

After the 1969 Children and Young Person's Act, the approved schools were transferred from home office to social service jurisdiction and renamed 'community homes with education' (CHEs). A more child-centred approach was advocated, notably through DHSS (1970), an important publication that stressed the sensitive meeting of physical needs, giving a sense of security, building self-esteem through achievement, and helping a healthy dependence grow into independence. 'Milieu therapy' and the creative use of 'life-space' were again to the fore. However, the hopes of this document were rarely to be realized in practice: rates of re-offending among leavers were now very high and more generous staffing increased costs. Within 20 years most of the CHEs had closed (Hyland, 1993). Young people who once could have gone to CHEs tended to enter the expanding special schools for the maladjusted, to which their staff also gravitated.

THE NATIONAL SURVEY OF ENGLAND, 1975–78

Wilson and Evans' (1980) and Dawson's (1980) major national study re-examined many of the issues discussed by the Underwood Report. The national system of schools' psychological services had been created. Many more day schools and special classes attached to mainstream schools existed, as well as more residential provision. Also, there was a growing number of special 'units' for the disruptive.

Perhaps in contrast to developing practice in the United States, most provision paid only limited attention to the psychodynamic approach and indeed, despite increasing publicity, to behaviour modification (Wilson and Evans, 1980). The majority favoured a humanistic (perhaps cognitive-behaviourist?) standpoint – what mattered was working through close relationships, attending to needs theory and reversing a child's expectancy of failure by ensuring that he or she achieved regular success in a range of activities which boosted low self-esteem. Talking and listening to children was crucial. Help targeted on underachievement in basic literacy and numeracy and a general educational approach was seen as important – even as therapy. Maladjusted children were also believed, by a clear majority of respondents to Dawson, Wilson and Evans, to appreciate steady routines and clear structures. The value of residential schools was also underlined.

EMOTIONAL AND BEHAVIOURAL DIFFICULTIES IN THE 1980s AND 1990s

In the latter decades of the twentieth century the themes and approaches already discussed continued to be central issues.

In England, the category of maladjustment – seen as stigmatizing and unsatisfactory – was abolished by the inclusionist 1981 Education Act. In the United States, the federal category of 'severe emotional disturbance', used at least since the first Individuals with Disabilities Education Act (IDEA) of 1978, continued although the term 'EBD' came to be favoured (Nelson and Pearson, 1991). In England, 'maladjustment' was soon unofficially replaced by the term 'EBD': some descriptor was necessary for policy construction and resource allocation and EBD (a phrase employed by the Underwood Report in 1955) seemed a step forward. The government's Circular 9/94 contained another vague 'catch-all' definition:

> Children with EBD are on a continuum. Their problems are clearer and greater than sporadic naughtiness or moodiness and yet not so great as to be classed as mental illness. (DFE, 1994b: 4)

The problems of children with EBD range from 'social maladaption to abnormal emotional stresses' (1994b: 7). They 'are persistent and constitute learning difficulties' (1994b: 7). Detailed amplification followed in which emotional factors, creating relationship problems, were counterpoised with externalized behaviour including truanting, aggression, violence and destructive behaviour. The causes were usually complex and ecosystemic, involving school and home factors. Whether a child had EBD depended on 'frequency, persistence, severity or abnormality and cumulative effect of the behaviour in context' compared to 'normal' children (1994b: 8). A small minority had clear psychiatric difficulties for whom close inter-agency working, with substantial input from specialist services, was especially important. This allusion to the need for close trans-disciplinary working was hardly new (see Underwood Report: Min of Ed., 1955), but was to be re-iterated with greater regularity in this decade on both sides of the Atlantic as the damage done by what the Americans Nelson and Pearson (1991) called 'the isolation and fragmentation of services' (1991: viii) was again stressed.

There were continuing and perhaps increasing concerns about the perceived threat posed to good order in mainstream American schools by children labelled EBD, sometimes following trades union campaigning or during media frenzy surrounding extreme events (for example, the Columbine massacre). In the United Kingdom, the Elton Report *Discipline in Schools* found teachers ground down by repeated minor disruption but rarely 'beaten up' (DES, 1989b). Again echoing advice being offered in the United States in the 1980s and 1990s (Skiba and Peterson, 2000), Elton advocated whole-school preventative approaches to behaviour management and the need for all teachers to learn and apply basic classroom techniques. These messages fed into Circular 8/94 *Pupil Behaviour and Discipline* (DFE, 1994a). Despite this advice, there was a four-fold rise in the number of students reported as legally excluded from schools before action from a government committed to promoting school and social inclusion helped to counter this. On both sides of the Atlantic, this was the period of an over-arching concern for 'inclusion' and the perhaps false assumption that this was best pursued by maintaining a minority of students against their wishes and perhaps against their interests in unresponsive, sometimes rejecting, mainstream schools (Cole, 1989; Kauffman, 2001; Cole et al., 2003). Despite the press for inclusion, the use of segregated provision for children with EBD increased in the United States in the 1990s (Kauffman, 2001) and was maintained at a similar level in Britain, where rapid expansion of off-site unit provision (under the name of 'Pupil Referral Units') off-set any closures of EBD schools (Cole, 2002; Cole et al., 2003).

While Her Majesty's Inspectors (HMI) criticized low standards of education and sometimes care and discipline in many EBD schools and special units in the 1980s (for example, DES, 1989a) and in the 1990s (OFSTED, 1995), the continuing usefulness of such provision was officially recognized in various government publications (for example, DFE, 1994b; DFEE, 1997; DFEE, 1998; OFSTED, 1999). Kauffman (2001) notes that federal American law (IDEA) and associated regulations continued to mandate a continuum of alternative placements including support in the mainstream, special classes and day schools and residential 'treatment centers'.

When a compulsory national curriculum was introduced to England after the Education Reform Act of 1988, EBD special schools were not exempted from its requirements. This had a dramatic effect on some schools who clearly placed therapy ahead of formal education. Some psychotherapists, such as Orr (1995), and some teachers (for example, Marchant, 1995) condemned the change. However, it was welcomed by a majority of headteachers and forced special schools to focus on the quality and range of teaching, making many abandon an easy-going, pastoral culture where nationally accredited courses were rare (Cole et al., 1998).

Key school improvement texts of this period, for example, Mortimore et al. (1983) and Ainscow (1991), were also influential. Charlton and David (1993) asserted that 'effectiveness' factors, taken from a wide British and American literature, tended to be present in schools that successfully managed difficult behaviour. These included:

- consultative and collaborative leadership which takes into account pupil and parent opinion;
- consistently applied school-wide policies on education and behaviour management;
- differentiated curricula;
- high but not unreasonable academic expectations;
- positive behaviour management stressing prevention and offering more rewards than sanctions;
- efficient and punctual staff offering skilful, responsive teaching;
- supportive and respectful relationships between all adults and pupils; and
- effective systems of pastoral care.

Research into mainstream and special school EBD provision in England (for example, Cooper, 1993; Cole et al., 1998; Daniels et al., 1998) and in Scotland (for example, Munn et al., 2000) underlined that such factors were indeed relevant. These factors also overlapped with the US government's seven strategic targets for children with EBD set in 1994 (Kauffman, 2001).

School improvement research also influenced the English government's advice (Circulars 8/94 and 9/94) on coping with difficult behaviour and the education of children with EBD in mainstream and other settings. The English government clearly wanted 'mainstream' type approaches to predominate in special schools and units. Staff were advised to 'establish firm boundaries of behaviour for all pupils. Good standards of behaviour should be the norm' (Circular 9/94, para. 68, p. 24). However, extra emphasis was needed on the affective needs of children to assist their personal and social development. Staff should look at the emotions beneath the surface behaviour, in short, to be aware of the theoretical perspectives to which allusion has been made in the pages above. Education (in the form of remedial help in literacy skills) was seen as building pupils' morale and self-esteem (para. 98). The 'triangle of needs' (Maslow, 1943) still held sway. Teaching style had to be carefully attuned to pupil learning style as adherents of behaviourist, cognitive/ behaviourist theory and ecosystemic approaches would advise (see Cooper et al., 1994; Cole et al., 1998): 'It is important to set short-term targets and goals which will stretch but not overwhelm them, to involve them in the formation of these learning goals and to establish high expectations of their performance' (Circular 9/94: 23). A collaborative approach to learning could help pupils to break out of negative cycles of pessimistic thinking about their abilities into which they were often locked.

The section on residential schooling worried about its high cost but again recognized that boarding can be beneficial where learning difficulties exist and/or 'where family support is lacking or inadequate, or family influence is damaging' (para. 73, p. 27). Where placement is essentially socially driven (as Cole et al., 1998, found), then social services should share the costs. Visser and Cole (1996) identified a marked reduction in the use of boarding in the 1990s.

Cole et al.'s national study, the first since Wilson and Evans (1980), and studies by government inspectors (OFSTED, 1999) found further support for the 'good practice' summarized in Circular 9/94. They also supported Cooper's (1993) finding that pupils in effective special schools were helped in three major areas – respite, relationships and re-signification. Children from stressful and disadvantaging family backgrounds and inappropriate mainstream schooling were provided with *respite* in special schools where they were able to form beneficial *relationships* with staff and peers. Here, they could be provided with appropriate, challenging learning experiences and emotional support which enabled them to cast off the negative labels with which they had been tagged and according to which they had lived, *re-signifying* themselves in a more positive light.

CONCLUSION

In this chapter, salient and still resonating developments and ideas from the past have been sketched. Kauffman rightly notes that the prominent dilemmatic issues at the start of the twenty-first century 'all have historical roots many decades deep and will likely remain problems for many decades to come' (2001: 86). From my perspective, there *are* 'lessons of history' and these include:

- the quality and commitment of the professionals serving children and youth with EBD matter more than the espousal of any particular conceptual or practical model;
- education, broadly defined, can indeed be therapy but the 'E' in 'EBD' must be given prominence;
- combined children's services, spanning the professions, should be given a real chance to prove themselves;
- mainstream schools should and can be made inclusive for more pupils with EBD (Cole et al., 2001);
- running effective 'alternative' provision is usually a difficult challenge; nevertheless –
- a range of contrasting forms of provision continues to be essential for some children with EBD.

Connected to this last point, about 1 per cent of American children and youth (Kauffman, 2001) and perhaps 0.5 per cent of British pupils

(Cole et al., 2003) receive specialist services for young people with EBD or deemed seriously disruptive. There are likely to remain another 1–5 per cent of the school population who perhaps should receive more specialist help (Cole et al., 2003; Kauffman, 2001). If in an imperfect world we are to respect some of these children's rights (and *their* wishes), then enforced and under-resourced 'mainstreaming' posing as 'inclusion' is less likely than responsive, well-run alternative provision to achieve meaningful *social* inclusion for them.

REFERENCES

Ainscow, M. (ed.) (1991) *Effective Schools for All*. London: David Fulton.

Bettelheim, B. (1950) *Love is Not Enough*. Glencoe, IL: Free Press.

Bridgeland, M. (1971) *Pioneer Work with Maladjusted Children*. London: Staples.

Carr, E.H. (1961) *What is History?* Harmondsworth: Pelican.

Charlton, T. and David, K. (eds) (1993) *Managing Misbehaviour in Schools*. London: Routledge.

Cole, T. (1989) *Apart or A Part? Integration and the Growth of British Special Education*. Milton Keynes: Open University Press.

Cole, T. (2002) 'Pupil Referral Unit Review', *AWCEBD Newsletter*, Autumn Edition. Maidstone: The Association of Workers for Children with EBD. pp. 7–9.

Cole, T. Daniels, H. and Visser, J. (2003) 'Patterns of provision for pupils with behavioural difficulties in England: a study of government statistics and behaviour support plan data', *Oxford Review of Education* 29 (2): 187–205.

Cole, T. and Visser, J. (1999) 'The history of special provision for pupils with EBD in England: what has proved effective?', *Behavioral Disorders*, 25 (1): 56–64.

Cole, T., Visser, J. and Daniels, H. (2001) 'Inclusive practice for pupils with emotional and behavioural difficulties in mainstream schools', in J. Visser, H. Daniels, and T. Cole (eds), *Emotional and Behavioural Difficulties in Mainstream Schools*. London: JAI. pp. 183–94.

Cole, T., Visser, J. and Upton, G. (1998) *Effective Schooling for Pupils with Emotional and Behavioural Difficulties*. London: David Fulton.

Cooper, P. (1993) *Effective Schooling for Disaffected Pupils*. London: Routledge.

Cooper, P., Smith, C. and Upton, G. (1994) *Emotional and Behavioural Difficulties*. London: Routledge.

Daniels, H., Visser, J., Cole, T., and de Reybekill, N. (1998) *Emotional and Behavioural Difficulties in Mainstream Schools*. Research Report RR90. London: DfEE.

Dawson, R. (1980) *Special Provision for Disturbed Pupils: A Survey*. London: Macmillan.

Department for Education (1994a) *Pupil Behaviour and Discipline*. Circular 8/94. London: DFE.

Department for Education (1994b) *Emotional and Behavioural Difficulties*. Circular 9/94. London: DFE.

Department for Education and Employment (1997) *Excellence for All Children: Meeting Special Educational Needs* (Green Paper). London: DfEE.

Department for Education and Employment (1998) *Meeting Special Educational Needs: A Programme of Action*. London: DfEE.

Department of Education and Science (1974) *The Health of the School Child, 1971–2*. London: HMSO.

Department of Education and Science (1989a) *Special Schools for Pupils with EBD*. Circular 23/89. London: DES.

Department of Education and Science (1989b) *Discipline in Schools: Report of the Committee of Enquiry Chaired by Lord Elton*. London: HMSO.

Department of Health and Social Security (1970) *Care and Treatment in a Planned Environment: Advisory Council on Child Care*. London: HMSO.

DES (1975) *Circular 2/75*. London: DES.

Eddy, J.M. and Gribskov, L.S. (1998) 'Juvenile justice and delinquency prevention in the United States: the influence of theories and tradition on policies and practices', in Gullota, T.P., Adams, G.R. and Montomayor, R. (eds), *Delinquent Violent Youth*. pp. 12–52.

Franklin, M. (1945) *The Use and Misuse of Planned Environmental Therapy*. London: Psychological and Social Services.

Grimshaw, R. with Berridge, D. (1994) *Educating Disruptive Children*. London: National Childrens' Bureau.

Hyland, J. (1993) *Yesterday's Answers; Development and Decline of Schools for Young Offenders*. London: Whiting and Birch/SCA.

Kauffman, J.M. (2001) *Characteristics of Emotional and Behavioural Disorders of Children and Youth*. 7th edition. Englewood Cliffs, NJ: Merrill, Prentice Hall.

Laslett, R. (1977) *Educating Maladjusted Children*. London: Granada.

Laslett, R. (1983) *Changing Perceptions of Maladjusted Children*. London: AWMC.

Marchant, S. (1995) 'The essential curriculum for pupils exhibiting emotional and behavioural difficulties', *Therapeutic Care and Education*, 4 (2): 36–47.

Maslow, A.H. (1943) 'A theory of human motivation', *Psychological Review*, 50: 370–96.

Millham, S., Bullock, R., Cherrett, P. (1975) *After Grace-Teeth*. London: Chaucer.

Ministry of Education (1946) *Boarding School Provision for ESN and Maladjusted Children*. Circular 79. London.

Ministry of Education (1953) *School Health Service and Handicapped Pupils' Regulations*. S. 1156, pt IIIg. London: HMSO.

Ministry of Education (1955) *Report of the Committee on Maladjusted Children* (the Underwood Report). London: HMSO.

Mortimore, P., Sammons, L., Stoll, L. and Ecob, R. (1983) *School Matters*. Wells: Open Books.

Munn, P., Lloyd, G. and Cullen, M. (2000) *Alternatives to School Exclusion*. London: Paul Chapman.

Nelson, C.M. and Pearson, C.A. (1991) *Integrating Services for Children and Youth with Emotional and Behavioral Disorders*. Reston: Council for Exceptional Children.

OFSTED (1995) *Annual Report of Her Majesty's Chief Inspector of Schools*. London: OFSTED.

OFSTED (1999) *Principles into Practice: Effective Education for Pupils with EBD*. London: OFSTED.

Orr, R. (1995) 'A prescription for failure', *Special Children*, September, 86: 24–5.

Polsky, H. (1967) *Cottage Six*. New York: Wiley.

Redl, F. and Wineman, D. (1952) *Controls from Within*. New York: Free Press.

Skiba, R.J. and Peterson, R.L. (2000) 'School Discipline at a Crossroads', *Exceptional Children*, 66 (3): 335–46.

Trieschman, A., Whittaker, J.K., Brendtro, L. (1969) *The Other Twenty-three Hours*. Chicago: Aldine.

Visser, J. and Cole, T. (1996) 'An overview of English special school provision for children with EBDs', *Emotional and Behavioural Difficulties*, 1 (3): 11–16.

Wills, D. (1971) *Spare the Child*. Harmondsworth: Penguin.

Wilson, M. and Evans, M. (1980) *Education of Disturbed Pupils*. London: Methuen.

4

Defining Emotional or Behavioral Disorders: The Quest for Affirmation

KENNETH A. KAVALE, STEVEN R. FORNESS
AND MARK P. MOSTERT

The high incidence, mild disabilities (specific learning disability (LD), mental retardation (MR), emotional disturbance (ED)) represent the largest group of students receiving special education in the United States. Yet, these categories have failed to acheive consensus about the way they should be defined. Both LD (see Kavale and Forness, 2000) and MR (see MacMillan et al., 1993) continue to experience contentious debate about definition. Similarly, ED is experiencing tensions about definition (see Kavale et al., 1996). Basically, the definitions offered lack precision and this creates vague boundary conditions among categories. Consequently, the high-incidence, mild disabilities tend to demonstrate more similarities than differences, which makes it difficult to reliably differentiate among them (Hallahan and Kauffman, 1977). The lack of clear definition means that any single classification does not possess validity because it will not yield groups whose characteristics are known from the assigned labels (Zigler and Hodapp, 1986).

For ED, definitional problems are compounded by the different social contexts where they are used. An ED label is assigned through cultural rules that demonstrate considerable variability across contexts and make the process inherently subjective (Forness, 1996). The result is a high degree of 'clinical judgment' in ED designation (Smith et al., 1988). At best, ED definitions describe a general population, but encounter difficulty when applied to individual cases because a uniform interpretation is lacking.

DEFINITIONS OF EMOTIONAL OR BEHAVIORAL DISORDERS

Many definitions of ED have been offered, but none has successfully resolved perceived problems and achieved consensus. Any ED definition stresses that the behaviors in question meet three criteria: severity, frequency, chronicity. Within the context of these criteria, the federal ED definition in the Individuals with Disabilities Education Act (IDEA) stipulates five characteristics:

1   An inability to learn which cannot be explained by intellectual, sensory, and health factors.
2   An inability to build or maintain satisfactory relationships with peers and teachers.
3   Inappropriate types of behavior or feelings under normal circumstances.
4   A general pervasive mood of unhappiness or depression.
5   A tendency to develop physical symptoms or fears associated with personal or school problems.

The characteristics stipulated in the ED definition have their origin in Bower's (1960) definition of 'emotionally handicapped'. From its codification in 1975, there was dissatisfaction with the IDEA definition because of its inherent vagueness and imprecision. The decision-making structure created was simply too subjective. For example, what is an inability to learn? Does it refer to only academic learning or can social learning be included? How exactly are satisfactory interpersonal relationships defined? What are normal conditions? When is unhappiness pervasive?

The IDEA definition possessed other difficulties. First, from 1975 to 1997, the condition being defined was 'seriously emotionally disturbed' (SED), which made it the only federal category to include an indication about severity level and potential problems when dealing with 'mild' problems (Forness, 1990). Second, an initial statement about characteristics being demonstrated over a long period of time and to a marked degree was extended to include 'which adversely affects educational performance'. This phrase seems unnecessary since the first stipulated characteristic deals directly with educational performance ('an inability to learn') (Forness, 1992a). Additionally, what if a student, for example, only manifests the 'inability to learn' criterion? The possible confounding with the LD classification seems evident (Forness et al., 1983). An emphasis on educational performance could potentially work against a student who, for example, demonstrated 'a general pervasive mood of unhappiness or depression' but no academic problems.

The most problematic aspect of the federal definition was a statement indicating who was included and who was excluded. The definition included children who were schizophrenic, which was compatible with the SED nomenclature. In subsequent reauthorizations, the federal definition was modified to exclude students with autism who were classified under 'Other Health Impairments' because of its presumed biophysical origin (Forness and Kavale, 1984). In 1990, autism was made a separate category.

Although schizophrenia was included, the SED definition 'does not include children who are socially maladjusted, unless it is demonstrated that they are seriously emotionally disturbed.' Since social maladjustment was not given specification in the law, it came to be defined in terms of disruptive and antisocial behavior (Forness, 1992b). Generally, such behavior is often equated with conduct disorder (CD) characterized by a persistent pattern of behavior violating basic rights of others or age-appropriate social rules (APA, 1994). Symptoms include a variety of aggressive, destructive, dishonest, or noncompliant behaviors (Kazdin, 1995). Given these parameters, it seems illogical to exclude students because their problems are considered to be 'merely' CD (Center, 1990) while the actual underlying emotional disorders may not be recognized because the more evident 'social maladjustment' is excluded (Forness, 1992b). Clearly, social maladjustment may be evidenced in the federal definitional criteria (especially b and/or c) which, in fact, were originally meant to be indicators of social maladjustment (Bower, 1982). Thus, strict adherence to the federal definition would seem to exclude children on the basis for which they might be included and thus enable schools to *not* serve children with significant behavioral problems (Cline, 1990).

An enduring problem continued to surround terminology. The Council for Children with Behavioral Disorders (CCBD) endorsed the term 'behavior disorder' in place of 'emotional disturbance'. The advantages were seen in a) focusing attention on clearly observable aspects of the problem (that is, disordered behavior), b) no suggestion about any particular theoretical perspective, and c) less stigma (Huntze, 1985). The concern about stigmatization was supported by findings that the label 'behaviorally disordered' implied less negative connotations to teachers than did 'emotionally disturbed' (Feldman et al., 1983). Nevertheless, the longstanding definition of emotional disturbance suggested that terminology should include the possibility that a student may have emotional or behavioral problems or both (Forness and Kavale, 1997).

In 1992, a definition of emotional or behavioral disorder (E/BD) was proposed by the National Mental Health and Special Education Coalition (see Forness and Knitzer, 1992). The definition reads as follows:

(i)   The term emotional or behavioral disorder means a disability characterized by behavioral or emotional responses in school programs so different from appropriate age, cultural, or ethnic norm that the responses adversely affect educational performance, including academic, social, vocational, and personal skills. Such a disability

(A)   is more than a temporary, expected response to stressful events in the environment.
(B)   is consistently exhibited in two different settings, at least one of which is school-related; and
(C)   is unresponsive to direct intervention in general education, or the child's condition is such that general education interventions would be insufficient.

(ii) Emotional and behavioral disorders can co-exist with other disabilities.
(iii) This category may include children or youth with schizophrenic disorders, affective disorder, anxiety disorder, or other sustained disorders of conduct or adjustment where they adversely affect educational performance in accordance with section (i). (Forness and Knitzer, 1992)

The definition resolves many problems by 1) recognizing that disorders of emotion and behavior can occur separately or in combination, 2) recognizing cultural and ethnic differences, 3) eliminating minor or transient problems, 4) recognizing that problems exhibited outside of school are important, 5) recognizing the possibility of multiple disabilities, and 6) eliminating arbitrary exclusions (Forness and Kavale, 2000).

Although the E/BD definition provides a more comprehensive perspective, eligibility remains predicated primarily on impaired educational performance. This places the definition in a special education context, but the E/BD phenomenon may also be the province of other agencies with different definitional perspectives (Forness, 1996). For example, the *Diagnostic and Statistical Manual of Mental Disorders-IV* (DSM-IV) focuses on the psychiatric bases of 'mental disorder' which is 'conceptualized as a clinically significant behavioral or psychological syndrome or pattern that occurs in an individual' (APA, 1994: xxi). The E/BD concept thus becomes far more generalized, which introduces greater problems in determining eligibility. Across agencies, there exists the possibility that a student might be found eligible in one system yet not meet criteria provided in a different agency definition (Forness and Kavale, 1997). School and mental health agencies thus operate in a parallel rather than a cooperative or interactive manner (Mattison and Forness, 1995). Consequently, special education and mental health diagnostic categories may not be concordant (Sinclair et al., 1985).

The problem of definition

The lack of precision in the ED definition creates potential confounding with other categories and LD provides a prime example. The LD definition clearly focuses on 'an inability to learn' manifested in significant academic underachievement (Kavale and Forness, 2000). Additionally, the LD definition also includes an exclusion clause indicating that the learning problems 'cannot be explained by intellectual, sensory, or health factors.' The definitions thus share many common features. In fact, large-scale evaluations have demonstrated the similarities in the academic deficits manifested by students with ED and LD (Stone and Rowley, 1964; Forness et al., 1983). Similarly, students with LD often tend to demonstrate behavioral difficulties closely resembling those found in students with ED (Epstein et al., 1983; McConaughy and Ritter, 1985). This is particularly the case for social skill deficits which are manifested by a majority of students with LD (Kavale and Forness, 1996) and led the Interagency Committee on Learning Disabilities definition of LD to include social skill deficits as a primary LD (see Kavanagh and Truss, 1988). Forness and Kavale (1991) pointed out the logical dilemma of diagnosing LD without the historically important academic deficits but, more importantly, the confounding it would cause with ED because social skill deficits are conceptually closer to ED than LD. Thus, the boundaries between ED and LD are imprecise and analyses generally fail to find clear distinctions between these categories (for example, Epstein and Cullinan, 1983; Fessler et al., 1991; Scruggs and Mastropieri, 1986).

Balkanization in special education

The difficulties in defining ED may not be related solely to a lack of precision, but rather in isolating the nature of a particular condition when there is a strong possibility that it may possess characteristics similar to other related conditions. The dilemma becomes one of how best to disentangle the conditions of interest from overlapping conditions (Achenbach, 1990/1991). For example, suppose that almost all individuals meeting criteria for condition X, 50 percent also meet criteria for condition Y, and

40 percent meet criteria for condition Z; substantial overlap exists between conditions Y and Z. Similarly, suppose there is also a high probability that almost all individuals who meet criteria for condition Z will meet criteria for condition X, while 25 percent will meet criteria for condition Y. Given these relationships, the question becomes: Do these relatively independent conditions represent phenotypic manifestations of the same underlying disorder or are they co-morbid conditions that co-exist in the same individual?

The tendency has been to view diagnostic categories as relatively independent conditions ignoring the possibility that they are co-morbid conditions (Tankersley and Landrum, 1997). This tendency has resulted in periodic calls to make each discrete disorder a separate category of special education.

The process of creating new special education categories has been likened to the geopolitical process of Balkanization where a region divides into smaller (and often antagonistic) units (Forness and Kavale, 1994). Balkanization generally begins with the recognition of a separate identity for an ethnic people, followed by movement to create a separate government to better accommodate the group's needs, and often introduces a process of 'ethnic cleansing' to ensure that only select individuals are included in the newly created state. Five disorders exemplify the Balkanization of special education because they either have become new categories or have seen serious efforts to establish them as separate categories. These disorders are: attention deficit hyperactivity disorder; traumatic brain injury; fetal alcohol syndrome; post-traumatic stress syndrome; and fragile X syndrome. When these 'new' behavior disorders are examined in relation to specific problem areas (for example, below-average IQ, language impairment, underachievement, inattention, conduct disorder, depressive disorder, anxiety disorder), significant overlap exists across the five disorders. In fact, there appears to be more symptom variability *within* disorders than across disorders. These 'new' disorders also demonstrate a great deal in common with the existing ED and LD categories. Consequently, confounding among disorders is probable and the Balkanization process may only waste valuable resources in attempting to determine eligibility for ever more circumscribed categories.

Attention deficit hyperactivity disorder

Among the 'new' behavior disorders, attention deficit hyperactivity disorder (ADHD) is perhaps most problematic because it illustrates how the issue of co-occurrence tends to be a confounding factor.

The ADHD concept emanated from the study of brain injury whose sequelae might include inattention, hyperactivity, and impulsivity

(Barkley, 1998). Over time, the ADHD concept has witnessed substantial changes in nomenclature and criteria, but the concept remains an ill-defined constellation of behaviors that calls into question its validity as a distinct diagnostic entity (Prior and Sanson, 1986).

The difficulty in defining ADHD creates the possibility of substantial overlap with related conditions (Silver, 1990). For example, the exact association between ADHD and LD is difficult to specify because co-morbidity rates have been found to range from 10 percent to 90 percent (for example, Biederman et al., 1991; Bussing et al., 1998; Marshall et al., 1997). A similar relationship exists between ADHD and CD (Gresham et al., 1998; Reeves et al., 1987). The situation is further complicated by a strong association between CD and LD (Hunt and Cohen, 1984). Cantwell and Baker (1987) found a large proportion of an LD sample also had some type of psychiatric diagnosis, with the most common being ADHD (40 percent) followed by CD (9 percent). Thus, although ADHD, LD, and CD can occur independently, there is a high probability that they may also co-occur, which raises questions about the nature of the associations: Are they subtypes of the same disorder? Does one predispose an individual to another? Do they share a common etiology that produces distinct syndromes? Until answers are forthcoming, precise definitions are not likely to be achieved (Forness and Kavale, 2002).

Emotional disorders and LD

There appears to be an association between emotional disorders (for example, anxiety, depression, mood disorders) and LD (Weinberg and Rehmet, 1983). For example, among LD samples, depressive symptoms can range from 26 percent to 36 percent (Wright-Strawderman and Watson, 1992). Forness (1988) found, in a sample of children diagnosed with depression, that 57 percent revealed co-morbidity in the form of a secondary diagnosis of ADHD, ED, or LD. Similar findings about co-morbidity were found when the primary diagnosis was ADHD (Sinclair et al., 1985) or CD (Forness et al., 1993). With respect to anxiety and mood disorders, in an LD sample, Cantwell and Baker (1987) found mood disorder more common than anxiety disorder at diagnosis (17 percent vs. 2 percent) but, at follow-up, anxiety was present at a higher rate than mood disorder (25 percent vs. 10 percent).

CD and ED

The co-morbidity issue is critical for ED because the failure to recognize co-occurrence may decrease the likelihood of a student being found eligible for special education. Recall that the federal definition stipulates that a student may not be considered for the ED category if the primary problem is viewed as social maladjustment. Yet, when social maladjustment is placed in the context of CD, it represents one of the most prevalent and most enduring of all psychiatric conditions (Offord and Bennett, 1994). Consequently, it would be advantageous to view CD as a 'complex' disorder where overt CD is co-morbid with other psychiatric disorders (Forness et al., 1993).

Forness et al. (1994) described how complex CD might be symptomatic of other underlying psychiatric disorders. There exists the possibility that the two major behaviors associated with CD (that is, not paying attention and disrupting classroom activities) may not be recognized as expressions of co-morbid disorders such as ADHD (Cantwell, 1996), mood disorder (Kovacs, 1996), anxiety disorder (Bernstein and Borchardt, 1991), or even schizophrenic disorder (Volkmer, 1996). For example, in mood disorder (such as depression) inattention may derive from diminished ability to concentrate, while disruptive behavior may derive from the primary symptom of irritability.

Forness et al. (1994) estimated the prevalence for 'complex' CD (that is, CD plus one of four psychiatric disorders) to be more than half (2.3 percent) of the prevalence for CD itself, which is generally viewed as approximately 4 percent. Complex CD may also be associated with other disorders, such as LD, especially if social skill deficits are present (San Miguel et al., 1996). Additional possible disorders include physical and sexual abuse (Cicchetti and Toth, 1995) and post-traumatic stress disorder (APA, 1994), whose sequelae often mimic CD symptomology. These possibilities were validated by findings showing that, in a large ED group, nearly two-thirds had a CD diagnosis and two-thirds of this group also had another co-morbid psychiatric diagnosis (Greenbaum et al., 1996). Thus, 'complex' CD may be more prevalent than 'simple' CD.

ED, LD, co-morbidity, and diagnostic validity

The failure to recognize co-morbidity may produce negative consequences related to the validity of individual diagnoses and the effectiveness of intervention efforts. Given the nature of the federal definitions for ED and LD, the issue of co-morbidity is not usually addressed in school assessments, which increases the potential for misclassification or no classification (that is, not being found eligible). On the intervention side, the treatment approaches suggested, although seemingly appropriate for the primary problem, may not be comprehensive or focused enough to effect possible disorders accompanying the primary symptomotology. For example, in a group of children diagnosed with depression or CD, special education eligibility was most likely when there was co-morbid LD (Forness, 1988; Forness et al., 1993). Thus, with depressive disorder or CD as a primary diagnosis, special education eligibility appears predicated, to a significant extent, on the presence of severely compromised educational performance (that is, LD).

The question of eligibility must be placed in the context of problems in identifying LD related primarily to the reliance on an IQ-achievement discrepancy, which means that the learning problems associated with psychiatric disorders may not actually be 'true' LD but are labeled as such (Kavale and Forness, 1995). For example, Forness et al. (1993) studied a group that was equally divided between a 'pure' ADHD group and a 'mixed' ADHD group (that is, concurrent with CD) and found them similar with respect to IQ levels, but the 'mixed' group was more impaired academically, which meant greater likelihood of an LD diagnosis because of the presence of a significant IQ-achievement discrepancy.

For ED, Duncan et al. (1995) found a significant delay before an ED classification was established. For a large ED sample, although some psychiatric intervention began at mean age 6.4 years, special education referral usually for LD did not begin until mean age 7.8 years, while the final ED placement did not occur until mean age 10.4 years. About half the sample had concurrent disruptive and anti-social behaviors which may have provided a barrier to appropriate identification because of the 'social maladjustment' exclusion found in the ED definition. Thus, the initial school action for an ED sample was usually for other problems (for example, LD), and perhaps five years passed until there was appropriate special education placement (that is, ED). Similarly, Del'Homme et al. (1996) found a relatively small proportion of referrals for students with solely behavior problems as opposed to combined (behavioral and academic) problems, suggesting that potential ED was under-identified either because the focus was on academic difficulties (that is, LD) or because the behavioral problems were related to disruptive and antisocial behavior (that is, CD) and hence excluded from ED consideration.

The potential for disregarding the significance of ED was also found by Lopez et al. (1996), who tracked 150 students in grades 2 to 4 meeting strict research-based criteria for ED, ADHD, and LD. Findings showed that 37 percent of ADHD and 50 percent of ED students were placed in an LD program, but only 9 percent of ADHD and none of the ED group were considered for ED placement. In fact, only *one* student out of 55 with ADHD or ED who might reasonably be expected to receive ED services actually received them. Why were 54 placed in a seemingly inappropriate program? It appears that the 'social maladjustment' exclusion criterion for

ED meant that such students were placed in LD programs in order to provide at least some special education services. The LD program, however, may be inappropriate because they usually lack an emphasis on remediating the behavior problems prominent in ED or ADHD (Forness et al., 1996).

CONCLUSION

The definition of ED in US federal law remains contentious. Although positive modifications have been made, the ED definition still does not provide a clear and unencumbered view of the phenomenon. Consequently, the ED definition has not been applied rigorously and systematically, resulting in much imprecision in the classification process.

A prime contributor to the imprecision is a failure to recognize co-morbidity, the co-occurrence of two or more conditions in the same individual. For ED, a major source of confounding is the LD category which possesses its own definitional problems, especially when social skill deficits are primary in discussing LD status. The situation for ED becomes further complicated by increasing recognition that ADHD, CD, and psychiatric diagnoses (for example, depressive disorder, mood disorder, anxiety disorder) may co-occur in complex associations that may cause one or more of these conditions to be overlooked.

The failure to acknowledge the co-existence of independent disorders has resulted in definitions of single disorders that are imprecise. The concurrent disorders may be primary or secondary, but not considering the many possibilities may adversely influence the diagnostic process by resulting in either misclassification or, more serious, no classification.

REFERENCES

Achenbach, T.M. (1990/1991) ' "Comorbidity" in child and adolescent psychiatry: categorical and quantitative perspectives', *Journal of Child and Adolescent Psychopharmacology*, 1: 271–8.

American Psychiatric Association (1994) *Diagnostic and Statistical Manual of Mental Disorders* (4th edn). Washington, DC: APA.

Barkley, R.A. (1998) *Attention Deficit Hyperactivity Disorder: A Handbook for Diagnosis and Treatment* (2nd edn). New York: Guilford.

Bernstein, G.A. and Borchardt, C.M. (1991) 'Anxiety disorders of childhood and adolescence: a critical review', *Journal of the American Academy of Child and Adolescent Psychiatry*, 30: 519–32.

Biederman, J., Newcorn, J. and Sprich, S. (1991) 'Comorbidity of attention deficit hyperactivity disorder with conduct, depressive, anxiety, and other disorders', *American Journal of Psychiatry*, 148: 564–77.

Bower, E.H. (1960) *Early Identification of Emotionally Handicapped Children in Schools.* Springfield, IL: Thomas.

Bower, E.M. (1982) 'Defining emotional disturbance: public policy and research', *Psychology in the Schools*, 19: 55–60.

Bussing, R., Zima, B.T., Belin, T.R. and Forness, S.R. (1998) 'Children who qualify for LD and SED programs: do they differ in level of ADHD symptoms and comorbid psychiatric conditions?', *Journal of Emotional Disorders*, 22: 85–97.

Cantwell, D.P. (1996) 'Attention deficit disorder: a review of the past 10 years', *Journal of the American Academy of Child and Adolescent Psychiatry*, 35: 978–87.

Cantwell, D.P. and Baker, L. (1987) *Developmental Speech and Language Disorders.* New York: Guilford.

Center, D.B. (1990) 'Social maladjustment: an interpretation', *Behavioral Disorders*, 15: 141–8.

Cicchetti, D. and Toth, S.L. (1995) 'A developmental psychopathology perspective on child abuse and neglect', *Journal of the American Academy of Child and Adolescent Psychiatry*, 34: 541–65.

Cline, D.H. (1990) 'A legal analysis of policy initiatives to exclude handicapped/disruptive students from special education', *Behavioral Disorders*, 15: 159–73.

Del'Homme, M., Kasari, C., Forness, S.R. and Bagley, R. (1996) 'Prereferral intervention and children at risk for emotional or behavioral disorders', *Education and Treatment of Children*, 19: 272–85.

Duncan, B.B., Forness, S.R. and Hartsough, C. (1995) 'Students identified as seriously emotionally disturbed in day treatment classrooms: cognitive, psychiatric and special education characteristics', *Behavioral Disorders*, 20: 238–52.

Epstein, M.H. and Cullinan, D. (1983) 'Academic performance of behaviorally disordered and learning disabled pupils', *Journal of special Education*, 17: 303–307.

Epstein, M.H., Cullinan, D. and Rosemeir, R. (1983) 'Behavior problem patterns among the learning disabled: boys aged 6–11', *Learning Disabilities Quarterly*, 6: 305–11.

Feldman, D., Kinnison, L., Jay, R. and Harth, R. (1983) 'The effects of differential labeling on professional concepts and attitudes toward the emotionally disturbed/behaviorally disordered', *Behavioral Disorders*, 8: 191–8.

Fessler, M.A., Rosenberg, M.S. and Rosenberg, L.A. (1991) 'Concomitant learning disabilities and learning problems among students with behavioral/emotional disorders', *Behavioral Disorders*, 16: 97–106.

Forness, S.R. (1988) 'School characteristics of children and adolescents with depression', *Monographs in Behavioral Disorders*, 10: 117–203.

Forness, S.R. (1990) 'Resolving the definitional and diagnostic issues of serious emotional disturbance in the schools', in S. Braaten and G. Wrobel (eds), *Perspectives on the Diagnosis and Treatment of Students with Emotional/Behavioral Disorders.* Minneapolis, MN: CCBD. pp. 1–15.

Forness, S.R. (1992a) 'Legalism versus professionalism in diagnosing SED in the public schools', *School Psychology Review*, 21: 29–34.

Forness, S.R. (1992b) 'Broadening the cultural-organizational perspective in exclusion of youth with social maladjustment', *Remedial and Special Education*, 13: 55–9.

Forness, S.R. (1996) 'School children with emotional or behavioral disorders: perspectives on definition, diagnosis, and treatment', in B. Brooks and D. Sabatino (eds), *Personal Perspectives on Emotional or Behavioral Disorders.* Austin, TX: PRO-ED. pp. 84–95.

Forness, S.R., Bennett, L. and Tose, J. (1983) 'Academic deficits in emotionally disturbed children revisited', *Journal of the American Academy of Child and Adolescent Psychiatry*, 22: 140–44.

Forness, S.R. and Kavale, K.A. (1984) 'Autistic children in schools: the role of the pediatrician', *Pediatric Annals*, 13: 319–28.

Forness, S.R. and Kavale, K.A. (1991) 'Social skill deficits as a primary learning disability: a note on problems with the ICLD diagnostic criteria', *Learning Disabilities Research and Practice*, 6: 44–9.

Forness, S.R. and Kavale, K.A. (1994) 'The Balkanization of special education: proliferation of categories for "new" behavioral disorders', *Education and Treatment of Children*, 17: 215–27.

Forness, S.R. and Kavale, K.A. (1997) 'Defining emotional and behavioral disorders in school and related services', in J.W. Lloyd, E.J. Kameenui and D. Chard (eds), *Issues in Educating Students with Disabilities*. Mahwah, NJ: Lawrence Erlbaum. pp. 46–62.

Forness, S.R. and Kavale, K.A. (2000) 'Emotional or behavioral disorders: background and current status of the E/BD terminology and definition', *Behavioral Disorders*, 25: 264–9.

Forness, S.R. and Kavale, K.A. (2002) 'Impact of ADHD on school systems', in P. Jensen and J.R. Cooper (eds), *Attention Deficit Hyperactivity Disorder: State of the Science and Best Practices*. Kingston, NJ: Civic Research Institute. pp. 24/1–20.

Forness, S.R., Kavale, K.A., King, B.H. and Kasari, C. (1994) 'Simple versus complex conduct disorders: identification and phenomenology', *Behavioral Disorders*, 19: 306–12.

Forness, S.R., Kavale, K.A. and Lopez, M. (1993) 'Conduct disorders in school: special education eligibility and co-morbidity', *Journal of Emotional and Behavioral Disorders*, 1: 101–108.

Forness, S.R., Kavale, K.A., MacMillan, D.L., Asarnow, J.R. and Duncan, B.R. (1996) 'Early detection and prevention of emotional or behavioral disorders: developmental aspects of systems of care', *Behavioral Disorders*, 21: 226–40.

Forness, S.R. and Knitzer, J. (1992) 'A new proposed definition and terminology to replace "Serious Emotional Disturbance" in Individuals with Disabilities Education Act', *School Psychology Review*, 21: 12–20.

Greenbaum, P.E., Dedrick, R.F., Friedman, R.M., Kutash, K., Brown, E.C., Lardieri, S.P. and Pugh, A.M. (1996) 'National adolescent and child treatment study (NACTS): outcomes for children with serious emotional and behavioral disturbance', *Journal of Emotional and Behavioral Disorders*, 4: 130–46.

Gresham, F.M., MacMillan, D.L., Bocian, K., Ward, S.L. and Forness, S.R. (1998) 'Comorbidity of hyperactivity-impulsivity-inattention and conduct disorders problems: risk factors in social, affective, and academic domains', *Journal of Abnormal Child Psychology*, 26: 393–406.

Hallahan, D.P. and Kauffman, J.M. (1977) 'Labels, categories, behavior: ED, LD, and EMR reconsidered', *Journal of Special Education*, 11: 139–49.

Hunt, R.D. and Cohen, D.J. (1984) 'Psychiatric aspects of learning disabilities', *Pediatric Clinics of North America*, 31: 471–97.

Huntze, S.L. (1985) 'A position paper of the Council for Children with Behavioral Disorders', *Behavioral Disorders*, 10: 167–74.

Kavale, K.A. and Forness, S.R. (1995) *The Nature of Learning Disabilities*. Mahwah, NJ: Erlbaum.

Kavale, K.A. and Forness, S.R. (1996) 'Social skills deficits and learning disabilities: a meta-analysis', *Journal of Learning Disabilities*, 29: 226–37.

Kavale, K.A. and Forness, S.R. (2000) 'What definitions of learning disability say and don't say: a critical analysis', *Journal of Learning Disabilities*, 33: 239–56.

Kavale, K.A., Forness, S.R. and Duncan, B.B. (1996) 'Defining emotional or behavioral disorders: divergence and convergence', in T.E. Scruggs and M.A. Mastropieri (eds), *Advances in Learning and Behavioral Disabilities* (Vol. 10). Greenwich, CT: JAI. pp. 1–45.

Kavanagh, J.F. and Truss, T.J. (eds) (1988) *Learning Disabilities: Proceedings of the National Conference.* Parkton, MD: York Press.

Kazdin, A.E. (1995) *Conduct Disorders in Childhood and Adolescence* (2nd edn). Newbury Park, CA: Sage.

Kovacs, M. (1996) 'Presentation and course of major depressive disorder during childhood and later years of the life span', *Journal of the American Academy of Child and Adolescent Psychiatry*, 35: 705–15.

Lopez, M., Forness, S.R., MacMillan, D.L., Bocian, K. and Gresham, F.M. (1996) 'Children with attention deficit hyperactivity disorder and emotional or behavioral disorders in the primary grades: inappropriate placement in the learning disability category', *Education and Treatment of Children*, 19: 286–99.

MacMillan, D.L., Gresham, F.M. and Siperstein, G.N. (1993) 'Conceptual and psychometric concerns about the 1992 AAMR definition of mental retardation', *American Journal of Mental Retardation*, 98: 325–35.

Marshall, R.M., Hynd, G.W., Handwerk, M.J. and Hall, J. (1997) 'Academic underachievement in ADHD subtypes', *Journal of Learning Disabilities*, 30: 635–42.

Mattison, R.E. and Forness, S.R. (1995) 'The role of psychiatric and other health services in special education placement decisions for children with emotional or behavioral disorders', in J.M. Kauffman, J.W. Lloyd, T.A. Asutuo and D.P. Hallahan (eds), *Issues in Educational Placement of Children with Emotional or Behavioral Disorders*. Hillsdale, NJ: Erlbaum. pp. 142–54.

McConaughy, S.H. and Ritter, D. (1985) 'Social competence and behavioral problems of learning disabled boys aged 6–11', *Journal of Learning Disabilities*, 18: 547–53.

Offord, D.R. and Bennett, K.J. (1994) 'Conduct disorder: long-term outcomes and intervention effectiveness', *Journal of the American Academy of Child and Adolescent Psychiatry*, 33: 1069–78.

Prior, M. and Sanson, A. (1986) 'Attention deficit disorder with hyperactivity: a critique', *Journal of Child Psychology and Psychiatry*, 27: 307–19.

Reeves, J.C., Werry, J.S., Ellkind, G.S. and Zametkin, A. (1987) 'Attention deficit, conduct, oppositional, and anxiety disorders in children: II. Clinical characteristics', *Journal of the American Academy of Child and Adolescent Psychiatry*, 26: 144–55.

San Miguel, S.K., Forness, S.R. and Kavale, K.A. (1996) 'Social skill deficits and learning disabilities: the psychiatric comorbidity hypothesis', *Learning Disability Quarterly*, 20: 215–24.

Scruggs, T.E. and Mastropieri, M.A. (1986) 'Academic characteristics of behaviorally disordered and learning disabled students', *Behavioral Disorders*, 11: 184–90.

Silver, L.B. (1990) 'Attention deficit-hyperactivity disorder: is it a learning disability or a related disorder?', *Journal of Learning Disabilities*, 23: 394–7.

Sinclair, E., Forness, S.R. and Alexson, J. (1985) 'Psychiatric diagnosis: a study of its relationship to school needs', *Journal of Special Education*, 19: 333–44.

Smith, C.R., Wood, F.H. and Grimes, J. (1988) 'Issues in the identification and placement of behaviorally disordered students', in M.C. Wong, M.C. Reynolds and H.J. Walberg (eds), *Handbook of Special Education: Research and Practice* (Vol. 2). New York: Pergamon. pp. 95–124.

Stone, F. and Rowley, V. (1964) 'Educational disability in emotionally disturbed children', *Exceptional Children*, 30: 422–6.

Tankersley, M. and Landrum, T.J. (1997) 'Comorbidity of emotional and behavioral disorders', in J.W. Lloyd, E.J. Kameenui and D. Chard (eds), *Issues in Educating Students with Disabilities*. Mahwah, NJ: Lawrence Erlbaum. pp. 153–73.

Volkmer, F.R. (1996) 'Childhood and adolescent psychosis: a review of the past 10 years', *Journal of the American Academy of Child and Adolescent Psychiatry*, 35: 843–51.

Weinberg, W. and Rehmet, A. (1983) 'Childhood affective disorder and school problems', in D.P. Cantwell and G.A. Carlson (eds), *Affective Disorders in Childhood and Adolescence: An Update*. New York: Spectrum. pp. 109–128.

Wright-Strawderman, C. and Watson, B.L. (1992) 'The prevalence of depressive symptoms in children with learning disabilities', *Journal of Learning Disabilities*, 25: 258–64.

Zigler, E. and Hodapp, R.M. (1986) *Understanding Mental Retardation*. New York: Cambridge University Press.

5

What do we Mean by 'EBD'?[1]

GARY THOMAS

Elsewhere (Thomas and Loxley, 2002), I have asserted that arguments for special education rest in particular ways of thinking and understanding. Those arguments have, I suggested, set on a pedestal certain kinds of theoretical and empirical 'knowledge' and favoured particular methodological avenues as routes to such knowledge. The putative character of this knowledge – stable, objective, reliable – has created a false legitimacy for the growth of special education and the activities of special educators. This chapter takes that theme forward, focusing on children who don't behave at school. It makes the point that the metaphors and constructs which are used to generate understanding about such difficult behaviour are often misleading, evoking as they do all kinds of quasi-scientific explanation – explanation which has popularly come to be known as 'psycho-babble'. While 'psycho-babble' is hardly a scholarly term to employ in a volume such as this, it is nevertheless an apt one. For the mélange of disparate metaphor and theory around which understanding of people's behaviour is popularly constructed – in both lay and professional circles – rests in the reification of what is little more than tentative psychological theory. Perhaps more scholarly than psycho-babble would be Crews's characterization of this knowledge, particularly that which rests in Freudian theory, as an 'ontological maze peopled by absurd homunculi' (1997: 298).

Whatever the register in which one chooses to discuss it, there have, I argue in this chapter, been some unfortunate consequences of this kind of discourse for schoolchildren. Further, in the more recent school-orientated approaches to helping avoid troublesome behaviour at school – approaches that put the emphasis on change by the school rather than the change in the child – are found merely a replication of the exclusionary phenomena of the past. Those phenomena are created by certain kinds of mindsets and professional systems which accentuate rather than attenuate difference – and these mindsets and professional systems themselves rest in the thinking about difference, of deficit and disadvantage.

I contend that a relatively recent concept, that of 'need', has come to reinforce these concepts of deficit and disadvantage. Intended to be helpful, to place emphasis on a child's difficulties rather than simply naming a supposed category of problems, the notion of need has instead come to point as emphatically as before at the child. It has allowed to remain in place many of the exclusionary practices associated with special education.

THE NOTION OF EMOTIONAL
AND BEHAVIOURAL DIFFICULTIES:
THE ROOT OF THE PROBLEM

A search through the last 10 years' issues of five leading national and international journals[2] finds not a single paper which discusses in any detail the provenance, status, robustness, legitimacy or meaning of the term 'emotional and behavioural difficulties' (EBD). This is surely a cause for concern. The term is widely and unquestioningly used in England (and other countries have their own equivalents) as an administrative and quasi-clinical category. Uniquely, it proffers a category that is specific to children, and which combines legal, medical and educational connotations and meanings.

Although EBD is not an official category in England, it exists as one in everything but name. Categories officially ceased to exist following the report of the Warnock Committee (DES, 1978) and the 1981 Education Act. Yet it would be clear to a Martian after five minutes' study of the English education system that for all practical purposes EBD is indeed a category and that it forms in the minds of practitioners, professionals and administrators one of the principal groups of special needs. It has been used as a category in the local statementing procedures which have followed from section 5 of the 1981 Education Act and the Education Acts which have succeeded it. It appears unquestioningly in papers in reputable academic journals (for example, Smith and Thomas, 1992), and it appears as a descriptor in official documents and papers (for example, DES, 1989a, 1989b; DfEE, 1995; Mortimore, 1997).

The term 'EBD', then, reveals no frailty; indeed it displays a peculiar resilience and this makes it particularly interesting and useful as an example of a special education concept. The resilience it shows is demonstrated in its ability to survive and prosper over the past few years, when attention has moved from the child to the institution, with, for example, the Elton Committee's (DES, 1989c) emphasis on whole-school approaches to discipline. Over the last decade or so, academics and policy-makers have proposed that in tackling the question of difficult behaviour at school, attention should be paid not only to analysis and treatment of the child's behaviour, but also to the operations and systems in the school which may cause or aggravate such behaviour.

But behind this sensible development in thinking there resolutely continues a powerful sub-text that the real causes of difficult behaviour lie in deficit and deviance in the child. Respected academics could, for example, as recently as 1994 frame their book (Chazan et al., 1994: 27) around section headings such as 'Identification of EBDs' and 'Factors associated with EBDs in middle childhood' (1994: 36). Another could entitle his book *Treating Problem Children* (Hoghughi, 1988). The agenda is of deficit, deviance and disadvantage in the child, and while school systems are usually mentioned in discourse such as this, they seem to appear almost as an afterthought. It is clear that the real problem is considered to be dispositional: that of the child – and the emphasis is thus on individual treatment. The term 'EBD' induces a clinical mindset from which it is difficult to escape.

This mindset operates within more all-encompassing ideas about need. The notion of need is seldom questioned. It is seemingly so benign, so beneficial to the child that it has become a shibboleth of special education thinking and policy. But I contend in this chapter that 'need' is less than helpful, and that it is a chimera when difficult behaviour is being considered. The notion of need here is based on a belief that a *child's* problems are being identified and addressed. 'Need' in this context, however, is more usefully seen as the school's need – a need for calm and order. The language of the clinic, though, invariably steers the response of professionals toward a child-based action plan.

This focus on emotional need substitutes a set of supposedly therapeutic practices and procedures for more down-to-earth and simple-to-understand sanctions. It also diverts attention from the nature of the environment which I expect children to inhabit. The ambit of the 'helping', therapeutic response invoked by the idea of EBD is unjustifiably wide, being called on neither at the request of the young person involved (or at least very rarely so), nor because of some long-standing pattern of behaviour which has demonstrated that the young person has a clinically identifiable problem, but rather because the behaviour is unacceptable for a particular institution. But because these therapeutic practices and procedures notionally constitute 'help', they are peculiarly difficult to refuse.

Likewise, it is difficult to refute the kindly, child-centred, humanitarian tenets on which they supposedly rest. The tenets on which therapeutic practice rest may be all these good things (kind, humanitarian, child-centred), but they have developed during an era when the intellectual climate eschewed – or, rather, failed even to consider as meaningful concepts – ideas about the rationality and rights of the child. In such a climate it was considered appropriate and necessary for decisions to be made about and for children by concerned professionals. Whereas systems for rule-breaking adults have come to incorporate strict procedures to protect rights, systems could develop in schools to deal with rule infraction which would incorporate no such protections – since the protection was considered to be automatically inherent in the beneficial action of the professionals acting on the child's behalf.

But those actors and advocates would often be the very same people who were offended by the child's behaviour. In the adult world, political and legal systems are particularly sensitive to the boundary between wrongdoing and mental illness, and it is a commonplace that in certain circumstances in certain political regimes it is only too convenient to brand wrongdoers and rebels 'mad'. In more favourable political circumstances, by contrast, fastidious care is taken to differentiate between law-breaking, rebellion and mental illness. Alongside this fastidiousness, there is a range of protections for both the wrongdoer and for the person who is depressed or schizophrenic – sophisticated protections against unfair conviction, or the too-convenient attribution of mental illness to unwelcome behaviour.

But for children and young people at school, because of assumptions about their vulnerability and their irrationality, and presuppositions about the beneficial actions of professionals acting on their behalf, those protections do not exist. Their absence has enabled in education a label like 'EBD' to be compiled out of a range of disparate ideas about order and disturbance. Those ideas are elided, yet their elision is rarely acknowledged or addressed.

The elision of ideas represented in the notion of EBD has done little, I contend, for the individual child. Yet it also exercises an influence even on supposedly whole-school approaches to behaviour management at school. The notion of EBD distorts the way that management or organizational issues at school are defined and handled. A whole school approach to behaviour difficulties existing in the same universe as a thriving notion of EBD means that behaviour difficulties are invariably seen through a child-centred, clinical lens. For this clinical lens is more convenient for everyone: it offers immediate response (often the removal of the child) rather than the promise of an improvement in a term or a year; it offers ready-made routes into existing professional systems which distract attention from possible shortcomings of the school, and it avoids the large-scale upheaval and expense of whole-school reform. Following episodes of difficult behaviour, traditional child-focused professional responses therefore tend to follow.

The language of need out of which we build ideas about problem behaviour therefore induces procedural responses whose main function is the appearance of doing something constructive. The mantra of need mechanically induces a set of reflexes from the school, but these are often little more than rituals – bureaucratic shows of willing. They constitute what Skrtic (1991) calls 'symbols and ceremonies'.

A different view about how to respond to difficult behaviour at school can emerge out of current thinking on inclusion. The inclusive school should best be seen as a humane environment rather than a set of pre-existing structures and systems for dealing with misbehaviour. These traditional structures and systems inevitably invoke already-existing professional responses. But my contention is that schools contain such an odd collection of rules and practices that unless these are themselves addressed and altered, misbehaviour from children is an almost inevitable consequence.

WHOSE NEEDS?

The blanket ascription of 'need' when behaviour is found difficult at school requires some examining. Whose needs are being identified and unravelled here? The route taken is nearly always to assume that the child needs something, and the assumptions about need proceed to imputations of intent, weakness and problem in the wrongdoer.

Foucault (1991) analysed this process as it has taken place in juridical practice over two centuries. According to his analysis, modern times have seen a transformation in society's response to wrongdoing. Because historically responses to wrongdoing were often so shockingly cruel, new 'kinder' techniques of control have supplanted them. Foucault's *Discipline and Punish* (1991) begins with an example. It begins with a picture of a savage punishment in pre-revolution France, where a prisoner, Damiens, has his limbs carved from his body. But it is not principally condemnation of this cruelty which follows from Foucault. Rather, he has drawn the picture to contrast it with the kinds of punishment which have come to succeed it. Because of the conspicuous savagery of punishment regimes in Europe until the mid-nineteenth century, Foucault says, a backlash forced attempts to be more gentle, to have 'more respect, more "humanity"' (1991: 16). It is these successors to the punishment of Damiens for which Foucault reserves his sharpest critique. For these systems – this 'gentle way in punishment' (1991: 104) – are quieter, more insidious. These new techniques, relying on the constructs and knowledge of the new social sciences, constructed various forms of understanding of the wrong-doer which made imputations of intent and assumptions about motive. This would not be so bad were it not for the fact that the understandings provided by the new sciences depended on tentative, fallible theories which were treated as though they were scientific fact.[3] In fact, they were merely making new kinds of judgement about misbehaviour, but judgements which were given added credence and respectability by their association with supposedly scientific thinking and understanding – understanding which had been so successful in the natural sciences. In short, what has occurred, the analysis of Foucault suggests, has been a movement from simple judgement and punishment of someone's disapproved-of act to complex and unjustified judgements about his or her 'soul'.

EBD provides an excellent case study of this elision from punishment to judgement. It provides a clear example of a category created from an intermingling, on one side, of certain systems of knowledge (like psychology and medicine) and, on the other, of a need for institutional order.

To make this proposition represents perhaps not too sparkling an insight, since a critical recognition of the place of the medical model in special education is hardly new. My specific focus here, though, is on the almost explicit conflation of administrative need with quasi-medical category; of the transition from naughty-therefore-impose-sanctions, to disturbed-therefore-meet-needs. It is the nature of the transition that I wish especially to examine: the gradient from punishment to 'help' down which the child tends to descend once 'need' has been established.

There are taken-for-granted assumptions of 'help' in the 'meeting need' mantra of contemporary special education protocols, and these 'needs' have been silently transmuted with the assistance of the constructs of academic and professional psychology from the *school's* needs for order calm, routine and predictability to the *child's* needs – supposedly for stability, nurture, security, one-to-one help or whatever.

In the unspoken assumptions behind special education procedures there is no acknowledgement of the manoeuvre which has occurred here – no recognition of the frailty of the idea of an 'emotional need' – and no willingness to entertain the possibility that emotional needs may be a fiction constructed to escape the school's insecurities about failing to keep order.

Table 5.1 distinguishes between two kinds of need: that of the school and that of the child. My intention is to point to the conflation of ideas and knowledges used in the notion of need and to suggest that the umbrella-use of the construct disguises different kinds of problem which school staff confront. But unacceptable behaviour is rarely a problem of the

Table 5.1   *What is meant by 'need'?*

School's needs	Children's needs	
'Juridical' needs (but expressed as children's psychological needs)	Educational needs (but 'identified' using psychological constructs and instruments)	Physical needs (which may sometimes result in educational needs)
category:	category:	category:
EBD	moderate learning difficulty (MLD)	physical disability hearing impairment visual impairment
Characterized by:	Characterized by:	Characterized by:
Questions of order for the school	Questions of how best to help children who are having serious problems with their work at school	Questions of how best to help children who have physical or sensory impairments

child. While this behaviour is a problem for the school, it rarely constitutes a clinical problem. Neither does it point to some abnormality or deficit.

An elevation in the status of psychological knowledge has meant that simple understandings about what is right or wrong have in themselves become insufficient to explain difficult behaviour. A new epistemology has emerged wherein a lexicon of dispositionally orientated words and phrases govern and mould the way unacceptable behaviour is considered. Thus, if children misbehave at school, education professionals are encouraged to examine the background, motivations and supposed traumas of the students rather than the simple humanity of the school's operation – its simple day-to-day processes and routines.

Foucault (1991) warns against the assumption that the knowledge of disciplines like psychology and sociology can inform the working practices of staff in schools and hospitals. It is not disinterested knowledge; in the context of prisons he says that it has acquired the status of an '"epistemological-juridical" formation' (1991: 23). It is the same perhaps as what Bourdieu calls 'doxa': a kind of taken-for-granted knowledge, naturalized knowledge, 'things people accept without knowing' (Bourdieu and Eagleton, 1994). In other words, the knowledge of psychology and psychiatry have infiltrated our everyday understanding of disorder and deviance so that they are now almost as one: disorder has somehow become melded with disturbance in such a way that thought about behaviour which is out-of-order at school can hardly be entertained without the collateral assumption of emotional disturbance and special need. This symbiosis of order and understanding is nowhere clearer than in the contemporary term 'EBD'.

MEETING NEED

In education, this last reconceptualization occurs under the cloak of *meeting individual need*. The 'meeting need' notion satisfies two conditions for the educationist. First, it enables the labelling of madness (a Bad Thing) to be transformed into the identification of a need in the child (a Good Thing). Thus, the educator, with a stroke of a wand, is changed from labeller (this child is maladjusted) to benefactor and helper (this child has special needs and I will meet them). Second, an institutional need for order is transformed to a child's emotional need. The child who misbehaves has special needs which are rooted in emotional disturbance, the vocabulary at once invoking psychological, psychoanalytic and psychiatric knowledge. Once need is established, the psychological genie has been released.[4]

It is strange that psychologists and educationists should have managed to pull off such a feat of alchemy, since a moment's thought discloses the fact that the things which children habitually do wrong at school rarely have any manifest (or indeed covert) association with their emotional makeup. They concern the school's need to regulate time (punishing tardiness and truancy), activity (punishing lack of effort or overactivity), speech (punishing chatter or insolence), and the body (punishing hairstyles, clothes, the use of make-up or the tidiness of the individual).[5] As Cicourel and Kitsuse put it, 'the adolescent's posture, walk, cut of hair, clothes, use of slang, manner of speech … may be the basis for the typing of the student as a "conduct problem"' (1968: 130). And the term 'conduct problem', or more likely 'conduct disorder', is still alive and well in special education.

But being unpunctual, lazy, rude or untidy were never, even by early twentieth-century standards, qualifications for madness, or even emotional difficulty. They concern, as Hargreaves et al. (1975) point out, rule-infractions. They have little or nothing to do with an individual's emotional need, but everything to do with the school's need to keep order. Maintaining order through the upholding of these codes is necessary, school managers would argue, for the efficient running and indeed for the survival of the school.

Few could disagree. Institutions which require the collecting together of groups of 20 or 30 in classes, and hundreds in assemblies, need ways of keeping order. The energy of young people must be kept in check if these assemblages are not to descend into scrums. To maintain order, there is a need for disciplinary methods through the regulation of the use of space and the control of activity. Mostly these work.

It is when they don't work, when children fail to conform and fail to respond to the 'gentle punishments', that the manoeuvre occurs in which need is passed from school to child. Unable to understand the stubbornness of the individuals concerned and fearful of the consequences for order, those responsible for order in the school then, following the precepts learned in teacher education and reinforced by the service-system provided by the local education authority, reconceptualize the students as having emotional and behavioural difficulties.

Although recent changes in discussion about policy (DfEE, 1997) have stressed the importance of an inclusive ethos in schools (that is, one in which the comprehensive ethos of the school is clearly articulated, and the systems of the school are established to ensure inclusion), there remains a firm resistance to such an ethos. Croll and Moses (2000: 61), for example, found that more than half of the 48 headteachers they interviewed felt that 'More children should attend special schools', and in the case of 'children with emotional and behavioural difficulties' this figure rose to two-thirds (see also Mousley et al., 1993). More serious, there is an unspoken acceptance of need as a means of securing the removal of the child – an unthinking collusion with the process of need attribution. It is the 'doxa' (Bourdieu and Eagleton, 1994) which is troublesome: the establishment almost without thinking of the child as having needs. In the language of attribution theorists, the problem is that of 'fundamental attribution error' (Ross et al., 1977) – the easy over-attribution of events to the disposition of individuals rather than to the failings of institutions. (It is worth noting that of Croll and Moses's sample, under 1 per cent of headteachers and only 2 per cent of teachers attributed 'emotional and behavioural difficulties' to 'school and teachers'.)

Once established as having emotional difficulties, children are diverted along a new path that separates them, and which ends in their being 'helped'. It shunts them sideways from a comprehensible and predictable system of practices and procedures which result in rewards and punishments, to an alternative set governed by alternative professional personnel – psychologists, counsellors, social workers, psychiatrists – who listen, analyse and understand.

The new world is stripped even of the procedural certainties of the mainstream school as groundrules change and parameters invisibly move. The arcane paraphernalia of assessment procedures confirm the diagnosis of emotional difficulties. Once so labelled, your every word becomes untrustworthy. Your complaints can be ignored, as the response to increasing irrationality is to pile on more and more 'help'.[6]

The result is incarceration by smothering: the entrapment of the child in a cocoon of professional help. One is launched on what Goffman (1987: 79) calls a 'moral career' in which both the individual's image of self and his or her 'official position, jural relations, and style of life' change in sequence as the child graduates through his or her career as sufferer and victim. Escape comes only by 'acknowledgement' and 'acceptance' of one's problems.[7] It helps if one can learn the vocabulary and the semiology of the therapeutic system and parrot it back to the therapeutic agent.

FROM SIMPLE WRONGDOING TO DISTURBANCE AND TREATMENT

How does all this happen? By a process not of judging the act or the behaviour in simple terms but by the judgement of what Foucault calls the 'passions, instincts, anomalies, infirmities, maladjustments, effects of environment …' (1991: 17). The impedimenta, vocabulary and constructs of the new professionals have come to invade the simple systems of judgement which preceded them. The act itself ceases to be condemned in simple terms; instead, it is an estimation of the *student* that is made. As Foucault puts it: 'behind the pretext of explaining an action, are ways of defining an individual' (1991: 18).

The delineation of emotional disturbance interrupts the procedure of simply judging whether an act is right or wrong, good or bad. Simple moral judgement is suspended. It is displaced by a morass of half-understood ideas about disturbance, a jumble of bits and pieces from psychoanalysis, psychology and psychiatry, a bricolage of penis envy and cognitive dissonance, of Freudian slip and standard deviation, of motivation and maternal deprivation, regression and repression, attention-seeking and assimilation, reinforcement and self-esteem – ideas corrupted by textbook-writers and mangled by journalists and the writers of popular culture. Ideas which, as Crews puts it, make 'an ontological maze peopled by absurd homunculi' (1997: 298). But these ideas are not only half-understood. Even if those who use the ideas in defining 'need' understood them as well as it is possible to understand them, they would be on shaky ground epistemologically and empirically (Nagel, 1959; Cioffi, 1975; Macmillan, 1997), for the models which stand behind notions of emotional disturbance are, as Crews points out, characterized by faulty logic, the manufacturing of evidence and facile explanation; they construct 'a cacophony of incompatible explanations' (1997: 297).

Explanatory and therapeutic currency is widely lauded by the psychological community in a small rainforest of 'scientific' journals, yet there is little sign of a diminution in unhappiness resulting from these supposed advances in understanding. Indeed, Smail asserts that 'There is certainly no evidence that the wider availability of psychological theories and techniques is leading to a decrease in psychological distress' (1993: 13). He suggests that in the burgeoning of psychological techniques to alleviate distress, there is far less a breakthrough in enlightened understanding, and more 'the success of an enterprise' (1993: 13). The mass of techniques make a bazaar in which plausible homily, mixed with large portions of psychoanalytic and psychological vocabulary, take the place of a rational consideration of children's behaviour at school. Nor is there much evidence in education of the successful impact of this burgeoning enterprise: numbers of children excluded from school continue to rise. Indeed, they continue to rise even in *special schools*, which have prided themselves on their supposedly therapeutic skills. There were over 600 permanent exclusions from special schools in 1996/97, an increase of 21 per cent in relation to the 500 permanent exclusions in the previous year (DfEE, 1998). Twenty-eight per cent of special schools reported at least one permanent exclusion in 1996/97. All this was in the context of other key indicators of deprivation and social exclusion – such as the proportion of children living in a workless household, or the proportion of children living in families of below-average income – which showed improving trends (Howarth et al., 1998).

It is strange that the therapeutic mindset behind notions of maladjustment and EBD should have been so resistant to suffocation in the absence of supporting evidence. Smail suggests that an ostensibly therapeutic approach survives first because people want it to, and second because it is impossible to demonstrate that it *isn't* effective. The result of this mock-scientific approach to behaviour is the sanctification of the agent of therapy (and even the agent of assessment), so that the whole assessment–therapy process surrounds itself with what Smail calls 'an aura of almost moral piety' in which to question putative benefits 'comes close to committing a kind of solecism' (1993: 16).

It is not only 'abnormal' psychology (as a sub-area of psychology) that plays a significant part in the 'clinicizing' of unacceptable behaviour. For educationists the notion of need *in the child* is reinforced by key psychological theories such as those of Piaget. Important for reports such as that of the influential Plowden (DES, 1967), these theories have stressed the genetic determinacy of development, leaving explanation for behaviour problems or learning difficulties to be made in terms of developmental defect or emotional deprivation, the vocabulary again invoking psychological or social explanation for behaviour at school.

Many have pointed to not only the tenuousness of the theories on which such educational and social policy is based (for example, Elkind, 1967; Gelman, 1982; Bryant, 1984; James and Prout, 1990; Rutter, 1995), but also to the way in which attention is distracted from the nature and significance of the school environment in itself constructing the difficulties

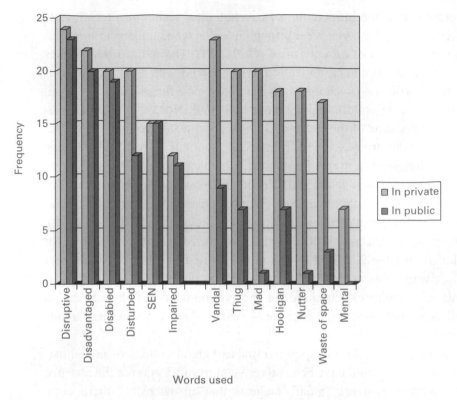

Figure 5.1   *Vocabulary used to describe children*

(for example, Walkerdine, 1983; Alexander, 1984). But frail as these theories are, they are perennially attractive (as the persistence of Piaget's theories in teacher education syllabuses demonstrates) and it is the ideas which stem from them that influence the professional as he or she works with the reconceptualized child: the child with needs.

An illustration of the clinicizing of unacceptable behaviour is given in Figure 5.1, which shows some of the vocabulary used to describe difficult children in one secondary school. Recorded by a teacher participant-observer (Sayer, 1993) in private settings (in informal conversation) and public settings (at a staff meeting or with parents), the recordings reveal not only a set of highly 'psychologized' labels about pupils, but also ones which are entirely focused on the disposition and character of the pupil.

Those labels used on the left of the figure (namely, 'disruptive' to 'impaired') are ones which the user is comfortable about using in public and in private, while those on the right ('vandal' to 'mental') may have been used more frequently but generally in private rather than in public. The public acceptability of terms such as 'disruptive', 'disadvantaged' and 'disabled' in the discourse of school life shows the extent to which the psychiatric and the psycho-social have become fused and converted into acceptable psycho-educational labels. 'Disturbed' and 'disruptive' supplant 'nutter' and 'mad'. These labels merely make more palatable for public consumption the sentiments and beliefs revealed by the words used privately for the same pupils ('vandal', 'thug', 'mad', 'nutter', 'mental'). The substitution of the former set for the latter set does nothing, however, to displace an even more firmly ingrained set of beliefs about the origins of these young people's difficulties at school. For aberrant behaviour to occur, there has, in Foucault's words, 'to be something wrong with him, and this is his character, his psyche, his upbringing, his unconscious, his desires' (1980: 44).

CATEGORIES FOR CHILDREN, NOT ADULTS

Ideas about psyche, motivation and background form the substrate out of which these new descriptors emerge. They also contribute to and exaggerate the unequal power balance between adult and child, for in no *adult* system is the official process of packaging and labelling aberrant behaviour as well-formed, sophisticated and widely accepted as it is in EBD for these minors. Concomitantly, the rules, punishment regimes and labelling tolerated within schools would not be tolerated within any adult organization (other than the prison). It is perhaps significant that although 25 years ago a ferment of discussion under the leadership of Laing (1965) and Szasz (1972) surrounded the issue of whether difficult behaviour constituted mental illness, little of the significance of that discussion was assimilated into debate about what was then called 'maladjustment' – perhaps because a central pillar of the superstructure of children's services and special education has been the taken-for-granted assumption of doing good, of acting in *loco parentis*, of guardianship. These ideas have flourished partly because of a tradition of seeing the child as not only vulnerable and helpless, but also as irrational.

The process of understanding children to be not only irrational but also emotionally disturbed effectively condemns them to voicelessness. Being seen as irrational (rather than simply stupid) is particularly damning, for it means that you are deemed unworthy even of consultation about what is in your best interests.

The system of soft categories (like EBD), spongy quasi-legal procedures – such as in the Code of Practice (DFE, 1994), quasi-medical diagnoses (like AD/HD) and mock-scientific assessments, though it doesn't stand up to rigorous scrutiny, has its effects insidiously. Partly because children are taken to be not only irrational, but also in need of protection, it has been possible for a network of special procedures – supposedly protective and therapeutic – to grow around them, in a way that they have not grown around adults.

For adults, unacceptable behaviour is punished – but a comprehensible (if less-than-perfect) system of procedures and protocols protects them. Even if the protection is written in legal jargon, it is at least in the language of straightforward relations: you have done wrong, we will punish you with x, but you are entitled to y. For children, by contrast, repeatedly unacceptable behaviour leads them into a set of arcane official and semi-official procedures (detention, exclusion, referral to the psychologist, statementing, placement in special education) in which their rights are unclear not only to them and their parents, but also to the administrators and professionals who work with them (and hence the need for the setting up of the Special Needs Tribunal). Ad hoc collections of people, such as governors in exclusions panels, decide about their rights to attend school, and decisions (unrestricted by anything so mundane as a time limitation) are made by teachers, psychologists and administrators about their lives. For children, protection takes on a wholly different meaning from the protection that the law gives to the adult suspected of law-breaking. The protection given to the child is a paternalistic protection, for example, in the 'protection' of a statement where supposed 'needs' are constructed and then met. It is far harder to argue against someone who is meeting your needs than someone who is accusing you of breaking the rules.

MAKING SCHOOLS MORE HUMANE AS ENVIRONMENTS: COMMON TALK IN HUMANE SCHOOLS

Lest it appears that I am endorsing misbehaviour, violence or abuse, let me stress that I am not. I do not seek in any way to condone violence or to romanticize difficult behaviour. Nor do I seek to play down or underestimate the school staff's need for disciplinary techniques to keep order. Instead I am seeking to point out that misbehaviour seems to be an endemic part of institutions that organize themselves in particular ways, and that if we seek to reduce such behaviour we have to recognize its provenance. We must recognize the possibility that the origins of misbehaviour lie less in children's emotions or even in their 'disadvantage' and lie more in the character of the organization which we ask them to inhabit for a large part of their lives. It is an organization staffed by professionals whose response when faced with trouble is necessarily a professional one. Here, Skrtic (1991) suggests, is its main problem since it operates as a 'professional bureaucracy' (and Weatherley and Lipsky, 1977, and Wolfensberger, 1990, point to similar processes). Professional bureaucracies are organizations which, far from being designed to think creatively about how to change for the better, think rather about how to direct their 'clients' toward some existing professional specialism. Or they may consider how the problem can be absorbed in the professional procedures defined in a local policy document. The mindset induced by the notion of disturbance fits happily into such a system, encouraging the view that specialized sets of professional knowledge exist to deal with misbehaviour.

It is odd that Skrtic's analysis occurs at a time when there has been optimism about the potential of school to influence 'outcomes' for children. For over the last decade or so, academics and policy-makers have proposed that in tackling the question of difficult behaviour at school, attention should be paid not only to analysis and treatment of the child's behaviour, but also to the operations and systems in the school which may cause or aggravate such behaviour. The positive arguments for such a shift in emphasis from child to institution rest in evidence and analysis from diverse sources. They rest in evidence about the significance of the school's role in influencing behaviour and achievement (for example, Edmonds, 1979; Neisser, 1986; Hallinger and Murphy, 1986; Rutter et al., 1979; Mortimore et al., 1988; Jesson and Gray, 1991; Sammons et al., 1993; Levine and Lezotte, 1995). They rest in recognition of the potentially damaging effects of labelling (in the work of theorists such as Cicourel and Kitsuse, 1968). And they rest in arguments about the invalidity of interpreting aberrant behaviour as disturbed (in the ideas of Szasz, Laing and others). Resulting models for intervention and help which thus attach significance to the impact of the wider environment, and particularly that of the school, have been given added impetus by the development of thinking in areas such as ecological psychology (following pioneers such as Kounin, 1967; Barker, 1968; Doyle, 1977; Bronfenbrenner, 1979) and systems theory (for example, Checkland, 1981).

In fact, though, only a small amount of the school effectiveness research has related specifically to behaviour (for example, Galloway, 1983; Galloway et al., 1985; McManus, 1987). The *Fifteen Thousand Hours* work (Rutter et al., 1979) looked at attendance and 'delinquency' but conceded that the process (independent) variables – that is, the school factors supposedly responsible for influencing outcomes – can contribute only in small measure to predictions concerning those outcomes. The authors say that other (unidentified) variables must be playing an important part in differences between schools on attendance and behaviour.

The tenuousness of the research evidence here has not prevented a widespread acceptance of the idea that schools make a difference when it comes to behaviour. Despite the clear caveat provided by Rutter and his colleagues about the generalizability of effectiveness findings when it comes to behaviour, there has been a near unanimous acceptance of the message which, it appears, policy-makers want to hear.

Optimism in the face of lack of evidence is interesting and perhaps related to the laudable desire to do whatever can be done to make schools more congenial places for all who inhabit them. But the general body of school effectiveness literature and research has pushed whole-school responses in the wrong direction. Consistent with the conclusions which would follow from Skrtic's (1991: 165) analysis, the particular professional vocabularies – psychological and psychiatric – induced by the label 'EBD' discourage a move to the necessary creativity. They induce merely what Skrtic calls 'an assortment of symbols and ceremonies' which look and sound like sensible action – things of the sort that appear in the *Elton Report* (DES, 1989c), like writing a bullying policy or improving liaison procedures – but in fact shift attention from characteristics of the environment to what Skrtic calls aspects of the 'machine bureaucracy': things that have the appearance (but only the appearance) of rational reaction to a problem (see also Weatherley and Lipsky, 1977, in this context).[8]

The system 'bureaucratizes deviance' (Rubington and Weinberg, 1968: 111), with a hierarchy of defining agents – and one may note how this hierarchy has been formalized over the years in the English system from Circular 2/75 to the 1981 Education Act to the Code of Practice (DFE, 1994).

The professional systems operating in schools to manage deviance in fact bureaucratize deviance as reliably today as they did when Rubington and Weinberg wrote about them 30 years ago. They now do so perhaps more sensitively and with more emphasis on the whole-school options suggested by Elton. However, the professional systems encourage and reinforce professional responses, thus diverting attention from ostensibly more mundane but potentially more significant aspects of the world that children have to inhabit. Thus, while a welcome move from the left-most column of Table 5.2 to the middle column has occurred in many circumstances, this move still represents attention to a narrow band of practices and activities which are professionally related. They ensure that the discourse is that of professionals, communicating in their habitual constructs. Discussion and debate about, for example, 'professional liaison' has more cachet than discussion about fair queuing systems at lunchtime, but the bullying policy thus engendered may be little more than an ineffectual sop, doing little to address the actual problems faced by pupils in the school. And liaison with the educational psychologist may do little to address the routine unfairnesses committed every day at school. As the great educator Rousseau (1993) noted more than two centuries ago, some

Table 5.2 *Approaches to misbehaviour*

Therapeutic emphasis	Whole-school emphasis	Humane environment emphasis
• Counselling	• Updating the bullying policy	• Having more pay phones for students to use
• Behaviour modification	• Ensuring better liaison with school psychologist	• Having more carpeted areas in the school
• Groupwork	• Rationalizing report card systems	• Ensuring that litter is regularly cleared
• Drugs (e.g. in AD/HD)	• Establishing clearer and more explicit guidelines for transfer from Code of Practice stage 3 to stage 4	• Ensuring that there is a plentiful supply of drinking fountains and that they are maintained regularly
• Family therapy	• Setting up a governor link with the learning support department	• Taking steps to discipline teachers who bully students
		• Staggering playtimes and school start and end times in large schools
		• Ensuring fair queuing systems at lunch in which staff don't automatically go to the front and older students can't routinely push in
		• Ensuring that the minutes of the School Council are routinely taken on the governing body agenda
		• Reducing the number of assemblies
		• Ensuring toilets are regularly cleaned and refurbished

observations are considered too trivial to be true.[9] They have to have a theoretical or professional spin to make them seem significant.

A nice example of simple, non-theoretical, a-professional thinking is given by Clarke as headteacher of a large urban comprehensive school. He notes:

> Some years ago, having taken issue with a teacher (male) for shouting at a student (female), I was invited at a staff meeting (under any other business!) to outline my 'policy on shouting'. Three points occurred to me:
>
> i. if mature adults disagree, they generally don't shout at each other;
> ii. it is hard to ask students to keep their voices down if the teachers shout;
> iii. it is impossible to say, hand on heart, that we do not have bullying if big, powerful men verbally assault small, powerless young women. (1997: 154)

This kind of intervention emerges from Clarke's values and beliefs as a teacher and as a person. It has nothing to do with any professional knowledge, theoretical archive or government code of practice. It is only this brave kind of thinking and action which emancipates one from the machine bureaucracy of which Skrtic writes.

An analogy can perhaps be drawn with successful action currently being taken on housing estates to manage the behaviour of unruly youngsters. This involves a deliberate move away from the pattern of response which would usually have taken place five or ten years ago – a response which involved 'understanding' the 'problems' of the young people involved, an understanding predicated on the theoretical assumptions of certain professional groups which imputed 'need' to certain kinds of behaviour. The move is toward more community action, which involves – on one side – increasing the likelihood that the perpetrators of misdemeanours will be caught, disapproved-of and, if necessary, punished, and – on the other – making systematic efforts to provide activity for the young people involved. It is through an engagement with the political (and a corresponding disengagement with the patronizing psycho-babble of 'understanding') that the patent truth of Postman's statement can shine out:

> There is no question that listlessness, ennui, and even violence in school are related to the fact that students have no useful role to play in society. The strict application of nurturing and protective attitudes toward children has created a paradoxical situation in which protection has come to mean excluding the young from meaningful involvement in their own communities. (1996: 103)

It is only by thinking in this way – outside the boundaries presented by the school walls – that genuinely inclusive solutions can emerge to the routine challenge presented by children's difficult behaviour. The champion of children's rights Eric Midwinter said something similar a quarter of a century ago:

> I gaze half-benignly on cuts in public expenditure. If those cuts can mean (it is a large 'if') the properly directed deprofessionalisation and deinstitutionalisation of our public services and the controlled mobilisation of community resources, then I am convinced the overall quality of services would be improved. (1977: 111)

The reflex response of education cannot, in other words, be a unilateral one using its familiar constructs and professional routes. Those constructs and routes inevitably involve separate action and sometimes segregated provision.

CONCLUSION

In the use of the term 'EBD' there is an indolent espousal of a term which too conveniently packages together difficult, troublesome children with emotional disturbance. In its use is an insidious blurring of motives and knowledges which imputes problems to children that in reality are rarely theirs. In the dispositional attributions which are therein made, unnecessarily complex judgements about putative need take the place of simple judgements about what is acceptable or unacceptable behaviour for a particular institution. Use of the term 'EBD' enables the substitution of the former for the latter – of the complex for the straightforward – and this in turn perpetuates a mindset about behaviour which distracts attention from what the school can do to make itself a more humane, inclusive place.

Recent understandings about the rights of the child have made little impact on the processes which formalize these attributions, fraught as those processes are with difficulties concerning the extra-judicial judgements being made on children's aberrant behaviour. Neither have questions which have been posed about the effectiveness and appropriateness of 'helping' services in adult clinical psychology and psychiatry been addressed to anywhere near the same extent in children's services. In fact, the professional services which exist notionally to support children exist often in reality to support the institution (a distinction which is sometimes overtly and unselfconsciously made) and may set in train routines and rituals which have the appearance of effective response, but in practice do little other than distract attention from significant aspects of the environment which children are being asked to inhabit.

By retaining and using the label 'EBD', sight is often lost of the fact that schools for many children present an environment with which it is difficult to come to terms. By packaging this difficulty as a problem of the children, we divert our own attention from ways in which schools can become more congenial and inclusive places.

SUMMARY

The legacy of the thinking behind special education is a set of ideas which perpetuate exclusion. In this chapter I focus on 'emotional and behavioural difficulties' (EBD), which I suggest represents a confused collation of notions. It rests on an unsteady foundation – a mélange of disparate ideas which nevertheless share one feature: the attribution of behaviour problems to the disposition of the child and his or her personal circumstances. Out of this mix of notions and attributions has emerged EBD – a category which substitutes quasi-clinical assessments about putative need for more straightforward judgements about right and wrong. It enables and legitimizes clinically orientated judgements about the causes of misbehaviour – 'emotional difficulties' – which allow the school to evade serious scrutiny of its own routines and procedures. Moreover, the judgements made about children occur in the absence of the panoply of protections which exist for adults who behave oddly or unacceptably. This difference between the way adults and children are treated is an increasingly untenable anomaly at a time when policy debate correctly pays more attention to children's rights. The predominantly clinical and child-centred mix of notions and attributions behind EBD influences also supposedly whole-school approaches to behaviour difficulties and distracts attention from ways in which schools can be made more humane, more inclusive places.

NOTES

1 This chapter is a development of a paper first published in *Discourse*, 21 (3), and I am indebted to the editor of that journal and its publishers, Carfax Publishing, members of the publishing group Taylor and Francis, London, for permission to use it in its amended form.

2 *The British Journal of Special Education*, the *Journal of Child Psychology and Psychiatry*, the *European Journal of Special Needs Education*, *Support for Learning* and the *British Educational Research Journal*.

3 Popper makes a similar point about the nature of psychoanalytic theory, saying, 'psychoanalysts of all schools were able to interpret any conceivable event as a verification of their theories' (1977: 264). The knowledge thus formed on such non-theory masquerading as theory is dangerous, disguising hunch and guesswork in the clothes of well-grounded science.

4 'Need' presents, in Corbett's thinking, far from a helpful idea, but rather 'sugar-coated poison' (1996: 3). Carson has also had something interesting to say about 'special needs' asserting that ordinary needs, concerned with children's humanity, are 'sacrificed on the altar of identifying and meeting their special needs' (1992: 217). Drawing from Murray, Fromm and Maslow, he points out that we all have needs to do with affection, security, belonging, fun, self-esteem and self-identity. These are ignored or downplayed in the obsession with special needs. The setting of the latter above the former can lead to the kind of 'solutions' to supposed learning difficulty which result in segregation.

5 Apologies to Miller (1993) for the paraphrase of his analysis of Foucault's position here.

6 It is worth noting the results of an increased willingness to listen to the child. The public enquiry into abuse at children's homes in Wales has disclosed 300 former residents who are now willing to testify in cases of abuse against 148 adults (Davies, 1998; Waterhouse, 2000). The abuse was physical and emotional, including sexual abuse, hitting and throttling children, bullying and belittling them. Punishments included being forced to scrub floors with toothbrushes, or to perform garden tasks using cutlery. The fact that these young people did not consider it worth complaining at the time attests to the fact that they themselves perceived the extent to which they were disenfranchised, to which they were considered not to be rational, believable people – not people who would be taken seriously. The scandal was exposed only after Alison Taylor, a children's home head in Gwynedd, pressed her concerns at the highest levels. When the police first investigated Ms Taylor's concerns in 1986–87, the authorities constructed a 'wall of disbelief' at the outset. The subsequent decision not to bring prosecutions was greeted, the Waterhouse enquiry concludes, with 'inappropriate enthusiasm' by social services. The fear must be that this was not an isolated incident; that it was not a pocket of evil in an otherwise broadly satisfactory system. The fear must be that such is the invalidity accorded to the child's view that it represents the tip of an iceberg. According to the Association of Child Abuse Lawyers, there are 80 police investigations into institutional abuse. It says each one

should prompt a public inquiry of its own. But the cost of the north Wales inquiry is put at £13.5m, and it is therefore almost certain to be the last of its kind.

7 The idea in the popular mind that acknowledgement and acceptance help in the process of 'healing' is linked to many and varied contributory ideas stemming from psychoanalysis in particular. But, as Macmillan (1997) indicates following a painstaking analysis of the original case notes of Breuer and Freud in the case of Anna O's talking cure, there was no empirical evidence for its success even in this bedrock case. One of the cornerstones of the almost universally held assumption that facing one's problems helps, is therefore on shaky ground.

8 Interestingly, Skrtic's analysis is similar to that of Toffler (1970: 364) who, before Skrtic, wrote of the need for a shift in schools from 'bureaucracy to Ad-hocracy', and likened the organizational system operating in schools to 'the factory model' (1970: 368), rather like Skrtic's analysis of it as 'machine bureaucracy'. The diagnosis of the likely consequences is similar, too. Nothing will change, asserts Toffler, if the basic machinery doesn't change – if the systems operating are not dismantled. As he puts it, '... much of this change [currently going on in schools] is no more than an attempt to refine the existent machinery, making it ever more efficient in pursuit of obsolete goals' (1970: 366).

9 Rousseau's comment was: 'There is nothing so absurd and hesitating as the gait of those who have been kept too long in leading-strings when they were little. This is one of the observations which are considered trivial because they are true' (1993: 49).

REFERENCES

Alexander, R. (1984) *Primary Teaching*. London: Holt.

Arnold, P., Bochel, H., Brodhurst, S. and Page, D. (1993) *Community Care: The Housing Dimension*. York: Joseph Rowntree Foundation.

Barker, R.G. (1968) *Ecological Psychology*. Stanford: Stanford University Press.

Bourdieu, P. and Eagleton, T. (1994) 'Doxa and common life: an interview', in S. Zizek (ed.), *Mapping Ideology*. London: Verso. pp. 265–77.

Bronfenbrenner, U. (1979) *The Ecology of Human Development*. Cambridge, MA: Harvard University Press.

Bryant, P.E. (1984) 'Piaget, teachers and psychologists', *Oxford Review of Education*, 10 (3): 251–9.

Carson, S. (1992) 'Normalisation, Needs and schools', *Educational Psychology in Practice*, 7 (4): 216–22.

Chazan, M., Laing, A.F. and Davies, D. (1994) *Emotional and Behavioural Difficulties in Middle Childhood*. London: Falmer.

Checkland, P. (1981) *Systems Thinking, Systems Practice*. Chichester: Wiley.

Cicourel, A.V. and Kitsuse, J.I. (1968) 'The social organisation of the high school and deviant adolescent careers', in E. Rubington and M.S. Weinberg (eds), *Deviance: The Interactionist Perspective: Text and Readings in the Sociology of Deviance*. London: Macmillan. pp. 124–36.

Cioffi, F. (1975) 'Freud and the idea of a pseudo-science', in R. Borger and F. Cioffi (eds), *Explanation in the Behavioural Sciences Confrontations*. Cambridge: Cambridge University Press.

Clarke, B. (1997) 'What Comprehensive Schools Do Better' in R. Pring and G.W. Binding (eds), *Affirming the Comprehensive Ideal*. London: Falmer Press.

Corbett, J. (1996) *Bad-Mouthing*. London: Falmer Press.

Crews, F. (1997) *The Memory Wars: Freud's Legacy in Dispute*. London: Granta.

Croll, P. and Moses, D. (2000) 'Ideologies and utopias: education professionals' view of inclusion', *European Journal of Special Needs Education*, 15 (1): 1–12.

Davies, N. (1998) 'The man who fought for the abused and was gagged', *Guardian*, 3 June, pp. 8–9.

DES (1967) *Children and their Primary schools*. The Plowden Report. London: HMSO.

DES (1978) *Special Educational Needs*. Report of the Committee of Enquiry into the Education of Handicapped Children and Young People, Cmnd 7212. London: HMSO.

DES (1989a) *Special Schools for Pupils with Emotional and Behavioural Difficulties*, Circular 23/89. London: HMSO.

DES (1989b) *Discipline in Schools* (The Elton Report). London: HMSO.

DES (1989c) *Discipline in Schools*. Report of the Committee of Enquiry. London: HMSO.

DFE (1994) *The Code of Practice on the Identification and Assessment of Special Educational Needs*. London: HMSO.

DfEE (1995) *Special Educational Needs in England, 1995*. London: HMSO.

DfEE (1997) *Excellence for all Children: Meeting Special Educational Needs*. London: DfEE.

DfEE (1998) http://www.coi.gov.uk/coi/depts/GDE/coi6201e.ok

Doyle, W. (1977) 'The uses of non-verbal behaviours: toward an ecological view of classrooms', *Merrill-Palmer Quarterly*, 23 (3): 179–92.

Edmonds, R. (1979) 'Effective schools for the urban poor', *Educational Leadership*, 37 (1): 15–23.

Elkind, D. (1967) 'Piaget's conservation problems', *Child Development*, 38: 15–27.

Foucault, M. (1980) 'Prison talk', in C. Gordon (ed.), *Power/Knowledge: Selected Interviews and Other Writings 1972–1977 – Michel Foucault*. London: Harvester Wheatsheaf. pp. 37–54.

Foucault, M. (1991) *Discipline and Punish* (trans. A. Sheridan). London: Penguin.

Galloway, D. (1983) 'Disruptive pupils and effective pastoral care', *School Organisation*, 13: 245–54.

Galloway, D., Martin, R. and Wilcox, B. (1985) 'Persistent absence from school and exclusion from school: the predictive power of school and community variables', *British Educational Research Journal*, 11: 51–61.

Gelman, R. (1982) 'Accessing one-to-one correspondence: still another paper about conservation', *British Journal of Psychology*, 73: 209–221.

Goffman, E. (1987) 'The moral career of the mental patient', in E. Rubington and M.S. Weinberg (eds), *Deviance: The Interactionist Perspective* (5th edn). New York: Macmillan. pp. 79–86.

Hallinger, P. and Murphy, J. (1986) 'The social context of effective schools', *American Journal of Education*, 94 (3): 328–55.

Hargreaves, D.H., Hestor, S.K. and Mellor, F.J. (1975) *Deviance in Classrooms*. London: Routledge and Kegan Paul.

Hoghughi, M. (1988) *Treating Problem Children: Issues, Methods and Practice*. London: Sage.

Howarth, C., Kenway, P., Palmer, G. and Street, C. (1998) *Key Indicators of Poverty and Social Exclusion*. York: Rowntree/New Policy Institute.

James, A. and Prout, A. (1990) 'A new paradigm for the sociology of childhood? Provenance, promise and problems' in A. James and A. Prout (eds), *Constructing and Reconstructing Childhood: Contemporary Issues in the Sociological Study of Childhood*. London, Falmer.

Jesson, D. and Gray, J. (1991) 'Slants on slopes: using multi-level models to investigate differential school effectiveness and its impact on schools' examination results', *School Effectiveness and School Improvement*, 2 (3): 230–71.

Kounin, J.S. (1967) 'An analysis of teachers' managerial techniques', *Psychology in the Schools*, 4: 221–7.

Laing, R.D. (1965) *The Divided Self*. London: Penguin.

Levine, D.U. and Lezotte, L.W. (1995) 'Effective schools research', in J.A. Banks and C.A. Banks (eds), *Handbook of Research on Multicultural Education*. New York: Macmillan.

Macmillan, M. (1997) *Freud Evaluated: The Completed Arc*. London: MIT.

McManus, M. (1987) 'Suspension and exclusion from high school – the association with catchment and school variables', *School Organisation*, 7 (3): 261–71.

Midwinter, E. (1977) 'The Professional–Lay Relationship: A Victorian Legacy', *Journal of Child Psychology and Psychiatry*, 18: 101–13.

Miller, J. (1993) *The Passion of Michel Foucault*. London: Harper Collins.

Mortimore, P. (1997) *The Road to Success: Four Case Studies of Schools which no Longer Require Special Measures*. London: DfEE.

Mortimore, P., Sammons, P., Stoll, L., Lewis, D. and Ecob, R. (1988) *School Matters: The Junior Years*. Exeter: Open Books.

Mousley, J.A., Rice, M. and Tregenza, K. (1993) 'Integration of students with disabilities into regular schools: policy in use', *Disability, Handicap and Society*, 8 (1): 59–70.

Nagel, E. (1959) 'Methodological issues in psychoanalytic theory', in S. Hook (ed.), *Psychoanalysis, Scientific Method and Philosophy*. New York: New York University Press.

Neisser, U. (ed.) (1986) *The School Achievement of Minority Children*. Hillsdale: Lawrence Erlbaum.

Popper, K.R. (1977) 'On hypotheses', in P.N. Johnson-Laird and P.C. Wason (eds), *Thinking: Readings in Cognitive Science*. Cambridge: Cambridge University Press.

Postman, N. (1996) *The End of Education*. New York: Alfred A. Knopf.

Ross, L.D., Amabile, T.M. and Steinmetz, J.L. (1977) 'Social roles, social control and biases in social-perception processes', *Journal of Personality and Social Psychology*, 35: 485–94.

Rousseau, J.-J. (1993 [1762]) *Emile*. Translated by Barbara Foxley. London: J.M. Dent and Sons.

Rubington, E. and Weinberg, M.S. (eds) (1968) *Deviance: The Interactionist Perspective; Text and Readings in the Sociology of Deviance*. London: Macmillan.

Rutter, M. (1995) 'Clinical implications of attachment concepts: retrospect and prospect', *Journal of Child Psychology and Psychiatry*, 36 (4): 549 71.

Rutter, M., Maughan, B., Mortimore, P. and Ouston, J. (1979) *Fifteen Thousand Hours: Secondary Schools and their Effects on Children*. London: Open Books.

Sammons, P., Nuttall, D. and Cuttance, P. (1993) 'Differential school effectiveness: results from a re-analysis of the Inner London Education Authority's junior school project data', *British Educational Research Journal*, 19 (4): 381–405.

Sayer, K. (1993) 'Language matters: the changing vocabularies of special needs'. Unpublished MA dissertation.

Skrtic, T.M. (1991) 'The special education paradox: equity as the way to excellence', in T. Hehir and T. Latus (eds) *Special Education at the Century's End: Evolution of Theory and Practice Since 1970*. Cambridge, MA: Harvard Educational Review No 23.

Smail, D. (1993) *The Origins of Unhappiness*. London: Harper Collins.

Smith, A.J. and Thomas, J.B. (1992) 'A survey of therapeutic support for children with emotional and behavioural disturbance (EBD) in special schools in the United Kingdom', *School Psychology International*, 13: 323–37.

Szasz, T.S. (1972) *The Myth of Mental Illness*. London: Paladin.

Thomas, G., and Loxley, A. (2002) *Deconstructing Special Education and Constructing Inclusion*. Buckingham: Open University Press.

Toffler, A. (1970) *Future Shock*. London: Pan Books.

Walkerdine, V. (1983) 'It's only natural: rethinking child-centred pedagogy', in A.M. Wolpe and J. Donald (eds), *Is There Anyone Here from Education?* London: Pluto.

Waterhouse Report (2000) *Committee of Enquiry into Abuse at Childrens' Homes*. London: HMSO.

Weatherley, R. and Lipsky, M. (1977) 'Street level bureaucrats and institutional innovation: implementing special educational reform', *Harvard Educational Review*, 47: 171–97.

Wolfensberger, W. (1990) 'Human service policies: the rhetoric versus the reality', in L. Barton (ed.), *Disability and Dependency*. London: Falmer.

6

The Forgotten 'E' in EBD

TONY BOWERS

AN EMOTIONAL WORLD

Our emotions shape the events in our lives. We typically seek out those things, people or activities we enjoy, that bring us happiness, and we avoid or minimize those that bring us discomfort or pain. Strong feelings or passions can extend not only to our relationships with others but to our moral, religious, professional and political convictions. Delight and disgust, pride and shame, joy and sadness, love and loathing all form part of the tapestry of human existence.

Ask someone to recall a particularly memorable film or play or sporting event and the chances are they won't relate the 'facts'; they'll tell you about the elements which touched them emotionally. They'll emphasize the really sad parts, maybe ('I was choking back the tears') or the really uplifting bit ('I nearly cried') or, in the case of the sporting event, perhaps the disappointment which turned to hope and then to joy ('I was on the edge of my seat'; 'I could hardly bear to look'; 'I was speechless by the end'). They may relate their behaviours, but they link them firmly to their feelings. People who sell things understand the power of our emotions and how they can influence our behaviour. Watch practically any television advertisement and note how little of it seeks just to convey factual information. Something which holds out the promise of popularity, enhanced status, increased attractiveness, better health, security or some other virtue, actually conveys the prospect, however fleeting or illusory, of emotional fulfilment. Touch the right emotions and it's likely to sell.

This doesn't mean that contentment is necessarily people's only goal. Some go to horror movies, seek out the most scary rides in theme parks or pay to bungee-jump in the anticipation of fear and the physiological effects which accompany that emotion. Whether or not we like it, some people gain pleasure from fighting and hurting others, enjoy the frisson which accompanies revenge, take satisfaction in their victory and another's defeat. For some these satisfactions are channelled vicariously (through television soap operas or through watching football, for example) or adopt simulated forms ('violent' computer games provide an example, as do some physical sports and activities such as 'paintballing'). Others may act them out more directly; they may become branded 'antisocial', but perhaps they gain admiration and prestige, at least from some. In short, we live in a world that is full of emotions, some which we approve of and some we'd prefer not to acknowledge. Everyone has them.

EBD AND EDUCATION

With this in mind, we can now look at what has been done for young people seen to experience 'difficulties' with their emotions. In UK educational circles, the term 'maladjusted' was in vogue until it became supplanted by the phrase 'emotional and behavioural difficulties' in the last quarter of the twentieth century. Laslett (1977) coined the phrase in his classic text for teachers and around the same time the government-convened Warnock Committee (DES, 1978) acknowledged, albeit reluctantly, that the word 'maladjusted' might stigmatize a child. The epithet 'maladjusted', of course, suggested that a young person was insufficiently adapted to the demands placed on him or her in particular situations. 'Emotional and behavioural difficulties' (EBD) on the other hand, covered two areas: the inner world of the child (his or her emotions) and the outer world of behaviour. The second of these might reasonably be expected to present more problems for the school and for those teaching the child. In spite of the Warnock Committee's warning that labelling of any kind should be avoided, and in the face of an increasingly radical challenge to discriminatory terminology, 'EBD' became the descriptor of choice. It remains with us today, even if the term 'social' has been bolted on along the way.

But not much else changed. Laslett (1977) in fact used the term 'EBD' interchangeably with 'maladjusted', as did Warnock (DES, 1978). It seems that it was actually too difficult to treat emotions and behaviour in separate and distinct ways. Some 10 years earlier, Hewett (1968) had acknowledged the same thing; he distanced himself from his book's title (*The Emotionally Disturbed Child in the Classroom*) on the first page, saying that the idea of 'emotional disturbance' was of little practical value in schools. Behaviourism and positivism were perhaps too heavily embedded in psychology, in whose province emotions appear to lie. Psychology has long sought to achieve scientific respectability; and scientific thinking, as Lazarus (1999) has pointed out, emphasizes objectivity. While we can observe behaviours (scientifically respectable), we can only assume or infer emotions (not so respectable). To understand feelings we must rely on subjective reports, and science has for a long time abhorred subjectivity. So the richness of accounts of states of mind and the behaviours they engender, which we find throughout literature, has never been even faintly matched by 'objective' research. Shakespeare might portray Hamlet's emotional turbulence and the thoughts accompanying it, Thomas Harris might engage us in the twisted mind of Hannibal Lecter. Somehow, though, emotions have offered too tricky a territory for those in the education system, with its ever-increasing emphasis on the gathering of seemingly objective data, to enter with much confidence.

EMOTIONS AND SCHOOLING

At the end of the 1980s, the government at the time commissioned a major report on pupil behaviour, stimulated in part by teacher unions' concerns and by the widespread popular concern with school bullying. The Elton Committee (DES, 1989) itself commissioned research from Sheffield University. There was plenty of opportunity for the researchers to engage with teachers' emotions and the affective (emotional) states of some of their more disturbing pupils. Unfortunately they touched only on the apparently observable: on behaviours which teachers found 'difficult' to deal with, on the sanctions they used and the kinds of problems (interrupting lessons, verbally abusing other children so on) they encountered during their working week. Although we can reasonably assume that emotions of many kinds (probably those of teachers and the politicians' emotions disturbed by their unions) led to the commissioning of this report, it focused solely on the 'B', not the 'E', of EBD. Its only contribution to the emotional lexicon can be found in its reference to the 'anxiety and paranoia' (1989: 151) engendered by the formal assessment process, although in doing this it also acknowledged that emotional problems can themselves constitute a special educational need.

The first Code of Practice on assessing children's special educational needs, published a few years later (DfE, 1994), embraced EBD as a learning difficulty. The relevant sections dwelt mainly on behaviour, although there was mention of four felt states or emotions: depression, fears, frustration and anger. The Code was intended to be followed by all those in education, although in fact it was given little priority by anyone other than educational psychologists, specialist education officers and schools' special educational need co-ordinators or SENCOs (Bowers et al., 1998). In many secondary schools, SENCOs paid little attention to matters classed as 'EBD', leaving these to the pastoral and disciplinary systems to deal with. The current Code of Practice (DfES, 2001) is considerably less forthcoming about emotions. Basing its categories of special educational need on those defined earlier by the English (not the British) government's Teacher Training Agency, this Code talks of 'development' rather than difficulties, adding 'social' to 'emotional and behavioural' (DfES, 2001: 7.60). The best we learn is that a child with what is now termed 'SEBD' may require 'help or counselling', 'flexible teaching arrangements', 'help with emotional maturity' and a few other anodyne provisions. It does nothing to enhance our knowledge of young people's emotional states and how they may influence their learning and behaviour at school.

Yet a visit to a government-inspired report from another era reveals far greater awareness of the importance of emotions than that demonstrated by the Code of Practice. Almost 50 years ago the Underwood Committee (MoE, 1955) presented a report on *Maladjusted Children*, which engaged far more fully with the emotional outcomes of relationships. It talked of 'a state of friction … in which each side becomes resentful, suspicious or cold' (1955: 93). It warned of the 'vicious cycle' (1955: 94) in which anxiety can lead to aggression, then to guilt and so to greater anxiety. The impact of insecurity and unhappiness on children's personal relationships was noted in this report, as was some children's apparent inability to respond to love and reassurance. Such topics as dread and the outcomes of inappropriately handled jealousy fell easily within the report's discourse. Unlike today's Code of Practice, the Underwood Report did not shy away from considering the link between emotions and behaviour or from accepting that presenting conditions such as anxiety or aggression may have differing emotional sources. Although the report was written long before 'emotional intelligence' (for example, Mayer and Salovey, 1993; Goleman, 1995) became an accepted part of everyday parlance, its recommendations on the qualities which teachers and others working with maladjusted children should possess suggest that its authors may well have had that characteristic in mind.

It seems, then, that emotions have been given a back seat where formally identified special educational needs are concerned. This doesn't mean that the words 'emotional' and 'emotionally', linked to 'difficulties', 'problems', 'disturbance' and 'disturbed', aren't still widely found. They are; but they tend to be non-specific. It's perhaps a bit like saying that a car has an 'engine problem' or a house has a 'structural difficulty.' It's doubtful whether the terms would be much good even to a motorist or a householder. They might cause a bit of worry, but they don't suggest what could be or ought to be done. When they come from a mechanic or a builder we could be forgiven for questioning their competence.

EMOTIONAL AWARENESS

While the Code of Practice on SEN (DfES, 2001) is thin on emotions, what has happened in individual schools has often been of richer quality. Over the past few years many schools have paid increasing attention to children's capacity to understand and express their feelings. Goleman (1995) put forward the notion that there is such a thing as 'emotional intelligence' which is independent of conventional definitions of intellect. At around the same time we saw the development of educational programmes intended to develop emotional competence in children. The Promoting Alternative Thinking Strategies (PATHS) curriculum (Greenberg et al., 1995), for example, set out to improve 'at risk' children's range of vocabulary and fluency in discussing emotional experience. It established agreed 'rules' for when and how particular emotions might be displayed. Understanding of emotions and management of certain emotions were also emphasized. PATHS has now been adopted in many schools in the United Kingdom; in some it is used with all students rather than with those considered emotionally vulnerable.

A range of primers has recently appeared, aimed at increasing students' or adults' 'emotional intelligence' (for example, Brearley, 2001) or 'emotional literacy' (Sharp, 2001). Despite their titles, emotions themselves seem to receive less prominence in these than they do in PATHS. Brearley (2001), for example, focuses on what appear to be dispositions (ambition, self-awareness, optimism, empathy, integrity), although these are described as 'emotional states'. A similar focus is provided by Sharp (2001), with self-awareness, resilience, motivation, interpersonal skills, influence and decisiveness given prominence. True emotions (happy, sad, 'mad' and so on) are of course mentioned, and there is little doubt that texts such as these promote emotional awareness. Anyone acquainted with counsellor training, management training or sales training will find a lot that is familiar in

Sharp's (2001) work, which is directed at the adults who teach and care for children.

So there are positive moves in many of our schools and classrooms. What, though, of the children whose emotional problems are sufficiently extreme for them to come to the attention of their local education authorities? When they are labelled EBD or SEBD, what actual feeling states are identified as causing difficulties? Given the title of this chapter, I propose to concentrate on emotions themselves rather than the personal characteristics which may promote or limit those emotions.

WHAT'S THE 'E' IN EBD?

I have just finished looking at the statements of 16 children (14 boys, 2 girls) which had been recently issued in three English local authorities. For those outside England, Wales and Northern Ireland, a statement is a legal document which indicates educational needs and sets out special arrangements to be made to meet those needs. It has similar force to the IEP (Individual Education Plan) in the United States. A statement is the product of a multiprofessional assessment involving, at the very least, detailed assessments and reports by teachers and an educational psychologist. The common feature of all 16 children was that their statements clearly related to EBDs.

So if these children were legally defined as having emotional as well as behavioural difficulties, we might reasonably expect to find the nature of those emotions and why they caused difficulties spelled out in Parts 2 and 3 of their statements (these are the sections dealing with special educational needs and the provision to be made to meet them). Certainly I found plenty of description of behaviour; terms such as 'restless', 'distractible', 'aggressive', 'verbally threatening', 'destructive', 'self harming', 'temper outbursts', 'impulsive', 'unmanageable' and 'abusive' provide some examples. Motivational attributions such as 'antisocial', 'defiant', 'demanding' and 'disaffected' also cropped up in some of the statements, as did the diagnostic categories ADHD (Attention Deficit Hyperactivity Disorder: five cases) and ODD (Oppositional Defiance Disorder: one case). 'Low self-esteem' and 'low self- confidence' also cropped up in 10 of these statements; we can reasonably discount these as emotions, however, even though they may be states of mind which give rise to emotions. Self-esteem is, as Apter (1997) points out, notoriously hard to assess with any accuracy; it is made up from a set of beliefs and expectations experienced by the child, and will inevitably be linked to his or her felt states (emotions). Low self-esteem is essentially a disposition and so unlikely to be of much help in either determining or changing 'emotional difficulties', even though its elements may well modify the way a person thinks about a situation.

If we remove descriptions of behaviours, attributions of motives and dispositional descriptions, we can concentrate on these students' emotions – the 'E' of the EBD which their local education authorities saw as sufficiently important to warrant both multidisciplinary assessment and specialist provision. Yet of the 16 statements, only nine could be found to say anything at all about emotions. Two mentioned 'anxiety', while another talked of 'frequent mood swings'. The latter, of course, isn't an emotion but it is suggestive of labile emotional states, so I counted it. Just one emotion was common to all the nine EBD statements which had any 'E' in them: unsurprisingly perhaps, it was *anger*. Such phrases as 'angry and frustrated,' 'angry outbursts' and 'needs help with managing anger' cropped up in all nine. Anger went with anxiety, with defiance, destruction and aggression. Although it was only mentioned in just over half the statements, it was implied in most of the others. Somehow it was the unifying emotion in these EBD statements.

This was a small sample and may be unrepresentative of all children with statements for EBD. Yet when I discuss emotions with those (teachers as well as education officers, advisers and psychologists) who work with young people seen to have social, emotional and behavioural difficulties, most of them suggest anger as the emotion most likely to be connected to those difficulties. This doesn't come as a surprise. Anger in others is likely not only to be hard to deal with; in schools it usually has to be dealt with in a very public way. It is an emotional state that both boys and girls recognize and can label equally effectively when they are as young as four (Hughes and Dunn, 2002), whereas awareness of another basic 'negative' emotion – sadness – develops rather later. Displays of anger, as Hughes and Dunn (2002) point out, are not only more dramatic than those of other emotions, they are also likely to be encountered more frequently. Manifestations of anger are also potentially threatening to the beholder. They can easily evoke fear and anxiety. The Greek philosopher Aristotle saw anger both as a 'boiling of the blood' and an 'appetite for returning pain for pain' (Barnes, 1984: 403); to be on the receiving end of anger can be an uncomfortable experience for school staff, children and parents. So it seems reasonable that anger should get top billing in EBD statements.

It seems reasonable, but in fact it's superficial. It is unworthy of the expensive, time-consuming and supposedly professional 'multidisciplinary' assessments that have led to the formulation of the statements. We all know about anger because we have experienced it lots of times in our lives. It's easy to recognize and difficult to deal with. It is intuitively easy to assume that if there was less of it, then life would be easier for teachers and pupils alike. It seems like the source of a lot of trouble. Averill has described anger as 'the holy ghost that … begets much aggression' (2001: 351), while at the same time pointing out that our knowledge of it is at best unsystematic. What we do know (Lazarus, 1999) is that the expression of anger depends heavily on the goal of preserving or increasing esteem: self-esteem, the esteem of others, or both. There has to be somebody or something to blame for some perceived harm to the individual. As we know, it doesn't have to be physical harm: some form of rebuke, put-down or 'disrespect' can be enough to stimulate it. The trouble with anger, as we will see later, is that it can so easily mask many other emotions which lie at its roots.

DISTURBANCE OR DIFFICULTY?

The problem with EBDs is that they present a problem for schools. Ask any teacher who the EBD children are (or the ones they find challenging, they're often the same) and they will be able to tell you. Ask them to define their emotional difficulties, though, and they may not find it so easy. Whether we choose the word 'difficulties' or opt for 'disturbance' to provide the 'D' in EBD, it is worth briefly considering what constitutes a difficulty or a disturbance where emotions are concerned. These days it is generally accepted by psychologists and philosophers alike (for example, Lazarus, 1999; Neu, 2000) that emotions and thoughts are inextricably intertwined. What we think about a situation (that is, how we perceive it) will affect how we feel – and how we feel will strongly affect our thoughts. There's nothing essentially 'disturbed' about a felt state (emotion); it simply flows from thoughts about people, problems and situations.

So where there are emotional 'disturbances' (or difficulties), these will go hand-in-hand with disturbed (or difficulty-inducing) thinking. Some things just don't seem the same to the young person with EBD as they do to most other children of similar age. They're experienced *more intensely* (or sometimes considerably less intensely) or simply *differently*. What most people see as faintly frustrating becomes deeply annoying. What most see as humorous becomes insulting. What most see as being a bit of a challenge becomes terrifyingly strange. These elements of cognitive intensity and cognitive difference lead children with EBD to demonstrate three things: *extremes of emotion* which seem somehow unusual or unreasonable; *abnormal displays of emotion* which run counter to those that we might expect in most similarly-aged young people; and sometimes an *apparent absence* of certain emotions which we see as normal (for example, compassion).

Although I haven't met any of the young people whose statements I referred to earlier, I suspect that their emotions alone didn't bring them to the attention of their local education authorities (LEAs). It was their behaviour. The 'B' of EBD is what bugs teachers and challenges schools. That's why anger is mentioned practically to the exclusion of any other emotional state. After all, what emotion other than anger are we likely to attribute to threatening or abusive behaviour? What can we safely assume underpins the actions of a student who regularly defies teachers, who repeatedly violates or destroys property or who consistently shows hostility to classmates and teachers alike? What extreme or unusual emotional state might we reasonably be expected to want most to modify or eliminate? Anger is just one of what Lazarus (1999) has called the 'nasty' emotions, but its behavioural accompaniments are more likely to upset the system of a school than others in the 'nasty' category. It seems a safe bet that the melancholy child or the nervous child won't challenge the smooth running of a school as much as a child who seems to show excessive anger or whose anger crops up when somehow we think it shouldn't.

A MASKING EMOTION

Starting with 135 separately named emotions, Shaver et al.'s (2001) research with young people ended up with just six core components (or 'prototypes') of emotion. These six – love, joy, surprise, anger, sadness and fear – are not far removed from Ekman and Friesen's (1975; 1976) earlier characterization of the emotion states which are recognizable from facial expressions. However, Shaver et al.'s analysis, based on the complexity of our language and its associated meanings, goes further. Within each one of the core emotions we can find a wide range of contributory emotions. Sadness, for example, has 36, while joy contains 33. Shaver et al's (2001) results indicate that within anger alone up to 30 different emotion states are traceable. To name just a few, we can locate such feelings as irritation, frustration, bitterness, vengefulness, contempt and revulsion within the over-arching prototype of anger. Since I've highlighted anger as the critical emotion in the (admittedly small) sample of children's statements I examined, I will focus on this in the ensuing sections.

So what does it mean when anger is seen as the predominant emotion with which a student has 'difficulty' or which is somehow 'disturbed'? Not very much when there are so many different emotions which can underpin or sustain it. Indeed, evidence from other research suggests that we can expand on the already long list that Shaver and his co-workers have compiled, certainly where the behaviour and discipline of young people are concerned. For example, Rutter et al. (1998) have pointed to the strong and consistent association between childhood antisocial behaviour of all kinds and depression and anxiety. Yet depression features under the general heading of 'sadness' in Shaver et al.'s (2001) six prototypes, while they put anxiety firmly under the heading of 'fear'. If we assume that antisocial behaviour is a fairly general feature of those children who are officially deemed to have 'social, emotional and behaviour difficulties', then the link with anger may be a tenuous one at anything more than a superficial level. Displays of anger and the surface emotionality associated with these will often cover up very different eliciting emotional states.

You may still find yourself wondering why I'm delving this deep. Surely an angry child is an angry child, whatever the emotional archaeology associated with that anger? And generally speaking, displays of anger in school or anywhere else aren't desirable. It's not hard for them to prove intolerable. Anger can beget violence. Exclusion from school often flows from incidents associated with anger. That's why we have anger management programmes (for example, Faupel et al., 1998) to help students to regulate it. That's why we have programmes aimed at increasing emotional intelligence (for example, Brearley, 2001). That's why counsellors are now employed in some schools and they will often work with children who are seen to have problems with their anger. Forget the rest of it – it's the anger and the behaviours that go with it that creates problems for most schools and for society as a whole.

That may be so. But we need also to remember the status of a statement which relates to 'emotional difficulties'. It indicates that the young person's affective state (not just his or her behaviour) is sufficiently problematic and intractable to interfere with his or her learning to the extent that special arrangements are necessary. Those arrangements (sometimes specialist provision or separate schooling, often the allocation of an additional person in class or at break times) are sufficiently resource-intensive to merit a statement. Multi-professional assessment and deliberation have gone into the decision-making process. Reports have been written not only by those in the school, but always by trained psychologists and often by social workers and medical professionals. The process can take six months or more. The purpose of a statement is to outline the young person's needs in some detail and set out what should be done, on the basis of those individual requirements, to meet them. Given all this, to end up so often with just one predominant emotion seems a bit thin when the sources of anger can be so different and when the emotions which support and sustain outward displays of 'temper' or anger can be so varied.

THOUGHTS AND FEELINGS

I have already mentioned that it is now generally recognized that thoughts and feelings go hand-in-hand. In simple terms, most 'therapeutic' interventions are aimed at changing thoughts; feelings, it is assumed, will then change or at least become less problematic. Yet an inadequate emotional foundation in early life, as Frankish (2000) has observed from her work with offenders with mental health and learning difficulties, leaves it difficult if not impossible to build an adequate thinking, feeling personality. This may be why both highly-critical and over protective parenting have been found to be associated with 'externalizing' (that is, aggressive) behaviours in young schoolchildren (Peris and Baker, 2000) and why inadequate knowledge of or recognition of others' emotions predict aggression and displays of anger in young children (for example, Denham et al., 2002).

What happens in early life when we contact others' emotions will affect our own ability to integrate those emotions into our own thinking. That very difficulty in thinking about emotions will make it hard to develop a full and appropriate range of feelings.

TOWARDS A TYPOLOGY OF ANGER

Just asking a young person why they seem constantly bad-tempered, 'short-fused' and easy to rouse to anger will probably not reveal the thinking that underlies their presenting emotional state. This may appear self-evident, but very few reports I read seem to explore the thinking and feeling states that could contribute to the emotional difficulties observed (or inferred to be present) in the student. It isn't always easy to do, yet because it is not easy doesn't mean it shouldn't be attempted. By now it will be apparent that anger alone does not offer a good descriptor of the emotions which it may conceal. I will turn to these shortly. But let's assume that we accept the description of anger as the sole emotion. Even then, we need to ask just what type of anger we are encountering.

Anger can take many forms. We are obviously familiar with rage, abuse, violence and so on: anyone demonstrating these seems pretty obviously angry. But what about the sullen, uncommunicative individual? What about the person who seems strained and icily polite when dealing with you? What about the individual who appears co-operative and compliant but then turns out not to have done what they were expected to do? When someone lets you down for no apparent reason, and perhaps does so on more than one occasion, is that just forgetfulness or is it maybe a demonstration of concealed anger? Lazarus (1999) helps us here by discriminating between five types of anger. While all are classifiable under one emotional heading, they take different forms. It isn't difficult to see, either, that different thought patterns are likely to accompany them. For brevity, they are set out in Table 6.1.

Table 6.1 Types of anger (after Lazarus, 1999) and accompaniments

Type of anger:	Prototypical anger	Righteous anger	Inhibited anger	Sulking	Hostility
Characterized by:	annoyance easily accelerating to rage; saying and doing things designed to hurt one or more others; ensuing retaliation; regret	self-justification; indignation; outrage; externalizing blame	distancing self from others; unintentional 'leaking' of anger through verbal utterances, expression or gesture	reproachful behaviour, lack of communication or co-operation; dependence on the other party not becoming unduly alienated; insecure anger	hatred; anger appears only when in the presence of (or at the thought of) the hated person(s); anger provoked by other persons will usually leave no residual hostility
Accompanying thoughts:	there is a slight or 'put down' indicating an absence of respect; damage has been done to me or those close to me	there has been an injustice which offers an excuse for anger; others' actions threaten my self-esteem; if others break the rules they should expect me to behave this way	fear of others' retaliation if anger is expressed; refusal to show feelings when they are negative; concern over revealing feelings and further damaging relationships	awareness of dependency; low estimation of own ability to deal with others	deep dislike of a person or persons becomes embedded as a dispositional feature

If these different kinds of anger aren't enough, we need to bear in mind also the range of emotions which can engender anger. It is too simple to assume that anger arises just because someone is angry. The emotional difficulties of many children who show anger and the aggression that goes with it are likely to have other deeper emotions underlying them. Space doesn't allow much elaboration, but we will look at just a few of these. Any attempt to 'manage' that anger (or effectively to reduce the behaviours which go with feelings of anger) will just scratch the surface without an appreciation of what lies beneath. We will all have experienced the emotions set out below. Remember, though, that what are related here will be experienced with a level of intensity and duration which will interfere with the ability to learn. In an educational context, these are the essential conditions of the 'E' in EBD or (since DfES, 2001) SEBD.

Jealousy

When someone is threatened by the loss of an important relationship with another person, jealousy ensues. If that loss has been experienced on previous occasions, perhaps painfully, then jealousy will be even more deeply felt. Insecurity and fear lie at the root of jealousy – and jealousy is a prime source of anger. Righteous anger, inhibited anger and hostility can all arise from jealousy. Although we often associate jealousy with romantic relationships, it can be found wherever the esteem of others is concerned. Neu (2000) sees the seeds of jealousy lying in a universal 'desire to be desired' (2000: 48) or need for affection and to be loved.

Incidents of bullying, particularly where they involve the social exclusion of a child, may have at their roots anger motivated by jealousy. Name-calling, sullying the reputation of the target child, getting that child into trouble and so on can often be driven by fear that the child in question will take something 'special' away from already valued relationships. More than many children realize, at a conscious level, their relationships with others confirm who they are: whether they are interesting, clever, witty, 'cool', good at games or whatever. A threat to those relationships is a threat to that confirmation. Jealousy and its associated emotion of fear – fear that something is about to be taken away that may not be recoverable – can often be found within aggression directed at members of a social group. In its extreme, jealous anger can be a very powerful force indeed. The sense of hurt which often accompanies it can lead both to angry feelings and sadness.

Depression/sadness

There is no shortage of literature reporting hostility and anger displayed by depressed adults and depressed children (Berkowitz, 2001). Typically, depression has been seen from a psychodynamic perspective (Hammen, 1997): anger is turned inward, rather than being directed outwards. Depression has therefore been associated with self-anger. It is widely reported that depressed individuals blame themselves when things go wrong and yet don't accept credit when they achieve; somehow self-confidence becomes inverted in the presence of feelings of sadness and depression.

Berkowitz (2001), however, has suggested that many 'sad' experiences, particularly those involving loss and the emotion of grief associated with that loss, lead to outward displays of anger and so to aggressive behaviour. He raises the reasonable argument that feeling very sad will make people angry, thereby making them quite likely to look for someone outside of themselves to blame and to project their aggression onto. From this perspective a child who is somehow on a 'hair trigger' for anger, whose unpredictability makes it likely that she or he will have outbursts of temper for no apparent reason, could well be a depressed child.

Shame and guilt

It is easy to think of these emotions as quite distinct from anger. Somehow they seem private and inward-directed emotions. Yet shame has been found to be closely linked to aggression in research by Tangney et al. (2001). Conventional wisdom has it that frustration of a desired goal (that is, not getting what you want) leads to aggression. However, Tangney and her co-workers reframed this. The problem, they suggested, lay not in the frustration itself but in the witnessing of that frustration. Shame, they suggested, can easily foster anger and so lead to aggression. Their research with older adolescents indicated that a *proneness to shame* was consistently correlated with measures of anger arousal, resentment, irritability and a tendency to blame others for negative events.

To be ashamed we need to be aware that others know of our shortcomings. Guilt, on the other hand, is a more private affair. Tangney et al. (2001) found that what they termed a *proneness to shame-free guilt* was unassociated with anger. Put quite simply, it seems that shame can very easily lead to anger, while guilt appears to be an inward-turning emotion. Guilty people often try to make things right with those they have wronged; humiliated people don't.

It is not hard to see how a student failing in school, or who fails to succeed socially, can develop a sense of shame which becomes continually reinforced by further frustrating (and therefore humiliating) experiences. We can expect anger to result. It would be easy to see that anger stemming from failure and in a way it does. But two conditions attach to any failure:

it must be witnessed and it must lead to a sense of shame in the student. Shame is a relatively fleeting emotion: resentment directed at the source of that shame is likely to be far longer lasting.

Envy

The philosopher Jerome Neu (2000) has distinguished two kinds of envy. The first is *malicious envy* (wanting to lower the other) and the second *admiring envy*, where the individual wants in some way to become like another person. Both can lead to anger.

At the centre of envy is invidious comparison. An envious person sees someone else as better off than they should be or they deserve to be. Envy can attach to qualities (good looks, popularity and so on) or to possessions or accomplishments. In school, openly expressed envy can lead to the destruction of property (clothes, books and so on) and to many of the facets of bullying with which we are familiar. However, there are potentially longer-term consequences. Envy, perhaps like other 'negative' emotions, can easily be repressed (Smith, 1991). It becomes what he terms an 'unsanctioned emotion' (1991: 92). Repressed feelings of envy now lead to a more pervasive condition: what Nietsche (1887/1967) has termed *ressentiment*. The essence of *ressentiment* is that it seeks out an external hostile world. 'It's not fair' is the key cognition that underpins it: what is envied cannot be attained and so the world is an unfriendly place. The philosopher Scheler (1915/1961), too, has addressed *ressentiment* as a condition resulting from repressed envy. He sees general negativity, accompanied by violent and apparently unsystematic rejection of people and situations, stemming from that condition.

If we look at Table 6.1, it is quite easy to locate the anger which may be shown by a student whose envy has been generalized into *ressentiment*. Inhibited anger and hostility seem good candidates. The shape of such anger may not always be obvious. Gossiping, denigrating, plotting, non-co-operation and so on all have their place in defining ill-will. We need, though, to remember that *ressentiment* and the anger accompanying it can, at times, bypass outward hostility (Smith, 1991). In that case resignation and apathy may actually mask the anger which accompanies envy.

EMOTIONAL PRECISION?

So if there are different kinds of anger and if many apparently angry episodes owe their existence to other emotional states, does that invalidate the notion of anger? No; it is an extremely common emotional prototype. But if we are to conclude that a student's special educational needs are somehow rooted in his or her emotional state, then we perhaps owe it to that student to delve more deeply into the important feelings which are masked by that prototype. It is just too simple to talk about anger.

Some 40 years ago, Gordon Allport drew attention to the common Latin root (*motum*) of two words: 'motive' and 'emotion'. Emotions, observed Allport (1963), move us, just like motives. Violent emotions, he suggested, are disruptive and seem not to have any adaptive purpose. For him, emotion was best defined as 'a stirred up condition of the organism' (1963: 198) and then left alone in his treatise on personality. Yet in his language we can find echoes of what many students will tell us: 'He's stirring me up' or 'I was stirred up' are phrases which indicate a common-sense understanding of what Allport viewed as a 'signal that things are not going right with us' (1963: 198).

Stirred up emotions are mixed emotions. We seldom just experience one emotion, even if we think we do. A sense of hurt can be accompanied by fondness for the person causing that hurt; a sense of fear or insecurity can easily accompany exhilaration or joy. Mixed emotions are an inevitable part of life; those who are unable to understand (or 'integrate') them are said to experience 'splitting' (Cole et al., 1994), and splitting in adults is seen as an indicator of personality disorder. Yet difficulty in integrating emotions, in achieving balance and understanding shades of feelings, is precisely what many young people labelled 'EBD' experience.

The ability to think and talk about emotion is an important dimension of self-regulation. Labelling, describing, conceptualizing and understanding one's feelings is a goal of many therapies. It is therefore disappointing to find such a one-paced approach to the 'emotional difficulties' of the young people whose statements I saw. It does not do justice either to them or to the assessment process that preceded the legal definition of their special educational needs.

EMOTION RESTRUCTURING

I remarked earlier that restricted ability to think about emotions will make it difficult to develop a full range of emotional experiences as the young person grows older. Learning to think and talk about emotional reactions is a goal of many therapies; the rise in attempts to develop emotional literacy in both students and teachers can therefore only be welcomed. Emotions don't usually come singly, though. Greenberg et al. (1995) recognized this in their work with younger students, placing an emphasis on the understanding of simultaneous emotions. At a simple level, we can be sad that we're deprived of something (for example, permission to go out, a valued toy and so on) and simultaneously 'mad' or annoyed with the person who won't let us have it. As we have seen, though, things can go deeper than that.

For a child to be formally labelled 'EBD' or 'SEBD', he or she will be seen to present considerable challenges at school. Abuse and neglect, particularly in early childhood, are associated with a cocktail of problems which include poor cognitive performance, low school attainment and delinquency (Perez and Widom, 1994). Risk factors which accumulate and overwhelm a child's capacity for coping, whether long-term (living in a violent home, violent community, protracted bullying and so on) or relatively immediate (exposure to a sudden traumatic event such as fire, homelessness and so forth) are known to cause energy needed for present conscious activities to be diverted to the replay of past extreme emotions (Melzak, 1997). Teasing out the emotional pathways which lead to a child's current simple 'anger' or 'sadness' (the prototypical emotions of EBD) will not necessarily be an easy activity. But the alternative, to ignore them or to define them in a simple or even banal way, dodges the complex motivating forces that generate the behaviours which are found difficult to handle.

The 'E' in EBD continues to be given little attention within our education system. Dispositional factors (self-esteem, social competence and so on) are sometimes seen as providing sufficient focus. There is a case to be made for working to enhance them; they are not, however, emotions. Emotions themselves can be worrying things; when others display them they can easily evoke strong emotions in us, and vice-versa. History has seen repeated attempts to reduce or eliminate young people's experience of particular emotions, with anger and fear high on the agenda at most times (Stearns, 1993). There isn't much evidence for their success. It's understandable, or course: seemingly unregulated emotions have always been scary and maybe not mentioning them is preferable to getting too involved with them. That is why it is often easier to use labels such as 'aggressive' or 'antisocial', or to ascribe to children such characteristics as 'low self-esteem' or 'poor emotional intelligence'.

But as I said at the start of this chapter, emotions are what drive us. They colour our lives, they fascinate us. The continuing popularity of television 'soap' dramas bears witness to this. Watch any one for a couple of episodes and you'll find a whole source of emotional literacy material: love, jealousy, fear, pride, envy, rage, vengefulness, trepidation, guilt, remorse, sorrow, greed and a whole host of others occupy our screens. Most importantly, the characters there have to cope with other people's displays of emotion; they also have to try (with varying success) to integrate their own mixed emotions in response to varying events. Plans and prescriptions for children which ignore the complexity of their emotional worlds yet indicate that somehow they have 'difficulties' with those emotions short-change them and indicate either lack of energy or lack of insight on the part of the professionals involved.

At a simple level, discourse on a child/young person's 'emotional difficulties' and what might be done about these should engage with at least the following:

- the prototypical emotion(s) shown (that is, how the child/young person seems a lot of the time or at times which cause concern);
- the ways in which those emotions are dysfunctional for the child/young person and others in school;
- from case history, the life events which may lie behind those dysfunctional emotions;
- how the child/young person currently regulates his or her emotions (that is, the things that are seen as extreme or inappropriate);
- what other emotions may underlie the prototypical emotion;
- what difficulties there may be for the child/young person in integrating mixed emotions;
- what emotions are seldom or never apparent;
- what language is needed to assist the child/young person in emotional understanding and integration; and
- how the child/young person can be moved closer to accessing a full range of emotions.

Many children we call 'EBD' seem 'stuck' with one emotional state which they replay vigorously and often. It isn't enough simply to cite the emotion that presents itself, however. We need to undertake the difficult task of understanding the complexity of an apparently simple emotional state. Otherwise we might as well drop the 'E' altogether in the typologies used by government, LEAs and schools.

REFERENCES

Allport, G. (1963) *Pattern and Growth in Personality.* London: Holt, Rinehart and Winston.

Apter, T. (1997) *The Confident Child.* New York: Norton.

Averill, J.R. (2001) 'Studies of anger and aggression: implications for theories of emotion', in W.G. Parrott (ed.), *Emotions in Social Psychology.* Philadelphia, PA: Psychology Press.

Barnes, J. (1984) *The Complete Works of Aristotle.* Princeton, NJ: Princeton University Press.

Berkowitz, L. (2001) 'On the formation and regulation of anger and aggression: a cognitive-neoassociationistic analysis', in W.G. Parrrott (ed.), *Emotions in Social Psychology.* Philadelphia, PA: Psychology Press.

Bowers, T., Dee, L., West, M. and Wilkinson, D. (1998) *Evaluation of the User Friendliness of the Special Educational Needs Code of Practice.* London: DfEE.

Brearley, M. (2001) *Emotional Intelligence in the Classroom: Creative Learning Strategies for 11–18s.* Carmarthen: Crown House.

Cole, P.M., Michel, M.K. and Teti, L.O'D. (1994) 'The development of emotion regulation and dysregulation: a clinical perspective', *Monographs of the Society for Research in Child Development*, 59, 73–100.

Denham, S.A., Caverly, S., Schmidt, M., Blair, K., DeMulder, E., Caal, S., Hamada, H. and Mason, T. (2002) 'Preschool understanding of emotions: contributions to classroom anger and aggression', *Journal of Child Psychology and Psychiatry*, 43 (7): 901–916.

Department for Education (1994) *Code of Practice on the Identification and Assessment of Special Educational Needs.* London: DfE.

Department for Education and Skills (2001) *Special Educational Needs Code of Practice.* London: DfES.

Department of Education and Science (1978) *Special Educational Needs: Report of the Committee of Enquiry into the Education of Handicapped Children and Young People* (The Warnock Report). London: HMSO.

Department of Education and Science (1989) *Discipline in Schools: Report of the Committee of Enquiry Chaired by Lord Elton.* London: HMSO.

Ekman, P. and Friesen, M.V. (1975) *Unmasking the Face.* Englewood Cliffs, NJ: Prentice-Hall.

Ekman, P. and Friesen, M.V. (1976) *Pictures of Facial Affect.* Palo Alto, CA: Consulting Psychologists Press.

Faupel, A., Herrick, E. and Sharp, P. (1998) *Anger Management: A Practical Guide.* London: Fulton.

Frankish, P. (2000) 'Thought and feeling – you can't have one without the other (presidential address to the British Psychological Society)', *The Psychologist*, 13 (8): 396–9.

Goleman, D (1995) *Emotional Intelligence.* London: Bloomsbury.

Greenberg, M.T., Kusche, C.A., Cook, E.T. and Quamma, J.P. (1995) 'Promoting emotional competence in school-aged children: the effects of the PATHS curriculum', *Development and Psychopathology*, 7: 117–36.

Hammen, C. (1997) *Depression.* Hove: Psychology Press.

Hewett, F.M. (1968) *The Emotionally Disturbed Child in the Classroom.* Boston, MA: Allyn and Bacon.

Hughes, C. and Dunn, J. (2002) '"When I say a naughty word". A longitudinal study of young children's accounts of anger and sadness in themselves and close others', *British Journal of Developmental Psychology*, 20: 515–35.

Laslett, R. (1977) *Educating Maladjusted Children.* London: Crosby Lockwood Staples.

Lazarus, R.S. (1999) *Stress and Emotion: A New Synthesis.* New York: Springer Publishing Company.

Mayer, J.D. and Salovey, P. (1993) 'The intelligence of emotional intelligence', *Intelligence*, 17: 433–42.

Melzak, S. (1997) 'The emotional impact of violence on children', in V. Varma (ed.), *Violence in Children and Adolescents.* London: Jessica Kingsley.

Ministry of Education (1955) *Report of the Committee on Maladjusted Children* (The Underwood Report). London: HMSO.

Neu, J. (2000) *A Tear is an Intellectual Thing: The Meanings of Emotion.* New York: Oxford University Press.

Nietzsche, F.W. (1967) *On the Genealogy of Morals*. Translated by W. Kaufmann and R.J. Hollingdale (original work 1887). New York: Vintage.

Perez, C.M. and Widom, C.P. (1994) 'Childhood victimization and long-term intellectual and academic outcomes', *Child Abuse and Neglect*, 18 (8): 617–33.

Peris, T.S. and Baker, B.L. (2000) 'Applications of the expressed emotion construct to young children with externalizing behavior: stability and prediction over time', *Journal of Child Psychology and Psychiatry*, 41 (4): 457–62.

Rutter, M., Giller, H. and Hagell, A. (1998) *Antisocial Behavior by Young People*. Cambridge: Cambridge University Press.

Scheler, M. (1961) *Ressentiment*. L.A. Coser (ed.), translated by W.W. Holdhein (original work 1915). Glencoe, IL: Free Press.

Sharp, P. (2001) *Nurturing Emotional Literacy: A Practical Guide for Teachers, Parents and those in the Caring Professions*. London: Fulton.

Shaver, P., Schwartz, J., Kirson, D. and O'Connor, C. (2001) 'Emotion Knowledge: further exploration of a prototype approach', in W.G. Parrott (ed.), *Emotions in Social Psychology*. Philadelphia, PA: Psychology Press.

Smith, R.H. (1991) 'Envy and the Sense of Injustice', in P. Salovey (ed.), *The Psychology of Jealousy and Envy*. New York: Guildford.

Stearns, P.N. (1993) 'Girls, boys, and emotions: redefinitions and historical change', *Journal of American History*, 80 (1): 36–74.

Tangney, J.P., Wagner, P., Fletcher, C. and Gramzow, R. (2001) 'Shamed into anger? The relation to shame and guilt to anger and self-reported aggression', in W.G. Parrott (ed.), *Emotions in Social Psychology*. Philadelphia, PA: Psychology Press.

Part Two

ROOTS AND CAUSES

7

Biology and Behaviour: The Educational Relevance of a Biopsychosocial Perspective

PAUL COOPER

Over recent years biology has come to play an increasing role in our understanding of human thought and behavioural processes. Educational discourses are beginning to acknowledge the relevance of biology in new ways (Geake and Cooper, 2003). This is particularly evident in the field of social emotional and behavioural difficulties (SEBD). There are difficult and, at times, controversial aspects to this topic. However, whilst we must address these challenges with care and caution, we must also avoid simplistic responses. A key assumption underpinning this chapter is that the more we understand about the nature of a child's difficulties the better placed we are to provide effective support. Crucially, we must find ways of incorporating biological insights with social and environmental understandings of SEBD. A biopsychosocial perspective, it is argued, will help us to do this. The chapter opens with examples of different types of SEBD, followed by brief accounts of the social psychological and behavioural explanations of how these difficulties develop. The chapter concludes with some examples of how these understandings can translate into approaches to intervention. Careful attention is given to the nature of and basis for biological claims and their value to educators in promoting the positive educational engagement of students' schools.

THE DEVELOPMENT OF SOCIAL, EMOTIONAL AND BEHAVIOURAL DIFFICULTIES

The prevalence of SEBD

It is estimated that at least 10 per cent of the school population in England is, at any one time, affected with SEBD. These students are distributed across the range of educational provision, though it is important to note that the overwhelming majority is to be found in mainstream schools (see Table 7.1).

Table 7.1   *The prevalence of SEBDs in England*

At least 10% (936,000) of children experience serious SEBDs (Source: *Young Minds* briefing paper.
  no. 1, March, 1999)
1% (93,500) of children are in special schools of various types, including those for SEBD
  (DfEE stats., 1998)
< 0.1% (8,000) are, over a year, excluded from school (DfEE stats., 2001)
< 0.1% (7,700) of children are in PRU's (DfEE stats., 1998)
(approximately) 90% of children with SEBDs are in mainstream schools.

Having said this, in spite of the overall increase in numbers of students with a wide range of special education needs (SEN) being educated in inclusive settings, the numbers of students with SEBD being educated in segregated settings in England has remained virtually static over the past 30 years (Norwich, 2003). This suggests that whilst SEBD is largely a pervasive problem faced by the majority of mainstream schools, there remains a significant problem in securing the access of members of this group to mainstream education.

Categories: caution and value

Although categorical approaches to SEBD (and other areas of SEN) are unpopular with some educationists, they can help us to appreciate the range of difficulties that fall under the vague umbrella term of SEBD. Categories should, however, be treated with caution. We should be wary about the negative consequences of indiscriminate labelling. It is helpful to think of these categories as applying to social, emotional and behavioural patterns that, rather than as labels to be applied to people. It is also helpful to see the patterns of behaviour defined by these categories as extreme variants of normal behaviour. As such, so-called deviant or disordered behaviour not only describes behaviour, but behaviour in relation to a particular situation. The situation will usually include the viewpoint of an individual (or shared by a group) that judges the behaviour to be deviant or disordered.

There is a further reason why a categorical approach to understanding SEBD might be useful. Studies suggest that teachers' pedagogical decision-making is strongly influenced by teachers' perceptions of pupils that are based on fairly limited interaction with and observation of pupils (Brown and McIntyre, 1993). A study of teachers in English secondary schools found that, after only seven weeks of year seven, teachers came to apparently stable decisions about the characteristics of their pupils in terms of pupils' levels of ability, whilst strong speculations were being made about pupils' behaviour, motivation and personal attributes (Cooper and McIntyre, 1996: 133). These decisions can be understood in terms of Hargreaves et al's (1975) theory of 'typing', by which the teacher places pupils into ready-made categories relating to pupils' perceived ability, behaviour and motivation, and other personal attributes (for example, appearance, gender and so on) (Cooper and McIntyre, 1996). These studies suggest that this 'typing' process is an important element in expert teachers' professional craft knowledge, enabling them to make speedy sense of complex circumstances and conditions in busy classroom settings in which there is limited time for extended reflection and analysis. If this is a general feature of the way in which teachers operate, then it would seem important that teachers employ sound theoretical knowledge. It is also important to note that whilst teachers can use research-based theoretical insights to inform their practice, it seems that this process is most effective when the theoretical knowledge can be assimilated through direct reference to their practical theorizing.

An outline typology of SEBD

Psychiatrists and psychologists commonly divide SEBDs into two main categories: *externalizing* difficulties and *internalizing* difficulties. It is also possible to think of these categories in terms of their *aetiology*, that is, the range of factors which influence the development of the difficulties. These aetiological factors can be thought of in terms of biological, psychological, social and cultural influences.

Externalizing difficulties I

These are patterns of behaviour and manners of self-presentation that are experienced by others as being disruptive, antisocial and/or confrontational.
  Sub-categories of externalizing will include:

• *Disaffection*: attitudes and behaviours that indicate discontent and an antipathy towards the formal values of the school and a consistent pattern of behaviour and discourse that challenge these values (for example, Cooper, 1993);

- *Conduct disorder*: aggression towards others, destruction of property; deceitfulness or theft; serious violation of rules (APA, 1994);
- *Delinquency*: as above, involving law-breaking;
- *Oppositional defiance*: 'a pattern of negativistic, hostile and defiant behaviour' (APA, 1994), including frequent loss of temper, arguing with adults, active defiance or refusal to comply with adult rules and requests, annoying others apparently deliberately; often blaming of others; touchy and easily annoyed by others; often angry and resentful; often spiteful and vindictive; this may include tantrum behaviour.

Some social and psychological influences on the development of externalizing SEBDs

Much of the research on these problems has focused on the search for *environmental* causes. For example, research by Patterson et al. (1992) on severely antisocial adult males found a particular pattern of social influences recurring in the life histories of these men. The men commonly came from families afflicted by social difficulties in the form of unstable and conflictual family circumstances, where patterns of care were unpredictable and discipline was enforced inconsistently, with corporal punishment being a recurrent feature in child management. Patterson et al.'s model has four main stages. The pre-school 'basic training' phase during which children's 'coercive' behaviour (for example, tantrums, crying, hitting, yelling) is unwittingly reinforced by carers, whilst more pro-social ways of expressing needs are not adequately reinforced. In the second phase, the child reaches school age, where his coercive behaviours receive a negative reaction from teachers and peers. As a result the child becomes increasingly marginalized. This paves the way to the third phase, which usually occurs in the junior/secondary years, in which the rejected child seeks out other similarly marginalized children with whom he forms an unholy alliance. They form a deviant subculture and reward each others' antisocial behaviour. The fourth stage is that of the 'career antisocial adult'. This stage is characterized by a replication of the social circumstances that gave rise to the initial difficulties. Individuals in this stage have difficulty forming relationships, obtaining and keeping employment. They drift into criminal behaviour and are at high risk of engaging in substance abuse and developing mental health problems.

This first set of externalizing problems can be seen largely in terms of *learned* patterns of behaviour. Negative, 'coercive' behaviour becomes the only tool that the individual has for getting needs met and alternative, more positive and pro-social patterns of behaviour are either taught ineffectively or simply not made available to the individual.

Another causative factor, sometimes associated with the social learning theory cited above, is concerned with the effect of attachment problems on social development (Bowlby, 1975). This theory suggests that some individuals experience unsatisfactory relationships with their primary carers in early infancy, and this deficiency can lead to feelings of insecurity and alienation, which in turn may manifest themselves in the form of internalized (see below) or externalized social, emotional and behavioural difficulties. This approach emphasizes the way in which SEBDs can sometimes be underpinned by deep, emotional problems. Where this is the case, the learning of pro-social behaviours is severely hampered by underlying emotional problems (for example, Bennathan and Boxall, 2000).

A further important psychological theory offering a powerful explanation for some SEBDs is attribution theory (for example, Weiner et al., 1971). This theory combines social learning and cognitive elements. It focuses on the explanations people give for their behaviour and places particular emphasis on the ways in which explanations either indicate individuals' belief that they are in control of their behaviour, or their belief that they are helpless in the face of external influences which cause their behaviour. The preference for external attributions is associated with the concept of 'learned helplessness', which is often the product of experiences in which individuals have been unsuccessful in controlling negative influences in their lives (Davison and Neale, 2001). This fatalism may render the individual passive in the face of antisocial or delinquent influences.

Externalizing difficulties 2

A second set of externalizing problems include:

- *Attention deficit/hyperactivity disorder* (APA, 1994): chronic, pervasive and debilitating problems in controlling attention and/or impulsivity and motor activity (hyperactivity) (see also *Hyperkinetic Disorder*, WHO, 1990).
- *Autistic spectrum disorders*: (including autism, Asperger's syndrome, Tourette's syndrome) debilitating impairments in the quality of the child's social interactions when compared to others of same developmental stage (for example, fails to make effective social relationships, shows lack of understanding of feelings of others; does not seek to share others' company spontaneously); communication problems; restricted and repetitive, and stereotypical behaviours. (This condition often has internalizing aspects as well.)

Some biological influences on the development of externalizing SEBDs

These problems, which are often referred to as 'developmental disorders', are characterized by the presence of biological factors in their causation, as well as evidence that for the most part there are genetic factors involved in the transmission of the disorders (Comings, 1990). In particular, neuro-psychological researchers have identified abnormalities in the brains of individuals with these conditions. In all three of these conditions the frontal lobes of the brains of affected individuals have been found to function differently from those of the general population. The frontal lobes are the part of the brain concerned with the regulation of attention and behaviour. In individuals with AD/HD, some studies have found marked 'under-activity' in this area of the brain (Tannock, 1998), leading to difficulties sustaining and directing attention and inhibiting behavioural responses. There are a number of theories as to the precise nature of the cognitive mechanisms involved in AD/HD. One widely-accepted view is that the neurological problems associated with AD/HD lead to cognitive impairments in the area of executive functions (Barkley, 1997). Executive functions include: short-term memory, internal dialogue, the appraisal of motivation and behavioural synthesis (that is, the recall of the consequences of behaving in a particular way). Executive functions come into play when we experience an impulse to behave in a particular way (for example, to call out, make a joke, or touch the surface of a painting in an art gallery). The impulse is filtered through the executive function system, and on the basis of this a decision is made whether or not to carry through the behavioural impulse. Where the executive function system is impaired, the filtering process does not take place, or is hampered in some way, leading us to act on the impulse in an automatic way.

In autism and Asperger's syndrome (sometimes referred to as 'high functioning autism'), cognitive impairments affect individuals' ability to attend to and monitor social elements in the environment. This gives rise to the 'theory of mind' hypothesis, which posits that the major difficulty experienced by individuals with these disorders is an impaired ability to interpret other people's thought states on the basis of their behaviour. These problems have been associated with dysfunctions of the frontal lobes, temporal lobes and the limbic system of the brain in individuals with these disorders (Klin et al., 2000).

In Tourette's syndrome, a dominant cognitive theory suggests that there is an impairment in the 'intention editor'. The intention editor is part of the executive function system (see above) and is responsible for controlling behaviour. These problems in Tourette's syndrome sufferers have been found, in some cases, to be associated with abnormalities in the basal ganglia and striatal regions of the brain, which are associated with sensory responding and the control of physical movement (Robertson and Baron-Cohen, 1998).

In each of these cases, the neurological impairments are sometimes associated with abnormalities in the physical structures themselves, as a result of abnormal development or brain injury, and sometimes with the neurochemical factors. In the latter cases the physical structures of the brain may be perfectly normal, but the chemicals responsible for stimulating activity in these regions (neurotransmitters) may be functioning in an inappropriate way, or present in insufficient quantities (Comings, 1990).

It is important to stress that the presence of biological factors should not be taken as an indication of a simple biological *cause* for the associated difficulty or disorder. Biology always interacts with the environment, so that even when there is a biological element present, the ways in which this biological element affects behaviour is often mediated by experience of the environment. This point is expanded upon below.

Internalizing difficulties I

This is the second sub-division of SEBD. These are difficulties of an emotional and/or behavioural nature that are not so much disruptive as disturbing to others. As with the first sub-division, however, these are problems that may well lead to serious under-performance in school, as well as impairment in social relationships.

Sub-categories of the internalizing sub-division of SEBD include:

- *Truancy and school refusal*: persistent and frequent failure to attend school for reasons unknown considered illegitimate by the school/in law.
- *Separation anxiety* (APA, 1994): 'developmentally inappropriate and excessive anxiety concerning separation from home or from those to whom the individual is attached' (1994: 75) as evidenced by, for example, excessive levels of stress, fear and/or worrying in relation to separation events.
- *Withdrawn behaviour*: excessive avoidance of contact with others to an extent that interferes with educational participation and progress as well as social functioning.
- *Elective/selective mutism* (APA, 1994): consistent and persistent failure to speak in specific social situations where speaking is expected to a degree that interferes with educational participation and progress.

Some social and psychological influences on the development of internalizing SEBDs

These problems, like the first set of externalizing problems, are generally seen as being primarily the product of environmental factors, similar in many ways to those associated with the first set of externalizing problems. Attachment theory, attribution theory and social learning theories apply to these conditions in much the same way as they do to externalizing problems. They are learned behaviours that have been programmed and reinforced by unfavourable social circumstances (Blau and Gullotta, 1996). Having said this, there is a body of evidence that relates extreme fear, shyness and social phobia in children to various biological mechanisms (Schmidt and Schulkin, 1999). It is noted, for example, that some children are, from birth, more reactive to environmental stressors than others, producing extreme fear and withdrawal responses in situations that other children find only mildly uncomfortable. Stansbury (1999) relates these physiological differences to differences in children's attachment behaviour.

Internalizing difficulties 2

A second set of internalizing problems includes:

- *Substance misuse and abuse*: problems of educational participation and progress which are related to the misuse through ingestion of alcohol, drugs or other substances.
- *Anxiety disorders* (APA, 1994): problems with panic attacks and agoraphobia (for example, fear of crowds) leading to problems of educational participation and progress; this can include various phobias, post traumatic stress disorder, obsessive-compulsive disorder.
- *Depression* (APA, 1994): suffering the majority of the following symptoms to an extent that seriously interferes with school performance and social functioning: depressed or irritable mood (self-reported or observed) most days; marked diminished interest or pleasures in all or most activities most days; significant weight loss when not dieting; insomnia or hypersomnia nearly everyday; observable psycho-motor agitation almost everyday; fatigue; delusional guilt; diminished ability to think and concentrate; preoccupation with death, suicide; suicidal behaviour.

Some biological influences on the development of internalizing SEBDs

Clearly, problems such as these are commonly associated with negative social circumstances (Davison and Neale, 2001). People sometimes turn to substance abuse as a form of self-medication when confronted with stressful circumstances. Similarly, anxiety and depression often follow in the wake of traumatic life experiences (2001). Having said this, there is a growing body of research pointing to the genetic underpinnings of some forms of depressive illness (2001). Other studies have implicated imbalances in particular neurotransmitters (mainly seratonin and norepinephrine) in the aetiology of a range of mood disorders and drug and substance abuse (2001). For example, low levels of seratonin have been found to be associated with depression and substance abuse, whilst unusually high levels of seratonin have been found to be associated with the presence of mania in some individuals (2001).

BIOLOGICALLY-BASED NEEDS: THE INTERTWINING OF EMOTION AND BEHAVIOUR

The importance of biologically-based drives in human development is well established. The psychologist Abraham Maslow (1970) theorized that all human beings are motivated by a set of biologically programmed 'needs'. He presents these needs in the form of a hierarchy, arguing that lower level needs must be met before needs further up the hierarchy can be addressed (see Table 7.2).

Table 7.2 *Maslow's (1970) hierarchy of needs (adapted from the original)*

- **Self-actualization** (the need to put one's talents to good use in the world and achieve success)
- **Self-esteem** (the need to be valued)
- **Affiliation** (the need to engage with other human beings in reciprocal, caring relationships)
- **Safety** (the need for a secure and predictable environment)
- **Physiological** (the need for clean air, food, warmth etc.)

The lower level needs of Maslow's hierarchy (physiological and safety) are concerned with individual survival. It is only once these needs are secured that the individual can begin to address the social world and show concern for interacting with others (affiliation). Once affiliation is established, then individuals become concerned with the quality of how they are perceived by others and make an effort to enhance their image by behaving in ways that encourage social approval (self-esteem). Only once healthy self-esteem is established can individuals become truly self-directing and operate as autonomous, responsible individuals in a pro-social but independent way. The implication of this theoretical framework for our understanding of SEBD is that if a particular category of need is left unmet, then the needs above it in the hierarchy are an irrelevance. For example, the student who is pervasively insecure and fearful is not going to be able to engage in pro-social affiliation behaviour until those security needs have been met. Furthermore, appeals to the student's supposed need to enhance his or her self-esteem through successful engagement with learning activities is likely to fail, this will only happen within a secure and affiliation-conducive environment.

Maslow's hierarchy resonates with Pringle's (1975) typology of children's needs. The important thing about Pringle's theory is that it is based on systematic analysis of data from the massive National Child Birth Study, which charted the lives of a very large cohort of people from birth through their childhood, teens and beyond. Pringle's theory relates to the school years. She concludes that 'healthy psychological development' (that is, emotional wellbeing, appropriate social engagement, and educational progress) are associated with four categories of need:

- the need for love and security;
- the need for praise and recognition;
- the need for new experiences; and
- the need to exercise responsibility.

Pringle's framework of needs bears many similarities to Maslow's, emphasizing the fundamental importance of security needs and the way in which social and cognitive competence are intertwined with basic emotional drives.

Glasser's (1993) 'control theory' takes our understanding of human needs a step further, citing the following set of biologically-based needs:

- to play and have fun;
- to be free to make choices;
- to exercise power and influence;
- to belong to a social group and love others; and
- to survive.

These 'needs' are best understood as a set of overlapping drives which should be held in balance. As the term 'control theory' suggests, a central feature of Glasser's needs framework is the idea that human beings are driven by a central need to exert control over their lives. Where there is an imbalance, problems occur. For example, the individual who does not achieve a sense of belonging to the social group may seek antisocial means of exerting power and influence over others, since the pro-social avenues which come with a sense of belonging are blocked.

An implication of Maslow's and Glasser's theoretical frameworks is that the kind of positive student engagement that schools seek to promote will only happen when schools and teachers understand and cater for these deeply embedded motivational drives. If we look back to Patterson et al.'s

(1992) four-stage model of how some people learn to become 'career antisocial adults' (see above), then we can see how the school experience sometimes interacts with individuals' basic needs in a way that promotes antisocial behaviour.

A common element of all three of these needs frameworks is the human paradox that the capacity for free and autonomous action is closely linked with the extent to which insecurity and dependency are effectively handled. This is also a central feature of attachment theory (see above). According to this view, SEBDs can often be located in relation to unmet security needs. The dysfunctional and challenging behaviour that is often associated with SEBDs, therefore, can be seen as a largely involuntary expression of deep-seated, unmet emotional needs. It follows from this theoretical approach that it is only when these basic needs are met that the individual finds himself or herself in the position to make more socially acceptable behavioural choices (so long as such positive options are available, of course).

INTERACTIONAL MODELS: BIOLOGY AND THE ENVIRONMENT

It has been shown how SEBD can be produced both environmentally and ways in which biological factors of two main kinds can sometimes influence the development of SEBD. The first set of biological factors is concerned with pathology or individual differences, often of a neurological and genetic nature. The second set of biological influences relate to common human needs, or drives. In this section consideration is given to how these various factors may interact.

The term 'biopsychosocial' is used to describe the way in which biological, psychological and socio-cultural factors interact with and influence one another (Norwich, 1990). In relation to social deviance and abnormal psychology, the 'diathes-stress paradigm' (Davison and Neale, 2001) describes the way in which individual, biologically-based constitutional (diathes) factors are affected by environmental stressors to produce social, emotional and behavioural difficulties. From this perspective, biological differences, which in some cases may be genetically based, take the form of risk factors which, when combined with a particular set of environmental conditions, lead to certain patterns of dysfunctional behaviour. In the absence of the necessary environmental conditions, the dysfunctional behaviour does not appear, or at least not to an extent that is severely disruptive to the individual or the social world inhabited by the individual. This paradigm has been used to explain a wide range of SEBDs, including anxiety, depression, conduct disorder and eating disorders.

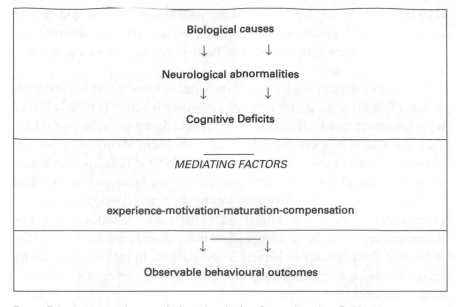

Figure 7.1   *Interaction between biological and other factors, based on Frith's (1992) model of developmental disorders*

Uta Frith (1992) has devised a model to show how developmental disorders (such as autism, Asperger's syndrome and AD/HD) can be understood in terms of the interaction between biological and other factors (see Figure 7.1). The extent to which brain-based differences lead to particular forms of behaviour is influenced by the individual's experience, level of motivation, maturation and their possession of compensatory skills and/or circumstances. Clearly, motivation to overcome difficulties will be influenced by the individual's sense of confidence, which in turn may well be influenced by their sense of security (see above). Skills, on the other hand, have to be learned. The point is that even biologically-based conditions, such as AD/HD, are not solely determined biological factors; they are the product of a combination of biological, psychological and social factors.

INTERVENTION ISSUES

Clearly, whether or not biological factors are implicated in a particular set of SEBDs, the role of educators is to respond to these difficulties with educational approaches. Educational approaches are always concerned with manipulating the environment in order to facilitate appropriate educational engagement by students and pupils. This begs the question: so what is the value of biological insights to teachers? There is a straightforward answer to this question. The role of biological understandings is to deepen the teacher's understandings of:

- why students behave as they do and the nature of specific difficulties;
- why different students sometimes respond differently to the same or similar situations and interventions;
- how to evaluate the appropriateness of different intervention approaches; and
- the importance, in some cases, of seeing educational intervention in the context of a co-ordinated multi-disciplinary intervention programme.

As we have seen, biological understandings emphasize the importance of social and emotional factors as crucial influences on SEBDs by showing the complex way in which these interact with biological factors. They help us to understand how the human biological subsystem interacts with the environmental/ecological system. This view challenges simplistic and inaccurate nature-versus-nurture arguments.

Systemic approaches

One way of converting this insight into an intervention approach is provided by the SALAD framework to dealing with SEBDs in schools (Cooper et al., 1994; Olsen and Cooper, 2001). This approach emphasizes the way in which SEBDs are embedded in complex, interacting individual and social factors, and attempts to shape this understanding into a school-based approach. The SALAD acronym stands for:

- *Systems*: the need for intervention and policy to be rooted in an ana-lytical understanding of the way in which individual psychological and biological factors interact with social circumstances, and how the views and understandings of different 'stakeholders' in relevant social subsystems need to be taken account of in the development and imple-mentation policy and intervention. The effectiveness of the rest of the SALAD approach depends upon the quality of the systemic analysis on which it is based.
- *Access*: the need for students who are the target for intervention (and other stakeholders) to have unimpeded access to knowledge about the interventions being used and their purpose. A central feature of access is *ownership*, whereby students become partners with other stakehold-ers in working towards making the intervention work on the basis of their understanding that the intervention serves their mutual interests.
- *Limits*: clear behavioural boundaries have to be in place. Appropriate behaviour should be defined and reinforced, whilst inappropriate behaviour should be identified and discouraged.
- *Acceptance*: interactions between stakeholders should be characterized by unconditional acceptance of persons as individuals. Condemnation

of unwanted behaviour should never be confused with condemnation of persons.

- *Direction*: support and guidance should be given to students to enable them to make progress through the intervention programme.

The SALAD approach attempts to combine clarity and comprehensiveness of approach with flexibility and the need to cater for individual differences. It can be seen as a school-based version of Henngeler's (1999) multisystemic therapy (MST), which is a community-based intervention programme for young people with SEBD, and in particular conduct disorder. The approach employs systemic analysis of problem behaviour (that is an analysis which looks at SEBDs in reaction to their social context), as well as individual analysis (that is, an exploration of 'within person' factors of psychological or biological nature). MST has been found to be one of the most effective forms of intervention for conduct disordered adolescent males in the United States (Kazdin, 1998). It is characterized by its multi-disciplinary focus, its comprehensiveness and its sensitivity to the full range of possible intervention strategies that may range from parent training to individual drug therapy, or include a combination systemic, behavioural, cognitive and medical therapies.

Behavioural approaches in context

When intervention is informed by the holistic biopsychosocial perspective presented in this chapter, the emphasis is placed on fitting the intervention to the specific circumstances of the SEBDs that we are targeting. Sometimes, it is found that simple behavioural interventions, such as positive or negative reinforcement, are all that is required. Such interventions include the use of points systems and 'time-out'. As we have noted, however, behaviour should not be seen in isolation from emotions. This means that the emotional climate in which a behavioural programme is introduced should always be seen as an important part of any behavioural intervention. For example, a climate of positive regard in which students are valued as individuals will enhance the effectiveness of behavioural interventions, whilst a climate of blame and negative labelling will undermine the behavioural intervention.

The importance of cognitive styles and learning styles

One of the practical outcomes of neuropsychological research has been the light it has shed upon the biological correlates of cognitive style.

Cognitive style refers to differences among people in the ways in which they engage with the world at an intellectual level. Learning styles relate to differences in the ways in which people go about learning new information and skills (Riding and Rayner, 1998). If cognitive and learning styles are influenced by the physical structure of the brain, then they are likely to be very resistant to change.

From an educational point of view, 'disorders', such as AD/HD and Asperger's syndrome, can be usefully seen as unusual cognitive style variants rather than in terms of cognitive deficit. When teachers take this perspective they question generalized assumptions about how pupils learn and acknowledge that different students might require quite different circumstances in order to learn the same content. Kolb (1984) identifies four main learning styles, each of which can be seen in terms of a set of preferences:

- *A preference for CONCRETE EXPERIENCE*
  Emphasizes: feeling over thinking; here-and-now complexity over theories and generalizations; intuitive over systematic.
- *A preference for REFLECTIVE OBSERVATION*
  Emphasizes: understanding over practical application; the ideal over the pragmatic; reflection over action.
- *A preference for ABSTRACT CONCEPTUALIZATIONS*
  Emphasizes: thinking over feeling; theories over here-and-now complexity; systematic over intuitive.
- *A preference for ACTIVE EXPERIMENTATION*
  Emphasizes pragmatic over ideal; doing rather than observing.
  (Based on Kolb, 1984: 68–9)

Pupils with AD/HD tend to favour the concrete experience and active learning styles. These learning styles are most useful in circumstances where tasks are experiential in nature: where the learning emerges from doing. Individuals with Asperger's syndrome, which is characterized by severe difficulties in reading social cues, often experience difficulty with metaphorical representations and are most comfortable with concrete, clear and logical representations of knowledge. The child with AD/HD is more likely than the child with Asperger's syndrome to thrive in a learning environment which values divergent and novel patterns of thinking.

An awareness of the implications of differences in cognitive and learning styles helps the teacher to plan learning experiences which play to the pupils' strengths. It also helps the teacher positively to reframe a pupil's apparent lack of interest or reluctance to engage in certain learning tasks.

CONCLUSION: BIOLOGY HELPS US TO UNDERSTAND – IT IS NOT AN EXCUSE

It is important to know when an individual's behaviour is accurately accounted for through reference to factors outside the immediate individual's conscious control. To hold people responsible for actions outside their control is wrong. This is not to say that biologically or socially induced behaviours cannot be brought under the control of the individual. An understanding of the ways in which biological, psychological and social factors sometimes interact to undermine an individual's power of self-control can open up opportunities from which positive, corrective and empowering interventions can be created. On the other hand, it is sometimes difficult for teachers to remain motivated and keen to support pupils whose difficulties are attributed to the pupil's own lack of enthusiasm for learning *per se*. In fact, such negative attitudes are likely to disempower individuals who are seeking to change the behaviour of others (Cooper and Ideus, 1996). After all, you can take a horse to water, but you can't make it drink … Furthermore, an acknowledgement of the complex interplay of different factors involved in shaping behaviour can lift the burden from the individual professional by leading them to the realization that they will benefit from sharing their expertise with that of other professionals.

A biopsychosocial perspective can help overcome the impulse to blame and condemn, but it must never be allowed to encourage anyone to escape from the responsibility to put effort into overcoming SEBD. A biopsychosocial understanding will not be useful if it is allowed to be employed as a means of excusing or ignoring SEBD. Almost any explanatory theory for SEBD can be misused in this way. The test of any theoretical approach will be the extent to which it gives rise to practical and humane forms of intervention that produce outcomes of benefit to the individual in relation to his or her social setting. The holistic and interactional features of a biopsychosocial approach make this a highly-persuasive tool when judged against these criteria.

REFERENCES

APA (American Psychiatric Association) (1994) *Diagnostic and Statistical Manual of Mental Disorders Vol. IV*. Washington, DC: APA.

Barkley, R. (1997) *ADHD and the Nature of Self Control*. New York: Guilford.

Bennathan, M. and Boxall, M. (2000) *Effective Intervention in Primary Schools: Nurture Groups*. London: Fulton.

Blau, G. and Gullotta, T. (1996) *Adolescent Dysfunctional Behavior*. London: Sage.

Bowlby, J. (1975) *Attachment and Loss,* Vol. 2. Harmondsworth: Penguin.

Brown, S. and McIntyre, D. (1993) *Making Sense of Teaching*. Buckingham: Open University.

Comings, D. (1990) *Tourette Syndrome and Human Behavior*. Duarte, CA: Hope Press.

Cooper, P. (1993) *Effective Schools for Disaffected Students*. London: Routledge.

Cooper, P. and Ideus, K. (1996) *AD/HD: A Practical Guide for Teachers*. London: Fulton.

Cooper, P. and McIntyre, D. (1996) *Effective Teaching and Learning: Teachers' and Students' Perceptions*. Buckingham: Open University.

Cooper, P., Smith, C., and Upton, G. (1994) *Emotional and Behavioural Difficulties: Theory to Practice*. London: Routledge.

Davison, N. and Neale, J. (2001) *Abnormal Psychology* (8th edition). New York: Wiley.

DfEE (1998) *Permanent Exclusions from Schools and Exclusion Appeals*. London: DfEE.

DfEE (2001) *Permanent Exclusions from Schools and Exclusion Appeals, England 1999/2000* (Provisional SFR 20/2001). London: DfEE.

Frith, U. (1992) 'Cognitive development and cognitive deficit', *The Psychologist*, 5: 13–19.

Geake, J. and Cooper, P. (2003) 'Implications of cognitive neuroscience for education', *Westminster Studies in Education*, 26 (10): 7–20.

Glasser, W. (1993) *Control Theory: A New Explanation of How We Control Our Lives*. New York: Perennial Library.

Hargreaves, D. Hester, D. and Mellor, F. (1975) *Deviance in Classrooms*. London: Routledge and Kegan Paul.

Henngeler, S. (1999) 'Multi-systemic therapy: an overview of clinical procedures, outcomes and policy implications', *Child Psychology and Psychiatry Review*. 4 (1): 2–10.

Kazdin, A. (1998) 'Psychosocial treatments for conduct disorder in children', in P. Nathan and J. Gorham (eds), *A Guide to Treatments that Work*. Oxford: Oxford University Press.

Klin, A., Schulz, R., and Cohen, D. (2000) 'Theory of mind in action: developmental perspectives on cognitive neuroscience', in S. Baron-Cohen, H. Tager-Flusberg and D. Cohen (eds), *Understanding Other Minds: Perspectives From Developmental Cognitive Neuroscience*. Oxford: Oxford University Press.

Kolb, D. (1984) *Experiential Learning. Experience as a Source of Learning and Development* Englewoods Cliffs, NJ: Prentice-Hall.

Maslow, A. (1970) *Motivation and Personality*. New York: Harper & Row.

Norwich, B. (1990) *Reappraising Special Needs Education*. London, Cassell.

Norwich, B. (2003) 'The meaning of inclusion', keynote address to the conference *Communication, Emotion and Behaviour*, University of Leicester, September.

Olsen, J. and Cooper, P. (2001) *Dealing with Disruptive Behaviour in Classrooms*. London: TES/Kogan-Page.

Patterson, G., Reid, J. and Dishion, T. (1992) *Anti-social Boys*, Vol. 4. Eugene, OR: Castalia.

Pringle, M. (1975) *The Needs of Children*, (2nd edition). London: Hutchinson.

Riding, R. and Rayner, S. (1998) *Cognitive Styles and Learning Styles*. London: Fulton.

Robertson, M. and Baron-Cohen, S. (1998) *Tourette Syndrome: The Facts*. Oxford: Oxford University Press.

Schmidt, L. and Schulkin, J. (1999) *Extreme Fear, Shyness and Social Phobia: Origins, Biological Mechanisms, and Clinical Outcomes*. New York: Oxford University Press.

Stansbury, K. (1999) 'Attachment, temperament and adrenocortical', in L. Schmidt and J. Schulkin (eds), *Extreme Fear, Shyness and Social Phobia: Origins, Biological Mechanisms, and Clinical Outcomes*. New York: Oxford University Press.

Tannock, R. (1998) 'AD/HD: advances in cognitive, neurobiological and genetic research', *Journal of Child Psychology and Psychiatry*, 39: 65–100.

Weiner, B., Frieze, L., Kukla., A., Reed, L., Rest, S. and Rosenbaum, R. (1971) *Perceiving the Causes of Success and Failure*. New York: General Learning Press.

World Health Organization (1990) *International Classification of Diseases* (10th edition). Paris. WHO.

Young Minds (1999) *Briefing Paper No.1*. London: Young Minds.

8

The Influences of the School Contexts and Processes on Violence and Disruption in American Schools

MICHAEL J. FURLONG,
GALE M. MORRISON AND EMILY S. FISHER

It is important to develop a better understanding of how school conditions and the relationship among and between students and adults increase or decrease safety on a school campus. Our interest is in those factors that schools have more control over because they emanate out of the formation of school policies and procedures and their implementation on a day-to-day basis. In this chapter, we first summarize the status of school violence in American schools based on recen US surveys and provide a commentary on some limitations in their use, then discuss the unique elements of the school context that contribute to or detract from the occurrence of aggression and other antisocial behavior, and finally outline principles of prevention and intervention that will assist schools in more effectively reducing violence and disruption on their campuses. An increased sensitivity to differentiate between violence and disruption is important because school is a place where aggressive, antisocial youth congregate versus aggression caused by or exacerbated by conditions of the school campus itself. In the former, aggression occurs at school as a place where youth gather, whereas in the latter aggression is, at least in part, caused by dynamics of the school. This is what we have previously referred to as focusing on the 'school' in school violence (Furlong and Morrison, 2000; Morrison et al., 1994). By this we mean those factors specific to the school culture, climate, and their contexts that contribute to the occurrence of aggression, both physical and relational.

STATUS OF SCHOOL VIOLENCE IN THE UNITED STATES

Despite the occurrence of notable and tragic school shootings, schools in the United States have made remarkable progress toward the reduction of measurable violence and disruption during the 1990s (Furlong et al., 2003a). At the same time, more recently there has been expanded attention given to lower, more chronic types of physical violence (Bear et al., 2000), relationship-based aggressive behavior (Crick and Grotpeter, 1995), and an increasing awareness that bullying as a class of school aggression is associated with particularly deleterious outcomes (Espelage and Swearer, 2003).

Trends in schools violence in the United States

National and regional surveys, conducted periodically, are essential sources of information about the occurrence of school violence and the progress that American communities are making toward its reduction. Until the mid- to late-1990s, attention to the topic of school violence was incomplete in the United States. Although some school violence data were collected as far back as the 1970s, it was not until 1999 that the first National Safe Schools report was issued (US Departments of Education and Justice, 1999). This national report was in response to an outburst of widely publicized shootings on secondary school campuses that resulted in multiple deaths, most notably the 15 deaths that occurred on April 20, 1999 at Columbine High School. This and other events also resulted in the development of US Federal Office of Education reports (Dwyer et al., 1998; Dwyer and Osher, 2000; Osher et al., 2003) meant to support efforts to stem the tide of what was widely perceived to be one of the most critical issues facing public education in the United States (for example, Rose and Gallup, 2000).

Although school violence was considered to be the primary problem facing American schools, there was no one specific mechanism with which to gather information about its occurrence. Consequently, what is now known has been cobbled from various sources (primarily a national *Youth Risk Behavior Surveillance Survey* (for example, Brener et al., 1999) administered by the United States Centers for Disease Control and Prevention, and the University of Michigan's *Monitoring the Future* survey (for example, Johnston et al., 1996) of high school students.

Prior to providing a summary of the most recent information about school violence, we note that in the United States, the topic of bullying, which has been a long-term interest in many countries, has only recently become a prominent concern among American educators. This interest has been influenced by studies completed by the US Federal Bureau of Investigation (O'Toole, 2000) and the US Secret Service (Fein et al., 2002) who found that some school shooters had a school history of being the victim of school bullying. One report even argued that these students fit a profile that was labeled the 'Classroom Avenger' (McGee and DeBernardo, 1999) – chronic bully victims rising up to seek revenge on their abusers. Although subsequent analyses have tempered discussion of the existence of a school shooter profile (Furlong et al., 2004; Reddy et al., 2001), this concern has led to an influx of state legislation to make bullying a recognizable discipline infraction. This legislation has not necessarily been based in sound scientific definitions of bullying and its essential elements: intentionality, repeated abuse, and a power differential (Furlong et al., 2003b; Limber and Small, 2003). Only recently have national US estimates of the occurrence of bullying been offered (for example, Nansel et al., 2001). These estimates indicated that 16 percent of boys and 11 percent of girls felt bullied, with 23 percent of boys and 11 percent of girls admitted to bullying other students. However, detailed studies of US bullying prevalence, as carried out by Solberg and Olweus (2003), have yet to be conducted.

What is known about the prevalence of school violence and disruption across American schools is summarized in Table 8.1. This Table shows that school violence has generally decreased during the 1990s. Despite the horrific shootings that have occurred on school campuses in recent years, the total number of school-associated deaths (including suicides) has decreased by 91.6 per cent between 1992–94 (119 deaths, including students and adults) and 2000–2002 (10 deaths) (Furlong et al., 2003b; Stephens, 2003). This encouraging trend has been accompanied by a decrease of weapon possession and physical fights on school campuses. In addition, the types of indicators collected identify male high-school students as being more prominently involved in school violence than female high-school students. Nonetheless, decreases in all types of school violence indicators are noted from 1993 to 1999 for males and females. With

Table 8.1   *Summary of US school violence trends*

Violence-related behaviors	Findings and trends	Comment
School-associated violent deaths are declining (Stephens, 2003)	• 91.6% decrease from 1992–94 (119 deaths; first two years' data available) through 2001–03 (10 deaths; last two years available)	This includes suicides and all violence-related deaths on school campuses regardless of the day or time of act. These involve adult victims (e.g., spouse shooting their teacher-wife on the school campus).
Physical fights on school property are declining (YRBS – Youth Risk Behavior Surveillance System; Brener et al., 1999; Kann et al., 2000)	• Physical fights on school property in past 12 months have declined by 12.3% • 1993: 16.2%; 1995: 15.5%; 1997: 14.8%; 1999: 14.2%	Rates by gender, racial/ethnic identification, and grade level have all been stable or decreasing. Hispanics reported an increase in physical fights (15.7% in 1999).
Possession of any weapon on school property is declining (YRBS; Brener et al., 1999; Kann et al., 2000)	• Any weapon possession in past 30 days has declined by 41.5% • 1993: 11.8%; 1995: 9.8%; 1997: 8.5%; 1999: 6.9%	Rates by gender, racial/ethnic identification, and grade level have decreased. Weapon possession at school is down for black males and white males.
Weapons are carried more often in the community than on school property (YRBS; Brener et al., 1999; Kann et al., 2000)	• Weapons are carried two times more often in the community than the school campus • Community – 1997: 18.3%; 1999: 17.3% • School: 1997: 8.5%; 1999: 6.9%	Weapon possession in the community and at school has declined steadily since 1991. Youths are exposed to more violence-related behaviors and experiences in the community than at school.
Level of concern about school safety is low and stable (YRBS; Brener et al., 1999)	About 1 in 20 students report they stayed home in the previous 30 days because of safety concerns at school and/or going to/from school	Concern about safety at school is not prevalent (Furlong et al., 1998) and it declines with age (Coggeshall and Kingery, 2001).
Males are most involved in school-associated violence (YRBS, 1999 survey, Kann et al., 2000)	• Physical fight on school property in past 12 months: 18.5% males vs. 9.8% females • Any weapon possession in past 30 days: 11.0% males vs. 2.8% females	School violence surveys have focused on overt physical behaviors and have not attended to patterns of behavior and aggression that might be more common among females (e.g., relational aggression).
Violent behaviors vary by grade level (YRBS, 1999 survey, Kann et al., 2000)	• Physical fights on school property in past 12 months: 18.6% 9th grade; 17.2% 10th grade; 10.8% 11th grade; 8.1% 12th grade • Any weapon possession in past 30 days: 7.2% 9th grade; 6.6% 10th grade; 7.0% 11th grade; 6.2% 12th grade	It is generally thought that violence-related behaviors decline with age because of the students' increased maturity and because high-risk youths are more likely to dropout, be expelled, or enroll in alternative school settings.

these promising trends, one would think that policymakers would conclude that school violence reduction efforts are working (at least to some extent) and that the general public would be less concerned about school safety. However, this does not appear to be the case (Breland, 2000), as evidenced by increases in federal funding of school violence prevention programs (for example, Furlong et al., 2003c) and the American public's continued perception that violence-related conditions on campuses are a primary problem facing its public schools (Rose and Gallup, 2000).

PREVENTION OF VIOLENCE
AND DISRUPTION: FOCUSING
ON THE STUDENT OR THE CONTEXT?

To date, efforts to understand the origins of violence in American schools have tended to focus on the individual student and his or her propensity for aggression and disruption. This framework is based in a traditional model of behavior disorders in which the origins of the problem are perceived to lie primarily within the youth, hence the most logical response is to develop intervention programs designed to help specific students modulate their aggressive tendencies and to increase their prosocial behaviors. Most of the programs being implemented in the United States have been identified as having sufficient empirical evidence to support their being classified as having proven effectiveness (see Furlong et al. (2002) for a review of these programs). Two of the comprehensive youth-focused approaches that have been broadly touted are Multisystemic Therapy (for example, Conoley and Conoley, 2001; Sheidow and Woodford, 2003) and Promoting Alternative Thinking Strategies Curriculum (PATHS) (Kusche and Greenberg, 1994), which have been included as an element in some of the US Federally-funded Safe School/Healthy Student Initiative projects (for example, Jefferson County Safe Schools/Healthy Students, 2003; Paige, 2002; Welsh et al., 2003).

These programs focus on social skills training and were designed to impart social decision-making skills, conflict management skills, and self-control in order to reduce the risk that a specific student would aggress. At the institutional level, local education agencies and legislative bodies passed what were called 'zero tolerance' school discipline mandates that required students to be suspended or expelled from school for various disciplinary infractions, but most notably carrying a weapon at school (Skiba and Knesting, 2001).

Continuing efforts have more recently begun to take a more balanced view that considers ecological or contextual influences in which school violence occurs (Conoley and Conoley, 2001; Osher et al., 2003). A special issue of *New Directions in Youth Development* was devoted specifically to the lack of empirical evidence to support schoolwide zero tolerance policies (Skiba and Noam, 2001). From this perspective, school discipline is considered to be part of a series of interactions or processes rather than a one-time event (Morrison et al., 2001). As such, recent efforts have encouraged the development of an understanding of the importance of how school conditions influence behavior, in addition to understanding psychological influences on a student's behavior. When it comes to school violence and disruption, there is also a need to focus on the role that the school as an organization and as a social setting plays in the occurrence of aggression and antisocial behavior. Efforts are needed to focus on ways that prevention programs can be assembled so that they truly are school violence prevention programs and not just youth violence prevention programs that are conveniently administered in school settings.

THE SCHOOL'S CONTRIBUTION TO VIOLENCE AND ITS PREVENTION

Schools as context for development of maladaptive behavior

Some researchers have begun to examine setting or contextual influences of aggression in school. In the school context, aggression is essentially a social event, especially as it supported by a culture of bullying (Unnever and Cornell, 2003). As such, in addition to understanding the psychological influences on a student's behavior, it is also important to understand how critical contexts influence behavior. When it comes to school violence and disruption, there is a need to focus on school and school-student interactions.

In the following paragraphs, we outline classroom, playground, peer, and schoolwide contexts that act as social influences on the development of or exacerbation on aggressive and acting out behavior by students who are at risk for emotional or behavior disorders. We choose to focus on 'at-risk' in recognition that these behaviors develop in concert with or in reaction to what happens in these selected contexts of school. That is, any one of these contexts involves a constructive and nonconstructive response; the more they experience nonconstructive responses, the worse things get.

The following contexts are described around the theme of school discipline as a powerful, overarching system that plays a major role in how students who are at-risk for or experiencing emotional and behavior disorders are treated within the educational system. In fact, students with emotional and behavior disorders are overrepresented in the suspension/expulsion statistics (Leone et al., 2000) despite protections provided by the provisions of the Individuals with Disabilities Education Act (IDEA). At each context level, we will highlight risk and protective factors that are associated with outcomes for students with or at risk for emotional and behavior disorders (EBD). A short case scenario will be presented to highlight how these situations are played out in the everyday reality of schools (these scenarios are taken from observations made in the context of a federally supported research project funded by the US Department of Education, Office of Special Education Program to G. Morrison).

Classroom context

A negative cycle of student/school interactions begins in the classroom where students experience academic failure. Overwhelmingly, students who experience EBD have a history of failing academic expectations (Scott et al., 2001). How the teacher responds to these difficulties is critical. Positive responses would include adjusting tasks demands and providing additional support (teacher's aide) for learning (Reinke and Herman, 2002). All too often students are allowed to fall behind; at some point their motivation sags and the possibility of catching up appears dim.

> Johnny is a third-grade student who has little support at home for doing homework and has been recommended for retention. His teacher is feeling the 'test score performance' pressure and is becoming frustrated with his lack of progress. She decides to 'bench' Johnny and three of his classmates at recess for not completing their work in class. They spend their recess at a lunch table trying to complete the work, with no adult available to answer their questions.

This scenario highlights the concerning trend for academic failure to be considered a 'disciplinary' offense in American schools. This trend is especially concerning for a student like Johnny who, in addition to struggling with his academic performance, is likely to show behavior problems.

Acting out, impulsivity, and socially aggressive behavior are also behaviors that can elicit constructive or destructive responses from teachers. Constructive responses might include positive behavior support strategies implemented as part of an overall classroom management plan (Blankemeyer et al., 2002; Reinke and Herman, 2002). Increasing the tolerance level for activity and 'noise' is a way to broaden the classroom norms to include rather than exclude students who struggle to be a quiet, 'still' student. Punitive responses from teachers include sending the student to the office or publicly reprimanding (yelling, scolding) the student, which serves to worsen the behavior and damage the relationship to the teacher (VanAcker et al., 1996).

> Javier is a student who has been identified for a local research project for presenting disciplinary challenges to the school. The researcher has arrived at the school numerous times to interview Javier and found him sitting in the office, having been sent out of the classroom by the teacher. Several of these times, the teacher has been a 'substitute' teacher, as this school has several teachers who are participating in a 'standards reform' project.

This scenario is a matter of concern for a several reasons. First, Javier is not learning about replacement behaviors. Second, Javier is missing the academic content of his educational program, causing him to fall further behind. Finally, it is ironic that school improvement efforts, which require American teachers increasingly to spend school days outside of their classroom, place behaviorally-challenged students at further risk for negative school outcomes.

Playground context

Playgrounds provide a time and space for respite for students from the structure and work of classrooms. Yet the playground, during recess and after lunch, is typically very unstructured and is staffed by non-teaching staff who rarely have the skills to intervene constructively with conflicts and inappropriate behavior (Colvin et al., 1997). As a result, children with behavioral challenges do not do well in these settings. Analysis of office referral data from elementary schools suggests that 50 per cent of referrals were for nonclassroom time (Taylor-Greene et al., 1997). These referrals result in additional exclusions for students and additions to already burgeoning discipline files for students with emotional and behavior challenges. Training of individuals who supervise these unstructured settings at school could reduce the risk in these situations for at-risk students.

> One creative school administrator initiated a program to engage some of the 'problem' students in more structured activities during recess and lunch; she appointed students as 'hallway monitors'. Students with this role would get a belt with a set of keys to open the doors for play equipment and restrooms. Another highly-coveted position was as a volunteer to help the janitor.

Schoolwide context

Zero tolerance for certain offenses on school campus, especially bringing weapons to school, has become commonplace in American schools (Morrison and D'Incau, 1997; Skiba and Knesting, 2001). Unfortunately, in some schools, zero tolerance policies have broadened to lesser offenses and are applied in a mechanistic and inflexible manner. This indiscriminant practice has led to many students, not all of them aggressive or violent, getting caught in the web of zero tolerance (Morrison and D'Incau, 1997). In fact, many students who get suspended or expelled from school have complex histories of school and family challenges that require solid educational practices and comprehensive support rather than exclusion from school, or in essence exclusion from the opportunity to learn more positive ways to adapt to life.

One school increased the number of suspensions from 12 percent to 21 percent from one year to the next (Morrison and Skiba, 2004). Closer examination of suspension data indicated that the increase was largely seen in suspensions for the use of foul language or profanity. Additionally, more students were being suspended just once; in other words, the web of zero tolerance expanded, but not necessarily for serious offenses or for intervention with students who were truly problematic or dangerous.

The existence of a schoolwide discipline plan is a key strategy used in American schools for preventing behavior problems that lead to student exclusion from school (Sugai and Horner, 1999). Such a plan includes a clear statement of rules and expectations, consistently communicated and applied consequences for rule-breaking behavior, concrete efforts to teach students appropriate behavior, and positive consequences available for positive behavior. With this system in place, consistently implemented by all staff, students have a better chance of behaving in ways that will maximize their inclusion into the activities of the school.

In summary, the various contexts within schools provide day-to-day opportunities to build positive behavior or exacerbate negative behavior for students. The school staff involved at the classroom, playground and schoolwide levels are key 'responders' and are critical forces in setting the stage for day-to-day interactions that will help or hinder the ability of students who are at risk for emotional and behavior disorders to participate fully in the life of the school.

SCHOOL VIOLENCE AND DISRUPTION PREVENTION PRINCIPLES

School violence literature addresses the need for schools to make systemic changes to prevent violent and aggressive acts among all students, including those with emotional and behavior problems (Burstyn et al., 2001; Furlong et al., 2002; Morrison et al., 2004.) Schools have tended to address violence prevention by implementing programs consisting of one-time interventions or interventions implemented at one grade-level (Burstyn et al., 2001). Schools often use packaged violence prevention programs that have shown some efficacy without considering the larger schoolwide factors that impact the success or failure of such programs (Furlong et al., 2002). Additionally, these programs do not take into account the unique needs of each school and the students in that school.

As experience and evidence mounts about what constitutes effective violence prevention programs, a number of themes have arisen that suggest program components that should be present in a high-quality program

(Greenberg et al., 1999; Henrich et al., 1999; Thornton et al., 2000). For example, an important beginning step in systematic change to prevent violence and aggression is to conduct a needs assessment to accurately identify the problems and risks that exist at each school. This includes gathering information on the current school climate, school policies, discipline procedures and referrals, and other school safety issues (Larson et al., 2002). The needs assessment provides information to all school staff about what is happening at their school, and provides an opportunity for staff to discuss their ideas, opinions, and philosophies about education, violence, and safe schools. As school personnel wrestle with the issues raised by the needs assessment, and integrate the information with their personal and professional beliefs, they should begin to determine the goals, objectives, and expectations they have for students, staff, and the school in terms of violence prevention. From this, a clear mission statement can be formed that will build cohesive educational and social goals. Involving the entire staff in the building of a mission increases staff buy-in and will empower teachers and other school personnel to take an active role in violence prevention at their school (Thornton et al., 2000).

After the school's mission regarding violence prevention has been clarified, the school must determine the logistics of how the mission will be accomplished. A large part of this is choosing a violence prevention program or series of programs that will meet the needs of all students, including those at risk for violence and those already engaging in violent behaviors. Violence prevention programs can be conceptualized on three different levels (Kazdin, 1996), as shown in Figure 8.1, the *primary* level, which includes the general needs of all students; the *secondary* level, which includes the needs of students who have been identified as at-risk for problem behaviors; and the *tertiary* level, which includes the needs of students who have already demonstrated aggressive and violent behaviors (Furlong et al., 2002). Although it is critical that all students participate in violence prevention programs in order to change the school climate, students at the secondary and tertiary level, like those with EBD, will need more intensive, targeted interventions to address their needs.

Furlong and colleagues (Furlong and Morrison, 2000) offer another method of conceptualizing the levels of violence prevention needed in schools using the ideas of reaffirming, reconnecting, reconstructing, repairing, and protecting school connectedness and bonding. Students who are already engaged in school will benefit from interventions that reaffirm their relationships with school personnel. Students who are more estranged from school are at risk for involvement in problem behaviors like aggression, and will benefit from interventions that will reconnect

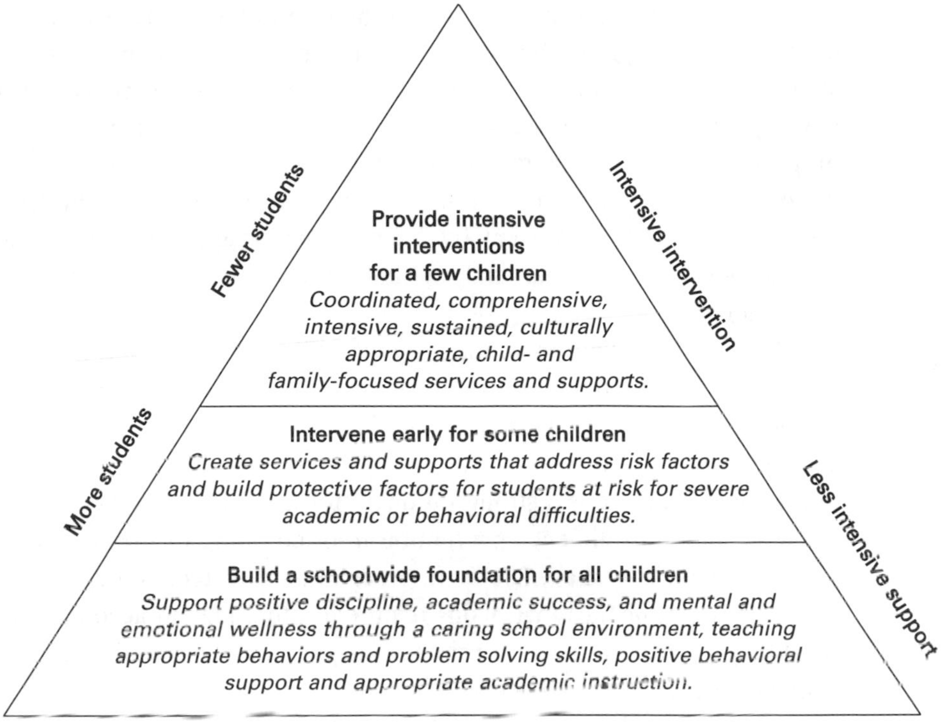

Fewer students

More students

Intensive intervention

Less intensive support

Provide intensive interventions for a few children
Coordinated, comprehensive, intensive, sustained, culturally appropriate, child- and family-focused services and supports.

Intervene early for some children
Create services and supports that address risk factors and build protective factors for students at risk for severe academic or behavioral difficulties.

Build a schoolwide foundation for all children
Support positive discipline, academic success, and mental and emotional wellness through a caring school environment, teaching appropriate behaviors and problem solving skills, positive behavioral support and appropriate academic instruction.

Figure 0.1   *Three levels of violence prevention programs*

them to school. Students who lack positive social bonds, who are disengaged from school academically, and who are likely to be engaging in aggression and other problem behaviors, need interventions that will reconstruct relationships with caring adults at the school. Students who are victims of aggression, and are therefore at a greater risk for committing future aggressive acts, need interventions that repair their 'violated social bonds within the school community' (2000: 135). Additionally, all students need to have their school relationships protected from community violence, and this involves having procedures in place to minimize student contact with dangerous people who may come onto campus. Furlong et al. suggest that comprehensive violence prevention plans will concurrently meet the engagement needs of all students. Students with EBD are likely to fall in the categories of students who need to reconnect, reconstruct, and repair their relationships with school. Not only are these students likely to engage in aggressive acts as a means of problem solving, but also they are also likely to be victimized because of their increased vulnerability.

Other than choosing an effective violence prevention program that meets the unique needs at each school, additional principles of violence prevention programming would be to attend to dosage and duration concerns (Greenberg et al., 1999; Henrich et al., 1999). How intensive and how long does the intervention need to be in order to produce significant change? The program should be comprehensive and intensive so that students' needs are met at different levels, and the programs should be developmentally appropriate so that skills build upon each other as students progress in school. In general, the earlier the intervention in students' lives, the more effective the intervention is likely to be and the more likely the program will act as a 'preventative' force. The program should also take into account environmental and cultural contexts of students and school personnel.

While the violence prevention literature has emphasized the above principles of effective practice, an often-ignored principle concerns the importance of integrating the program into the mainstream of the school and its educational program. 'Add-on' programs may work for the short term; however, there is a strong rationale for integrating the practice and implementation of violence prevention into the fabric of the educational program (Morrison et al., 2004). In order to do this, recognition must be given to the challenges that mainstream educators face in accomplishing what they perceive to be their primary mission, to attend to the academic achievement of their students. Thus, the question becomes, how do schools integrate the content and process of violence prevention into their broader educational mission?

This question may be answered partially by attending to school reform and school change literature (Levine and Lezotte, 1990; Teddlie and Reynolds, 2000). This literature suggests that educators who are attending to effective schools and positive change will attend to factors such as:

- productive school climate and culture;
- effective instructional arrangements and implementation;
- focus on student acquisition of central learning skills;
- high operationalized expectations and requirements for students;
- appropriate monitoring of student progress;
- practice-oriented staff development at the school site;
- outstanding leadership; and
- salient parental and community involvement.

These factors have some overlap with the principles of violence prevention; the key is how to integrate the dual mission of academic progress and development of personal-social skills in the context of violence prevention.

As a start, the program chosen should be based on theories that match the school's mission statement, and should simultaneously focus on changes within the students and the school environment, with the best programs being holistic in nature. As previously discussed, sustainability is a critical factor in choosing and implementing a program because change occurs over time. Administrators and teachers must be committed to implementation over several years, with frequent feedback to make adjustments and ongoing evaluation to monitor progress (Domitrovich and Greenberg, 2000).

A major factor in lasting systemic change in violence prevention in schools is the active participation of the school administrators (Morrison et al., 2004). As the school leaders, administrators provide vision, guidance, and support for the entire school in violence prevention efforts, and help secure resources (for example, release time for teacher training, incentives for teachers and students, needed supplies, and so on) necessary for efforts to be successful (Osher et al., 2004). Administrative leaders must be committed to change and can model flexibility and willingness to accept feedback as discipline policies and other school-level policies are discussed and critiqued in an examination of the school environment. Additionally, it is necessary that the school leaders take an active role in conducting a needs assessment, choosing and implementing quality violence prevention programs, and evaluating and providing feedback on program success.

CONCLUSION

Students with emotional and behavior disorders are at risk of being estranged from the schooling process and of becoming involved with the school discipline process. How the school responds to the challenges presented by these youths is critical. As suggested by Osher and colleagues (Osher et al., 2003), the prevention of school disruptions and violence required a multi-level strategy that targets students at their specific level of need. The vast majority of students are inclined to take school seriously, to study hard, and this is reflected in their number one worry about school: getting good grades. Other students are less involved with school and may be poorly engaged. They may not fully adhere to the school educational mission, may question their own purpose in school, and may from time to time engage in antisocial behaviors that lead to office referrals. These youth will require a more intensive program that builds on their personal strengths and which utilizes their remaining social bonds at school as resources to rekindle positive school connections and to teach them positive social and academic skills. Unfortunately, most schools are also likely to have a much smaller, but more challenging group, those who are disconnected from the traditional schooling process, have or are on a trajectory toward dropping out of school, and involved in both school and community behavioral disorder. These youth will require a more intensive intervention that will typically require more resources than a given school has available. These youth will need to have coordinated school–community–family strategies that seek to reform the positive social bonds that have been severely strained by their history of anti-social behavior. However, as we have argued in this chapter, these efforts hold the greatest promise when they not only focus on the social-emotional development of the individual student, but also initiate a balanced strategy that examines how the school itself fosters or hinders the expression of aggressive and disruptive behavior.

Our emphasis on the importance of school context in the existence or exacerbation of school disruption and violence is echoed by Osher et al. (2004), who extend the 'warning signs' rubric (Dwyer et al., 1998) to indicate signs at the school, classroom, and family context levels that are associated with and could reflect danger signs within a school. They make the critical point that these contexts are important in how they interact with students within the school. That is, the precursors to violence and disruption are not static individual, or even static contextual, factors. Individual and contextual characteristics will interact in a dynamic, changing, and evolving way. Therefore, as schools adopt prevention and intervention strategies, they need to be constantly aware that 'one size does not fit all.' Some strategies will work to reduce aggressive behavior from high-risk students, while others will assist to reduce low-level disruption. Finally, reduction in *school* violence can be achieved when schools recognize their role not only in the reduction of misbehavior and disruption, but in its creation; use a variety of strategies to target different groups of students; and integrate these efforts into the overall mission of their school, making these strategies everyday practice.

REFERENCES

Bear, G., Webster-Stratton, C., Furlong, M.J. and Rhee, S. (2000) 'Prevention of school violence', in G. Bear and C. Minke (eds), *Preventing school problems – Promoting School Success: Strategies that Work.* Washington, DC: National Association of School Psychologists. pp. 1–70.

Blankemeyer, M., Flannery, D.J. and Vazsonyi, A.T. (2002) 'The role of aggression and social competence in children's perceptions of the child-teacher relationship', *Psychology in the Schools*, 39 (3): 293–304.

Breland, A.M. (2000) 'The "true" perpetrators of violence: The effects of media on public perceptions of youthful violent offenders', in D.S. Sandhu and C.B. Aspy (eds), *Violence in American Schools: A Practical Guide for Counselors.* Alexandria, VA: American Counseling Association. pp. 109–120.

Brener, N.D., Simon, T.R., Krug, E.G. and Lowry, R. (1999) 'Recent trends in violence-related behaviors among high school students in the United States', *Journal of the American Medical Association,* 282: 440–46.

Burstyn, J.N., Bender, G., Casella, R., Gordon, H.W., Guerra, D.P., Luschen, K.V., Stevens, R. and Williams, K.M. (2001) *Preventing Violence in Schools: A Challenge to American Democracy.* Mahwah, NJ: Lawrence Erlbaum Associates.

Coggeshall, M.B. and Kingery, P.M. (2001) 'Cross-survey analysis of school violence and disorder', *Psychology in the Schools*, 38: 107–116.

Colvin, G., Sugai, G., Good, R.H. and Lee, Y. (1997) 'Using active supervision and precorrection to improve transition behavior in an elementary school', *School Psychology Quarterly*, 12 (4): 344–63.

Conoley, J.C. and Conoley, C.A. (2001) 'Systemic interventions for safe schools', in J.N. Hughes and A.M. La Greca (eds), *Handbook of Psychological Services for Children and Adolescents*. London: Oxford University Press. pp. 439–53.

Crick, N.R. and Grotpeter, J.K. (1995) 'Relational aggression, gender, and social-psychological adjustment', *Child Development*, 66: 710–22.

Domitrovich, C.E. and Greenberg, M.T. (2000) 'The study of implementation: Current findings from effective programs that prevent mental disorders in school-aged children', *Journal of Educational and Psychological Consultation*, 11 (2): 193–221.

Dwyer, K. and Osher, D. (2000) *Safeguarding our Children: An Action Guide*. Washington, DC: US Departments of Education and Justice, American Institutes of Research. Retrieved June 29, 2003, from http://cecp.air.org/guide/actionguide.htm

Dwyer, K., Osher, D. and Warger, C. (1998) *Early Warning Timely Response: A Guide to Safe Schools*. Washington, DC: US Department of Education, Retrieved June 29, 2003, from www.air-dc.org/cecp/guide/annotated.htm

Espelage, D.L. and Swearer, S.M. (2003) 'Research on school bullying and victimization: What have we learned and where do we go from here?', *School Psychology Review*, 32: 365–83.

Fein, R., Vossekuil, B., Pollack, W., Borum, R., Modzeleski, W. and Reddy, M. (2002) *Threat Assessment in Schools: A Guide to Managing Threatening Situations and to Creating Safe School Climates*. US Department of Education, Office of Elementary and Secondary Education, Safe and Drug-Free Schools Program and US Secret Service, National Threat Assessment Center, Washington, DC.

Furlong, M.J., Bates, M.P., Smith, D.C. and Kingery, P.E. (eds) (2004) *Appraisal and Prediction of School Violence: Methods, Issues, and Contexts*. Hauppauge, NY: NovaScience Publishers.

Furlong, M.J., Jimenez, T.C. and Saxton, J.D. (2003a) 'The prevention of adolescent homicide', in T. Gullotta and M. Bloom (eds), *The Encyclopedia of Primary Prevention and Health Promotion*. New London, CT: Kluwer Academic/Plenum Publisher. pp. 575–82.

Furlong, M.J., Morrison, G.M. and Greif, J.L. (2003b). 'Reaching an American consensus: Reactions to the special issue on school bullying, *School Psychology Review*, 32: 456–70.

Furlong, M.J., Paige, L. and Osher, D. (2003c) 'The safe schools/healthy students (SS/HS) initiative: Lessons learned from implementing comprehensive youth development programs', *Psychology in the Schools*, 40: 447–56.

Furlong, M.J., Pavelski, R. and Saxton, J. (2002) 'School violence prevention', in S. Brock, P. Lazarus and S. Jimerson (eds), *Best Practices in School Crisis Prevention*. Alexandria, VA: National Association of School Psychologists. pp. 131–49.

Furlong, M. and Morrison, G. (2000) 'The school in school violence: Definitions and facts', *Journal of Emotional and Behavioral Disorders*, 8: 71–82.

Furlong, M.J., Morrison, R., Chung, A. and Bates, M. (1998) 'School violence and victimization among secondary students in California: Grade, gender and racial-ethnic group incidence patterns', *California School Psychologist*, 3: 71–87.

Greenberg, M.T., Domitrovich, C. and Bumbarger, B. (1999) *Preventing Mental Disorders in School-age Children: A Review of the Effectiveness of Prevention Programs*. University Park, PA: Prevention Research Center for the Promotion of Human Development.

Henrich, C.C., Brown, J.L. and Aber, J.L. (1999) 'Evaluating the effectiveness of school-based violence prevention: Developmental approaches', *Social Policy Report: Society for Research in Child Development*, 13 (3): 2–17.

Jefferson County Safe Schools/Healthy Students (2003) *Project Shield*. Retrieved September 8, 2003, from http://www.sshsevaluation.org/initiative/sitedata.cfm?siteID=21

Johnston, L.D., O'Malley, P.M. and Bachman, J.G. (1996) *National Survey Results on Drug Use from Monitoring the Future Study, 1975–1995: Volume I Secondary School Students*. Washington, DC: US Government Printing Office, NIH Publication No. 96–4139.

Kann, L., Kinchen, S.A., Williams, B.I., Ross, J.G., Lowry, R., Hill, C.V., Grunbaun, J.A., Blumson, P.S., Collins, J.L. and Kolbe, L.J. (1998) 'Youth risk behavior surveillance – United States, 1997', *Journal of School Health*, 68: 355–69.

Kann, L., Kinchen, S.A., Williams, B.I., Ross, J.G., Lowry, R., Hill, C.V., Grunbaun, J.A. and Kolbe, L.J. (2000) 'Youth risk behavior surveillance – United States, 1999', *Morbidity and Mortality Weekly Report*, 49 (SS05): 1–96.

Kazdin, A. (1996) *Conduct Disorders in Childhood and Adolescence* (2nd edn). Thousand Oaks, CA: Sage.

Kusche, C.A. and Greenberg, M.T. (1994) *The PATHS Curriculum: Promoting Alternative Thinking Strategies*. Seattle, WA: Developmental Research Programs.

Larson, J., Smith, D.C. and Furlong, M.J. (2002) 'Best practices in school violence prevention', in A. Thomas and J Grimes (eds), *Best Practices in School Psychology IV*. Washington, DC: National Association of School Psychologists. pp. 1081–98.

Leone, P.E., Mayer, M., Malmgren, K. and Meisel, S.M. (2000) 'School violence and disruption: Rhetoric, reality, and reasonable balance', *Focus on Exceptional Children*, 33 (1): 1–20.

Levine, D.U. and Lezotte, L.W. (1990) *Unusually Effective Schools: A Review and Analysis of Unusually Effective Schools*. Madison, WI: National Center for Effective Schools Research and Development.

Limber, S. and Small, M. (2003) 'Laws and policies to address bullying in US schools', *School Psychology Review*, 32: 445–55.

McGee, J.P. and DeBernardo, C.R. (1999) 'The classroom avenger', *The Forensic Examiner*, 8: 5–6.

Morrison, G.M., Anthony, S., Storino, M., Cheng, J., Furlong, M.J. and Morrison, R.L. (2001) 'School expulsion as a process and as an event: Before and after effects on children at-risk for school discipline', in R.J. Skiba and G.G. Noam (eds), *New Directions in Youth Development – Zero Tolerance: Can Suspension and Expulsion Keep Schools Safe?* pp. 92, 45–72.

Morrison, G.M. and D'Incau, B. (1997) 'The web of zero-tolerance: Characteristics of students who are recommended for expulsion from school', *Education and Treatment of Children*, 20 (3): 316–35.

Morrison, G.M., Furlong, M.J., D'Incau, B. and Morrison, R.L. (2004) 'The Safe School: Integrating the School Reform Agenda to Prevent Disruption and Violence at School', in J.C. Conoley and A.P. Goldstein (eds), *School Violence Intervention: A Practical Handbook* (2nd edn). New York: Guilford.

Morrison, G.M., Furlong, M.J. and Morrison, R.L. (1994) 'From school violence to school safety: Reframing the issue for school psychologists', *School Psychology Review*, 23: 236–56.

Morrison, G.M., Peterson, R. and O'Farrell, S. (2004) 'Using office referral records in school violence research: Possibilities and limitations (or of fables and foibles)', *Journal of School Violence*, 3: 39–61.

Morrison, G.M. and Skiba, R. (2001) 'Predicting violence from school misbehavior: Promises and perils', *Psychology in the Schools*, 38: 173–84.

Morrison, G.M. and Skiba, R.J. (2004) 'School discipline indices and school violence: An imperfect correspondence', in M.J. Furlong, M.P. Bates, D.C. Smith and P.E. Kingery (eds), *Appraisal and Prediction of School Violence: Methods, Issues, and Contexts*. Hauppauge, NY: NovaScience Publishers.

Nansel, T.R., Overpeck, M., Pilla, R.S., Ruan, W.J., Simons-Morton, B. and Scheidt, P. (2001) 'Bullying behaviors among US youth: Prevalence and association with psychosocial adjustment', *Journal of the American Medical Association*, 285: 2094–2100.

Osher, D., VanAcker, R., Morrison, G.M., Gable, R., Dwyer, K. and Quinn, M. (2004) 'Warning signs of problems in schools: Ecological perspectives and effective practices for combating school aggression and violence', *Journal of School Violence*, 3: 13–37.

Osher, D., Dwyer, K. and Jackson, S. (2003) *Safe, Supportive, and Successful Schools: Step by Step*. Longmont, CO: Sopris West.

O'Toole, M.E. (2000) *The School Shooter: A Threat Assessment Perspective*. Quantico, VA: National Center for the Analysis of Violent Crime, Federal Bureau of Investigation.

Paige, L.Z. (2002) 'Writing a safe schools/healthy students grant', *NASP Communiqué*, 29 (6): Retrieved September 8, 2003, from http://www.nasponline.org/publications/cq296sshsgrant.html

Reddy, M., Borum, R., Berglund, J., Vossekuil, B., Fein, R. and Modzeleski, W. (2001) 'Evaluating risk for targeted violence in schools: Comparing risk assessment, threat assessment, and other approaches', *Psychology in the Schools*, 38: 157–72.

Reinke, W.M. and Herman, K.C. (2002) 'Creating school environments that deter antisocial behaviors in youth', *Psychology in the Schools*, 39 (5): 549–60.

Rose, L.C. and Gallup, A.M. (2000) The 32nd Annual Phi Delta Kappa/Gallup Poll of the Public's Attitudes Toward Public Schools. Retrieved September 8, 2003, from http://www.pdkintl.org/kappan/kpol0009.htm#1a

Scott, T., Nelson, C.M. and Liaupsin, C.J. (2001) 'Effective instruction: The forgotten component in preventing school violence', *Education and Treatment of Children*, 24 (3): 309–322.

Sheidow, A.J. and Woodford, M.S. (2003) 'Multisystemic therapy: An empirically supported, home-based family therapy approach', *Family Journal – Counseling and Therapy for Couples and Families*, 11 (3): 257–63.

Skiba, R.J. and Knesting, K. (2001) 'Zero tolerance, zero evidence: An analysis of school disciplinary practice', *New Directions for Youth Development: Theory, Practice, Research*, 92: 17–44.

Skiba, R.J. and Noam, G.G. (eds) (2001) 'Zero tolerance: Can suspension and expulsion keep schools safe?', *New Directions in Youth Development*, 92 (entire issue).

Solberg, M.E. and Olweus, D. (2003) 'Prevalence estimation of school bullying with the Olweus Bully/Victim Questionnaire', *Aggressive Behavior*, 29: 239–68.

Stephens, R. (2003) *National School Safety Center School-associated Death Database*. Thousand Oaks, CA: National School Safety Center. Retrieved September 8, 2003, from www.nssc1.org

Sugai, G. and Horner, R. (1999) 'Discipline and behavioral support: Practices, pitfalls, and promises', *Effective School Practices*, 17 (4): 10–22.

Taylor-Greene, S., Brown, D., Nelson, L., Longton, J., Gassman, X., Cohen, J. and Swartz, J. (1997) School-wide behavioral support: Starting the year off right', *Journal of Behavioral Education*, 7: 99–112.

Teddlie, C. and Reynolds, D. (eds) (2000) *The International Handbook of School Effectiveness Research*. London: Falmer.

Thornton, T.N., Craft, C.A., Dahlberg, L.L., Lynch, B.S. and Baer, K. (2000) *Best Practices of Youth Violence Prevention*. Atlanta, GA: Center for Disease Control and Prevention.

Unnever, J.D. and Cornell, D.G. (2003) 'The culture of bullying in middle school', *Journal of School Violence*, 2: 5–27.

US Departments of Education and Justice (1999) *1999 Annual Report on School Safety*. Retrieved August 1, 2003, from http://www.safetyzone.org/pdf/schoolsafety2.pdf

VanAcker, R., Grant, S.H. and Henry, D. (1996) 'Teacher and student behavior as a function of risk for aggression', *Education and Treatment of Children*, 19 (3): 316–34.

Welsh, J., Domitrovich, C.E., Bierman, K. and Lang, J. (2003) 'Promoting safe schools and healthy students in rural Pennsylvania', *Psychology in the Schools*, 40 (5): 457–72.

9

The Problem is not the Problem: Hard Cases in Modernist Systems

TIM O'BRIEN AND DENNIS GUINEY

In this chapter we argue that children who experience emotional and behavioural difficulties (EBD) are largely a product of modernist systems. We assert that these systems create and sustain generalized, personalized and internally or socially focused labels such as 'problem children', 'disturbed and disturbing children', 'troubled and troubling children' or 'challenging children'. We then set out our understanding of the terms and relationship between modernism and postmodernism in order to argue for a refocusing and development of our critical awareness, away from group or individual labels that highlight problems, onto multiple discourses and modes of discourse about problem systems, and the epistemologies that currently underpin them and the assumptions, values, beliefs, interests and motives that are upheld and transmitted by them. We see the epistemologies as having an emotional, cognitive and sociocultural context rather than incorporating definitions located solely within cognitive processes.

In turn we believe that problem systems are the result of an erroneous premise, which believes that modernist applications can solve all problems. From where we stand, to continue treating modernist 'problems' with modernist 'solutions' is largely a waste of time. In making this case we also aim to promote thinking about emotional and behavioural difficulties with regard to the current debate about inclusion and pedagogy.

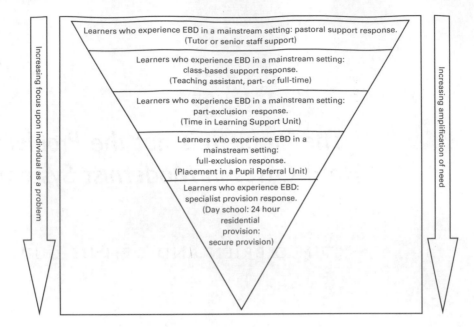

Figure 9.1   *The modernist systemic response to EBD*

MODERNIST LABELS

These learners, those described as having or being 'EBD', may be felt to form a distinct group, yet as with many labels in modernist systems it is the label that confers the similarities, not the characteristics or individual dispositions of the learners being described. Consequently it is important to be more specific about who we are talking about. Figure 9.1 offers a brief description of the continuum of need as we see it in this area, presented as distinct yet related groups with differing emphases within the EBD label. It also highlights modernist responses and the current 'quest for categorization' (Garner, 1999). The triangle symbolizes a decreasing population, yet with increasing amplification of need, at each level.

We believe that this population of learners who experience emotional and behavioural difficulties and who are often caught up in the interactions of multiple modernist agencies, such as education, social services, medical services and youth justice, for example, become defined as 'hard cases'. For this reason our use of the term 'EBD' throughout this chapter refers to those hard case learners situated towards the tip or the sharp end of this pyramid of exclusion, rather than those located towards the top of the model.

HARD CASES ... AND HARD PLACES

Learners who experience EBD, those who inhabit the exclusion clauses of the modernist social contract, represent and occupy the spaces between the interstices of modernist systems. They exist on and at the margins. For this reason we conceptualize them and the perceived challenges that they present to modernist systems as 'hard cases' (O'Brien, 2001). Hard cases highlight the tensions and dilemmas that exist within and between systems and force us to look at the goals and values of those systems. Though our examples will be drawn from education in general and EBD in particular; we could equally have drawn examples from elsewhere. In educational settings hard cases challenge us to confront the manner in which we balance attitudes, values and beliefs within complex systems. They also enable us to reflect upon how we construct meaning. They help us to bring a progressive focus onto the inherent risks of making decisions that focus on identifying the *differences* between individuals, especially when difference is conceptualized as being more threatening than sameness. From one perspective, difference challenges conformity and can highlight how individuals or groups actively reject what is on offer to them as the norm. However, we propose that differences do not have to be a threat to commonality. Within the current education system differences are referenced to where learners should be taught, what they should be taught and how they should be taught. The framework for referencing must also come under scrutiny. This is why a consideration of difference as part of the solution and not as part of the problem is important: it offers opportunities to reflect upon different meanings, understandings, needs, dispositions and goals.

Difference can be constructed differently within different frameworks. Frameworks can be constructed differently too – some are comfortable with plurality and some are not. Some include a form of mutuality that incorporates difference and some do not. Some see difference as disconnected from what learners share in common and some do not. Our assertion is that difference itself is constructed within systems – it can be constructed so that identifying difference is seen as discriminatory or emancipatory – and hard cases enable us to understand such constructions and the frameworks in which they thrive. Hard cases also present contraindicating variables that challenge the epistemology upon which systems are founded and thus problematize knowledge, its construction and its application. Clearly this has implications for pedagogy, which we will consider at a later point. Our contention is that hard cases – be they individuals, groups or systems – should not be ignored or labelled as 'problems' simply because they raise tensions. Tensions can generate reflection upon ontology and epistemology. We assert that we can, should and must learn from the hard cases.

We also characterize, by association, the margins of modernist systems in which hard cases exist as 'hard places'. Hard cases and hard places can be found in all modernist systems and share similar characteristics, whether they be in health, housing, transport or social policy. As such they usefully illuminate the often blurred and unlit areas of our social world: those areas that are situated at the cusp of social exclusion and which are the outcome of an essentially reductionist and rigid paradigm. The assertion here is that this paradigm lacks flexibility because political responses – the actions of national and local government – are rooted in modernism and are consequently unable, despite the development of various rapid-response strategies, to apply solutions that are radical enough for our postmodernist times. Therefore solutions to the problems that hard cases/places illuminate are often doomed to fail. This is because such solutions often only serve to relocate problems within and between the various systems that we have identified. Thus a focus on the control of street crime results in stringent targets being set for schools and local education authorities by way of a reduction in truancy and school exclusions.

A lack of responsivity occurs first because at present hard cases can only be perceived negatively – they are problematical. Problems demand and warrant action from mass pluralistic modernist systems, which, in order to move to action and resolution, have to overcome the weight of systemic inertia that necessarily sustains them. Second, because of almost pre-set systemic responses, modernist 'solutions' are being applied to modernist 'problems'. This action, or non-action, occurs within a fundamentally absolutist paradigm that limits the possibility of formulating hard cases and hard places as part of the solution, rather than part of the problem.

PROBLEMS HAVE SOLUTIONS

If hard cases are framed as a problem, then why are we proposing that they are part of the solution? This is because they demand new ways of conceptualizing and re-conceptualizing that will result in the development of new postmodern epistemologies. Such epistemologies could offer the possibility of rejecting over-simplification of complexity and can steer us away from dichotomous or oppositional stances that often emerge through an over-reliance on modernist epistemology. A useful example of this is the current debate in education about inclusion, elements of which can be typified as 'inclusion is good, exclusion is bad'. This complexity-made-simple approach promotes dichotomous positioning. Such separatism and polarization is a cause for concern and has major implications for how inclusion is defined (Lunt and Norwich, 1999). Hornby (1999) considers whether the confusions surrounding the definition and application of inclusion have clouded the focus upon whether, in reality, all educational needs can be met in so-called 'mainstream' settings. He is right to assert that the 'Can one size fit all?' question has to be confronted and the debate surrounding such questioning is necessary and valid. However, we propose that there are inherent dangers and limitations if such an important debate takes place solely within a modernist framework. If this occurs, then the existing parameters of the debate will only deal with issues such as location, speed, funding, processes, definitions and criteria. The essence of this discourse is modernist and it does allow some models of inclusion to be driven by authoritarianism, thus enabling 'concealed interests to take up supposedly very humane ideals' (Norwich, 2000: 110).

We assert that the development of postmodern epistemologies could promote a fusion of conceptual perspectives and allow for the development of new discourses. In turn this would allow for movement away from polarized stances and inflexible systems onto those that can accommodate the concept of ideological impurity proposed by Norwich (1996). In this way, solutions that include multiple values, such as practicability, caring (Noddings, 1992), quality of life (Robertson, 1998) and equity can be sought, as can a focus upon related outlooks and methods. This moves us away from the modernist context where hard cases and places are always reframed and negatively connoted as 'problems' in order that they can be incorporated into existing modernist structures. The danger of this is that it has made it possible largely to ignore the task of developing a critical gaze with, for and by those who feel – and those who are – excluded. Furthermore, it is now essential to develop and deploy new ways of looking. We have to be comfortable with multiple perspectives and a plurality of voice in order to help us define and better understand the strengths and weaknesses of modernist structures so that they may be analysed and developed beyond their existing parameters. Hard cases can help to generate new paradigms. They must not be undervalued or oversimplified by being defined as problem children or as problems within systems that require more effective management. This mindset will simply continue to constrain and limit our thinking and responses so that the debate about inclusion is ultimately reduced to a consideration of how to solve the problem within current models. In this way we will simply repeat current thinking; the thinking that forms the lifeblood of modernism and prevents us from engaging in conceptualization that incorporates and enables 'border crossing' (Giroux, 1997).

MODERN TIMES

We see modernism as incorporating a spirit of optimism in humankind's ability to control and plan the environment in a manner which can define, ensure and sustain the 'public good'. However, its meta-narratives are based upon suppositions about what the public good is and the dominant values, beliefs and actions needed to secure this. In modernist states the universal application of macro- theoretical interpretations have typically been defined and managed by the intervention, intrusion and assumptions of the political elite. The theoretical approach of Bernstein (1996) is founded upon a belief that such assumptions are applied as modalities of control and uphold unequal distribution of privilege. We see 'EBDness' as a case in point here. The notion of public good can be seen as both the drive and justification underlying mass social ideals, which in turn are based upon notions such as certainty, need, predictability, planning, clarity of purpose and a single and knowable truth. It is through these means by which modernism establishes and consolidates its epistemological security.

This sense of 'the knowing of the truth' is apparent in the development of the curriculum and the curriculumization of knowledge in modernist approaches to education. Modernist principles, driving a notion of a common education for all, could be summarized – or perhaps over-summarized by us – as follows:

- Mass education is socially desirable/essential between the ages 5–16.
- Key knowledge/skills/understanding and values can be identified and imparted via mass education systems.
- Key developmental stages in the client population can be identified and matched to the curriculum base.
- Homogeneity of experience within the curriculum is desirable/essential.
- Homogeneity of response within the curriculum is desirable/essential.
- Homogeneity of teaching strategies within the curriculum is desirable/ essential.

Such principles of course beg many essential questions. These will include questions about who defines and controls the knowledge, values and skills base that is seen as being the necessary fundamentals in forming the curriculum. Skrtic (1991), adopting a postmodernist framework of reference, claims that knowledge is antifoundational: that it does not have fixed foundations and it is reliant upon community dialogue and discourse. This is opposed to a foundational conceptualization, which defines knowledge as being monological and validated by elites.

We believe that foundational knowledge only serves to reinforce existing structures and systems. It does not encourage us to engage in collaborative reflective critique to enable change or enable inclusion. Foundational knowledge is less fluid and more fixed than antifoundational knowledge. It results in certain groups and individuals becoming the throwaways of modernist systems, which we contend are not open to deconstruction and are unresponsive to practitioner feedback. This is a critical way of reflecting upon curriculum content and development in education in the United Kingdom over recent decades – who and what is being legitimized either singularly or in combination. The learner? The teacher? The curriculum? The pedagogy? The status quo? This also raises associated questions about the process of reflection itself and whether it occurs within communities where knowledge is socially constructed, creates new meanings and is seen as being grounded in antifoundational theories, or whether it occurs in isolation. It should also cause us to question the power relations between learners and systems and to question whether knowledge is being used as a tool of control (Freire, 1972).

By definition the group of learners labelled as 'EBD' have struggled, amongst other things, with foundational knowledge in modernist systems and the power that such systems exert over them. These are systems that must continue to support universal applications of modernist systems and solutions, rather than responsive, flexible and coherent postmodernist applications. These applications consider individuals and minorities as well as majorities, localized democracy rather than centralized control and equity as well as equality. An inability to respond flexibly results in varying forms of exclusion as a modernist response to individual difference. There is a debate to be engaged in about the 'who' and 'how' of this process of exclusion, but this does not occur within the boundaries of this chapter. Instead we are interested in challenging the view that the content, rather than the location, of the education of this group of learners should be the same as that which would have been afforded to them had they remained in the mainstream system. These are the EBD hard cases who are excluded from the mainstream system that manages to retain other learners who are given the same EBD label. More than this, there is now a gathering momentum to include this group into a standards and targets-driven mainstream education system, as far as is possible. A human rights perspective largely drives this momentum. Not only is it viewed, and largely accepted, that there is a human right to an education but modernist systems appear to have transformed this through an equality agenda that now asserts that all learners have a right to the *same* education. In our view this does not appear to have been established as a goal of what is termed 'inclusive education'. We support the principle that everyone has a right to an education within a diverse community of learners where individuality is not subordinated to concepts of community, built upon a notion of the wider public good. What appears to be still unresolved is what that education should be and what it should be for. This is an example of how hard cases can be used to help us generate solutions rather than problems, for in considering such questions with regard to learners who 'act out' – those 'with EBD' who feature at the sharp end of Figure 9.1 – we are also equally obliged to consider them in relation to learners who act-in, those who are more likely to appear at the broader levels of Figure 9.1. We have to consider learners as individuals as well as members of groups.

MARGINALIZED BY MODERNISM

In positing a critique of modernism we now consider this EBD sub-group further and explore some of the reasons how and why learners who experience emotional and behavioural difficulties are marginalized by modernism. Typical interpretations in the form of judgements stated in the modernist voice are added at the end of each of the statements that we provide. They are added to highlight how language reflects ideology and interpretation of experience, as well as to show how such statements affirm and uphold modernist perspectives:

- This sub-group serves to reinforce the citizenship of the majority whom modernism strives to convince have absolute morality and certainty of values:
  'Anyone who is not like them is obviously better than them.'
- This sub-group refuses, by choice or necessity, to be incorporated or integrated into modernist systems:
  'They are immoral.'
- This sub-group challenges the fundamental premise of modernist systems by continually raising epistemological questions such as those about adult–child relationships, social order and causality of difficulty:
  'They have a deficit. There is something wrong with them.'
- The modernist discourse is about them, not with them:
  'We know what is best for them.'
- Modernist educational goals are problematized by individual and group disposition:
  'They deserve what they get because it is their fault.'
- Dissenting voices challenge the tenets of modernism:
  'What do you expect? They have all got EBD.'

These judgements emerge from and sustain a modernist reality, but we are now coming to believe that reality is more complex than that. If we do not search beyond this reality we are liable to be stuck within it – hence the problem is the problem. In terms of our proposition, modernist systems are reductionist in their application of inputs and outcomes – stifling individuality and diversity for a greater good, or perhaps the wider goal, of social conformity and the predictability that emanates from the knowledge of an absolute truth. Modernism creates curriculum reductionism. Ultimately, what the curriculum adds in terms of content it must lack in terms of process, because its primary drive tends to make it over-focus on control. Modernist reductionism therefore has to provide a system to deliver the bulk of a common, foundational, monological curriculum content, to a mass clientele at a standard level of competence. This is the description of a bureaucracy. It is not the description of a responsive and reflective education system that serves localized community needs in a flexible manner. Bureaucratic pedagogy and bureaucratic inclusion have already destroyed respon-siveness to diversity and difference.

TIME FOR IMPURITY

In contrast to modernism we are using the term 'postmodernism', whilst at the same time recognizing the potential lack of coherence about what this term means. Postmodernism, even if incoherent in definition, springs from a grounded review of the applications of modernist systems. Whilst this review recognizes the progress such systems have afforded, it also recog-nizes where these systems have not and cannot work. We do not see modernism and postmodernism as antithetical – they are not in opposition. Nor do we propose that each is ideologically unconnected with the other, a form of ideological purity. They are interconnected – they both use moder-nity as a reference point – but they are also distinct. Postmodernism is the logical transmutation of the processes unleashed by modernist applications, thinking and structures. It offers fluid methods of enquiry and knowledge creation, but we acknowledge that it also has its limitations in that some of its assumptions may be fallible. We do not see postmodernism as a panacea that incorporates modes of magical thinking. However, it does recognize the breakdown in consensus arising in society not only from threats that emanate from outside of that society, but also from the erosion of the elite power base within society due to the very success of modernism.

Postmodernity springs from a growing maturity and realization that the world is complex and interconnected and made up not of one naturally occurring over-riding singular and universal truth, but of many socially constructed truths. Here we have a realization that everything cannot be resolved and understood by adopting the principles and thought processes that underpin modernism and its emphasis upon fixed realities. We therefore see postmodernism challenging the modernist notion that we can have a clearly defined mass education with an associated curriculum for all. It is becoming increasingly clear that we need to take radical steps towards conceptualizing curriculum and curriculum entitlement in terms of common principles for all but with different content for some (O'Brien and Guiney, 2001). This would force us to confront reductionist principles and ask ourselves whether curriculum adaptations for the majority are necessarily beneficial for the minority, and in turn whether they are actually beneficial for the majority, for we are arguing that the one must provide a continuous reiterative and reflective reference for the other. It would challenge us to analyse the epistemological basis and usefulness of terms such as 'EBD'. It also demands that we not only accept, but positively connote, the existence of hard cases and the solutions they can help us to generate. One such area that may benefit from this type of reflective response is that of the conceptualization of pedagogy.

DEVELOPING GROUNDED PEDAGOGY

In our view the inclusion debate, occurring within paradigms and social goals that are modernist, has largely avoided dealing with the realities of individuals' lives and the effect that inclusion has upon individual lives. Nor has it incorporated sufficient theorizing about responsive and transformative pedagogies that can relate to individuals as well as groups. Whilst there are many exceptions to this generalization, such as in the thinking of Slee (1999) and Daniels (2001), the debate has too often only been about structural changes. We propose that the development of a grounded pedagogy, which seeks to integrate social, emotional and psychobiological factors and where the focus is on learning not labelling, is now essential. Postmodernist perspectives on diversity and difference, individuality, subjective reality and culture and community, for example, provide routes to a grounded pedagogy for individuals and groups and also reflective and responsive systems. In recognizing individuality we are also asserting that learning is a psychosocial activity: learning is culture dependent. Lave and Wenger (1991), following in the tradition of Vygotsky (1978), remind us that learning takes place within a social world. They propose that learning should be analysed and understood in terms of 'legitimate peripheral participation'. Participation is 'peripheral' because it changes; it is a dynamic process. Teaching and learning activity is never complete, and nor are the domains of knowledge within and beyond 'participation' ever complete. A defining characteristic that makes it 'legitimate' is the knowledge that emanates from and belongs to a learning community. By contrast with modernist education systems, legitimate peripheral participation can never be enabled by a rigid and reductionist paradigm, especially for those labelled as experiencing EBD (O'Brien, 2002).

Lave and Wenger also refer to 'arenas of practice', which are participatory in nature. What arenas of practice do the excluded belong to? Existing arenas of practice are those formulated within modernist systems, but we must now find, develop and validate new arenas outside or peripheral to existing structures in order to accommodate difference. We also propose that pedagogy has to be directly related to the goals of the systems and flexible enough to deal with a fusion of approaches – it should be able to incorporate 'top-down' and 'bottom-up' approaches, for example – as well as diversity of curriculum content. We must also define how such arenas can be validated in a manner that is principled, ethical, flexible, practical and able to uphold the right to education – whilst at the same time recognizing and delivering pedagogical diversity. In this way, social identities are constructed and validated and the implications for pedagogy and the resourcing of teaching to enable situated learning becomes clearer. The establishment of the relationship between definitions of knowledge – what is considered as valid in terms of knowledge, content and pedagogy – can result in curriculum models that are experimental and fluid and which can offer risk-taking experiences for learners and teachers. It can also provide a questioning context to those who would seek to inhibit ambiguity, those who seek to set finite and prescriptive boundaries about what is to be known and what is to be taught – those who would seek to limit opportunities for learners and teachers to question what is being offered to them as objective truth. Pedagogy is not neutral – it can emancipate or oppress consciousness. It can enable learners to develop their own epistemological grounding through interaction with a world that is constantly changing and developing. Learners can gain knowledge and be transformed through pedagogies that see theory and practice as interconnected, enable dialogue and create a sense of belonging to arenas of practice – not by excluding individuals into out-groups. It is also possible for pedagogy to be used to constrain human development and uphold social structures rather than alter them.

LEARNING NOT LABELLING

In this chapter we have structured our propositions in an iterative manner. We have proposed a redefinition of prevailing epistemological tools, a recasting and validation of new arenas of educational participation and practice, the democratization of the curriculum and the enabling of a critical dialogue and gaze which moves us beyond imprecise labelling processes and bureaucratic inclusion. We have used hard cases as a reference point for doing so. At the same time we recognize that it is not possible to present over-simplified prescriptions for how such change is to be achieved. Our task now is to engage in radical thought and action in order to promote conceptual models and associated practice that is accepting of individuality, complexity, diversity and ambiguity. Models that combat foundationalism, conceptualize enquiry as situated, knowledge as localized and tentative and inclusion in education as a concept that references individuals, groups, systems and policies within existing and newly-developed and validated arenas of participation. This enabling process allows us to seek to integrate and develop pedagogies that are grounded and responsive. By doing this we can see that modernism is not the solution and the problem is not the problem.

REFERENCES

Bernstein, B. (1996) *Pedagogy, Symbolic Control and Identity: Theory, Research, Critique*. London: Taylor and Francis.
Daniels, H. (2001) 'Activity theory and knowledge production: twin challenges for the development of schooling for pupils who experience EBD', *Emotional and Behavioural Difficulties*, 6 (2): 113–24.
Freire, P. (1972) *Pedagogy of the Oppressed*. London: Sheed and Ward.
Garner, P. (1999) *Pupils With Problems: Rational Fears ... Radical Solutions?* Stoke-on-Trent: Trentham Books.
Giroux, H. (1997) *Pedagogy and the Politics of Hope: Theory, Culture and Schooling*. Boulder, CO: Westview.
Hornby, G. (1999) 'Inclusion or delusion: can one size fit all?', *Support for Learning*, 14 (4): 152–7.
Lave, J. and Wenger, E. (1991) *Situated Learning: Legitimate Peripheral Participation*. Cambridge: Cambridge University Press.
Lunt, I. and Norwich, B. (1999) *Can Effective Schools be Inclusive Schools? Perspectives on Education Series*. London: Institute of Education.
Noddings, N. (1992) *The Challenge to Care in Schools: An Alternative Approach to Education*. New York: Teachers College Press.
Norwich, B. (1996) 'Special needs education or education for all? Connective specialisation and ideological impurity', *British Journal of Special Education*, 23 (3): 100–104
Norwich, B. (2000) 'Profile', in P. Clough and J. Corbett, *Theories of Inclusive Education*. London: Chapman.

O'Brien, T. (2001) 'Learning from the Hard Cases', in T. O'Brien (ed.), *Enabling Inclusion: Blue Skies ... Dark Clouds?* London: The Stationery Office.

O'Brien, T. (2002) 'As chaotic as a box of frogs? Teaching learners who experience emotional and behavioural difficulties', in B. Rogers (ed.) *Teacher Leadership and Behaviour Management*. London: Chapman.

O'Brien, T. and Guiney, D. (2001) *Differentiation in Teaching and Learning: Principles and Practice*. London: Continuum.

Robertson, C. (1998) 'Quality of life as a consideration in the development of inclusive education for pupils and students with learning difficulties', in C. Tilstone, L. Florian and R. Rose (eds), *Promoting Inclusive Practice*. London: Routledge.

Skrtic, T.M. (1991) 'The Special Education Paradox: Equity as the Way to Excellence', *Harvard Educational Review*, 61 (2): 148–206.

Slee, R. (1999) 'Identity, difference and curriculum: a case study in cultural politics', in L. Barton and F. Armstrong (eds), *Difference and Difficulty: Insights, Issues and Dilemmas*. Sheffield: University of Sheffield.

Vygotsky, L.S. (1978) *Mind in Society: the Development of Higher Psychological Processes*. Cambridge, MA: Harvard University Press.

10

Academic Achievement and Behaviour: An Axiomatic Link?

TOM NICHOLSON

What do you call someone who is disruptive in class, does not do any work, gets into fights, shouts at the teacher and fails school exams? Or a student who is shy, antisocial, withdrawn, depressed, does not have friends and likely to take drugs? The term for students exhibiting these behaviours is emotional and behavioural difficulties (EBD). Depending on the behaviour, this type of student is likely to be stood down, suspended or even expelled from school. In New Zealand, a stand-down is exclusion from the school for a specified period, no more than 10 days a year, for disobedience or physical assault. A suspension is for more serious behaviour, for example drugs, and can be for an unspecified period (Ministry of Education, 2002).

How many students are excluded from school each year? As an example, New Zealand statistics for the year 2001 showed 17,421 stand-downs and 4,872 suspensions, about 2.6 per cent of the total school roll (Ministry of Education, 2002). Three out of four excluded pupils were boys, and four out of ten were Maori, even though Maori represent only 20 per cent of the school population. About half of those stood down or suspended (10,000 students) were 13 to 15 years of age, which is 4 per cent of the secondary school population. The percentage of students excluded from school for poor behaviour is not high, but the actual numbers are far from small, even in a little country like New Zealand with only 4 million people.

What is the long-term prognosis for such students? In the United States, it has been found that 58 per cent of students with emotional and behavioural difficulties (EBD) leave school without formal qualifications, 20 per cent have been arrested at least once before they leave school, compared with only 6 per cent of the normal school population, and 35 per cent will be arrested within two years of leaving school (Stanford Research Institute International, 1990). More than just about any other students, those with EBD are at risk for negative outcomes both in school and in life (Levy and Chard, 2001). If we could help these children, it would not only benefit them, it would benefit society as well.

Why are EBD students so disruptive and antisocial, and what can be done about it? This is a hard question and there are differences of opinion. One thing that stands out, though, is that many students with EBD have reading problems. The overlap between behavioural difficulties such as attention deficit hyperactivity disorder (ADHD) and reading problems ranges from 60 to 90 per cent (Rowe and Rowe, 1999), that is, between six and nine out of ten students with these behavioural difficulties are also likely to have reading difficulties.

A number of studies indicate that teachers regard behavioural difficulties as a major issue, due to the large numbers of students involved and the problem of managing their behaviour (Osher et al., 1994; Elam and Rose, 1995; McDaniel, 1984). Even trivial problems such as talking out of turn are regarded seriously by teachers (Merrett and Wheldall, 1984). Teachers seem to regard behavioural difficulties as a result of factors outside the school, such as the home, or factors internal to the child, and not due to the school (Mavropoulou and Padeliadu, 2002). Yet, it may be a mistake to disassociate the school from behavioural difficulties since there is considerable research to show that the school can do a great deal to change the negative behaviour of children. In particular, progress in learning to read may play a key role in ameliorating behavioural difficulties in the classroom.

A problem for EBD students is that much of the special education help available to them in schools concentrates on modifying their negative behaviours and improving their social skills rather than helping them with their academic problems, especially reading. In one American study that compared the progress of EBD students with learning disabled (LD) students over a five-year period found that EBD students made hardly any progress in reading compared with LD students, even though they received more special education services (Anderson et al., 2001).

What should get more attention, behavioural difficulties or reading problems? Do behavioural difficulties cause reading problems, or vice versa? This is the chicken-and-egg problem in this field of study. There are several possibilities about the link between reading failure and EBD:

- behavioural difficulties cause reading problems;
- reading problems cause behavioural difficulties;
- there is a reciprocal effect, where both problems exacerbate each other, so that behaviour gets worse and reading gets worse as well; and
- reading problems and behavioural difficulties are caused by other factors, such as home background, poverty, genetic inheritance and so on.

If you are a teacher in the classroom, the fact that EBD students have reading problems might seem the last thing to worry about. When students are running wild in the classroom, you will want them quietened down or taken out of class. There is no way they are likely to sit quietly and let you teach them to read. The teacher is most likely to subscribe to the view that the behavioural difficulties prevent learning. If you change the behaviours you will get more learning. However, this is not the only way to think about the problem. It may be that not learning to read is causing the poor behaviour. So focusing on the symptoms (that is, negative behaviour) of the problem (that is, inability to read) is not going to solve anything in the long term. A behaviour modification programme can only deal with the symptoms. It will not get to the root of the problem. A better approach in the long term is to focus on fixing the reading problem. Success in this basic skill can make students feel more confident and happier, and encourage them to behave better.

Support for improving behaviour by giving students a sense of accomplishment comes from a study of excluded pupils in England. The researchers surveyed a number of special learning programmes designed to build self-esteem in these pupils (Kinder et al., 2000). The programmes were for pupils who had been permanently excluded from schools, who had negative attitudes to education, aggression, low self-esteem, and behavioural and learning difficulties. The focus of the learning programmes was on achievement and recognition through completion of practical certificates (for example, power boat driving certificate). The survey results indicated that successful experiences in the programme made pupils more confident and more willing to learn. For example, one probation officer reported, 'They know they haven't achieved academically in the past ... and I think that, in itself, is always in the back of their head and they think "I'm not going to be able to do this" ... But, by the time they've gone through the project, they know they can, and I think it's like a steady build up of self-esteem, self-confidence and, like, personality building' (2000: 17). A parent commented about his son, who had learning difficulties, 'You need something like this, 'cos children with special needs have very low self-esteem and generally children who are excluded have very low self-esteem and [the provision] has helped bring his self-esteem up … that he is worth something, that he can do something, that there is a good side to him' (2000: 16–17).

In the school situation effective academic interventions, especially in reading, will also boost self-esteem and improve learning behaviours. To give another example, my own University of Auckland has a special reading programme for failing readers that has been operating during summer and after-school (Nicholson, 2003a). Our data indicate that improvements in reading are accompanied by more positive attitudes and behaviours. This is reflected in students' improved attitudes to reading and in their parents' feedback to us. Many children have entered the programme with very negative attitudes to reading, yet left the programme feeling more positive and were better behaved. For example, when the programme first started we enrolled a 7-year-old pupil called Elliot in the summer school. He was already two years behind in reading. At first, he was so badly behaved we had to insist that one of his parents remain present at each lesson. A year later, after weekly lessons of extra tuition in the after-school programme that ran as a follow-up to the summer school, his reading had improved and his behaviour had changed for the better. When the *New Zealand Herald* (Middlebrook, 2002) interviewed his parents, they said that their son used to slouch at his desk, face downcast, when his classmates opened their books for reading lessons. The mother was told to medicate her 'naughty' son to improve his behaviour at school. Yet the reading programme had made him more confident and willing to learn. When the boy himself was interviewed he said he still found reading 'really hard'. On the other hand, his attitude to reading had changed, as shown in his comment, 'But I can read more books than yesterday now' (2002: A2). This case study does not mean that reading improvement by itself is sufficient to improve all the negative behaviours of EBD students, but it seems to reduce them. This would support the third possibility listed earlier, that there is a reciprocal relationship between reading failure and EBD.

WHAT DOES THE RESEARCH SAY?

Many studies have found that reading problems and EBD go hand-in-hand, but the findings tend to be correlational. For example, Kulekowskis (1996) surveyed 128 second grade children in one American school. The ethnic composition of the school was 50 per cent Hispanic, 34 per cent white and 16 per cent African-American. Half of the student population were considered 'low income'. According to school records, 51 children had 'troubling behaviour' and 77 had 'good behaviour'. Kulekowskis randomly selected 30 children from each of these groups and compared their reading scores on a standardized test. The results showed that the 'troubling behaviour' group had an average reading score of 23 and the 'good behaviour group' had an average reading score of 64. There was a very large and significant reading gap between the two groups. The finding, however, still leaves open the question of whether one causes the other, or whether they are independent of each other.

A study by Prochnow et al. (2002) suggests that problem behaviours, especially among boys, are not necessarily the cause of poor reading achievement. They reported a 3-year longitudinal reading study of 152 children from 5 years of age through to 8 years of age. By the end of the study 123 children remained. The researchers assessed classroom behaviours at the end of the third year by asking teachers to rate children in the study on the Child Behavior Checklist (CBCL) (Achenbach and Edelbrock, 1984). The results at the end of Year 3 showed that boys were more likely than girls to show externalizing behaviours such as aggression and delinquency, even though boys and girls did not differ at school entry in reading-related skills, and even though the reading scores of boys and girls did not differ through the three years of the study. Although they found gender differences in externalizing behaviours, they found no gender differences in internalizing behaviours, for example, withdrawal, anxiety, depression. This result supports the view that externalizing behaviour problems are not necessarily related to later academic underachievement, except that they may result in boys being over-selected as having reading problems because on the surface they appear to be not achieving as well as girls.

However, other longitudinal studies have come to the conclusion that early disruptive behaviours do predict later academic underachievement. Rabiner (2000) reported a longitudinal study of 387 children from kindergarten through to fifth grade and concluded that attention problems predicted the development of reading difficulties even after controlling for prior reading achievement, IQ and other kinds of behavioural difficulties. In Christchurch, New Zealand, Fergusson and Horwood (1997) reported similar findings. A longitudinal study showed that behavioural difficulties among boys predicted later poor reading achievement. They also found that girls with behavioural difficulties were likely to achieve poorly. Velting and Whitehurst (1997) tracked the relation between inattention-hyperactivity and reading achievement in a sample of 105 preschool children enrolled in Head Start, a programme designed for children from low-income backgrounds. They found that attention problems did not interfere with early reading development in the early years of schooling, as in preschool and kindergarten when the demands of learning to read were small, but that there was interference as the demands of learning to read increased.

It appears that the jury is still out on whether behavioural difficulties cause reading problems or vice versa. There is also the possibility that behaviour and reading problems interact with a third factor, such as lack of pre-reading skills on entry to school. Some studies (for example, Juel, 1988, 1994; Nicholson, 1999, 2003a; Stanovich, 1986) have found that children who are at risk for reading and behaviour problems are likely to start school with low levels of pre-reading skills, such as lack of knowledge of the alphabet and lack of phonological awareness (that is, the ability to break spoken words into their component sounds). A child who starts school with behaviour problems as well as a deficit in pre-reading skills would be even more at risk.

If the school focused its efforts on targeting children who appear to show problem behaviours and ensure that they receive effective and additional reading instruction, they might reduce and ameliorate existing behavioural difficulties and reduce the possibility of other later behavioural difficulties such as delinquency, smoking, drugs and so on. Reading achievement is so central to school learning that failure in this area can have cascading negative effects on many other aspects of a child's development, both social and academic. Success in reading, however, encourages children to try harder and to focus on academic tasks. Lack of success in reading discourages children from learning and causes them to engage in negative classroom behaviours.

These positive and negative snowball effects are part of the literature on Matthew effects, that is, rich-get-richer and poor-get-poorer effects that influence not just reading but a range of other behaviours as well (Stanovich, 1986). Positive Matthew effects derive from positive experiences in learning to read (that is, 'the rich get richer'). In contrast, children who experience difficulty in learning to read aren't as likely to want to read, or to want to engage in reading tasks or other school academic work. They experience negative Matthew effects (that is, 'the poor get poorer'). Children who learn to read quickly are likely to improve more quickly in vocabulary and general knowledge. They are likely to be ranked highly by teachers and attend schools with other students who read well and achieve well. In contrast, children who do not learn to read quickly fall behind, lose the motivation to read, lose opportunities to build vocabulary and general knowledge, and end up in classrooms with other 'problem' children who are likely to avoid learning and be disruptive, which in turn makes it even harder to make progress in reading. Stanovich (1986) has argued that even small deficits in pre-reading skills on entry to school, especially in the area of phonological awareness, will have negative Matthew effects on reading, classroom behaviour and many other things.

Juel (1988, 1994) reported Matthew effects in her 4-year longitudinal study. She found that by fourth grade, poor readers did much less after-school reading than did good readers. She reported that 'The poor readers rarely correctly read even 80 per cent of the words' (1988: 442). Reading had become an unpleasant activity, as was revealed by interview questions: one question was, 'Would you rather clean your room or read?'. Only 5 per cent of the good readers said they would rather clean their room, but 40 per cent of the poor readers opted to clean their room. One poor reader said, 'I'd rather clean the mould around the bathtub than read' (1988: 442). Another question was, 'Do you like to read?'; of the 30 good readers, 26 said 'yes'; of the 24 poor readers, only five said 'yes'. Several of the poor readers said they hated reading; most said it was boring. Juel (1994) found a near-90 per cent probability (a correlation of 0.88) that a poor reader after the first year of school would still be a poor reader four years later.

In New Zealand, where children start school at age 5, Clay (1979) reported a similar dismal probability, arguing that where a child was placed in relation to classmates at the end of the first year of school was about where the child would be at age 7 or 8. In Sweden, where instruction starts at age 7, Lundberg (1984) reported that 40 out of 46 low-achieving readers in 1st grade were still poor readers in 6th grade. That was a 0.87 probability. Juel (1994) argued that there has to be intervention for children who are not moving forward, by mid-1st grade at the very least. As she put it, 'To prevent the cycle of failure, early intervention in first grade is mandatory' (1994: 126).

Nicholson (1999, 2000, 2003a, 2003b) reported Matthew effects in a 5-year longitudinal study of low- and high-socioeconomic status (SES) New Zealand children. A comparison of the reading scores of children from low-SES and high-SES backgrounds, through the first five years of school, showed that initial disparities in pre-reading skills at school entry escalated into larger and larger gaps in reading and other literacy skills.

The survey of 111 5-year-old children in year 1 of school showed major discrepancies between low- and high-SES children at school entry in pre-reading skills, such as knowledge of the alphabet, phonemic awareness, invented spelling and decoding skills. For example, while low-SES children could identify on average 10 out of 26 letters of the alphabet, high-SES children could identify 20 out of 26 letters. Similar gaps occurred in other pre-reading skills, such as phonemic awareness and invented spelling. These major gaps in pre-reading skills at school entry may play a strong role in later behavioural difficulties simply because of the negative effects of reading failure on self-esteem and feelings of confidence.

During these studies, interviews with children revealed that some had already acquired the feeling that they were failures, even though it was only their first year of school. For example, one child was asked, 'How often do you read at home?' The answer was, 'Never. I hate reading now.' Another child was asked, 'Would you rather clean up your room or read?' The child said, 'Clean up my room, because I can clean up my room, but I can't read.' Another child was asked, 'Do you like to read?' The child said, 'No. Mum likes me to read, but I read ugly. 'Cause I don't know how to read.'

There is evidence to suggest that children's classroom behaviours, as perceived by their teachers, can improve when reading tasks are easy for them. Jorgenson (1977) studied the classroom behaviours of 71 second-through sixth-grade students. First, he assessed the reading abilities of the students. Second, the teachers of these pupils were asked to make a note of the pages of the books these pupils were reading at that time. Third, he calculated the readability levels of the pages. Finally, teachers were asked to rate the classroom behaviours of the pupils. Teachers rated behaviours like the extent to which each pupil was disruptive, impatient, disrespect-ful, defiant, blamed others for failure, failed to understand what he or she was reading, lacked creativity, and relied on being close to and friendly with the teacher. The study found that pupils were better behaved if the readability levels of reading materials were below their reading ability levels, that is, relatively easy to read. Pupils who were placed with diffi-cult text materials were more likely to be rated by teachers as disruptive, impatient and demanding of teacher time. Teachers also rated them as having less understanding of what they read, and being less creative. The results indicated that pupils are better behaved if they are given materials that they can read.

Improving the reading levels of pupils who are disruptive in the class-room can have positive effects on their classroom deportment. Ialongo et al. (2001) randomly assigned 630 first-grade children to two experimental groups and a control group. The first experimental group was placed in a 'good behaviour' programme where children were allocated to three teams in each classroom, and the teams competed against each other to gain points for specific good behaviours. To encourage children who were shy to be less shy, they were appointed as team leaders. The classroom teams were balanced for gender and levels of aggressive behaviour. The teacher listed specific behaviours that would lose each team points, such as shout-ing, talking out of turn and teasing. There were material rewards such as pencils, erasers and so on. Later, there were also social rewards, such as praise. The games were played for 10 minutes a day initially, and for longer periods later. The teacher kept each team's score on the board. If each team showed good behaviour, then all teams could win a reward. There was also a prize for the weekly winning team. In addition to this intervention, the children received an enhanced reading and maths curriculum. The second experimental group received a broader treatment where their teachers were taught more effective communication techniques with parents, and parents were taught behaviour modification strategies and strategies for helping their children with schoolwork at home. The results showed that both treatments were effective, but that the first treatment was more effective. Children who received the combination of behaviour modification and curriculum enhancement improved their reading and maths, and exhibited lower levels of conduct problems. Follow-up studies found that these positive effects were still evident in sixth grade. It appears that improved reading achievement is a protective factor that reduces the likelihood of later conduct problems. It also reduces levels of depression in young children who are vulnerable to depression (Kellam et al., 1999). These are important findings in that there are strong correlations between feelings of depression conduct disorders and school achievement.

The effects of any reading intervention, however, need to be monitored in order to ensure that children do actually make real progress. Failure to do this adequately was shown in a study by Chapman et al. (1998). They looked at the effects of reading failure on children's self-concept about reading and their classroom behaviours. The sample was made up of 26 children who had completed the reading recovery program, 20 poor readers who had not received reading recovery, and 80 average or better readers. The aim of reading recovery is to bring children who are below classroom average in reading up to average classroom levels (Clay, 1993). The children in the study all had similar reading self-concepts in year 1 of school (5-year-olds) before the reading recovery program. But by the end of the second year of school, the poor readers in the sample, including those who had completed reading recovery, had lower reading self-concepts and worse classroom behaviour than children in the study who were average or better readers. Why these negative results for the children who had received extra reading tuition? The reason was that the tuition had not succeeded in its aims. The reading recovery children had not been brought up to average reading levels for their age. Their reading levels were still similar to those of the poor readers who had not received the extra reading recovery tuition.

Reading interventions for children at risk of EBD need to be put in place at preschool level since many children begin school with very low levels of pre-reading skills (Nicholson, 2003a, 2003b). Children who leave kindergarten with low levels of pre-reading skills are at risk for EBD. This applies especially to males, as well as low-SES and minority children (Levy and Chard, 2001). Since this is the case, effective preschool interventions will be especially important for them. For other children who are not succeeding, then the school system needs to think outside the square, to provide additional instruction for children who have fallen behind, as well as after-school programmes that are free and provide specialist reading tuition (Nicolson, 2003a).

CONCLUSION

There does not have to be an axiomatic link between behaviour problems and underachievement in school. Children with behaviour problems are almost certain to have reading and other academic problems, but in order to ameliorate this linkage the classroom focus should be broader than just the prevention of behaviour problems. Instead, it should focus on ensuring that all children do well in reading. The literature on reading suggests that children who begin school with low levels of pre-reading skills, especially phonemic awareness, are at risk of later behavioural and reading difficulties. While survey data suggest that teachers regard behavioural difficulties as caused by the home rather than the school, it may well be that this is not the whole story. It could be argued that the school is also responsible for behavioural difficulties since it has a major role in teaching all children to read. Although classroom discipline is a major problem, perhaps it would be less of a problem if all children could be helped to succeed academically in the classroom, especially in the basic skill of reading.

REFERENCES

Achenbach, T.M. and Edelbrock, C.S. (1984) *Child Behaviour Checklist – Teacher's report.* Burlington, VT: University Associates in Psychiatry.

Anderson, J., Kutash, K. and Duchnowski, A. (2001) 'A comparison of academic progress of students with EBD and students with LD', *Journal of Emotional and Behavioural Disorders*, 9: 81–144.

Chapman, J.W., Tunmer, W.E. and Prochnow, J.E. (1998) *Reading recovery in relation to language factors, reading self-perceptions, classroom behavior difficulties and literacy achievement: A longitudinal study.* Paper presented at the meeting of the American Educational Research Association, April, at San Diego, CA.

Clay, M.M. (1979) *The Patterning of Complex Behaviour.* Auckland, NZ: Heinemann.

Clay, M.M. (1993) *Reading Recovery: A Guidebook for Teachers in Training.* Auckland, NZ: Heinemann.

Elam, S. and Rose, L. (1995) 'The 27th annual Phi Delta Kappa/Gallup poll', *Phi Delta Kappa*, 77: 41–9.

Fergusson D.M. and Horwood, L.J. (1997) 'Gender differences in educational achievement in a New Zealand birth cohort', *New Zealand Journal of Educational Studies*, 32: 83–96.

Ialongo, N., Poduska, J., Wethamer, L. and Kellam, S. (2001) 'The distal impact of two first-grade preventive interventions on conduct problems and disorder in early adolescence', *Journal of Emotional and Behavioral Disorders*, 9: 146–60.

Jorgenson, G.W. (1977) 'Relationship of classroom behavior to the accuracy of the match between material difficulty and student ability', *Journal of Educational Psychology*, 69: 24–32.

Juel, C. (1988) 'Learning to read and write: A longitudinal study of 54 children from first through fourth grades', *Journal of Educational Psychology*, 80: 437–47.

Juel, C. (1994) *Learning to Read in One Elementary School.* New York: Springer-Verlag.

Kellam, S.G. Koretz, D. and Moscicki, E.K. (1999) 'Core elements of developmental epidemiologically-based prevention research', *American Journal of Community Psychology*, 27: 463–82.

Kinder, K., Halsey, K., Moor, H. and White, R. (2000) *Working Out Well: Effective Provision for Excluded Pupils.* Paper presented at the British Educational Research Association Conference, September, at Cardiff University, Wales.

Kulekowskis, J. (1996) *The Effect of Student Behaviour on the Reading Achievement of Second Grade Students.* Educational Resources Information Centre (ERIC), ED 397 398.

Levy, S. and Chard, D.J. (2001) 'Research on reading instruction for students with emotional and behavioural disorders', *International Journal of Disability, Development and Education*, 48: 317–26.

Lundberg, I. (1984) 'Learning to read', *School Research Newsletter.* August. National Board of Education of Sweden.

Mavropoulou, S. and Padeliadu, S. (2002) 'Teachers' causal attributions for behaviour problems in relation to perceptions of control', *Educational Psychology*, 22: 191–202.

McDaniel, T. (1984) 'School discipline in perspective', *The Clearing House,* 59: 369–70.

Merrett, F. and Wheldall, K. (1984) 'How do teachers learn to manage classroom behaviour? A study of teachers' opinions about their initial training with special reference to classroom behaviour management', *Educational Studies*, 19: 91–102.

Middlebrook, L. (2002) 'Holiday help brushes up reading skills', *The New Zealand Herald*, 18 January, pp. A2.

Ministry of Education (2002) *Report on Stand-downs and Suspensions.* Wellington, NZ: Author.

Nicholson, T. (1999) 'Literacy in the family and society', in G.B. Thompson and T. Nicholson (eds), *Learning to Read: Beyond Phonics and Whole Language.* New York: Teachers College Press. pp. 1–25.

Nicholson, T. (2000) *Reading the Writing on the Wall: Debates, Challenges and Opportunities in the Teaching of Reading.* Palmerston North, NZ: Dunmore.

Nicholson, T. (2003a) 'Risk factors in learning to read, and what to do about them', in B. Foorman (ed.), *Preventing and Remediating Reading Difficulties: Bringing Science to Scale.* Timonium, MD: York.

Nicholson, T. (2003b) 'Phonemic awareness and learning to read: A developmental perspective', in R.M. Joshi and P.G. Aaron (eds), *Handbook of Orthography and Literacy.* Hillsdale, NJ: Lawrence Erlbaum.

Osher, D., Osher, T. and Smith, C. (1994) 'Toward a national perspective in emotional and behavioural disorders: A developmental agenda', *Beyond Behaviour*, 6: 6–17.

Prochnow, J.E., Tunmer, W.E., Chapman, J.W. and Greaney, K.T. (2002) 'A longitudinal study of early literacy achievement and gender', *New Zealand Journal of Educational Studies*, 36: 221–36.

Rabiner, D. (2000) 'Early attention problems and children's reading achievement: A longitudinal investigation', *Journal of the American Academy of Child and Adolescent Psychiatry*, 39: 859–67.

Rowe, K.J. and Rowe, K.S. (1999) 'Introduction: effects and context. Investigating the relationship between inattentiveness in the classroom and reading achievement', *International Journal of Educational Research*, 31: 1–16.

Stanford Research Institute International (1990) *National Longitudinal Transition Study of Special Education Students*. Menlo Park, CA: Author.

Stanovich, K.E. (1986) 'Matthew effects in reading: Some consequences of individual differences in the acquisition of literacy', *Reading Research Quarterly*, 20: 360–406.

Velting, O.N. and Whitehurst, G.J. (1997) 'Inattention-hyperactivity and reading achievement in children from low-income families: a longitudinal model', *Journal of Abnormal Child Psychology*, 25: 321–31.

11

Juvenile Delinquency and Emotional and Behavioural Difficulties in Education

PAUL O'MAHONY

The classification emotional and behavioural difficulties (EBD) provides an omnibus term, embracing difficulties resulting from 'abuse or neglect, physical or mental illness, sensory or physical impairment or psychological trauma', which manifest themselves in a wide variety of forms, including 'withdrawn, depressive or suicidal attitudes; obsessional eating habits; school phobias; substance abuse; disruptive, antisocial and uncooperative behaviour; and frustration, anger and threat of or actual violence' (UK Dept. of Education 1994). The concept of emotional and behavioural difficulties in education is deliberately multifactorial and holistic, promoting a contextualized and relational, and not merely an individual-centred, understanding of the child. The broad focus on family, community and peer group influences and on the school environment itself parallels a similar concern in research into the roots of juvenile delinquency.

The area of juvenile offending is one of the most researched and theorized topics in criminology. This work provides important insights into who becomes delinquent and why. Numerous studies have linked possible explanatory variables from diverse domains, including brain dysfunction, parenting style, school experience and social environment, with later outcome measures of delinquent and criminal behaviour based on self-reports, observation or official records.

In particular, prospective, longitudinal studies, which examine children and their social situations at various stages of their development, have provided compelling evidence for the central role of school failure in the development of persistent juvenile offending and adult criminality. Consequently, the study of the causes and correlates of juvenile delinquency is much concerned with the study of the kind of emotional and behavioural difficulties that impede a child's education, with a particular focus on uninhibited, aggressive and antisocial behaviours from the externalizing end of the spectrum.

THE ROLE OF INTELLIGENCE AND SCHOOL FAILURE IN THE DEVELOPMENT OF JUVENILE DELINQUENCY

The evidence for the centrality of school failure in the development of criminality comes from three main sources: cross-sectional studies of identified criminal groups; prospective longitudinal studies; and the long-term evaluations of the impact of early intervention educational programmes on later criminal outcomes.

It is well known from studies in many countries that incarcerated juvenile and adult offenders show very high rates of educational failure (Rutter and Madge, 1970; Hirschi and Hindelang, 1977). For example, in a random sample survey of Ireland's largest prison it was found that 80 percent of respondents had left school before the legal leaving age of 16, and one-third had not attended school beyond the primary or special school level. Twenty-nine percent of the sample claimed to have some difficulty with reading, including 21 percent who admitted to functional illiteracy. Only 4 percent had progressed to the Leaving Certificate level or beyond, in a country where almost 80 percent of each age cohort completes the Leaving Certificate (O'Mahony, 1997). The results for the United States' national survey of state prison inmates are similar, if less dramatic (US Dept. of Justice, 1993). This survey indicated that in 1991, 66 percent of inmates had not graduated from high school and 19 percent had dropped out before high school. The English National Prison Survey (Dodd and Hunter, 1992) showed that 46 percent of all prisoners aged under 21 had left school before the age of 16, compared with only 10 percent of the equivalent general population. Thirty percent of prisoners of all ages claimed that they had mainly truanted from rather than attended school, compared with just 3 percent of the general population.

Early childhood intervention programmes such as the Abecedarian (Ramey and Campbell, 1991) and Perry Preschool (Berruatta-Clement et al., 1984) projects, are primary prevention initiatives that aim to increase school readiness and academic achievement in at-risk children. The fact that these projects are of proven value not only in increasing academic performance but also in reducing offending and the likelihood of criminal convictions (Zigler et al., 1992) is further evidence for the central role of educational failure in juvenile delinquency.

Given the paramount importance of education in modern life as a primary agent of socialization and as a pathway to employment, social status and economic success, the significance of school failure is undeniable. An Irish study (NESF, 1998) has estimated that the risk of poverty is five times greater for someone with no educational qualifications than for someone with the Leaving Certificate.

It is a reasonable assumption that a comparatively low level of intelligence plays a role in the widespread educational failure of offenders. Indeed, according to Binder (1988), there is consensus in the international literature that the imprisoned have, on average, a lower IQ than the population at large. Indeed, Hirschi and Hindelang (1977), on the basis of their review of relevant scientific studies, estimate that the deficit is in the region of nine IQ points, or approximately half a standard deviation. Moffit (1990) reports that a consistent finding of investigations of delinquents is a relatively greater weakness in the area of verbal intelligence compared to performance or visuo-spatial intelligence and, as Luria (1961) points out, a deficit in verbal skills has crucial implications for the child's capacity for self-regulation. The ability to recall instructions and to use language to think through the consequences of actions, which are mediated by verbal intelligence, are vital ingredients in the effective self-regulation of emotion and behaviour (Hill, 2002).

On the other hand, there is also substantial evidence to support the view that high levels of educational failure amongst offenders relate as much to adverse factors in their background as to inherent low intelligence. For example, Eilenberg (1961), in a study of detained juvenile delinquents, found that 39 percent of subjects equalled or bettered the population average in terms of measured intelligence, but only 10 percent were at or above the average in terms of scholastic attainment. Conversely, while only 20 percent were substantially below normal on IQ tests, 64 percent were educationally retarded by at least three school years. In short, although offenders as a group tend to be of lower than average intelligence, it appears that other factors in their personal, family and social background, including emotional and behavioural difficulties emerging at school, often cause them not to achieve their true educational potential.

CONTINUITY OF ANTISOCIAL PROBLEMS
FROM PRESCHOOL TO ADULTHOOD

Farrington has stated that 'the antisocial child tends to become the antisocial teenager and the antisocial adult, just as the antisocial adult then tends to produce another antisocial child' (Farrington, 1995: 61). This is undoubtedly an overstatement, which does not do justice to the potential to intervene with and help change all sorts of troubled children. For example, Loeber and LeBlanc (1990) argue that 'about half of at-risk children do not reach the serious outcomes of chronic offender, sociopath or drug abuser.' As they develop, many children find relatively constructive solutions to their problems and it is, therefore, essential not to assume that early aggressive or antisocial behaviour sets an inevitable pattern for later life. However, Farrington's statement conveys an important kernel of truth about the continuity of problem behaviour, since it is now well established that antisocial and aggressive behaviour patterns emerging at an early age are the best predictor of chronic delinquency and adult criminality and violence.

Retrospective and prospective studies alike confirm a major degree of continuity of childhood antisocial problem behaviour into adulthood. Robins (1978), summarizing the results of an empirical study, states that 'antisocial personality rarely or never arose *de novo* in adulthood.' Magnusson (1987) concludes from a large-scale prospective study that 80 to 90 percent of violent criminals have been highly aggressive in adolescence. Scott (1998) reports that 90 percent of a group of recidivist juvenile delinquents had been diagnosed as conduct disordered at 7 years of age. Follow-up of children diagnosed as attention deficit hyperactivity disorder (ADHD) also indicates that the majority continue to have significant social problems in adulthood, including low self-esteem and difficulties in interpersonal relationships (Hechtman, 1991).

Moffit has drawn a distinction between early onset or 'life-course' and 'adolescent limited' problem behaviour. There is compelling evidence that early onset of problem and illegal behaviour is an important marker for later serious chronic delinquency. For example, Farrington (1988, 1995) found that males in the Cambridge study who were first convicted at ages 10 to 13 tended to commit large numbers of offences at high rates over a long period and that this held both for official convictions and self-reports. Farrington also reports that all eventual chronic offenders in the study had been convicted by the age of 15. In a study of a prison population, O'Mahony (1997) found that prisoners who had left school at 11 or 12 years had a mean age of first conviction almost four years earlier than that of prisoners who had left school when 16 or older, and had accumulated more than twice the number of convictions.

A recent trend in research is to examine continuities between conduct problems in early childhood and later criminal outcomes. For example, in the Dunedin study, Henry et al. (1996) found that 'lack of control' at 3 and 5 years, along with the number of changes of parental figures up to the age of 13, is a strong predictor of convictions for violent offences at 18 years. Similarly, Tremblay et al. (1994) found that measured impulsivity in the kindergarten period carries the highest risk of later delinquent behaviour, and Bartusch et al. (1997) found that antisocial behaviour at 5 years was significantly associated with convictions for violence at 18. These finding are impressive, especially since self-regulatory problems in the preschool period, such as temper tantrums and management difficulties, have been linked to adult criminality even when factors such as maternal depression, family stress and social disadvantage are controlled (Stevenson and Goodman, 2001).

Research of this kind, which pushes the timeframe back to infancy and early childhood and finds significant continuities enduring through middle childhood, teenage and adulthood, appears to lend support to the view that there is a significant, independent, biogenetic component to many of the forms of EBD that become highly salient in school. However, it needs to be borne in mind that learning environment, parenting styles and other social processes are very potent factors in early childhood, which have the potential to, on the one hand, alleviate or aggravate self-regulatory problems related to inborn temperament or frontal lobe dysfunction and, on the otherhand, to generate their own forms of EBD.

CAUSES, CORRELATES AND CONSEQUENCES OF SCHOOL FAILURE AND EBD

According to Bailey, 'school has the potential to offer positive outlets to satisfy needs for belonging and recognition and acceptance through non-violent means' (Bailey, 2002: 98). School failure and associated isolation from peers at school leaves the child seeking other means to satisfy these needs. Children at a competitive disadvantage because of low verbal IQ or other related difficulties that impede their performance may well struggle with school tasks and find that school becomes more and more unrewarding. School life can become a highly aversive succession of reminders of personal failure and inadequacy rather than a positive source of self-esteem and support. Some children are at risk of rejecting their rejectors, that is, of turning away from the values of school, peers and mainstream society towards deviant and oppositional subcultures (Cohen, 1955). Ultimately, failure to benefit from the educational system brings in its wake the additional burdens of socially inferior status, restricted employment opportunities and greater risk of poverty, all of which exert their own independent pressure towards adopting illegal and antisocial means to satisfy basic material, social and psychological needs.

While some children resolve their school crisis by truanting and dropping out of school, others may satisfy their need for a postive sense of self and for social status within the school itself. They may adopt the role of bully (Olweus, 1993), embrace a 'macho' culture of toughness and indifference or turn their talent for disruption into a permanent attitude of rebelliousness against authority. A background of social deprivation potentiates and aggravates these processes because, as Straub (1996) states, 'poverty creates frustration and feelings of relative deprivation, injustice, and anger as well as self-devaluation and hopelessness.'

Low intelligence is neither a necessary nor a sufficient cause of school failure. As Skinner et al. (1998) note, motivation and self-regulation are associated with academic achievement independently of measured intelligence. School readiness, academic achievement and social acceptance all presuppose a modicum of self-control and motivation in the child, including at the most basic level the ability to sit still and listen attentively. Intelligence in the absence of these qualities will not prevent school failure, just as the presence of these qualities will greatly improve the chances of success for the less intelligent child.

Motivation to engage in educational pursuits is directly influenced by intelligence, but neighbourhood subcultural values, parental attitudes and the home environment are also significant determinants. Poverty and social deprivation have a very significant role in setting conditions that undermine the kind of home-based emotional support and cognitive stimulation that enhances the school readiness and performance of the child. Indeed, White (1982) shows that family income is the highest single correlate of academic achievement, followed by parental occupation and parental education. Hess and Holloway (1984) identify a number of relevant factors and processes that are far more common in impoverished families and impact negatively on the child's motivation for education and school-based achievement. These include an attitude of devaluation of education, low parental expectations for achievement, a lack of positive affective relations between parents and children, a lack of verbal interactions between mothers and children and a failure to teach effective self-discipline and control strategies. McLoyd (1998) points out that poverty also has a negative impact on a child's school achievement because it is strongly linked to risks that diminish the physical and mental health of the child, such as low birth weight, prematurity, maternal alcohol, tobacco and drug use, poor diet and lead contamination in the local environment.

ADHD and conduct disorder (CD), especially disruptive and aggressive behaviour, represent problems from the externalizing pole of the continuum of EBD. It is these kinds of apparently individual-focused problems, possibly but not necessarily in conjunction with low intelligence, that are most obviously implicated in both school failure and the development of persistent delinquent behaviour. Given the preponderance of males amongst juvenile offenders, it is noteworthy that the male:female ratio for ADHD in clinical samples ranges from 4:1 to 9:1 (American Psychiatric Association, 1994), and that it is the aggression and non-compliance of ADHD children that best predicts their unpopularity with peers (Erhardt and Hinshaw, 1994).

ADHD and CD are to some extent controversial categories because of their uncertain aetiology. Many writers are convinced that there is a neurological basis to these problems (for example, Kewley, 1998; Blair, 2002), but others emphasize the significant role of family processes and social conditioning in the development of attentional and conduct disorders. For example, Olson et al. (2002) argue that hostile care-giving and harsh discipline create or exacerbate attentional difficulties and impulsivity because they fail, at a critical time, to promote the internalization of parental rules.

Self-regulatory competence involves a set of functions, often termed 'the executive functions', which include the capacity to delay immediate gratification, to inhibit impulsive behaviour and to anticipate and respond to tasks in a planned manner. The child's effective self-regulation of emotion and behaviour is an essential foundation for prosocial behaviour as well as for academic success and is subserved by the frontal lobe of the brain. Blair (2002) argues that frontal lobe dysfunction can leave general intelligence largely intact while impairing planning, self-monitoring, attention and responsivity to impending reward or punishment.

It is probable that there is a biological basis to ADHD and some conduct disorders. However, this basis may be no more than an inborn temperamental tendency toward high activity, distractibility and irritability, which can be amplified and transformed into a pattern of serious problem behaviour by inappropriate learning environments and inadequate parental reponse. For example, Olson et al. (2002) describe how a 'difficult' temperament child is exposed to an increased number of coercive transactions with parents and other socializing agents. These transactions in turn tend to evoke and eventually stabilize antisocial patterns of behaviour in the child.

Adoption studies confirm the existence of a largely heritable temperament vulnerable to criminality. For example, Mednick et al. (1987) studied over 14,000 children separated from their parents at birth and found that children were at heightened risk for criminal conviction if their biological parents, but not if their adoptive parents, had been convicted. Individual differences in genetically-based temperament, self-regulatory competence and intelligence provide a plausible explanation for why some siblings do and others do not become criminal despite largely similar, adverse family and social situations. They do not, on the other hand, in any way affirm that 'biology is destiny' with respect to criminality. For example, Bohman (1996) has examined the criminal outcomes for children with criminal or non-antisocial biological parents placed in either low-risk or high-risk adoptive families. Of the children with non-antisocial biological parents, 3 percent in low-risk adoptive families, compared to 6 percent in high-risk adoptive families, gained criminal records. Of the children with criminal biological parents, 12 percent in low-risk adoptive families, compared to 40 percent in high-risk adoptive families, gained criminal records. These results point to the relatively modest effect of criminality in the biological family, but appear to confirm a very powerful interaction between inheritence and environment.

There can be little doubt that, even in the absence of frontal lobe dysfunction or temperamental predisposition, inadequate home environment and especially certain forms of abuse and neglect and modelling by caregivers can generate enduring patterns of aggressive and disruptive behaviour in children. These EBDs are largely indistinguishable from clinically diagnosed ADHD and CD. Dodge et al. (1995), in a study of 507 children recruited from kindergarten, found that 28 percent of physically abused children had clinically significant conduct problems at 8 and 9 years, compared with 6 percent of non-abused children. Widom (1989) reviewed evidence on the intergenerational transmission of violence and concluded that children physically abused up to the age of 11 years were significantly more likely to become violent offenders later in life. Patterson (1982) has described a 'coercive family' pattern, which helps explain how familial dynamics can foster and reinforce aggressive behaviour in some children, whether the child's initial aggression is biogenetically or situationally based. Patterson argued that parents' responses to aggressive child behaviours tend to follow an escape-avoidance paradigm. In order to escape their own discomfort and avoid escalation of a child's aggression, parents often fall into the 'reinforcement trap' of giving in to the child's aggression. Whatever the original source of the aggression, the child learns that aggression pays off and is encouraged to use it as an effective bargaining technique.

Olweus (1979) and Baumrind (1991), among many others, have adduced evidence that it is possible for previously non-aggressive youth to acquire aggressive behaviour patterns through their victimization by other people both within and outside the family. Athens (1989) concludes, from his own studies of adult serious violent offenders, that almost all instances of uncontrolled, excessive, criminal violence against other people have their roots in the perpetrator's childhood experience of utter powerlessness when exposed to extreme violence. Underscoring the critical role of poverty and social deprivation in the abuse and neglect of children, it has been found in the US that fatal child abuse is 60 times more common in families with an income under $15,000 than in families with an income over $30,000 (Sedlock and Broadhurst, 1996).

AN HOLISTIC THEORY OF THE GENESIS OF JUVENILE DELINQUENCY

Of course, variables such as school failure, though often used in research as independent predictors of delinquency, are themselves complex outcomes of biogenetic determinants, parenting style and social and cultural processes. There is obviously a need for an holistic model for the genesis of criminal behaviour, as much as for an holistic model of the origin of EBDs Such models must fully acknowledge the inextricable interplay of biological, psychological, family, peer group, community and cultural variables. An holistic approach presupposes a mutifactorial, multilevel analysis, but also requires a central focus on the individual actor. The individual person is the complex product of a myriad of diverse influences, but the person is also a self-organizing agent whose actions, motives and attitudes can never be entirely reduced to the influences of brain function, family relationships, environmental conditioning, social opportunities or any combination of these.

West and Farrington (1973, 1977) in their Cambridge study, one of the most influential longitudinal surveys of the causes and correlates of juvenile offending, have followed up, from 8 to 32 years of age, more than 400 children from a working-class area of London. This study and other similar studies, such as the Philadephia birth cohort study (Wolfgang et al., 1972), the Dunedin study in New Zealand (White et al., 1990) and the more recent linked studies in Denver, Rochester and Pittsburgh (Huizinga et al., 1994), provide compelling evidence that, while a very large proportion of young people occasionally offend, a small minority of them account for the majority of more serious offences, most especially violent offences. This small group is identifiable at an early age and demonstrates considerable continuity in offending, extending into adulthood. They accumulate the majority of convictions handed down to their cohort and frequently go on to establish serious criminal careers. The Cambridge study established school failure and large family size in particular, but also low family income, poor housing and criminal parents and siblings as important correlates of membership in this qualitatively distinct, highly delinquent subgroup.

But West and Farrington (1973) argue from their data that individual characteristics, such as aggressiveness, immoderation in the pursuit of immediate pleasure, irregular work habits and lack of conventional social restraints, also play a large part. West and Farrington conclude that their findings point to a susceptible temperamental type identified by such traits as low intelligence, high impulsiveness, daring, sensation-seeking, hyperactivity and attention deficit. These variables probably reflect both temperamental, brain function and social learning influences, but they paint a clear picture of a syndrome akin to ADHD and CD and falling into the general category of externalizing EBDs.

Research such as that by the McCords (1956, 1988) and Snyder and Patterson (1987) focuses more closely on the role of the caregiver and the home environment. This research has identified the important role of specific forms of parenting style as precursors of delinquency, including lax supervision, inconsistent discipline, maternal rejection, parental example and parental disharmony. Punitive, power-assertive methods of discipline, especially when they are used inconsistently, have been associated with poorer outcomes, as has a generally permissive, but cold, unengaged and unsupportive style of child-rearing. A lack of rules in the family setting, or inconsistent rules, or a lack of enforcement of rules, especially when combined with harsh treatment, can also lead to aggressiveness and can undermine an individual's capacity for self-control. Analysis has indicated that these parenting factors work to promote delinquent behaviour irrespective of social class, or indeed of whether a family is intact, a lone-parent family or a disrupted family.

Patterson (1982) has tied these key determinants at the level of family interaction into a more holistic model. He shows that there are significant correlations between poor parenting, of a type that can foster delinquency, poverty, social disadvantage, a parental history of exposure to poor parenting skills in their own family of origin, a child with a 'difficult' temperament, and major stressors in daily life, such as substance abuse, unemployment or marital disharmony or separation. The key role of social deprivation is further underlined by research, such as the 30 year follow-up study of 1,142 children born in 1947 in Newcastle, UK (Kolvin et al., 1988). This found that 60 percent of males from a multiply deprived background ended up with a criminal record, compared with only 17 percent of those from a non-deprived background.

Research, then, unequivocally confirms the complex, multifactorial causation of offending behaviour. Putative causal factors, operating singly or more frequently in interactive combination, range from frontal lobe impairment linked to poor self-regulatory competence to low intelligence, lack of motivation for learning, neglectful, abusive or inadequate parenting style, poverty and neighbourhood attitudes that are tolerant of antisocial behaviour. Given this diversity of possible causal factors, it is perhaps surprising that it is possible to identify probable members of the group of serious, chronic delinquents from quite an early age. In fact, school failure is one of the most significant markers for this group. However, research strongly suggests that school failure itself is rarely a sufficient cause of delinquency. Rather, it is the presence of multiple adverse factors in the background of a child, almost invariably including school failure and factors that predispose to school failure, that best predicts future persistent offending.

School failure is a key variable of pre-eminent importance because it is often a sign of: underlying EBDs in the child; failures in the socialization of the child by family and others; and low intelligence, especially in the verbal domain – all of which have a broad negative impact on aspects of behaviour other than academic achievement. But school failure is also key because it is itself an independent source of new criminogenic pressures.

However, social deprivation and poverty are of even more fundamental importance within an holistic model of the origin of juvenile offending because they greatly increase the risk of occurrence of almost all the direct causal factors linked to delinquency and crime, including both school failure and EBDs. Furthermore, the child's personal experience of poverty, deprivation and inequality, which intensifies with age, can itself become a direct cause of crime, since, on the one hand, it promotes frustration, anger and resentment and so fuels psychological readiness for crime and, on the other hand, it provides material motivation for self-gain crime.

Finally, the important role of labelling and expectational processes must be recognized. The commission of certain disapproved acts, the joining of a delinquent gang, the initiation of drug use, expulsion from school or official classification as a delinquent can represent the crossing of a major threshold which, almost immediately, profoundly alters social reaction to the child. Labelling effects, expectational processes and the deployment of scripts, which govern interactions with the peer group and authority figures, can amplify and stabilize deviant behaviour (Lemert, 1972). These processes further isolate the child from prosocial influences and reinforce the alternative, antisocial influence of delinquent peer groups. At the same time, the delinquent label can furnish the child with a negatively glamorous reputation, which confers substantial social and psychological benefits within the wider peer group.

CONSTRUCTIVE INTERVENTIONS

It is obvious that any intervention that can prevent school failure and delay school dropout or can alleviate the EBDs associated with these outcomes can be beneficial in the prevention of later serious offending. For example, Head Start and other similar early intervention programmes that improve the school readiness of at-risk children have a long-term, positive impact on both academic achievement and the diminution of juvenile offending (Zigler et al., 1992).

Useful interventions can be broadly targeted or specifically aimed at children with EBDs (Peters and McMahon, 1996; Greenwood et al., 1996). They can be directed at family support, improving parenting skills, enriching the learning environment, or providing a more positive, inclusive and responsive school environment (see, for example, Olweus, 1991; Tucker, 1999; O'Donnell, 1992; Gottfredson, 1997). Alternatively, they can be directed at the child. The latter programmes, by employing cognitive-behavioural strategies (Meichenbaum, 1977) and other techniques, can aim to help at-risk children understand and express their own emotions, increase their self-regulatory competences, improve their ability to empathize and their readiness to take the role of others and better manage their anger in conflict situations (McCord and Tremblay, 1992).

Given the pervasive importance of social deprivation and adversity in the background of those who go on to become chronic offenders, there is much to be learned from the study of resilient children, which, according to Masten (2001), 'has overturned many negative assumptions and deficit-focused models about the development of children growing up under the threat of disadvantage and adversity'.

Masten argues that resilience is an ordinary phenomenon and that if basic adaptational systems are protected and in good working order, development will be robust, even in severely adverse circumstances. This suggests that schemes that help troubled children to develop a stable, positive sense of identity and to establish secure attachments to positive adult role models or to institutions like school will be beneficial. A focus on building up the assets and internal resources of children, including their intellectual meta-skills, social and study skills, sense of self-efficacy and sense of pleasure-in-mastery can lay a solid foundation for future progress and impact positively on the child's motivation to learn and engage with the environment.

REFERENCES

American Psychiatric Association (1994) *Diagnostic and Statistical Manual of Mental Disorders: DSM-IV*. Washington, DC: APA.

Athens, L. (1989) *The Creation of Dangerous Violent Criminals*. London: Routledge.

Bailey, S. (2002) 'Violent children: a framework for assessment', *Advances in Psychiatric Treatment*, 8: 97–106.

Bartusch, D., Lynam, D. and Moffit, T. (1997) 'Is age important? Testing a general versus a developmental theory of antisocial behaviour', *Criminology*, 35: 13–48.

Baumrind, D. (1991) 'Effective parenting during the adolescent transition', in P. Cowan and M. Hetherington (eds), *Family Transitions*. Hillsdale, NJ: Erlbaum.

Berruatta-Clement, J., Schweinhart, l., Barnett, W., Epstein, A. and Weikart, D. (1984) *Changed Lives: The Effects of the Perry Preschool Program on Youths Through Age 19*. Ypsilanti, MI: High/Scope Press.

Binder, A. (1988) 'Juvenile delinquency', *Annual Review of Psychology*, 39: 253–82.

Blair, C. (2002) 'School readiness: Integrating cognition and emotion in a neurobiological conceptualization of children's functioning at school entry', *American Psychologist*, 57 (2): 11–27.

Bohman, M. (1996) 'Predisposition to criminality: Swedish adoption studies in retrospect', in G. Brock and J. Goode (eds), *Genetics of Criminal and Antisocial Behaviour*. Chichester: Wiley.

Cohen, A. (1955) *Delinquent Boys: The Culture of the Gang*. Glencoe. Free Press

Dodd, T. and Hunter, P. (1992) *The National Prison Survey of 1991*. London: HMSO.

Dodge, K.A., Pettit, G., Bates, J. and Valente, E. (1995) 'Social information-processing patterns partially mediate the effect of early physical abuse on later conduct problems', *Journal of Abnormal Psychology*, 104: 632–43.

Lilonberg, M. (1961) 'Remand home boys: 1930–55', *British Journal of Criminology*, 2: 111–31.

Erhardt, D. and Hinshaw, S. (1994) 'Initial sociometric impressions of attention deficit hyperactivity disorder and comparison boys – Predictions from social behaviours and from non-behavioural variables', *Journal of Consulting and Clinical Psychology*, 62 (4): 833–42.

Farrington, D. (1988) 'Studying changes within individuals: the causes of offending', in Rutter (ed.), *Studies of Psychosocial Risk*. Cambridge: Cambridge University Press.

Farrington, D. (1995) 'The development of offending and antisocial behaviour from childhood: key findings from the Cambridge study in delinquent development', *Journal of Child Psychology and Psychiatry*, 36: 929–64.

Gottfredson, D.C. (1997) 'School-based crime prevention', in L. Sherman (ed.), *Preventing Crime: What Works, What Doesn't Work, What's Promising*. Report to the US Congress, US Dept. of Justice, Washington, DC.

Greenwood, P., Model, K., Hydell, C. and Chiesa, J. (1996) *Diverting Children from a Life of Crime: Measuring Costs and Benefits*. Santa Monica, CA: Rand.

Hechtman, L. (1991) 'Resilience and vulnerability in long-term outcome of attention deficit hyperactive disorder', *Canadian Journal of Psychiatry*, 36 (6): 415–21.

Henry, B., Caspi, A., Moffit, T. and Silva, P. (1996) 'Temperamental and familial predictors of violent and non-violent criminal convictions: From age 3 to age 18', *Developmental Psychopathology*, 32: 614–23.

Hess, R. and Holloway, S. (1984) 'Family and school as educational institutions', in R.D. Parke (ed.), *Review of Child Development Research*. Chicago: University of Chicago Press. pp. 7, 179–222.

Hill, J. (2002) 'Biological, psychological and social processes in the conduct disorders', *Journal of Child Psychology and Psychiatry*, 43 (1): 133–64.

Hirschi, T. and Hindelang, M. (1977) 'Intelligence and delinquency', *American Sociological Review*, 42: 571–87.

Huizinga, D., Loeber, R. and Thornberry, T. (1994) *Urban Delinquency and Substance Abuse: Initial Findings*. Washington, DC: Office of Juvenile Justice and Delinquency Prevention.

Kewley, G.D. (1998) 'Attention deficit hyperactivity disorder is underdiagnosed and undertreated in Britain', *British Medical Journal*, 316: 1594–5.

Kolvin, I, Miller, F., Fleeting, M. and Kolvin, P. (1988) 'Social and parenting factors affecting criminal offence rates', *British Journal of Psychiatry*, 152: 80–90.

Lemert, E. (1972) *Human Deviance, Social Problems and Social Control*. Englewood Cliffs, NJ: Prentice-Hall.

Loeber, R. and LeBlanc, M. (1990) 'Towards a developmental criminology', in M. Tonry and N. Morris (eds), *Crime and Justice: An Annual Review of Research*, Vol. 12. Chicago: University of Chicago Press.

Luria, A.R. (1961) *The Role of Speech and the Regulation of Normal and Abnormal Behaviour*. New York: Basic Books.

Magnusson, D. (1987) 'Adult delinquency and early conduct and physiology', in D. Magnusson and A. Ohman (eds), *Psychopathology: An International Perspective*. New York: Academic Press.

Masten. A.S. (2001) 'Ordinary magic: Resilience processes in development', *American Psychologist*, 56 (3): 227–38.

McCord, J. (1988) 'Parental behaviour in the cycle of aggression', *Psychiatry*, 51: 14–23.

McCord, J. and McCord, W. (1956) *Psychopathology and Delinquency*. New York: Grune and Stratton.

McCord, J. and Tremblay, R. (eds) (1992) *Preventing Antisocial Behaviour – Interventions from Birth through Adolescence*. New York: Guildford.

McLoyd, V.C. (1998) 'Socioeconomic disadvantage and child development', *American Psychologist*, 53 (2): 185–204.

Mednick, S.A., Gabrielli, W. and Hutchings, B. (1987) 'Genetic factors in the etiology of criminal behaviour', in S.A. Mednick, T. Moffit and S. Stark (eds), *The Causes of Crime: New Biological Approaches*. New York: Cambridge University Press.

Meichenbaum, D. (1977) *Cognitive-Behaviour Modification: An Integrative Approach*. New York: Plenum.

Moffit, T.E. (1990) 'The neuropsychology of delinquency: a critical review of theory and research', in N. Morris and M. Tonry (eds), *Crime and Justice: An Annual Review of Research*. 12 Chicago: University of Chicago Press. pp. 99–169.

NESF (1998) *National Economic and Social Forum, Report No. 11, Early School Leavers and Youth Unemployment*. Dublin: Government Stationery Office.

O'Donnell, C.R. (1992) 'The interplay of theory and practice in delinquency prevention: From behaviour modification to activity settings', in J. McCord and R. Trembley (eds), *Preventing Antisocial Behaviour: Interventions from Birth through Adolescence*. New York: Guildford.

Olson, S., Bates, J., Sandy, J. and Schilling, E. (2002) 'Early developmental precursors of impulsive and inattentive behaviour: From infancy to middle childhood', *Journal of Child Psychology and Psychiatry* 43 (4): 435–47.

Olweus, D. (1979) 'Stability of aggressive reaction patterns in males: A review', *Psychological Bulletin*, 86: 852–75.

Olweus D. (1991) 'Bully/victim problems among schoolchildren: Basic facts and effects of a school based intervention programme', in D. Pepler and H. Rubin (eds), *The Development and Treatment of Childhood Aggression*. Hillsdale, NJ: Erlbaum.

Olweus, D. (1993) *Bullying at School: What we Know and What we Can Do*. Oxford: Blackwell.

O'Mahony, P. (1997) *Mountjoy Prisoners: A Sociological and Criminological Profile*. Dublin: Government Stationery Office.

Patterson, G. (1982) *Coercive Family Process*. Eugene, OR: Castilia.

Peters, R. and McMahon, R. (1996) *Preventing Childhood Disorders, Substance Abuse and Delinquency*. London: Sage.

Ramey, C. and Campbell, F. (1991) 'Poverty, early childhood education and academic competence: The Abecedarian experiment', in A. Huston (ed.), *Children in Poverty*. New York: Cambridge University Press.

Robins, L.N. (1978) 'Sturdy childhood predictors of adult antisocial behaviour: replications from longitudinal studies', *Psychological Medicine*, 8: 611–22.

Rutter, M. and Madge, N. (1970) *Cycles of Disadvantage*. London: Heinemann.

Scott, S. (1998) 'Aggressive behaviour in childhood', *British Medical Journal*, 316: 201–206.

Sedlock, A. and Broadhurst, D. (1996) *Executive Summary of the Third National Incidence Study of Child Abuse and Neglect*. Washington, DC: Department of Health and Human Services.

Skinner, E.A., Zimmer Gembeck, M. and Connel, J. (1998) *Individual Differences and the Development of Perceived Control*. Monographs of the Society for Research in Child Development 63 (2–3, Serial Number 254).

Snyder, J. and Patterson, G. (1987) 'Family interaction and delinquent behaviour', in H. Quay (ed.), *Handbook of Juvenile Delinquency*. New York: Wiley.

Stevenson, J. and Goodman, R. (2001) 'Association between behaviour at age 3 years and adult criminality', *British Journal of Psychiatry*, 179: 230–35.

Straub, E. (1996) 'Cultural-societal roots of violence', *American Psychologist*, 51: 117–32.

Trembley, R., Pihl, R. and Vitaro, F. (1994) 'Predicting early onset of male antisocial behaviour from pre-school behaviour', *Archives of General Psychiatry*, 51: 732–9.

Tucker, C.M. (1999) *African American Children: A Self-empowerment Approach to Modifying Behaviour Problems and Preventing Academic Failure*. Needham Heights, MA: Allyn and Bacon.

UK Dept. of Education (1994) *Code of Practice on the Identification and Assessment of Special Educational Needs*. London: HMSO.

US Department of Justice (1993) *Survey of State Prison Inmates (1991)*. Washington, DC: Bureau of Justice Statistics.

West, D. and Farrington, D. (1973) *Who Becomes Delinquent?* London: Heinemann.

West, D. and Farrington, D. (1977) *The Delinquent Way of Life*. London: Heinemann.

White, K. (1982) 'The relation between socioeconomic status and academic achievement', *Psychological Bulletin*, 91: 461–81.

White, J., Moffit, T., Earls, F., Robins, L. and Silva, P. (1990) 'How early can we tell? Predictions of childhood conduct disorder and adolescent delinquency', *Criminology*, 27: 507–533.

Widom, C.S. (1989) 'Does violence beget violence? A critical examination of the literature', *Psychological Bulletin*, 106 (1): 3–28.

Wolfgang, M., Figlia, R. and Sellin, T. (1972) *Delinquency in a Birth Cohort*. Chicago, IL: University of Chicago Press.

Zigler, E., Taussig, C. and Black, K. (1992) 'Early childhood intervention: A promising preventative for juvenile delinquency', *American Psychologist*, 47: 997–1006.

12

Television and Viewers' Behaviour: Real or Elusive Links?

TONY CHARLTON AND CHARLIE PANTING

Learned behaviour is the product of complex connections between individuals' biological make-up (non-genetic and genetic) and their environment. For most children, elements of this learning equip them with the personal and social skills essential for a healthy adjustment to their surroundings. Thus, for instance, they become able to forge – and to sustain – satisfactory relations with others. Lacking these 'life skills', youngsters can encounter difficulties with their socialization efforts. Along these lines, some have cautioned that there may be an alarming increase in the number of people:

> … entering adulthood with serious personal and social deficits, including fragile ties to parents, difficulties in maintaining intimate relationships, weak community attachments … (Amato and Booth, 2001: 210)

More specific sources of individuals' personal and social problems are heeded, too. For example, television is regularly accused of provoking antisocial behaviour among youngsters (a claim just as frequently challenged). With this allegation in mind, this chapter considers the role that television may play in adversely affecting young viewers' behaviour. In doing so, it reflects upon particular areas commonly accepted as mediating any television viewing effects (identification, perceptions of content reality, amount/type of viewing, social controls). The highlighting of these areas illustrates how vulnerable viewers' personal, social and viewing characteristics are often shared by youngsters evidencing serious behaviour problems. To conclude, reference is made to factors which should be utilized to help reduce antisocial behaviour among vulnerable viewers as well as others evidencing serious problem behaviour.

Whilst the authors are mindful of the semantic confusion in the literature concerning terms such as aggression, violence and antisocial behaviour, these terms are used interchangeably in this chapter in order to reflect particular usages across different studies.

SOME CAUSES OF ANTISOCIAL BEHAVIOUR

Efforts to extend our understanding of the aetiology of antisocial behaviours commonly reflect upon factors within and outside the individual. The 'within person' perspective considers factors including 'the state of the nervous system and certain glandular functions, heredity and genetic considerations' (Charlton and George, 1993: 17) and symptoms such as stress, loss of hope and self-esteem, anxiety, stigma and powerlessness (Cattell, 2001). The 'outside the person' viewpoint generally pays attention to the family, neighbourhood, community and school inquiring what it is about 'respective social structures and cultures' (Laub and Lauritsen, 1998: 128) that helps generate antisocial behaviour.

In reality, learned behaviour is the outcome of an elaborate interplay between what Laub and Lauritsen refer to as the result of 'interactions between individual development and social contexts' (1998: 128). Thus, youngsters with a low self-concept may engage in vandalism and violence in order to exact revenge upon those whom they see as neglecting – or, perhaps, precipitating – their needs. Even so, antisocial and other behaviours can be acquired in a relatively elementary manner; for example, through observational learning.

LEARNING BY OBSERVING

Observational learning is a process through which individuals imitate – intentionally or otherwise – the behaviour of those they observe (that is, models). A plenitude of potential models is readily available (for example, family members, peers, celebrities) from whom individuals can learn skills, attitudes, values, habits and emotions, for instance, although at times this learning is neither desirable nor beneficial to the individual or the wider society.

Utilizing real-life and filmed models, laboratory research – chiefly in the United States – has demonstrated the particular conditions which encourage observers to imitate (or otherwise) observed behaviour (for example, Bandura and Walters, 1963). More latterly, research of this kind has tended to focus upon television programme content and its influence upon viewers.

REAL OR ELUSIVE LINKS?

Since television's availability, arguments have raged about whether television viewing – and violence viewing, in particular – incites viewers to behave antisocially. Some have found that youngsters became more anti-social after exposure to media violence (for example, Williams, 1986; Huesmann et al., 2003; Boyatzis et al., 1995). Others have failed to repli-cate these findings (for example, Weigman et al., 1992; Gunter et al., 2000), and some have claimed that television violence viewing can lessen view-ers' aggression (for example, Berkowitz and Rawlings, 1963). Elsewhere, Huesmann and colleagues (2003) have contended that substantial evidence exists that media violence is a 'long-term predisposing and short-term precipitating factor' (2003: 201), whilst Gauntlett (1997) has expressed doubts about the existence of any such links.

More refined conceptual models have also emerged (Berkowitz and Heimer, 1989), where the viewer is seen as 'playing a cognitively more active role in the context of media content interpretation and choice of response to media stimuli (Gunter et al., 2000: 66). Another viewpoint on these seemingly 'elusive' links makes an important distinction between the *learning* and *practising* of antisocial behaviours. So, environmental controls – or the lack of them – are largely responsible for permitting or prohibiting the practising of behaviours acquired through observational learning. Thus:

> ... where environments actively check on and correct children's behaviour, television's capacity to adversely affect young viewers' social behaviour is lessened or removed, in general. (Charlton et al., 2002: 131)

The non-practising of learned aggression may stem from a variety of sources, including a fear of rebuke or other punishment, a sensitivity to being watched over and – with some older individuals – a well-developed value system.

MEDIATING LINKS BETWEEN TELEVISION AND VIEWERS' BEHAVIOUR

Potential links between television viewing and viewers' behaviour are complex, and can be mediated by a range of factors including the amount and type of television viewed, how television programme content is perceived (that is, as fact or fiction) and the degree to which viewers identify with television characters. A further factor concerns the extent to which healthy control is exercised over young viewers' social behaviour together with their television viewing.

Identification with television characters

According to Hake (2001), the identification process is about relations between the viewer and a media character whereupon the viewer wishes that he or she was like that person. The identification drive is a simplistic one. It's about the pursuit of desired attributes or qualities (for example, attitudes, dress, values, speech and actions). However, whilst the identification process can promote 'good' behaviour, antisocial behaviours can be acquired, too. Whilst earliest 'identifications' usually involve parents, the absence of 'appealing' models at home can encourage young viewers to look elsewhere. Merlo-Flores, for example, talked about the screen magically solving 'the situation by presenting heroes who never die, who everybody knows and accepts' (1998: 175).

There is evidence that the identification process is associated with the amount – and types – of viewing undertaken. Whilst some characters, for instance, can foster altruistic behaviour, the influence of others is less pleasing. For example, children (mostly boys) who identify with aggressive television characters tend to be heavy 'television violence' viewers (Huesmann et al., 1984). Even so, the differentiation between desirable and less desirable models is not simplistic for:

> Good characters frequently are the perpetrators of aggression on TV. A full 40 per cent of the violent incidents are initiated by characters who have good qualities that make them attractive role models to viewers. Not only are attractive characters often violent, but physical aggression is frequently condoned. (Wilson et al., 1998: 71)

Perceptions of content realism

Reeves (1978) claimed that television effects can be understood better by attending to viewers' perceptions of content realism. The reasons why these perceptions are considered important derive:

... from convictions that realistic portrayals of vicariously reinforced behaviour have greater instructional potential for performing vicarious, aggressive sequences ... because the expected likelihood of actually achieving rewards or avoiding punishment can be more accurately assessed. (Atkin, 1984: 615)

This thinking has been reinforced by empirical research. For example, children were found to respond more aggressively to television aggression when they were informed the programming was real, compared to those told the programming was fictional (Feshbach, 1976). Likewise, Hapkirwitz and Stone (1974) reported that non-realistic programmes had less impact than realistic ones, and in Atkin's (1984) study viewers became more aggressive when violent incidents were presented as realistic news rather than fantasy. Last but not least, from a meta-analysis of over 200 studies, Hearold (1986) concluded that the degree of realism in television programmes was a major variable affecting the amount of anti-social behaviour practised by viewers.

Cognitive development plays a weighty role in children's ability to differentiate between reality and unreality. Thus, younger viewers seem more vulnerable to untoward viewing outcomes (van Evra, 1998, Chandler, 1997). For example, UK primary school children were often unsure about the realism of television characters attending a fictional secondary school *Grange Hill*. They tended to use the programme's content about what to expect once they (themselves) transferred to secondary school, whereas secondary school children were often critical of the *Grange Hill* story lines, as their own real-life experience had taught them that they wrongly portrayed secondary school life (Gunter et al., 1991).

Social control and social capital

More recently, the term 'social control' has permeated the television effects' debate. Laub and Lauritsen construed the term being about 'community norms regarding acceptable and unacceptable behaviour' (1998: 138). Lacking these controls, youngsters can feel free to misbehave with little fear of retribution. A related term is 'social capital', which refers to the extent to which individuals have others to rely upon for assistance and support. Thus:

... in terms of family management, increased social capital means residents share information about children and others in the neighbourhood, thereby establishing community norms regarding acceptable and unacceptable behaviour. (Laub and Lauritsen, 1998: 138)

Moreover, Cattell talked about it as 'a resource produced when people cooperate for mutual benefit' (2001: 1052).

Some young viewers become vulnerable to untoward television viewing effects due to deficient social controls. They include those from homes where healthy parental supervision is lacking and there is insufficient supervision over youngsters' viewing, and few – if any – rules about television viewing (Abelman et al., 1991). Singer and Singer (1986), for example, reported that low parental mediation of children's viewing combined with high levels of viewing predicted high levels of aggressive behaviour a year later. In a similar vein, Charlton et al. (2002) talked about youngsters becoming vulnerable to untoward viewing effects where homes, neighbourhoods and communities are unable, or unwilling, to watch over and healthily influence youngsters' social behaviour. Along lines demonstrated by Bandura and Walters (1963), Charlton and colleagues (2002) argued that whilst children can learn antisocial behaviours from their viewing, environmental influences chiefly determined whether or not they are practised. In like manner, Korzenny et al. (1979) argued that parental discipline and adult–child interactions affect children's expression of the antisocial behaviour 'taken' from their viewing. Desmond et al. (1990) wrote similarly, suggesting that general family communication style may be more important than specific television rules and discipline for mediating television effects. They stressed the import of discussing moral judgements and providing explanations about television programmes. Supportive of this reasoning, Singer and Singer found a more overall emphasis by parents on 'physical discipline and power assertion all predict greater aggressive behaviour by the children' (1986: 86).

The erosion of the 'traditional family' has left many children separated from watchful and careful eyes of grandparents, aunts and uncles, for example (Amato and Booth, 2001). Fontana reflected upon the extended family of past times who:

> ... tended to live near each other, and the child often saw as much of other relatives as he did of his own parents, with the result that he was subject to a broad range of influence. This influence is sometimes seen by modern sociologists as being all to the good in that it engendered more of a sense of community into a neighbourhood and provided checks upon antisocial behaviour in the young. (1981: 44)

This loss is worrying, given that an increasing number of children are replacing the extended family with the television set (Singer and Singer, 1986).

Amount and type of viewing

Singer and Singer claimed that the amount and type of viewing is an important predictor of behaviour, arguing that heavy viewing places the child at serious risk of 'greater restlessness and more aggression, all contributory to poor behavioural adjustment when the child is beginning at school' (1986: 88). Huesmann and colleagues have also stressed the increased risk of aggressive and violent behaviour occurring in later life when youngsters 'view a high and steady diet of violent television shows in early childhood' (2003: 218). Additionally, there is the risk that heavy viewing limits children's opportunities to acquire and practise the social skills that under-pin healthy functioning. Heavy viewers have been found to be more socially inept when interacting with peers and parents (Schramm et al., 1961), although the causal direction is unclear. Does viewing displace time from activities which help enhance social skills' development, or do those bereft of such skills turn to the 'set' for the comfort and company unobtainable elsewhere (Abelman, 1991)?

BLUEPRINT FOR THE VULNERABLE VIEWER

Although the television effects' debate rages, laboratory research has yielded persuasive evidence that television viewing *can* adversely affect viewers' behaviour, although personal and social/contextual factors assume a key role in determining whether untoward outcomes become manifest. Accordingly, the research outcomes referred to in earlier pages suggest the following profile for those at risk of becoming vulnerable viewers. Those:

- who identify with aggressive characters;
- with difficulty differentiating between real and fictional characters;
- who are heavy viewers, especially of television violence;
- whose viewing is unsupervised; and
- whose social behaviour is largely unchecked.

THE VULNERABLE VIEWER AND CHILDREN WITH EMOTIONAL AND BEHAVIOUR PROBLEMS

Huesmann and colleagues' (2003) claim that the television effects' debate is settled appears both untimely and reckless. The literature remains bedevilled by dissension. Yet, there may be a plausible explanation for the lack of consensus, one to do with context. Charlton et al. (1998) suggested that youngsters' antisocial behaviour could be discouraged where respon-sible supervision is available, whereas the likelihood of antisocial behav-iour occurring is heightened by its absence. Many children with emotional and behaviour difficulties grow up adversely affected by deviant families, deviant peer groups, socio-economic inequality, poverty, high population turnover and environments generally short on social capital as well as healthy social controls. Unsurprisingly, many of these youngsters share a number of television-related characteristics with the vulnerable viewer (see Sprafkin et al., 1992), including:

- heavy television use;
- heavy viewing of television violence;
- confusion between reality and fantasy;
- identification with aggressive characters; and
- a lack of 'guardianship' behaviour over their viewing, and social behaviour, in general.

Thus, many youngsters evidencing emotional and behavioural difficulties become exceptionally vulnerable viewers not only in the sense that they are exceptional children, but also because their environments together with their viewing habits heighten their vulnerability to adverse viewing effects. The nature of the overt and covert problems of vulnerable and exceptionally vulnerable viewers suggests some similarity in the resolutions required to ameliorate them.

LOOKING FOR SOLUTIONS

Arguably, central to the predicament of many vulnerable young viewers, and others with emotional and behavioural problems, is the dwindling amounts of both healthy attention and sensible support made available by families, individuals and the wider community. This parsimony includes a widespread laxity in checking and steering youngsters' social behaviour in ways that help them to sustain healthy relationships and function responsibly within families, neighbourhoods and communities. Lacking this care and guidance, youngsters can learn antisocial behaviours from their viewing (and elsewhere) and freely practise them, for checks upon their social behaviour are uncommon. In contexts like these, given that antisocial behaviour frequently attracts neither contingent rebuke nor healthy suggestions for alternative desirable behaviour, the (mis)- behaver can readily construe that such behaviour is condoned.

A plenitude of plausible solutions exists to help vulnerable viewers; some tried, others not. They include the 'watershed' (that is, in the United Kingdom, only material suitable for family viewing can be broadcast before 21.00 hrs), the V-chip technology, electronic programme guides (EPGs) as well as in-school interventions (see Sprafkin et al., 1992). Arguably, a more practicable solution (with implications for youngsters with severe behaviour problems) is inextricably linked to the breakdown of the nuclear and extended family, of neighbourhood support networks and of communities, the consequences of which have left many children exposed to 'not good enough' parenting and 'inadequate supervision'. It is remarkable – some say iniquitous – that this critical aspect of children's social development is given insufficient attention in school. Davie (1996) drew attention to the futility of the arguments made to redress this neglect at the time of constructing the National Curriculum (NC) for England and Wales. He argued that the promotion of sensible 'good-enough' parenting needed to be given greater priority within schools. Since then, addenda to the NC have provided an enhanced focus upon 'education for parenthood' and 'citizenship' for example, although it is too early to evaluate the impact of these changes. However, the import of such matters remains clear.

A FOCUS FOR FURTHER RESEARCH

The television effects' debate persists, unabated. Even so, laboratory studies – which are well placed to analyse the processes through which television can affect viewers – have demonstrated that viewing aggression, for example, can make viewers behave more aggressively. Moreover, differential conditions were shown to encourage or discourage the practising (yet not the learning) of this aggression. A highly influential condition was found to be the context. Some contexts provoked aggressive behaviour, others prevented it. Arguably, however, the tendency for media research to be overly focused upon the 'television' has been at the expense of 'context'. Clearly, the television is a 'risk' factor in terms of abetting antisocial behaviour, but no more.

If 'context' matters in the laboratory, it should matter also in real life (that is, in the naturalistic setting). Thus, conflicting findings from naturalistic research may well, on occasions, reflect differential contexts (for example, Williams, 1986; Charlton et al., 2002). Deviant families and peer groups, families under stress, poor parenting and 'broken' communities can all too easily bring about problem behaviour. On the other hand, a supportive context which helps children to become better parents, more responsible citizens and more effective contributors to their community offers more pragmatic ways for limiting pernicious outcomes from television viewing (and from other risky environmental influences).

Contexts should be considered more earnestly in quests to add to an understanding of the role that television plays in creating problem behaviours, and ways in which such problems can be prevented, resolved or minimized. Even so, such thinking remains speculative until a body of naturalistic research is able to assemble sufficient evidence to challenge the assumptions of those under the illusion that links between media violence and antisocial behaviour are proven. Until such times, the media effects' debate will persist in questioning whether these links are real or elusive.

REFERENCES

Abelman, R. (1991) 'Parental communication style and its influence on exceptional children's television viewing', *Roeper Review*, 14 (1): 23–7.

Abelman, R., Sprafkin, J. and Gadow, K.D. (1991) *Television and Exceptional Children.* Hillsdale, NJ: Erlbaum.

Amato, P.R. and Booth, A. (2001) *A Generation at Risk: Growing up in an Era of Family Upheaval.* Cambridge, MA: Harvard University Press.

Atkin, C. (1984) 'Effects of realistic TV violence vs fictional violence on aggression', *Journalism Quarterly*, 34 (2): 615–21.

Bandura, A. and Walters, R.H. (1963) *Social Learning and Personality Development.* New York: Halt, Rinehart and Winston.

Berkowitz, L. and Heimer, K. (1989) 'On the construction of the anger experience: Aversive events and negative priming in the information of feelings', in L. Berkowitz (ed.), *Advances in Experimental Psychology.* New York: Academic Press. pp. 22, 1–27.

Berkowitz, L. and Rawlings, E. (1963) 'Effects of film violence on inhibitions against subsequent aggression', *Journal of Abnormal and Social Psychology*, 66 (5): 405–12.

Boyatzis, C.J., Matillo, G.M. and Nesbitt, K.M. (1995) 'Effects of the "Mighty Morphin Power Rangers" on children's aggression with peers', *Child Study Journal*, 25 (1): 45–55.

Cattell, V. (2001) 'Poor people, poor places, and poor health: the mediating role of social networks and social capital', *Social Science and Medicine*, 52: 1501–1516.

Chandler, D. (1997) 'Children's understanding of what is "real" on television: a review of the literature', *Journal of Educational Media*, 23 (1): 65–81.

Charlton, T., Davie, R., Gunter, B. and Thomas, P. (2002) 'Children's social behaviour before and after the availability of broadcast television: Findings from three studies in a naturalistic setting', in T. Charlton, B. Gunter and A. Hannan (eds), *Broadcast TV Effects in a Remote Community.* Hillsdale, CA: Erlbaum. pp. 107–134.

Charlton, T. and George, B. (1993) 'The development of behaviour problems', in T. Charlton and K. David (eds), *Managing Misbehaviour in Schools* (2nd edition). London: Routledge.

Charlton, T., Gunter, B. and Coles, D. (1998) 'Broadcast television as a cause of aggression? Recent findings from a naturalistic study', *British Journal of Emotional and Behavioural Difficulties*, 2: 5–13.

Davie, R. (1996) 'Preface', in K. David and T. Charlton (eds), *Pastoral Care Matters: in Primary and Middle Schools.* London:Routledge.

Desmond, R.J., Singer, J.L. and Singer, D.G. (1990) 'Family mediation: Parental communication patterns and the influence of television on children', in J. Bryant (ed.), *Television and the American Family.* Hillsdale, CA: Erlbaum.

Feshbach, S. (1976) 'The role of fantasy in the response to television', *Journal of Social Issues*, 32 (4): 71–85.

Fontana, D. (1981) *Psychology for Teachers.* London: British Psychological Society and Macmillan.

Gauntlett, D. (1997) 'Why no clear answers on media effects?', in T. Charlton and K. David (eds), *Elusive Links: Television, Video Games and Children's Behaviour.* Tewkesbury: Park Published Papers.

Gunter, B., Charlton, T., Coles, D. and Panting, C. (2000) 'The impact of television on children's antisocial behaviour in a novice television community', *Child Study Journal*, 30 (2): 65–90.

Gunter, B., McAleer, J.L. and Clifford, B.R. (1991) *Children's Views About Television*. Aldershot: Avebury.

Hake, K. (2001) 'Five-year-olds' fascination for television: A comparative study', *Childhood*, 8 (4): 423–41.

Hapkirwitz, W.G. and Stone, R.D. (1974) 'The effect of realistic versus imaginary aggressive models on children's interpersonal play', *Child Study Journal*, 4 (2): 47–57.

Hearold, S. (1986) 'A synthesis of 1043 effects of television on social behaviour', in G. Comstock (ed.), *Public Communications and Behaviour*, Vol. 1. New York: Academic Press, pp. 65–133.

Huesmann, L.R., Lagerspetz, K. and Eron, L.D. (1984) 'Intervening variables in the TV-Violence–aggression relation: Evidence from two countries', *Developmental Psychology*, 20: 746–75.

Huesmann, L.R., Moise-Titus, J., Podolski, C. and Eron, L.D. (2003) 'Longitudinal relations between children's exposure to TV violence and their aggressive and violent behaviour in young adulthood: 1977–1992', *Developmental Psychology*, 39 (2): 201–221.

Korzenny, F., Greenberg, B.S. and Atkin, C.K. (1979) 'Styles of parental disciplinary practices as a mediator of children's learning from antisocial television portrayals', in D. Nimmo (ed.), *Communications Yearbook 3*. New Brunswick, NJ: Transaction.

Laub, J.H. and Lauritson, J.L. (1998) 'The Interdependence of school violence with neighbourhood and family conditions', in D.S. Eliot, B. Hamburg and K.R. Williams (eds), *Violence in American Schools: A New Perspective*. New York, NJ: Cambridge University Press.

Merlo-Floroo, T. (1998). 'Why do we watch television violence?', in U. Carlsson and C. von Feilitzen (eds), *Children and Media Violence*. Goteborg, Sweden: UNESCO.

Reeves, B. (1978) 'Perceived TV Reality as a predictor of children's social behaviour', *Journalism Quarterly*, 55 (4): 682–9.

Schramm, W., Lyle, V. and Parker, E. (1961) *Television in the lives of Our Children*. Stanford, CK: Stanford University Press.

Singer, J.L. and Singer, D.G. (1986) 'Television-viewing and family communication style as predictors of children's emotional behaviour', *Journal of Children in Contemporary Society*, 17 (4): 75–91.

Sprafkin, J., Gadow, K.D. and Abelman, R. (1992). *Television and the Exceptional Child: A Forgotten Audience*. Hillsdale, CA: Erlbaum.

Van Evra, J. (1998) *Television and Child Development*. Hillsdale, NJ: Erlbaum.

Weigman, O., Kuttschreuter, M. and Baarda, B. (1992) 'A longitudinal study of the effects of television viewing on aggressive and prosocial behaviours', *British Journal of Social Psychology*, 31: 147–64.

Williams, T.M. (ed.) (1986) *The Impact of Television: A Natural Experiment in Three Communities*. New York: Academic Press.

Wilson, B.J., Kunkel, D., Linz, D., Potter, J., Donnerstein, E., Smith, S.L., Blumenthal, E., Berry, M. and Federman, J. (1998) 'The nature and context of violence on American television', in U. Carlsson and C. von Feilitzen (eds), *Children and Media Violence*. Goteborg, Sweden: UNESCO.

13

Racial/Ethnic Representation across Five Public Sectors of Care for Youth with EBD: Implications for Students in School Settings[1,2]

MAY YEH, KRISTEN MCCABE,
KATINA LAMBROS, RICHARD HOUGH,
JOHN LANDSVERK, MICHAEL HURLBURT,
AND SHIRLEY CULVER

Studies estimate that among children as a whole, a substantial proportion of youth with emotional or behavioral problems are not receiving necessary mental health services (Burns et al., 1995; Realmuto et al., 1992; Tuma, 1989). In addition, some have suggested that ethnic minority children who suffer from emotional or behavioral problems may be further underserved (Burns, 1991; Cross et al., 1989). However, little is known about the actual rates of ethnic minority child mental health service use. While such information is available for adults (Cheung and Snowden, 1990; Sue, 1977), there is a gap in the knowledge about racial/ethnic service representation rates for children.

Information about ethnic minorities is particularly important, given the growth of this population. The US Bureau of the Census (1997a) estimates that by the year 2050, less than 53 percent of the US population will be of non-Hispanic white background. As the US population continues to diversify ethnically and racially, it is important to provide cross-culturally responsive services. This is especially salient given findings from the

Surgeon General's report on *Mental Health: Culture, Race and Ethnicity* (US DHHS, 2001), indicating that the disability burden from unmet mental health needs is disproportionately high for racial and ethnic minorities in comparison to Caucasian Americans. In order to improve access to services, develop services that are culturally responsive, and begin to understand how racial, ethnic and cultural factors affect service utilization patterns, we must start by closely examining the delivery of currently existing services.

Although most studies of services for youth with emotional and behavioral problems have focused on traditional specialty mental health treatments (for example, psychotherapy and psychotropic medication), youth with such problems can enter into services provided by a variety of professionals, agencies, and organizations (Burns et al., 1992). In the public behavioral health domain, these services have been referred to collectively as the 'public system of care' (Stroul and Friedman, 1986). The public system of care is made up of publicly-funded services that serve large numbers of children with emotional and behavioral problems. The system of care contains many smaller 'sectors' of care, including mental health, child welfare, primary physical health care, juvenile justice, alcohol and drug treatment, and services for children with emotional disturbance (ED), formerly referred to as serious emotional disturbance (SED), in the public schools (Burns et al., 1995). While all of these sectors serve large numbers of children with emotional or behavioral problems (Stroul and Friedman, 1986), the highest prevalence rates of diagnosable mental disorders are found in children served in ED special education settings, as compared to other sectors (Garland et al., 2001). Schools, in particular, have special education supports and services that are tailored to meet the complex needs of students with severe emotional and behavioral problems that interfere with educational achievement. While the current study examines service representation patterns across several sectors, specific emphasis will be placed on students receiving ED services in the school sector.

Children and youth identified with ED in school settings are undoubtedly a heterogeneous group of youth who present with a complex range of disabilities and disorders (Forness et al., 1994). Nationally, the identification rate for emotional disturbance has remained stable at approximately 0.9 percent, which is significantly lower than current estimated prevalence rates, which range from 4 to 10 percent of school-age youth (Brandenburg et al., 1990; Kauffman, 1997). Within the state of California, rates of ED are at 0.4 percent, which is lower than the national identification rate (0.9 percent), illustrating the extent of underidentification of this population within schools (US DoE, 2000). Within the ED disability category, males outnumber females by a ratio of 5 to 1 or more – the highest proportion of males to females in any of the federal disability categories (Hallahan and Kauffman, 2000; Marder and Cox, 1991). African Americans appear to be overrepresented in this category as well (US DoE, 2000). Additionally, students with ED are more likely to be economically disadvantaged (Hallahan and Kauffman, 2000). Students with ED commonly have more than one disorder, which typically intensifies maladaptive behaviors and functional impairment (Caron and Rutter, 1991; Friedman et al., 1996). They also fail more courses, earn lower grade point averages, have more absences, and experience more grade retentions than students with other disabilities (Wagner et al., 1993). Fifty-five percent of ED students drop out of school before graduating (Wagner, 1995). Furthermore, students with ED come into more frequent contact with the juvenile justice system (Gilliam and Scott, 1987; Leone, 1991), and are more likely to live in single parent homes, or foster care (Cullinan et al., 1992; Marder, 1992; Wagner, 1995). As may be expected, these students frequently require assistance from a variety of agencies and providers, increasing the likelihood of multi-sector service use.

The factors that determine which sector of care a particular child with emotional or behavioral problems will enter are complex, poorly understood, and not limited to the clinical characteristics of the child (Garland and Besinger, 1997). Various gatekeepers, including parents, schools, police, courts, and others, have a major impact on which sectors of care the child will enter (Lindsey, 1991; Westendorp et al., 1986). For instance, in schools, the Student Study Team (SST), or any other pre-referral student assistance team, is typically the first opportunity in which children are moved into a pathway to receive school services (Hallahan and Kauffman, 2000). More specifically, the SST is a multidisciplinary team composed of school personnel and parents who work with the classroom teacher to design academic and/or behavioral interventions for children preceding formal evaluation for special education eligibility. Variables impacting teacher, school staff and parent referrals to this initial service mechanism and those subsequent (that is, assessment by a multidisciplinary team, qualification by team for special education services) must be examined in order to reveal possible reasons for the occurrence of racial and ethnic disparities.

An understanding of how racial and ethnic factors impact children's use of services would be impossible without examining multiple sectors of care. Investigation of service representation patterns across sectors of care is particularly important because studies have demonstrated that receiving services from one sector of care may affect the likelihood that services will be received from other sectors of care. For instance, several authors

(Gunter-Justice and Ott, 1997; Westendorp et al., 1986) have found that minority children were more likely to be placed in the juvenile justice sector than the mental health sector compared with majority children, even when other demographic and offense characteristics were held constant. Thus, overrepresentation of one group in juvenile justice may be mirrored by underrepresentation of that group in the mental health sector. Clearly, the mental health sector is not independent of other public service sectors, and representation across these sectors must be examined to understand fully how minority children access public services that target emotional and behavioral problems. Examination of cross-sector service representation may be essential and quite telling for minority children receiving ED services within the public schools. As mentioned previously, it is common for students with emotional disturbance to be at heightened risk for a host of negative outcomes such as comorbidity, substance abuse, school drop-out, contact with juvenile justice, foster care, and so on (Caron and Rutter, 1991; Wagner, 1995; Gilliam and Scott, 1987; Leone, 1991; Cullinan et al., 1992). This suggests that multiple service sectors may be needed to address the diverse problems suffered by this population, and that entry into one service sector may result in referrals to other sectors for additional services. Exploration of this possible hypothesis must also occur in order to understand more fully service access and use by minority children with emotional and behavioral problems.

Attention to minority representation has been highly variable across sectors. Studies have generally focused exclusively on one sector, limiting our ability to draw broad conclusions about cross-sector service use or to examine overlap between sectors. However, some data do exist about individual racial/ethnic groups in individual sectors. The literature on representation of four racial/ethnic groups (African American, Asian/Pacific Islander American, Caucasian American, and Latino) in five public sectors of care (mental health, juvenile justice, child welfare, alcohol/drug treatment, and ED services in schools) will be reviewed below. Although there are a number of ways to operationalize over- or underrepresentation, the literature reviewed here has generally compared the representation of a particular racial/ethnic group in a service sector to the representation of that group in the general population, catchment area population, or, in some instances with ethnic minorities, to the representation of Caucasian Americans in the sector.

With reference to the ED school service sector, data reported from the Office of Civil Rights (OCR) within the US Department of Education on enrollment of students in special education programs delineated by racial/ethnic group will be presented below. The OCR data reviewed will provide two slightly different perspectives on representation rates (MacMillan and Reschly, 1998). The first calculation will give the percentage of students in the ED disability category who are members of a given racial/ethnic group (that is, the percentage of students classified as ED that are African American), as compared to their representation in the total school population. In addition, a second perspective will provide the percent of racial/ethnic group in a category or program (that is, the percent of African American students that are identified as ED). While this data reported by OCR is considered informative to the review of individual school sector information, a cautionary note must be given when interpreting representation rates. The OCR aggregates data on disability by race/ethnicity across counties and states and does not take other socio-demographic variables into account.

AFRICAN AMERICANS

African American children and adolescents have been found to be overrepresented across several sectors of care: child welfare, juvenile justice, mental health, and school ED services. In the child welfare sector, Courtney et al. (1996) reviewed the literature and concluded that African Americans were three to five times more likely to enter the child welfare sector than Caucasian Americans. They further concluded that African American children who enter the child welfare sector were less likely to be offered additional support services, were more likely to be placed out of the home, and were more likely to stay in care longer, even controlling for entry characteristics (Courtney et al., 1996).

Similarly, African American youth have been found to be overrepresented in the juvenile justice sector. Studies of minority representation have found that African American youth are overrepresented at either some or all stages of the detention process (for example, arrest, intake, detention, probation, and incarceration; Conley, 1994; Pope and Feyerherm, 1995; Wordes et al., 1994). The reason for the overrepresentation of African American youth has been debated in the literature. However, recent analyses have concluded that the disparity is due at least in part to discrimination (Pope and Feyerherm, 1990). African American youth have been found to be convicted more often and receive harsher sentences than Caucasian American youth, even after controlling for severity of the crime and past offenses. African American youth are also more likely to be detained in public, rather than private facilities compared with Caucasian American youth (Krisberg et al., 1992).

Although fewer studies have examined identification of African American children for ED services in the public schools, national rates of representation indicate that African American children are more likely to receive ED services from the public schools than are Caucasian Americans. Data from the 1994 Office of Civil Rights *Elementary and Secondary School Compliance Report* on race and ethnicity indicate that African American children are overrepresented in classrooms for ED children: 24.5 percent of all ED children are African American, compared with 16 percent of the total school population (US DoE, 1994). Overall, 1.1 percent of all African American students are identified as ED. African American students are at higher risk for ED identification than any other group (US DoE, 1994).

Extensive controversy has ensued in explaining this overrepresentation of African American youth in the ED category and several reasons for this disparity have been suggested. Research indicates that the ED handicapping condition is highly 'subjective' in its definitional criteria, limited by a paucity of culturally and linguistically appropriate assessment tools, and confounded by stigma and concern over labeling effects (US House of Representatives, 1997). In addition, lack of culturally appropriate prevention and early intervention services for this population may also contribute to racial/ethnic disparities in referral and identification rates. Data from the National Longitudinal Transition Study suggest that race/ethnicity is not the primary contributor to the overrepresentation of African Americans in special education. Rather, in most cases it is caused by the overrepresentation of poor students in special education (Wagner, 1995). Although a portion of racial/ethnic disparity may be eliminated by developments in unbiased and culturally appropriate assessment and intervention practices, the larger issue of child poverty must come to the fore (Wagner, 1995). Undoubtedly, poverty reduces the quality of life in all children, regardless of race or ethnicity (Hodgkinson, 1995). However, few studies have examined racial/ethnic disparity while taking socioeconomic status into account.

Few studies have considered child and adolescent representation in the mental health sector. In addition, the studies that have been conducted have used different methodologies and have produced conflicting results. One study examined the racial/ethnic breakdown of adolescents in mental health services in a large, metropolitan area and found African American adolescents to be overrepresented (Bui and Takeuchi, 1992). However, others conclude that African American youth use mental health services at a rate lower than that of Caucasian Americans (US DHHS, 2001).

Very little attention has been given to utilization of substance abuse treatment services among African American adolescents. Research on adult substance abuse treatment utilization has been mixed, with some studies suggesting underutilization by African American adults, and others finding representation at the expected rate (Longshore et al., 1992).

A body of epidemiological research, however, suggests that African American youth abuse substances less frequently than do Caucasian and Latino youth (Bachman et al., 1991; Maddahian et al., 1986). For example, the multi-site Youth Risk Behavior Survey found that African American youth were less likely to have used a variety of substances (Center for Disease Control, 1998). However, these studies have been criticized for conducting surveys in schools, given that minority group members may be more likely to drop out of school, and this dropout group may be the group at highest risk for substance abuse (Bachman et al., 1991; Swaim et al., 1997). Additionally, minority adolescents have been found to be more vulnerable to the negative consequences of substance abuse than Caucasian American adolescents given the same amount of substance use (Barnes and Welte, 1986; Welte and Barnes, 1987). Therefore, it is difficult to draw firm conclusions about the extent to which African American adolescents utilize alcohol and drug treatment.

In summary, research to date indicates that African Americans are overrepresented in the juvenile justice, child welfare, and school ED sectors, with mixed findings for the mental health sector. While this research provides meaningful individual sector data, it is also important to examine representation rates across multiple sectors for a single population and also to investigate the reasons for any differential representation rates found.

ASIAN/PACIFIC ISLANDER AMERICANS

Although there is a scarcity of data concerning Asian/Pacific Islander American populations, available data show underrepresentation across most sectors. Courtney et al. (1996) report that there is less known about Asian/Pacific Islander Americans in the child welfare sector compared with other racial/ethnic groups. However, once having entered the sector, Asian/Pacific Islander American youth appear to be placed out of home less often than Caucasian Americans and are equally as likely to be provided with support services (Olsen, 1982). Very few studies of the juvenile justice sector have examined representation of Asian/Pacific Islander American youth. However, available data indicate that Asian/Pacific Islander American youth are underrepresented in juvenile detention facilities (Krisberg et al., 1992). Bui and Takeuchi (1992) have also found that Asian/Pacific Islander American youths' mental health service patterns parallel the underutilization of Asian/Pacific Islander American adults. Asian/Pacific Islander students comprise 0.9 percent of the school identified ED population and 3.7 percent of the total student population

(US DoE, 1994), indicating underrepresentation in this group as compared to their student population percentage. Overall, 0.2 percent of all Asian/Pacific Islander students are identified as ED.

Finally, there has been some suggestion that Asian/Pacific Islander Americans underutilize substance abuse treatment services (Zane and Kim, 1994). However, empirical evidence is lacking. Epidemiological surveys suggest that Asian/ Pacific Islander American youth are less likely to use and abuse all major classes of substances in comparison with Caucasian American youth (Center for Disease Control, 1998), but the extent of service use for substance abuse is unknown.

In general, Asian/Pacific Islander Americans tend to be underrepresented across a range of service sectors. However, because many studies of racial/ethnic variation have excluded this group, more work is necessary before service utilization patterns can be described accurately for children and adolescents.

CAUCASIAN AMERICANS

Caucasian Americans have often been used as the 'standard' for comparison of representation rates in studies of racial/ethnic representation in service sectors. This practice, while having the conceptual appeal of allowing one to examine the effects of discrimination or differential treatment, has led to diminished information about the representation of Caucasian American groups relative to their representation in the population. We do know, however, that Caucasian Americans are less likely to enter the child welfare sector than African Americans, and equally as likely to enter as Latinos. Once Caucasian Americans have entered the child welfare sector, they are less likely to be placed out of home than African Americans, and are more likely to receive mental health services, to leave care earlier, and to be adopted than both African Americans and Latinos (Courtney et al., 1996; Garland and Besinger, 1997). Further, Pope and Feyerherm (1995) found that Caucasian Americans are less likely to be arrested, detained, and given harsh sentences than African American youth and are detained less often than Latino youth.

In terms of the mental health sector, very little data about the utilization rates of Caucasian American youth exists. Bui and Takeuchi (1992) focused on minority populations and thus did not directly address the representation of Caucasian Americans in the mental health sector; however, their data suggest that Caucasian Americans were represented at a rate similar to their proportion in the community. Caucasian Americans appear to be represented at the expected rate among ED services in public schools. According to data from the 1994 Office of Civil Rights *Elementary and Secondary School Compliance Report* on race and ethnicity, Caucasian Americans made up 65.5 percent of the total student population nation-wide, and comprised 65 percent of the total ED population (US DoE for Civil Rights, 1994). Overall, the schools identified 0.8 percent of all Caucasian American students as ED.

In short, less information about absolute rates of representation is available for Caucasian Americans. However, existing evidence suggests that they are likely to be underrepresented or represented at the expected rate across most sectors.

LATINOS

Latinos have demonstrated a variable pattern of service use across sectors. Latinos were found to enter the child welfare sector at the same rate as Caucasian Americans, but, once having entered, they were offered fewer support services (such as psychotherapy), stayed in care longer, and were less likely to be adopted, even controlling for entry characteristics (Courtney et al., 1996). Studies of the juvenile justice sector have found that, although Latino youth have not experienced bias to the same extent as African American youth, Latino youth are detained at a rate higher than Caucasian American youth (Wordes et al., 1994).

Latino youth appear to be underrepresented in ED services in the public schools. In 1994, Latinos made up 16 percent of the total student population and represented 7.8 percent of the total ED population in schools (US DoE, 1994). Overall, 0.5 percent of all Latino students were identified by schools as ED. Latino adolescents are also underrepresented in the mental health sector (Bui and Takeuchi, 1992).

Similar to other groups, little is known about the utilization of substance abuse treatment programs by Latino adolescents. As with African Americans, the literature on adult treatment utilization has been mixed, with some studies indicating underutilization by Latino adults, and others finding representation at the expected rate (Longshore et al., 1992). Epidemiological data has found Latino adolescents to be the group that is most similar to Caucasian Americans in drug use patterns (Bachman et al.,1991; Center for Disease Control, 1998; Maddahian et al., 1986). However, these findings are also confounded by the relatively high dropout rate of Latino high school students and therefore may underestimate substance use and abuse in this population (Bachman et al., 1991).

Latinos' overall service use patterns seem to reflect overrepresentation in high level, restrictive care for adolescents (juvenile justice), with underrepresentation in less restrictive, more voluntarily entered service sectors (mental health and ED services). Further research to elucidate the reasons for these findings is necessary.

UNDERREPRESENTED COMPARED WITH WHOM? THE QUESTION OF COMPARISON GROUPS

Researchers who wish to determine whether a particular racial/ethnic group is over-or underrepresented in a particular sector of care must first determine how the expected rate of representation will be defined. Studies of the mental health sector have largely considered the expected rate of representation in a given sector to be the rate of representation in the population as described by Census data. For example, if 12 percent of the public mental health sector users in a given city were Latino, and 20 percent of the general population of that city was Latino, the conclusion that Latinos are underrepresented in the mental health sector would be drawn.

Although the Census provides an important point of comparison, it has some serious limitations when examining racial/ethnic representation in public sectors of care (Stolp and Warner, 1987). Public system service users are more likely to be of low-income than the general population. Minority children in general are overrepresented among the impoverished (US Bureau of the Census, 1995). Therefore, comparing rates of representation within public service systems to Census data is likely to underestimate the expected rate of utilization for minority children, while overestimating the expected rate of utilization for Caucasian American children. It may be impossible to identify the perfect comparison group for each public sector, as numerous factors affect the likelihood of a particular child accessing a particular service. However, the current investigation attempts to provide insight into this issue by identifying three distinct comparison groups and examining the conclusions that may be drawn from each comparison.

The current investigation adds to our knowledge and understanding of ethnic minority service use by examining representation rates across four racial/ethnic groups and five service sectors simultaneously in a large population of service users. This allows us to generate hypotheses about explanations for observed service use patterns that take into account multiple sectors. Although our data does not allow us to draw conclusions about causal factors that produce differential service representation, it provides information about existing patterns that must be identified before causal explanations can be explored and may generate hypotheses about causal factors that should be explored in future research. Finally, the current investigation introduces a unique methodology for determining the relative over- and underrepresentation of racial/ethnic groups in each sector by providing comparisons to three different sets of census data: 1996 Full Census estimates of youth aged 0–18 in San Diego County (the usual comparison point); 1996 Census estimates of youth at or below 200 percent of poverty level in San Diego County (a comparison group taking into account socioeconomic status); and 1997 San Diego County School Enrollment Census.

METHOD

Sample

The sample was drawn from the Patterns of Youth Mental Health Care in Public Service Systems Project (POC) enumeration of youth who were active to one or more of five public sectors of care (alcohol/drug treatment, child welfare, juvenile justice, mental health, and ED services in public schools) in San Diego County during a six-month period in the 1996–97 fiscal year ($N = 11,515$). In order to include all sectors to which each youth was active, multiple sector representation was recorded (for example, a youth who entered the juvenile justice sector and the alcohol/drug treatment sector would be represented in both sectors). However, if one youth had more than one episode in a single sector (for example, a youth entered the mental health sector in January, terminated care in February, and re-entered in March), that youth would be represented a single time in that sector. Representation in each of the sectors was defined as follows:

- Alcohol/Drug Treatment (ADT): youth received any county-contracted service from an alcohol/drug treatment provider.
- Child Welfare (CW): records indicated that youth was a dependent of the Juvenile Court because of protective issues.
- Juvenile Justice: youth was under jurisdiction of the juvenile court as a ward because of a true finding on a criminal charge.
- Mental Health (MH): youth received any service through a county mental health service program[3] (for example, psychological assessment, therapy, medication consult, and so on).
- School services for youth with Emotional Disturbance (ED): youth was designated as having the handicapping condition 'Emotional Disturbance' or as previously designated 'Serious Emotional Disturbance', as defined by the Individuals with Disabilities and Education Act (IDEA) and the California Education code.

This database was used to determine the proportion of the population served by each sector in the entire 1996–97 fiscal year that were of four racial/ethnic backgrounds: African American, Asian/Pacific Islander American, Caucasian American, and Latino. This data was derived from the management information system (MIS) databases for each of the sectors. Race/ethnicity categories were not always consistent across the MIS databases, and thus, rules were implemented to integrate the databases and create a uniform racial/ethnic classification. African Americans were those coded as 'Black or African American'. The Asian/Pacific Islander American group was the most complicated to integrate due to a lack of uniformity across MIS database variables. These included those identified as being of a member of an Asian/Pacific Islander racial/ethnic group, including, amongst others, Cambodian, Chinese, Filipino, Japanese, Korean, Filipino, Laotian, Pacific Islander, and Vietnamese. When databases did not allow for identification of various Asian/ Pacific Islander American groups to be differentiated from the 'Other/Unknown' categories, other means for determining racial/ethnic group were employed (for example, cross-checking race/ethnicity with another sector in instances of multiple sector use, examining subject names). Caucasian Americans included all those who were identified in the sector databases as being White or Caucasian, but not belonging to any Latino or Hispanic group. Latinos were all those who had been identified as belonging to a Hispanic or Latino ethnic group and included, amongst others, those who were recorded as Cuban, Mexican, Puerto Rican, and South American. Based on San Diego County demographics, it is estimated that 87 percent of the Latino sample were of Mexican background (SANDAG, 1995). The database included 4,642 Caucasian Americans (40 percent), 2,539 African Americans (22 percent), 546 Asian/Pacific Islander Americans (5 percent), and 3,421 Latinos (30 percent). 'Other' and 'Unknown' categories contained 367 children (3 percent), and due to uncertainty about the racial/ethnic background of these children, they were not included in further analyses.

Comparison groups

For the current investigation, we will present data on three different comparison groups. This method allows us to examine the differences between rates of representation when socioeconomic status (SES) is or is not taken into account. Each comparison group is described below:

1996 Census Estimates: Full Census

Census data were obtained from the 1990 Census of Population and Housing: Public Use Microdata Sample (PUMS), 5 percent sample

(US Bureau of the Census, 1992). The PUMS data is a 5 percent sample of detailed information collected by the Census Bureau. Comparisons were computed using the PUMS 5 percent sample to determine the racial/ethnic composition of children between the ages of 0 and 18 in San Diego County without regard to household income. These numbers were updated for 1996 using estimates of population growth derived by the San Diego Association of Governments (SANDAG, 1995) to reflect current population trends. This comparison point is equivalent to the Census data used by the majority of recent studies investigating racial/ethnic representation.

1996 Census Estimates At or Below 200 Percent of the Poverty Level

The PUMS 5 percent sample (US Bureau of the Census, 1992), described above, was used to determine the racial/ethnic distribution of children between the ages of 0 and 18 that lived in households where income was at or below 200 percent of the poverty level during 1989. This is a population that has been labeled 'low-income' by the US Bureau of the Census (1997) and is likely to approximate the socioeconomic status of the public service system subjects in our data. The PUMS data was then updated for 1996 using SANDAG projections (SANDAG, 1995). This provided a comparison group that controlled for socioeconomic status.

1997 San Diego County Public School Enrollment Census

Racial/ethnic breakdowns of San Diego County Public School Enrollment Census were also used for comparison. This school enrollment data represents the full universe from which ED children are drawn, and thus is the best comparison group for that particular service sector. It also provides a fairly up-to-date estimate of the current San Diego population of children, particularly given the fact that Census data may underestimate the number of ethnic minorities (Aponte and Crouch, 1995).

Analyses

The analyses tested the hypothesis that the racial/ethnic group representations across the five sectors of care in the POC sample were different than those of the following three comparison groups: 1996 Full Census Estimates; 1996 Census Estimates At or Below 200 percent of the Poverty Level; and 1997 San Diego County School Enrollment data. (For convenience, these groups will be referred to as the Full Census, 200 percent Poverty Census, and the School Enrollment data, respectively, for the remainder of the paper.) Tests for the differences between proportions were used to detect instances in which service sector proportions differed from proportions in the comparison groups. A strict correction for multiple analyses was used to reduce the likelihood of Type I errors ($p = 0.05/60 = 0.0008$). When significant differences in the proportions were present, a service sector proportion larger than the comparison group proportion was interpreted as overrepresentation and a service sector proportion smaller than the comparison group proportion was interpreted as underrepresentation.

Results

The patterns of representation varied greatly, depending on the racial/ethnic group as well as the comparison group. In order to facilitate understanding of racial/ethnic patterns across the five sectors, the data will be summarized for each racial/ethnic group, with differences between comparison groups noted accordingly. The results of the study are summarized in Table 13.1.

African Americans
African Americans were overrepresented in four of the five service sectors (child welfare, mental health, juvenile justice, and ED), regardless of the comparison group. However, they were present at expected rates in the alcohol/drug treatment sector across comparison groups. It should be noted that in all cases, the rates of overrepresentation were reduced when socioeconomic status was taken into account by using the 200 percent Poverty Census comparison group.

Asian/Pacific Islander Americans
For each of our comparison groups, Asian/Pacific Islander Americans were underrepresented in the child welfare, mental health, and ED sectors. However, they were present at the expected rate in the alcohol/drug treatment sector for all three comparison groups and also in the juvenile justice sector when compared to the Full Census and 200 percent Poverty Census estimates.

Caucasian Americans
Patterns shifted dramatically for the Caucasian Americans depending on the comparison group. When looking at the Full Census data, Caucasian Americans were underrepresented in child welfare, mental health, and juvenile justice, represented at the expected rates in alcohol/drug treatment, and overrepresented in ED. However, when using the 200 percent Poverty Census, this pattern nearly reversed, with overrepresentation indicated in the alcohol/drug treatment, child welfare, mental health, and ED sectors, and representation at expected rates in the juvenile justice sector. The comparisons with School Enrollment data roughly followed the

Table 13.1   Racial/ethnic sector representation with three comparison groups

Racial/ethnic group by sector	Racial/ethnic sector N over total sector N	Proportion of sector from racial/ethnic group	Proportion of racial/ethnic group in 1996 Full Census Estimates	Proportion of racial/ethnic group in 1996 200% Poverty Census Estimates	Proportion of racial/ethnic group in 1997 School Enrollment Data
African Americans (N = 2539)					
Alcohol/Drug	26/305	.09	.07	.11	.09
Child Welfare	1230/4272	.29	.07↑	.11↑	.09↑
Mental Health	770/4227	.18	.07↑	.11↑	.09↑
Juvenile Justice	726/3639	.20	.07↑	.11↑	.09↑
SED	485/1980	.25	.07↑	.11↑	.09↑
Asian/Pacific Islander Americans (N = 546)					
Alcohol/Drug	33/305	.11	.09	.10	.11
Child Welfare	107/4272	.03	.09↓	.10↓	.11↓
Mental Health	192/4227	.05	.09↓	.10↓	.11↓
Juvenile Justice	319/3639	.09	.09	.10	.11↓
SED	43/1980	.02	.09↓	.10↓	.11↓
Caucasian Americans (N = 4642)					
Alcohol/Drug	128/305	.42	.49	.30↑	.45
Child Welfare	1759/4272	.41	.49↓	.30↑	.45↓
Mental Health	1789/4227	.42	.49↓	.30↑	.45↓
Juvenile Justice	1030/3639	.28	.49↓	.30	.45↓
SED	1129/1980	.57	.49↑	.30↑	.45↑
Latinos (N = 3421)					
Alcohol/Drug	115/305	.38	.32	.48↓	.34
Child Welfare	1064/4272	.25	.32↓	.48↓	.34↓
Mental Health	1305/4227	.31	.32	.48↓	.34↓
Juvenile Justice	1460/3639	.40	.32↑	.48↓	.34↑
SED	294/1980	.15	.32↓	.48↓	.34↓

Note:
- Column 3 contains the proportion of each sector that was from a particular racial/ethnic group. This number is compared to the proportions of that racial/ethnic group in each comparison group (Full Census, 200% Poverty Census, and School Enrollment). If the comparison is significant at the 0.0008 level, the direction of the difference is noted (↑ indicates significant overrepresentation and ↓ indicates significant underrepresentation).
- Columns do not add to 100% due to the exclusion of children whose race/ethnicity was not known or of a group outside of those examined in this study.

trends found with the Full Census data: underrepresentation in the child welfare, mental health, and juvenile justice sectors, representation at expected rates in the alcohol/drug treatment sector, and overrepresentation in the ED sector. The only consistent trend across comparison groups was that of overrepresentation in the ED sector.

Latinos

The comparisons for Latinos using the Full Census and School Enrollment data were similar, reflecting underrepresentation of Latinos in the child welfare and ED sectors, overrepresentation in the juvenile justice sector, and representation at the expected rate in the alcohol/drug treatment sector. In the mental health sector, Latinos were represented at the expected rate compared with Full Census, but were underrepresented compared with School Enrollment data. When the 200 percent Poverty Census was used, Latinos were underrepresented in all five service sectors.

DISCUSSION

This study indicates that patterns of child service representation vary widely between racial/ethnic groups across five public service sectors. Further, it demonstrates that findings regarding the issue of over- or underrepresentation can be altered considerably depending on the comparison group used to determine representation. For example, Caucasian Americans in the child welfare sector were underrepresented when compared to the Full Census estimates and School Enrollment Data, and overrepresented when using the 200 percent Poverty Census estimates. Striking differences in findings depending on the comparison group used illustrate the importance of selecting appropriate comparisons that control for factors that may affect utilization, such as poverty status, insurance coverage, and relative youth of the ethnic group (Stolp and Warner, 1987). Future studies should carefully consider the implications of the comparison group chosen, as this appears to have a strong influence on the conclusions drawn about service use patterns.

As stated above, a rationale exists for each of the three comparison groups included in this study. However, we place the greatest confidence in the findings obtained when using the 200 percent Poverty Estimates for most sectors, because children who utilize the public system of care are more likely to be of low socioeconomic status than children in the general population. Because SES is highly confounded with ethnicity (Hewlett, 1991; US Census, 1990), using full Census data as the comparison group is likely to cause us to overestimate expected use by the 'majority' and underestimate expected service use by 'minority' children in this population. The one exception to this is the ED sector, where school enrollment data may provide a more appropriate comparison group because all ED children in the public schools are drawn from the larger universe of children enrolled in the public schools. Therefore, the discussion of racial/ethnic representation across all sectors will focus on the racial/ethnic proportions found in the 1996 200 percent Poverty Census estimates and additional information will be provided about representation within the ED sector compared with 1997 School Enrollment Data.

African Americans

Using the 200 percent Poverty Census estimates as a comparison point, African Americans were overrepresented in four of the five public sectors in this study. The finding of overrepresentation in the juvenile justice sector was not surprising, given reports that African Americans are overrepresented at various stages of the detention process (Conley, 1994; Pope and Feyerherm, 1995; Wordes et al., 1994). The higher than expected rates of mental health service use are consistent with studies on adult populations, suggesting similar processes may be present for both adults and children in this sector (Sue et al., 1991). In the child welfare sector, which has no adult parallel, African American children were present at 264 percent of the expected rate. The possibility that over-identification is occurring with this population should be considered, as these findings are consistent with those of other studies. African American children were also represented at 227 percent of the expected rate in the ED service sector. When representation of this group was compared with the School Enrollment Census, similar results were obtained, with African American children being represented at 278 percent of the expected rate in ED services. These findings point to the need for information about how children are referred and identified for school services. More specifically, the question of 'where' in this process disproportion occurs must be asked. Is there racial/ethnic disproportion among the population initially referred to SST by teachers? Are there disparities in those students referred from SST for special education evaluation? Is there disparity in the population of students that qualify as ED based on the special education assessment? Last, are there racial and ethnic disparities in the placement of students with ED into classrooms/programs and differences in service access and service use?

Research has suggested that overrepresentation of African Americans in the ED disability category may be the result of teacher expectations regarding normative behavior (Horowitz et al., 1998; Metz, 1994). For instance, patterns of eye contact, physical contact, use of language, and ways of responding to authority figures may differ among ethnic groups (Hallahan and Kaufman, 2000). It is clear that teachers are the primary gatekeepers in the referral and identification process, and they are more likely to refer and identify students who exhibit externalizing behaviors over students with internalizing types of behavior (Gresham et al., 1996). In addition, the paucity of culturally sensitive and linguistically appropriate assessment instruments has also been identified as a possible cause of racial/ethnic disparity (Harry, 1994). More pressing still is the question of whether the number of African American students identified as ED is in proportion to those whose achievement or behavior indicates a need for special supports and services (Donovan and Cross, 2002).

The one exception to the general trend of overrepresentation was in the alcohol/drug treatment sector, where African Americans were present at the expected rates. Possible explanations for this finding include that of lower epidemiological rates of problematic alcohol and/or drug use in the African American population as compared to youth in general, or a lower rate of referral to alcohol/drug treatment services by particular gatekeeping or referral agencies.

Asian/Pacific Islander Americans

The Asian/Pacific Islander American group displayed an interesting pattern of service representation compared with the 200 percent Poverty Census estimates. This population was represented at the expected rate in both alcohol/drug treatment and juvenile justice sectors that contain adolescents with serious behavioral problems and underrepresented in all other sectors. In fact, representation in the sectors most often associated with voluntary entry was extremely low: 50 percent of the expected rate for the mental health sector, and 20 percent of the expected rate for ED programs (findings for ED representation were similar when compared with School Enrollment data). Asian/Pacific Islander American presence in the child welfare sector was also very low, at approximately 30 percent of the expected rate.

These findings suggest that Asian/Pacific Islander Americans in this community are indeed experiencing difficulties, as evidenced by their presence in the alcohol/drug treatment and juvenile justice sectors. However, it is possible that they may not be entering voluntary services in the early stages of problem development due to factors such as cultural barriers. In addition, our finding that Asian/Pacific Islander American youth are represented at the expected rate in the juvenile justice and alcohol/drug treatment sectors is surprising, given that past investigations have found this group to be underrepresented across sectors. This may be due to the fact that the Asian/Pacific Islander American community in San Diego includes a substantial South East Asian population that has endured war and refugee-related traumas and whose acculturation level may be low. Exposure to war-related violence and trauma may increase the risk of problem behaviors among these youth. Future studies are needed to address the specific service use patterns of these and other Asian/Pacific Islander American subgroups in this sample.

Caucasian Americans

Using the 200 percent Poverty Census estimates as a comparison, Caucasian Americans were found to be overrepresented across four of the five sectors of care. Caucasian Americans were also overrepresented in ED services when compared with the School Enrollment data. These findings make intuitive sense when cultural factors are taken into consideration. Caucasian Americans as a group may be more familiar with the concept of mental health services, and this familiarity may facilitate greater use of mental health and ED programs when compared to other racial/ethnic groups. The overrepresentation in the alcohol/drug treatment sector is consistent with epidemiological studies that find a high rate of drug use for this racial/ethnic group (Center for Disease Control, 1998). However, the presence of Caucasian Americans at higher than expected rates in the child welfare sector has not been found in other investigations and bears further exploration (Courtney et al., 1996). It should be noted that this overrepresentation is only apparent when SES is taken into account by using the 200 percent Poverty Census estimates as a comparison point.

Latinos

Latinos were present at lower than expected rates across all five sectors when compared with the 200 percent Poverty Census. This finding was anticipated for more voluntary services such as mental health and ED programs, where past studies of Latino adults (Hough et al., 1987; Padgett et al., 1994; Sue et al., 1991) and adolescents (Bui and Takeuchi, 1992) point to mental health care underuse. Many barriers to mental health service utilization have been identified for Latinos, including lack of insurance or mental health coverage, lack of bilingual and bicultural therapy providers, culturally-based negative attitudes towards mental health treatment, and lack of provider sensitivity to culturally diverse populations (Woodward et al., 1992). It was not surprising, then, that Latinos were present at about 65 percent of the rate that would be expected in the mental health sector. The extent to which Latinos were underrepresented in ED services in the public schools was also dramatic: Latinos were present at 31 percent of the expected rate in the ED sector compared with the 200 percent Poverty Census and at 44 percent of the expected rate compared with the School Enrollment Census. Also surprising was the fact that Latino youth were also underrepresented in the juvenile justice sector, given evidence of arrest bias (Wordes et al., 1994; Pope and Feyerherm, 1995). Latino youth were underrepresented in alcohol/drug treatment, which is disconcerting given that epidemiological findings indicate a need for services that is as great or greater than that of Caucasian Americans (Bachman et al., 1991; Center for Disease Control, 1998; Maddahian et al., 1986; Welte and Barnes, 1987).

Further research is necessary to explain the factors responsible for the patterns found by this study. It is possible that prevalence rates of emotional/behavioral disorders and/or child maltreatment may vary across racial/ethnic groups, thus accounting for differential service use patterns based upon need. For example, one racial/ethnic group may experience higher levels of psychological distress than another due to a unique stressor (for example, refugee status, discrimination) or a racial/ethnic group may differ from others in the incidence of a particular psychological problem (for example, high rates of drug abuse or major depression). Differential exposure of one racial/ethnic group over another to living environments which are less supportive of early cognitive and emotional development (lead exposure, poor nutrition), or perhaps entrance into disadvantaged settings (low income schools, fewer experienced teachers, lack of high-quality instruction) may also influence the types of care needed and used.

Another possibility is the existence of racial/ethnic variation in the use of alternative mental health services (for example, religious personnel, spiritual healers, and so on). In this case, disorder prevalence rates may be similar across racial/ethnic groups, but representation across sectors would differ due to varying use of these resources. Alternatively, referral patterns for services may differ across racial/ethnic groups. For example, parents of varying cultural backgrounds may have differing cultural thresholds for symptomatology (Weisz et al., 1988), varying beliefs about mental health and the causes of mental illness (Araneta, 1993; Griffith and Baker, 1993; Kim, 1993; Martinez, 1993), varying parenting practices and beliefs about what constitutes child abuse (Yamamoto et al., 1993), and differing levels of tolerance for substance abuse (Perez-Arce, 1994), that may influence the chances of entering a service sector. Additionally, service sector gatekeepers such as school personnel, health care workers, law enforcement personnel, and social workers may refer or detain children from certain racial/ethnic groups differentially due to discrimination or other factors such as the perception that families will not be receptive to referrals. With respect to the school sector, there exists great variability in how children are classified by individual schools into the disability categories (MacMillan and Reschly, 1998). Identification rates of ED may differ substantially from state to state, and district to district, due to ambiguity of the federal definition of ED, financial constraints of school districts, and hesitation to use pejorative labels such as ED, which results in classification in the learning disabilities category instead (Duncan et al., 1995; Gresham et al., 1996; Lambros et al., 1998; Lopez et al., 1996). It appears that in schools disproportion becomes more common when the disability categories are more subjective in nature (for example, emotional disturbance, mild mental retardation) compared with those that are biologically determined (MacMillan and Reschly, 1998). Finally, even if a referral is made, access to services may also vary for each racial/ethnic group (Takeuchi et al., in press) and cultural factors may dictate acceptance of voluntary services or the ability to negotiate legal and school systems. For example, the general trend of overrepresentation for Caucasian Americans in voluntarily entered sectors of care (that is, mental health and school ED) may reflect greater familiarity with and cultural acceptance of mental health and related services in this group. A similar trend of representation in these sectors at higher than expected rates was present for African Americans, who are also likely to be familiar with services. In contrast, the two racial/ethnic groups studied with general trends of underrepresentation across voluntarily entered sectors are those where a higher proportion of immigrant families may be present. Further exploration of cultural factors in service use patterns is needed, taking into account potential differences in service access and delivery across sectors.

CONCLUSION

It is interesting to note that when using the 200 percent Poverty Census for comparisons, no racial/ethnic group showed both under- and overrepresentation in different sectors, each racial/ethnic group tended to be either over- or underrepresented across the five sectors when representation was not at expected rates. The reasons for these general patterns of representation require further examination. A possible hypothesis in need of further study is that entry into one service sector may open the door to other sectors and lead to referrals for additional services.

Several limitations to this study bear mention. First, although great effort was made to find an appropriate comparison group that took into account socioeconomic status, other factors such as insurance status (Stolp and Warner, 1987) were not controlled. Second, many children may enter services through the primary care sector (Burns et al., 1992), and this study would have been enhanced by the availability of such data. Third, the racial/ethnic categories in this study did not allow for examination of the heterogeneity within each group. For example, although the Latino group can be largely characterized as Mexican American (SANDAG, 1995), this group also included individuals from other national groups including Cuban, Puerto Rican, South American, and so on. The Asian/Pacific Islander American population is even more heterogeneous, with individuals from numerous countries including the Philippines, Vietnam, Laos, Cambodia, China, Korea, India, Samoa, and Japan, among others. This data does not allow for the examination of representation rates for ethnic 'subgroups' in the various sectors. Research conducted by Phinney concluded that it may be insightful to 'unpack the variable of ethnicity' (1996: 918) and differences in social class, income, education, generation of immigration, geographical region, and family structure that are present in families with the same ethnic label. Regarding the issue of over- and underrepresentation, isolating the specific aspects of ethnicity that impact referral, identification and placement into services may be valuable. This limitation may be particularly relevant for minority students in school sectors, where ethnicity determination is haphazardly made and there exists no uniform district or state guidelines (MacMillan and Reschly, 1998). Typically, on school forms, only one box can be checked and multi-racial children are often checked as 'Other', which further confounds analyses for this population of students. As the population continues to diversify racially and ethnically, the use of ethnicity as a variable will be ever more complicated and perplexing. Fourth, the lack of measures of important characteristics that may mediate the relationship between ethnicity and service use, such as acculturation, prevalence rates, referral patterns, cultural beliefs, and provider characteristics, prevents us from drawing conclusions about the factors that account for the observed patterns. Fifth, insufficient information about those in the 'Other' or 'Unknown' categories led to their exclusion from this study. Sixth, researchers must consider that an accurate understanding of the problem of disproportionate representation requires desegregation by gender (Coutinho et al., 2002), especially for the ED category which predominately consists of males. In addition, examination of age differences in gender/ethnic disproportionality rates is also suggested (Coutinho et al., 2002) and may shed light on how racial/ethnic disparities arise (in preschool, elementary, or middle school, and so on). Finally, our data did not include private service sectors, limiting the generalizability of our findings to public service system users. Future studies addressing these issues are needed.

This study provides information important to understanding racial/ethnic representation for children in public care sectors, when compared to a census estimate of comparable socioeconomic status. Racial/ethnic patterns of representation were examined in a large database with comprehensive data from multiple sectors, with a greater understanding of these patterns possible due to the breadth of sectors studied. The heterogeneity and size of the population allowed for comparisons between racial/ethnic groups. Further, this study illustrates the need to use comparison groups that take into account salient factors of the population. Future research is needed to elucidate the factors leading to the patterns of representation found in this study in order to facilitate the delivery of services to children in need.

NOTES

1 Portions of this chapter are from 'Racial/ethnic representation across five public sectors of care for youth', by K.M. McCabe, M. Yeh, R.L. Hough, J. Landsverk, M.S. Hurlburt, S.W. Culver and B. Reynolds (1999) *Journal of Emotional and Behavioral Disorders*, 7: 72–82. Copyright 1999 by PRO-ED, Inc. Reprinted with permission.

2 The research presented in this chapter was supported by National Institute of Mental Health (NIMH) Grant U01 MH55282. The preparation of this chapter was supported by NIMH Research Scientist Development Awards KO1 MH 01767 and KO1 MH 01924.

3 The state-funded Fee For Service Medicaid program data are not presented in this study because race/ethnicity could not be determined for a substantial number of youth (33%), due in large part to missing data. Separate analyses conducted with the inclusion of this database yielded results similar to those excluding Fee for Service data.

REFERENCES

Aponte, J. and Crouch, R.T. (1995) 'The changing ethnic profile of the United States', in J.F. Aponte, R.Y, Rivers and J. Wohl (eds), *Psychological Interventions and Cultural Diversity*. Needham Heights, MA: Allyn and Bacon, pp. 1–18.

Araneta, E.G., Jr. (1993) 'Psychiatric care of Filipino Americans', in A.C. Gaw (ed.), *Culture, Ethnicity, and Mental Illness*. Washington, DC: American Psychiatric Press. pp. 377–411.

Bachman, J.G., Wallace, J.M., O'Malley, P.M., Johnston, L.D., Kurth, C.L. and Neighbors, H.W. (1991) 'Racial/ethnic differences in smoking, drinking, and illicit drug use among American high school seniors', *American Journal of Public Health*, 81: 372–7.

Barnes, G.M. and Welte, J.W. (1986) 'Adolescent alcohol abuse: Subgroup differences and relationships to other problem behaviors', *Journal of Adolescent Research*, 1: 79–94.

Brandenburg, N., Friedman, R. and Silver, S. (1990) 'The epidemiology of childhood psychiatric disorders: Prevalence findings from recent studies', *Journal of the American Academy of Child and Adolescent Psychiatry*, 29: 76–83.

Bui, K. and Takeuchi, D.T. (1992) 'Ethnic minority adolescents and the use of community mental health care services', *American Journal of Community Psychology*, 20: 403–417.

Burns, B.J. (1991) 'Mental health service use by adolescents in the 1970s and 1980s', *Journal of the American Academy of Child and Adolescent Psychiatry*, 30 (1): 144–50.

Burns, B.J., Angold, A. and Costello, E.J. (1992) 'Measuring child, adolescent, and family service use', in L. Bickman and D. Rog (eds), *Evaluating Mental Health Services for Children*. San Francisco, CA: Jossey Bass. pp. 17–30.

Burns, B.J., Costello, E.J., Angold, A., Tweed, D., Stangl, D., Farmer, E.M.Z. and Erkanli, A. (1995) 'Children's mental health service use across service sectors', *Health Affairs*, 14 (3): 147–59.

Caron, C. and Rutter, M. (1991) 'Comorbidity in child psychopathology: Concepts, issues and research strategies', *Journal of Child Psychopathology and Psychiatry*, 32: 1063–80.

Center for Disease Control (1998) *Youth Risk Behavior Surveillance: United States, 1997.* MMWR Volume 47, #SS3. pp. 1–92.

Cheung, F.K. and Snowden, L.R. (1990) 'Community mental health and ethnic minority populations', *Community Mental Health Journal*, 26: 277–91.

Conley, D.J. (1994) 'Adding color to a black and white picture: Using qualitative data to explain racial disproportionality in the juvenile justice system', *Journal of Research in Crime and Delinquency*, 31: 135–48.

Courtney, M.E., Barth, R.P., Berrick, J.D., Brooks, D., Needell, B. and Park, L. (1996) 'Race and child welfare services: Past research and future directions', *Child Welfare*, 75: 99–135.

Coutinho, M.J., Oswald, D.P. and Forness, S.R. (2002) 'Gender and socio-demographic factors and the disproportionate identification of culturally and linguistically diverse students with emotional disturbance', *Behavioral Disorders*, 27 (2): 109–25.

Cross, T.L., Bazron, B.J., Dennis, K.W. and Isaacs, M.R. (1989) *Towards a Culturally Competent System of Care: A monograph on effective services for minority children who are severely emotionally disturbed*. Washington DC: National Institute of Mental Health, Child and Adolescent Service System Program.

Cullinan, D., Epstein, M.H. and Sabornie, E.J. (1992) 'Selected characteristics of a national sample of seriously emotionally disturbed adolescents', *Behavioral Disorders*, 17 (4): 273–80.

Donovan, M.S. and Cross, C. (2002) *Minority Students in Special and Gifted Education*. Washington, DC: National Academy Press.

Duncan, B.B., Forness, S.R. and Hartsough, C. (1995) 'Students identified as seriously emotionally disturbed in school-based day treatment: Cognitive, psychiatric, and special education characteristics', *Behavioral Disorders*, 20 (4): 238–52.

Forness, S.R., Kavale, K.A., King, B.H. and Kasari, C. (1994) 'Simple versus complex conduct disorders: Identification and phenomenology', *Behavioral Disorders*, 19 (4): 306–312.

Friedman, R.M., Kutash, K. and Duchnowski, A.J. (1996) 'The population of concern: Defining the issues', in B. Stroul and R. Friedman (eds), *Children's Mental Health: Creating Systems of Care in a Changing Society*. Baltimore, MD: Brookes. pp. 69–96.

Garland, A. and Besinger, B. (1997) 'Racial/ethnic differences in court referred pathways to mental health services for children in foster care', *Children and Youth Services Review*, 19: 1–17.

Garland, A.F., Hough, R.L., McCabe, K.M., Yeh, M., Wood P.A. and Aarons, G.A. (2001) 'Prevalence of psychiatric disorders in youth across five sectors of care', *Journal of the American Academy of Child and Adolescent Psychiatry*, 40 (4): 409–418.

Gilliam, J.E. and Scott, B.K. (1987) 'The behaviorally disordered offender', in R. Rutherford, C. Nelson and B. Wolford (eds), *Special Education in Correctional Education*. Columbus, OH: Merrill.

Gresham, F.M., MacMillan, D. and Bocian, K. (1996) 'Behavioral earthquakes: Low frequency, salient behavior events that differentiate students at-risk for behavioral disorders', *Behavioral Disorders*, 21 (4): 277–92.

Griffith, E.E.H. and Baker, F.M. (1993) 'Psychiatric care of African Americans', in A.C. Gaw (eds), *Culture, Ethnicity, and Mental Illness*. Washington, DC: American Psychiatric Press. pp. 147–73.

Gunter-Justice, T.D. and Ott, D.A. (1997) 'Who does the family court refer for psychiatric services?', *Journal of Forensic Science*, 42: 1102–1104.

Hallahan, D.P. and Kauffman, J.M. (2000) *Exceptional Learners: Introduction to Special Education* (8th edn). Boston, MA: Allyn and Bacon.

Harry, B. (1994) *The Disproportionate Representation of Minority Students in Special Education: Theories and Recommendations*. Alexandria, VA: Project FORUM, National Association of State Directors of Special Education.

Hewlett, S.A. (1991) *When the Bough Breaks: The Cost of Neglecting Our Children*. New York: Basic Books.

Hodgkinson, H.L. (1995) 'What should we call people? Race, class, and the Census for 2000', *Phi Delta Kappan*, 77: 173–9.

Horowitz, S.M., Bility, K.M., Plichta, S.B., Leaf, P.J. and Haynes, N. (1998) 'Teacher's assessments of behavioral disorders', *American Journal of Orthopsychiatry.*

Hough, R.L., Landsverk, J.A. and Karno, M. (1987) 'Utilization of health and mental health services by Los Angeles Mexican-American and Non-Latino Whites', *Archives of General Psychiatry*, 44: 702–9.

Kauffman, J.M. (1997) *Characteristics of Emotional and Behavioral Disorders of Children and Youth* (6th edn). Columbus, OH: Prentice-Hall.

Kim, L.I.C. (1993) 'Psychiatric care of Korean Americans', in A.C. Gaw (eds), *Culture, Ethnicity, and Mental Illness*. Washington, DC: American Psychiatric Press. pp. 347–75.

Krisberg, B., DeComo, R. and Herrera, N. (1992) *National Juvenile Custody Trends 1978–1989*. (OJJDP Publication No. NCJ 131649) Washington DC: US Department of Justice.

Lambros, K.M., Ward, S.L., Bocian, K.M., Macmillan, D. and Gresham, F. (1998) 'Behavioral profiles of children at-risk for emotional and behavioral disorders: Implications for assessment and classification', *Focus on Exceptional Children*, 30 (5): 1-16.

Leone, P.E. (1991) *Alcohol and Other Drug Use by Adolescents with Disabilities*. (ERIC Document Reproduction Service No. ED 340 150). Reston, VA: Council for Exceptional Children.

Lindsey, D. (1991) 'Factors affecting the foster care placement decision: An analysis of national survey data', *American Journal of Orthopsychiatry*, 61: 272–81.

Longshore, D., Hsieh, S., Anglin, M.D. and Annon, T.A. (1992) 'Ethnic patterns in drug abuse treatment utilization', *Journal of Mental Health Administration*, 19: 268–77.

Lopez, M.F., Forness, S.R., MacMillan, D.L., Bocian, K.M. and Gresham, F.M. (1996) 'Children with attention deficit hyperactivity disorder and emotional or behavioral disorders in primary grades: Inappropriate placement in the learning disability category', *Education and Treatment of Children*, 19 (3): 286–99.

MacMillan, D. and Reschly, D. (1998) 'Overrepresentation of minority students: The case for greater specificity or reconsideration of the variables examined', *Journal of Special Education*, 32 (1): 15–24.

Maddahian, E., Newcomb, M.D. and Bentler, P.M. (1986) 'Adolescents' substance use: Impact of ethnicity, income, and availability', *Advances in Alcohol and Substance Abuse*, 5: 63–78.

Marder, C. (1992) 'Secondary school students classified as seriously emotionally disturbed: How are they being served?' Paper presented at the meeting of the American Educational Research Association, April, San Francisco, CA.

Marder, C. and Cox, R. (1991) 'More than a label: Characteristics of youth with disabilities', in M. Wagner, L. Newman, R. D'Amico, E.D. Jay, P. Butler-Nalin, C. Marder and R. Cox (eds), *Youth with Disabilities: How are they doing? The first comprehensive report from the National Longitudinal Transition Study of Special Education Students*. Menlo Park, CA: SRI International.

Martinez, C., Jr. (1993) 'Psychiatric care of Mexican Americans', in A.C. Gaw (eds), *Culture, Ethnicity, and Mental Illness*. Washington, DC: American Psychiatric Press. pp. 431–66.

Metz, M.H. (1994) 'Desegration as necessity and challenge', *Journal of Negro Education*, 63 (1): 64–76.

Olsen, L. (1982) 'Services for minority children in out of home care', *Social Service Review*, 572–85.

Padgett, D.K., Patrick, C.P., Burns, B.J. and Schlesinger, H.J. (1994) 'Women and outpatient mental health services: Use by Black, Latino, and White women in a national insured population', *Journal of Mental Health Administration*, 21: 347–60.

Perez-Arce, P. (1994) 'Substance abuse patterns of Latinas: Commentary', *International Journal of the Addictions*, 29: 1189–99.

Phinney, J.S. (1996) 'When we talk about American ethnic groups, what do we mean?', *American Psychologist*, 51: 918–27.

Pope, C.E. and Feyerherm, W.F. (1990) 'Minority status and juvenile processing', *Criminal Justice Abstracts*, 22: 327–36.

Pope, C.E. and Feyerherm, W.F. (1995) *Minorities and the Juvenile Justice System* (OJJDP Publication No. NCJ 145849). Washington, DC: US Department of Justice.

Realmuto, G.M., Bernstein, G.A., Maglothin, M.A. and Pandey, R.A. (1992) 'Patterns of utilization of outpatient mental health services by children and adolescents', *Hospital and Community Psychiatry*, 43: 1218–23.

SANDAG: San Diego Association of Governments (1995) *Population Estimates by Age, Sex, and Ethnic Group*, 1 January.

Stolp, C. and Warner, D. (1987) 'Mental health service utilization of California hospitals by age, ethnicity, and sex, in 1983', in R. Rodriguez and M.T. Coleman (eds), *Mental Health Issues of the Mexican Origin Population in Texas: Proceedings of the 5th Robert Lee Sutherland Seminar in Mental Health*. Austin, TX: The Hogg Foundation for Mental Health. pp. 116–33.

Stroul, B.A. and Friedman, R.M. (1986) *A System of Care for Severely Emotionally Disturbed Children and Youth*. Washington, DC: CASSP Technical Assistance Center.

Sue, S. (1977) 'Community mental health services to minority groups: Some optimism, some pessimism', *American Psychologist*, 32: 616–24.

Sue, S., Fujino, D.C., Hu, L., Takeuchi, D.T. and Zane, N.W.S. (1991) 'Community mental health services for ethnic minority groups: A test of cultural responsiveness hypothesis', *Journal of Consulting and Clinical Psychology*, 59: 533–40.

Swaim, R.C., Beauvais, R., Chavez, E.L. and Oetting, E.R. (1997) 'The effect of school dropout rates on estimates of adolescent substance use among three racial/ethnic groups', *American Journal of Public Health*, 87: 51–5.

Takeuchi, D., Uehara, E. and Maramba, G. (in press) 'Cultural diversity and mental health treatment', in A. Horwitz and T. Scheid (eds), *The Sociology of Mental Health and Illness*. New York: Oxford. pp. 550–65.

Tuma, J.M. (1989) 'Mental health services for children: The state of the art', *American Psychologist*, 44: 188–9.

US Bureau of the Census (1990) *Census '90*. Washington, DC: Census Bureau.

US Bureau of the Census (1992) *Census of the Population and Housing 1990: Public Use Microdata Samples*. US (machine-readable data files)/prepared by the Bureau of the Census. Washington, DC: Author.

US Bureau of the Census (1995) *Statistical Abstracts of the US* (115th edn). Washington, DC: Author.

US Bureau of the Census (1997) 'Number and percentage of children under 19 years of age, at or below 200 percent of poverty, by state: Three-year averages for 1994, 1995, and 1996. *Current Population Surveys* (on-line). Available at: http://www.census.gov/ftp/publ/hhes/hlthins/lowinckid.html.

US Department of Education (1994) *Sixteenth Annual Report to Congress on the Implementation of the Individual with Disabilities Education Act*. Washington, DC: Author.

US Department of Education (2000) *Twenty-second Annual Report to Congress on the Implementation of the Individual with Disabilities Education Act*. Washington, DC: Author.

US Department of Education Office for Civil Rights (1994) *Elementary and Secondary School Compliance Report*. Washington, DC: Author.

US Department of Health and Human Services (2001) *Mental Health: Culture, Race and Ethnicity – A Supplement to Mental Health: A Report of the Surgeon General*. Rockville, MD: US Department of Health and Human Services, Substance Abuse and Mental Health Services Administration, Center for Mental Health Services.

US House of Representatives (1997) *Report No. 105–95*. Washington, DC: Author.

Wagner, M. (1995) 'Outcomes for youths with serious emotional disturbance in secondary school and early adulthood', *The Future of Children: Critical Issues for Children and Youths*, 5 (4): 90–112.

Wagner, M., Blackorby, J. and Hebbeler, K. (1993) *Beyond the Report Card: The Multiple Dimensions of Secondary School Performance of Students with Disabilities*. Menlo Park, CA: SRI International.

Weisz, J.R., Suwanlert, S., Chaiyasit, W., Weiss, B., Walter, B. R. and Anderson, W.W. (1988) 'Thai and American perspectives on over- and undercontrolled child behavior problems: Exploring the threshold model among parents, teachers, and psychologists', *Journal of Consulting and Clinical Psychology*, 56: 601–609.

Welte, J.W. and Barnes, G.M. (1987) 'Alcohol use among adolescent minority groups', *Journal of Studies on Alcohol*, 48: 329–36.

Westendorp, F., Brink, K.L., Roberson, M. and Ortiz, M.K. (1986) 'Variables which differentiate placement of adolescents into juvenile justice or mental health systems', *Adolescence*, 21: 23–30.

Woodward, A.M., Dwinell, A.D. and Arons, B.S. (1992) 'Barriers to mental health care for Latino Americans: A literature review and discussion', *Journal of Mental Health Administration*, 19: 224–36.

Wordes, M., Bynum, T.S. and Corley, C.J. (1994) 'Locking up youth: The impact of race on detention decisions', *Journal of Research in Crime and Delinquency*, 31: 149–65.

Yamamoto, J., Silva, J.A., Justice, L.R., Change, C.Y. and Leong, G.B. (1993) 'Cross-cultural psychotherapy', in A.C. Gaw (eds), *Culture, Ethnicity, and Mental Illness*. Washington, DC: American Psychiatric Press. pp. 101–124.

Zane, N., and Kim, J.H. (1994) 'Substance use and abuse', in Zane, N., Takeuchi, D. and Young, K.N.J. (eds), *Confronting Critical Health Issues of Asian and Pacific Islander Americans*. Thousand Oaks, CA: Sage. pp. 316–43.

Part Three

STRATEGIES AND INTERVENTIONS

14

Working with Children and Young People with Social, Emotional and Behavioural Difficulties: What Makes What Works, Work?

JOHN VISSER

Coming towards that stage in one's career when retirement is a whole lot nearer than the start of one's career, I have been reflecting on a professional life spent working with and for children and young people with social, emotional and behavioural difficulties (SEBD). That professional life has involved a lot of reading, visits to a great many and wide variety of institutions providing for these pupils, and the privilege of observing many gifted practioners successfully meeting their needs and the joy of dealing with the students themselves.

This period of reflection revealed a common question underlying many adults' questions when faced with children and young people with SEBD, and one which has been a common strand in my own professional development. That question is: 'What makes for the most proficient approach to meeting the needs of children and young people with social, emotional and behavioural difficulties?' Put succinctly: 'Why does what works, work?'

Preparation for this chapter also involved looking back through a multitude of conference papers, journal articles and books, as well as videos and DVDs, all of which purported to give if not *the* answer, then *an* answer as to what do to meet the needs of pupils with SEBD. This chapter doesn't aim to add to this plethora of advice but seeks to provide a contribution that looks at aspects of the medium rather than the means for successful working with these children and young people.

I want to use this chapter to explore the notion of there being 'eternal verities'; that is, core factors that must be present if any intervention is to meet successfully the needs of children and young people with SEBD. I will clarify my use of the terms 'approaches', 'SEBD' and 'pedagogue' in this chapter. I will then highlight some changes and developments illustrative of wheel reinvention, before going on to explore what could possibly constitute eternal verities and their importance.

CLARIFICATIONS

When working with colleagues, both in national or international contexts, I have always endeavoured to ensure that the terms we use have a shared understanding. This is particularly important in the field of SEBD: a professional arena that is littered with terms, such as 'delinquent', 'challenging', 'disaffected', 'phobic', 'disturbed', 'disordered', 'challenging', which each of us believes has a meaning shared by colleagues. This is a dangerous assumption to make, even between members of the same professional agency let alone the multi-professional readership of this chapter.

APPROACHES

The term 'approaches' is used to encompass policies, practices and provision in relation to children and young people and SEBD. To repeat endlessly the terms 'policy, practice and provision' would be a little tiresome. I have avoided the terms 'interventions' and 'treatment', both of which have connotations of adult power over youngsters. One of the keys to my success has, I believe, lain in the way I approach the child, which has been more important than the particular form of 'intervention' or 'treatment' I have decided to use.

DEFINING SEBD

Defining SEBD is at the best of times fraught with difficulties, as is pointed out in Daniels et al. (1998). Despite discussion by various writers (amongst them Warnock, 1978; Upton, 1978; Smith and Thomas, 1993;

and Cooper, 1996 in the United Kingdom; and Kauffman, 2001; Rosenburg et al., 1997, and Forness and Kavale, 2000 in the United States), SEBD remains an imprecise but professionally useful concept. David Wills (1971) referred to these pupils as the 'frightened, wounded, damaged and inadequate'. The definition within Circular 9/94 (DfE, 1994) seems to meet with the greatest consensus within England (Cole et al., 1999), that is, children and young people with SEBD range from:

> ...social maladaptation to abnormal emotional stresses ... are persistent and constitute learning difficulties, involve emotional factors and/or externalised disruptive behaviours; and general difficulties in forming 'normal' relationships. Social, psychological and sometimes biological factors, or commonly interactions between these three strands, are seen as causing pupils' EBD. (Circular, 1994: 7)

That definition covers those pupils I am concerned with in this chapter.

PEDAGOGUES

There are many different professional groups who work with pupils with SEBD; amongst them are educational psychologists, care workers, teachers, social workers and classroom assistants. All have a pedagogic role; they are pedagogues. Pedagogues are those whose role, according to Hayden Davis Jones, is to be concerned 'for the physical, emotional and educational well-being of the child' (Cole, 1997) For example, administrators and policymakers, parents, psychologists, social workers, and school advisors all contribute to a child's physical, emotional and educational well-being. As pointed out elsewhere, the important pedagogic role of support staff, care workers and classroom assistants needs to be emphasized (Cole et al., 1998). The term 'pedagogue' here, then, refers to all those working with and for children and young people with SEBD.

ETERNAL VERITIES

Arguing for eternal verities is not to argue that approaches in the past were always good and that there is no need for change and development. There is much to question, both in past as well as in current approaches. Many of the changes and developments made over the past 30 years have benefited children and young people with SEBD. Some changes have been subtle, yet reflect important shifts in the understanding of special educational needs and disabilities. As an example, it would now be inappropriate to use the descriptor 'the maladjusted child', implying as it does that maladjustment is a within-child 'condition' requiring 'treatment'. Given the increased awareness of the range of factors that are associated with SEBD, it is more appropriate to separate the child from the special educational need and talk of pupils *with* SEBD, ensuring that pedagogues at least see the child first and the descriptor afterwards. Another example of positive development would be the increased emphasis on working in partnership with parents and pupils; listening to the voice of the child. The latter something that Wills (1968, 1971) advocated and others (Cooper, 1993; Wise, 2000; Davie and Galloway, 1996) have shown is refulgent in arriving at approaches that effectively meet the needs of pupils with EBD as well as developing the skills, knowledge and understanding of pedagogues. The *Revised Code of Practice for the Identification and Assessment of Special Educational Needs* (DfES, 2001) requires the inclusion of the child in the assessment, identification and provision made for meeting his or her educational needs.

Nor should the concentration upon eternal verities be taken as a statement that there is no need for further research into the causes of and approaches needed by children and young people with SEBD. There is an increasing recognition of what constitutes 'good practice', particularly within England where schools have been subject to a rigorous inspection process. However, there remain many gaps in the knowledge and understanding of approaches as well as the reasons why there are children and young people with SEBD who continue to be a marginalized group within schooling and society. I am arguing that in any future changes and developments of approaches, if they are effective in meeting the needs of children and young people with SEBD you will find the eternal verities present.

DEVELOPMENTS AND CHANGES IN TERMINOLOGY AND APPROACHES

In England, 'maladjustment' served as the official descriptor for pupils with SEBD from around the time of the 1944 Education Act and gained further professional credence with publication of the Underwood Report (Ministry of Education, 1955) in the 1950s. It had some 40 years of useful life until it was replaced by emotional and behavioural difficulties (EBD) following the Warnock Report (1978). SEBD in its turn has served the field (in England) for over 20 years, and the winds of change are blowing with the draft revised SEN Code of Practice (DfES 2001) using the term 'social, emotional and behavioural difficulties' (SEBD). Maladjustment and SEBD are generic terms encompassing many other descriptors, such as 'delinquent', 'disaffected', 'disturbed', 'troublesome', 'challenging', each of which has come to the fore in the past as different aspects of SEBD have been focused upon. If the descriptors, and along with them the policies, practices and provisions, are changeable and yet the children and young people remain the same, the danger arises that in seeking 'new' solutions for new descriptors the essential factors in what works are lost sight of. The newly advocated approach is seen as the means by which successful outcomes can be achieved; all too often too little attention is paid to the medium through which those means are actioned.

Paralleling changes in descriptors have been changes in approaches. The last 20 years have seen an increase in the rate of that change and development with a seemingly constant stream of research, guidance, literature, policies and publication of strategies all purporting to give if not *the* answer, then certainly *an* answer on how best to meet the needs of children and young people with SEBD. Many of these changes and developments in approaches have been driven more by enthusiasm for the means than by evidence-based practice and with little or no attention drawn to the eternal verities which I will argue are embedded in the medium. Each change and development in approach is heralded as 'new'. Too often pedagogues accept these 'new' approaches without reference to their past incarnations. Their focus is usually seeking to replicate the structure and systems of the approach, not upon its underlying driving force, rather than melding the approach to the eternal verities that sustain any successful approach. What then happens is that when the success of the approach begins to fall away because it is not sustained by the verities, the approach is dumped and the stage is set for wheel reinvention.

WHEEL REINVENTION

There is within many of the changes and developments in approaches a strong tendency towards wheel reinvention (Dyson, 2001). When reinventing wheels, there is more focus upon the structure of the wheel than the reasons why wheels go round. The wheel often gets renamed, but basically it is the same wheel or a reincarnation of a previous one. The changes and developments in approaches are accepted by most pedagogues who see differences in terminology, structures and physical forms as more easily absorbed and capable of being put into practice than seeking to understand the metaphysics of the approach. The eternal verities are a part of the metaphysics of approaches. They are the pedagogues' motive force for making the approach work.

Each succeeding generation of pedagogues faces what they believe is an increase in either the severity of SEBD, or its incidence, or a mixture of both. They seek new answers. In doing so they begin with examining the cart that the wheel is attached to, seeking ways of improving that. Witness much of the school effectiveness literature (Sammons et al., 1995; McGilchrist et al., 1997). The interactions between the cart's driver, the cart's passengers and the motive force for moving the cart forward are often not examined to ensure that eternal verities are in place or in need of renewal.

Let us assume that the cart represents the approach advocated, the cart's drivers the pedagogues and the passengers are the children and young people. Redesigning the cart, developing better cart driving skills and enhancing the ability to be more precise over the identification of the passengers' needs will be important. But if little or no attention is paid to the source and reasons for movement, then little will be achieved in the long term. This is particularly so if no evidence base is drawn upon for deciding what makes for optimum performance in terms of achieving forward movement. Wheel reinvention, illustrated by these metaphors, is an expedient solution rather than a strategically planned tactic for the long-term resolution of the challenges that pupils with SEBD face.

As an example of wheel reinvention, examine the manner in which concern regarding children and young people's behaviour in schools and classrooms, as well as society at large, finds expression. This concern is perennial. Sometimes it has a generic focus and gives rise to documents such as the Elton Report (DES, 1989) and chapter seven in the English government's Green Paper (DfEE, 1997). At other times it has a particular focus, such as bullying (Galloway, 1994; Olweus, 1994; Sian et al., 1993) and exclusions (Hayden and Ward, 1997; Parsons, 1999). The former rose to prominence in the early 1990s and the latter as this century dawned.

As each generation of pedagogues takes to the field there appears to be a crescendo of such concern that usually sees expression in the national and educational press and is expressed as a decline in some notion of standards. The following sentence, or one very much like it, is repeated in the educational press as well as the wider media at least once every seven to ten years:

For the past __A__ a rising concern facing __B__ because of __C__ is a lack of __D__.

Where for A you insert a period of time, for B a particular group of pedagogues, for C insert any recent change in educational approaches, and for D insert one of the following: standards, behaviour, discipline, respect, order.

The reactions to these concerns usually result in searches for the 'answer' by teachers, administrators and politicians. This process usually takes the form of someone or body with a pedagogue's authority indicating that:

> While the concern expressed is real there are pockets of 'good practice' here or abroad which do not have this difficulty or do not have it in such abundance.

This 'pocket' is hailed as a *new* approach and is then put forward as either the answer or more cautiously as an answer. A recent example in England is the *Social Inclusion: Pupil Support* (SIPS) Circular 10/99 (DfEE, 1999). It has many admirable qualities and strengths in the guidance it gives. However, it puts forward as exemplars of good practice some approaches as though they are new approaches. For example, in-school centres and pupil referral units are advocated as an answer to halting the social exclusion of young people, without so much as a backward glance to their previous incarnations. Centres and Units were approaches in England that were tried and tested in the 1970s (ACE, 1980; Galway, 1979; HMI, 1978; Jones, 1973). There are accounts in the Underwood Report (Ministry of Education, 1955) of them being in place in the 1950s within London as 'tutorial units'. The evidence from these earlier incarnations points to their potential strengths and to the limitations of their ability to meet the needs of all pupils with SEBD. Perhaps this lack of reference to earlier incarnations is deliberate, as it would appear that these approaches are not seen as having a long life expectancy. As with so many other exemplar approaches, particularly those espoused by central policymakers, they are only funded for short periods through mechanisms such as the English Government's 'Standard Funds' (Cole et al., 2000). A similar argument could be advanced for the guidance offered to use Assertive Discipline. Short-term funded projects do little to encourage the application of the eternal verities since they are aimed at achieving narrow short-term goals, such as reducing truancy over three years. Inevitably such short-termism begs the question 'And then what?'.

The literature as a whole pays little attention to the 'how' of an approach; the focus is rather on the 'what' and 'when' of the approach. Research particularly has a tendency to seek evidence that focuses upon the identification of structures and systems, missing out the part played by the eternal verities which sustain them. There is a propensity for commissioned research to deliver quick, uncomplicated headline 'answers' to what are complex questions. This research often focuses upon what sort of 'wheel' is required in terms of structures and systems and how they are to be replicated. Seldom, if ever, are the underlying eternal verities explicitly part of the research brief. They are frequently left to be inferred by the reader, and at worst are not seen as important to the achievement of successful outcomes. Acknowledging the importance of eternal verities in achieving successful outcomes might go some way to stopping the need for wheel reinvention.

As I hope to show, asking how the eternal verities are a part of the approaches utilized might enable these to be more readily assimilated by pedagogues. At the very least, a restatement of eternal verities should form part of any dissemination of 'new' and current approaches. This might produce wheels that are capable of a more proficient forward movement. It might also provide pedagogues with a set of criteria against which they can assess the value of different approaches and thus build up an evidence base of what works for them.

'Eternal verities' is not a term that is often seen in educational publications. Wills (1968) referred to the need for the pedagogue to have a faith based upon 'the unchanging and eternal verities' if he or she is to survive the stresses involved in working with pupils with SEBD. As with so many other professional terms, I am unclear where I first came across it. Somewhere in the mists of my professional work I heard it used and assimilated it into my professional thoughts. It is a term used more in oral discourses than in the literature. As such it is associated with the language of interactions, rather than systems and structures.

The term resonates with a personal quest for an underlying set of unifying principles within all approaches. Is there a set of principles that are seldom enunciated, associated with good practice, which, to quote Whelan and Kauffman (1999), are the field's 'memory banks', subliminally passed on to each succeeding generation of proficient pedagogues?

As a teacher of pupils with EBD I faced contradictions, as I perceived them, between the various approaches put forward as ways of meeting these pupil's needs. Some of the approaches seemed to me to be diametrically opposed to each other. As a young teacher struggling to do what was right for the pupils in my charge, which should I choose? What could ensure that the approach chosen would work?

Amongst the many institutions I have visited over the years, two are vividly imprinted because the visits occurred close together. One espoused a behavioural approach and one had a psychodynamic basis for its work. Both were perceived at that time as schools of good practice. It was evident that they were both successful in meeting the needs of pupils with SEBD. Which should I choose to use in my own approach to working with pupils with SEBD? Were there common underlying factors/ principles/beliefs that accounted for this success? Are there eternal verities which are a part of all successful approaches? The DNA of approaches? Just as cells within the human body perform different functions but contain the same DNA, are there eternal verities which are to be found in all proficient approaches?

WHAT IS AN ETERNAL VERITY?

Verities are truths that are apparent in the web and weave of approaches. They are eternal in as much as they are necessary to the proficiency of all approaches regardless of the timeframe in which the approaches are being developed and applied. They are the strongest links between different approaches and the achievement of successful outcomes. As such they carry values and beliefs about the human condition and the quality of life to which we, and especially pupils with SEBD, are entitled. They are rarely made explicit, often emerging implicitly from literature, discussion and research. They are observable, but their quantification is seldom helpful and may ultimately be impossible. Having more or less of them is not so much the issue as their quality and presence within an approach. They sustain pedagogues in times of stress and good practice flows from them.

The list that follows is not a definitive one. It is a list in the making. It is idiosyncratic and needs to be tested out by pedagogues if it is to be of use in the future. The list may not coincide with one that the reader may draw up in a particular national or cultural setting, though I would be surprised if there were no overlaps.

This list of eternal verities has drawn on three sources. The first is experiences as a pedagogue in a variety of settings: from the classroom to researcher and provider of staff development programmes, and from parent to foster parent. The second is from involvement with pedagogues in a number of research and consultancy projects. The third comes from a review of the literature, which describes the various understandings and perspectives of emotional and behavioural difficulties. Among these I have drawn particularly on the work of Ayers et al. (2000), ERIC (1997), Laslett et al. (1998), Whelan and Kauffman (1999), Porter (2000) and Kauffman (2001). These writers offer the reader a comprehensive view of the variety of approaches to be found in SEBD work, both in England and the United States, and thus provide one basis for seeking possible eternal verities. The SEBD research team of which I am a member has also provided summaries of perspectives and approaches in the research reports we have published (see, for example, Daniels et al., 1998; Daniels et al., 1999; Visser and Bedward, 1999; Cole et al., 1999; Cole et al., 2000; Cole et al., 2001; Daniels et al., 2003; and Visser, 2003).

A possible list of eternal verities would include the following, discussed in detail below:

- Behaviour can change; emotional needs can be met.
- Intervention is second to prevention.
- Instructional reactions.
- Transparency in communications.
- Empathy and equity.
- Boundaries and challenge.
- Building positive relationships.
- Humour.

Behaviour can change; emotional needs can be met

It may seem axiomatic that approaches are premised upon a belief that behaviour can change, social and emotional needs can be met. However, it is dangerous to assume that this is so. Meeting the needs of pupils with SEBD absorbs a large slice of any agency's budget, particularly in education. If approaches cannot meet needs and produce change, then should they be funded?

Having a belief in the ability of even the most damaged child's ability to change and develop into an acceptable adult (maybe with a great deal of support) sustains pedagogues' uses of any approach.

Behaviour is perceived by proficient pedagogues as capable of change, whether viewed as learnt behaviour or the result of internal, intra-physic forces or resulting from a medical condition or derived from interactions within a social context. This eternal verity views the actor as being capable of altering actions and it is the actions and their consequences for him or her that are seen as the focus of the approach. There is an understanding that to be human is not to be at the mercy of instincts or genetic make-up. This is apparent even in the re-emerging medical perspectives of aspects of SEBD, such as ADHD (Cooper, 2001). Nurture and the social context of the child or young person are viewed as important in the literature published over the past 30 years. Actors are seen as being able to attain control over their actions and emotional needs that have caused the SEBDs.

This belief in the possibility of change provides pedagogues with the ability to continue to work with children and young people when so often they reject the pedagogues' attempts to meet their needs. This quality, of going 'the extra half mile' because the behaviour can change the child, is held in high esteem even when their actions are not and is one seen as being necessary in pedagogues (Cole et al., 1998; Daniels et al., 2003). As Rodway pointed out:

However much (the child) wounds his own self-esteem (the child) cannot change the esteem in which (the pedagogue) holds him (if the approach is to be successful). (1993: 379; Rodway's parentheses)

Intervention is second to prevention

The history of nearly all approaches indicates that they have been derived from the identification of a 'difficulty' presented by a group of children or young people. The difficulties are identified before the approaches are developed. The interventions seek to meet the challenge presented by the identified difficulties. Publicizing the success of the intervention inevitably leads to the identification of 'fault lines' within the child's environment, be that school, home or community. At some, usually early, stage aspects of the approach are highlighted as being able to contribute to the prevention of SEBD in other children and young people. There is a sense of compensation in the approach, which suggests that had this or that aspect of the approach been present in the first instance, then this child or young person would not have 'developed' SEBD. All proficient approaches underscore the proverb 'Prevention is better than the cure.'

Much of the literature on how to manage classes well is derived from studies of the factors that make for poor classroom management (Visser, 2000; DES, 1989). Concerns about classroom management and pupils' behaviour have given rise to a number of manuals, training opportunities and administrative strategies which set out to correct poor teaching. Ensuring that teachers become aware of good classroom management strategies and skills during their teacher training has only recently come to the fore in England.

Approaches which ensure that preventive strategies are at least as strongly explicit as intervention strategies within the overall approach seem to me to have the greater possibility of achieving successful outcomes for pupils with SEBD (Visser, 2000).

Instructional reactions

Pupils with SEBD often do not understand the relationship between their behaviours and the reactions those behaviours cause. Few children set out with malice aforethought to be the disturbed and disturbing characters many of them become. When they do, it is to achieve some gratification or status that protects them. Proficient approaches recognize this and work consistently to portray to the child what the relationship is between cause and effect, and how they can achieve different reactions, which meet their needs. Just remonstrating with SEBD pupils or issuing sanctions for inappropriate behaviours has little effect, except perhaps to persuade the child not to get caught next time. Pedagogues who give the child the reasons why the behaviour is inappropriate together with alternative ways to react appropriately achieve more successful outcomes. Approaches which do not provide the child with alternative ways of behaving, making a desired social skill achievable or giving ways in which the emotion can be more appropriately expressed, haven't in my experience had very much success.

Transparency in communications

A consistent finding reported in the University of Birmingham's SEBD research team's work is the degree to which clear, consistent, coherent communications is an aspect in good practice schools (see, for example, Daniels et al., 1998; Cole et al., 1998; Daniels et al., 2003). Pedagogues in a variety of approaches always ensured that these aspects were there between all the players in given situations. Together they provided a transparency in communications. This in turn supports the development of a caring, learning and sharing school ethos in meeting the needs of pupils with EBD (Visser et al., 2002).

Empathy and equity

Approaches devoid of empathy seem to me to have had less effect than those that incorporate it. Proficient approaches encourage the development by pedagogues of a robust empathy with the children and young people. It forms a central plank on which relationships can be built. This is not as easy as some would make out. The case histories of most pupils with SEBD reveal significant family trauma, poverty in their range of positive experiences, a paucity of expectations, an absence of the emotional capacity to make and sustain relationships and, sadly, all too often physical, emotional and sexual abuse. Though some pedagogues may have personal experience of one or more of these, few have experienced them in the depth and range experienced by the pupil with SEBD. It is not necessary to have the experience in order to have empathy with the person who has experienced it.

Empathy, that ability to begin to see the world through the eyes of the child's experience, is an important component in any approach's success. Does the approach at the very least allow for empathy if it does not see it as an essential component? Empathy provides the pedagogue with the question, which needs to be asked continuously when working with the child with SEBD, 'Why has this child behaved in this way at this time and what does that mean for the approach I use?' It provides the basis upon which the pupil can begin to feel valued and understood. Being empathic should not lead to excusing the SEBD, that is the province of sympathy; rather it provides an understanding as to why the SEBD has occurred. This provides the basis upon which an approach can equitably meet the needs of the child.

Boundaries and challenge

Most approaches speak of the need for structure, particularly of the need to provide the child with boundaries. The lack of self-imposed or acknowledgement of boundaries has a co-morbidity with SEBD. This is hardly surprising, given that it is the constant lack of being able to behave and display emotions within boundaries that most frequently triggers the identification of a pupil as having SEBD. The boundaries need to be set by the pedagogues, but must have a flexibility which bends but never breaks what Amos called 'rubber boundaries' (cited in Cole et al., 1998). In other words, approaches that have a rigid structure in meeting the needs of pupils are very unlikely to be effective. As Royer (2001) points out, the inflexible approach fails because it ends up identifying all difficulties as nails because the only tool in the pedagogue's kit is a hammer. A single approach to meeting the needs of pupils has little chance of overall success in my experience. Advocates of such single approaches come and go through the literature. Bentley (1997) identifies this eternal verity as being necessary if pupils with SEBD are to avoid being further marginalized.

With the boundaries should go high, achievable expectations of behaviour and educational achievement (Cole et al., 1998; Daniels et al., 1998; OfSTED, 1999a). The therapeutic effect of being set challenging achievable targets, even when initially a great deal of support is required, is noted by Wilson and Evans (1980) and others (Greenhalgh, 1994; Cooper, 1993). OfSTED (1999b) reported low expectations as a contributory cause in many of the schools in England for pupils with SEBD being placed in special measures or serious weakness following inspection.

Building positive relationships

Bentley (1997) writes that 'social networks are powerful determinants of an individual's life chances'. He goes on to indicate that having access to a range of adults as role models is an indispensable resource for young people. Daniels (2001) and Ryan (2001) reinforce this with their view that the ability to develop genuine caring and learning relationships, and knowing where to go to make them, is an important skill for pupils to acquire if they are to be integrated members of their community. Children and young people with SEBD are not good at making and sustaining positive relationships; they constantly test out the adults they come across (Laslett, 1977). Porter (2000) indicates that for pupils with SEBD relationships need to provide emotional safety and protection, personal involvement and trust, and acceptance from others. Approaches that are successful emphasize the need to develop such relationships. Cooper (1993) shows that it is when pupils with SEBD gain a positive relationship with an adult they begin the process of what he calls re-signification, an important 'stage' on the way to 'losing' one's social, emotional and/or behavioural difficulties. The extent to which an approach allows for, sustains and maintains the abilities of adults to build positive relationships is, for me, a measure of the extent to which the approach will be successful.

Humour

As Cole et al. (1998), Visser (2000) and Porter (2000) point out, having a sense of humour has been seen since the early 'pioneers' in SEBD work as a vital component in any approach. But humour is rarely mentioned in descriptions of approaches and yet, as one of our studies (Cole et al., 1998) found, it is consistently placed as one of the top three characteristics of the effective pedagogue working with pupils with EBD. Humour is a great stress reliever, and not only for the pupils concerned!

THE RANGE OF ETERNAL VERITIES

We work in an age where there has been an information explosion and with it has gone some of the old certainties of testing the veracity of what we are told. The pattern, shape and accessibility of information is radically changing. It is not always easy, for example, to know the extent to which information on the Internet is objective, valid or reliable in the way that you might be able to examine an article published in a peer-reviewed journal. If pedagogues are to develop and change their abilities to meet the needs of pupils with SEBD, then having a set of eternal verities may provide a sound base upon which to test the information available.

Are these the only eternal verities? Though not using the term, Greenhalgh (1999), analysing David Wills' written contributions to the field of SEBD, lists six characteristics he saw as constant in successfully working with pupils with SEBD. Laslett (1977) gives those he saw as

Table 14.1 *Essential characteristics of successful practice*

Greenhalgh (1999)	OfSTED (1999a)	Laslett (1977)	Whelan and Kaufman (1999)
Children's experience as basis for intervention.	Well-defined structure.	Good relationships.	Interpersonal relationships.
Human relationships at heart of the approach.	Explicit rules consistency.	Caring, warm, informal ethos. High tolerance.	Competent teaching. Evaluative intervention.
Importance of boundaries.	Consequences for behaviour.	Avoidance of punishment.	
Dual task of care and confrontation.	Preventative feedback.	Importance of restitution/reparation	
Non-authoritarian organization.	High expectations.	Clear structures.	
Importance of loving concern.		Behaviour modelled.	
		Reflective reactions.	
		Participation.	
		Good quality teaching.	
		Creative work.	

common to the early pioneers. OfSTED (1999a) indicates six features consistently associated with good practice, and Whelan and Kauffman (1999) have three. Table 14.1 sets these out for comparative purposes. Further work needs to be completed to ascertain the degree to which a consensus set of eternal verities could be achieved. Acknowledging and agreeing that eternal verities exist could help to establish an evidence base from which to assess the potential of new approaches and the worthwhileness of current ones.

WHAT WE NEED ARE 'BETTER' APPROACHES

Approaches in and of themselves do not make the difference when working with pupils with EBD. Pedagogues make the difference; the approaches support or hinder the process. This is particularly so in relation to physical structures (Visser, 2001), but it is equally true when applied to the variety of strategies which derive from the various perspectives and understandings of SEBD. I will illustrate this point by reference to a recent English television series. *The Office* is a spoof documentary about the office of a paper supply company. It has all the right structures and systems. Amongst them are good office space, which is well lit and warm, and a manager who has obviously recently completed his MBA in management and attends all the updating courses. There are team-building exercises, appraisals, staff development programmes, and an open approach to decision making. Relationships are seen as important, work behaviour is seen as capable of change, intervention is seen as second to prevention, appropriate targets are set, and communications appear transparent. But, and it is a big but, in the hands of this manager the eternal verities are at best seen as crass and at worst potentially damaging. The key is that the eternal verities are espoused but not believed and lived.

Eternal verities do not 'grow over night nor to order' (Wills, 1971). They cannot, as Mains and Robinson (1983) point out, be put on like a suit of armour just before you meet the child or young person. They are not amenable to short-term approaches which at best only put a 'patch' on the pupil with SEBD which 'falls off' as soon as the pupil and the approach part. They can be explained and taught, but not in a 'tips for teachers' sense. That oft-asked question by pedagogues as they meet up with the 'expert' in SEBD, 'So what should I do with pupil x?' cannot be answered by just reciting the eternal verities, but neither will the approaches suggested by the 'expert' work without an understanding on the pedagogue's part of the importance of eternal verities to a successful outcome.

At the risk of being controversial, let me move to a conclusion by indicating how acknowledgement of eternal verities might go some way to taking the heat and stress out of many professional debates regarding the 'correctness' of a particular approach.

A modern equivalent of the dilemma of deciding what is the 'right' approach is the controversy over ADHD. Much of the debate has focused on two questions: 'Does it exist?' and 'Is Ritalin the best treatment?' The extent to which it is necessary to identify ADHD behaviours against non-ADHD behaviours is an interesting issue because it adds to our knowledge on human behaviour. Whatever your views on the existence of ADHD and the use of Ritalin, it is a fact that there are children and young people with SEBDs who display behaviours which some pedagogues term ADHD. Perhaps the debate should focus more upon the extent to which the set of approaches espoused by those advocating the existence of ADHD and the use of Ritalin have enshrined the set of eternal verities? If pedagogues who believe that ADHD 'exists' adopt approaches that have most, if not all, of the eternal verities, then I predict they will have successful outcomes.

CONCLUSION

That a set of agreed criteria such as described as eternal verities in this chapter needs to be established is, for me, beyond dispute. Currently, evidence for the effectiveness of the approaches utilized in meeting special education needs is at best equivocal and at worst non-existent (Dyson, 2001). The evidence base in SEBD is similarly poor for what works and why. Beside the need to halt the circle of wheel reinvention, establishing a set of eternal verities may also provide a brake on the increasing categorization of pupils within SEBD. It will not negate the need for pedagogues to use their independent and professional judgements (Pirrie, 2001), rather it may provide the basis upon which to make that judgement.

David Wills said approaches 'are all useless without the genuine loving concern for the child' (1971: 152). To this I would add 'and a faith in the potential for goodness in the developing child and young person.' The reason to go that 'extra half mile' (Cole et al., 1998).

I finish with a story from the *Peanuts* cartoon that illustrates this. Over the years these cartoons have impressed me with their ability to reveal the EBDs that exist both in children and adults. In this story Charlie Brown wants to improve his football kick. His sister Lucy offers to help by holding the ball in position. As Charlie Brown approaches the ball, Lucy whisks it away and Charlie Brown inevitably falls with a thump onto his back. Lucy has done this many times and each time she renews her offer of help, Charlie Brown believes her. Charlie believes each time that the process of resignification (Cooper, 1993) has begun to occur. Not so, but Lucy has recognized in Charlie Brown one of the necessary eternal verities – the belief that behaviour can change. As she concludes this particular strip, 'I admire you, Charlie Brown, you have such faith in human nature.'

REFERENCES

ACE (1980) 'Disruptive units', *Where* 158. London: Advisory Centre for Education.

Ayers, H., Clarke, D. and Murray, A. (2000) *Perspectives on Behaviour: A Practical Guide to Effective Interventions for Teachers* (2nd edn). London: Fulton.

Bentley, T. (1997) 'Learning to belong', *Demos Collection*, 12: 44–6.

Cole, T. (1997) Personal communication.

Cole, T., Daniels, H. and Visser, J. (1999) *Patterns of Educational Provision Maintained by Local Authorities for Pupils with Behaviour Problems*. Birmingham: University of Birmingham.

Cole, T., Sellman, E., Daniels, H. and Visser, J. (2001) *The Mental Health Needs of Children with Emotional and Behavioural Difficulties in Special Schools and Pupil Referral Units*. Birmingham: University of Birmingham.

Cole, T., Visser, J. and Daniels, H. (2000) *An Evaluation of In-School Centres In Dudley LEA*. Birmingham: University of Birmingham.

Cole, T., Visser, J. and Upton, G. (1998) *Effective Schooling for Pupils with EBD*. London: Fulton.

Cooper, P. (1993) *Effective Schools for Disaffected Pupils*. London: Routledge.

Cooper, P. (1996) 'Giving it a name: the value of descriptive categories in educational approaches to emotional and behavioural difficulties', *Support for Learning*, 3 (1): 37–43.

Cooper, P. (2001) 'Medical con-trick or new paradigm for emotional and behavioural difficulties: the case for attention deficit/hyperactive disorder', in J. Visser, H. Daniels and Cole, T. (eds), *International Perspectives on Inclusive Education: Emotional and Behavioural Difficulties in Mainstream Schools*. Amsterdam: JAI.

Daniels, H. (2001) 'Activity theory and knowledge production: twin challenges for the development of schooling for pupils who experience EBD', *Emotional and Behavioural Difficulties*, 6 (2): 113–24.

Daniels, H., Cole, T., Sellman, E., Sutton, J. and Visser, J. with Bedward, J. (2003) *Study of Young People Permanently Excluded from School*. London: Department for Education and Skills.

Daniels, H., Visser, J., Cole, T. and de Reybekill, N. (1998) *Emotional and Behavioural Difficulties in Mainstream Schools*. Research Report 90. London: Department for Education and Employment.

Daniels, H., Visser, J., Cole, T., de Reybekill, N., Harris, J. and Cumella, S. (1999) *Educational Support for Children with Mental Issues Including the Emotional Vulnerable*. Birmingham: University of Birmingham.

Davie, R. and Galloway, D. (1996) *Listening to Children in Education*. London: Fulton.

DES (1989) *Discipline in Schools* (The Elton Report). London: Department for Education and Science.

DfE (1994) *The Education of Children with Emotional and Behavioural Difficulties*. Circular 9/94. London Department for Education.

DfEE (1997) *Excellence for All Children: Meeting Special Educational Needs*. London: Department for Education and Employment.

DfEE (1999) *Social Inclusion: Pupil Support*. Circular 10/99. London: Department of Education and Employment.

DfES (2001) *Revised Code of Practice for the Identification and Assessment of Special Educational Needs*. London: Department of Education and Skills.

Dyson, A. (2001) 'Special needs education as the way to equity: an alternative approach?', *Support for Learning*, 16 (3): 99–104.

ERIC (1997) 'Common features of school-wide behaviour management', *ERIC Research Papers*, 1: 1.

Forness, S. and Kavale, K. (2000) 'Emotional or behavioral disorders: background and current status of the E/BD terminology and definition', *Behavioral Disorders*, 25 (3): 264–9.

Galloway, D. (1994) 'Annotation: bullying at schools: basic facts and effects of a school based intervention programme', *Journal of Child Psychology and Psychiatry*, 35 (7): 1171–90.

Galway, J. (1979) 'What pupils think of special units', *Comprehensive Education*, 39: 18–20.

Greenhalgh, P. (1994) *Emotional Growth and Learning*. London: Routledge.

Greenhalgh, P. (1999) 'The 1998 David Wills Lecture: Integrating the legacy of David Wills in an era of target setting', *Emotional and Behavioural Difficulties*, 4 (1): 46–53.

Hayden, C. and Ward, D. (1997) *Children Excluded from Primary School: Debates, Evidence and Responses*. Buckingham: Open University Press.

HMI (1978) *Behavioural Units: A Survey of Special Units for Pupils with Behavioural Problems*. London: Department of Education and Science.

Jones, N. (1973) 'Special adjustment units in comprehensive schools: I needs and resources, II structure and function', *Therapeutic Education*, 1 (2): 23–31.

Kauffman, J.M. (2001) *Characteristics of Emotional and Behavioural Disorders of Children and Youth* (7th edn). Englewood Cliffs, NJ: Merrill Prentice-Hall.

Laslett, R. (1977) *Educating Maladjusted Children*. London: Granada.

Laslett, R., Cooper, P., Maras, P., Rimmer, A. and Law, R. (1998) *Changing Perceptions: Emotional and Behavioural Difficulties Since 1945*. Maidstone: AWCEBD.

Mains, B. and Robinson, G. (1983) *A Bag of Tricks*. Bristol: Lucky Duck.

McGilchrist, B., Myers, K. and Reed, J. (1997) *The Intelligent School*. London: Chapman.

Ministry of Education (1955) *The Report of the Committee on Maladjusted Children* (The Underwood Report). London: HMSO.

OfSTED (1999a) *Principles into Practice: Effective Education for Pupils with Emotional and Behavioural Difficulties*. London: OfSTED.

OfSTED (1999b) *Lesson Learnt from Special Measures*. London: OfSTED.

Olweus, D. (1994) 'Annotation: Bullying at School: Basic facts and effects of a school based intervention program', *Journal of Child Psychology and Psychiatry and Allied Disciplines*, 35: 1171–90.

Parsons, C. (1999) *Education, Exclusion and Citizenship*. London: Routledge.

Pirrie, A. (2001) 'Evidenced-based practice in education: the best medicine?', *British Journal of Educational Studies*, 49 (2): 124–36.

Porter, L. (2000) *Behaviour in Schools: Theory and Practice for Teachers*. Buckingham: Open University Press.

Rodway, S. (1993) 'Children's rights: children's needs. Is there a conflict? The 1993 David Wills Lecture', *Therapeutic Care*, 2 (2): 375–91.

Rosenberg, M., Wilson, R., Maheady, L. and Sindelar, P. (1997) *Educating Students with Behavior Disorders* (2nd edn). Boston: Allyn and Bacon.

Royer, E. (2001) 'The education of students with emotional and behavioural difficulties: one size does not fit all', in J. Visser, H. Daniels and T. Cole (eds), *International Perspectives on Inclusive Education: Emotional and Behavioural Difficulties in Mainstream Schools*. Amsterdam: JAI.

Ryan, K. (2001) *Strengthening the Safety Net: How Schools Can Help Youth with Emotional and Behavioural Needs*. Burlington, VT: School Research Office University of Vermont.

Sammons, P., Hillman, J. and Mortimore, P. (1995) *Key Characteristics of Effective Schools: A Review of School Effectiveness Research*. London: OfSTED.

Sian, G., Callaghan, M., Lockhart, R. and Lawson, T. (1993) 'Bullying: teachers' views and school effects', *Educational Studies*, 19 (3): 307–321.

Smith, A. and Thomas, J. (1993) 'What's in a name: some problems of description and intervention in work with emotionally disordered children', *Pastoral Care*, 29: 3–7.

Upton, G. (1978) 'Definitions and terminology – an old issue in need of further examination', *Therapeutic Care*, 7 (2): 3–13.

Visser, J. and Redward, J. (1999) *An Evaluation of the Work of the Zaacheus Centre*. Birmingham: University of Birmingham.

Visser, J (2000) *Managing Behaviour in Classrooms*. London: Fulton.

Visser, J. (2001) 'Aspects of physical provision for pupils with EBD', *Support for Learning*, 16 (2): 64–8.

Visser, J. (2003) *A Study of Young People with Challenging Behaviour*. London: Office for Standards in Education.

Visser, J., Cole, T. and Daniels, H. (2002) 'Inclusion for the difficult to include', *Support for Learning*, 17 (1): 23–5.

Warnock, M. (1978) *Report of the Committee of Enquiry into the Education of Handicapped Children and Young People* (The Warnock Report). London: HMSO.

Whelan, R.J. and Kauffman, J.M. (1999) *Educating Students with Emotional and Behavioral Disorders: Historical Perspective and Future Directions*. Arlington, VA: CEC.

Wills, D. (1968) 'Closing address at the AWMC conference at St Mary's College Cheltenham'. Unpublished.

Wills, D. (1971) 'Obituary for Marjorie Ellen Franklin', *Journal of the Association of Workers for Maladjusted Education*, 3 (2): 93–4.

Wilson, M. and Evans, M. (1980) *Education for Disturbed Pupils: Schools Council*. Working Paper 65. London: Methuen.

Wise, S. (2000) *Listen to Me! The Voices of Pupils with Emotional and Behavioural Difficulties*. Bristol: Lucky Duck.

15

Teaching Students with Emotional Behavioural Disorders

BILL ROGERS

NARROWING THE FOCUS OF ENQUIRY

This chapter quite deliberately 'steps back' from any explicit theoretical consideration of emotional and behavioural difficulties (though the reader will inevitably discern something of the author's orientation, which is more explicitly expressed elsewhere in Rogers, 2000b, 2000c). Rather, the account that follows narrows the focus of the lens with which we view student behaviours, to look firstly at some actual phenomena of emotional behaviour disorder (EBD), and then at the actual, explicitly practical ways in which teachers can *manage contexts of behaviour* so as to minimize, if not actually prevent, inappropriate behaviours. This is not to eschew theory by any means, but rather to insist on its realization in practical and demonstrable ways. Although not explored at any length here, a primary claim of the paper is that *causative pathologies* – such as attributing certain behaviours to genetic or environmental factors outside the compass of the classroom – cannot in themselves generate effective solutions to contextual difficulties.

This chapter thus addresses EBD in terms of the contextual *frequency, generality* and *durability* of distracting and disruptive behaviour present in students in 'mainstream' school contexts. Notwithstanding causative pathologies which are often attached to students' behaviours at school, many teachers have taught effective behaviours for learning and social relationships to students who present with EBD. This chapter discusses how teachers use strategies to teach positive behaviours to such students.

SUE AND NATHAN: A CASE SKETCH

Sue has been teaching for 15 years; Nathan (one of her pupils) is 6 years old – it's still week one in Sue's class. Whenever the children sit, *en masse*, on the mat Nathan rolls around at the back of the group, 'hides' under the computer table and makes 'attentional' noises. Sue directs him to join the others – she is pleasant and appropriately firm. He grins, grunts, holds on to the top of the table then the legs of the table … The other children naturally laugh at Nathan's behaviour, and – likewise – are naturally distracted from their teaching and learning. Most children become annoyed. Sue has tried the characteristic 'mix' of encouragement and positive discipline. Nathan sometimes joins with others after several reminders. On days when he is too distracting, Sue uses supported 'time-out' measures, at times having Nathan calmly escorted from her class group (part of his 'audience').

As a mentor-teacher, part of my role was to support Sue in developing a longer-term management approach to help Nathan – described as EBD (and suspected ADDH – Attention Deficit Disorder with Hyperactivity) – understand his behaviour and develop self-control for learning time. Whilst teachers are increasingly used to behaviour being categorized and 'labelled' (ADD – Attention Deficit Disorder, ADDH, ODD – Oppositional Deficit Disorder, Asperger's syndrome, Tourette's syndrome and the more generic EBD …) in these ways, the terminologies do not in themselves point to ways out of immediate situations of difficulty. To find these 'ways out' we need, surely, to be cognizant of special conditions and circumstances relative to behaviour disorders, but more importantly to focus specifically on the behaviour *in context* at school.

INTERROGATING THE CONTEXT

The key questions we ask about any EBD behaviour are:

- How *frequent* are behaviours such as calling out, inappropriate noise levels, wandering around the room, hassling and irritating other students, pushing and shoving while lining up, significant task-avoidance (not related to ability) …?
- How *durable* are such behaviours? Is such behaviour occasional 'bad-day' syndrome or several times each lesson, each day? The combination of *frequency* and *durability* is what teachers find stressful (as do the class group).

In developing a more whole-school approach to addressing EBD, it is also important to be aware of the *generality* of distracting/disruptive behaviour. Some children are *selectively* disruptive according to which adults they are with during the day; they may be frequently distracting in one setting and co-operative in another. Such children would not be 'termed' EBD. Students with ADD do not always present as troublesome, difficult or challenging. A key issue for teachers is whether a student's behaviour presents as frequent, durable and generally distracting or disruptive, not necessarily a behavioural 'label'.

BEHAVIOUR IS LEARNED IN CONTEXT

While my colleagues are very aware of, and empathetic about, a child's predisposing circumstances affecting behaviour at school they are also aware that behaviour is learned in context. Children 'learn' – or fail to learn – co-operation, confidence; how to manage frustration and how to develop workable relationships with others (and much more) in their home environments. But similarly, children who present with EBD often have maladaptive coping behaviours ensuing from non-school settings, and causative pathologies – such as family dysfunction, abusive child management practices, structural poverty, long-term unemployment, substance abuse and so on – are commonly and often uncritically adduced to 'explain' them. My colleagues are realistically aware that they have little ability to affect (or control) such predisposing factors. It is crucial, though, that teachers do not 're-victimize' a child at school from a mindset that effectively says '… well, what can you expect when he comes from a home like that …!' or 'How can we hope to help him with a mother or father who …' (of course, teachers are often surprised and encouraged how sane, focused and resilient some students can be, given difficult non-school settings).

School has to be a safe place for children; a place where they can find a positive sense of belonging – a place where they can feel emotionally and psychologically safe. Teachers, like Sue, also make a conscious effort to *teach* children who present with patterns of EBD some new and appropriate coping behaviours at school.

COLLEAGUE SUPPORT

In many countries currently espousing inclusive ideoogy, teachers are at the demanding (and often stressful) end of government policy: policy which may be unquestionably morally and politically desirable, but frequently lacks the resource of meaningful support really to bring about inclusive practice. Teachers frequently seek consciously – and conscientiously – to assist and support students like Nathan with behaviour at school, and most do so with great goodwill and patience. They do not, however, always get the acknowledgement (and affirmation) of how difficult, demanding and taxing that role is.

As well as normative moral support among the teaching team, it is essential to establish 'structural' support (Rogers, 2002a), dependable 'forms', 'processes', 'plans' to support them in stressful management contexts. For example, when a child is *repeatedly* disruptive or behaving in dysfunctional or dangerous ways, it is essential that teachers have access to school-wide time-out support. It is also essential that such 'structural' support has a clear psychological and pedagogic basis for its policy and practice (see Rogers, 1998, 2002a).

DEVELOPING INDIVIDUAL BEHAVIOUR SUPPORT PLANS

Early intervention is crucial in supporting students with patterns of 'attentional' and maladaptive behaviours. Such behaviours significantly affect learning, peer-acceptance and positive peer-socialization (not to mention teachers' stress levels!).

When any pattern of *frequency*, *durability* and *generality* of distracting and disruptive behaviour is noted, teachers will need to set up personal behaviour support for the child in question. In this sense the child is perceived as having 'special needs' – in a literal and everyday, rather than technical sense – instead of simply as a child who is difficult and naughty (they are that, too!). In these contexts my colleagues (and I) work with the child directly to *teach academic and social survival behaviours*. We see these behaviours as skills that can be learned in the school context. These are skills as deceptively basic as: entering the classroom without 'grandstanding' (pushing, shoving, loud noises); hands up *without* calling out; sitting on the mat *without* turning round and touching others, or calling out, or rolling on the mat or making inappropriate noises …; using a 'partner voice' for work time (instead of a playground voice) and so on. Other behaviour skills address frustration: tolerance; how to be a good loser; how to use your manners (please, thanks, excuse me); positive language (instead of put-downs and swearing 'language') and so on.

Many of these behaviours seem deceptively basic and thankfully a majority of students (say, 70 to 80 percent) will display such behaviours most of the time. Students who present with EBD will need this extra behaviour support on a long-term basis within the school from the teaching team. And a vital and integral part of any such support is the development of a *personal* behaviour support plan.

KEY ELEMENTS AND FEATURES OF A BEHAVIOUR-SUPPORT PLAN

The emphasis of any behaviour-support plan, or programme, is educational; the aim is to teach key behaviour skills essential for academic and social 'survival' in the school context. Any counselling (particularly with at-risk children) runs parallel to the educational emphases of a behaviour support plan.

The central person in engaging and developing such a plan is the grade (or classroom) teacher supported by teacher aides. At the secondary-age phase a senior teacher takes on a 'case supervision' role, working with the student one-to-one and co-ordinating with subject teachers in consistent support of a school-wide (but individualized) plan for students who present with EBD.

The several elements of such a plan are sketched in Figure 15.1. The aim is to support, teach and encourage a child to develop a confident sense of self-control and coping behaviour relative to learning and social interaction. Since many of these children have known failure and discouragement in their schooling journey, it is essential that the case supervisor adopt a supportive approach with the student and not, in any sense, associate the process with normative and necessary discipline or consequences. The key to any success with such programmes is the ongoing one-to-one attention and encouragement of the mentor teacher[1] within the individual plan.

RAISING INITIAL SELF-AWARENESS

All teaching sessions are conducted one-to-one with the child (often in non-contact time in a busy primary school).

Picture cueing

To help raise the child's initial self-awareness about his pattern of disruptive behaviour, the teacher will prepare a simple drawing of the child illustrating their 'calling-out', or 'loudness', or 'pushing and shoving', or 'wandering',

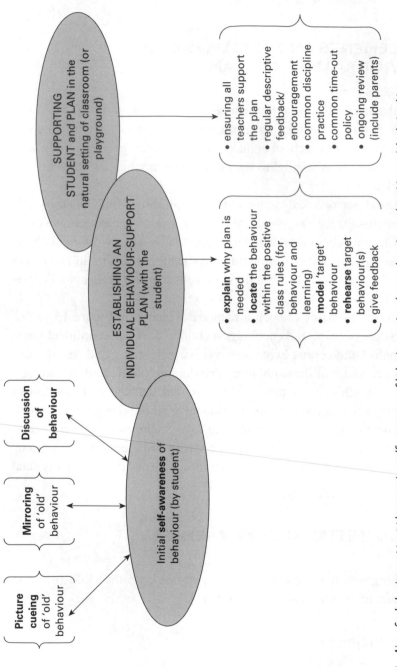

Figure 15.1 *Aim of a behaviour-support plan: ongoing self-awareness of behaviour as it enhances learning and positive social relationships*

or 'bad language' and so on. In Nathan's case (above), Sue and I showed him a simple drawing that illustrated him lying under the table. The faces of Sue (his teacher) were shown reading to the class, and the children sitting around him had sad looks to indicate social annoyance and disapproval. These simple drawings can be as basic as stick figures on an A4 sheet. Children at any age at primary level always immediately recognize themselves, their teacher and their peer-group. To add verisimilitude to these visual cues, the child's hair can be more authentically curly, his face freckled, his overall size positionally larger. Later in the session a second drawing is introduced, displaying the appropriate, or new, or required behaviour.

Whenever my colleagues ask the child *what* they are doing in the picture (for example, rolling on the carpet, annoying other students, time-off-task behaviour) they will initially say they are 'being naughty', or older children (boys) will often say they're 'just mucking around'. Some students will discount their behaviour ('I'm not the only one who does stuff like that!') or they will claim their 'right to silence'. In these cases it is important for the teacher simply to describe what they note in the illustration and reframe (where necessary). For example, 'When you roll on the mat like that (teacher indicates on the picture/illustration) other children get annoyed because they can't listen properly to their teacher ,,,' or '... if other children call out like this (teacher points to picture/illustration) I'll speak to them as well. For the moment, I want you and I to talk about what happens many times in class when you call out ...'

A sense of 'social place' and 'belonging' are central needs of children at school. These simple pictures help to cue that reality.

Initially the plan will focus on a key 'target' behaviour, such as with Nathan, sitting on the mat (*without* touching or pushing others), eyes and ears facing the front and the teacher, waiting his turn in questions, hands up (without calling out) when he wants to ask a question or contribute, and so on. Even in a deceptively basic behaviour such as 'sitting on the mat (during whole-class instruction/discussion) there are several aspects to positive, attentive behaviour.

Mirroring of frequent, distracting/ disruptive behaviour

To aid self-awareness my colleagues and I often 'mirror back' to the child his typical and frequent distracting/disruptive behaviour. For example, when discussing classroom behaviour with Nathan I rolled under the computer table, briefly imitating (mirroring) what I had seen Nathan do many times in class (I stress this was one-to-one, with my colleague present). Nathan laughed as I briefly imitated his behaviour; most students do.

When we hold up a 'behavioural mirror' like this it is important to:

- Conduct such sessions in a one-to-one relaxed (discursive) supportive setting.
- Ask the student's permission (even at infant age): '... Nathan, I want to show you what I see you do when we're all having story time on the carpet ...' It is also important to consider the ethical probity of any one-to-one setting with the child, particularly a male teacher and a female student. In such cases a female teacher would sit in on the session (at secondary level the case supervisor/mentor-teacher would be a female). If a student is reluctant, or refuses the teacher's request to 'show them what it looks like when you ...' (the mirroring), it is apposite quickly to re-cue to the picture and use the accompanying discussion to raise self-awareness. However, it must be said that it is rare that a student will refuse a teacher's *supportive* request.

  It is also important to note that we would never mirror aggressive behaviour (like throwing a chair – though picking up a chair and simulating a 'throw' is sufficient to gain a brief 'kinaesthetic connection'). When mirroring the behaviour of a child who frequently engages in pinching, poking, pushing or shoving behaviours, the teacher will pinch, poke, push, shove an 'imaginary child', briefly created in kinaesthetic space as it were.
- Keep the mirroring *brief*; along with the picture cue, the mirroring assists the child's self-awareness about their typical (and frequent) behaviour.
- Keep the tone of the mirroring supportive (it should *never* be used to embarrass the child). Most children laugh when their teacher mirrors the student's loudness, their simulated pushing and shoving, their wanderings, their rolling on the carpet and so on: 'That's what it looks like, Nathan, when you ... It looks funny when I do it, Nathan, but in class it's not funny because ...' (here the teacher can briefly refer back to the face, on the picture/illustration, that indicates social disapproval/annoyance).
- Having 'mirrored' the student's distracting/disruptive behaviour, the teacher will physically step back (from their brief 'role-play') – creating a psychological distinction between adult and recreated child behaviour. It is important to re-establish quickly the supportive, adult role.

ESTABLISHING A PLAN WITH THE CHILD

When developing a 'behaviour plan' with a student, the teacher is highlighting a key academic or social behaviour skill. The teacher will emphasize to the student why the child needs to behave 'like this' if they are going to enjoy school, learn well and get on with his classmates (and make mum happy too – notwithstanding the teacher's relative happiness!). In establishing such a plan the teacher is emphasizing *achievable*, positive behaviour(s).

The plan will include rehearsal and practice sessions where the mentor teacher will:

- *identify* what behaviours (skills) the child needs to develop and why;
- *model* the behaviour skill (the target behaviour);
- encourage the child to *rehearse* the target behaviour (in the safety of the one-to-one session); and
- *explain* how their plan fits in with the classroom/school rules (always emphasizing that it is the student's plan). It is important that the student sees the direction of their behaviour as the normal expectation of his peers; of 'all of us in our classroom'.

When developing a plan for behaviour change a simple picture cue can – again – be a useful *aide-mémoir* for the student. The target behaviour is identified by a simple drawing or even a photo of the child engaged in the desired behaviour. For example, a drawing of Nathan sitting on the mat, with classmates around him smiling (social approval); the teacher, too, is shown in the picture, also smiling.

In one recent plan (for a 6-year-old student), one of my colleagues took a digital photograph of the whole grade coming into class normatively and considerately. She had explained to the child (with whom she was developing a behaviour plan) that she wanted him to come into class 'like the others' so that she could have a 'reminder photo' to use in his plan. The other students merely thought the teacher was taking a general photo (this photo was also displayed in the class alongside the class rules about 'How we come into our class and settle for learning time ...'). Many teachers use digitally scanned photos to develop positive visual reminders of students 'sitting on the mat considerately ...', raising their hand without calling out ...' or 'working at their table group/desk (in a thoughtful, focused, way ...').

If photographs are used in such plans/programmes, it is necessary (for probity) to ask the parents' permission and explain that this photo is an important part of the child's plan to assist his learning in class time. It should always be emphasized to parents that any 'behaviour programme' is to assist the student's learning.

When I was developing a behaviour plan with Nathan, I asked him what was different about *this* drawing – a drawing which illustrated him sitting positively, like the other students. I had previously explained why we sit on the mat during class teaching/story/discussion time (without behaviours like those shown in the first picture … the rolling, the pushing, the touching others). Initially he noted that he was sitting listening to his teacher. I asked him what else he was doing and he replied 'Nothing.' It is important to prompt supportively the student's line of thinking with something like: 'Are you poking anyone with your finger?' 'No.' 'Are you pushing anyone in their back?' 'No.' 'Are you hiding under a table?' 'No.' 'So what are you doing with your hands …? Eyes …? Where are you looking …? How are you sitting?'

Supportive prompting – again – raises self-awareness about the inappropriate behaviour illustrated in the first illustration in contrast to that of the second illustration (the positive, target behaviour). 'How do you think your teacher feels when you listen like that?' ' … when you put your hand up without calling out and wait your turn?' The teacher then briefly discusses the social approval on the faces of his peers (and teacher) illustrated in the picture, linking this to the 'new', target behaviour.

MODELLING THE BEHAVIOUR

It is important that the teacher then model the required target behaviour to the child, for example, how to:

- line up (without pushing, shoving, beating the rest …);
- sit on the mat/at your desk (without hassling others …);
- raise your hand for questions, or help, (without calling out, clicking fingers or…);
- use a partner voice (instead of a playground voice at work time …);
- come to a work task and know what to do, *how to* start, *how to* continue and *how to* (fairly) get teacher help …; and
- manage frustration and angry feelings/thoughts.

If a behaviour (plan) cannot be modelled, it may simply not be clear enough to the student what the teacher is focusing on in terms of expected, required behaviours. The teacher will therefore need to identify and explain the behaviour skill to the child and reinforce it by modelling and student rehearsal.

REHEARSAL/PRACTICE

My colleagues and I have practised many, many times with many children (one-to-one), 'how to line up'; 'use partner voices'; 'develop time-on-task skills'; 'manage their frustration and anger' and so on. We always emphasize that practice is the way we get better at *anything* (football, swimming, playing an instrument, chess).

Some children will be a little hesitant at the invitation to practise, but with encouragement (and not infrequent laughter generated by the teacher's goodwill) most children will have a go. With older children even cognitive rehearsal can help consolidate the future change in their behaviour. Cognitive rehearsal can also include teaching children to sub-vocalize a more constructive self-talk relative to their behaviour (Rogers, 1994; Bernard and Joyce, 1985; Wragg, 1989; Seligman, 1990). Rehearsal of self-talk begins with an explanation, and discussion, of 'how we all talk inside our heads' and the *effect* of how, and what, we typically (characteristically) say to ourselves when we feel frustrated, angry or anxious. The teacher then develops, with the student, new self-talk patterns; rehearses the new 'patterns' aloud (by modelling first); and rehearing sub-vocally (the norm). Students are encouraged to keep a personal copy of their self-talk/coping statements as a personal, visual *aide-mémoir.*

DEVELOPMENT AND MAINTENANCE OF 'THE PLAN'

The teacher lets the student know that all the teachers (and support teachers) who work with him during the day will get a copy of his plan to help them, encourage, remind and support the student.

It is crucial that all the teaching team be aware of the plan, in particular, and support the concept of behaviour teaching generally. In this sense the individual plan becomes the whole-school approach.

Encouragement and feedback

Self-esteem is often linked to other-esteem. It is crucial that the teacher(s) acknowledge, affirm, encourage and give feedback to the student when he begins to behave within the aims and goals of his plan. This will mean a conscious effort to notice the direction of behaviour change and any approximation, by the student, to new and desired behaviour.

When encouraging a student some teachers will often over-praise: 'That was great, Nathan' 'Fantastic!' 'Marvellous!' 'Wonderful!' 'Brilliant!'

Brilliant? – Why? Because a student suddenly starts to 'sit on the mat positively' or 'puts his hand up without calling out'? Some children cannot effectively handle such global praise and may become attentionally silly, even rejecting the well-meaning intent of such praise. Those among the student's peers may also see such overly ebullient praise to a (perceptually) difficult student as 'unfair'.

When encouraging students:

- Keep the encouragement specific and focused in, and on, the behaviour itself. 'Nathan, you remembered your plan; you ...' (and here describe *what* the student did that made a difference to his behaviour); for example, 'You sat on the mat and kept your hands and feet safe; you looked at your teacher, and the board, and you remembered to put your hand up without calling out' (in this sense the encouragement has a feedback element).

- Keep it 'private' wherever possible; a brief word aside from his peers, or even a quiet word in the student's ear during on-task time, is more apt than a grand, public affirmation. This is particularly important with older children in upper-primary or secondary school settings.

  It can even help to give feedback on how the student responded to any necessary discipline: 'When I reminded you with that signal (here the teacher models a private non-verbal cue practised by the teacher and student in the one-to-one rehearsal session) to keep your hands and feet to yourself you remembered, and you turned again to face the front. I'm pleased you're remembering your plan, Nathan.'

- Avoid qualifying any praise or encouragement, for example: 'You put your hand up without calling out or clicking your fingers' (the positive feedback element); 'Why can't you do that all the time?' (the unnecessary qualifying element).

- Ask the student to self-reflect on their progress. At a brief one-to-one session after class or (more commonly at non-contact time) ask the student:

  - 'What's the easiest part of your plan at the moment – and why?'
  - 'What's the hardest part of your plan – and why?'
  - 'What can we do to improve this week?'
  - 'How can we help?'

Discipline

It is important in the maintenance of the plan/programme that the teaching team use positive discipline practice as the norm. Discipline can often be exercised by a quiet reminder or question, directed to the student, about his plan. For example, if a student is using a loud voice (instead of a 'partner voice' during on-task learning time), his teacher walks over and says (as a quiet aside), 'Nathan, what's your plan?' 'What are you supposed to be doing now?' Teachers will often discreetly show the student a copy of their plan (as a visual *aide-mémoir*, one-third of an A4 size). Non-verbal cues are also useful disciplining 'encouragers' (the teacher indicates with thumb and forefinger the 'turning down of volume control'; the teacher indicates with four fingers, extended downwards, that the student needs to have his chair 'four on the floor'; the teacher puts her hand up and finger to lips to indicate hands up without calling out and so on).

I have seen some early progress in a student's personal behaviour plan thwarted by some teachers who insist on unreasonable compliance with the plan. It is important to remember that the discipline of students who present with EBD is not fundamentally different, in precept and practice, from normative positive discipline. Thus:

- Avoid unnecessary confrontation, embarrassment, public *over-focusing* on the distracting or disruptive behaviour.
- Keep the *focus* of any corrective discipline on the 'primary' issue/behaviour; avoid getting drawn into 'secondary' issues such as 'sulky looks', whingeing, moaning, whining, 'tut-tutting', sighing and so on. Such 'secondary behaviours' are not untypical when teachers address a student's distracting or disruptive behaviour. Much of this 'secondary behaviour' can be *tactically* ignored (in the emotional moment) and addressed at a later stage. If it does need to be addressed, it is more appropriate to do so *briefly* – with a focus on the inappropriate or offensive *behaviour*.
- Use positive corrective language (wherever possible) and avoid *easy use*, or overuse, of 'don't', 'mustn't', 'no' or interrogatives such as 'why?' (for example, 'Why aren't you sitting on the mat with the others' 'Why are you calling out?' 'Haven't you started work yet?'). Interrogatives can be restated, more positively, as descriptive reminders with *focused* questions as directions, for example: 'I noticed you haven't started work yet … how can I help?' or 'What are you supposed to be doing now?' or 'What's your plan?' or even a brief *directional* statement 'What you need to be doing now is …'.
- Always balance any necessary correction with appropriate encouragement.

As with all progress in behaviour change, the creative tension in one's leadership between encouragement, reminder, positive discipline and appropriate *tactical* ignoring is essential (Rogers, 1998, 2002b).

'Rewards'

Some teachers link a student's progress with such a plan to 'rewards'. Approximations to target behaviours are noted (ticked on a reminder card), shared with the child one-to-one as a form of encouragement, and celebrated when a nominal target is reached.

The 'celebration' can range from stickers and items such as pens, rulers, books or free time. Some teachers even link a student's progress into a 'token economy'. With any such approaches the emphasis is best centred on acknowledging, affirming and celebrating effort, rather than 'rewarding' – or worse, 'bribing': 'If you do this I'll give you a special reward such as …'.

Review and generalization and 'norming' of behaviours

Many children, like Nathan, do respond well (and positively) to such an individual programme. The teacher's special attention and behaviour teaching (one-to-one outside of the classroom) and thoughtful encouragement within the classroom are central to any success.

All 'plans' have to be regularly reviewed by the teaching teams and senior staff. Time-out records are noted and the frequency, generality and durability of the new (target) behaviours are noted and discussed by the team.

Most students do respond well and show improvement. As one primary school teacher wrote to me recently, 'Joel has hardly been in time-out since we've been doing this programme. He's keen to do well (and I think he's keen to make me feel better too!). The rest of the class, too, are behind him; I think their behaviour has improved as well. This was an unintended bonus!'

A small percentage of students present with ongoing resistant behaviour; attentional or power-seeking behaviours that – effectively – 'hold a class to ransom' in terms of learning, a sense of safety or the teacher's ability to teach functionally. In these cases it is essential to pursue due process and work with parents and local authorities for alternative placement.

CONCLUSION

At the end of the day it is not drawings, discipline, encouragement, even 'rewards' that see changes in behaviour with students who present with EBD; rather, it is the quality of the ongoing relationship between teacher and student. Any 'programme' or 'plan' has to have aims, objectives and goals – in this case increasing self-control (by the student) in relation to learning and relationships at school. Those aims are only realized, however, when the sorts of approaches tabled here are exercised with collegial goodwill and a professional desire to enable and support the child to 'own his own behaviour'.

NOTE

1 Or adult-mentor – while there are different 'terms' used for such a role it is the ability of the 'mentor-teacher' to teach and supportively encourage children that really matters.

REFERENCES

Bernard, M. and Joyce, M. (1985) *Rational Emotive Therapy with Children and Adolescents: Theory, Treatment Strategies, Preventative Methods*. New York: Wiley

Rogers, B. (1994) *Behaviour Recovery (A whole-school program for mainstream schools)*. Camberwell: Australian Council for Educational Research. (Published in the UK by Pittman, London. Reprinted 2000.)

Rogers, B. (1998) *You Know the Fair Rule and Much More*. Camberwell: Australian Council for Educational Research. (Published in the UK by Pittman, London.)

Rogers, B. (2002a) *I Get By with a Little Help: Colleague Support in Schools*. Camberwell: Australian Council for Educational Research.

Rogers, B. (2002b) *Classroom Behaviour: A Practical Guide to Effective Teaching, Behaviour Management and Colleague Support*. London: Chapman.

Rogers, B. (ed.) (2002c) *Teacher Leadership and Behaviour Management*. London: Chapman.

Seligman, M. (1990) *Learned Optimism*. Sydney: Random House.

Wragg, J. (1989) *Talk Sense to Yourself: A Program for Children and Adolescents*. Camberwell: ACER.

16

Reducing Problem Behavior through School-wide Systems of Positive Behavior Support[1]

TIMOTHY J. LEWIS AND LORI L. NEWCOMER

One of the greatest challenges confronting educators is to provide a positive learning and teaching environment in schools with high rates of discipline problems (Shinn et al., 2002). A recent study indicated that general education teachers reported on average one in five of their students exhibited disruptive/off-task behavior and one in twenty exhibited aggressive behaviors to the point intervention was necessary (Myers and Holland, 2000). Unfortunately, educators routinely rely on traditional discipline practices that generally involve punishment and exclusionary options. The assumption is punishment-based discipline actions taken in response to rule violations will both deter future occurrences and somehow teach and promote more prosocial skills (Sugai and Horner, 2001). However, the current 'zero tolerance' approach to discipline has proven ineffective in reducing problem behavior (Skiba, 2002). In fact, relying exclusively on reactive, consequent-based discipline policies are actually associated with increases in problem behavior (Mayer, 1995). Not surprising, students with emotional or behavioral disorders (EBD), given their high rates of externalizing behavior, are often frequent recipients of ineffective discipline practices (Skiba, 2002).

While outcomes for students identified as EBD remain poor, compounding the problem is the fact that many students who may be eligible to receive special education and related services specifically targeted for children and youth with EBD actually do not, due to current under-identification or misidentification. For example, in the United States, less than 1 percent of children and adolescents are identified as having EBD. Yet professionals are in agreement that approximately 10 percent of school-age children and youth manifest EBD significant enough to warrant support (Walker et al., 1995). Forness and colleagues point out that students are typically identified late in elementary school at a point many feel is beyond the critical developmental window in which the disorder may have been prevented or effectively remediated (Forness et al., 1996). Thus, it has long been acknowledged that prevention is perhaps the best strategy we have to significantly impact children and youth who present challenging behaviors, including aggression and violence, in schools (Conduct Problems Prevention Research Group, 1992; Elliot, 1994; Walker et al., 1995).

The field of EBD faces two pressing issues as outlined above. The first is the high rate of removal of children and youth with challenging behavior from the general education environment. As noted elsewhere in this *Handbook*, research has clearly pointed to the benefit of quality academic instruction as an effective strategy for addressing EBD. The second challenge is the poor prognosis children and youth with EBD face in school and beyond. Compounding this challenge is the fact that the majority of children and youth with EBD are not identified to receive specialized education and therefore face a general education environment that is not prepared to educate or address the behavioral and emotional needs of these children and youth. In an attempt to address both of these challenges, researchers and educators have begun work in building school-wide systems of positive behavior support (PBS) (Sugai et al., 2000). School-wide PBS incorporates empirically validated practices into a system designed to support all students and all staff within schools. School-wide PBS is designed to prevent chronic behavioral challenges; provide early intervention for children and youth displaying minor but repeated patterns of problem behavior which if left untreated may eventually manifest into EBD; and provide proactive supports to children and youth at-risk and those with EBD to allow them to successfully remain in the general education environment.

POSITIVE BEHAVIOR SUPPORT

Positive behavior support (PBS) is a general term that refers to the application of an applied science that uses proactive and effective educational methods, behavioral interventions, environmental redesign, and systems change methods to support individuals who exhibit disruptive and/or dangerous behaviors in school, work, social, community, and family settings. PBS has emerged as an outgrowth of applied behavior analysis, building on an operant conceptual framework for behavior change, assessment and intervention strategies (Carr et al., 2002). PBS emphasizes proactive, data-based decision making to teach and support appropriate and functional behavior through an integration of behaviorally-based systems that place greater emphasis on correcting problem contexts than the problem behavior. Desired outcomes should be articulated, measurable and should guide the adoption of practices. Moreover, the articulated outcomes, curricula, strategies and interventions must have a good contextual fit with the values of the school, teachers and family members to sustain use and maximize achievement.

School-wide PBS

The emerging literature on building PBS plans for students with disabilities clearly points to a need to build larger overall school systems of support both to insure that individual PBS plans are implemented with a high degree of integrity and to prevent problem behaviors from developing into chronic patterns that will ultimately require special services. School-wide systems of PBS are an extension of the core features of individually developed PBS plans and are applied to all students and staff within schools and school districts. The OSEP Center on Positive Behavioral Interventions and Supports has defined school-wide PBS as a set of 'strategies and systems designed to increase the capacity of schools to (a) reduce school disruption, and (b) educate students with problem behaviors' (Sugai et al., 2000: 6).

Like individually developed PBS plans, school-wide PBS focuses on providing regular, predictable, positive learning and teaching environments, positive adult and peer models, and a place to achieve academic and social behavioral competence. Added within the school-wide PBS perspective is the inclusion of all adults and students, not just specialists and students with disabilities, and shaping school systems to allow essential features to work naturally within and across the school day. Common components of these practices include a systemic proactive approach across school settings; providing all school personnel with ongoing training and support; effective academic/pre-academic instruction; home–school collaborations; and school–agency collaborations.

Schools represent an intricate mix of professionals, policies, programs, and practices that interact in complex ways. Sugai and Horner refer to systems as 'processes, routines, working structures, administrative supports needed to ensure consideration of valued outcomes, research validated practices, and data-based decision makings' (2002: 31). PBS considers and organizes these working structures (for example, committees), policies, operating routines (for example, faculty meetings, communication, action planning), resource supports (for example, families, special education, community resources, counseling), staff development, and administrative leadership to increase their efficiency, effectiveness and relevance to create a comprehensive 'host environment,' a prerequisite for the adoption, extension and sustained use of best practices (Zins and Ponti, 1990).

Essential features of school-wide PBS

School-wide PBS provides an organizational infrastructure for managing the interplay between three necessary implementation elements. The first is the application of empirically validated practices. Second, data are used to guide the adoption and evaluation of all practices. Finally, systems must be in place to support staff's learning, implementation, and efficacy evaluation of all student-based practices.

Practices

An instructional-based perspective is applied through a continuum of supports for all students. Because problem behavior occurs along a continuum, from the occasional mild misbehavior to behavior that is chronic, severe, and disruptive to the learning environment, school-wide PBS emphasizes a parallel continuum of instructional and environmental supports in which the intensity of practices and interventions increases to match the intensity and complexities of the presenting problem behaviors. Research validated practices are implemented across all school settings, focus on all students, and include all building personnel. Implementation activities occur at three levels: universal; small group or targeted; and individual or intensive (Lewis and Sugai, 1999). All three levels are built on a central theme of teaching appropriate behavior, building multiple opportunities to practice appropriate behavior, and altering environments to promote success.

The universal level of prevention/intervention serves to build a foundation for all other practices and establishes a system 'designed to increase the capacity of the school' (Sugai et al., 2000: 6). Research has shown that approximately 20 percent of children within a school building will need behavioral supports beyond universal group strategies (Sugai and Horner, 1999). Small group/targeted level of prevention/intervention serves to meet the needs of students who continue to display behavioral challenges that place them 'at risk' for establishing chronic patterns of problem behavior leading to a host of later life difficulties. Finally, individual/intensive strategies are developed for those students who demonstrate clear chronic patterns of challenging behavior. Research has shown that approximately 5 percent of students within a school building will require more intensive individualized behavioral interventions (Sugai et al., 2002). For these students, who often represent a combination of both students with EBD and those who are not identified, a functional behavioral assessment (FBA) is conducted. Based on assessment outcomes, specific replacement behaviors that result in the same outcome (that is, function) for the student are targeted and taught and needed environmental supports are identified and implemented.

Data-based decisions

Prevention and intervention procedures emphasize: assessment; a function-based approach; and data-informed decision making. All students and staff within school are viewed as part of the assessment process to redesign environments and curriculum across a continuum to support all students. Colvin, Sugai and colleagues (Colvin et al., 1993; Tobin et al., 1996) demonstrated that valid, reliable information regarding student and adult behavior patterns can be obtained through the collection and analysis of commonly collected school data, such as behavioral incident reports. Data are used to identify types of problem behaviors, settings, and at-risk students. Data also provide continuous feedback to evaluate whether practices and interventions are effective and to guide modifications in processes and practices.

Systems of support

School-wide PBS organizes efforts within four common school systems: school-wide (all students, staff, and settings); classroom; non-classroom (for example, playground, cafeteria, hallways); and individual and small groups of students (Lewis and Sugai, 1999). Contextual variables that predict and influence the occurrence of student behavior and the structures and routines to improve the academic and social behavioral outcomes are considered across contexts. School-wide systems focus on clearly defined expectations and procedures to teach and encourage desired behavior. Classroom setting systems incorporate the school-wide features and procedures in addition to classroom management practices, routines, and effective instruction (Colvin and Lazar, 1997). Non-classroom setting systems (for example, hallway, cafeteria, playground, restroom) add precorrection and active supervision to the behavior instruction and management practices employed in the school-wide and classroom systems (Colvin et al., 1997). Individual systems of PBS focus on comprehensive, integrated processes for team-based problem solving, functional assessment and behavior intervention planning, case management, and staff training and implementation delivered through small group instruction and individual behavior support plans (Lewis, Newcomer et al., 2000).

EMPIRICAL FOUNDATIONS OF SCHOOL-WIDE PBS

Reviews of the literature on prevention and reduction of challenging behavior indicate that the technology to change behavior is available (Walker et al., 1995). School-wide systems of PBS are firmly grounded in empirically validated practices such as social skills instruction, academic and curricular restructuring, proactive management, and individualized behavioral interventions.

Social skill instruction

Social skill instruction involves direct and planned instruction designed to teach specific social behavior that promotes social competence (Sugai and Lewis, 1996). The literature recommends that schools provide direct instruction using a 'model lead test' format through role-play and rehearsal and include multiple examples and practice across settings, involving a variety of people to maximize successful acquisition and generalized responding (Gresham, 1998). At the heart of all school-wide PBS practices is an emphasis on teaching pro-social behavior. School-wide PBS also provides an environment that is structured to be responsive to individual and small group social skill instruction. While the literature is clear that social skills can be taught to students with challenging behavior (for example, McIntosh et al., 1991), the generalized outcomes of training have been extremely weak (DuPaul and Eckert, 1994). However, researchers have built a case that poor generalization is primarily a function of environments not supporting newly-learned skills while allowing previous inappropriate patterns of behavior to continue to access social needs (Gresham, 1998; Gresham et al., 2001). School-wide PBS provides an environment that matches small group and individual strategies, thereby potentially increasing the likelihood of generalized responding through an emphasis on teaching social skills, a common language around expectations across school environments, and multiple adults reinforcing skill use.

Academic and curricular restructuring

Creating and adapting curriculum to insure that children are successful learners increases self-esteem and reduces correlated problem behavior (Colvin et al., 1993). The literature also associates effective instruction, academic engagement, and success with a reduction in problem behaviors (Cotton, 1999). Sugai and Horner (2002) suggest the adoption of curriculum that is empirically supported, culturally and developmentally appropriate and modified to accommodate individual differences.

Proactive management

Recent studies provide evidence that school-wide preventative management strategies can reduce the occurrence and escalation of problem behavior (Colvin and Fernandez, 2000; Nakasato, 2000; Taylor-Greene and Kartub, 2000). Practices such as precorrection and active supervision (Colvin et al., 1997) and frequent positive contacts with students promote positive climates and improvement in social behavior.

Individual behavioral interventions

Approximately 1 to 5 percent of students account for the majority of problem behavior in school settings (Sugai and Horner, 1999). Teams of educators must be fluent in functional assessment and the development of individualized interventions that build and extend the larger school-wide system to accommodate individual differences. Individual systems of PBS focus on integrated, team-based planning and problem solving to design individual support plans to prevent, reduce, and replace problems and to develop, maintain, and strengthen socially desirable behaviors. School-wide systems of PBS increase the likelihood that individual support plans are implemented with a high degree of integrity (Lewis, Colvin and Sugai, 2000).

CURRENT AND FUTURE DIRECTIONS

To date, a body of research has provided evidence to support the component features of school-wide PBS. In addition, an emerging database has shown that implementing universal systems of school-wide behavior support will impact overall rates of problem behavior in school. Findings from preliminary research show improvements in behavior, academic gains, and increases in instructional time (Horner et al., in press). Schools implementing a universal system of school-wide PBS report reductions of 40 to 60 percent in discipline reports (Sugai et al., 2002). For example, over a one-year period Taylor-Greene and her colleagues (1997) demonstrated a 42 percent reduction in behavioral offenses by clearly defining school-wide expectations and teaching students how to meet each expectation. More important, Taylor-Greene and her school team continue to report declines in behavioral problems (Taylor-Greene and Kartub, 2000). Likewise, Nakasato (2000) demonstrated drops in daily office referrals across six elementary schools through the development of universal PBS strategies. Finally, Scott (2001) demonstrated 65 to 75 percent reductions in out-of-school suspensions and in-school detentions, which allowed students to be more successful in class to the point of increased standardized test scores.

A related recommended universal strategy is to build systems of support in specific non-classroom settings such as the cafeteria, hallway, and playground. At this level, in addition to teaching positive expectations, routines and supervision are essential. For example, Kartub et al. (2000) demonstrated reductions in transition-related problem behaviors in the hallways of a middle school through a simple feedback system to the students. Lewis et al. (1998), through a combination of social skill instruction, active supervision, and group contingencies, demonstrated reductions in problem behaviors across the cafeteria, playground, and hallway within an elementary school. Colvin et al. (1997) demonstrated that through simple routine restructuring consisting of increased adult supervision, problem behaviors during the start of the school day were significantly reduced. Lewis et al. (2002) demonstrated similar reductions in problem behavior on the playground with instruction in rules, routines, and desired behaviors, and implementation of a group contingency reinforcement system.

While the data show the efficacy of school-wide PBS systems on reducing overall rates of problem behavior displayed by the general school population, less is known about the impact that school-wide PBS has on supporting at-risk and identified students. What is emerging from the field is that PBS may increase the capacity of schools to deliver more systematic and intensive targeted small group (Crone et al., 2001) and individual interventions (Horner et al., in press). Preliminary data from pilot studies are showing that functional-based interventions are outperforming traditional behavioral interventions (Ingram, 2002; Newcomer, 2002) and that plans are of higher quality if linked to school-wide PBS systems (Newcomer and Powers, 2002). More research is needed to show what additional benefit school-wide systems of PBS 'value add' to small group and individual student support plans.

IMPLICATIONS FOR PRACTICE AND RESEARCH

Practice

School-wide systems of PBS have the potential to prevent the occurrence of problem behaviors, to reduce the frequency of problem behaviors, and to increase the likelihood that individual support plans designed to support students with chronically challenging behavior are implemented with a high degree of integrity. Schools that have implemented school-wide systems of PBS increase their capacity to support students who present challenges by shifting away from traditional punishment-based responses to an approach that emphasizes the development of proactive, positive interventions. This trend in education is a shift away from pathology based models and places greater emphasis on personal competence and environmental integrity (Carr et al., 2002). In doing so, the roles and responsibilities of educators and all school personnel have been redefined in accountability for promoting an agenda of prevention and positive behavioral interventions.

The shift will also be evident as practioners move away from reliance on an 'expert' consultant model and a list of specific intervention techniques to one of collaboration with administrators, teachers, parents, and other professionals and become more involved as active intervention agents as part of a broad network of support (Lewis and Newcomer, 2002). As members of collaborative teams, educators will be responsible for goal setting, intervention selection, and programmatic changes that are embedded and integrated into broader support infrastructures.

Research

As research addressing PBS has moved from controlled laboratory and clinical environments to the more naturalistic environment of school, new challenges arise in assessment and methodology. Because multiple interacting variables come into play in application, it is difficult to measure the impact of individual variables. As an applied science, analysis must take into consideration multi-component interventions. This calls for greater flexibility in correlational analyses, data sources, and case studies (Carr et al., 2002).

Carr and colleagues (2002) point out that as schools take a more multi-dimensional approach to prevention and intervention, research is needed to identify variables and decision rules regarding how to combine multiple components into comprehensive packages. They further encourage the field to move toward a more preventative approach through investigation of specific skill and environmental deficiencies that lead to problem behavior.

NOTE

1 Development of this manuscript was supported in part by a grant from the Office of Special Education Programs, US Department of Education (H324T000021). Opinions expressed herein are those of the authors and do not necessarily reflect the position of the US Department of Education, and such endorsements should not be inferred.

REFERENCES

Carr, E.G., Dunlap, G., Horner, R., Koegel, R., Turnbull, A.P., Sailor, W., Anderson, J., Albin, R.W., Koegel, L. and Fox, L. (2002) 'Positive behavior support: Evolution of an applied science', *Journal of Positive Behavior Interventions*, 4 (1): 4–16, 20.

Colvin, G. and Fernandez, E. (2000) 'Sustaining effective behavior support systems in an elementary school', *Journal of Positive Behavior Interventions*, 2: 251–3.

Colvin, G., Kame'enui, E.J. and Sugai, G. (1993) 'Reconceptualizing behavior management and school-wide discipline in general education', *Education and Treatment of Children*, 16 (4): 361–81.

Colvin, G. and Lazar, M. (1997) *The Effective Elementary Classroom: Managing for Success.* Longmont, CO: Sopris West.

Colvin, G., Sugai, G., Good, R.H. and Lee, Y. (1997) 'Using active supervision and precorrection to improve transition behavior in elementary school', *School Psychology Quarterly*, 12 (4): 344–63.

Conduct Problem Prevention Research Group (1992) 'A developmental and clinical model for the prevention of conduct disorders: The FAST Track Program', *Development and Psychopathology*, 4: 509–527.

Cotton, K. (1999) *Research You Can Use to Improve Results.* Alexandria, VA: Association for Supervision and Curriculum Development.

Crone, D.A., Horner, R.H. and Hawken, L.S. (2001) *The Behavior Education Program (BEP) Handbook: A School's Systematic Guide to Responding to Chronic Problem Behavior.* Unpublished manuscript. Eugene, OR: University of Oregon.

DuPaul, G. and Eckert, T. (1994) 'The effects of social skills curricula: Now you see them, now you don't', *School Psychology Quarterly*, 9: 113–32.

Elliot, D.S. (1994) *Youth Violence: An Overview.* Boulder, CO: Center for the Study and Prevention of Violence.

Forness, S.R., Kavale, K.A., MacMillan, D.L., Asarnow, J.R. and Duncan, B.B. (1996) 'Early detection and prevention of emotional or behavioral disorders: Developmental aspects of systems of care', *Behavioral Disorders*, 21: 226–40.

Gresham, F.M. (1998) 'Social skills training: Should we raze, remodel, or rebuild?', *Behavioral Disorders*, 24 (1): 19–25.

Gresham, F.M., Sugai, G. and Horner, R.H. (2001) 'Interpreting outcomes of social skills training for students with high-incidence disabilities', *Exceptional Children*, 67 (3): 331–44.

Horner, R.H., Sugai, G., Todd, A.W. and Lewis-Palmer, T. (in press) 'School-wide positive behavior support: An alternative approach to discipline in schools', in L. Bambara and L. Kern (eds), *Positive Behavior Support.* New York: Guilford.

Ingram, K. (2002) *Comparing Effectiveness of Intervention Strategies that are Based on Functional Behavioral Assessment Information and those that are Contra-indicated by the Assessment*. Unpublished doctoral dissertation. Eugene, OR: University of Oregon.

Kartub, D.T., Taylor-Greene, S., March, R.E. and Horner, R.H. (2000) 'Reducing hallway noise: A systems approach', *Journal of Positive Behavior Interventions*, 2: 179–82.

Lewis, T.J., Colvin, G. and Sugai, G. (2000) 'The effects of pre-correction and active supervision on the recess behavior of elementary students', *Education and Treatment of Children*, 23 (2): 109–121.

Lewis, T.J. and Newcomer, L.L. (2002) 'Examining the efficacy of school-based consultation: Recommendations for improving outcomes', *Child and Family Behavior Therapy*, 24 (1/2): 165–81.

Lewis, T.J., Newcomer, L., Kelk, M. and Powers, L. (2000) 'One youth at a time: Addressing aggression and violence through individual systems of positive behavioral support', *Reaching Today's Youth*, 5 (1): 37–41.

Lewis, T.J., Powers, L.J., Kelk, M. and Newcomer, L.L. (2002) 'Reducing problem behaviors on the playground: An investigation of the application of schoolwide positive behavior supports', *Psychology in the Schools*, 39 (2): 181–90.

Lewis, T.J. and Sugai, G. (1999) 'Effective behavior support: A systems approach to proactive schoolwide management', *Focus on Exceptional Children*, 31 (6): 1–24.

Lewis, T.J., Sugai, G. and Colvin, G. (1998) 'Reducing problem behavior through a school-wide system of effective behavioral support: Investigation of a school-wide social skills training program and contextual intervention', *School Psychology Review*, 27: 446–59.

Mayer, G.R. (1995) 'Preventing antisocial behavior in the schools', *Journal of Applied Behavior Analysis*, 28 (4): 467–78.

McIntosh, R., Vaughn, S. and Zaragoza, N. (1991) 'A review of social studies interventions for students with learning disabilities', *Journal of Learning Disabilities*, 24: 451–8.

Myers, C.L. and Holland, K.L. (2000) 'Classroom behavioral interventions: Do teachers consider the function of the behavior?', *Psychology in the Schools*, 37 (3): 271–80.

Nakasato, J. (2000) 'Data-based decision making in Hawaii's behavior support effort', *Journal of Positive Behavior Interventions*, 2 (4): 247–51.

Newcomer, L.L. (2002) *Functional Assessment: An investigation of assessment reliability and treatment validity and the effectiveness of function-based interventions compared to non-function based interventions*. Unpublished doctoral dissertation. Columbia, MO: University of Missouri.

Newcomer, L.L. and Powers, L. (2002) *A Team Approach to Functional Behavioral Assessment-Based Positive Behavioral Support Plans*. Paper presented at Midwest Symposium for Leadership in Behavior Disorders, February, Kansas City, MO.

Scott, T.M. (2001) 'A school-wide example of positive behavioral support', *Journal of Positive Behavioral Interventions*, 3: 88–94.

Shinn, M., Stoner, G. and Walker, H.M. (eds) (2002) *Interventions for Academic and Behavior Problems: Preventive and Remedial Approaches*. Silver Springs, MD: National Association of School Psychologists.

Skiba, R.J. (2002) 'Special education and school discipline: A precarious balance', *Behavioral Disorders*, 27 (2): 81–97.

Sugai, G. and Horner, R.H. (1999) 'Discipline and behavioral support: Practices, pitfalls and promises', *Effective School Practices*, 17: 10–22.

Sugai, G. and Horner, R.H. (2001) 'The evolution of discipline practices: School-wide positive behavior supports', *Child and Family Behavior Therapy*, 24 (1/2): 23–50.

Sugai, G., Horner, R., Dunlap, G., Hieneman, M., Lewis, T.J., Nelson, C.M., Scott, T., Liaupsin, C., Sailor, W., Turnbull, A.P., Turnbull, H., Wikham, D., Wilcox, B. and Ruef, M. (2000) 'Applying positive behavior supports and functional behavioral assessment in schools', *Journal of Positive Behavior Interventions*, 2: 131–43.

Sugai, G., Horner, R., Lewis, T.J. and Cheney, D. (2002) *Positive Behavioral Supports*. Invited presentation at the OSEP Research Project Directors' Conference, July, Washington, DC.

Sugai, G. and Lewis, T.J. (1996) 'Preferred and promising practices for social skills instruction', *Focus on Exceptional Children*, 29 (4): 1–16.

Taylor-Greene, S., Brown, D.K., Nelson, L., Longton, J., Gassman, T., Cohen, J. Swartz, J., Horner, R.H., Sugai, G. and Hall, S. (1997) 'School-wide behavioral support: Starting the year off right', *Journal of Behavioral Education*, 7: 99–112.

Taylor-Greene, S.J. and Kartub, D.T. (2000) 'Durable implementation of school-wide behavior support: The high five program', *Journal of Positive Behavior Interventions*, 2: 233–5.

Tobin, T., Sugai, G. and Colvin, G. (1996) 'Patterns in middle school discipline referrals', *Journal of Emotional and Behavioral Disorders*, 4 (2): 82–94.

Walker, H. M., Colvin, G. and Ramsey, E. (1995) *Antisocial Behavior in School: Strategies and Best Practices*. Pacific Grove, CA: Brooks/Cole.

Zins, J.E. and Ponti, C.R. (1990) 'Best practices in school-based consultation', in A. Thomas and J. Grimes (eds), *Best Practices in School Psychology – II*. Washington, DC: National Association of School Psychologists. pp. 673–94.

17

Building School-wide Behavior Interventions that Really Work

BOB ALGOZZINE AND KATE ALGOZZINE

Effective school-wide interventions that meet the needs of all students are well recognized as essential in improving educational outcomes and results for children and youth, especially those with emotional and behavioral disabilities (EBD) (see, for example, Algozzine and Kay, 2001). Unfortunately, many children currently being served under the Individuals with Disabilities Education Act (IDEA) are typically identified too late to receive full benefit from those interventions. This problem is most prominent with two groups of children – those identified for special education and related services under the categories 'emotional disturbance' (ED) and 'specific learning disabilities' (LD). Children with ED, sometimes referred to as those with 'behavior disorders' (BD), are among the most difficult for many teachers to teach because their behaviors challenge even the most experienced professionals (Kauffman, 1999). These children are often not identified as being eligible for special education and related services until after their problems and disabilities have reached serious levels. These are children who, very early in their education, exhibit behaviors that lead to discipline problems as they get older.

There currently exists a substantial and compelling body of research describing how to help these children. For instance, research indicates that children with ED:

- can be assessed and identified early with relative ease and accuracy;
- often fall behind because they do not receive appropriate interventions earlier;
- can make tremendous gains when provided with effective services during early childhood; and
- may need individually tailored interventions because one approach may not fit all children. (see, for example, Algozzine and Kay, 2001)

Without effective interventions, these students are at high risk for failing in school, becoming discipline problems, and dropping out of school. A key step in building effective school-wide programs for students with emotional and behavior problems is identifying those requiring assistance and providing them with a menu of proactive interventions.

IDENTIFYING STUDENTS REQUIRING INTERVENTION

A key feature of promising school-wide behavior interventions is their emphasis on the inclusion of all students in the school. Effective support for behavior begins by attending to all students and identifying those requiring more intensive instruction and intervention. Providing such support, in turn, requires understanding the range of behavioral problems that students present in schools and knowledge of effective strategies and practices for addressing those difficulties and challenges. To meet these varied needs, interventions need to be systemic and address a range of needs across three groups representing three levels of intervention intensity (see Figure 17.1):

1 Primary prevention involves universal instruction to avert the onset of behavior problems.
2 Secondary prevention refers to strategies and procedures that address small groups of students who need additional support or assistance to successfully acquire new behavioral skills.
3 Tertiary prevention involves more intense, specialized interventions, such as one-on-one interventions, for individual students who, despite previous instruction and intervention efforts, experience chronic behavior problems.

PROMOTING PROMISING PRACTICES

School administrators face daily and continuous challenges in efforts to establish and maintain safe and orderly classroom environments where

Primary intervention	Secondary intervention	Tertiary intervention
All students participate in the same system with or without the benefit of referral for or identification of special education needs.	Subgroups of students participate in more intensive system with or without the benefit of referral for or identification of special education needs.	Individual students participate in most intensive system with or without the benefit of referral for or identification of special education needs.
[Unified Discipline]	[Self-Monitoring] [Self-Management] [Contracts]	[Functional Behavioral Assessment] [Individual Behavior Plan]

A key feature of a multi-level intervention model is that as the level of intensity increases the number of students requiring services decreases.

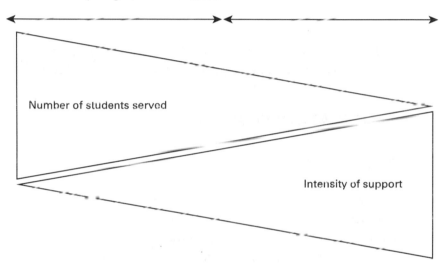

Number of students served

Intensity of support

Figure 17.1   *Components of effective school-wide behavior interventions*

teachers can teach and students can learn (Brooks et al., 2000; Leone et al., 2000; Nelson et al., 1998; Sugai, Sprague et al., 2000). Prevention strategies for controlling problem behaviors are preferred to general behavior management approaches because of the potential to reduce the development of new (incidence) and current cases (prevalence) of school-related problems. A well-crafted approach to prevention improves the efficiency and effectiveness with which school, classroom, and individual behavior support systems operate. Some models are difficult to implement and maintain because many students are unresponsive to generalized interventions, have a dominant impact on classroom functioning, respond slowly even to targeted interventions, and often demand intensive, ongoing, individualized behavior support (Sugai, Sprague et al., 2000). Preventing and reducing behavior problems requires a plan that:

- uses a team-based approach to identify, implement, and evaluate best practices, includes administrators, teachers, school psychologists, other support personnel, and parents, and supports improvement efforts with budget, personnel, and resource allocations;
- uses research-validated practices;
- makes behavioral instruction proactive by modeling and teaching appropriate social behavior, giving students opportunities to practice and become fluent at expected behavior, and providing plenty of positive feedback;
- provides a continuum of behavioral support, increasing the intensity of the intervention as the intensity of the problem increases;
- uses data-based systems to guide decisions and keep staff informed as to what is currently in place as well as what is working and not working; and
- uses data on behavior as part of the school's goals. (Algozzine and Kay, 2001; Safran and Oswald, 2003; Sugai, 2000; Sugai and Horner, 2001; Sugai, Horner et al., 2000; Turnbull et al., 2002)

ILLUSTRATION FROM PRACTICE

These facets of effective school-wide behavior interventions are integrated into the four interrelated objectives that drive efforts to implement *unified discipline* (Algozzine et al., 2000). Effective use of this school-wide behavior intervention requires that all participating school staff master each of these objectives: unified attitudes, unified expectations, unified correction procedures, and unified team roles.

Effective discipline requires active monitoring that is firm and caring without overly-emotional responses. The ability to interact with misbehaving students using appropriate voice tones, without responding in kind and without becoming emotionally upset, is a key behavior that is shared by those who practice unified discipline (see, for example, White, Algozzine et al., 2001). These *unified attitudes* are supported by the following beliefs: instruction can improve behavior; behavioral instruction is part of teaching; personalizing or becoming tangled up in misbehavior makes matters worse rather than better; and, mental and emotional poise and toughness make discipline methods work. Measurable behaviors associated with unified attitudes include use of warm voice tone when giving teacher direction or correction and active monitoring of classroom activities.

Consistency and positive, *unified expectations* for successful behavioral instruction are a hallmark of an effective school-wide discipline plan (Colvin et al., 1993; White, Algozzine et al., 2001). Clearly described school and classroom rules, procedures, and consequences define the expectations

Definition: Unified discipline is a positive approach for school-wide discipline that brings all
                     school staff together as a team with a consistent, common, shared approach to
                     managing behavior.

Focus: Administrators, teachers, and staff are 'on the same page' philosophically and act as
                     a cohesive team in creating and enforcing school and classroom rules; students
                     know what they are expected to do and realize that everyone is 'refereeing with the
                     same rules.'

Key components:

Unified *Attitudes*	• Good behavior can be taught, just like reading, writing, and math. • We can teach appropriate behavior in a positive manner. • We are all in this together.
Unified *Expectations*	• Represented by rules and procedures. • Rules and procedures are curriculum for teaching behavior.

Unified
Management
	• Use more do's than don'ts to teach students academics *as well as* behavior.
	• Monitor rule violations.
	• Use warm, assertive, and firm voice tones.
	• Use a consistent correction procedure as needed.
	   • State problem behavior.
	   • State rule violated.
	   • State unified consequence.
	   • Provide direction to self-correct.
	   • Reinforce self-correction.
	   • Provide encouragement for expected behavior.

Unified roles	• School personnel have clear responsibilities. • Faculty support administrators and administrators support faculty. • Faculty's role is to follow procedures as a job requirement. • Principal's role is to take best action when students are sent to the office.

Figure 17.2   *Definition, focus, and key components of unified discipline*

for success in schools using unified discipline (see Figure 17.2). Having
clear-cut expectations does not mean every school practicing unified discipline looks the same. Administrators and teachers in each school define
their particular expectations based on architectural arrangements, prior
history, and staff and community concerns. Regardless, some fundamental
characteristics are evident in each school.

First, rules are set without equivocation. Rules form the basis for
describing expectations; following rules is a major objective of behavioral
instruction. Rules implemented correctly depersonalize conflict and protect teachers and administrators (that is, conflict is between student and an
expectation, not a teacher or administrator). Rules provide a basis for
establishing and maintaining a consistent, safe and orderly environment.

Second, clear, specific, and reasonable expectations are evident within four
categories: school rules, classroom rules, school procedures, and classroom

procedures. School rules apply across all locations and activities within the school, at all times and with all personnel. Major school rules describe actions that threaten the safety and well being of people in the school (for example, 'Verbal or physical threats are prohibited in this school.'). School procedures describe actions that promote the orderly flow of the instructional process and are time, place or activity specific (for example, 'Walk in the hallways at all times.'). Classroom rules apply across all activities within the classroom, at all times and with all personnel. Areas typically addressed by classroom rules are teacher–student talk, student–student talk, student movement, and student work. Classroom procedures apply to specific times or activities, or places (for example, where to turn in work, when to sharpen pencils, where to find free-time activities, where to find transition activities).

When school rules, school procedures, classroom rules, or classroom procedures are violated, professionals practicing unified discipline respond similarly and consistently with correction procedures. When everyone handles infractions with *unified correction procedures*, students learn that what happens when they misbehave is procedural, not personal. Teachers gain competence (I know what to do) and confidence (I know that what I do is respected and practiced by my colleagues). Inconsistent consequences represent broken promises, non-assertive behaviors, opportunities for student distrust, and invitations for rule infractions. Consistent correction procedures build trust, provide opportunities for change over time, and represent consistent consequences illustrating a commitment to students and colleagues within the school.

Unified correction procedures involve actively monitoring student behavior and applying consequences consistently, in a warm, assertive, firm voice using four observable steps: state the behavior, state the violated rule, state the unified consequence, and offer encouragement to prevent future violations. In unified discipline, faculty members act as referees. They 'call the fouls' every time and they maintain their poise and composure. If players get upset, they remind players that rules are part of the game, and they deliver the promised consequences. The particular consequences applied vary by school. At the elementary level, teachers pull colored tickets, change colors on a stoplight, or turn happy faces on a board to unhappy faces. Often, the faculty unify on a system currently used by one of their respected and effective colleagues.

Reinforcement is not unified within the model by design. In contrast to correction, teachers are encouraged to provide personal versus procedural reinforcement that is also genuine and performance-based reinforcement. Teachers are encouraged to provide high ratios of reinforcement to correction, particularly for those with higher frequencies of rule or procedural violations.

In a school where unified discipline is practiced, clear *unified roles* and responsibilities are described for all school personnel. This aspect of the model promotes faculty support of administration and administration support of faculty, and eliminates second-guessing when disciplinary and classroom actions are taken. Unified roles also develop collegial participation in unified discipline programs. For example, the principal's role is to reinforce teachers when they follow the unified discipline procedures correctly. Reinforcement is based on teacher performance, not student response to correction or improvement. When the procedures are followed correctly, second-guessing is not allowed, regardless of a student's response to them. Principals are also expected to make flexible and individualized decisions about discipline when students are referred to the office for school rule violations. This means principals make decisions on student needs and reinforcement history, not on a 'one size fits all,' inflexible policy. For example, 'students who violate a major school rule will receive three days out-of-school suspension' is an inflexible policy that puts principals in a straightjacket. There really is no decision making. The principal is forced to suspend, even if suspension is reinforcing to the student (Thank you. I want to go home!). Under unified discipline, the principal is free to do what is best for the student, and is assured of faculty support, no matter what action is taken. Similarly, the faculty's role is to follow the procedures as a job requirement. Each teacher should expect support for a correction done accurately. No longer is support defined as the principal providing harsh punishment for a student offense. Second-guessing of principal decisions for office referrals is not allowed, regardless of student response. An 'I do my job and you do your job' attitude is encouraged. Since office referrals are only used for school rule violations within unified discipline, data can be collected on percentage of appropriate versus inappropriate teacher referrals.

DATA ON EFFECTIVENESS

The effects of using unified discipline have been evaluated; the value of this research is the demonstration that what goes on in classrooms containing students with disruptive behavior can be improved with the application of a systematic, consistent school-wide discipline model. For example, Marr et al. (2002) compared data from students in classrooms of two groups of teachers (that is, Project and Comparison). The Project group ($n = 12$) met three criteria: teachers used unified discipline for at least one year; served as models or lead teachers for new teachers; and taught the same grade while participating in the evaluation project. Students in classrooms of a random sample of other teachers were included in the Comparison group ($n = 15$). With the exception of reading, students in Project classrooms demonstrated more positive on-task behavior and less negative off-task behavior than students in Comparison classrooms. Total on-task behavior was significantly higher in Project classrooms than in Comparison classrooms. Significant specific on-task differences were indicated in question answering and hand-raising behaviors, as well as paying attention. Significant off-task differences were indicated in time spent looking around, talking inappropriately, and engaging in appropriate tasks. An additional effectiveness comparison was completed using summary observations from these and other classrooms in comparisons of behaviors over time. At the beginning of the project, on-task behavior was significantly lower in model classrooms than in other rooms. Significant improvements in on-task behavior were evident in the Spring observations conducted in the model classrooms, while Fall and Spring on-task observations were similar in comparison classrooms. At the beginning of the project, off-task behavior was significantly higher in model classrooms than in other rooms. Significant improvements in on-task behavior were evident in the Spring observations conducted in the model classrooms, while Fall and Spring off-task observations were similar in comparison classrooms. In a related study, classroom observations supported the integrity of teachers' use of the model discipline program and numbers (per school, classroom, and child) of office referrals dropped consistently from unacceptably high levels prior to the intervention to reasonable and acceptable levels throughout the course of the project (White, Marr et al., 2001).

WHAT WE NEED TO KNOW

Efforts to improve general learning conditions at school revolve around preventing inappropriate behavior and teaching appropriate behavior. Effective behavior instruction is as important as effective academic instruction. For example, Nelson et al. argued that 'students will behave according to social norms if [teachers] take the trouble to teach those students those norms and supervise them in a consistent way' (1998: 4). They proposed a model that emphasized direct interventions within and across all school settings (ensuring that disruptive behavior did not occur or become entrenched (that is, *preventative* focus) or was corrected (that is, *remedial* focus). They argued that different types of students (that is, typical, at-risk, target), varying according to the nature of their problems, need different types of interventions. School-wide interventions (for example, effective teaching, school-wide discipline) are appropriate for students who are not at risk for problems. Targeted interventions (for example, conflict resolutions, anger management) are appropriate for students at risk of developing disruptive behavior problems. Intensive, comprehensive interventions (for example, community-based service linkages, school and community partnerships) are appropriate for students exhibiting persistent disruptive behavior patterns.

Preventing and reducing behavior problems is not the responsibility of any one group or individual. Administrators need assistance identifying, implementing, and supporting effective interventions. Teachers need help teaching behavior as well as teaching academics. Students need to be taught appropriate social, behavioral, and academic norms and supervised in their learning and demonstration of them. Parents need assistance participating as partners in making schools safer, more positive places to send their children.

Research makes it clear that there is no single program or method that is effective in teaching all children to behave. Rather, successful efforts to improve behavior emphasize identification and implementation of *evidence-based* practices that educators can use to promote success among students with diverse behavioral needs.

The term 'evidence-based instruction' means that an educational practice has a tested and proven record of success; that is, there is reasonable evidence to suggest that when the practice is used, success is expected. Other terms that are sometimes used to convey the same idea are 'research-based instruction' and 'scientifically-based research.'

In general, interventionists (that is, teachers, psychologists, school counselors) agree that such evidence should be:

- *Objective*: data would be identified and interpreted similarly by any evaluator.
- *Valid:* data adequately represent the tasks that children need to accomplish to succeed.
- *Reliable*: data will remain essentially unchanged if collected on a different day or by a different person.
- *Systematic*: data were collected according to a rigorous design of either experimentation or observation.
- *Peer reviewed*: data have been approved for publication by a panel of independent reviewers.

The challenge that confronts interventionists is the need to evaluate methods and programs through the lens of their particular school and classroom settings. They must determine if the practices they are reviewing or using are a good match for the children they teach.

It is imperative now and in the future that interventionists have access to the knowledge base of findings supporting effective behavior interventions. Just as important is the challenge of helping these individuals to understand and use what is known about improving behavior and involving them in ongoing efforts to study these methods in a variety of classroom and clinical settings. In most cases, this means developing 'reality-based' practices by 'fine-tuning' effective instructional practices through reflective and systematic use in schools and other field-based environments. Engaging in 'reality-based' research means extending the knowledge base by carefully observing, generating, and testing hypotheses, collecting data, and drawing conclusions. The extent to which interventionists extend 'reality-based' practices with 'reality-based' research will be the test of future efforts to build school-wide behavior interventions that really work.

REFERENCES

Algozzine, B., Audette, B., Ellis, E., Marr, M.B. and White, R. (2000) 'Supporting teachers, principals and students through unified discipline', *Teaching Exceptional Children*, 33 (2): 42–7.

Algozzine, B. and Kay, P. (2001) *Preventing Problem Behaviors: A Handbook of Successful Prevention Strategies*. Thousand Oaks, CA: Corwin.

Brooks, K., Schiraldi, V. and Ziedenberg, J. (2000) *School House Hype: Two Years Later*. Washington, DC: Justice Policy Institute. (Available online at http://www.jjic.org/pdf/shh2.pdf)

Colvin, G., Kame'enui, E.J. and Sugai, G. (1993) 'Reconceptualizng behavior management and school-wide discipline in general education', *Education and Treatment of Children*, 16: 361–81.

Kauffman, J.M. (1999) 'Comments on social development research in EBD', *Journal of Emotional and Behavioral Disorders*, 7: 189–91.

Leone, P.E., Mayer, M.J., Malmgren, K. and Meisel, S.M. (2000) 'School violence and disruption: Rhetoric, reality, and reasonable balance', *Focus on Exceptional Children*, 33 (1): 1–20.

Marr, M.B., Audette, R., White, R., Ellis, E. and Algozzine, B. (2002) 'School-wide discipline and classroom ecology', *Special Services in the Schools*, 18: 55–73.

Nelson, J.R., Crabtree, M., Marchand-Martella, N. and Martella, R. (1998) 'Teaching behavior in the whole school', *Teaching Exceptional Children*, 30 (4): 4–9.

Safran, S.P. and Oswald, K. (2003) 'Positive behavior supports: Can schools reshape disciplinary practices?', *Exceptional Children*, 69: 361–73.

Sugai, G. (2000) 'Instituting school-wide behavior supports', *CEC Today*, 6 (7): 5.

Sugai, G. and Horner, R.H. (2001) *School Climate and Discipline: Going to Scale*. Paper presented at the National Summit on the Shared Implementation of IDEA, Washington, DC.

Sugai, G., Horner, R.H., Dunlap, G., Hieneman, M., Lewis, T., Nelson, C.M., Scott, T., Liaupsin, C., Turnbull, A., Turnbull, R., Wickham, D., Ruef, M. and Wilcox, B. (2000) 'Applying positive behavioral supports and functional behavioral assessment in schools', *Journal of Positive Behavior Intervention*, 2 (3): (Available online at http://www.pbis.org/files/TAG1.doc)

Sugai, G., Sprague, J.A., Horner, R.H. and Walker, H.M. (2000) 'Preventing school violence: The use of office discipline referrals to assess and monitor school-wide discipline interventions', *Journal of Emotional and Behavioral Disorders*, 8: 94–101.

Turnbull, A., Edmonson, H., Griggs, P., Wickham, D., Sailor, W., Freeman, R., Guess, D., Lassen, S. McCart, A., Park, J., Riffel, L., Turnbull, R. and Warren, J. (2002) 'A blueprint for schoolwide positive behavior support: Implementation of three components', *Exceptional Children*, 68: 376–402.

White, R., Algozzine, B., Audette, R., Marr, M.B. and Ellis, E.D. Jr. (2001) 'Unified discipline: A school-wide approach for managing problem behavior', *Intervention in School and Clinic*, 37 (1): 3–8.

White, R., Marr, M.B., Ellis, E., Audette, B. and Algozzine, B. (2001) 'Effects of schoolwide discipline on office referrals', *Journal of At-Risk Issues*, 7 (2): 4–12.

18

Advocacy for Students with Emotional and Behavioral Disorders

CARL R. SMITH

The notion of advocacy is a concept familiar to those who work with youth with disabilities and their families or other youngsters who may be considered as having special needs. After all many, if not most, of the services and programs that are in place today are there as a result of the committed work of advocates who *may* have been challenging the status quo of their time to seek and secure services for a population of individuals who may have been perceived by many as undeserving of special considerations (Gray and Noakes, 1998). The readers of this volume represent different countries of our world in which advocacy struggles have reflected different social and timing contexts that affect the critical moments in which advocated changes became possible. Also variable are the committed individuals who were 'there' to provide the energy, passion and vision to provoke and sustain needed change and the identified mechanisms for accomplishing the social and structural change required in order to take promises and dreams to a level of implementation.

Within special education in the United States we saw the results of advocacy efforts in the passage in 1975 by the US Congress of the Education of All Handicapped Children Act (later to be entitled the Individuals with Disabilities Act). This particular piece of legislation put forth the notion that *all* children and youth with disabilities are entitled to a free and appropriate special education program, regardless of severity of their disabilities, and are also to be provided with other program dimensions such as an appropriate evaluation, an individualized educational program, an education in the least restrictive environment, guarantees regarding parental participation and procedural safeguards extending beyond those offered for students in general education (Turnbull and Turnbull, 2000). This final product of advocacy reflected a complex series of social forces, historical context and political leadership; dimensions we will be discussing within this chapter.

Yet in the midst of this social policy progress in meeting the needs in the United States has loomed another perspective critical of these special education rights that has not been as readily apparent. This specifically relates to those students who have behavioral disorders (designated as students with emotional disturbance within IDEA). In an influential policy document developed to set the scene for the upcoming amendments to the IDEA the following is asserted regarding the continued eligibility for students with behavioral disorders who fail to respond to school-and system-wide interventions:

> For those students who persist in defying rules despite such interventions, it is questionable whether they should be included within the framework of special education at all. It is a fine line between a psychiatric disorder that can be treated and criminal behavior that should be adjudicated ... (Horn and Tynan, 2001: 44)

As recently suggested by Scheuermann and Johns (2002), this report, and specifically the content illustrated above, seems to set the scene for serious discussion of which students 'belong' or 'don't belong' in our schools.

In the mid 1990s this perspective also came up in the intense debate, in the US Congress and across the country regarding the means by which students with disabilities should be disciplined in the schools. From the early implementation of the federal special education legislation until 1995 the application of disciplinary outcomes for students with disabilities had been considered as a matter to be dealt with on an individualized basis, all the while considering the relationship of any behavior necessitating disciplinary measures to a student's disability condition. This individualized approach was being attacked as protecting the rights of a few at the risk of the general wellbeing of the many (Stanfield, 1995).

Thus, in the United States there continues an ongoing debate over the extent to which students with behavioral disorders should be dealt with differently in the basic eligibility for services domain as well as in the area of discipline. Such debate points to the importance of advocacy efforts on behalf of these youth. These students are more at risk to be excluded from our school systems, more likely to become involved with the juvenile justice system, and tend to have negative long-term outcomes following their school experiences (US DoE, 1998; Valdes et al., 1990; Walker and

Sprague, 1999). These data suggest the complexity of the challenges we face in advocating for these students and their families.

In meeting the needs of these students we need to keep in mind both specific (micro) and broad based (macro) perspectives in our advocacy efforts (Walker and Sprague, 1999). This should remind us that we are truly dealing with the needs of these students from a systems perspective, with our schools being merely one element, albeit a critical one, in meeting the needs of these students. Walker and Sprague, in discussing the practice of functional behavioral assessments, describe how we need to be open to both specific and broad views of behavior:

> The functional behavioral assessment approach is viewed as having great value for analyzing and understanding the social contingencies and contextual factors that sustain maladaptive behavior within specific settings. The risk factors exposure model is more macro in nature and is useful for understanding and predicting the development of maladaptive behavior across time and settings in a longitudinal, developmental sense. The integration of the two approaches is viewed as necessary in order to gain a comprehensive, complete understanding of the origins and dynamics of maladaptive behavior patterns among at-risk children and youth. (1999: 335)

From a micro perspective we, as advocates, need to be committed to providing an appropriate educational program for each of these students. Within the recent US federal legislation the use of a functional behavioral assessment approach is suggested, including a careful analysis of any per-ceived problem behaviors, their context and the forces that appear to be maintaining the behavior of concern within specific settings. We also need to be committed to using such information to design effective behavioral intervention strategies leading to positive behavioral changes for the student, including the contextual elements that need to be changed in order for the student to benefit. The term 'positive behavioral supports' has come into both policy directions (Sugai et al., 1999) and advocacy vocabulary (Children's Behavioral Alliance, 2003) as the organizing schema for developing such a support system for all youth, particularly those with behavioral disorders. But this micro perspective, as important as it may seem, only takes us part of the way in our advocacy efforts on behalf of these students.

From a macro perspective we need to realize that there are critical and complex factors beyond the school setting that strongly influence the eventual outcomes for these students. The professional literature in areas such as juvenile justice (Coalition for Juvenile Justice, 2000) refers to the balance of risk and protective factors that ultimately impact the outcome for students with behavioral disorders. From an advocacy perspective this macro domain should remind us all that our efforts of advocating within the school realm needs to be complemented with advocacy efforts beyond our school settings to those broader community and societal arenas in which change needs to occur in order to meet the needs of our students.

This macro perspective also needs to attend to the importance of the perspective taken by the persons we serve, namely the children and their families, regarding the extent to which they 'buy-in' and value the programs, services and/or interventions for which we are advocating. We, in professional roles, may easily fall into the trap of assuming that the persons for whom we are advocating see their needs in the same manner in which we do. Obviously, this leads to the importance of our ability to effectively and authentically communicate with the persons for whom we are advocating, with a constant reminder to ourselves that we have not necessarily walked in their shoes. This writer is reminded of a situation a number of years ago involving a youngster in rural Iowa whose behavior had reached such a point that school officials were convinced that he required residential treatment in order to bring his behavior under control. School officials had also been involved in a series of conversations with the mother of this student in which the mutual concerns of the school and home had been identified and appeared to be relatively consistent. On the day of a particular serious incident at school the mother was called from work to meet with staff, including the school principal, the boy's teacher, the school psychologist, the school social worker, and this writer, who was serving as a consultant to the school. The mother, a hard-working woman with a strong demeanor and a no-nonsense way about her, broke down into tears shortly after our meeting started. At this point, the school social worker, in a sincere attempt to comfort the mother, innocently stated, ' I know how you feel, this is a difficult decision.' To this statement the mother paused, glared at the social worker and asserted, 'Don't tell me you know how I feel – you have never had to send your child away.'

As much as we advocate for students and causes, we don't necessarily *know* how it feels to be the person we are trying to serve, and we best remember so! This dynamic reinforces the importance of the humility we should all shoulder in working with those for whom we advocate. This should also remind us of the importance of considering the *acceptability* of the interventions we are proposing for students to both the student and their families. As Jensen describes, the selection process for choosing evidence-based interventions in medical decision making the treating physician must:

> … not only consider the 'evidence,' but all evidence must be evaluated in the context of the provider's clinical skills and past experiences, his/her ability to evaluate the patient/consumer's health care status and needs, identifying all available treatment options, coupled with the simultaneous consideration of patient/consumer preferences, concerns, expectations, and values. (2001: 50)

DIMENSIONS OF ADVOCACY

There are several dimensions of advocacy that impact our work with students with behavioral disorders. This includes areas we may want to refer to as legal/policy as well as our professional responsibility to advocate. While the power of overall advocacy frequency depends on the extent to which these two forms overlap, it would seem beneficial to speak briefly about each of these dimensions.

Legal/policy advocacy

A primary focus of these volumes is on various aspects of meeting the needs of students with behavioral disorders. An essential element is the extent to which the institutional structures serving these youth, are, in fact, meeting the intent of their missions. Added to this complexity is the extent to which each of the institutional structures has been given a mandate and formal expectation for serving these youth. Other, additional mandates or rules may go to the quality of the services to be provided by the respective entities. At the core of each of these bureaucracies is an elected body that provides direction regarding what the agency must provide versus what it is able to provide. This is true whether we are speaking at the local level, regional, state or national levels.

Driving the momentum of these structures are the citizens to which the structures are accountable. In the area of serving students with behavioral disorders, our most important legal and policy mandates have occurred as a result of advocacy efforts impacting those legislative bodies, which enact laws and direct rule making. In the area of behavioral disorders in the United States and other countries (Didaskalou and Millward, 2002; Gray and Panter, 2000), we have often been swept along in this policy advocacy by other constituencies representing students with disabilities. Indeed, had we been given the task of beginning from 'scratch' on behalf of students whose behaviors may challenge the very core of what many may consider the civility expectation of our schools and communities, we may have fallen far short of our current policy directives. Within the context of this 'piggy-back' dynamic there does emerge certain dimensions of program needs that seem particularly important for these youth and their families from the policy perspective.

For example, a major policy lynchpin in the entire realm of providing programs and services for these youth is what is determined to be an 'appropriate' program to meet the basic needs of these youth. Under the IDEA requirements in the United States it is expected that every child who qualifies as a student with special education needs will be provided a *free, appropriate, public education (FAPE)*. According to the US Supreme Court (*Board of Education v. Rowley*, 1982), this 'basic floor of opportunity' is required in special education. This is, in this writer's opinion, a powerful mandate that has yet to be achieved for many students with behavioral disorders. Yet, despite these apparent failings, this expectation does establish the foundation from which many individual and collective advocacy efforts can progress.

Dyson, from a British perspective, points to another policy challenge in reviewing the progress that has been made in serving special populations. He points to the dilemma we all face in whether to put our efforts toward improvements for the greater good of all versus placing most of our advocacy efforts toward assuring the rights of individual learners who may need assistance. Dyson describes this as the 'commonality-difference' dilemma and challenges all of us to carefully examine the fault-lines of either position taken to its extreme:

> I fully realize that this is a difficult message to give to an audience of practitioners and policy-makers who cannot avoid the necessity to act – and frequently to act quickly and decisively in complex situations, with minimal opportunities for reflection and debate. ... However, in a field such as ours, which is shot through with ethical and political questions, it seems doubly important to resist this desire. If looking at our past enables us to do that, then it will indeed be a worthwhile exercise. (2001: 28)

Professional advocacy

An important adjunct to the dimension of legal/policy advocacy is the role played by professionals who serve students with behavioral disorders. In this author's opinion, the relative importance of professional advocacy is, in large part, dependent on the extent to which the professional interests in serving students with behavioral disorders is clearly articulated, has professional champions who can take the message to a broad range of consumers, has a reasonable support base within the professional discipline and, perhaps most important from an advocacy standpoint, is aligned with a comparable position being taken by consumer or parent groups. The various roles taken by professionals and others in such a movement has recently been described by Malcolm Gladwell (2000) in an insightful social commentary titled *The Tipping Point*. Gladwell presents several examples of ideas, products or social movements that were unexpectedly successful and not dependent on the traditional measures of empirical research, market surveys or the like. He asserts that the success of any efforts in creating what he refers to as epidemic change is dependent on our ability to use the 'right' people (content experts, knowledge brokers, and communicators) with a powerful manner of capturing the message for the change we are advocating:

> … we're trying to change our audience in some small yet critical respect: we're trying to infect them, sweep them up in our epidemic, convert them from hostility to acceptance. That can be done through the influence of special kinds of people, people of extraordinary personal connection. That's the Law of the Few. It can be done by changing the content of communication, by making a message so memorable that it sticks in someone's mind and compels them to action. That is the Stickiness Factor. (2000: 166)

As we look at advocacy needs in the field of behavioral disorders, we perhaps should attend to specific sub-examples of where advocacy efforts have appeared to be most successful with Gladwell's analysis in mind.

An example of where professional interests have melded into a successful advocacy movement, using the above criteria would be meeting the needs of young children with autism. Even during times of limited resources and calls for reduction in spending in special education, advocacy efforts in educational programming, research, and public awareness regarding the needs of these students have seemed to flourish. I would suggest that a significant reason for such is the extent to which alliances have been formed among parents, providers and various professionals with expertise across research, policy development, and communication to speak to the needs of such youth. In impacting policy development, advocates in the area of autism have been able to point to specific interventions and professional practices that suggests more positive outcomes for their children. Legal advocates have been able to take this professional work and mold a threshold in providing meaningful benefit for children served and thus led to appropriate programs. All of these efforts have aligned themselves and thus have led to new programs and services that would not have been delivered if the school bureaucracy alone had defined what policymakers considered to be required for these children EBD and youth.

This example of *successful advocacy* leading to new and needed programs for students with behavioral disorders is being duplicated, to some extent, in other areas such as attention deficit/hyperactivity disorder (AD/HD). This author has, for the last several years, been active with the primary family-led organization representing children and adults with this condition (Children and Adults with Attention Deficit/Hyperactivity Disorder – CHADD). A large difference between the AD/HD condition and autism is the sheer number of students who have been or could be identified as having such a condition. While there have been numerous reports regarding the increase in the number of children with a diagnosis of autism, the numbers still do not come close to projections regarding the prevalence of students with AD/HD, which seems to hover around 3–5 percent of all children.

The successful advocacy efforts in securing needed programs for students with AD/HD seems to be the result of a compatible alignment of the professional research, policy advocacy (which includes an active cadre of attorneys), and grassroots supports from parents and other family members. And, in trying to capture a powerful message advocating an AD/HD agenda, CHADD has taken its message to a broad constituency through publications, meetings, and political advocacy.

Contrast the two examples from above with other groups of students with behavioral disorders, whose numbers, severity, and outcomes may actually tower over these first examples. For example, students with a diagnosis of oppositional defiant disorder and conduct disorder may be among the highest risk students in our countries today (Walker et al., 1995). Although we do realize that the complexity of factors in these disorders and the array of potential services needed implicate the need for the coordination of such services and the complexity of meeting the full needs of these students (Hoagwood, 2001), we also have research suggesting that we do know of interventions that will make a difference in the lives of these children. Yet, students with these behavioral patterns are still quite prone to be denied services in special education, or worse yet, be excluded altogether from our schools (Children's Behavioral Alliance, 2003).

What's the difference here? One critical element is the differences in the social capital available to parents of these students in seeking and securing services for their children. These families are often dealing with significant issues themselves, including significant challenges in meeting their everyday needs. But I would suggest that another factor contributing to the relative lack of success in assuring appropriate services for these students rests with the lack of *alignment* among the parties involved with these students, including researchers, policy advocates, parents and families, and professional service providers. In fact, in this case, we may be frequently dealing with conflicting opinions across these stakeholders as to the remedies needed to serve such youth that will lead to a more positive outcome. This misalignment and perhaps even *contradictory directions* seems to continue to interfere with the possibility of securing needed programs and subsequently more positive outcomes for a significant number of young people! And tied to this is the cost to society in our inability to meet the needs of these youth.

These examples of specific behavioral conditions requiring our need for advocacy efforts should also remind us of two salient themes that should guide our advocacy efforts. First, similar to the physician's oath, we should first commit ourselves to 'do no harm.' In serving students with behavioral disorders this should, in this writer's opinion, convert to the commitment we make our intervention decisions based on the best and most complete assessment procedures that we have available. While this conclusion may seem obvious, earlier studies (for example, McGinnis et al., 1984; Smith et al., 1984) have questioned whether those involved in behavioral programming do, in fact, use relevant, behaviorally-based data in designing programs for these youth. With the recently enacted amendments to the IDEA that seems to reinforce the need for using important assessment strategies such as functional behavioral assessments, we also find significant shortfalls in meeting the expectations of such practices (Smith, 2000).

Following this assessment expectation is the logical need to use these data to design needed interventions for the youth targeted for intervention and to base these interventions on what research suggests to be the most promising interventions for dealing with such behavior. This focus on research-based practices in education is specifically addressed in the most recent amendments to the Elementary and Secondary Education Act in the US (commonly referred to as 'Leave No Child Behind') in 2001. This act, which appears similar to earlier legislation enacted in Great Britain (Didaskalou and Millward, 2002; Gray and Noakes, 1998) establishes the expectation that teaching methods used in the schools are based on research findings. While the obvious first applications of this expectation is in areas such as reading and mathematics, we are expected to apply such methods across all areas – including behavior.

This speaks to the importance of choosing interventions that reflect the most recent findings regarding practices that are likely to lead to meaningful benefit for the students with behavioral disorders who we serve. In making judgements regarding evidence-based interventions we also need to keep in mind the differences that may need to be weighed regarding macro versus micro approaches to this evidence-based challenge.

A concept related to the choices we make regarding evidence-based interventions is the role that the use of specific diagnostic or categorical designations are or are not a prerequisite to arriving at such intervention decisions. In the medical and mental health areas the designation of a diagnosis appears to be a universally agreed upon practice (US Department of Health, 1999), although some recent reports (National Advisory Mental Health Council Workgroup, 2001) have seemed to suggest that both context and personal traits need to be considered:

> Developing measurement systems that blend symptom-based indicators with process-based indicators would allow for a richer understanding of the individual child and his/her context, thereby allowing a better scientific understanding of the complex interplay of process and symptom and the development of finer-grained intervention approaches. (2001: 46)

In the arena of special education in the United States, there has been considerable discussion in recent years regarding the extent to which special education programs and services should be delivered on the basis of categorical designations versus being designed and delivered based solely on the basis of presenting problems. This latter approach, often referred to as a non-categorical approach, is said to be more empirically supported and is asserted by proponents to lead to less stigmatization of the students served. Furthermore, proponents of this approach assert that there are little, if any, meaningful instructional implications by virtue of labeling a child as having a learning disability, mental disability or behavioral disorder (Reschly et al., 1998).

So we seem to be facing somewhat of a conundrum here! On the one hand we have research suggesting that meaningful interventions are, at least partially and perhaps greatly, contingent on our ability to focus on the specific *type* of behavioral disorder being presented by the child, and the differentiation of programming options for students with behavioral disorders versus other students with disabilities; a categorical approach. On the other hand, other professionals seem to insist that such differentiations are relatively meaningless and may, in fact, drain valuable time and resources away from the more meaningful process of delivering behaviorally-focused interventions; a non-categorical approach.

This author would suggest that this labeling discussion does have direct implications in the advocacy domain. First, it would appear that it is important to carefully consider the professional literature base correlating specific behavioral conditions of students with needed interventions. To lightly dismiss the importance of such designations would seem to be selling short our advocacy responsibilities. At the same time it seems crucial that we always pose the critical question of the way in which any use of labels or categorical designations are relevant in planning a youngster's program.

A final element within the professional advocacy area is the importance of ongoing progress monitoring of any student we are serving. Particularly important here is the responsibility to demonstrate that a student is receiving meaningful educational benefit and is not being merely 'maintained' in the current program. Such a maintenance philosophy may have been dominant in the past but would, in this author's opinion, fall well short of our responsibility. The successful completion of this program element would also seem to be the ultimate measure of the importance of the categorical versus non-categorical differentiations discussed above!

SUCCESSFUL ADVOCACY: A LOOK TOWARD THE FUTURE

This overall discussion leads us to perhaps the primary questions we should be asking regarding advocating for students with behavioral disorders. What are the ways in which we define successful advocacy? I would suggest that three broad-band questions should be posed. These include:

1   To what extent are our advocacy efforts geared toward a better outcome for the youth for which we are advocating?
2   Are our efforts based on timely interventions that offset any downside to the use of such interventions?
3   To what extent do our interventions address the major needs of the caretakers, particularly the families of these students?

The first of these questions asks us to carefully consider the issue of ultimate functioning for students with behavioral disorders. As noted earlier, the current data on long-term outcomes for these students is not promising. To what extent can we assure the students and families we serve and the public to whom we need to communicate the particular program elements for which we are advocating will, in fact, produce meaningful results?

The second question gets to the notion of a *trajectory* of behavior patterns. Current research suggests that problem behavioral patterns seem to develop a trajectory pattern that foreshadows future serious problems. To what extent can we comfortably assert that the interventions we are advocating can demonstrate the potential to interrupt this negative trajectory pattern and replace such with a more positive pattern of development?

The third question interacts with the second by asking us to remember that the extent to which we are successful in turning a child's behavior around, particularly with younger children, may be contingent on the extent to which we are able to support those who work most closely with a child, rather than just with the child themselves.

In looking at these questions we can look to promising practices (even evidence-based!) that provide a firm foundation from which to launch our advocacy efforts. For example, the Regional Intervention Program (Strain and Timm, 2001) has provided data demonstrating the power of a parent-driven intervention program on a group of students with significant behavioral concerns in a 25-year follow-up study. The concepts surrounding the implementation of school-wide positive behavioral supports (Sugai et al., 2000) are demonstrating the impact of creating and maintaining more behavioral coherent schools on practices such as office referrals and student perceptions regarding the predictability of their school environments. Finally, research on broad-based interventions such as *wrap-around services* (Eber et al., 2002) are demonstrating the importance of comprehensive planning for students whose needs reflect macro perspectives and who benefit from coordinated planning that involves, but is not limited to, the school.

Successful advocacy is generally a collective enterprise, but is also heavily dependent, in this writer's mind, on the individual passions carried forth by the persons who collectively form a cause on behalf of children and their families. Parker Palmer speaks eloquently to the energy that emerges when those involved with a cause are no longer divided in their individual existences or collectively. He states:

> The decision to live an undivided life, made by enough people over a long period of time, may eventually have social and political impact. But this is not a strategic decision, taken to achieve some political goal. It is a deeply personal decision, made for the sake of one's own identity and integrity. To decide to live divided no more is less a strategy for attacking other people's beliefs than an uprising of the elemental need for one's own beliefs to govern and guide one's life. The power of an authentic movement lies in the fact that it originates in naming and claiming one's identity and integrity – rather than accusing one's 'enemies' of lacking the same. (1998: 168)

More recently Gardner et al. (2001) have begun the inquiry into what factors lead various professionals to combine the qualities of high competence in their work with a high level of integrity. According to these authors, 'good work' is based on our ability to support the fulfillment of individual needs and potential with the harmonious growth of other individuals and groups. This challenge to our personal work seems to complement the definition of integrity as proposed by Carter (1996) that challenges us to: always ask what is 'right' in given situations; decide to act accordingly, even with the danger of negative personal outcomes; and be willing to publicly state our course of action.

By meeting our advocacy efforts with students with behavioral disorders we truly are practicing enlightened self-interest. As Hill Walker and colleagues (Walker et al., 1995) have noted in relation to the consequences of excluding students from our schools who subsequently are prone to vandalize our neighborhoods during the afternoon school hours, we can apply this concept generally to our self-interests in serving students with behavioral disorders and perhaps breaking a cycle or interrupting a behavioral trajectory that is likely to lead to an unsuccessful life and the ripple effect to society of a lack of success in a life that perhaps could be much more than it is. The decision is ours – as well as the subsequent consequences.

REFERENCES

Board of Education v. Rowley, 458 U.S. 176 (1982).
Carter, S.L. (1996) *Integrity*. New York: Basic Books.
Children's Behavioral Alliance (2003) *In the Best Interests of All*. Landover, MD: Children and Adults with Attention-Deficit/Hyperactivity Disorder (CHADD).

Coalition for Juvenile Justice (2000) *Handle with Care: Serving the Mental Health Needs of Young Offenders*. Washington, DC: Coalition for Juvenile Justice.

Didaskalou, E.S and Millward, A.J. (2002) 'Breaking the policy jog-jam: Comparative perspectives on policy formulation and development for pupils with emotional and behavioural difficulties', *Oxford Review of Education*, 28 (1): 109–21.

Dyson, A. (2001) 'Special needs in the twenty-first century: Where we've been and where we're going', *British Journal of Special Education*, 28 (1): 24–9.

Eber, L., Sugai, G., Smith, C.R. and Scott, T. (2002) 'Wraparound and positive behavioral interventions and supports in the schools', *Journal of Emotional and Behavioral Disorders*, 10 (3): 171–80.

Gardner, H., Csikszentmihalyi, M. and Damon, W. (2001) *Good Work: When Excellence and Ethics Meet*. New York: Basic Books.

Gladwell, M. (2000) *The Tipping Point: How Little Things Can Make a Big Difference*. Boston, MA: Little, Brown.

Gray, P. and Noakes, J. (1998) 'Current legislation for pupils with emotional and behavioural difficulties: A clear way forward?', *Support for Learning*, 13 (4): 184–7.

Gray, P. and Panter, S. (2000) 'Exclusion or inclusion? A perspective on policy in England for pupils with emotional and behavioural difficulties', *Support for Learning*, 15 (1): 4–7.

Hoagwood, K. (2001) 'Evidence-based practice in children's mental health services: What do we know? Why aren't we putting it to use', *Emotional and Behavioral Disorders in Youth*, 1: 84–90.

Horn, W.F, and Tynan, D. (2001) 'Time to Make Special Education "Special" Again', in C.E. Finn, A.J. Rotherham and C.R. Hokanson (eds), *Rethinking Special Education for a New Century*. Washington, DC: Thomas B. Fordham Foundation and the Progressive Policy Institute.

Jensen, F.V. (2001) *Bayesien Networks and Decision Graphs*. New York. Springer–Verlag.

McGinnis, E., Kiraly, J. and Smith, C. R. (1984) 'The types of data used in identifying public school students as behaviorally disordered', *Behavioral Disorders*, 9: 239–46.

National Advisory Mental Health Council Workgroup on Child and Adolescent Mental Health Intervention Development and Deployment (2001) *Blueprint for Change: Research on Child and Adolescent Mental Health*. Washington, DC. Author.

Palmer, P.J. (1998) *The Courage to Teach*. San Francisco, CA: Jossey-Bass. pp. 183.

Reschly, D.J., Tilly, W.D. and Grimes, J. (eds) (1998) *Functional and Noncategorical Identification and Intervention in Special Education*. Des Moines, IA: Iowa Department of Education.

Scheuermann, B. and Johns, B. (2002) 'Advocacy for students with emotional or behavioral disorders in the 21st century', *Behavioral Disorders*, 28 (1): 57–69.

Smith, C.R. (2000) 'Behavioral and discipline provisions of IDEA 97: Implicit competencies yet to be confirmed', *Exceptional Children*, 66 (3): 403–412.

Smith, C.R., Frank, A.R. and Snider, B.F. (1984) 'School psychologists' and teachers' perceptions of data used in the identification of behaviorally disordered students', *Behavioral Disorders*, 10: 27–32.

Stanfield, R.L. (1995) 'Devolution – Holding the Bag?', *National Journal*, 27 (9): 2006–9.

Strain, P.S. and Timm, M.A. (2001) 'Remediation and prevention of aggression: An evaluation of the Regional Intervention Program over a quarter century', *Behavioral Disorders*, 26 (4): 297–313.

Sugai, G., Horner, R.H., Dunlap, G., Hieneman, M., Lewis, T.J., Nelson, C.M., Scott, T., Liaupsin, C., Sailor, W., Turnbull, A.P., Turnbull, H.R., III, Wickham, D., Reuf, M. and Wilcox, B. (2000) 'Applying positive behavioral support and functional behavioral assessment in schools', *Journal of Positive Behavioral Interventions*, 2: 131–43.

Sugai, G., Horner, R. and Sprague, J. (1999) 'Functional-assessment-based behavior support planning: Research to practice to research', *Behavioral Disorders*, 24 (3): 253–7.

Turnbull, H.R. and Turnbull, A.P. (2000) *Free Appropriate Public Education: The Law and Children with Disabilities* (6th edn). Denver, CO: Love.

US Department of Education (1998) *Twentieth Annual Report to Congress on the Implementation of the Individuals with Disabilities Education Act*. Washington, DC: Author.

US Department of Health and Human Services (1999) *Mental Health*: *A Report of the Surgeon General*. Rockville, MD: US Department of Health and Human services.

Valdes, K.A., Williamson, C.L. and Wagner, M. (1990). *The National Longitudinal Transition Study of Special Education Students. Vol. 3: Youth Categorized as Emotionally Disturbed*. Palo Alto, CA: SRI.

Walker, H.M., Colvin, G. and Ramsey, E. (1995) *Antisocial Behavior in School: Strategies and Best Practices*. Pacific Grove, CA: Brooks/Cole.

Walker, H.M. and Sprague, J. (1999) 'The path to school failure, delinquency, and violence: Causal factors and potential solutions', *Intervention in School and Clinic*, 35: 67–73.

19

Voices from the Margins: The Perceptions of Pupils with Emotional and Behavioural Difficulties about their Educational Experiences

JOHN DWYFOR DAVIES

Consulting 'consumers' regarding the services they receive is relatively recent in England. Within education, the idea began to make an impression with the introduction of 'Records of Achievement' in 1991, aimed at emphasizing pupils' successes and encouraging them to discuss their progress with teachers. But evidence suggests that only a minority of professionals practise consultation with pupils, the majority seeing it as irrelevant (Wade and Moore, 1993). This is especially so in cases where the pupil experiences emotional and behavioural difficulties (EBD).

Until professionals learn to listen to the views of all pupils, legislation alone will not achieve the goal of greater social or educational inclusion for disaffected or alienated pupils. In this chapter I draw on existing, published research, whilst also using my own, emerging findings of a study of pupils' views of school (Davies, 2004). This ongoing personal research suggests that listening to what these pupils have to tell us holds the key to subsequent action to help combat social exclusion. This principle has widespread application, and is being adapted to differential national or cultural contexts.

EXPLORING THE VIEWS OF
DISAFFECTED PUPILS: THE BACKGROUND

A substantial body of research emerged during the 1990s in England concerning how mainstream pupils perceive the learning process (see, for example, Keyes and Fernandes, 1993; Blatchford, 1996). Less work has been undertaken to ascertain the perceptions of pupils whose behaviour causes concern. This is understandable from the perspective of the researchers, since the problems confronting those conducting enquiry in this field – discussed elsewhere in this *Handbook* – are not insignificant. The subjects are often resentful, defensive, alienated and, in some cases, disturbed. Their educational careers have invariably involved individual and family stress, and invitations to discuss them are not always welcomed. This is unfortunate, since a failure to find out what these pupils really think is likely to perpetuate their negative experiences of school.

This is unfortunate from a policy perspective, too. Garner noted that: 'With some notable exceptions the student's voice has been the least influential in the formulation of strategies for dealing with problems in these areas' (1993). This view is endorsed by Gersch et al. (1993), who point out that there has been a traditional professional scepticism concerning advocacy for pupils with special needs, and in particular those referred to as 'disruptive'. Wade and Moore (1993) also found that less than one-third of the teachers in their study took account of the views of their pupils. Teachers commented that consultation with pupils was largely seen as a waste of time and mainly irrelevant.

Cooper (1993) drew attention to the importance of supporting all pupils to express their views as 'a moral obligation to enable pupils to articulate their views as effectively as possible' (1993: 129). In addressing the needs of pupils 'on the margins', this imperative becomes particularly significant. Cooper argues that in order to modify behaviour, pupils' perception of self needs to be supported if they are to change from a negative self-perspective to a positive one – what he terms 'resignification'.

Brannen develops this view, arguing that 'This resignification goes beyond the need for pupils to see themselves as different but requires them to construe the role of the teaching staff in different ways' (1996: 58). For many disaffected pupils, previous experience will have resulted in an interpretation of the relationship between themselves and their teachers as one in which they are seen as inferior and insignificant by those in authority. It therefore seems logical that to achieve resignification for themselves, these pupils also need to achieve a resignification of the identities that others hold of them. If this is to be realized, teachers have an obligation to explore the pupils' perception of their experiences in school, thus supporting this process of resignification.

Moreover, amidst the growing imperative for schools to demonstrate greater effectiveness, there has been a particular focus on pupils with special educational needs, including those experiencing EBD (Cooper, 1993; Cole and Visser, 1998; Spalding et al., 2001). It is noteworthy, in this respect, that Rutter (1980), in his work on school effectiveness, identified successful schools as those which provided ample opportunities for children to take responsibility for and to participate in the running of their school lives. This theme is a feature of subsequent – EBD specific – literature (Cole and Visser, 1998).

For those involved with children with special educational needs, including EBD, the original Code of Practice in England (DfE, 1994a) provided the benchmark by which effectiveness is measured. It recommended that schools consider how they involve children in decision-making relating to assessment and identification, individual education plans and in the process of monitoring and review. The subsequent Circular 8/94, relating to 'pupils with problems' (DfE, 1994b), confirmed the desirability of involving children in behaviour management by suggesting that 'pupils can play a positive role'. In the discrete circular relating to EBD (DfE, 1994c), the advice is more forthright: 'there is a positive association between pupils' involvement and greater motivation and feelings of self-worth on their part' and that, consequently, they 'should be encouraged and guided in setting and organising learning goals according to their age and understanding'.

The revised Code of Practice (DfE, 2001) emphasizes the importance of providing opportunities for pupils (from an early age) to be supported in making decisions, and provides guidance for teachers and others as to how to this process can be facilitated. Section 3 of that document is entirely devoted to this. Paragraph 3.13 is explicit about the structures that can be instigated to facilitate better access to pupils in the broader management of curriculum and the wider life of the school. It must be remembered, however, that the Code is a tool that offers guidance only and does not represent a statutory obligation. It should also be remembered that the Code of Practice locates the majority of its focus on enabling pupils to participate in the process of assessment and review and is less forthcoming about their broader role in the life of the school.

The principles of the Code and of the circulars are enshrined in the arrangements for the inspection of schools, undertaken in England by the Office for Standards in Education (OFSTED, 1995a; 1995b; 1995c). Inspectors are advised to look for evidence of 'pupils' involvement in the daily routines of the school' and the extent to which schools are presenting 'scope for pupils to take responsibility' and the encouragement for them 'to articulate their own views and beliefs' (OFSTED, 1995c). More recently, guidance for inspectors remind them of the value of involving pupils in the inspection process, encouraging them to hold 'Discussions with pupils [since this] provide[s] a good way into their views of the subject [being inspected]' (OFSTED, 2001). This suggests that the school inspectorate in England is now recognizing the significance of pupil voice, accepting the view expressed by Kuorelahiti (2001) that such a perspective enables a better evaluation of the education provided for all pupils, including those experiencing EBD.

WHAT PUPILS WITH EBD TELL US ABOUT THEIR EXPERIENCES OF SCHOOLING

There are many studies that focus on pupils' perceptions of mainstream schooling (for example, Davie et al., 1996), but few authors have focused specifically on pupils with EBD. Those that do (for example, Garner, 1993; Wise, 1999; Jahnukainen, 2001) provide a rich insight not only into the way that marginalized pupils perceive and reflect on their educational experiences, but also, even more fundamentally, on the factors that play an important part in the process of marginalization itself.

Received wisdom might suggest that disaffected pupils invariably offer negative perspectives of their education career, and there is some evidence to support this (Garner, 1995). Recently one year 11 pupil presently attending a special school did reveal to me that his recollection of mainstream primary education had been so traumatic that he was unable (or refused) to recall any aspect of that period of his life. These early difficulties have had a lasting impact: when asked what aspect of his present schooling he find enjoyable, his response was immediate – 'What do I like about school? Nothing … School is just not enjoyable … Learning's boring.' In contrast, many studies which explore how disruptive pupils view their educational experiences do indicate a recognition of some positive features of schooling. My own recent research, for example, clearly identifies aspects of mainstream schooling that these pupils valued – irrespective of the fact that they were subsequently rejected and excluded by the system. William, a 15-year-old, currently in a day special school, recalled his time in mainstream primary school with affection and said 'Harfield primary [school]? I used to love it … It's the best school I've ever been to.' It is perhaps timely, therefore, to dispel the myth that *all* marginalized pupils view their educational experience negatively.

Pupils with behaviour problems frequently find difficulty in forging and sustaining positive relationships. The process of labelling these pupils – both by teachers and other pupils – can itself create additional, relationship difficulties. Pupils frequently draw attention to the significance of labelling, commonly practised once a young person exhibits resistance to authority, confirming the view that such labels impact adversely on pupil's experience of schooling (Habel et al., 1999). They also highlight the part that such labels plays in affirming 'difference', further supporting and enhancing their 'disaffected' status.

Some proponents of inclusive approaches in education (for example, Ainscow, 1999: Rustemier, 2002), however, have cited the negative consequence of labelling, and the associated stigma, as a significant factor in favour of educating all pupils in mainstream schools and the cessation of alternative educational provision. But from the pupils' perspective, many feel stigmatized once identified as 'different' – irrespective of the setting they are educated in. The label 'EBD' signifies difference in the mind of the pupil (Guterman, 1995; Jahnukainen, 2001). Indeed, for some pupils, the stigma associated with the label is often felt more acutely whilst they remain in the mainstream schools (Jahnukainen, 2001), where they are seen as particularly 'different' and less valued by peers.

Such findings are indicative of the over-arching importance of listening to the views of disaffected pupils. At a more micro level, Wise (1999) identifies factors that pupils describe as having influenced their behaviour at school. Notable amongst these are the size of mainstream schools and classes, and the nature and content of the curriculum and its delivery.

School and class size

School and classroom size is frequently cited by many marginalized young people, particularly by those who have also been the subject of bullying, as the underling cause of their 'problems' (Wise and Upton, 1998; Wise, 1999; Jahnukainen, 2001). They claim that large impersonal school environments are a major contributing factor to their unhappiness, leading to truanting and antisocial or disruptive behaviour. Data gathered in my current research includes a statement by James, a 14-year-old who, when asked what specifically made it difficult for him to manage in mainstream schools, readily identified the size of the school as of prime importance: 'The amount of kids that were there ...', and when asked what he would choose to change about the schools he'd attended, he was in no doubt that creating smaller, less threatening environments would be his priority. Pupils I have interviewed often claim that large settings make it difficult for teachers and others in authority to provide them with the safe environment that they require in order to thrive and develop. Malcolm claimed that 'I just don't get on in big classes ...' This was seen as a major factor at the point of transition from primary to secondary education. Fifteen-year-old Mary drew attention to this by saying that 'Everything was too big ... the jump from primary to secondary school was a big shock.' Pupils in Jahnukainen's study (2001) reflecting on the difference between their experience of mainstream and special provision also make reference to the size of the environment in which they were educated. Smaller institutions such as special schools, they stated, met their needs more appropriately than large impersonal mainstream settings. The inference, therefore, is that the bigger the school, and the classes within it, the more difficult it is to offer support and protection, whilst providing potential for negative social interaction. Similarly, the larger the classes, the more difficult it becomes for teachers to find the space and time to listen and relate to individuals.

Curriculum

Researchers have long drawn attention to the correlation between behaviour difficulties and limited academic success (Epstein et al., 1989) and how an inappropriate curriculum can exacerbate behavioural difficulties (Fogell and Long, 1997; Porter, 2000; Hamill and Boyd, 2002). Frustration at the failure to achieve will frequently result in antisocial behaviour, often in an attempt to compensate for low academic status. O'Brien graphically describes such an example: 'Godwin can perform sophisticated task evasion, which might include threatening or abusive behaviour. It is clear that his challenging behaviour is a consequence, not a causatory component, of his learning difficulty – his behaviour is not independent of his learning' (1998: 35–6). The DfES has recently acknowledged this reality (2003b), admitting that many pupils '... do not have the motivation to continue with any formal education or training. For some, this is reflected in poor behaviour and regular truancy' (2003b: 1.4 p. 10).

Similarly, White (1982) demonstrated the centrality of the curriculum to the way that pupils behave. Many pupils choose not to attend school, or to misbehave whilst they are there, not because they dislike the school but because they do not appreciate particular lessons and they way they are taught. Many fail to recognize the relevance of what they have to do in particular subject areas or that the curriculum is inaccessible to them. This leads to resentment and potential misbehaviour. William, who was 15 at the time, recently reminded me of this when he expressed the view that the main thing he would change in school was 'the stuff you do in lessons. You use English but there are things we've got to do in English that you'll never use – why do it? I know we need to do English and maths but things like science – when will I ever need to use dangerous chemicals? They need to make them relevant.'

Kauffman (1997) emphasizes the importance of finding ways to ensure that pupils appreciate the relevance of the compulsory curriculum. But the weight of evidence from pupils themselves is that it is the content and delivery of the curriculum which results in them adopting unacceptable strategies – including truancy and lesson disruption – to combat boredom and to avoid the stigma they feel associated with curriculum failure.

Analysing what pupils experiencing EBD say about the curriculum is complicated by the tendency to conflate their experience of the subject matter with the way that it is taught. Teacher-related factors tend to blur responses. Hence, statements made to me such as 'French is boring and a waste of time', or 'I always try to skip maths 'cos all you do is work through a book' would suggest that this is more a reflection on teaching style as opposed to being subject specific. Stephen told me that 'If I get on well with the teacher, I get on with the work. If I get on with the teacher, I'll ask for help – but not the others.' Turner notes a similar point and cites John, a 9-year-old pupil with behaviour problems who reports that 'he takes time to settle to work depending on the activity. If he finds the work fun then he settles quickly and without distraction … If he does not like the activity he takes his time, talks to others and shouts out' (2000: 15). In such cases, Richmond suggests that a negotiated approach is necessary, which 'enables learners to learn what they need to learn, in a way which suits them and in a way which means that they are involved in and have some responsibility for the process' (1993: 20). A negotiated approach appears to be particularly important for EBD pupils (Davies, 1996).

Crowley (1993) and Habel et al. (1999) demonstrate that disaffected pupils appreciate the opportunity to engage with a flexible academic programme as opposed to a rigid approach to curriculum management. Recently I visited a special school in the south of England that has recently introduced a negotiated, flexible arrangement. In this the pupils play a significant part in choosing what aspect of the curriculum they work on at any given time, with guidance from teachers. Pupils told me that they particularly valued the autonomy this gave them: 'It's good now it's flexible and we have a say in what we do and when.' Staff at the school had also noticed a significant change in pupil attitude to the curriculum following this initiative. It is worth remembering that the value of involving pupils more actively in planning their educational experiences has been recognized for a long time (Gersch, 1990), but such practice appears not to be commonplace in 2003. This is not surprising, given the constraints placed on teachers by the rigidity of the national curriculum in the United Kingdom and a series of related initiatives such as national literacy and numeracy strategies. Indeed, it can be argued that strict compliance to existing official frameworks are a significant barrier to addressing disaffection and behaviour difficulties.

What is not constrained, however, are the teaching approaches used. Moody et al. (2000) argue that the way teachers deliver the curriculum is of prime importance if pupils with learning needs (including EBD) pupils are to benefit form their educational experiences. They suggest that unless teachers modify their approach to teaching to meet the needs of individuals, any advantage gleaned from other adaptations, such as the opportunity to work in small classes, will be negated. The same point is emphasized by De Pear (1997), who stresses the importance of offering opportunities for pupils 'at risk'of learning failure to talk about their difficulties, and for teachers to respond appropriately. Her informants were firmly of the opinion that had they been allowed to voice their views about preferred learning and teaching styles at an earlier stage, the likelihood of disaffection and exclusion would have been significantly reduced.

WHAT PUPILS TELL US ABOUT TEACHERS

Of all the factors that pupils view as significant in shaping their perceptions of schooling, their views of teachers as authority figures is arguably the most influential. This is perhaps not surprising since, as Neel et al. (1997) discovered when compared to other pupils, pupils with EBD often spend more time with their teachers than they do socializing with peers. This, however, does not imply that they view all authority figures in a positive light. Armstrong and Galloway (1996), for instance, found that it was not uncommon for pupils experiencing EBD to view their referral to the psychologist as an expression of the power the school had over them. Jahnukainen (2001) drew similar conclusions, suggesting that EBD pupils frequently have a long history of negative experiences with adults generally and with those in authority positions (such as teachers) in particular.

Evidence also suggests that pupils are particularly adept at analysing their teachers and tend not to view all teachers as the same. They construe identities for teachers on an individualized basis as opposed to generating a collective identity. Such identities are crucial to the way that they subsequently interact with the teachers and in the degree to which teachers respond, thereby helping to support or frustrate development and change. Brannen (1996) identifies three key features that pupils use to group teachers: those who are 'powerful' compared to pupils; those who are 'supporters' of the pupil; and those who are viewed as less powerful than pupils. The way that the pupil perceives the teacher, and the relationship that ensues, is seen to impact significantly on their professional effectiveness when working with EBD pupils. The frail persona of many pupils with EBD is readily exposed by teachers who fail to take account of the impact that personal interaction can play. For such pupils, the importance of teachers listening to them and understanding them as individuals is considerable.

Teachers and teaching styles are seen as hugely significant by the pupils interviewed by Wise (1999). This research reveals that the teacher's skills and abilities in curriculum presentation and classroom management were every bit as significant for the pupils as the content of the curriculum. So important is the relationship between pupil and teacher that for some pupils, the main barrier to learning may well be dislike of the teacher as opposed to the curriculum area (Turner, 2000).

Consistency and fairness are also seen as essential teacher qualities, as is the willingness – and ability – to provide support at the point of need. De Pear (1997) confirms the importance of providing timely opportunity for pupils to voice their anxieties and draws on the views of pupils excluded from mainstream education. Her research concludes that many pupils felt that opportunities to express their anxieties and concerns at an earlier stage could well have resulted in reducing subsequent difficulties; the pupils in her study felt that such opportunity had been denied them. Russell (1996) advocates the need to support young people in expressing their views and suggests that in order to enable pupils to speak for themselves before a crisis occurs, they must be given time and a framework within which to acquire the necessary skills to do so. The same point is made by De Pear (1995).

Summarizing his analysis of the teacher qualities seen as significant by disaffected pupils, Garner (1993) identified five teachers who are seen as:

- a source of help;
- having a charismatic personality;
- patient;
- motivators; and
- disciplinarians.

Interestingly, the way that marginalized pupils describe 'good' teachers are not dissimilar to the views expressed by more successful pupils and reported by Raymond (1987), echoing work by Rudduck et al. (1996) who identified respect for pupils, fairness, autonomy and intellectual challenge as important teacher qualities from pupil perspectives.

The literature makes recurrent reference to the weight that 'disruptive' pupils place on teacher fairness and respect for pupils (Scarlett, 1989;

Getzels and Smilansky, 1983; Garner, 1993; Cruddas et al., 2000). My recent interviews with disaffected pupils further underlines this point. Emily was adamant that this was the most important quality in teachers and that it impacted significantly on her perception of schooling. In comparing two schools that she had attended, she recalls that the significant difference between the two was that in one 'teachers in Fairway wouldn't listen to you. They just listened to one person and then give the other boy detention.' This sentiment reinforces what Hamill and Boyd (2002) discovered, that pupils with EBD in particular feel that their views are often disregarded as invalid.

On the issue of fairness and equity, Crozier and Anstiss (1995) found that disruptive girls resent the attention and time that teachers seem to devote to boys in the classroom. The statistical data generated by this research seems to confirm the intuitive impressions held by girls, who expressed considerable resentment about teachers' preoccupation with the behaviour of boys. The same point is amplified in the findings of Cruddas et al. 'I think boys get more support than girls. I think it's sad, they get it before us … They want attention, don't they, and will do anything to get it' (2000: 16). The main concerns for girl informants in this research exercise seems to have been a desire to be listened to, feeling that they often went unheard at school (and at home) and that this was a factor that led to low motivation and frustration – and in turn, disruptive behaviour and/or withdrawal.

Humour features significantly as a teacher characteristic in comments by disaffected pupils (Garner, 1993, 1995). When recently interviewing David, who had been identified by his teachers as a particularly challenging individual, he told me 'I like it when I work with Miss Johnston. We have a laugh in maths while doing our work – and listen to music – it helps to relax and to concentrate.' Such findings are not new. Redl and Wineman (1965) made much of the importance of humour in facilitating appropriate working relationships with challenging pupils, drawing attention to the important difference between the positive use of humour in the classroom as opposed to the use of sarcasm.

The value placed by pupils on a teacher's ability to use humour might seem to contradict other equally important teacher qualities identified by pupils at risk. The ability to impose discipline and control the learning environment is a teacher quality much appreciated by vulnerable young people (Garner, 1993). These pupils seem to appreciate a clear structure and fair management (Davies, 1973; Woods, 1990; Davies, 1996) within which they can feel comfortable, knowing that the teacher is both fair and 'in control'.

An important element in providing such an environment is that of establishing a discipline policy that is also seen as fair by the pupils. Pupils suggests that it is not that they resent discipline *per se*, but rather that they question its appropriateness and fairness. This was a point raised by the majority of the pupils interviewed in my recent survey: 'Some teachers punish me but don't listen to me ... But here, they listen to what I think before giving me detention. I don't mind if they [the teachers] let me explain why I've done something. If I deserve detention, I get detention.'

EBD pupils also suggest that considerable gains can accrue from their wider involvement in whole-school discipline policies (Lucas, 1991). Mounton et al. (1996), cited by Habel et al. (1999), demonstrate that the extent to which pupils are encouraged and supported in developing a sense of identifying with school at an early age largely dictates their attitudes to their teachers, and to the education system thereafter. They argue that to be successful, schools must foster an environment within which pupils can develop a sense of belonging, a network of relationships with peers and staff, and an appreciation of the learning that is experienced at school. Building such an environment poses a real challenge if the inclusion of disaffected pupils in mainstream settings is to be realized. These, after all, are the pupils at the margins, whose very behaviour is likely to alienate both their peers and their teachers (Elias, 1989), leading to more general social exclusion.

IMPLICATIONS FOR PROFESSIONAL DEVELOPMENT

Ever since the 1981 Education Act, which raised 'special educational needs' to the top of the policy agenda in England, the need for training mainstream teachers in better managing and providing for the individual educational needs of pupils has been paramount in importance. But resources have tended to be directed at supporting professional development programmes that respond to centrally-driven 'targets' and initiatives. The introduction of the 1988 Education Act, for instance, resulted in national in-service programmes to equip teachers with the skills necessary to 'deliver' a prescribed national curriculum. And whilst the DfEE (1997) in its influential document *Excellence for all Children: Meeting Special Educational Needs*, was explicit in reaffirming the aim of the Department to support teachers in accessing further professional development opportunities, it was equally explicit about the direction that that support would be targeted: 'We will encourage all teachers to develop further skills in planning, teaching and assessing pupils with SEN' (1997: 63). Subsequent documents have outlined the content and nature of such skill development (TTA, 1999).

Professional development in England has largely been preoccupied with supporting teachers to manage a plethora of directives and guidance addressing new initiatives within a context of standards driven reform, including SureStart, national literacy and numeracy strategies, a national behaviour and attendance strategy and citizenship education. All are accompanied by a raft of 'standards' that teachers are required to demonstrate. So, whilst at face value the publication of *Meeting Special Educational Needs: A Programme for Action* (DfEE, 1998) seemed to provide support for teachers' professional development, the document served only to promote areas prescribed by central government – notably, curriculum management and pupil assessment.

The direction that professional development has taken over recent years in England has not escaped the attention of observers such as Lee (1997) who, in reviewing 22 years' of articles published in the *British Journal of In-service Education*, noted that there has been a progressive emergence of articles that focused on 'competence' and an agenda for professional development dictated by the Teacher Training Agency, moving professional development increasingly towards a skills competence model. Teaching, however, is an intuitive and responsive business, as has been argued elsewhere (Davies and Lee, 2001). It is as much concerned with the affective as the cognitive, as researchers such as Nias (1989) have demonstrated. For those working with EBD pupils, the affective element is even more significant than for most. Yet the prescriptions set by the DfES and the TTA in England have offered, until recently, little opportunity for critical reflection concerning personal beliefs and decision-making or to take account of what children themselves tell us about their experiences. There is also no mention in official guidance of the emotive aspect of the teaching role and little attention given to developing the substantial skills necessary to engage effectively with challenging and/or disaffected pupils. As Lee (1997) demonstrates, these so called 'softer', affective aspects of professional functioning have hence been ignored in terms of professional development opportunities for far too long (Davies and Lee, 2001). And yet it is greater focus on the affective aspects of professional practice that is likely to serve best the needs of the growing number of EBD pupils that in turn would result in more effective schools and classrooms – an issue picked up at various points in this *Handbook*.

Those pupils exhibiting EBD, in the various studies referred to in this chapter, have emphasized the importance of whole systems and individual teachers respecting and 'listening', highlighting the importance of this in enhancing their self-concept and self-esteem (Summerskill, 2000). This is also important from the teacher's perspective, since listening to the pupil's views can result in a greater understanding of pupil behaviour, which in itself can lead to adopting more appropriate teaching approaches necessary to engage *all* pupils in the educational process in schools.

It would be naïve and irresponsible to think that all teachers instinctively possess the skills necessary for effective listening – or to assume that the skills-dominated initial teacher training programmes will have equipped them for this. This is amply reflected in the literature (Garner, 1993; Cooper et al., 1994; Wise, 1999). It is a reality which has been further reinforced for me when reading an account reported by Lewis (1996), which argues that too often pupils grow to believe that teachers rarely recognize and respect those things that are of importance to them but are more concerned with the mechanics of generating 'correct' work. He recalls a child who drew a gravestone and wrote underneath 'I wish I was dead'. The work was returned with only one modification, the teacher having crossed out and replaced the word 'was' with 'were' (1995: 56). All this signals the importance of professional development, to enhance teacher awareness and to refine the important skills of effective listening and support and to 'reframe' teacher perception and understanding of the undesirable behaviour exhibited by the pupil.

Equally, the evidence that many EBD pupils find difficulty in articulating their views is also convincing and provides a further professional development priority. Lewis (1996) draws attention to the fact that many EBD pupils have become accustomed to having decisions made on their behalf – particularly in cases of those who are formally ascertained as having a 'statement of special educational need'. It is incumbent on teachers to find strategies and structures that will support these pupils in (re)discovering the skills needed to voice their views. This implies the formulation of a specific and complex agenda of staff development that facilitates teachers with the skills necessary to empower pupils to communicate openly and freely, expressing their concerns and anxieties.

Armstrong and Galloway remind us that 'gaining access to children's perspectives requires skill in communicating meanings to children and understanding the meanings embedded in children's language and behaviour' (1996: 112). Despite the caution advised by the National Curriculum Council (1989) in drawing attention to the dangers inherent in overemphasizing professional development that is located in training teachers to *manage* behaviour at the expense of attempting to understand children's feelings, little professional development opportunities have been provided to help teachers effect this, although more recent developments in the United Kingdom are encouraging (TTA, 2004).

Brannen (1996) demonstrates that the way individual teachers are identified by pupils plays a critical role in the influence that they have when supporting learning. Teachers themselves need support in identifying the way that they adopt a particular identity from the pupil's perception and in learning how to move between roles as appropriate. This implies what has been argued for elsewhere (Davies and Lee, 2001), that opportunities for staff development lead to a more sophisticated version of the reflective practitioner in which reflection does not ignore the emotional context in which professional development takes place.

As yet, however, the government's obsession with ensuring a 'coherent approach to teaching and learning' (DfES, 2003a: 19) means that such support is the exception. The powerful forced of the TTA and other government agencies in driving the professional development agenda remains relatively oblivious to the significance of this need, resulting in an imbalance in terms of the focus of provision and opportunities.

My own research and that reviewed for this paper indicates that teachers and others are slowly beginning to acknowledge the importance of 'listening to young people' and appreciate the value that this can bring to refining and developing practice. It is perhaps unfortunate that official advice and guidance on this issue tend at best to be ambivalent. Whilst it encourages the professional to consider drawing on pupil perceptions, it leaves the final decision to the individual's professional judgement.

As the government agenda moves to promote greater pupil participation in the educative process, teachers may well reap a series of benefits from adopting a more collaborative approach to teaching and learning. To achieve this, opportunities for professional development play a key part. This signals the imperative for institutions of higher education and local education authorities to work collaboratively on designing the kind of professional development programmes that would enable teachers better to provide for their disaffected pupils.

CONCLUSION

Tisdall and Dawson (1994) suggest that as a consequence of recent legal requirements, professionals are becoming increasingly aware of the importance of listening to the perspective of the pupils about whom concern is being expressed. It is worth noting, however, that the obstacles to developing a 'listening culture' for children exhibiting challenging behaviour in mainstream schools are considerable. Davie and Galloway (1996) remind us that the pressures on teacher time is such that they may be reluctant to give further attention to the very pupils that tax them most.

It is important to note that many children identified by teachers as 'disruptive' express a refreshing sense of optimism about what is happening to them in school. There is a tendency, at least on the part of the general education community, to view 'EBD children' as almost entirely oppositional to schools, to learning and to teachers as a professional group. The evidence from a significant and growing research database generated from what pupils themselves have to say suggests that the contrary is often the case, expressing a desire to be included, to be controlled and to experience respect, and they are able to do so by recounting a high proportion of positive events from their own experiences of education.

Moreover, what is being said by the children in the more recent studies of the views of EBD pupils simply reinforces much of what has been said by such young people in earlier literature on the subject (Willis, 1977; Everhart, 1983). It should also be stressed that the views of this discrete group of children have many similarities with the views expressed by their teachers and by their 'ordinary' peers, again a parallel drawn from earlier work in this field (Raymond, 1987).

Finally, it is salutary to note that the observations made about schools and teaching by these children frequently coincide with the competencies expected of a 'good' teacher, as prescribed by the present government and other political observers. The future for children who are referred to as 'EBD' and those who work with them can best be secured by a recognition that both have traditionally functioned as a marginalized and segregated part of the educational community. Just as 'EBD children' have never really been listened to on a widespread or statutory basis, so, too, little attention has formerly been given to the views of those working with 'EBD children'. Whilst there has been an interesting shift in this situation in recent times, it remains essential that *all* concerned in this field of education strengthen their position by 'telling it like it is'.

Given the challenges faced by young people in the new millennium, it is essential that the views of children are used proactively to inform policy and practice, rather than as a means by which such children can be further patronized by an education system whose Pavlovian response has been to reject them. Only by incorporating the views of this group of 'educational outsiders' can schools genuinely be termed effective and democratic.

REFERENCES

Ainscow, M. (1999) *Understanding the Development of Inclusive Schools*. London: Falmer.
Armstrong, D. and Galloway, D. (1996) 'How children with emotional and behavioural difficulties view professionals', in R. Davie and D. Galloway (eds), *Listening to Children in Education*. London: Fulton.

Blatchford, P. (1996) 'Pupils' views on school work and school from 7 to 16 years', *Research Papers in Education*, 11: 263–88.

Brannen, R. (1996) 'Teacher identities: Hearing the voice of pupils with special educational needs', *Support for Learning*, 11 (2): 57–61.

Cole, T. and Visser, J. (1998) 'How should the 'effectiveness' of schools for pupils with EBD be assessed?', *Emotional and Behavioural Difficulties*, 3 (1): 37–44.

Cooper, P. (1993) *Effective Schools for Disaffected Students: Integration and Segregation*. London: Routledge.

Cooper, P., Smith, C. and Upton, G. (1994) *Emotional and Behavioural Difficulties: From Theory to Practice*. London: Routledge.

Crowley P. (1993) 'A qualitative analysis of mainstreamed behaviourally disordered aggressive adolescents', *Exceptionality*, 4: 131–51.

Crozier, J. and Anstiss, J. (1995) 'Out of the spotlight: Girls' experience of disruption', in M. Lloyd-Smith and J.D. Davies (eds), *On the Margins: The Educational Experience of 'Problem' Pupils*. Stoke-on-Trent: Trentham.

Cruddas, L., Dawn, S., Freedman, E., Pierre-MacFarlane, G. and Smith, J. (2000) *Girls Voices: Are They on the Agenda?* London: Newham Education.

Davie, R. and Galloway, D. (eds) (1996) *Listening to Children in Education*. London: Fulton.

Davie, R., Upton, G. and Varma, V. (1996) *The Voice of the Child*. London: Falmer.

Davies, J.D. (1973) 'The re-integration of maladjusted children into a society that has rejected them', *New Era*, 54 (3): 65–7.

Davies, J.D. (1996) 'Pupils' views on special educational needs provision', *Support for Learning*, 11 (4): 157–61.

Davies, J.D. (2004) 'The views of pupils with problems about schools and schooling'. Unpublished research, ongoing.

Davies, J.D. and Lee, J. (2001) 'Learning from experience or just meeting standards? The future of continuing professional development provision for special educational needs coordinators', *Journal of In-service Education: International Journal of Professional Development*, 27 (2): 261–74.

Department for Education (1994a) *Code of Practice on the Identification and Assessment of Special Educational Needs*. London: DfE.

Department for Education (1994b) *Pupil Behaviour and Discipline* (Circular 8/94). London: DfE.

Department for Education (1994c) *The Education of Children with Emotional and Behavioural Difficulties* (Circular 9/94). London: DfE.

Department for Education (2001) *Revised Code of Practice on the Identification and Assessment of Special Educational Needs*. London: DfE.

Department for Education and Employment (1997) *Excellence for All Children: Meeting Special Educational Needs*. London: The Stationery Office.

Department for Education and Employment (1998) *Meeting Special Educational Needs: A Programme for Action*. London: The Stationery Office.

Department for Education and Skills (2003a) *14–19: Opportunity and Excellence*. London: DfES.

Department for Education and Skills (2003b) *Truancy Sweep: Press Notice 2003/0013*. London: DfES.

De Pear, S. (1995) 'Perceptions of exclusion by pupils with special needs', in M. Lloyd Smith and J.D. Davies (eds), *On the Margins: The Educational Experience of 'Problem' Pupils*. Staffordshire: Trentham.

De Pear, S. (1997) 'Excluded pupils' views of their educational needs and experiences', *Support for Learning*, 12 (1): 19–22.

Elias, M.J. (1989) 'Schools as a source of stress to children: An analysis of causal and ameliorative influences', *Journal of School Psychology*, 29: 393–407.

Epstein, M.H., Kinder, D. and Burnsuck, B. (1989) 'The academic status of adolescents with behavioural disorders', *Behavioural Disorders*, 14 (3): 157–65.

Everhart, R. (1983) *Reading, Writing and Resistance: Adolescence and Labour in a Junior High School*. New York: Routledge and Kegan Paul.

Fogell, J. and Long, R. (1997) *Spotlight on Special Educational Needs – Emotional and Behavioural Difficulties*. Tamworth: NASEN.

Garner, P. (1993) 'What disruptive students say about the school curriculum and the way it is taught,' *Therapeutic Care and Education*, 2 (2): 404–415.

Garner, P. (1995) 'Schools by scoundrels: the views of "disruptive" pupils in mainstream schools in England and the United States', in M. Lloyd-Smith and J.D. Davies (eds), *On the Margins: The Educational Experience of 'Problem' Pupils*: Stoke-on-Trent: Trentham.

Gersch, I. (1990) 'Pupils' views', in M. Scherer, I. Gersch and L. Fry (eds), *Meeting Disruptive Behaviour*. London: Macmillan.

Gersch, I., Holgate, A. and Sigston, S. (1993) 'Valuing the child's perspective: A revised student report and other initiatives', *Educational Psychology in Practice*, 9 (1): 36–45.

Getzels, J. and Smilansky, J. (1983) 'Individual differences in pupil perceptions of school problems', *British Journal of Educational Psychology*, 5: 307–316.

Gill, N. (1990) 'Are the rights of children being respected in the National Curriculum?', *Education*, 175 (17): 407.

Guterman, R.R. (1995) 'The validity of categorical learning disabilities services: The consumer view', *Exceptional Children*, 62: 111–24.

Habel, J., Bloom, I.A., Ray, M.S. and Bacon, E. (1999) 'Consumer reports: What students with behaviour disorders say about school', *Remedial and Special Education*, 20: 93–105.

Hamill, P. and Boyd, B. (2002) 'Equality, fairness and risks – young person's voice', *British Journal of Special Education*, 29 (3): 111–17.

Jahnukainen, M. (2001) 'Experiencing special education. Former students of classes for the emotionally and behaviourally disordered talk about their schooling', *Emotional and Behavioural Difficulties*, 6 (3): 150–66.

Kauffman, J.K. (1997) *Characteristics of Behaviour Disorders of Children and Youth*. Columbus, OH: Merrill.

Keyes, W. and Fernandes, C. (1993) *What do Students Think About School?* Slough: NFER.

Kuorelahiti, M. (2002) 'Experiencing special education: Former students of classes for the emotionally and behavioural disordered talk about their schooling', *Emotional and Behavioural Difficulties*, 6 (3): 105–166.

Kuorelahiti, M. (1998) 'Quality of School Life in Finnish Special Educational Settings (EBD)', in A. Anttila and A. Uusitalo (eds), *Contemporary Marginalisation and Exclusion of Young People. Whose Reality Counts?* Helsinki: NUORA Publications, pp. 47–50.

Lee, M. (1997) 'The development of in-service education as seen through the pages of British Journal of In-service Education', *British Journal of In-service Education*, 23: 9–22.

Lewis, J. (1996) 'Helping children find a voice', in K. Jones and T. Charlton (eds), *Overcoming Learning and Behaviour Difficulties: Partnership with Pupils*. London: Routledge.

Lucas, P. (1991) 'A neglected source for reflection in the supervision of student teachers', *New Era in Education*, 72 (1): 2–6.

Moody, S.W., Vaughn, S., Hughes, M.T. and Fisher, M. (2000) 'Reading instruction in the resource room: Set-up for failure', *Exceptional Children*, 66: 305–316.

Mounton, S.G., Hawkins, J., McPherson, R.H. and Copley, J. (1996) 'School attachment: Perspectives of low-attached high school students', *Educational Psychology*', 16: 297–304.

National Curriculum Council (1989) *Curriculum Guidance 2: A Curriculum for All*. York: NCC.

Neel, R.S., Alexander, L. and Meadows, N.B. (1997) 'Expand positive learning opportunities and results', *Journal of Emotional and Behavioural Disorders*, 5: 6–14.

Nias, G. (1989) *Primary Teachers Talking*. London: Routledge.

O'Brien, T. (1998) *Promoting Positive Behaviour*. London: Fulton.

Office for Standards in Education (1995a) *Guidance on the Inspection of Primary Schools*. London: HMSO.

Office for Standards in Education (1995b) *Guidance on the Inspection of Secondary Schools*. London: HMSO.

Office for Standards in Education (1995c) *Guidance on the Inspection of Special Schools*. London: HMSO.

Office for the Standards of Education (2001) *Evaluating Educational Inclusion*. London: HMSO.

Porter, L. (2000) *Behaviour in Schools –Theory and Practice for Teachers*. Buckingham: Open University Press.

Raymond, J. (1987) 'An educational psychologist's intervention with a class of disruptive pupils using pupil perceptions', *Educational Psychology in Practice*, 3 (2): 16–22.

Redl, F. and Wineman, D. (1965) *Children who Hate*. London: Macmillan.

Richmond, T. (1993) 'Making learning flexible', *British Journal of Special Education*, 20 (1): 20–23.

Rudduck, J., Chaplain, R. and Wallace, G. (1996) *School Improvement: What Can Pupils Tell Us?* London: Fulton.

Russell, P. (1996) 'Listening to children with special educational needs', in R. Davie and D. Galloway (eds), *Listening to Children in Education*, London: Fulton.

Rustemier, S. (2002) *Social and Educational Justice: The Human Rights Framework for Inclusion*. Bristol: CSIE.

Rutter, M. (1980) *Changing Youth in a Changing Society*. London: Nuffield Provincial Hospital Trust.

Scarlett, P. (1989) 'Discipline: Pupil and teacher perceptions', *Maladjustment and Therapeutic Education*, 7 (3): 169–77.

Spalding, B., Kastirke, N. and Jennessen, S. (2001) 'School improvement in the context of the special school for children with emotional and behavioural difficulties', *Emotional and Behavioural Difficulties*, 6 (1): 7–18.

Summerskill, B. (2000) 'All the advantages? They'll fail without self-esteem', *Observer*, 24 September, p. 3.

Teacher Training Agency (1999) *National Standards for Special Educational Needs (SEN) and Specialist Teachers*. London: TTA.

Teacher Training Agency (2004) *Initial Teacher Training Professional Resource Network (Behaviour)*. London: TTA.

Tisdall, G. and Dawson, R. (1994) 'Listening to the children: Interviews with children attending a mainstream support facility', *Support for Learning*, 9 (4): 197–83.

Turner, C. (2000) 'A pupil with emotional and behavioural difficulties perspective: Does John feel that his behaviour is affecting his learning?', *Emotional and Behavioural Difficulties*, 5 (4): 13–18.

Wade, B. and Moore, M. (1993) *Experiencing Special Education*, Milton Keynes: Open University Press.

White, R. (1982) *Absent with Cause*. London: Routledge and Kegan Paul.

Willis, P. (1977) *Learning to Labour: How Working-class Kids get Working-class Jobs*, Farnborough: Saxon House.

Wise, S.F. (1999) 'Improving success in the mainstream setting for pupils with emotional and behavioural difficulties. *Pastoral Care*, September, 14–20.

Wise, S.F. and Upton. G. (1998) 'The perception of pupils with emotional and behavioural difficulties of their mainstream Schooling,' *Emotional and Behavioural Difficulties*, 3 (1): 3–12.

Woods, P. (1990) *The Happiest Days*. London: Falmer.

20

Involving Students with Emotional and Behavioural Difficulties in their Own Learning: A Transnational Perspective

BARRY GROOM AND RICHARD ROSE

The United States and England have historically had both significant similarities and differences in the development of their respective special educational needs (SEN) policy and practice. Over the last 30 years both countries have systemically reviewed their national responses to SEN provision culminating in major legislation, in the United States, the IDEA (1997) and in England, the SEN Code of Practice (DfES, 1994, Revised 2001). Within both legislative reforms is a key shift in emphasis away from segregated provision for students with special educational needs towards inclusive schooling (England) and 'least restrictive environments' (US).

The primary focus for both countries has been in addressing the *processes* and *procedures* for identifying and assessing SEN and planning appropriate programmes, with the individual education plan or programme (IEP) being central to contributing to a developing process of accountability (LeRoy and Simpson, 1996; Tod, 1999). Within the SEN Code of Practice (DfES, 2001), specific weight has been given to the pupil's own direct involvement in the assessment and learning process, including the recording of their views, providing support to enable students to identify their own needs and moving towards greater involvement in decision-making processes. These demands have inevitably challenged schools to examine their policies and procedures and to reconsider the teacher–student relationship.

The voice and opinion of the student in decision making and planning is seen as an important and valuable contribution to the development of more effective teaching approaches. However, although this development is promoted in England in the procedures outlined in the SEN Code of Practice and in the United States through individual responses to IDEA (for example, Massachusetts Department of Education, 2001), Rose and his colleagues (1996, 1999) and Fletcher (2001) have identified that student participation has generally received much less attention from educators. The narrower focus in practice being the drive to implement effective management and planning systems that address curriculum demands and assist teachers through a technocratic approach to planning.

THE IMPACT OF POLICY ON STUDENTS WITH EMOTIONAL AND BEHAVIOURAL DIFFICULTIES (EBD)

Concurrent with and influencing these SEN developments has been a sustained market-led approach to the management of English and US educational systems that has produced inherent tensions between policy and practice in both countries as identified by Lange and Riddell (2000). Of particular significance deriving from this tension has been the increase in the number of students with the label of 'emotional and behavioural difficulties' (EBD) and the continued worrying rates of exclusion, truancy and drop-out from school.

In England, the central drive of general education policies continues to be the emphasis on standards, assessment tests and league tables (Booth et al., 1998). Consequently, as the Office for Standards in Education (OfSTED) found in its review of effective education for students with emotional and behavioural difficulties:

> There have also been some undesirable and unintended side-effects of more general educational policies. For example, with the advent of Local Management of Schools (LMS), published examination and test results, growing competitiveness between schools and generally reduced levels of funding, mainstream schools have become less prepared to retain and support students who exhibit disturbed and disturbing behaviour and who do them no public credit. (OfSTED, 1999: para. 18)

Muscot (2000) has identified that although there is an 'extensive practice base with strong empirical support' in the area of positive behaviour management, students with emotional and behavioural difficulties continue to underachieve in both social and academic dimensions. In comparison with other special needs groups, students with EBD have lower graduation rates, lower reading and maths scores and are less likely to continue their education post-16 years of age.

It is also likely that students with EBD will have a greater involvement in the criminal justice, mental health, welfare and public health systems than other special needs groups. As a response to a perceived problem of growing youth social disorder, England has adopted many aspects of the 'tough love' rights and responsibility agenda first developed in the United States. A range of policy interventions has been introduced aimed directly at impacting upon antisocial behaviour, disaffection and truancy. Included among these interventions are tougher sanctions for parents of truants, community curfew orders for young people who display antisocial behaviours, a more prominent role for the police, both in school and in tackling truancy, and the withdrawal or holding back of welfare benefits.

The national concern in the United States for children who have mental health problems was expressed by The Surgeon General (US DHHS, 1999) for the need further to develop effective interventions to address their multiple needs. Identifying the 'joined-up' nature of social problems is one of the key factors underlying the concept of social exclusion with its focus on the links between the contexts of unemployment, poor skills, high crime, poor housing and family breakdown. The Social Exclusion Unit (2001) in England was set up to co-ordinate policymaking on linked social problems, such as school exclusion and truancy, rough sleeping, teenage pregnancy, youth at risk and inadequately serviced communities. This link has been further identified by Parsons (1999), whose detailed analysis found that it was the most vulnerable families and social groups who are most likely to experience exclusion from school. These risk factors are also identified by Kay (1999) as contributing to mental health problems in children, lessening their resilience to risk and uncertainty, lowering their self-esteem and inhibiting their ability to deal with change and adaptation.

MOVING FROM ALIENATION AND PASSIVITY TO PARTNERSHIP

Muscott (2000) found that teachers frequently voiced concern that students with EBD were not motivated to learn or complete schoolwork, particularly in areas in which their interest level was low or they were performing below the level of attainment of their peers. O'Flanagan (1997) reported that students with EBD often perceived themselves as 'damaged goods', rarely having structured opportunities to change either their own or other people's negative perceptions of them. These strong feelings of isolation and rejection lead inevitably to disengagement from the education process itself. Maeroff (1998) identified these students – experiencing social and personal disempowerment – as having a 'lack of social capital', disenfranchised from the mainstream of educational opportunity. Further alienation is often experienced by students with SEN when they are required to take only a 'passive' role in the learning process – wherein they are the receivers of planned education programmes that are focused on their difficulties, rather than on their talents, experiences and achievements (Munby, 1995; Armstrong and Galloway, 1996). The consequences of this approach is that students with EBD are inevitably defined by their difficulties and feel limited by the school system to a narrow range of educational experiences and expectations. Lewis (1999) argues for a curriculum for pupils with EBD to have as its focus the development of resilience-building skills to counteract student's strongly held perceptions of helplessness. Lewis states that 'sadly it takes a great deal of effort to maintain a negative motivational style, the challenge is to tap and redirect that energy, rather than suppress or contain it' (1999: 16).

In support of a pedagogical argument for increased pupil participation in their own learning, Brendtro (1994) advocates a philosophical shift in emphasis from a curriculum of control and compliance to that of a 'reclaiming environment' that promotes attachment, achievement, autonomy and altruism.

When students' voices are heard and given credence, as in Poplin and Weeres's (1992) major study, then fresh insights are given into students' perceptions, expectations and aspirations. In their work, Poplin and Weeres reveal that students have a clear perception of those factors which influence their own ability to learn. What comes across clearly and strongly from this study is the wish to be involved actively in school processes and for teaching and learning to be meaningful and dynamic. Wade and Moore's (1993) account of the views and experiences of students with SEN from a range of countries provides valuable understanding of the phenomenological experience of special needs. The use of students' own voices in providing unique views of their experiences and perceptions has been undertaken further by Johnson (1991), Gersch (1996), Garner (2000), Cooper (1999) and Jelly et al. (2000). Each of these writers report improved self-esteem and enhanced educational attainment in students who are encouraged to play a full role in determining assessment and learning processes.

The benefits to the learning experience for students with EBD in the assessment and management of their own learning has been stressed by Cooper (1993), who emphasizes the promotion of a positive self-image and developing self-confidence. The process of negotiation immediately provides a statement about the way in which the teacher values the pupil's opinions and creates a climate for the promotion of self-esteem. Jelly et al. details a range of interventions undertaken in EBD schools to promote active pupil participation, and states that:

> Teaching that fails to take into account factors that enhance or inhibit individual learning is unlikely to result in sustained achievement for the majority of students. (2000: 12)

THE ROLE OF THE TEACHER

One of the potential difficulties faced in schools developing the use of step-by-step targets for pupils with SEN is that this group of pupils will be perceived to require only basic instruction and intensive concentration on a narrow range of objectives and curriculum areas. The traditional special education approach of focusing upon individual needs has at times resulted in a concentration upon developing planning and assessment procedures which fail to recognize the potential of pupils to give some direction to their own learning. There is evidence (Griffiths and Davies, 1995) that pupils at the earliest stages of formal education are capable of identifying their own learning strengths and needs. However, there is a clear perception on the part of some teachers that students who have a label which indicates a learning or behavioural difficulty are unlikely to be either motivated or capable of making effective decisions about their own learning. Gersch (1996) has asserted that many teachers may feel with some justification that they have a good idea about what is best for a student in terms of their learning. However, he suggests that in their experience many students who are described as having SEN respond positively to being fully involved in decision-making processes. Furthermore, those students who may have EBD need to enhance their skills of negotiation and to be encouraged to see the point of view of others. This will not be achieved unless educational opportunities are provided for them to express their views in the security of a classroom environment. Paradoxically, as Jelly et al. note, 'there has been a growth of interest in empowering individual learners alongside an attainment-driven agenda that seeks wide scale achievement of nationally set targets' (2000: 12). Jolivette et al. (2002), Munk and Repp (1994) and Gunter et al. (1994) show in their different case studies how presenting choice and decision-making opportunities in classroom tasks promotes and increases the appropriate behaviours of students with EBD.

Rose (1999) states that teachers need to have a range of teaching styles and techniques at their disposal, and have the confidence and skills to move between them as situations change and in relation to pupil need. Such confidence will not be gained easily and requires that teachers develop a good understanding of how to recognize the preferred learning styles of individual pupils and how these may be addressed in a range of teaching situations. Furthermore, a recognition that some pupils with EBD have learning styles which differ greatly from those of their peers means that teachers must equip themselves with a broad spectrum of differentiation strategies and an understanding of when these may be most appropriately deployed. Jelly et al. recognize that promoting real partnership with pupils in the classroom involves the teacher in risk-tasking:

> Being a risk-taker does not align itself easily with being a teacher. Prescriptive curriculum structures, proliferation of rules, systems, checks and controls along with the need to be effective at maintaining discipline and an orderly community lead many teachers to favour a direct, didactic style which demands relatively little response from the pupil. The emphasis on the maintenance of power and control lies firmly with the teacher but often restricts the creative aspects of teaching and learning and most certainly restricts the learner. (2000: 16)

Where the opinions of pupils with EBD have been sought, they reveal interesting perceptions of the teachers and the climate of the schools that they attend. Cooper, questioning students with EBD about their views of teachers, found that they were generally regarded as:

> … too strict, too formal, intolerant, humourless, uninterested in pupils' personal welfare, guilty of labelling some pupils with negative identities and insufficiently helpful to students with learning difficulties (1993: 144).

Similar findings from a study conducted by Wise and Upton (1998) identified a perception on the part of students that their disruptive and disaffected behaviour was caused by one or more of the factors highlighted by Cooper. This reveals how difficult it is for teachers to gain positive assent from some students who are disaffected, and emphasizes the need for teachers to review their image and relationships with such students.

Cole (2003) emphasizes the need to develop what he describes as an inclusive culture within schools. He suggests that feelings of disaffection can be minimized in those schools where students feel that their opinions and beliefs are most valued. In Cole's view, form tutors must perform a vital pastoral role as mentors and supporters in whom students have confidence. This will only be achieved through a process of dialogue and where students feel that they are working in a climate of mutual respect and understanding. For many pupils with EBD, figures of authority present a challenge and are seen as oppressive and controlling. Teachers who have regular contact with these students have a unique opportunity to present authority in a manner which demonstrates that this can be accompanied by respect for individuals and the ability to recognize difference and culture.

SCHOOL IMPROVEMENT FOR PUPIL PARTICIPATION

Models of school improvement have dominated much of the inclusion literature in recent years (Porter, 1995; Giangreco, 1997; Ainscow, 1999) and an emphasis has been placed upon creating a climate for changes in school practices which facilitate greater opportunities for learning for all students. A common theme that runs through much of the research into school improvement is a recognition of the gains in effectiveness to be made through ensuring that the self-esteem of all members of the school community is raised. It has been suggested (Rouse and Florian, 1996; Ainscow, 1999) that self-esteem in both teachers and students is most effectively raised when they are encouraged to play a full role in decision-making and policy processes.

Much can be gained through listening to the voices of young people with SEN who have experienced both the positive and negative aspects of the education system. Writing of her personal experiences in both mainstream and special education, Noble (2003) suggests that many of her teachers had low expectations of what they could achieve. This led to frustration, which was at times exhibited through poor behaviour. She believes that a lack of willingness on the part of schools to provide students with an opportunity to express their opinions and be involved in decision-making processes is a major inhibitor of pupil progress. However, she is also conscious of the fact that what often passes for pupil involvement is little more than tokenism.

Pupil involvement in the setting of targets through IEP procedures or during meetings to review their progress needs to be founded upon an awareness of the skills and understanding necessary to become a successful participant. Developing the ability to understand the point of view expressed by others, to negotiate and to predict the consequences likely to follow personal actions taken in school, is not easy for all students. These are skills that need to be taught and demand that schools give a commitment to student involvement right from the start. School improvement must start from an audit of existing school procedures in order to gauge where there are opportunities to promote practices which will encourage greater pupil participation. Self-advocacy and participation in planning for personal progress must become an embedded part of everyday school life, rather than an additional component or an optional extra. Barth (1990) emphasizes the need for teachers and students to learn from each other. He suggests that the culture of a school is dependent upon the quality of personal relationships, which can be developed only through mutual respect and dialogue. The opinions of pupils as cited above would tend to suggest that this has become the norm in only a limited number of schools.

School structures must provide opportunities for pupil participation at all levels. This should begin with policies for which students feel some ownership through consultation and discussion. Such policies must be followed by the provision of transparent procedures whereby students can see that their opinions and concerns are being addressed. Where, for example, students feel a true ownership of their IEP they are more likely to engage fully in the assessment of their own progress and in discussions related to improvement of their performance. By contrast, where targets and requirements are perceived by students as having been imposed by persons in authority, we are more likely to witness resentment and consequent antisocial behaviours.

Models of school improvement must be founded upon the creation of communities which are committed to personal development and shared values. Too often the cultural beliefs and expectations that students described as having EBD bring with them into schools are remote from the perceived requirements for the development of orderly school communities. Efforts to achieve conformity simply by bringing students into line are likely to lead to conflict and increase the stress of all parties. Sharing perceptions and beliefs, even when these begin from opposing viewpoints, must be an important starting point in developing a climate that is conducive to learning. Good models of improvement will have a goal of creating a school that is respected by all of its community and to which all members feel they can make a valued contribution.

REFERENCES

Ainscow, M. (1999) *Understanding the Development of Inclusive Schools*. London: Falmer.

Armstrong, D. and Galloway, D. (1996) 'The voice of the child with special educational needs', in R. Davie and D. Galloway (eds), *Listening to Children in Education*. London: Fulton.

Barth, R.S. (1990) *Improving Schools from Within*. San-Francisco, CA: Jossey Bass.

Booth, T., Ainscow, M. and Dyson, A. (1998) England: Inclusion and exclusion in a competitive system, in T. Booth and M. Ainscow (eds), *From Them to Us*. London: Routledge.

Brendtro, L.K. (1994) 'Tapping the strength of oppositional youth: Helping Kevin change', *Journal of Emotional and Behavioural Problems*, 3 (2): 41–5.

Cole, T. (2003) 'Policies for positive behaviour management', in C. Tilstone and R. Rose (eds), *Strategies to Promote Inclusive Practice*. London: Routledge Falmer.

Cooper, P. (1993) *Effective Schools for Disaffected Students*. London: Routledge.

Cooper, P. (1999) 'Emotional behavioural difficulties and adolescence', in P. Cooper (ed.), *Understanding and Supporting Children with Emotional and Behavioural Difficulties*. London: Jessica Kingsley.

Department for Education and Skills (2001) *The SEN Code of Practice*. London: DfES.

Fletcher, W. (2001) 'Enabling students with severe learning difficulties to become effective target setters', in R. Rose and I. Grosvenor (eds), *Doing Research in Special Education*. London: Fulton.

Garner, P. (2000) *Teachers and Students Voices on Inclusion: Preferred Practice for Children who are Regarded as Having Emotional and Behavioural Difficulties*. Paper given at International Special Needs Congress, (ISEC) Manchester.

Gersch, I. (1996) 'Listening to children in educational contexts', in R. Davie, G. Upton and V. Varma (eds), *The Voice of the Child*. London: Falmer.

Giangreco, M.F. (1997) 'Key lessons learned about inclusive education: summary of the 1996 Schonell memorial lecture', *International Journal of Disability*, 44 (3): 193–206.

Griffiths, M. and Davies, C. (1995) *In Fairness to Children. Working for Social Justice in the Primary School*. London: Fulton.

Gunter, P.L., Shores, R.E., Jack, S.L., Denny, R.K. and DePaepe, P. (1994) 'A case study of the effects of altering instructional interactions on the disruptive behavior of a child identified with severe behavior disorders', *Education and Treatment of Children*, 17: 435–44.

IDEA (USA Federal Law) (1997) *Individuals with Disabilities Education Act, Amendments of 1997*.

Jelly, M., Fuller, A. and Byers, R. (2000) *Involving Students in Practice*. London: Fulton.

Johnson, J.H. (1991) 'Student voice: Motivating students through Empowerment', *OSSC Bulletin*, (Special issue) 35 (2).

Jolivette, K., Sticher, J. and McCormack, K. (2002) 'Making choices – improving behaviour – engaging in learning', *Teaching Exceptional Children*, Jan./Feb.: 24–9.

Kay, H. (1999) *Bright Futures. Promoting Children and Young People's Mental Health*. London: Mental Health Foundation.

Lange, C. and Riddell, S. (2000) 'Special educational needs policy and choice: tensions between policy development in the USA and UK contexts.' in M. McLaughlin and M. Rouse (eds), *Special Education and School Reform in the United States and Britain*. London: Routledge.

LeRoy, B. and Simpson, C. (1996) 'Improving student outcomes through inclusive education', *Support for Learning*, 11 (1): 32–6.

Lewis, J. (1999) 'Research into the concept of resilience as a basis for the curriculum for children with EBD', *Emotional and Behavoural Difficulties*, 4 (2): 11–22.

Maeroff, G.I. (1998) *Altered Destinies: Making Life Better for School Children in Need*. New York: St. Martin's.

Massachusetts Department of Education (2001) *IEP Process Guide*. Malden, MA: Author.

Munby, S. (1995) 'Assessment and pastoral care: sense, sensitivity and standards', in R. Best, P. Lang, C. Lodge and C. Watkins (eds), *Pastoral Care and Personal Social Education*. London: Cassell.

Munk, D.D. and Repp, A.C. (1994) 'The relationship between instructional variables and problem behavior: A review', *Exceptional Children*, 60: 390–401.

Muscott, H.S. (2000) 'A review and analysis of service-learning programs involving students with emotional/behavioral disorders, *Education and Treatment of Children*, 23: 346–68.

Noble, K. (2003) 'Personal reflection of experiences of special and mainstream education', in M. Shevlin and R. Rose (eds), *Encouraging Voices*. Dublin: National Disability Authority.

Office for Standards in Education (OfSTED) (1999) *Principles into Practice: Effective Education for Students with Emotional and Behavioural Difficulties*. London: Ofsted.

O'Flanagan, B. (1997) 'Building purpose through service', *Reclaiming Children and Youth*, 5: 223–5.

Parsons, C. (1999) *Education, Exclusion and Citzenship*. London: Routledge.

Poplin, M. and Weeres, J. (1992) *Voices from the Inside: A Report of Schooling from Inside the Classroom*. Claremont, CA: The Claremont Graduate School, Institute for Education in Transformation.

Porter, G.L. (1995) 'Organisation of schooling: achieving access and quality through inclusion', *Prospects*, 25 (2): 299–309.

Rose, R. (1999) 'The involvement of students with severe learning difficulties as decision makers in respect of their own learning needs', *Westminster Studies in Education*, ' 22 (2): 19–29.

Rose, R., McNamara, S. and O'Neil, J. (1996) 'Promoting the greater involvement of students with special needs in the management of their own assessment and learning processes', *British Journal of Special Education*: 23 (4): 166–71.

Rouse, M. and Florian, L. (1996) 'Effective inclusive schools, a study in two countries', *Cambridge Journal of Education*, 26 (1): 71–85.

Social Exclusion Unit (2001) *Preventing Social Exclusion: Report of the Social Exclusion Unit*. London: SEU.

Tod, J. (1999) 'IEPs: Inclusive educational practices?', *Support for Learning*, 14 (4): 184–8.

US Department of Health and Human Services (1999) *Mental Health: A Report of the Surgeon General*. Rockville, MD: Department of Health and Human Services.

Wade, B. and Moore, M. (1993) *Experiencing Special Education*. Milton Keynes: Open University Press.

Wise, S. and Upton, G. (1998) 'Perceptions of pupils with emotional and behavioural difficulties of their mainstream schools', *Emotional and Behavioural Difficulties*, 3 (3): 3–12.

21

Directions in Teaching Social Skills to Students with Specific EBDs

HELEN MCGRATH

Gresham (1997) has argued that a lack of social competence virtually defines an emotional and behavioural disorder (EBD). Social competence is the extent to which a student can initiate and maintain positive relationships with both classmates and teachers, gain social acceptance from their peers, make satisfying friendships, and terminate negative or disadvantaging social associations (Gresham, 2000). This chapter focuses on the identified specific social learning needs of students with the EBDs of attention deficit/hyperactivity disorder, conduct disorder, or one of the several anxiety disorders. The effectiveness of teaching social skills to students with EBDs as a supportive intervention is also discussed. A feature of the chapter is the manner in which detailed use has been made of the literature in order to scope the extent of work in this aspect of EBD – but also to exemplify its complexity.

Students with EBDs are more likely to demonstrate negative, withdrawn, conflicted or otherwise ineffective patterns of social interaction. Their social behaviour often leads those with whom they interact socially to respond initially with discomfort, anger or avoidance and, eventually, with rejection (Shores and Wehby, 1999). Ongoing peer rejection then places those students at greater risk for adverse social, academic and mental health consequences. The likely short-term outcomes of unsatisfying peer relationships include increased aggression and antisocial behaviour, truancy, substance abuse, low academic achievement, depression and dropping out of school (Kupersmidt et al., 1995; Walker et al., 1995). Possible longer-term outcomes include depression, unsatisfactory employment experiences, criminality and poor marital success. In general those with poor relationship skills are more likely to have less satisfactory, less independent, less successful and unhappier lives (Blackorby and Wagner, 1996).

Their social difficulties also adversely impact on their development of friendships. These students may make friends initially, but often lack the skills needed to keep them (Miller-Johnson et al., 1999). Gresham et al. (1997) found that only about 20 percent of children in grade 3 who were designated as 'at risk' for EBDs had one or more friends in a typical classroom, compared to 50 percent in a matched control group. A lack of satisfying friendship experiences not only leads to a decreased frequency of positive social interactions, but also to lower levels of academic task completion (Newcomb and Bagwell, 1995). Lack of opportunities to engage in ongoing friendship behaviours also has implications for students' socio-moral development. Friendship provides opportunities for the participants to disagree more in a 'safe' way, learn about perspective-taking, debate socio-moral issues and make decisions about moral dilemmas, all of which provokes changes in socio-moral thinking (Schonert-Reichl, 1993).

NEW DIRECTIONS

Sugai et al. (2000) have argued for the replacement of the more typical punitive and exclusionary approach to the management of the behaviour of students with EBDs with one characterized by a school-wide programme of positive behaviour support. Such an approach focuses more on positive interventions, such as rewards for appropriate behaviour, improved teaching strategies to maximize student engagement, environmental changes (for example, furniture and room reorganization), the creation of a prosocial classroom culture, and the direct teaching of social skills (Sugai and Horner, 2002). The direct teaching of social skills has been the most researched of these initiatives.

Most reviewers of studies investigating the effectiveness of social skills programmes in improving social outcomes for 'at-risk' students have concluded that there is much empirical support for the positive impact of a great variety of social skills training programmes (Gresham, 1998; Hepler, 1998; Hermann and McWhirter, 1997). However, Gresham (1997) has also noted that there is an enormous variation in the effect sizes (0.20 to 0.50) across more recent meta-analyses of research on the effectiveness of social skills programmes. In general, research has also suggested that social skills programmes seem to have been more effective at *teaching* the skills than at ensuring that they generalize across settings and maintain over time (Ogilvy, 1994).

A MODEL OF SOCIAL BEHAVIOUR

Several social information processing models have been proposed to explain social behaviour (Dodge and Price, 1994). Dodge's (1986) model was initially developed more to explain aggressive behaviour in children, rather than all social behaviour. The five processes in his model are:

- the encoding of social cues;
- their interpretation;
- the generation of potential responses;
- their evaluation; and
- the enactment of the selected response.

An alternative, more general model of social behaviour is proposed below to explain the process of general social behaviour. Students with specific EBDs may have deficits in one or more of the following processes:

- accessing social knowledge/social memory;
- applying personal values;
- social cognition (that is, recognition of social cues, intention detection, empathy, emotional regulation, goal selection, social problem solving consequential thinking, and social self-efficacy assessment);
- social skill enactment; and
- social self-reflection (monitoring of immediate responses and later analysis and reflection).

Accessing social knowledge and social memory

The student accesses their current knowledge of culturally appropriate social expectations and social rules, and of the social skills which are consistent with those expectations and rules. They also access their memory of previous similar social encounters.

Applying personal values

The student recalls and applies their personal socio-moral values (or lack thereof) to the social situation. Values are predominantly:

- *Prosocial* (that is, focused on enhancing relationships and respecting the rights and feelings of others).
- *Antisocial* (that is, focused on personal gain in violation of the rules and social expectations of the community and irrespective of the negative impact on others).
- *Non-social* (that is, focused on personal gain but not necessarily through the violation of societal rules or the violation of rights).

Social cognition

Many different social cognitive processes are then applied as part of the student's analysis of the social cues and resultant selection of response. Some of these are:

- *Recognition of social cues:* the student identifies and integrates the social cues in the situation, that is, any combination of the context and other people's words, actions and non-verbal features such as voice tone and facial expression.
- *Intention detection:* the student decides whether the other person's intentions towards them are hostile (for example, they want to make me look stupid or beat me at the game no matter what it takes) or benign (for example, they want to be friends or they want to get to know me).
- *Empathy:* the student takes the perspective of the other person to try to understand their views and feelings in order to respond appropriately (for example, are they feeling lonely? Do they seem nervous that I might not like them?).
- *Emotional regulation:* the student recognizes and names the feelings they are experiencing in response to the social cues and the social setting (especially anger and anxiety) and finds ways to regulate them (that is, calm down) so that they don't overwhelm rational thought and inhibit appropriate social responses.
- *Social goal selection:* on the basis of their personal values and the reading of the social situation, the student decides what they want to achieve from the social encounter. Possible *positive* and *prosocial* goals are: getting on well with the other person, having a good time, maintaining a positive social reputation, keeping out of trouble, getting to know someone, finding a peaceful solution and maintaining a friendship. Possible *negative* and *antisocial* goals are: retaliation, winning at all costs, manipulating someone to get what you want, and maintaining a reputation as someone socially dominant and/or tough and intimidating. Possible *self-protective* or *non-social* goals are: safety and avoidance, and controlling everything that happens in the encounter.

- *Social problem solving*: the student generates possible alternative social responses and strategies to achieve their goal using their social knowledge and social memory as the data base.
- *Consequential thinking*: the student predicts the potential positive and negative outcomes of each possible response before deciding on the most effective one to use.
- *Social self-efficacy assessment*: the student assesses whether or not they have enough skill and confidence to enact the selected skill.

Social skill enactment

The student enacts the chosen social skill to achieve their selected goal. A skill involves a combination of words and actions as well as non-verbal features, such as smiling (or lack of it), type of eye contact, and facial expressions.

Monitoring of responses and social self-reflection

There are two parts to this process. The first is *immediate self-reflection,* in which the student monitors and interprets the reactions of others and adjusts their next response accordingly. The second is *long-term self-reflection,* in which, at a later point, the student mentally 'replays' (or talks to others about) the social encounter and evaluates the effectiveness of their own performance in terms of the goals they selected. At this later point they also make attributions for the success or failure of the social enactment (for example, a rebuff or humiliation is attributed to either internal factors (for example, ability) or external factors (for example, the other person's bad mood). This information is then added to their store of social knowledge and their social memory, and becomes part of the data base for the next similar social skill enactment.

ATTENTION DEFICIT HYPERACTIVITY DISORDER (ADHD)

ADHD is characterized by a persistent pattern of inattention and/or hyperactivity/impulsivity that is more frequent and severe than is typically observed in individuals at a comparable level of development (APA, 1994).

- *Inattention* refers to difficulties in focusing and sustaining appropriate attention. It contributes to distractibility, high rates of off-task behaviour, disorganization and a lack of persistence on tasks (Barkley, 1990).
- *Impulsivity* refers to behavioural disinhibition and reflects difficulties in controlling both behaviour and thoughts. It results in difficulties such

as not waiting for a turn, speaking without thinking, intruding on others' boundaries, and the seeking of immediate gratification (Barkley, 1990). Impulsivity also contributes to off-task behaviour, rule breaking and higher levels of risk-taking or sensation-seeking behaviours (Dulcan and Benson, 1997).

• *Hyperactivity* involves excessive and inappropriate levels of activity, such as moving around, fidgeting and talking.

Students with ADHD are usually not appealing to classmates or friends and are often unpopular (Farmer et al., 1999). They evoke negative reactions from peers and teachers because of their annoying, boisterous, intractable and irritating social behaviour (Landau and Moore, 1991) and classmates are more aware of them than other peers in a negative way (Grizenko et al., 1993). Their emotional volatility and behaviour often create frequent conflicts and confrontations. Their reputation amongst peers is often one of aggression and immaturity, characterized by relatively uninhibited behaviour and non-compliance with rules of both classroom and playground (Dulcan and Benson, 1997).

The social picture of a typical student with ADHD (combined type) is based more on boys than girls, because research has focused almost exclusively on boys, most likely as a result of the disproportionately high number of boys with ADHD compared to girls (Barkley, 1990). Studies suggest that approximately 50 per cent of students with ADHD have poor social functioning and are rejected by their peers (Hinshaw et al., 1997). Peer rejection of students with ADHD tends to be maintained across new peer groups and time (Guevremont, 1990), and many of their social difficulties persist into young adulthood, affecting both their heterosocial competencies and their employability.

The ADHD subtype predicts significant differences in social outcomes. Three subtypes of ADHD have been identified. The first type is characterized predominantly by inattention, the second by hyperactive/impulsivity, and the third is a combined type that has features of all three, that is, inattention, impulsivity and hyperactivity (APA, 1994). The majority of students diagnosed with ADHD are in the category of combined type (APA, 1994).

Students who are predominantly inattentive are more likely to have a deficit of positive social skills and are more likely to be socially withdrawn and ignored or neglected (Dumas, 1998). On the other hand, students with ADHD who are characterized by either just impulsiveness or impulsivity plus inattentiveness appear to be at greater risk of peer rejection than students with just attention difficulties (Carlson et al., 1987). Such students are more likely to display an excess of negative social behaviours and hence become socially uncomfortable for peers to associate with. It may take only one demonstration of uncontrolled anger or inappropriate aggression on the part of an impulsive student for peers to make up their minds to avoid and/or reject them. Such social rejection appears to be bi-directional (Hymel et al., 1990), with rejected students responding with even more aggression to their rejected status than do those who are socially neglected (Carlson et al., 1987).

Students in the combined type category are also more likely to have a co-morbid conduct disorder than those who are just inattentive and disorganized. Adolescents with a dual diagnosis of ADHD and conduct disorder experience even greater social problems than adolescents with only ADHD (Biederman et al., 1996). In one study, Weiss et al. (1985) found that parents of children with ADHD reported that 30 percent of their children had few steady friends.

Their frequency of social interaction of students with ADHD appears to be much the same as for their peers (Cunningham and Siegal, 1987; Hinshaw et al., 1989, but they are more likely to exhibit verbal and physical aggression towards peers, be less compliant with rules, be loud and disruptive, talk rapidly and excessively (especially when on-task behaviour is required), be argumentative and stubborn, show lower levels of co-operation and peer compliance, offer less assistance to peers, and be less able to share and wait patiently for their turn (Barkley, 1990). They are also more likely to be more domineering and controlling with peers (Clark et al., 1988) and be more critical of and negative towards others (Dumas, 1998). They use ineffective and less reciprocal communication, often to the point of ignoring peer overtures (Dumas, 1998). They tend to be more oppositional and defiant with teachers and other adults (Dumas, 1998). Their impulsivity often leads to their speaking without thinking and hence saying thoughtless or negative things to peers or teachers, and intruding on others' boundaries (Barkley, 1990).

The negative social behaviour of students with ADHD appears to have a 'contagion' effect on their non-ADHD classmates. Classmates are less likely to co-operate and more likely to be off-task when in the company of students with ADHD. They also respond to classmates with ADHD with their own counter-controlling and noncompliant responses. Cunningham and Siegal (1987) have speculated that classmates start to avoid students with ADHD partly to avoid responding with negative behaviours of their own and getting into trouble when doing so.

The specific social difficulties of students with ADHD

Table 21.1 (column 1) outlines possible strategies for each area of social difficulty experienced by students with ADHD, after applying the social behaviour model mentioned earlier in the article.

Table 21.1 *Directions in teaching social skills to students with specific EBDs*

	Attention Deficit/Hyperactivity Disorder (ADHD)	Conduct Disorder	Anxiety Disorders (especially social phobia)
Social knowledge	Teach facts about skills and expectations in regard to: • co-operation • conflict management • conversation • being positive • being a good friend • fair playing in games	Teach facts about skills and expectations in regard to: • co-operation • conflict management	Teach facts about skills and expectations in regard to: • taking turns in conversation and making contributions in discussions
Personal values	Teach the prosocial values of: • respect for the rights and feelings of others • co-operation • support for others	Teach the prosocial values of: • respect for the rights and feelings of others • co-operation • honesty	
Social cognitions: • Recognizing social cues • Intention detection and empathy • Emotional regulation • Goal selection Social problem solving • Consequential thinking	Teach: • accurate intention detection • anger management • the selection of relationship-enhancing goals (instead of retaliation and winning) • social problem-solving skills • consequential thinking	Teach: • accurate intention detection • the selection of relationship-enhancing goals (instead of retaliation and winning) • consequential thinking • empathic responding	Teach: • accurate monitoring of social cues • the selection of relationship-enhancing goals (instead of avoidance and safety) • anxiety management • evidence-based social self-efficacy
Performance of social skills	Teach and practise skills for: • conversation effectiveness • conflict management • co-operation • being positive	Teach and practise skills for: • conflict management • social entry • conversation	Teach and practise skills for: • assertiveness • fluent conversation (minimizing pauses) • effective eye contact
Social self-reflection	Teach: • accurate social monitoring of others' responses to their social behaviour • accurate (and less self-serving) social attribution for social failure	Teach: • accurate social monitoring of others' responses to their social behaviour	Teach: • accurate (and less self-critical) social attribution for social failure • accurate social monitoring of others' responses to their social behaviour

Social knowledge and social memory

Students with ADHD display less knowledge about socially appropriate and agreeable behaviour (especially the importance of being positive, co-operative and compliant and being fair in games and activities). They also have less knowledge about effective communication and conversation and conflict management (Carlson et al., 1987; Grenell et al., 1987).

Personal values

ADHD students are less likely to demonstrate behaviours which reflect an endorsement of the prosocial values of co-operation and respect for the rights and feelings of others.

Social cognition

Students with ADHD who are aggressive tend to have poor intention detection skills and misattribute hostile intentions to others, especially in ambiguous social situations (Milich and Dodge, 1984). Such a bias increases the likelihood that peers will retaliate aggressively and deliver defensive rejecting responses. Impulsivity and inattention often lead to a failure on the part of the ADHD student to collect all the relevant information and social cues and to then jump to conclusions. Students with ADHD also show high levels of uncontrolled emotionality, explosiveness and moodiness (Barkley, 1990), and it is less satisfying to have a friendship with someone whose behaviour is unpredictable (Dumas, 1998). Poor social problem-solving ability is also a common characteristic of these students (Dodge and Coie, 1987; Guevremont and Foster, 1993), as is a reduced ability to accurately anticipate the consequences of using socially coercive behaviour (Dodge and Coie, 1987). They are more likely to choose goals of retaliation and winning at all costs over goals of relationship enhancement or staying friends.

Social skill enactment

The three broad areas of socially skilful behaviour that have been identified as problematic for students with ADHD are: peer social communication, peer co-operation, and conflict management. Although these skills may in part arise from a poor social knowledge base, they are also likely to reflect poor skill enactment.

Students with ADHD are likely to use ineffective general social communication. For example, they show low levels of verbal reciprocity and often do not respond to peer verbal initiations (Dumas, 1998). They tend to use less co-operative communication (Bickett and Milich, 1990) and are less competent at explaining things to others (Carlson et al., 1987). In particular they use poor conversational skills, with their style of conversation being characterized by poor listening, interruptions, monopolizing of the conversation, a disorganized style of thoughts and responses, and constant changing of the topic of conversation (Carlson et al., 1987). Dumas (1998) has suggested that ADHD symptoms may contribute even more to a student's social interaction problems when they become a young adolescent because of the greater importance at that age of social reciprocity and conversation as an aspect of making and keeping friends. A lack of effective communication may contribute significantly to a student's negative social reputation from around about the age of 10 onwards (Pope et al., 1989). Foster et al. (1986) have also identified conversational skills as one of the strongest predictors of peer acceptance in adolescence. In particular, talking too quickly and monopolizing conversations have been shown to be related to disliking in the teenage years (Jackson and Bruder, 1984). Poorly developed skills for managing conflict in a relationship-enhancing way are also characteristic of students with ADHD (Dulcan and Benson, 1997).

Social self-reflection

Students with ADHD appear to have a more inflexible social style. They are less able to adjust what they say and do to the demands of the situation (Landua and Milich, 1988), suggesting that they are inattentive, do not monitor others' responses and social cues well and hence do not rethink and adjust their social behaviour as they go. They are more likely to blame social failure on external factors, such as the other person's perceived ill-intended behaviour (Dodge, Bates and Pettit, 1990).

CONDUCT DISORDER

Students with conduct disorder exhibit a persistent pattern of behaviour that violates the basic rights of others and major age-appropriate social norms. They are frequently engaged in antisocial behaviours such as aggression, stealing, fighting, lying, cheating, bullying and destruction of property (APA, 1994). Some students with a diagnosis of conduct disorder are aggressive and hostile. Others are glib and charming and more difficult to detect (McGrath and Edwards, 2000).

Students with conduct disorders who are also aggressive have particular difficulties in forming and maintaining friendships with peers and are more likely than other students to experience peer rejection (Coie, 1990). Hinshaw et al. (1997) found that antisocial behaviours such as stealing and property destruction also predicted peer rejection. Such difficulties appear still to be apparent in adolescence (Campbell, 1990).

The social picture of a conduct disordered student who is aggressive is one characterized by lack of co-operative behaviour, attempts to dominate and intimidate peers, verbal and physical aggression towards peers, bullying, lying, stealing from peers, and destruction of peer property. On the other hand, the glib and manipulative conduct disordered student may, on the surface, have a range of seemingly positive behaviours which are designed to persuade others to become involved in their antisocial behaviours (often to the point of acting on behalf of the student with the conduct disorder) or to protect them from consequences from adults.

Table 21.1 (column 2) outlines possible strategies for each area of social difficulty experienced by conduct disordered students after applying the social behaviour model mentioned earlier in this chapter.

Social knowledge and social memory

Young children with conduct disorders have fewer positive social skills, engage in more destructive conflict and have limited knowledge of social expectations and skills related to co-operation, shared play and conflict management (Webster-Stratton and Lindsay, 1999). They also have less knowledge about effective strategies for social entry. These deficits appear to continue over time (Campbell, 1990).

Personal values

Antisocial values are reflected in the behaviour of students with a conduct disorder and the social goals they select.

Social cognitions

Aggressive conduct disordered students are limited in their perspective taking skills and, hence, in empathy (Webster-Stratton and Lindsay, 1999). They also tend to misattribute hostile intentions to others (Coie, 1990) and to selectively attend to aggressive social cues more than to nonaggressive cues (Milich and Dodge, 1984). They have access to fewer social problem-solving strategies. They are more likely to choose the goal of retaliation or dominance and hence enact coercive responses or solutions. Chung and Asher (1997) found that aggression was the preferred strategy of conduct disordered students to deal with a hypothetical conflict situation if retaliation was selected as the prime goal. However, when they select aggression as the social option, they usually fail to anticipate the negative consequences of their choice. Lochman, Coie et al. (1993) demonstrated that boys who chose dominance and revenge as their main goals in hypothetical social situations went on to have a stronger history of criminal activity and substance misuse. Erdley and Asher (1999) have argued that conduct disordered students are more likely to choose as their first goal, the one for which they have already developed a set of strategies and for which they have a strong sense of self-efficacy, that is, aggression and coercion.

Social skill enactment

Students with conduct disorders are more likely to lack the skills of approaching and joining peers in a positive way (Dodge et al., 1983), giving positive feedback and starting a conversation (Coie et al., 1990). Younger children with a conduct disorder lack positive play skills, such as offering assistance and playing co-operatively (Ladd et al., 1990).

Social self-reflection

Lynam (1996) has suggested that conduct disordered students fail to attend to shifts in social cues. For example, if a peer moved from conflict to placation (for example, by apologising or acting in a friendly manner) they would be likely to continue in a confrontational manner. They also overestimate their own social competence with peers (Webster-Stratton and Lindsay, 1999). Their tendency not to report being lonely perhaps reflects their inability to accurately detect the negative social response of others (Webster-Stratton and Lindsay, 1999).

ANXIETY DISORDER

Students with a generalized anxiety disorder worry excessively about many areas of their life, such as school work, family, friends, health, travel and any new situation (APA, 1994). Students with social phobia are very anxious about social or performance situations in which they are exposed to unfamiliar people and evaluation. They fear that they will act in a way that will result in humiliation or embarrassment and hence negative evaluation from others (APA, 1994). Children with separation anxiety disorder have excessive anxiety about separation from parents, especially their mother (APA, 1994).

Children with internalizing disorders, such as social phobia, generalized anxiety or separation anxiety, also tend to have impaired social relationships, have difficulty making friends, are socially withdrawn and have a lower frequency of social interactions than their peers. They tend to be socially ignored rather than rejected, but their anxiety often leads to their becoming the targets of bullying (Olweus, 1991; Rigby and Slee, 1992).

Table 21.1 (column 3) outlines possible strategies for each area of social difficulty experienced by anxious students (especially those with social phobia) after applying the social behaviour model mentioned earlier in this chapter.

Social knowledge/social memory

Anxious students do not appear to have specific social knowledge deficits. However, their social memories are more likely to emphasize their own social failures more than any social successes (Morris et al., 2002).

Personal values

This does not seem to be particularly relevant for the social difficulties of anxious students.

Social cognition

Anxious students tend to select the goal of avoidance or safety rather than relationship-enhancing goals. Whilst they do not misattribute hostile intention to others, they do tend to perceive that others are evaluating them negatively, and selectively attend to cues suggesting the other person is critical or contemptuous of them. They have great difficulty in regulating their anxiety in social situations, especially those students with social phobia.

Social skill enactment

Maag (1992) has advocated the use of stress inoculation training to help anxious students to improve their social effectiveness. Baker and Edelmann (2002) concluded that adults with social phobia had two major enactment deficits, which are possibly present also in students with the same disorder – they displayed excessive gaze aversion and had many more filled (for example, 'er' and 'um') and unfilled (silent) pauses during conversation.

Social self-reflection

Poorly-accepted anxious students tend to attribute social successes to external factors (for example, the friendliness of the other person), and social failures to internal factors, such as their own social ineptitude (Kendall and Chu, 2002; Morris et al., 2002). They are highly self-critical and many become depressed because of what they perceive to be their social failures and lack of confidence. Their readiness to withdraw from an uncomfortable social situation instead of monitoring the responses and persisting with new strategies makes it less likely that they develop social flexibility.

CO-MORBIDITY

Emotional and behavioural problems tend to co-occur (Tankersley and Landrum, 1997). Between 50 to 80 percent of students diagnosed with ADHD also suffer from a co-morbid condition, usually another externalizing disorder such as conduct disorder or oppositional defiant disorder (ODD) or both (Scahill et al., 1999). Approximately 25 percent of students with ADHD also have a co-morbid anxiety disorder (Angold et al., 1999). So for many students the social difficulties are more complex.

SOCIAL SKILLS PROGRAMMES

The outcomes of recent research studies suggest the following guidelines for incorporating programme features that are most likely to lead to the success of social skills programmes:

- Social skills programmes should be whole-class based, taught by teachers and embedded in the regular curriculum.
- The most effective model is one based on a direct social skills training (DSST) model, with some elements of social cognitive training (SCT).
- Social skills programmes need to be appealing and acceptable to teachers.
- Restructuring the classroom culture and physical environment to make them more prosocial is also a necessary element.
- Cultural sensitivity is necessary.
- The teaching of social skills should start as early as possible.
- There should be some match between the social skills and social cognitions taught in the programme and the specific social difficulties of at-risk students.
- There should be plans for the generalization of learned social skills across settings and maintenance over time.
- Social skills programmes are an additional component to a preventative treatment plan, not a complete replacement.
- Strategies for changing a student's negative social reputation should be included in any social skills programme.
- Developing positive associations with non-deviant peer groups is important for students with ADHD or conduct disorder.

- Peer-mediated strategies can add power to an intervention.
- Other behaviour management strategies need to be incorporated.

Although many of the earlier research studies into the teaching of social skills investigated programmes delivered in small groups by non-school personnel, there is now a strong push for programmes to be whole-school based and embedded in the regular curriculum. There are many powerful arguments for the idea that social skills programmes are best implemented by teachers in the school setting, preferably in a non-withdrawal context (Hops and Greenwood, 1988). Schools are the most significant places in which students develop the type of social skills which are particularly important for peer acceptance at different ages and stages (Gresham, 1988) and it makes little sense to decontextualize the teaching of social skills (Gresham, 1997).

Classroom-based programmes are also more attractive to children than infrequent interactions on a withdrawal basis with an unfamiliar counsellor or specialist, and the stigmatization which is often associated with outside referral is avoided (Weissberg et al., 1981). A school-based programme is also more cost-effective, in that, once trained, teachers can continue to use newly-acquired skills with other students (McGrath, 1996).

Walker et al. (1995) have argued that the 'selected' model of social skills training, in which children are trained in small withdrawal groups, inhibit generalization and does not address the issue of reputation. A classroom-based social skills programme offers a greater likelihood of producing generalization and maintenance of programme effects through the provision of naturalistic opportunities to practise and receive naturalistic reinforcement from real-life peers and a wide range of teachers (Maag, 1990). Gresham (1997) has, however, noted that it might be more effective for some students to start with a selected programme (that is, small group programme) and then move to a whole-class 'universal' programme (that is, one taught to all students) where the same skills are reinforced.

One significant factor that must be considered in the implementation of whole-class social skills programmes is whether or not the programmes selected are acceptable to teachers in terms of appropriateness, fairness, time and effort required, and intrusiveness (Witt and Elliott, 1985). Unacceptable interventions are less likely to be implemented or implemented correctly (1985). There needs to be some realistic expectation that the social outcomes for the at-risk students will be worth the time, cost and effort. Outcomes need to be socially important or valid, that is, make a difference to a student's overall social behaviour with classmates and teachers, create a more positive social reputation, lead to perceptions of greater social competence by teachers, produce improved peer acceptance, and enhance friendships (Gresham, 1997).

Teacher commitment must be ensured if a programmes is to succeed (McGrath, 1996), and substantial school support and resources are required (Rotheram-Borus et al., 2001). Teachers need training to acquire skills to teach the programme and need to be reasonably socially competent themselves (2001). They also need to be aware of the theoretical framework that underpins a social skills programme.

THE DIRECT SOCIAL SKILLS TRAINING (DSST) AND SOCIAL COGNITIVE TRAINING (SCT) MODELS

The most researched programmes for teaching social skills are direct social skills training (DSST) programmes and social cognitive training (SCT) programmes. In DSST programmes, social skills are directly taught by a process which usually involves an initial discussion of the skill which stresses why it is a useful skill to have, verbal rehearsal of the steps of the skill, structured opportunities to practise the newly-learned skill (usually through role plays), and corrective feedback and reinforcement for correct usage of the skill (Ladd and Mize, 1983). On the other hand, SCT programmes have predominantly focused on the teaching of social problem-solving skills using mostly hypothetical social situations.

Overall, most researchers have found that a DSST model produces the most socially valid changes (for example, McGrath and Francey, 1988), and that an SCT intervention is the least likely to produce such changes (for example, Zaragoza et al., 1991). Many researchers have suggested that one reason for the relative ineffectiveness of SCT programmes is that the way in which children respond in hypothetical situations of social problem solving, which allows time for reflective cognition, may be very different from the ways in which they actually respond in real-life or semi-naturalistic situations when emotional arousal factors and self-interest factors are more likely to be present (for example, Richard and Dodge, 1982).

However, there should be *some* component of social cognitive training in any programme. This should focus not only on social problem solving as in the past, but also on the teaching of such social cognitive skills as emotional regulation, intention detection, empathy, consequential thinking and positive self-efficacy. Erdley (1996) has suggested that it is especially important to teach positive and relationship-enhancing goal selection, and to try to eliminate the retaliation goal, as this has been shown to be the strongest predictor of aggression. Since about one half of the attempts by most children to join others in a typical day are rebuffed (Corsaro, 1981; Putallaz and Gottman, 1981), there also needs to be a focus on teaching students to be more persistent, optimistic and resourceful in the face of a social failure, rather than to respond with aggression or withdrawal (Goetz and Dweck, 1980).

Programmes which are predominantly based on a DSST model but which include a diverse range of social cognitive strategies can be packaged in a relatively structured and clearly outlined curriculum to make them attractive and user-friendly for teachers (for example, McGrath and Francey, 1991; McGrath and Noble, 2003).

Poor peer acceptance is a function of both the behaviour of an individual student and the social system in which they interact (La Greca, 1993; Schneider, 1993). Higher levels of classroom cohesion can create a context of acceptance that allows students more comfortably to change their behaviour. A more relationship-enhancing classroom culture can be developed through the use of co-operative learning classroom meetings, alternative seating arrangements and so on. The teaching of prosocial moral values, such as co-operation, support and concern for others, acceptance of differences, inclusion, respect, honesty, fairness and responsibility, should also be a component of this process (McGrath and Noble, 2003). There are only a few research studies in this area so far (for example, Tyron and Keane, 1991), few of which have yet demonstrated that changing the social ecology of a classroom affects more direct measures of social behaviour or peer acceptance. However, it is not logical to attempt to teach students social behaviour which is not encouraged by the social ecology of the classroom and school (Ogilvy, 1994). It is also important to ensure that the teaching of social skills is culturally sensitive, as social interactions are always value-laden.

KEY ISSUES IN THE TEACHING OF SOCIAL SKILLS

Early identification

Severson and Walker (2002) have argued strongly that early identification is essential for children who demonstrate patterns of aggressive, inappropriate or withdrawn social behaviour that suggest that they are at-risk for later problematic behaviour and peer rejection. They suggest that this should begin at age four or five so that early prevention can be started. Many learning and social/behavioural problems are progressive in nature, and schools need to focus strongly on prevention and early intervention (O'Shaughnessy et al., 2002).

Misattribution of intentions has been identified in children as young as four (Webster-Stratton and Lindsay, 1999). Patterson et al. (1992) suggest that children with emotional and behavioural problems can be identified as early as three. Walker et al. (1995) and Kazdin (1987) point out that anti-social behaviour patterns are highly resistant to change if intervention does not occur before the age of eight. Currently it is estimated that although many children are showing high-risk behaviours at age six, they do not receive any intervention until the age of 11 or 12 (Duncan et al., 1995). Children who use predominantly coercive social behaviour by grade 3 are likely to continue displaying some degree of antisocial behaviour throughout their lives (Loeber and Farrington, 1998). Kauffman (2001) has argued that educators' apprehensions about stigmatizing children by trying to identify those at risk for EBDs has led to a system that actually 'prevents prevention'.

Match between social skills and cognitions taught and the social difficulties of the EBD student

The social difficulties, and hence the social learning needs, of students with EBDs are not homogeneous. A 'one size fits all' approach is less likely to be effective. There needs to be some match between the social learning needs of the 'at-risk' student and what is taught (Gresham, 2002). In their review of research, McIntosh et al. (1991) concluded that those studies that had matched the teaching intervention to each students' spe-cific social skills deficits were more likely to produce positive results.

Generalization of learned social skills across settings and maintenance over time

Students need enough practice to ensure that they become so fluent in those newly-learned social skills that they becomes a reliable part of their repertoire (Gresham, 1997). Opportunities should be planned and orga-nized for students to practise across a variety of settings and peers. This may involve mixing up small groups of students within the same class, working and playing with other classes or schools, using buddy systems and so on.

Social skills programmes should be an *additional* component to a preventative treatment plan

In the case of some students, there will still be a need to address academic needs too, as these can affect social behaviour (Gresham, 1997). There should also be plans to analyse competing behaviours (for example, social withdrawal or aggression) which provide secondary rewards and then reduce them by rearranging situations so that using the more effective social behaviour is more rewarding than not (1997). The newly-learned social skill may be overpowered by older and stronger competing behaviours, or older competing behaviours may more efficiently (or equally efficiently) produce a desired outcome for the student (1997). The social benefits of the newly-learned social skills must be able to overpower competing negative social behaviours, and the social benefits of the competing behaviours must be diminished.

Strategies for changing negative social reputation should be included

A student's reputation can best be described as the social expectations others hold of them. However, labelling by peers can have the effect of maintaining negative peer status and social reputation, even when behavioural patterns that in the past have contributed to that reputation have been eliminated (Asher, 1991). The same social behaviour can also receive a positive response when exhibited by a high-status student, but a negative response when exhibited by a low-status student (Dodge, 1983). Rejected children are more likely to be held to be personally responsible for their negative peer interactions, which are seen by peers as intentional and as the results of stable personal dispositions (Waas and Honer, 1990). How much change does there need to be for classmates and teachers to notice and then slowly change their opinion of a child's reputation (Gresham, 1997)? Sechrest et al. (1996) argue that the difference needs to be large enough to be noticed by others without prompting. Putallaz (1982) has suggested training poorly accepted children to anticipate and cope with potential rejection from peers when they attempt to practise newly-learned social skills. Another approach would be to directly teach a student's peers to perceive others in more differentiated and positive ways, or arrange successful and repeated opportunities for positive social interaction (Hymel et al., 1990).

Positive associations with peer group

One of the reasons why students do not generalize a newly-learned social skill into a different but relevant social context may be because they continue to affiliate with like-minded students who support their antisocial or nonsocial goal selections and perceptions (Mathur and Rutherford, 1996). Several researchers have demonstrated that aggressive children with either ADHD or conduct disorder tend to associate with a more 'deviant' peer group (Wehby et al., 1997). Strategies need to be identified for involving such students with more prosocial peers as models and affiliates (Erdley and Asher, 1999). This can also help them to create new positive social histories (1999).

Peer-mediated strategies can support teacher intervention

Peer-mediated social skills strategies involve creating a classroom social environment which encourages and promotes positive interactions between classmates by structuring activities and instructing students to interact in particular ways with isolated or disruptive students. Involving peers in a naturalistic social environment is an effective strategy for developing generalization and maintenance of newly-learned social behaviours (Gresham, 1997). Peers can also be taught to reinforce the practice of prosocial behaviours by peers. In one study, a peer-monitoring procedure was used by five-year-old children who gave tokens to eight classmates for following classroom rules, such as cleaning up after play and waiting their turn. Children with three tokens a day could vote on and participate in play activities (Carden-Smith and Fowler, 1983).

Other behaviour management strategies should be incorporated

The use of group contingencies means that the improved social behaviour of certain class members determines the consequences received by the entire group (Williamson et al., 1992). This works best when the rest of the class is well behaved. For example, when a targeted student has earned five points, then the whole class gets a 10-minute free-conversation time.

CONCLUSION

Positive peer relations, social acceptance and the resulting positive self-image play an important role in self-control of aggressive impulses and the internalization of societal morality as well as increasing resilience (Dumas, 1998). Research so far suggests that significant positive changes in social behaviour and peer relationships can be made if an effective social skills intervention is used and if it is located in a prosocial and positive learning culture.

REFERENCES

American Psychiatric Association (APA) (1994) *Diagnostic and Statistical Manual of Mental Disorders* (4th edn). Washington, DC: Author.

Angold, A., Costello, E.J. and Erkanli, A. (1999) 'Comorbidity', *Journal of Child Psychology and Psychiatry and Allied Disciplines*, 40 (1): 57–87.

Asher, S.R. (1991) *Loneliness and Self-referral Among Aggressive-rejected Withdrawn-rejected Children*. Paper presented at the biennial meeting of the International Society for the Study of Behavioral Development, Minneapolis, MN.

Baker, S.R. and Edelmann, R.J. (2002) 'Is social phobia related to lack of social skills? Duration of skill-related behaviours and ratings of behavioural adequacy', *British Journal of Clinical Psychology*, 41: 243–57.

Barkley, R.A. (1990) *Attention-Deficit Hyperactivity Disorder: A Handbook for Diagnosis and Treatment*. New York: Guilford.

Bickett, L. and Milich, R. (1990) 'First impressions formed of boys with learning disabilities and attention deficit disorder', *Journal of Learning Disabilities*, 23 (4): 253–9.

Biederman, J., Farone, S. and Chen, W.J. (1996) 'Social adjustment inventory for children and adolescents. Concurrent validity in ADHD children', *Journal of the American Academy of Child and Adolescent Psychiatry*, 5: 1059–64.

Blackorby, J. and Wagner, M. (1996) 'Longitudinal outcomes for youth with disabilities: Findings from the National Longitudinal Transition Study', *Exceptional Children*, 62 (5): 399–413.

Campbell, S.B. (1990) 'The Socialisation and Social Development of Hyperactive Children', in M. Lewis and S.M. Miller (eds), *Handbook of Developmental Psychopathology*. New York: Plenum, pp. 77–91.

Carden-Smith, L.K. and Fowler, S.A. (1983) 'An assessment of student and teacher behavior in treatment and mainstreamed classes for preschool and kindergarten', *Analysis and Intervention in Developmental Disabilities*, 3: 35–57.

Carlson, C.L., Lahey, B.B., Frame, C.L., Walker J. and Hynd, G.W. (1987) 'Sociometric status of clinic-referred children with attention deficit disorders and without hyperactivity', *Journal of Abnormal Child Psychology*, 15: 537–47.

Chung, T. and Asher, S.R. (1997) *Children's Conflict Resolution in Different Relational Contexts: The Linkages Between Goals and Strategies*. Paper presented at the annual meeting of the American Educational Research Association, Chicago.

Clark, M.L., Cheyne, J.A., Cunningham, C.E. and Siegel, L.S. (1988) 'Dyadic peer interactions and task orientation in attention deficit disordered boys', *Journal of Abnormal Child Psychology*, 16: 1–5.

Coie, J.D. (1990) 'Toward a theory of peer rejection', in S.R. Asher and J.D. Coie (eds), *Peer Rejection in Childhood*. Cambridge: Cambridge University Press. pp. 365–402.

Coie, J.D., Dodge, K.A. and Kupersmidt, J.B. (1990) 'Peer group behavior and social status', in S.R. Asher and J.D. Cole (eds), *Peer Rejection In Childhood*. Cambridge: Cambridge University Press. pp. 17–59.

Corsaro, W.A. (1981) 'Friendship in the nursery school: Social organization in a peer environment', in S.R. Asher and J.M. Gottman (eds), *The Development of Children's Friendships*. New York: Cambridge University Press. pp. 207–241.

Cunningham, C.E. and Siegal, L.S. (1987) 'Peer interactions of normal and attention deficit disordered boys during free-play, cooperative task, and simulated classroom situations', *Journal of Abnormal Child Psychology*, 15: 247–68.

Dodge, K.A. (1983) 'Behavioral antecedents of peer social status', *Child Development*, 54: 1386–9.

Dodge, K.A. (1986) 'A social information processing model of social competence in children', in M. Perlmutter (ed.), *Cognitive Perspectives on Children's Social and Behavioral Development: The Minnesota Symposia on Child Psychology* (Vol. 18). Hillsdale, NJ: Erlbaum.

Dodge, K.A., Bates, J.E. and Pettit, G.S. (1990) 'Mechanisms in the cycle of violence', *Science*, 250: 1678–83.

Dodge, K.A. and Coie, J.D. (1987) 'Social information-processing factors in reactive and proactive aggression in children's playgroups', *Journal of Personality and Social Psychology*, 53: 1146–58.

Dodge, K.A. and Price, J.M. (1994) 'On the relation between social information processing and socially competent behavior in early school-aged children', *Child Development*, 65: 1385–97.

Dodge, K.A., Schlundt, D.G., Schocken, I. and Delugach, J.D. (1983) 'Social competence and children's sociometric status: The role of peer group entry strategies', *Merrill-Palmer Quarterly*, 29: 309–336.

Dulcan M.K. and Benson, R.S. (1997) 'AACAP Official Action: Summary of the practice parameters for the assessment and treatment of children, adolescents, and adults with ADHD', *Journal of the American Academy of Child and Adolescent Psychiatry*, 36 (9): 1311–17.

Dumas, M.C. (1998) 'The risk of social interaction problems among adolescents with ADHD', *Education and Treatment of Children*, 21 (4): 447–61.

Duncan, B.B., Forness, S.R. and Hartsough, C. (1995) 'Students identified as seriously emotionally disturbed in school based day treatment: Cognitive, psychiatric, and special educational characteristics', *Behavioral Disorders*, 20 (4): 238–52.

Erdley, C.A. (1996) 'Motivational approaches to aggression within the context of peer relationships', in J. Juvonen and K.R. Wentzel (eds), *Social Motivation: Understanding Children's School Adjustment*. New York: Cambridge University Press. pp. 98–125.

Erdley, C.A. and Asher, S. (1999) 'A social goals perspective on children's social competence', *Journal of Emotional and Behavioral Disorders*, 7 (3): 156–67.

Farmer, T.W., Rodkin, P.C., Pearl, R. and Van Acker, E. (1999) 'Teacher-assessed behavioural configurations, peer assessments, and self concepts of elementary students with mild disabilities', *Journal of Special Education*, 33: 63–80.

Foster, S.L., DeLawyer, D.D. and Guevremont, D.C. (1986) 'A critical incidents analysis of liked and disliked behavior in children and adolescents', *Behavioral Assessment*, 6: 84–103.

Goetz, T.E. and Dweck, C.S. (1980) 'Learned helplessness in social situations', *Journal of Personality and Social Psychology*, 39: 246–55.

Grenell, M.M., Glass, C.R. and Katz, K.S. (1987) 'Hyperactive children and peer interactions: Knowledge and performance of social skills', *Journal of Abnormal Child Psychology*, 15: 1–13.

Gresham, F.M. (1988) 'Social skills: Conceptual and applied aspects of assessment, training, and social validation', in J.C. Witt, S.N. Elliott, and F.M. Gresham (eds), *Handbook of Behavior Therapy in Education*. New York: Plenum. pp. 523–46.

Gresham, F.M. (1997) 'Social competence and students with behavior disorders: Where we've been, where we are, and where we should go', *Education and Treatment of Children*, 20: 233–49.

Gresham, F.M. (1998) 'Social skills training: Should we raze, remodel, or rebuild?', *Behavioral Disorders*, 24 (1): 19–25.

Gresham, F.M. (2002) 'Social skills assessment and instruction for students with emotional and behavioral disorders', in K.L. Lane, F.M. Gresham and T.E. O'Shaughnessy (eds), *Interventions for Children With or At Risk for Emotional and Behavioral Disorders*. Boston: Allyn and Bacon. pp. 242–58.

Gresham, F.M., MacMillan, D.L., Bocian, K.M. and Ward, S.L. (1997) *Friendship Relations of Students At-Risk for Academic and Behavioral Difficulties in School.* Unpublished manuscript.

Grizenko, N., Papineau, D. and Sayegh, L. (1993) 'Effectiveness of a multimodal day treatment programme for children with disruptive behavior problems', *Journal of the American Academy of Child and Adolescent Psychiatry,* 32 (1): 127–34.

Guevremont, D.C. (1990) 'Social skills and peer relationship training', in R.A. Barkley (ed.), *Attention Deficit Hyperactivity Disorder: A Handbook for Diagnosis And Treatment.* New York: Guilford. pp. 540–72.

Guevremont, D.C. and Foster, S.L. (1993) 'Impact of problem-solving on aggressive boys: Skill acquisition, behavior change, and generalization', *Journal of Abnormal Child Psychology,* 21: 13–27.

Hepler, J.B. (1998) 'Social integration of children with emotional disabilities and nonhandicapped peers in a school setting', *Early Child Development and Care,* 147: 99–115.

Hermann, D.S. and McWhirter, J. (1997) 'Refusal and resistance skills for children and adolescents: A selected review', *Journal of Counseling and Development,* 75 (3): 177–87.

Hinshaw, S.P., Henker, B., Whalen, C.K., Erhardt, D. and Dunnington, R.E. (1989) 'Aggressive, prosocial, and nonsocial behavior in hyperactive boys: Dose effects of methylphenidate in naturalistic settings', *Journal of Consulting and Clinical Psychology,* 57: 636–43.

Hinshaw, S.P., Zupan, B.A., Simmel, C., Nigg, J.T. and Melnick, S. (1997) 'Peer status in boys with and without attention deficit hyperactivity disorder: Predictions from overt and covert antisocial behavior, social isolation, and authoritative parenting beliefs', *Child Development,* 68 (5): 880–96.

Hops, H. and Greenwood, C.R. (1988) 'Social skill deficits', in E.J. Mash and L.G. Terdal (eds), *Behavioral Assessment of Childhood Disorders* (2nd edn). New York: Guidford. pp. 263–314.

Hymel, S., Wagner, E., and Butler, L.J. (1990) 'Reputational bias: View from the peer group', in S. Asher and J. Coie (eds), *Peer Rejection in Childhood.* New York: Cambridge University Press. pp. 156–86.

Jackson, H.J. and Bruder, J.N. (1984) 'Social validation of nonverbal behaviors in social skills training with adolescents', *Journal of Consulting and Clinical Psychology,* 13: 141–6.

Kauffman, J.M. (2001) *Characteristics of Emotional and behavioural Disorders of Children and Youth.* Englewood Cliffs, NJ: Prentice-Hall.

Kazdin, A. (1987) *Conduct Disorders in Childhood and Adolescence.* Beverly Hills, CA: Sage.

Kendall, P.C. and Chu, B.C. (2002) 'Retrospective self reports of therapist flexibility in a manual based treatment for youths with anxiety disorders', *Journal of Clinical Child Psychology,* 29 (2): 209–220.

Kupersmidt, J.B., Burchinal, M. and Patterson, C.J. (1995) 'Developmental patterns of childhood peer relations as predictors of externalizing behavior problems', *Development and Psychopathology,* 7: 825–43.

Ladd, G.W. (1990) 'Having friends, keeping friends, making friends, and being liked by peers in the classroom: Predicators of early school adjustment?', *Child Development,* 61: 312–31.

Ladd, G.W. and Mize, J. (1983) 'A cognitive-social learning model of social skills training', *Psychological Review,* 90: 127–57.

Ladd, G., Price, J. and Hart, C. (1990) 'Pre-Schoolers' behavioural orientations and patterns of peer contact: Predictive of peer status?', in S.R. Asher and J.D. Coie (eds), *Peer Rejection in Childhood.* New York: Cambridge University Press, pp. 90–115.

La Greca, A.M. (1993) 'Social skills training with children: Where do we go from here?', *Journal of Clinical Child Psychiatry*, 22 (1): 288–98.

Landau, S. and Milich, R. (1988) 'Social communication patterns of attention-deficit-disordered boys', *Journal of Abnormal Child Psychology*, 16: 69–81.

Landau, S. and Moore, L.A. (1991) 'Social skills deficits in children with attention deficit hyperactivity disorder', *School Psychology Review*, 20: 235–51.

Lochman, J.E., Coie, J.D., Underwood, M.K. and Terry, R. (1993) 'Effectiveness of a social relations intervention program for aggressive and nonaggressive, rejected children', *Journal of Consulting and Clinical Psychology*, 61: 1053–8.

Loeber, R. and Farrington, D.P. (1998) *Serious and Violent Juvenile Offenders: Risk Factors and Successful Interventions*. Thousand Oaks, CA: Sage.

Lynam, D. (1996) 'The early identification of chronic offenders: who is the fledgling psychopath?', *Psychological Bulletin*, 120: 209–34.

Maag, J.W. (1990) 'Social skills training in school', *Special Services in the School*, 6 (1–2): 1–19.

Maag, J. (1992) 'Integrating consultation into social skills training: Implications for practice', *Journal of Educational and Psychological Consultation*, 3 (3): 233–58.

Mathur, S.R. and Rutherford, R.B. (1996) 'Is social skills training effective for students with emotional or behavioral disorders? Research issues and needs', *Behavioral Disorders*, 22: 21–8.

McGrath, H.L. (1996) *An Evaluation of Three School-based Whole Class Social Skills Intervention Programmes*. Unpublished Ph.D manuscript. Melbourne: Monash University.

McGrath, H.L. and Edwards, H. (2000) *Difficult Personalities: A Practical Guide to Managing the Hurtful Behaviour of Others (and Perhaps Your Own!)*. Sydney: Choice.

McGrath, H.L. and Francey, S. (1988) *An Evaluation of a school-based Social Skills Training Program*. Paper presented at the Bicentennial conference of the Australian Behaviour Modification Association, May, Adelaide, South Australia.

McGrath, H.L. and Francey, S. (1991) *Friendly Kids, Friendly Classrooms*. South Melbourne: Longman Cheshire.

McGrath, H. and Noble, T. (2003) *Bounce Back! A Classroom Resiliency Program*. Sydney: Pearson Education.

McIntosh, R., Vaughn, S. and Zaragoza, N. (1991) 'A review of social interventions for students with learning disabilities', *Journal of Learning Disabilities*, 24: 451–8.

Milich, R. and Dodge, K.A. (1984) 'Social information processing in child psychiatric populations', *Journal of Abnormal Child Psychology*, 12: 471–89.

Miller-Johnson, S., Coie, J.D., Maumary Gremaud, A., Lochman, J. and Terry, R. (1999) 'Relationship between childhood peer rejection and aggression and adolescent delinquency severity and type among African American youth', *Journal of Emotional and Behavioral Disorders*, 7 (3): 137–46.

Morris, R.J., Shah, K. and Morris, Y.P. (2002) 'Internalizing behavior disorders', in K.L. Lane., F.M. Gresham and T.E. O'Shaughnessy, *Interventions for Children with or At Risk for Emotional and Behavioral Disorders*. Boston: Allyn and Bacon. pp. 223–42.

Newcomb, A.F. and Bagwell, C.L. (1995) 'Children's friendship relations: A meta-analytic review', *Psychological Bulletin*, 117: 306–347.

Ogilvy, C.M. (1994) 'Social skills training with children and adolescents: A review of evidence on effectiveness', *Educational Psychology*. 14 (1): 73–8.

Olweus, D. (1991) 'Bully/victim problems among school children: Basic facts and effects of a school-based intervention program', in K. Rubin and D. Pepler (eds), *The Development and Treatment of Childhood Aggression*. Hillside, NJ: Erlbaum. pp. 411–48.

O'Shaughnessy, T.E., Lane, K.L., Gresham, F. and Beebe-Frankberger, M.E. (2002) 'Students with or at risk for emotional-behavioural difficulties', in K.L. Lane,

F.M. Gresham and T.E. O'Shaughnessy (eds), *Interventions for Children with or At Risk for Emotional and Behavioral Disorder.* Boston: Allyn and Bacon. pp. 3–18.

Patterson, G.R., Reid, J.B. and Dishion, T.J. (1992) *Antisocial Boys*, Eugene, OR: Castalia.

Pope, A.W., Bierman, K.L. and Mumma, G.H. (1989) 'Relations between hyperactive and aggressive behavior and peer relations at three elementary grade levels', *Journal of Abnormal Child Psychology*, 17: 253–67.

Putallaz, M.F. (1982) 'Predicting children's sociometric status from their behavior', *Dissertation Abstracts International*, 42 (11 B): 4589.

Putallaz, M. and Gottman, J.M. (1981) 'An interactional model of children's entry into peer groups', *Child Development*, 52: 986–94.

Richard, B.A. and Dodge, K.A. (1982) 'Social maladjustment and problem solving in school-aged children', *Journal of Consulting and Clinical Psychology*, 50: 226–33.

Rigby, K. and Slee, P.T. (1992) *Bullying in Schools.* Melbourne: ACER.

Rotheram-Borus, M.J., Bickford, B. and Milburn, N.G. (2001) 'Implementing children's social skills training programs in schools', *Journey of Educational and Psychological Consultation*, 12: 91 111.

Scahill, L., Schwab-Stone, M., Merikangas, K.R., Leckman, J.F., Zhang, H. and Kasl, S. (1999) 'Psychosocial and clinical correlates of ADHD in a community sample of school age children', *Journal of the American Academy of Child and Adolescent Psychiatry*, 38 (8): 976–84.

Schneider, B.H. (1993) *Children's Social Competence in Context.* New York: Pergamon

Schonert-Reichl, K.A. (1993) 'Empathy and social relationships in adolescents with behavioral disorders', *Behavioral Disorders*, 18: 189 204.

Sechrest, L., McKnight, P. and McKnight, K. (1996) 'Calibration of measures for psychotherapy outcome studies', *American Psychologist*, 51: 1065–71.

Severson, H.H. and Walker, H.M. (2002) 'Proactive approaches for identifying children at risk for sociobehavioral problems', in K.L. Lane., F.M. Gresham and T.E. O'Shaughnessy (eds), *Interventions for Children with or At Risk for Emotional and Behavioral Disorders.* Boston: Allyn and Bacon. pp. 33–53.

Shores, R.E. and Wehby, J.H. (1999) 'Analyzing the classroom social behavior of students with EBD', *Journal of Emotional and Behavioral Disorders*, 7 (4): 194–8.

Sugai, G. and Horner, R. (2002) 'The evolution of discipline practices: School-wide positive behavior supports', *Child and Family Behavior Therapy*, 24 (12): 23–50.

Sugai, G., Sprague, J.R., Horner, R.H. and Walker, H.M. (2000) 'Preventing school violence: The use of office discipline referrals to assess and monitor school-wide discipline interventions', in H.M. Walker and M.H. Epstein (eds), *Making Schools Safer and Violence Free: Critical Issues, Solutions, and Recommended Practices.* Austin, TX: Pro Ed. pp. 50–57.

Tankersley, M. and Landrum, T.J. (1997) 'Comorbidity of emotional and behavioural disorders', in J.W. Lloyd, E.J. Kameenui and D. Chard (eds), *Issues in Educating Students with Disabilities*. Mahwah, NJ: Erlbaum. pp. 153–73.

Tyron, A.S. and Keane, S.P. (1991) 'Popular and aggressive boys' initial social interaction patterns in co-operative and competitive settings', *Journal of Abnormal Child Psychology*, 19: 395–406.

Waas, G.A. and Honer, S.A. (1990) 'Situational attribution and dispositional inferences: The development of peer reputation', *Merrill-Palmer Quarterly*, 36 (2): 239–60.

Walker, H.M., Colvin, G. and Ramsey, E. (1995) *Antisocial Behavior in Schools: Stages and Best Practices.* Montere, CA: Brooks-Cole.

Webster-Stratton, C. and Lindsay, D.W. (1999) 'Social competence and conduct problems in young children: Issues in assessment', *Journal of Clinical Child Psychology*, 28 (1) : 25–44.

Wehby, J.H., Symons, F.J. and Hollo, A. (1997) 'Promote appropriate assessment', *Journal of Emotional and Behavioral Disorders*, 5 (1): 5–54.

Weiss, G., Hechtman, L., Milroy, T. and Perlman, T. (1985) 'Psychiatric status of hyperactives as adults: A controlled prospective 15-year follow-up of 63 hyperactive children', *Journal of the Academy of Child Psychiatry*, 24: 211–21.

Weissberg, R.P., Rapkin, B.P., Cowen, E.L., Davidson, E., Flores De Apodaca, R., and McKim, B.J. (1981) 'Evaluation of a social-problem-solving training program for surburban and inner-city third grade children', *Journal of Consulting and Clinical Psychology*, 49: 251–61.

Williamson, S.H., Williamson, D.A., Watkins, P.C. and Hughes, H.H. (1992) 'Increasing cooperation among children using, dependent–group orientated reinforcement contingencies', *Behaviour Modification*, 16: 400–13.

Witt, J.C. and Elliott, S.N. (1985) 'Acceptability of classroom intervention strategies', in T.R. Kratochwill (ed.), *Advances in School Psychology* (Vol. 4). Hillsdale, NJ: Erlbaum. pp. 251–88.

Zaragoza, N., Vaughn, S. and McIntosh, R. (1991) 'Social skills interventions and children with behavior problems: A review', *Behavioral Disorders*, 16: 260–75.

22

The Pupil Support Base in the Scottish Secondary School: An Alternative to Exclusion

PAUL HAMILL

Young people whose special needs arise as a result of social, emotional and behavioural difficulties (SEBD) are often excluded from mainstream schools or from classes within the school because their behaviour is deemed to be challenging and disruptive. The body of research literature in relation to inclusive education has grown considerably in the last few years and voices promoting inclusion are now heard increasingly (Ainscow, 1999; Allan, 1999; Mittler, 2000). However, most of the research done in this area concludes that for many young people inclusion is still not a reality.

In Scotland as elsewhere in the United Kingdom, and indeed globally, the issue of social inclusion is currently high on the educational agenda. It has been challenging policymakers since 1978 when the Warnock Report first introduced the concept of 'need' (Warnock, 1978). In 2000 the Standards in Scottish Schools (Scotland) Act (SEED, 2000) made it clear that as far as possible the mainstream school would be presumed to be the environment in which all young people should be educated. This means that the presumption of mainstreaming is now enshrined in Scottish law and local authorities and schools must face up to the challenges this poses.

It would be naive, however, to suggest that all schools in Scotland have embraced this inclusive philosophy. While supporting the principle of inclusion, many professionals still express concern in relation to how these principles are being translated into practice. The main concern relates to one particular group of young people whose behaviour is deemed to be consistently challenging.

In response to these concerns, the education minister in Scotland set up a discipline task force to examine the reasons for this perceived decline in behavioural standards. The subsequent report entitled *Better Behaviour – Better Learning* (SEED, 2001) indicated, as one would expect, that there were no easy solutions. Among its recommendations, this report advocated that there should be flexibility in provision for young people whose behaviour can be disruptive and who are in danger of exclusion, and this provision should include in-class support and support out- with the normal classroom environment. Several local authorities concerned about the increase in exclusion rates had already taken the initiative, encouraging their schools to think about alternatives to exclusion, and many schools responded by setting up pupil support bases (PSB) aimed at including young people whose behaviour was deemed to be disruptive. The discipline task force encouraged local authorities and schools to consider this approach, and consequently most schools in Scotland have now established some form of PSB provision.

As support bases became established, several local authorities were keen to evaluate their effectiveness. Consequently in session 2000–01 and 2002–03 two Scottish authorities commissioned a research team from the University of Strathclyde to conduct an evaluative study of support systems for young people (SEBD), with a particular focus on the PSB. Twenty secondary schools took part in the study, and each had set up a PSB designed to:

- promote inclusion and helped lower exclusion rates;
- encourage young people to develop their full potential; and
- reduce the sense of alienation, marginalization and disaffection among some young people.

The research team kept these aims at the forefront of their study and the main thrust was the extent to which they were being met. The researchers examined the support systems in place from the perspective of all of the significant stakeholders including pupils, teachers, parents and key personnel in other agencies including social work, community education and psychological services.

THE RESEARCH

The concept of quality permeates all levels of the Scottish education system and underpins planning, particularly school development planning. The report *'How good is Your School?' – Self-evaluation Using Performance Indicators* (SOEID, 1997) placed emphasis upon the need for schools to analyse their practice in relation to meeting pupil needs. Within this context inclusion was given some priority and it was recommended that schools make every effort to ensure that they promote an inclusive culture. The Strathclyde researchers therefore highlighted the qualitative dimension of their research and were particularly keen to ascertain how behaviour support systems in schools impact upon the quality of experience young people receive. Mason (1996) and Seale (1997) provide a comprehensive overview of qualitative research, and this helped to provide a focus and direction for the research team. The emphasis was placed upon qualitative evidence, which was gathered by using a range of strategies.

Questionnaires were completed by 1,200 teachers across the 20 schools, and the senior management team and PSB staff in all schools were interviewed. Fifty parents whose children accessed the PSB and 150 parents whose children did not were interviewed. In addition 75 pupils who had been excluded and 150 who had not were interviewed, as were 80 professionals from other agencies. Interviews were conducted using a semi-structured interview schedule and use was also made of focused group interviews. A sample of 25 of the excluded pupils were observed in school for one day using an observation schedule, and use was also made of a pupil support grid designed by the research team to gather data on the range of pupils being referred to the PSB.

The process of translating an inclusive vision into practice was viewed as a social phenomenon and the emphasis was placed upon how individuals understand, accept and interact with this process. At the same time an action research perspective underpinned the study, providing opportunities for collaboration with those who had the task of making inclusion work. A cycle of feedback was built in, ensuring that all participants felt that the key to the research process was partnership.

The qualitative data was analysed in a way that accurately described and reconstructed it into a recognizable reality using the descriptive narrative approach (Strauss and Corbin, 1990). This strategy was also described by Belenky (1992) as the interpretative-descriptive approach, which allows all of the significant players a voice that is blended into a series of themes and related issues shared by a number of people.

Greenwood and Morten (1998) emphasize that researchers must at all times adhere to their role as objective impartial outsiders who ask hard questions. The research team therefore remained totally unbiased, while at the same time balancing this with the process of participatory evaluation as presented in the work of Patton (1986), Brunner and Guzman (1989) and Fine (1996). Thus the possibility of mutual learning was opened up, and by internalizing the philosophy underpinning participatory evaluation the research team were able to engage in a professional dialogue with all of the key players.

THE THEORETICAL CONTEXT

The research team placed a high priority on ensuring from the outset that the study was located firmly within a sound theoretical context. This provided a framework in which the team could plan and evaluate the research strategy, reflect upon the research process and critically analyse the evidence. Three key questions were used within this framework in order to extend understanding, enhance awareness and provide valuable insights.

What is inclusion?

Early in 2003 the report *Count Us In* (SEED, 2003) examined the issue of inclusion in Scottish schools and highlighted the importance of establishing a shared understanding and belief in the concept of inclusion. Inclusion was presented as a complex issue, with no single blueprint automatically fitting all schools. This report considered the additional support needs of all young people, but one group was identified as presenting a particular challenge to schools. This group was described as 'pupils who present severely disruptive behaviour or who are generally alienated from school' (2003: 34). A strong case was made for inclusion, but it was also acknowledged that establishing a set of principles is fairly easy though putting them into practice can be challenging.

Mittler (2000) makes an important point when he presents inclusion as a process of reform capable of transforming schools so that they offer genuine social and educational opportunities for all. This view has also been described by others (Ainscow and Muncey, 1988; Westwood, 1997; Armstrong et al., 2000) who see inclusion as having the power to restructure schools, making them more responsive to the diversity of learning needs. However, some writers paint a different picture and conclude that in reality inclusion has simply resulted in the setting up of separate colonies of young people in mainstream schools as opposed to transforming them (Dyson, 1997). All writers do, however, recognize that inclusion involves schools in the process of fairly radical change if they are to embrace all young people.

In their study *From Them To Us,* Booth and Ainscow (1998) outline the dangers inherent in adopting a narrow restrictive view of inclusion, and caution professionals not simply to equate it with special education. Catering for the diverse needs of these young people is, of course, a major part of inclusion, but as described by Booth and Ainscow (1998) inclusion is a diverse concept extending beyond this particular group to include all regardless of ability, gender, sexual orientation, religion or race. This wider definition helps to clarify the concept and provides a clearer under-standing of inclusion.

Who are excluded?

There is ample research evidence to suggest that that when the concept of inclusion focuses upon young people whose behaviour can be challeng-ing, the issues become more highly charged (Cooper, 1993; O'Brien, 1998; Porter, 2000) These young people pose problems for their schools, and for many the response is exclusion. Barber refers to this group as 'the disadvantaged, the disaffected and the disappeared' (1996: 20) and alludes to a vicious circle which begins with underachievement fuelling disaffec-tion and exclusion leading to detachment from the education system. Labelling these young people as SEBD is in itself problematic, tending to set them apart from others recognized as having additional support needs. There has, of course, in Scotland as elsewhere in the United Kingdom, been a move away from identifying need in terms of a deficit model. However, research evidence still suggests that in relation to young people with (SEBD), this model is alive and well and this group are often perceived in terms of problems – their own and those they pose to their teachers and their peers. Many writers argue that an over-emphasis upon the deficit model results in less attention being paid to the wider ranging sources of behav-ioural difficulty, such as an inappropriate curriculum (Garner and Gains, 1996; Montgomery, 1998; O'Brien, 1998).

The difficulties these young people experience often have their source rooted deeply in early childhood when they had no access to appropriate role models and lacked the opportunity to learn appropriate behavioural responses (Thomas, 1992; Herbert, 1993; Evans and Lunt, 1994). Cooper (1993) argues that seriously disaffected young people often come from socially and economically disadvantaged families and are likely to experience inconsistent and ineffectual parental discipline and a lack of parental interest in schooling. It is all too easy to blame parents and one must be extremely careful, as the situation is generally more complex. Cooper reminds us that to understand why some young people are disruptive we must take full account of 'the complex interaction between contextual factors and aspects which the individual brings to the situation' (1993: 9).

There is in reality no objective definition of the term 'social, emotional and behavioural difficulties'. Essentially it must be understood as a product of the relationship between the young person, his home environment, his community and his school. Fundamentally, however, these young people have special needs and require additional support. The Education Act (1993) states that a young person has special needs if he or she has significantly greater difficulty in learning than the majority of his or her peers. Difficulty in learning must be viewed from a fairly wide perspective to include both the cognitive and affective dimensions. Young people who are consistently excluded from school have difficulty in developing social competence and adjusting to social contexts, and they often struggle to follow normal and accepted patterns of behaviour. Thus within this wider definition many excluded young people can be seen to have special needs.

What is an inclusive school?

Catering for diversity is at the core of inclusive education. In 1996 the CSIE described an inclusive school as being barrier free, community based, promoting collaboration and equality (CSIE, 1996). Such a school should be accessible to all, should not be exclusive or rejecting, and above all should be democratic providing opportunity for all. In Scotland over the past few years there has been an increasing focus on those factors which characterize an effective school. These include inter-professional collaboration, co-operative teaching and learning, differentiation, meeting individual need and parental involvement. Not all schools, however, are equally effective and where these factors tend to be seen as peripheral, then the school culture is less likely to respond to the principle of inclusion (Sebba and Ainscow, 1996).

The curriculum is also a powerful tool in promoting inclusion and it is through the curriculum that messages are sent and received about individual status (Swann, 1988).

It can be painful for teachers to realize that some young people may not learn effectively and behave badly because of what they are taught and the way they are taught. Planning and delivering an inclusive accessible curriculum is a complex and skilled process (Solity, 1993), and additional challenges emerge when professionals adhere to deep-rooted attitudes and expectations. Cullingford (1999) reinforces this point when he suggests that all too often in schools exclusion is seen as an automatic response to disruptive behaviour. Effective inclusion involves professional reflection and critical analysis of current practice, and once again the *Count Us In* report (SEED, 2003) provides some helpful guidance. In inclusive schools the senior management internalize and convey a clear vision of inclusion, the curriculum meets the needs of all pupils, teaching is interactive and appropriate and there is a strong commitment to equality and opportunity for all.

THE PUPIL SUPPORT BASE – AN ALTERNATIVE TO EXCLUSION

As one would expect, there is some diversity across schools in the way the PSB operates, and this reflects the particular needs of the pupil population and the community the school serves. In general, however, the aims of all the PSBs are similar, and the researchers used these aims as a framework in which to evaluate the PSB. In the following section some of the emerging issues are presented and discussed.

Good practice

Overall, the evidence suggests that there is a considerable amount of good practice in schools. The majority of parents interviewed whose children accessed the PSB commented favourably in relation to the quality of support provided and felt that they were involved as partners. They consistently gave credit to the behaviour support staff working in the base with their child: 'If the base was not here my son would be permanently excluded.' 'The teachers in the base are different and help me and my son a lot.'[1] These sentiments were echoed by the young people supported in the PSB who were keen to express the view that the base helped them assess and to some extent control their behaviour. The mainstream class teachers emphasized their view that disruptive behaviour was a major issue for them and felt that the PSB was a vital part of the school's support systems. The main focus was upon the need to remove young people from class who were perceived to be hindering the education of their peers. Although the majority of teachers saw the PSB as an essential part of the school's strategy for supporting young people, there was also evidence to suggest that the PSB was often perceived as a 'sin bin' for young people constantly referred to by some teachers as 'the bad pupils'.

Ownership

At local authority level, emphasis was placed upon the fact that setting up base provision in schools was a new and innovative venture, and the consultative process was recognized as very important if the PSB was to be seen as a whole-school initiative owned by all staff. This was conveyed to the senior managers in schools, who were encouraged to do everything they could to ensure that all staff felt some ownership of the new system. In reality, however, the researchers found that many class teachers did not understand the rationale underpinning the base provision, nor the internal working of the PSB. Teachers tended to feel they had not been involved as partners in developing the PSB and very few expressed any sense of ownership. One member of the PSB staff summed this up by saying, 'Once the pupil is sent to the base most teachers refer to him as one of yours. It's as if the class teacher no longer has responsibility for him.' Thus in most schools the role and function of the base was not as well understood as it might be. As a result, misunderstandings, suspicion and mistrust can occur, based on lack of information and ineffective communication. The PSB staff can all too easily become isolated and this affects their ability to be recognized as a whole-school resource as opposed to individuals who operate with a few pupils on the periphery of school life.

Meeting needs

The research team were keen to ascertain the extent to which the young people accessing the PSB were seen to have special educational needs. In reality, the majority of class teacher's felt that young people who were excluded from school because of disruptive behaviour forfeited the right to education in the mainstream. They were viewed as individuals who were responsible for their disruptive behaviour and who were often rewarded rather than punished for this behaviour. One teacher conveyed this view clearly by saying, 'These pupils manipulate the system, they don't deserve to be included. They get rewarded for their bad behaviour, not punished.' In the teacher questionnaires, most teachers made a clear distinction between young people who experience SEBD and those with special needs. Young people with SEBD were to a large extent seen as a group apart, whose difficulties result because of deficiencies which reside within them. These young people are perceived as making a conscious choice to be disruptive, and the deficit model is still frequently used by teachers as a means of understanding their difficulties. The research team also analysed the documentation in schools which related to the process whereby pupils are referred to the PSB and teacher comments were consistently negative, for example, 'virtually illiterate and attention seeking', 'totally unreasonable', 'lacking concentration and aggressive'.

This conflicts with the message communicated by the Scottish Office Education Department (SOED) in the report *Effective Provision for Special Educational Needs* (SOEID, 1994) which emphasized that the concept of special needs was complex and diverse and included young people with SEBD. The majority of parents interviewed in the study whose children did not access the PSB were keen to convey that their understanding of the term 'special educational need' did not cover young people with SEBD who were excluded from school. The general view expressed was that young people with special educational needs experienced sensory, physical and learning difficulties, whereas 'the disruptive kids are a totally different issue from kids with special need.' It is difficult to see how the PSB can operate as an effective support system aimed at meeting individual need if teachers and parents continue to perceive the source of these needs as relating directly to individual inbuilt deficiencies.

Accessing an appropriate curriculum

Garner and Gains (1996) emphasize that the inappropriate or antisocial behaviour of some young people may deflect attention away from their attendant learning difficulties. Several other research studies have highlighted the strong link between disruptive behaviour and an inappropriate curriculum (Booth and Coulby, 1987; Montgomery, 1998; Cole, Visser and Upton, 1998). In the Strathclyde study this link was also raised as an important issue by parents and young people in particular. It would be unfair to say that teachers did not make this connection, but the evidence suggests that many do not see it as a priority when thinking about why some young people are disruptive. As one would expect, the majority of young people referred to the PSB were underachieving and around half were identified by the researchers as having learning difficulties. Most conveyed the message that one of the reasons they were disruptive was because they could not cope with the inappropriate demands made on them. One boy made this view very clear: 'He [teacher] kept asking me to do the work but I couldn't read the worksheet. He said I should be able to and started shouting so I swore and he threw me out of class.'

All of the PSBs aimed to maximize learning potential and raise the attainment. However, a picture emerged which showed that this aim was consistently interpreted from a fairly academic viewpoint. Evidence to support this came from the teachers in the PSB: 'When children come here they bring with them the work they are doing in class. We make it clear at all times that the child is here to work.' This concept of work was given high priority and showed that a fairly narrow cognitive view is often taken in relation to what constitutes attainment. There was less evidence to suggest that the affective dimension was being addressed effectively, and although teachers and senior managers emphasized the importance of the non-cognitive dimension in relation to meeting need, in practice this tended to be seen as a secondary issue. Ainscow (1991) discusses the importance of that dimension of schooling which focuses upon self-esteem, interpersonal skills and relationships and shows how this is particularly relevant to young people who are excluded. Most PSBs had not managed to strike the correct balance between the cognitive and the affective dimension.

Inter-professional collaboration

One approach which was highly commended by the local authorities was the need for all professionals to work together and pool their skills and expertise in order to meet the needs of young people with SEBD holistically. In order to test out if this principle was evident in practice, the researchers gathered data from professionals in external agencies who had knowledge and experience of the PSB system. These professionals indicated that good practice existed in most schools and that there was generally a good foundation on which to build. Collaborative working was viewed as a positive experience which benefited pupils, but there were also some vital issues to be resolved if the PSB system was to be seen as professionally integrated. It was evident that all professionals did not necessarily share or agree upon the philosophy underpinning inclusion. A common view held by many of those interviewed was expressed by one community education worker: 'It's all about saving money – kids come second, budgets first. Inclusion is, in my opinion, just fine words and the so-called child-centred ethos is seldom evident in practice.' All professionals are people who need to feel valued. This study reveals that professionals who work in schools often feel that they are perceived as lower down the professional hierarchy and their input is somewhat devalued. One educational psychologist described this as: 'My input depends very much on the school: in one I feel valued as a member of the extended team, in another I feel like a second-class citizen.'

Hamill and Boyd (2001) conclude that no professional group have all of the skills required to meet the needs of young people with SEBD. The behaviour exhibited by these young people affects all aspects of their lives, including home, school and the community, and if their needs are to be addressed holistically within the context of a PSB, then it is very important that all professionals are able to share skills and expertise while at the same time retaining the unique dimension of their role. Thus the focus is upon complementary as opposed to interchangeable skills. It would appear, however, that here is room for improvement and this can be exemplified if one looks in particular at two models often used by professionals to explain how they work. Teachers, for example, often use an educational model and social workers a therapeutic model. These models are often rigidly adhered to as the correct approach, and the result can be professional tension as opposed to partnership. When this happens, young people are caught in the middle and do not benefit.

Contextual issues

The PSB operates within a wider-school context and some issues emerged which related to whole-school policy and practice but which also had a particular impact upon the role and function of the PSB. In 1996 the Scottish Office report *Achievement for All* made it clear that one of the most important decisions a school has to make relates to how it organizes young people into classes. Three commonly used forms of organization were presented: setting, streaming and mixed ability. The Strathclyde research team found that schools were increasingly moving away from mixed ability classes and resorting to setting and streaming as a means of raising attainment. It is important to remember that these developments can have negative as well as positive effects on young people, and there was evidence to suggest that some of the more vulnerable young people were suffering. As the majority of young people being excluded from school were underachieving, most of them were to be found in what was described as the lower ability sets alongside their peers who were not disruptive but who had difficulties in learning. The researchers found that in reality the disruptive young people took up an inordinate amount of the teacher's time and this situation worsened as young people moved up the school. The researchers interviewed a number of young people in these lower sets who knew that they required learning support and were keen to learn, but found this an uphill task faced constantly with those who were challenging and who demanded the teacher's attention. When asked what they could do about this, one young man replied despondently, 'You can't do anything, you just have to put up with it.' This theme was echoed by several young people, and it would appear that the challenging behaviour impacts most seriously on these more vulnerable learners who find themselves in these lower sets with their disruptive peers. This can be directly linked to the forms of organization adopted by schools, which may not be in the best interests of all young people.

Senior managers in schools were generally aware of this situation, but found it difficult to resolve because of the curricular framework in place The national curriculum does not exist in Scotland; however, there are clear curricular guidelines in place, which in reality impact on the senior manager's ability to make decisions based on what they perceive to be the needs of the young person. In relation to disaffected young people who are excluded from schools, the senior managers in many schools thought that the fairly rigid curricular guidelines in place were, to say the least, unhelpful. The focus was seen to be too academic, and this was supported by the researchers when they observed young people in class. Some schools had responded by setting up an alternative curriculum for these disaffected young people which balanced their academic, vocational, social and emotional needs. Initiatives like this were at the early stages, but the young people involved, their teachers and their parents saw it as a possible way forward. The research team felt that it was an initiative worthy of further investment and appeared to be a more effective way of meeting the needs of these young people.

Two final issues relate to the gender and the age of the young people attending the PSB. Around 80 per cent of young people being excluded and accessing the base were boys, echoing concerns throughout Scotland in relation to the general decline in attainment among males. Thus the Strathclyde research provides further evidence of the strong link between disruptive behaviour and gender. It would also appear that the needs of many of these young people are not being identified early enough. The Strathclyde team found that the majority of young people who were most often excluded in third and fourth years had also been excluded in their primary schools. However, the resources put in to support them were focused more directly at the secondary school. Although the PSBs were generally fulfilling an important function, they were usually working with young people who had become seriously disaffected rather than focusing their efforts in the early stages of secondary education and the upper primary.

DEVELOPING INCLUSIVE SCHOOL CULTURE

The Strathclyde study has a lot to say about how schools can develop inclusive cultures. One factor that emerged constantly was the importance of the teacher who was seen by the young people who were frequently excluded as the key to inclusion. These young people proved to be extremely perceptive and just as teachers see them as different, they see teachers as a very diverse group, especially when it comes to their ability in creating inclusive classrooms. There was widespread understanding among young people that the teacher's job was often difficult and stressful. Nonetheless, they also provided valuable insights into what they perceived to be 'good teachers'. They did not talk about inclusive teachers, but in reality the good teacher displays the same qualities as the inclusive teacher. These young people spoke very highly of teachers who listen to them, treat them fairly, see everyone as equal and are strict but have a sense of humour. On the other hand, some teachers do not appear to have these qualities. They are seen as believing they are always right, authoritarian and subject- as opposed to child-centred. The Standards in Schools (Scotland) Act emphasizes that schools must give all young people a voice in relation to decisions which affect them, and realize that the decision to exclude a young person can have a major impact upon their life both at present and in the future. If this decision has to be made, it is important that these young disaffected people have their say. Their view must be recognized as valid, and this may be difficult when it does not correspond with the teacher's view (Hamill and Boyd, 2002).

Inclusion can never become a reality unless teachers want it to. The present study showed that teachers find no difficulty in supporting the principle of inclusion. Problems arise when theory has to be translated into practice. The majority of teachers felt that inclusion was something which was forced upon them, and constantly raised issues in relation to resourcing, inadequate staff development, policy imposition, health and safety and the incompatibility of the drive to raise attainment and to include. There was also overwhelming evidence to indicate that teachers tended to relate the concept of inclusion directly to young people who are disruptive. This narrow interpretation, while understandable, impacts upon schools actively striving towards inclusion. Inclusive schools need inclusive teachers, and first and foremost these teachers need to understand and accept that inclusion is a diverse and complex concept, extending well beyond those with behavioural difficulties to include all regardless of ability, gender, race, religion, social class, sexual orientation or language. In schools where this understanding has not been internalized by staff, it will be very difficult to develop a genuine inclusive ethos.

Most teachers favour inclusion but will continue to resist policies which in their view are imposed upon them by government, local authorities and educationalists who don't have to face the challenges inclusion brings. Inclusive schools must listen to teachers and support them in their efforts to identify and resolve issues which emerge in making inclusion a reality.

Within an inclusive culture, parents are valued and feel included. The Strathclyde study identified good practice in this area, but also highlighted some issues which need to be addressed. Research evidence has consistently emphasized the importance of this parent/teacher partnership and in 1996 Armstrong hit at the heart of the matter when he said that partnership implies mutual respect, complementary expertise and a willingness to learn from each other. All of the parents involved in the study expressed their support for the schools and were able to give concrete examples of feeling included. However, several of the group of parents whose children accessed the PSB felt that too often class teachers who referred their child to the base blamed them for their children's misbehaviour. Most parents acknowledged that they played a crucial part in this, but felt that some teachers laid the blame at their door rather than seeing behavioural difficulties as a complex issue that also involved how young people were treated in school. One parent spoke for many when she said, 'At parents night some teachers make no attempt at all to try and understand my problems. I am a single parent bringing up four kids and it's not easy. I do my best and I know it's sometimes not good enough, but blaming me for all of X's bad behaviour just makes things worse.' Inclusive schools listen to all parents, understand their needs and avoid creating blame cultures.

Finally, inclusive schools strive to enhance self-esteem and value everyone. This study showed that all individuals did not always feel they were accorded this sense of worth. This was true of many of the young people, but it was also an issue raised by professionals from external agencies who came into the school to support them. For these young people an integrated approach involving all professionals in partnership cannot simply be an option, it must become a reality. This can be easier said than done and if inclusive schools are to convert the rhetoric into reality, the barriers to professional collaboration must be recognized and overcome.

CONCLUSION

The *Count Us In* report (SEED, 2003), emphasized that an inclusive approach to education does not imply conformity amongst schools which must reflect the nature of the community they serve. The inclusiveness of a school can only be measured by looking at its aims and values, its climate and the extent to which the needs of all pupils are met. An inclusive school commits itself to providing opportunity for all and fair treatment regardless of sex, ethnic origin, religion, social, economic and linguistic background. The Strathclyde study reveals that this all-embracing definition is not as well established in schools as it might be. Many professionals and parents still simply equate inclusion with young people who can be challenging and are often excluded. There is ample evidence from the research that many teachers in particular see this as the priority and think that if these young people were excluded permanently, then schools would automatically become inclusive. The evaluative study of the PSBs shows that the issues are much more complex, and although specialist provision like this plays an important role within the whole school support system, in itself it is not the solution.

Inclusion has the power to transform schools. At present, however, the evidence reveals that putting the principle of inclusion into practice is challenging. Fundamentally, inclusion is about confronting firmly entrenched attitudes and expectations. It is in the final analysis about people, those who experience exclusion and those who strive to make inclusion a reality. Meeting the needs of the most disaffected will continue to be a challenge for schools, and the PSB will continue to play an important role in helping to lower exclusion rates, develop the potential of young disaffected people and reduce their sense of alienation. There is, however, as always room for improvement and schools must strive to be more proactive. In particular they should continue to evaluate the effectiveness of the PSB as an alternative to exclusion and take on board the emerging issues.

NOTE

1 Throughout I have used quotes from children, teachers and other professionals. These have been gathered from research evidence which is published in the following two reports:

Hamill, P. and Boyd B. (2001) *Striving for Inclusion – The Development of Support Systems for Pupils with Social, Emotional and Behavioural Difficulties in Secondary Schools.* Glasgow: University of Strathclyde.

Hamill, P., Grieve, A. and Boyd, B. (2003) *Inclusion – Principles into Practice: Developing Integrated Support Systems for Young People with Social, Emotional and Behavioural Difficulties.* Glasgow: University of Strathclyde.

REFERENCES

Ainscow, M. (1991) *Effective Schools for All.* London: Fulton.

Ainscow, M. (1999) *Understanding the Development of Inclusive Schools.* London: Falmer.

Ainscow, M. and Muncey, J. (1988) *Meeting Individual Needs in the Primary School.* London: Fulton.

Allan, J. (1999) *Actively Seeking Inclusion.* London: Falmer.

Armstrong, D. (1996) *Power and Partnership, Children and Special Educational Needs.* London: Routledge.

Armstrong, F., Armstrong, D. and Barton, L. (2000) *Inclusive Education – Policy Contexts and Comparative Perspectives.* London: Fulton.

Barber, M. (1996) *The Learning Game.* London: Indigo.

Belenky, M.F. (1992) *Bringing Balance to the Classroom or Workplace.* Paper presented at the Wisconsin Women's Studies Conference Green Bay W1.

Booth, T. and Ainscow, M. (eds) (1998) *'From Them to Us' – An International study of Inclusion.* London: Routledge.

Booth, T. and Coulby, D. (eds) (1987) *Producing and Reducing Disaffection.* Milton Keynes: Open University Press.

Brunner, I. and Guzman, A. (1989) 'Participatory Evaluation: A Tool to Assess Projects and Empower People', in R.F. Connor and M. Hendricks (eds), *International Innovations in Evaluation Methodology: New Directors for Programme Evaluation.* San Francisco, CA: Jossey Bass.

Cole, T., Visser, J. and Upton, G. (1998) *Effective Schooling for Pupils with Emotional and Behavioural Difficulties.* London: Fulton.

Cooper, P. (1993) *Effective Schools for Disaffected Students: Integration and Segregation.* London: Routledge.

CSIE (Centre for Studies in Inclusive Education) (1996) *The Inclusive School.* Bristol: CSIE.

Cullingford, C. (1999) *The Causes of Exclusion.* London: Kogan Paul.

Dyson, A. (1997) 'Social and Educational Disadvantage: Reconnecting Special Needs Education', *British Journal of Special Education*, 24 (4): 152–7.

Evans, J. and Lunt, I. (1994) *Collaborating for Effectiveness.* Buckingham: Open University Press.

Fine, M. (1996) *Talking Across Boundaries: Participatory Evaluation Research in an Urban Middle School.* New York: City University of New York.

Garner, P. and Gains, C. (1996) 'Models of Intervention for Children with Emotional and Behavioural Difficulties', *Support for Learning*, 11 (4): 141–5.

Greenwood, D.J. and Morten, L. (1998) *Introduction to Action Research – Social Research for Social Change.* London: Sage.

Hamill, P. and Boyd, B. (2001) 'Rhetoric or reality? Inter-agency provision for young people with challenging behaviour', *Emotional and Behavioural Difficulties*, 6 (3): 135–49.

Hamill, P. and Boyd, B. (2002) 'Equality, fairness and rights – the young person's voice', *British Journal of Special Education*, 29 (3): 111–17.

Herbert, M. (1993) *Working with Children and the Children Act.* London: BPS.

Mason, J. (1996) *Qualitative Researching.* London: Sage.

Mittler, P. (2000) *Working towards Inclusive Education – Social Contexts.* London: Fulton.

Montgomery, D. (1998) *Reversing Lower Attainment – Developmental Curriculum Strategies for Overcoming Disaffection and Underachievement.* London: Fulton.

O'Brien, T. (1998) *Promoting Positive Behaviour.* London: Hodder and Stoughton.

Patton, M.Q. (1986) *Utilization – Focused Evaluation.* Beverley Hills, CA: Sage.

Porter, L. (2000) *Behaviour in Schools – Theory and Practice for Teachers.* Buckingham: Open University Press.

Seale, C. (1997) 'Ensuring rigour in qualitative research', *European Journal of Public Health*, 7: 379–84.

Sebba, J. and Ainscow, M. (1996) 'International developments in inclusive schooling: mapping the issues', *Cambridge Journal of Education,* 26 (1): 5–18.

SEED (Scottish Executive Education Department) (2000) *Standards in Schools (Scotland) Act.* Edinburgh: HMSO.

SEED (Scottish Executive Education Department) (2001) *Better Behaviour – Better Learning*: *Report of the Discipline Task Group.* Edinburgh: HMSO.

SEED (Scottish Executive Education Department) (2003) *Count Us In – Achieving Inclusion in Scottish Schools – A Report by HM Inspectors.* Edinburgh: HMSO.

SOEID (Scottish Office Education and Industry Department) (1994) *Effective Provision for Special Educational Needs.* Edinburgh: HMSO.

SOEID (Scottish Office Education and Industry Department) (1997) '*How Good Is Your School?*' – *Self-Evaluation Using Performance Indicators.* Edinburgh: HMSO.

Solity, J. (1993) *Special Education.* London: Cassell.

Strauss, A. and Corbin, J. (1990) *Qualitative Analysis for Social Scientists.* Cambridge: Cambridge University Press.

Swann, W. (1988) 'Learning difficulties or curricular reform – integration or differentiation', in G. Thomas and D. Feilder (eds), *Planning for Special Needs: A Whole School Approach.* Oxford: Basil Blackwell.

Thomas, G. (1992) *Effective Classroom Teamwork – Support or Intrusion.* London: Routledge.

Warnock, M. (1978) *Special Educational Needs: Report of the Committee of Enquiry into the Education of Handicapped Children and Young People.* London: HMSO.

Westwood, P. (1997) *Commonsense Methods for Children with Special Needs.* London: Routledge.

Part Four

SOME POINTS OF TENSION AND DEVELOPMENT

23

The Gap Between Research and Practice: Achieving Effective In-service Training for Teachers Working with EBD Students

EGIDE ROYER

Pre-service and in-service training of teachers and other school staff is not a new topic and has long been an important preoccupation for schools as well as for university Schools of Education. We nevertheless deem it necessary to address the specific problems related to the poor quality of today's teacher training with regard to the educational needs of emotionally and behaviourally disordered (EBD) students. This issue is extremely important, particularly in terms of the academic achievement and social adaptation of EBD students and its relevance to the quality of intervention research conducted in the school setting.

Over the last 15 years, I have taught many courses on this very subject at the School of Education at Université Laval, Québec, and have also given numerous in-service training seminars and presentations on school intervention with EBD students in Belgium, England, France, Canada, Thailand and Brazil. One conclusion from these activities is obvious: when attending an in-service training session, our teachers are most often receiving pre-service training they had not received while at university. Most of the school staff attending these sessions or listening to the presentations at other times are often learning something totally new. Clearly, the basic training in how to teach behaviourally disordered students has not been part of their initial training. This situation may be best summarized by a comment made recently by a soon-to-be-retired teacher following one of the seminars I had presented: 'If only I had known that when I began to teach ... 25 years ago!'

Our field is seriously deficient in terms of pre-service and in-service teacher training in educating EBD students. To say the least, the relationship between research and practice is also difficult. The present chapter therefore seeks to address the following questions:

- What is our knowledge base concerning the most effective practices used in educating EBD students and how visible is it in the classroom?
- How significant is the gap between research and practice in this aspect of education?
- How can we best describe excellence in pre- and in-service training in teaching EBD students?

A SAMPLE OF OUR KNOWLEDGE BASE OF THE BEST EDUCATION PRACTICES WITH EBD STUDENTS AND ITS VISIBILITY IN THE CLASSROOM

Our current knowledge base on the education of EBD students reflects many important developments of the last 25 years. To assess the quality of pre- and in-service training in teaching EBD students, we may use a sample of this 'knowledge' as a reference or standard which will serve as a basis for comparison and help us to determine what must be considered in the professional development of our teachers. For each element, an observation is made to evaluate the integration of this specific knowledge in the professional practice of teachers who work each day with EBD students.

Knowledge 1: When teaching an EBD student, the school must address the child as a whole

We know that in order to be effective, educators of EBD students must consider an holistic school approach that uses a strong inter-agency component based on collaboration. This requires expanding the intervention to include each setting in which the child evolves (particularly home and school), within the notion that education is necessary, yet not sufficient in effectively helping these children. The mission and structure of the school therefore provides the ideal setting for the integration of health care and education into comprehensive, community-based, wrap-around services for these students.

Observation

There remains a very strong tendency to target the EBD student or his family as being the problem. The school is not perceived as a base for the integration of the many inter-agency services required by the child and his family (Cheney and Barringer, 1995). Too often we see multiple agencies offering services to EBD children, their family and their school, with no effective dialogue. The school philosophy is thus often limited to one of 'cure the child and his family, then we will be able to teach him.'

Knowledge 2: Many EBD students break rules to enhance their reputation

Lacking academic success, some students seek to compensate by adopting a non-conforming behaviour. To achieve this, they use the school's behaviour management strategies to ensure that their non-conforming activities are all very public and visibly displayed. They also see to it that how teachers respond is also highly visible to peers. Punishment and admiration from peers is then equated with success. Therefore, a school's intervention strategies actually may assist some children in achieving the goal of establishing a non-conformist reputation.

Observation

What we are seeing is the overly-visible response to individual inadequate behaviours. The management methods currently used by teachers actually reinforce this non-conformist reputation (Houghton and Carroll, 1996). Teachers and other school staff do not realize that their interventions are, in fact, helping to sustain the behaviour problems of some EBD students.

Knowledge 3: Academic achievement is an important intervention goal with EBD students

We know that it is imperative that these students develop academic skills that will enable them to do well academically, as a definite connection exists between school achievement and behaviour disorders (Ruhl and Berlinghoff, 1992). Academic and behavioural interventions must therefore be synchronized. Attempting to encourage a child's self-esteem in school while he is failing academically is increasingly considered to be a doomed effort.

Observation

Many teachers, principals and professionals continue to believe that we must 'fix' the behaviour of students before being able to teach them. Many still view the two processes – academic achievement and social behaviour in school – as two independent realities (Levy and Vaughn, 2002).

Knowledge 4: When teaching EBD students, some interventions are more effective than others

Using punishment as the sole method of intervention to make education happen simply does not work. It ignites the cycle of coercion and increases the probability of problem behaviours. The first line of intervention in schools should not be repression, but an overall improvement of the environment and disciplinary practices. Skiba and Peterson (2000), among others, recommend conflict resolution/social instruction, classroom strategies for disruptive behaviours, parent involvement, school-wide discipline and behavioural planning, functional assessment and individual education plans. For teachers, the following elements are critical when educating students with EBD:

- structure and routine;
- positive teacher-student interaction with sufficient encouragement and systematic response to inappropriate behaviour; and
- organized teaching that solicits a high level of academic commitment and student response.

Observation

These interventions are not often observed, even in the specialized EBD classroom (Wehby et al., 1998). Preferred interventions most often remain based on a philosophy of control and the use of punishment to suppress problem behaviour (Royer, 1995).

Knowledge 5: Students affect their teacher's behaviour

We know that child behaviour influences the way in which adults interact with them (Patterson, 1982). For example, teachers' efforts to work with EBD students are often received negatively and contribute to teacher antipathy: the teacher gives a lesson, the student responds aggressively, and the teacher reacts by teaching him less often. This avoidance behaviour by the teacher results in an unpleasant classroom environment, which explains why they teach less and less to EBD students.

Observation

Most teachers do not recognize the significant impact caused by the student's behaviour. Despite the fact that this transactional aspect of dealing with EBD students is extremely important in developing effective classroom intervention, it is not part of the usual assessment of EBD students made by teachers, principals and other school employees (Wehby et al., 1998).

Knowledge 6: Setting limits and having positive expectations are essential when teaching EBD students

We have long known some basic truths about successful teaching practices with EBD students. As stated by Visser (2002), the field of educating EBD students has pointed out some 'eternal truths' or core factors which must be present in any intervention with children with EBD needs, such as maintaining consistent and coherent communication, setting boundaries and providing challenges, which appear to have been effective with EBD students for as long as one can remember.

Observation
There is often the incoherent application of rules and a lack of consensus in the expectations educators have with regard to the behaviour and achievement of EBD students. Few seem to realize that a predictable school environment and consistent adult supervision not only contribute to diffuse anxiety, but also to help these students develop self-control and a greater understanding of their emotions and behaviour.

Knowledge 7: Assessment is a direct component of intervention

We know that diagnostic categories, be they educational or psychiatric in nature, are poor predictors of intervention responsiveness (Strain, 2001; Tremblay and Royer, 1992). Recent developments in functional analysis support the importance of tailored interventions for EBD students. The ability to determine the functions of behaviour and to teach replacement behaviour are essential elements of a successful intervention.

Observation
Teachers and principals continue looking for the 'one size fits all' solution, which will somehow solve the complex and long-lasting problems of EBD children, regardless of the nature and function of their behaviour (Royer, 2001).

Knowledge 8: The practitioner must have a plan, a representation, and a reference to be able to work with EBD students

We know that to be effective, teachers require a model to explain, to predict, and to provide a better understanding of what is happening in their interactions with difficult students and how they should organize their interventions. As an example, the social learning model (Kauffman, 1997; Bandura, 1986, 1997) proposes a comprehensive method to explain and predict behaviour, with sound recommendations regarding intervention that support the use of, for example, rules, teacher encouragement, positive reinforcement, verbal feedback, modelling, systematic social skills training and self-monitoring.

Observation

We note a definite lack of paradigms or intervention models in the practice of most teachers, school directors and even professionals, when educating EBD students. What is observed is often completely improvisational, based more on personal beliefs than on research-based models (Vaughn et al., 1998).

Knowledge 9: A staff value system is a crucial element in successfully educating EBD students

As stated by Cole et al., 'Good practice in relation to EBD pupils will not happen without the existence of strong and appropriate staff value systems which shape the ethos of a school' (1999: 13). Good schools thus appear to be a great place to learn. Their philosophy is to support the positive development of their students and staff. They promote positive and high-quality, differentiated teaching by enhancing staff skills and problem-solving abilities. Their behaviour policy is to help students not only learn, but also to maintain positive social behaviours.

Observation

Many schools continue to reinforce a 'curriculum of control' (Osher et al., 1994), where everything is fine when behaviour problems are suppressed, not visible.

Knowledge 10: Individualized intervention is necessary to make education happen for EBD students

Following a careful functional analysis, a multi-modal, multi-environmental intervention must be planned and tailored to the needs of the EBD student. Each case must be considered on an individual basis and with a carefully designed intervention. This consumes both time and energy, but it nevertheless has a direct relationship with the complex behaviours many of these children and youth manifest in school. It does justice to their individuality as well as to the complexity of every human being.

Observation

One of the favoured methods in education continues to be the grouping together of students with the same problem in the same class with some kind of omnibus intervention or treatment. As we all know, a special class does not an individualized intervention make. For instance, I have witnessed the proposed creation of a special EBD class for adolescents expelled from regular school for having sold drugs. The primary criterion to be part of this special education placement was to be 'in the business'!

The preceding are examples of what may be assumed to be folk-knowledge, but strongly supported and well documented by researchers in the field. Yet as a body of knowledge it does not really appear to be part of the professional expertise of teachers working with EBD students. So what explains this discrepancy between research and practice?

THE GAP BETWEEN RESEARCH AND PRACTICE

There are admitedly very few scientific endeavours that compare to the use by educators of the knowledge base developed by the researchers in the field of behaviour problems in school (Schiller, 1995). As stated by Greenwood (2001), compared to science, education is not impressively effective. Empirical evidence does not support decision making. Practice is often based on a popular way of doing things and is not in the main scientifically tested for its contribution to students' learning or achievement. Government policies themselves are a mixture of ideology and politics occasionally supported by research.

The lack of knowledge and skills of our teachers in their interactions with EBD students is problematic, to say the least. More often than not, teachers have no crisis intervention plan or procedure to rely on when things start to go wrong, which tends for many reasons to make even special EBD classes unsafe. In this context, many researchers question the ability of regular teachers to deal with EBD students in inclusive classroom settings (Cheney and Barringer, 1995). What is apparent, however, is that even the most effective behavioural strategies are not well implemented in mainstream education (Skiba et al., 1997; Wehby et al., 1998).

Many teachers continue to choose less effective methods of managing behaviour because the impact of introducing research-supported interventions is not immediately visible to them. Very often, changing their practice – as proposed by research – is not in itself rewarding and can even be viewed to be threatening. Another significant impediment is time. Teachers are reluctant to implement practices that take too much time, regardless of the promising results (Vaughn et al., 1998). Some issues may be related to a cost–benefit ratio for certain teachers. If the cost of change is high and the benefits low or only positive to one student (the EBD student), teachers may be unwilling to change how they deal with problem behaviours in their classroom in general (Malouf and Schiller, 1995).

We must bear in mind that teachers and schools are rarely, if ever, sued for failure to apply the most effective instructional intervention or to change a practice that is not working or is found to be detrimental to a student's learning. The common explanation for a student's failure to learn is based largely on characteristics such as poverty, disability, ethnicity/language and family, and rarely on the use of ineffective or inappropriate practices (Carnine, 1995).

Considering the quality of our knowledge base on the preferred teaching practices with EBD students and the significant problems these students face during and after their school years, *not* using the best practices available to help them succeed in school truly represents an ethical problem. The situation also has an impact on the quality of research undertaken in the school setting. When researchers present a new intervention programme for the purpose of evaluation, an assumption is made that teachers already possess the core of basic skills required to implement and test this programme. As an analogy, when testing with a new drug in pharmacology to assess its potential to cure a specific illness, medical researchers assume that the doctors applying the research protocol are able successfully to give a patient an intravenous injection or check their blood pressure. In short, medical researchers trust that the practitioner participating in a study is able to administer the treatment with integrity by referring to a background of basic medical skills. We cannot be so sure when implementing and evaluating a new education programme to help EBD students succeed academically. This is another reason why we must bridge the gap between knowledge and practice (Carnine, 1997).

One cannot reflect on the problematic relationship between research and practice without directly considering the teachers' pre-service and inservice training on how to work specifically with EBD students. As stated by Sugai et al. (1997), the initial training given to teachers fails to prepare them adequately to educate these students. In this regard, if we are to deal effectively with the quality of education offered to EBD students, the fundamental issue of adequate pre- and in-service teacher training must be examined.

PRE-SERVICE AND IN-SERVICE TRAINING FOR TEACHERS OF EBD STUDENTS: PROMOTING EXCELLENCE

Many would now acknowledge that Schools of Education must revise their pre-service, curriculum (for specific knowledge and abilities, see Bullock et al., 1994) in order better to train new teachers on how to educate EBD students and alleviate conflict. It is imperative that we introduce courses and training seminars that are coherent with the latest knowledge of our field and are precisely designed to address practical teaching problems in today's classroom. What are the characteristics of an effective pre-service training programme pertaining to the education of EBD students?

Pre-service training must support the development and use of proactive rather than reactive intervention in dealing with EBD students. It must be clear to every teacher that two levels of intervention – universal and specific – must exist within the school. Universal interventions are offered to each student by means of school rules, classroom rules and social skills teaching. Specific interventions are tailored, individualized interventions for EBD students, consisting of consultations, individual educational plans, self-control and aggression management training and so on. As proposed by Walker (2000), this pre-service training should focus on solving problems and developing intervention strategies that will truly work in the school setting. Therefore, following the initial training received in their teacher-preparation programme, new teachers should:

- be actively involved in the needs assessment of their students and not rely solely on the diagnosis of someone who is not a teaching specialist (Cooper, 1996);
- possess the necessary knowledge base with which to address the different manifestations of behaviour disorders before they are encountered, rather than be unprepared and face these specific needs as they are occur in their classroom;
- have a practical understanding of which services can be applied in the regular classroom and which should be reserved for specialized settings;
- focus on reinforcing learning and academic achievement in EBD students instead of targeting their problem behaviours (Levy and Vaughn, 2002; Ruhl and Berlinghoff, 1992);
- be responsible for the curriculum and teaching components of the individual education plan (IEP) developed for these students and not merely the executor of decisions taken by other professionals;
- be conscious of the importance of remaining in tune with the development of the EBD student, continue to strive for the development of

the best EBD education practices, and avoid practices that are crystallized around knowledge learned in pre-service training;

- be able to read a recent research paper related to innovative approaches in the field;
- be able to use a model or a paradigm to explain, predict and offer suggestions to help EBD students;
- always focus on the reinforcement of positive behaviour;
- be aware that maintenance and generalization must be planned and not left to chance;
- prefer the teaching of replacement behaviour over the use of punishment;
- possess a clear model of reference to deal with crisis intervention, and in particular with the cycle of coercion that is so prevalent when dealing with aggressive students;
- know how to organize the classroom environment by establishing clearly defined rules, with foreseeable consequences when these rules are not adhered to;
- have developed the necessary skills to establish a confident and trusting relationship with parents; and
- focus on approaches that enhance the strengths that each child brings to the classroom (Bullock, 1999).

In-service training must enable teachers to enhance these baseline capabilities in order that they might integrate new knowledge and skills supported by research and demonstrably effective practices (Royer, 2001). This training must become part of the school staff's mission and be an ongoing career project. We know now that isolated training sessions may be inspiring or increase awareness, yet these limited, occasional workshops rarely alter classroom practices. In-service training must therefore be encouraged by the school administration and will have a better chance of producing change if some kind of entrapment effect takes place. Should this up-graded training lead to a more productive classroom environment as a whole for EBD students – and no doubt decrease the stress felt by teachers – then these new approaches will be better welcomed as part of the preferred intervention practices of these teachers. In so doing, direct consultation and supervision of teachers should become one of the best ways to train in-service practitioners in the use of behavioural intervention (Nelson and Rutherford, 1987; Veillet and Royer, 2001).

Pre- and in-service training related to EBD students must, in themselves, be research-based (Gable et al., 1992). It is therefore imperative that we continue to support further research in this area itself. Longitudinal studies on how newly-certified teachers begin in the profession, adjust, implement and maintain new practices raise important questions which must be addressed if our understanding is to evolve.

REFERENCES

Bandura, A. (1986) *Social Foundation of Thought and Action: A Social Cognitive Theory*. Toronto: Prentice Hall.

Bandura, A. (1997) *Self-efficacy: The Exercise of Control*. New York: Freeman.

Bullock, L.M. (1999) *Understanding, Reaching and Teaching Today's Youth*. Keynote address, Second Canadian Conference on Educating Students with Emotional and Behavioral Disorders, Québec, QC, Canada.

Bullock, L.M., Ellis, L.L., and Wilson, M.J. (1994) 'Knowledge/skills needed by teachers who work with students with severe emotional/behavioral disorders: A revisitation', *Behavioral Disorders*, 19 (2): 108–125.

Carnine, D. (1995) 'The professional context for collaboration and collaborative research', *Remedial and Special Education*, 16: 368–71.

Carnine, D. (1997) 'Bridging the research-to-practice gap', *Exceptional Children*, 63: 513–21.

Cheney, D., and Barringer, C. (1995) 'Teacher competence, student diversity, and staff training for the inclusion of middle school students with emotional and behavioral disorders', *Journal of Emotional and Behavioral Disorders*, 3 (3): 174–82.

Cole, T., Visser, J., and Daniels, H. (1999) 'A model explaining effective practice in mainstream schools', *Emotional and Behavioural Difficulties*, 4 (1): 12–18.

Cooper, P. (1996) 'Giving it a name: The value of descriptive categories in educational approaches to emotional and behavioural difficulties', *Support for Learning*, 11: 146–50.

Gable, R.A., Hendrickson, J.M., Young, C.C., and Shokoohi-Yekta, M. (1992) 'Pre-service preparation and classroom practices of teachers of students with emotional/behavioral disorders', *Behavioral Disorders*, 17 (2): 126–34.

Greenwood, C.R. (2001) 'Science and students with learning and behavioral problems', *Behavioral Disorders*, 27 (1): 37–52.

Houghton, S. and Carroll, A. (1996) 'Enhancing reputations: High school adolescent males' effective use of teacher behavior intervention strategies', *Scientia Paedagogica Experimentalis*, 33 (2): 227–44.

Kauffman, J.W. (1997) *Characteristics of Emotional and Behavioral Disorders of Children and Youth* (6th edn). Toronto: Merrill.

Levy, S. and Vaughn, S. (2002) 'An observational study of teachers' reading instruction of students with emotional or behavioral disorders', *Behavioral Disorders*, 27 (3): 215–35.

Malouf, D. and Schiller, E. (1995) 'Practice and research in special education', *Exceptional Children*, 61: 414–24.

Nelson, C.M., and Rutherford, R.B. (1987) 'Behavioral interventions with behaviorally disordered students', in M. Wang, M. Reynolds and H. Walberg (eds), *Handbook of Special Education: Research and Practice* (Vol. 2) New York: Pergamon pp. 125–53.

Osher, D., Osher, T. and Smith, C. (1994) 'Toward a national perspective in emotional and behavioral disorders: A developmental agenda', *Beyond Behavior*, 6: 6–17.

Patterson, G.R. (1982) *A Social Learning Approach: Cohercive Family Process*. Eugene, OR: Castilia.

Royer, E. (1995) 'Behavior disorders, suspension and social skills: Punishment is not education', *Therapeutic Care and Education*, 4: 32–6.

Royer, E. (2001) 'The education of students with emotional and behavioral difficulties: One size does not fit all', in J. Visser, T. Cole and H. Daniels (eds), *Emotional and Behavioural Difficulties in Mainstream Schools*. London: Elsevier Science. pp. 127–40.

Ruhl, K.L. and Berlinghoff, D.H. (1992) 'Research on improving behaviorally disordered students' academic performance: A review of the literature', *Behavioral Disorders*, 17: 178–90.

Schiller, E.P. (1995) 'The missing link in special education research: The practitioner', *CEC Today*, August, p. 14.

Skiba, R.J. and Peterson, R.L. (2000) 'School discipline at a crossroad: From zero tolerance to early response', *Exceptional Children*, 66 (3): 335–47.

Skiba, R.J., Peterson, R.L. and Williams, T. (1997) 'Office referrals and suspension: Disciplinary intervention in middle schools', *Education and Treatment of Children*, 20 (3): 1–21

Strain, P.S. (2001) 'Empirically-based social skill intervention: A case for quality-of-life improvement', *Behavioral Disorders*, 27 (1): 30–36.

Sugai, G., Bullis, M. and Cumblad, C. (1997) 'Providing ongoing skill development and support', *Journal of Emotional and Behavioral Disorders*, 5 (1): 55–64.

Tremblay, R. and Royer, E. (1992) 'Pour une perspective éducationnelle dans l'évaluation des élèves en trouble du comportement', *Sciences et comportement*, 22: 253–62.

Vaughn, S., Hughes, M.T., Schumm, J.S. and Klingner, J.K. (1998). 'A collaborative effort to enhance reading and writing instruction in inclusion classrooms', *Learning Disability Quarterly*, 21 (1): 57–74.

Veillet, M. and Royer, E. (2001) 'Los problemas de comportamento na escola secundaria : Avaliaçao de um modelo de formaçao pragmatica por acompanhamento de professores. Les problèmes de comportement à l'école secondaire: évaluation d'un modèle de formation pragmatique par accompagnement des enseignants', *Revista Portuguesa de Pedagogia*, 34: 651–72.

Visser, J. (2002) 'Eternal verities: The strongest links', *Emotional and Behavioural Difficulties*, 7 (2): 68–84.

Walker, H.M. (2000) 'Investigating school-related behavior disorders: Lessons learned from a thirty-year research career', *Exceptional Children*, 66 (2): 151–61.

Wehby, J.H., Symons, F.J. and Canale, J.A. (1998) 'Teaching practices in classrooms for students with emotional and behavioral disorders: Discrepancies between recommendations and observations', *Behavioral Disorders*, 24 (1): 51–6.

24

Researching a Marginalized Population: Methodological Issues

ANN LEWIS

This chapter is about how, as part of research methodologies, we might go about accessing the views of marginalized child populations. It will not attempt to review the nature of those views as that is done elsewhere in this volume. An initial caution is that despite our good intentions in accessing pupils' views, children and young people retain a right to silence, privacy and solitude.

I take conducting research to be about 'The production of knowledge pursued by the employment of systematic and rigorous methods of data collection and analysis' (Foster, 1999), 'the results of which are available for public scrutiny' (Pring, 2000). Thus whatever researchers' individual value positions about the nature of truth and reality (and hence their preferred methodologies, methods of data collection and analyses), they need to address publicly a series of overarching issues. These issues relate, first, to the ethics of data collection and, second, to optimizing the authenticity, credibility and trustworthiness of data.

I relate these issues to interviewing/having conversations with children and young people from marginalized populations as that is a popular, probably the predominant, method of data collection with this group (for example, Wise and Upton, 1998). Styles of research interviews in this context include the highly-structured, reflecting clinical interview methods.

For example, the psychiatrist Sula Wolff (1995), in her account of 'loners', describes interviews based on the use of a large number of pre-specified and specific questions (for example, re: solitariness, impaired empathy, emotional detachment, rigidity, increased sensitivity, single mindedness), with responses scored according to written definitions.

A much less structured interview style is given by Paul Cooper (1993) in his account of research with disaffected pupils. He describes the process as a conversation rather than an interview; beginning with a 'lead' question and then inviting elaboration. Where directive questions were asked, these were often based on material provided by the interviewee.

A very unstructured approach is illustrated by Jo Crozier (Crozier and Tracey, 2000; respectively teacher and pupil in an alternative school unit) in her report of a reciprocal process in which each responded to the other's oral and written interpretations of events. This reflects Tom Billington's (2000) approach of building up 'narratives of difference'; itself reminiscent of Virginia Axline's powerful account of working with a child 'in search of self' (Axline, 1964).

The research criterion, above, of public scrutiny requires that ethical issues as well the authenticity, credibility and trustworthiness of data are addressed explicitly and fully in research accounts, whatever their methodological orientation. The points made in this chapter are not specific to research involving marginalized populations, but are heightened in that context because of the possible vulnerability of those populations; by definition, outside the 'mainstream' and beyond the intended protection of procedures there.

ETHICAL CONCERNS IN RELATION TO ELICITING THE VIEWS OF CHILDREN AND YOUNG PEOPLE WITH EBD

There are concerns about the ethical aspects of interviewing children (Moore and Beazeley, 1998; Lindsay, 2000; Alderson and Morrow, in press). These may be heightened when children with emotional and behavioural difficulties (EBD) are involved because of the perceived characteristics of those children. The term 'emotional and behavioural difficulties' is a broad label for which definitions are contested (EPPI, 2003). However, a UK government document (DfES, 2001) described these children as being possibly withdrawn, disruptive, disturbing, hyperactive, lacking concentration, having immature social skills, presenting challenging behaviour and/or requiring counselling. Thus such children (the broad reference group for this chapter) may be seen as challenging interviewees (Armstrong et al., 1998).

Ethical concerns of research with children have revolved around six main areas:

- access/gatekeepers;
- consent/assent;
- confidentiality/anonymity/secrecy;
- recognition/feedback;
- ownership; and
- social responsibility.

These may operate slightly differently in research, compared with professional, contexts. For example, in the professional context, the professional's position will lead to the involvement of a particular group; for researchers who are based outside the context, sampling issues and access become more critical and may shape findings significantly. The researcher perspective has relevance for professionals as it may highlight otherwise unexamined issues, such as the distinctions between informed consent, assent, failure to dissent and informed dissent.

There are additional ethical issues arising from involving in research children with EBD. First, the process may, by definition, draw attention to those difficulties because it is the main research focus. This may be disturbing to the children. Second, they may inadvertently be misled into believing that involvement in the research will change events in their lives.

Access/gatekeepers

1st level – e.g. Parent
2nd level – e.g. Ethics: Committee
                             Headteacher
                             Other children

Unless the researcher is interviewing their own child, then someone acts as a *gatekeeper*, providing or withholding *access*, to the child to be interviewed. In most cases this direct (1st level) gatekeeper will be the parent or carer. Somebody else may in turn act as an indirect (2nd level) gatekeeper to the parents and carers. In school contexts this may be the headteacher, school governors or local education authority; but depending on the focus of the research it may also, or instead, be health, legal, and/or social service agencies.

There are ethical committees and protocols designed to protect children from unwarranted intrusion by potential researchers. These procedures and their interpretation will shape the nature of the group of children interviewed and hence the range of views ultimately collected. A clear illustration in the integration/inclusion context occurs when a school chooses to opt out of involvement in an evaluation, consequently removing a particular group from those whose views are accessed. This may also occur through tangential circumstances rather than by design, as when a school withdraws from the study due to, for example, staff illness or prioritizing of inspection arrangements. Decisions about sample have repercussions for access (and vice versa), with consequent implications for the interpretation of the findings of the work.

Consent/assent

The importance of obtaining consent is a prominent topic in the literature concerning research with children (Alderson and Morrow, in press). In contrast with the United Kingdom, Morrow and Richards (1996) reported that in the United States, by law, written parental consent must be obtained if children are to be asked to participate in sensitive social research. This is a stronger position than that currently taken in the United Kingdom.

The continuum from informed consent – through assent to failure to object – highlights the distinction between consent and assent. Consent may be given by the child or by another on the child's behalf for either the child to be interviewed or the researcher to ask the child to be interviewed. *Assent* is generally taken to refer to the child's agreement to participation in the process when another has given consent. In the more conventional context of interviewing adults these two aspects are conflated, that is, the adult being interviewed both consents and assents to the interview.

Consent is not in itself sufficient; *informed consent/assent* is needed. In order to give informed consent, the person giving this has to have:

- information about the chance to participate;
- know about a right to withdraw from the activity;
- know what the participant's role will be; and
- know what the outcomes are intended to be.

To be able to respond to all the above four aspects of informed consent the participant (or someone on their behalf) has to receive the information, understand it and respond to it (Alderson, 1995). Spelt out in this way, it can be seen that obtaining informed consent may be a considerable undertaking and daunting to achieve. Some writers have argued that, while involving children and young people in research and evaluation is important, it may be very difficult genuinely to obtain their informed consent (McCarthy, 1998; Clegg, 2001; Homan, 2001).

An unusual study (Hurley and Underwood, 2002) tested claims about children's giving of informed consent. The study involved 178 children, ages 8, 10 and 12. Children's understanding about confidentiality and degree of understanding of the information on which they based their consent was assessed. For example, 69 per cent of 8-year-olds, 36 per cent of 10-year-olds and 22 per cent of 12-year-olds could not explain the reasons for the project. Guarantees of confidentiality were also not understood: 40 per cent of 8-year-olds, 14 per cent of 10-year-olds and 18 per cent of 12-year-olds believed that the experimenter would, if asked, pass on information to people in the child's family or school.

There is strong agreement among commentators that allowing *informed dissent* is crucial. Children have a right to privacy that researchers have a moral responsibility to acknowledge (Homan, 2001). A child's expression of informed dissent may not be easy to recognize. For example, there may be disagreement among adults about whether a particular behaviour by a child with severe or profound and multiple learning difficulties reflects dissent. Keeping an open dialogue with the network of people around the child helps to sustain checks on whether the child is continuing to assent to involvement (Kellett and Nind, 2001; Porter et al., 2001). Explicit continuation of assent enables a corresponding and genuine right to withdraw at any point.

In the legal context, much stress is placed on whether a person is competent to give consent: 'A child who has the capacity to understand fully a decision affecting his or her life automatically has the capacity to make that decision unless statute law states otherwise' (Masson, 2000: 39). This is referred to, in short, as the Gillick competence test after the Gillick 1985 case, concerning under 16-year-olds' right to contraception without the permission of their parents. The court found in favour of the general practitioner. This set a precedent in that it allowed under 16-year-olds to consent to medical treatment providing they could show 'sufficient understanding' and 'competence to make wise choices'. Lengthy debate has ensued around how such competence is to be defined (for example, Corey et al., 2002), and this seems likely to become an even greater concern of both researchers and service providers (Lewis, 2004). Regardless of the legal debate, lack of competence does not remove the right to express a view.

Confidentiality/anonymity/secrecy

Formal guidance on research methods usually stresses the importance of *confidentiality*. This seems right, proper and uncontroversial. However, it may be more difficult to sustain in practice, particularly if small or atypical groups are involved, than exhortations to sustain confidentiality suggest. Confidentiality may also not be sustained for different reasons – that is, if the child reveals information that the interviewer feels should be passed on in the child's best interests. It might be felt that it is preferable to exclude a particular type of data collection if its collection might place the researcher in an invidious ethical position (and hence jeopardize the relationship with the child) (see Oakley, 2000, for an example).

A researcher may attempt to guarantee *anonymity* in any written documentation (that is, comments or views are not attributed in a way that could be traced back to a specific individual). This may mean that some views have to be excluded from the report (for example, if only one child with cerebral palsy is included in mainstream schools in the sample, then any comment reflecting that particular perspective could be traced back to an individual).

Another issue about confidentiality arises from procedures concerning conducting interviews; privacy has to be balanced with child protection procedures. Whether parents should be present at interviews with their children has been much debated and it has been argued that parents may want, but not need, to know what happens. Relevant bodies produce ethical guidelines for researchers (see, for example, BPS, 1991: BERA, 2003), although the detail of these varies widely (see Lindsay, 2000). Clegg (2001) argued that when interviews are conducted in a spirit of openness, then privacy/confidentiality is not an issue and the very notion of gatekeepers (see above) betrays a lack of trust between those involved with the children.

> People with a range of learning disabilities have relationships of dependence with close carers ... Having decided it is neither necessary nor useful to wish most carers away, many problems of 'confidentiality' disappear because there are fewer secrets to guard. (Clegg, 2001)

There is a distinction between confidentiality, given to people participating in the research, and *secrecy*. Secrecy applies to procedures and in most cases such secrecy would probably be deemed inappropriate in educational research. However, there might be contexts in which it was felt legitimate to keep procedures secret (for example, observation to monitor suspected bullying).

Recognition/feedback

> Research subjects need to be able to distinguish between providing information as part of receiving services and providing information without any quid pro quo ... The absence of anything for the research subject is the key element. (Masson, 2001)

Often when children are interviewed in schools, this is presented as part of routine school activities with no specific 'reward' for participating. However, small token gifts such as holographic stickers given to all the children in a class whether or not interviewed seem to be popular and provide a modest 'thank you'. Alternatively, a group 'treat' such as a party may be organized. In more substantial projects researchers may give children gift vouchers or token payment in exchange for their involvement (with parental agreement). The basis of this exchange is respect for the children's time and efforts.

It is now widely recognized that participants should have the opportunity to receive *feedback* from researchers about the outcomes of the study. However, some sample groups move around geographically and this makes sustained links difficult or impossible over a longer-term project. With children, feedback may be done through adults known to them. Little seems to have been written on this topic in published accounts of children's views about inclusion, and it is potentially a sensitive area.

Ownership

In educational research *ownership* of data is generally presumed to belong to the researcher (although data protection measures apply, giving participants rights to access electronic data under certain conditions). Kellett and Nind (2001) propose the researcher as a banker, retaining data/information (for example, video material or interview narrative) but giving others access to it. In the inclusion context, it might be argued that schools should have access to such information and the right to use it in certain contexts. One might make a distinction here between data and information. Information refers to what is collected (for example, a piece of video film), while the process of conversion or extraction from information generates data – the units or material analysed. Thus the data are a subset of the information.

There may be unintended outcomes of using protocols intended to safeguard the interests of children interviewed. For example, notions of ownership whereby materials are returned to children interviewed may be interpreted as a rejection or failure. Jean Ware (personal communication) has noted that destroying confidential materials at the close of a project may be read as discounting of the material by some children, particularly perhaps those with difficulties in learning. 'Valuable' material would have been retained or even displayed.

Professional groups may take contrasting views, sometimes arising from particular legislative constraints, about what constitutes an authentic way to obtain children's views. A particular issue here is the use of facilitators. Ideally, facilitators should be chosen by the child. Facilitators act as intermediaries conveying, or translating, the views of those interviewed. For example, a facilitator may interpret Makaton or BSL signs for the researcher. This enables views to be collected from people who might otherwise be excluded from those whose views are accessed. However, the filter of the facilitator may unwittingly distort the views held. If they are used, then any report needs to acknowledge how views were collected so that the reader/listener can make a judgement about whether the conduit for views may have distorted the evidence. Ware (submitted) suggests that taking into account a range of structured assessment information (for example, through observations of the child) may be preferable to methods which involve a high degree of inference. Her point relates to children with profound and multiple learning difficulties, but may be applicable also to children with EBD.

Social responsibility

One of the intellectual virtues embodied in the process of carrying out research is the pursuit of truth. This links with Lindsay's (2000) discussion about the *social responsibility* of the researcher. The strong rights arguments around inclusion and the strength with which personal value positions are held may make it difficult to sustain research endeavours that threaten to produce findings at odds with the prevailing orthodoxy. Researchers have a responsibility to acknowledge both their own value positions and whatever truth emerges from the research process. The integrity of the research (Pring, 2000) is an over-arching principle.

PRINCIPLES UNDERLYING THE RESEARCH PROCESS IN RELATION TO ELICITING THE VIEWS OF CHILDREN AND YOUNG PEOPLE WITH EBD

Authenticity

The potency of research is in its authenticity. Research involving children with difficulties in learning increasingly seeks to check for the authenticity of the context in which views are collected; that is, these should be true to the child. Part of these checks are likely to be awareness of features that may distort the child's response in unhelpful ways (for example, reflecting who else is present; their relationship with the child; the child's tendency to be acquiescent; features of the context such as noise and so on).

Validity/credibility

Validity, or in a similar vein credibility, draws attention to the fairness of the particular process leading to a child's response. This includes seeking responses that are about what we think they are about; for example, if we ask children about which schools they prefer when seeking *educational* preferences, we may instead be obtaining comments about friendship patterns as children tend to prefer the schools to which friends go. A loss of validity may arise more subtly when a child's interpretation of the situation leads them to make a particular (untrue) response. For example, when Nesbitt (2000) talked with children about religious beliefs, she noted that the children sometimes applied terms from one sect to their own (for example, a Baptist girl, against her normal practice, termed her church minister a 'vicar'), possibly reflecting what she believed the researcher would expect or understand. Such nuances are often lost but were highlighted here through the researcher's sensitivity and the use of language as distinctive markers.

Validation concerns ways of checking that responses are being interpreted in a fair way. There has been increasing discussion about validation of responses in interviews with children. Some researchers have used peers as interviewers or involved people with learning difficulties in validation (see projects by Triangle/NSPCC, Save the Children, the Children's Society and Joseph Rowntree Foundation, for example, Ward, 1996). Accounts in which researchers have sustained contact through friendships with those interviewed also help to show, through longer-term and personal involvement, whether interpretations were valid (Crozier and Tracey, 2000; Booth, 1998).

Reliability/trustworthiness

Reliability, or trustworthiness, encompasses the idea that the response is representative or typical of what the child believes. Two aspects of the many ways in which we may unwittingly distort children's responses to questioning are summarized here: questioning style and ways of prompting (elaborated in Lewis, 2002, 2004).

A range of work with children has shown the value of making statements that prompt a response, rather than a direct question, to elicit views. The tendency for adults, particularly teachers, to use question–answer–feedback routines has been described by some writers as reflecting power relationships (Edwards and Westgate, 1994). Through the use of questions, the adult keeps the 'upper hand'. Thus in the context of an interview, the use of questions rather than statements also reflects an implied power relationship. However, the use of statements as prompts (less overtly 'powerful') can occur naturally in small group interviews with children when one child's comment may naturally trigger a response from another child in the group (Dockrell et al., 2000).

How much to prompt children, and the effects of this on the reliability of what is said, has been examined by various researchers. In summary, children with difficulties in learning seem to respond best to general open-ended questions, for example, 'What did you do in the playground?' (rather than free recall, for example, 'Tell me about playtime', or specific questions, for example, 'Did you play with Pokemon cards at playtime?'). The level of general open-ended questions parallels the function of the cue cards described in the following section which are somewhat, but not overly, specific. More generally, children have a bias towards confirming what is put to them, so it is important to ask about both sides of an issue (for example, not presuming a wish to stay in/leave the current school).

TECHNIQUES IN RELATION TO ELICITING THE VIEWS OF CHILDREN AND YOUNG PEOPLE WITH EBD

The ways (modes, medium and structure) through which the child responds in an interview (or less formal discussion) can be varied in a wide number of ways so that all children can potentially make an authentic, credible and trustworthy response. An increasingly wide range of techniques are being developed to access children's views. Several points about methods of data collection, drawing on the implications of the preceding material, are made here.

The importance of using multiple approaches to elicit pupils' views is increasingly recognized

Clark and Moss (2001) describe their 'Mosaic' approach which combines observation, child conferencing, use of cameras, mapping and role play as well perspectives from parents and professionals. Although this work was developed with young children, it has application to other contexts and is referenced to principles of participation, reflexivity, adaptability and relevance. Interviews may be supplemented with other approaches including drawings, photographs, diaries, simple questionnaires, grids for completion, multi-media and web-based approaches, or observational records.

The use of drawings (and to a lesser extent photographs), while intuitively attractive, needs to be considered carefully as it is easy to misinterpret such information (Thomas and Silk, 1990; Lange-Kuttner and Edelstein, 1995). This danger is lessened if drawings are an adjunct to other methods.

For some pupils it may be particularly important to minimize over-stimulation

Bourg et al. (1999) warn against using too many props as this may cause children to become over-excited. They suggest hiding props from the child's eye before they are needed and interviewing the child in short bursts rather than a single longer interview.

Narratives (as in Crozier and Tracey, 2000) tend to be more valid and reliable as responses than are answers to a series of questions

A possible strategy here is in the cue card approach (Lewis, 2001) which, by presenting children with pictures to which they respond and without giving question prompts, encourages a flow of uninterrupted talk from the child.

Several specific strategies are associated with more accurate responses

Linked with fostering narratives, the avoidance of probing questions, open rather than closed questions, and questions that are neither too general nor too specific (Lewis, 2001, 2004), have all been found to limit children's responsiveness to implied suggestions or bias.

Emotional states may limit or distort responses in various ways

First, the recall of emotions is often inaccurate. There is a tendency to overstate one's initial emotional state. Further, emotional states are recalled as more intense if the individual has successfully overcome them (Dockrell, 2002). Second, pupils with EBD may inhabit a cultural world foreign to that of the interviewer. This has clear implications for terms used by the interviewer (for example, using the child's terms for 'bullying') but, more subtly, in relation to not making assumptions about the child's emotional world. Armstrong et al. (1998) describe their interviews with young people about mental health issues. They found that the sub-group of children with identified emotional, psychological and/or psychiatric problems were far less likely than other children to admit to, or acknowledge, negative feelings. The researchers concluded that these children were not 'covering these up'; 'They simply did not seem to associate their feelings or behaviour with negative emotions' (1998: 38).

CONCLUSION

The approaches described in this chapter reflect the growing interest in participatory research in which research is with, not on, participants – in this context, children with EBD. That position is signalled in Clough's comment that:

> The research act of listening to voice must always involve the broadly defined processes of both mediation and translation … in the case of special educational needs these functions may be particularly indicated where there are doubts about the capacity of the subject to express an intention that is about his/her powers of articulation (1998: 129).

Marginalized groups are, by definition, often excluded from mainstream studies. The greater the difficulties in reflecting the views of those marginalized groups, the greater the concomitant danger (particularly in a policy context which is increasingly recognizing children's right to be heard (Lewis, 2004) that the loudest voices obliterate those of the unheard. This places a responsibility on researchers to develop methodologies and methods which recurrently open the research process.

REFERENCES

Alderson, P. (1995) *Listening to Children: Children, Ethics and Social Research.* Barkingside: Barnardo's.

Alderson, P. and Morrow, G. (in press) *Ethics, Social Research and Consulting with Children and Young People.* London: Barnardo's.

Armstrong, C., Hill, M. and Secker, J. (1998) *Listening to Children.* London: Mental HealthFoundation.

Axline, V. (1964) *Dibs: In Search of Self.* Harmondsworth: Penguin.

BERA (2003) *Draft – Revised Ethical Guidelines for Educational Research.* Edinburgh: BERA/SCRE.

Billington, T. (2000) *Separating, Losing and Excluding Children.* London: Routledge.

Booth, W. (1998). 'Doing research with lonely people', *British Journal of Learning Disabilities,* 26: 132–6.

Bourg, W., Broderick, R., Flagor, R., Meeks Kelly D., Lang Ervin, D. and Butler, J. (1999) *A Child Interviewer's Handbook.* Thousand Oaks, CA: Sage.

BPS (1991) *Code of Conduct, Ethical Principles and Guidelines.* Leicester: BPS.

Clark, A. and Moss, P. (2001) *Listening to Young Children: the Mosaic Approach.* London: Joseph Rowntree Foundation/ National Children's Bureau.

Clegg, J. (2001). *Healthcare Ethics from a Hermeneutic Perspective.* Paper presented at the seminar series 'Methodological issues in interviewing children and young people with learning difficulties', Funded by ESRC 2001–3, University of Birmingham, School of Education.

Clough, P. (1998) 'Differently articulate? Some indices of disturbed/disturbing voices', in P. Clough and L. Barton (eds), *Articulating with Difficulty.* London: Chapman. pp. 128–45.

Cooper, P. (1993) *Effective Schools for Disaffected Students.* London: Routledge.

Corey, G., Callahan, M.S. and Corey, P. (2002) *Issues and Ethics in the Helping Professions* (6th edn). Pacific Grove, CA: Brooks/Cole.

Crozier, J. and Tracey A. (2000) 'Falling out of school: A young woman's reflections on her chequered experience of schooling', in A. Lewis and G. Lindsay (eds), *Researching Children's Perspectives.* Buckingham: Open University Press. pp. 173–86.

DfES (2001) *Code of Practice on the Identification and Assessment of Pupils with Special Educational Needs.* London: DfES.

Dockrell, J. (2002) *How can studies of memory and language enhance the authenticity, validity and reliability of interviews?* Paper presented at the ESRC seminars, School of Education, University of Birmingham.

Dockrell, J., Lewis A. and Lindsay G. (2000) 'Researching children's perspectives – a psychological perspective', in A. Lewis and G. Lindsay (eds), *Researching Children's Perspectives.* Buckingham: Open University Press. pp. 46–58.

Edwards, A.D. and Westgate, D.P.G. (1994) *Investigating Classroom Talk* (2nd edn). Lewes: Falmer.

EPPI (2003) *Supporting Pupils with Emotional and Behavioural Difficulties (EBD) in Mainstream Primary Schools: a Systematic Review of Recent Research on Strategy Effectiveness (1999–2000).* London: EPPI Centre, University of London Institute of Education.

Foster, P. (1999) '"Never mind the quality, feel the impact": A methodological assessment of teacher research sponsored by the Teacher Training Agency', *British Journal of Educational Studies,* 47 (4): 390–8.

Homan, R. (2001) 'The principle of assumed consent: the ethics of gatekeeping', *Journal of Philosophy of Education,* 35 (3): 329–43.

Hurley, J.C. and Underwood, M.K. (2002) 'Children's understanding of their research rights before and after debriefing: Informed assent, confidentiality and stopping participation', *Child Development,* 73: 132–43.

Kellett, M. and Nind, M. (2001) 'Ethics in quasi-experimental research on people with severe learning disabilities: Dilemmas and compromises', *British Journal of Learning Disabilities,* 29: 51–5.

Lange-Kuttner, C. and Edelstein, W. (1995) 'The contribution of social factors to the development of graphic competence', in C. Lange-Kuttner and G.V. Thomas (eds), *Drawing and Looking.* London: Harvester Wheatsheaf. pp. 159–72.

Lewis, A. (2001) 'Reflections on interviewing children and young people as a method of inquiry in exploring their perspectives on inclusion', *Journal of Research in Special Educational Needs,* 1 (3): ejournal. www.nasen.uk.com/ejournal.

Lewis, A. (2002) 'Accessing, through research interviews, the views of children with difficulties in learning', *Support for Learning,* 17 (3): 110–16.

Lewis A. (2004) '"And when did you last see your father?" Exploring the views of children with learning difficulties/disabilities', *British Journal of Special Education,* 3 (1): 4–10.

Lindsay, G. (2000) 'Researching children's perspectives: ethical issues', in A. Lewis and G. Lindsay (eds), *Researching Children's Perspectives.* Buckingham: Open University Press. pp. 1–20.

Masson, J. (2000) 'Researching children's perspectives: legal issues', in A. Lewis and
   G. Lindsay (eds), *Researching Children's Perspectives*. Buckingham: Open University
   Press. pp. 34–44.

Masson, J. (2001). *Ethical Issues from a Legal Perspective*. Paper presented at the
   seminar series 'Methodological issues in interviewing children and young people with learning difficulties', Funded by ESRC 2001–3, School of Education, University of Birmingham.

McCarthy, M. (1998) 'Interviewing people with learning disabilities about sensitive
   topics: A discussion of ethical issues', *British Journal of Learning Disabilities, 26*: 140–45.

Moore, M. and Beazeley, S. (1998) *Researching Disability Issues*. Buckingham: Open
   University Press.

Morrow, V. and Richards, M. (1996) 'The ethics of social research with children: An
   overview', *Children and Society, 10*: 90–105.

Nesbitt, E. (2000) 'Researching 8–13 year olds' experience of religion', in A. Lewis and
   G. Lindsay (eds), *Researching Children's Perspectives*. Buckingham: Open University
   Press. pp. 135–49.

Oakley, M. (2000) 'Children and young people and care proceedings', in A. Lewis and
   G. Lindsay (eds), *Researching Children's Perspectives*. Buckingham: Open University
   press. pp. 73–85.

Porter, J., Ouvry, C. Morgan, M. and Towry, C. (2001) 'Interpreting the communication
   of people with profound and multiple learning difficulties, *British Journal of Learning
   Disabilities, 29* (1): 12–16.

Pring, R. (2000) *Philosophy of Educational Research*. London: Continuum.

Thomas, G.V. and Silk, A.M. (1990) *An Introduction to the Psychology of Children's
   Drawings*. Hemel Hempstead: Harvester Wheatsheaf.

Ward, L. (1996). *Seen and Heard: Involving Disabled Children and Young People in
   Research and Development Projects*. York: Joseph Rowntree Foundation.

Ware, J. (submitted) 'Interviewing people with profound and multiple learning difficulties –
   contextual issues.

Ware, J. (personal communication).

Wise, S. and Upton, G. (1998) 'The perceptions of pupils with emotional and behavioural
   difficulties of their mainstream schooling', *Emotional and Behavioural Difficulties,
   3* (3): 3–12.

Wolff, S. (1995) *Loners: The Life Path of Unusual Children*. London, Routledge.

25

Attention Deficit Hyperactivity Disorder: Concerns and Issues

MARJORIE MONTAGUE AND
MARCELO CASTRO

Before we embark on a discussion of the concerns and issues surrounding attention deficit hyperactivity disorder (ADHD), it seems important to provide some background on the changes that have occurred over the past two decades in the conceptualization of the disorder. It is generally agreed that the estimated prevalence rate of ADHD among school-aged children is between 3 percent and 5 percent. Research supports this prevalence rate, although studies vary considerably in the percentages reported (APA, 1994; Barkley, 1998). Safer and Malever's study (2000) reported that about 3 percent of school children in Maryland were on medication for ADHD. Given that not all diagnosed children are on medication, the percentage of children with ADHD probably exceeds that rate. Additionally, ADHD is no longer considered a childhood disorder. Indeed, longitudinal studies have found that approximately 75 percent of children continue to display symptoms of ADHD into adulthood (for example, Biederman et al., 1996). Because ADHD is a lifelong condition that is manifested differently over the various developmental stages, consideration must be given to differential diagnosis and treatment.

Definitions and diagnostic criteria have been re-examined several times since symptoms were first noted in the second edition of the *Diagnostic and Statistical Manual of Mental Disorders* (DSM-II) (APA, 1968) as hyperactive-impulsive behavior. The condition was renamed 'attention deficit disorder' (ADD) when the DSM-III was published (APA, 1980). The DSM-III actually specified two distinct subtypes based on the presence (ADDH) or absence (ADDnoH) of hyperactivity. The 1987 revision, the DSM-III-R (APA, 1987), eliminated the distinction between ADD with and without hyperactivity, but maintained the three primary behavioral indicators: inattention, impulsivity, and hyperactivity. This edition again changed the term to be more inclusive, that is, ADHD. In the fourth and latest edition of the manual, the DSM-IV (APA, 1994), extensive national field trials and consensus meetings delineated three subtypes of ADHD: ADHD – predominately inattentive type; ADHD – predominately hyperactive-impulsive type; and ADHD – combined type. Because there is no established educational definition of ADHD, general and special educators must rely on the DSM-IV criteria and its latest revision (DSM-IV-TR, 2000) for identifying individuals with ADHD. The primary characteristics of ADHD continue to be inattention, hyperactivity, and impulsivity. Behavioral characteristics associated with these three constructs are listed in the DSM-IV.

Inattention means that an individual has difficulty sustaining attention when effort is required. Behaviors associated with inattention include carelessness, difficulty staying on task, not listening, disorganization, failure to finish schoolwork and chores, distractibility, losing things, and forgetfulness. Inattention may be less or more noticeable depending on contextual factors. Children with ADHD seem to have an attentional bias toward novelty because they generally respond favorably to novel and stimulating activities and frequently are able to sustain attention in these situations. Hyperactivity implies an inordinate activity level. Impulsive individuals seem unable to control their behaviors and appear to act without thinking. Impulsivity implies a problem with self-regulation. Hyperactive and impulsive behaviors include fidgeting and squirming, constant movement, inability to stay seated for a reasonable time, talking excessively, difficulty waiting or taking turns, and interrupting and intruding on others.

For diagnosis of ADHD, not only must individuals display at least six of the symptoms associated with either inattention and/or impulsivity/hyperactivity, but they must also meet the following criteria regarding persistence, time of onset, pervasiveness, and severity. Persistence relates to the length of sustained time an individual has exhibited symptoms of inattention and/or hyperactivity-impulsivity. The DSM-IV requires that symptoms be present for at least six months. Age of onset refers to the age of the individual at which the behaviors were first evident. The DSM-IV states that an individual must have displayed symptoms prior to seven years of age. Pervasiveness refers to the number of settings and situations in which the symptoms are evident. The DSM-IV requires that symptoms be severe enough to cause clinically significant problems for individuals in at least two settings (for example, school, home, and/or work situations). That is, the symptoms must seriously impede functioning in a developmentally appropriate manner academically, socially, personally, or occupationally and must not be due to other developmental or personality disorders.

Thus, for diagnosis of ADHD, individuals must display at least six of the symptoms of inattention and/or display at least six of the symptoms of hyperactivity/impulsivity for at least six months in a developmentally inappropriate manner. There are three possible subtypes:

- For the ADHD: Predominately Inattentive Type, individuals will display symptoms of inattention but display less than six of the hyperactivity/impulsivity symptoms.
- For the ADHD: Predominately Hyperactive-Impulsive Type, individuals will display symptoms of hyperactivity/impulsivity but display less than six of the inattention symptoms.
- For the ADHD: Combined Type, individuals will display at least six symptoms of inattention and six of the hyperactivity/impulsivity symptoms.

Individuals with the Combined Type or Predominantly Hyperactive-Impulsive Type have more behavioral and acting-out problems, whereas those with the Predominately Inattentive Type seem to have more learning problems and often qualify for learning disabilities programs.

School performance problems seem to characterize all students with ADHD because the behaviors associated with ADHD interfere with a student's productivity in school. In other words, students with ADHD may fail not because they cannot do their schoolwork, but because they do not finish their work and perform poorly on tests. In addition to production problems, students with ADHD may have learning and/or serious behavioral and emotional problems (McKinney et al., 1993). ADHD co-occurs with learning disabilities in at least 10 percent to 20 percent of the students when stringent identification criteria are applied for both conditions. Students with ADHD and learning disabilities are often described as inattentive and distractible, but not necessarily hyperactive. ADHD can also co-occur with behavioral disorders. Approximately 30 percent to 50 percent of these students are seriously aggressive, oppositionally defiant, or conduct disordered. Students with ADHD who have serious emotional problems may be withdrawn, depressed, moody, or anxious. Regardless of the type of ADHD diagnosis, research has consistently reported that students with ADHD are at significantly greater risk than other children for poor academic, social, personal, and vocational outcomes (Barkley, 1998).

ADHD is perhaps one of the most controversial developmental disorders because the prevalence rate seems to be on the increase, the etiology is not well understood, the diagnosis is subjective, and the treatments vary considerably. One of the most controversial issues is the use of stimulant medication with children (for example, Ritalin, Adderall). This chapter will examine issues related to theoretical perspectives and current thinking about ADHD, definitions and diagnostic criteria, assessment and identification procedures, and treatment/intervention practices.

THEORETICAL PERSPECTIVES

Neuropsychological model

Research at various centers, for example, The University of Virginia (UVA) Health Sciences Center (2002a), is accruing scientific evidence that ADHD is a biologically-based disorder and that the primary component of ADHD, attention, is a neuropsychological function having a strong genetic link.

Evidence supporting this view is accumulating through methodologies and procedures, including anatomic studies, positron emission scanning, blood flow analysis, clinical correlation studies, and ongoing twin studies. The UVA Center (2002b) has developed a neurochemical model of ADHD to more fully understand the effects of stimulant medication on the brain. Stimulants have been very effective in alleviating the symptoms of ADHD in many individuals. The thinking is that the medication modulates the release and levels of neurotransmitters such as dopamine, noradrenaline, and serotonin that are associated with various functions in the central nervous system (CNS) and that presumably operate in an interrelated manner.

Based on knowledge of the locales of the brain in which these neurotransmitters are influential in CNS functions, such as attention and response inhibition and the clinical variation among individuals with ADHD, researchers have posited a model of at least three ADHD subtypes that suggest differential origins and possible differential pharmacological interventions. At the risk of oversimplification, the first type, inattentive, is characterized by impaired sensory filtering and cognitive processing. Dopamine is the primary neurotransmitter for this function located in the right hemisphere of the brain and the prefrontal cortex. The second type, hyperaroused, is characterized by abnormal levels of activity. Located near the brain stem is the locus ceruleus, which is the norepinephrine containing nucleus that has as its primary function the inhibition of spontaneous activity. The third type, impulsive, is associated with the neurotransmitter, serotonin, which seemingly has to do with representing and integrating motivating events within a complex sensory network.

Barkley (1997) takes a different perspective by postulating ADHD not as an attentional disorder, but rather as a behavioral inhibition disorder. His theoretical perspective is also based on neuropsychological research, but his interpretation of the research and conceptualization of the disorder depart considerably from the traditional notions of ADHD as primarily an attention deficit. He contends that, particularly, neuroimaging studies in which certain parts of the brain are smaller and less active in individuals with ADHD support this perspective. The research strongly suggests the disorder results from abnormalities in the brain's prefrontal areas, particularly the right orbital-prefrontal region, the executive functioning region that presumably controls the ability to self-regulate. Barkley concluded that deficits in this region may indeed be the source of ADHD.

In Barkley's Hybrid Model of Executive Functions, the prefrontal lobe controls the ability to inhibit behavior, and this ability can be broken down into four separable executive functions: nonverbal working memory, verbal working memory, self-regulation of affect/motivation/arousal, and reconstitution. All four functions are connected with a motoric response system. A deficit in behavioral inhibition has to do with a delay in the ability to internalize behavior to the extent that an individual can reflect on the past, present, and future, that is, reflect on and appropriately inhibit present responses based on consequences of past responses and the anticipation of future activity. This inhibitory deficit leads to an inability to control goal-directed motor behavior. The executive functions are negatively affected, as evidenced by faulty neuropsychological functioning. Figure 25.1 lists the characteristics associated with each executive function.

Notwithstanding the differences in neuropsychological models, they serve to provide an explanation of the etiology of ADHD, the characteristic deficits associated with the affected regions of the brain, and the resulting behaviors that interfere with functioning in school, at work, and at home. Brain research promises not only explanations of behavior, however; it also offers the promise of neurologically-based prevention and intervention specific to the neurological dysfunctions that may be unique to an individual with ADHD.

Developmental model

In contrast to earlier views of ADHD as a condition affecting young children who typically 'outgrow' the symptoms, the current view is that

Nonverbal working memory

   1 Inability to hold events in mind
   2 Unable to manipulate or act on the events
   3 Impaired imitation of complex sequences
   4 Defective hindsight
   5 Defective forethought
   6 Poor anticipatory set
   7 Limited self-awareness
   8 Diminished sense of time
   9 Deficient nonverbal rule-governed behavior
  10 Delayed cross-temporal organization

Limited verbal working memory

   1 Reduced description and reflection
   2 Poor self-questioning/problem solving
   3 Deficient rule-governed behavior
   4 Less effective generation of rules/meta-rules
   5 Impaired reading comprehension
   6 Delayed moral reasoning

Immature self-regulation of affect/motivation/arousal

   1 Limited self-regulation of affect
   2 Less objectivity/social perspective taking
   3 Diminished self-regulation of motivation
   4 Poor self-regulation of arousal in the service of goal-directed action

Impaired reconstitution

   1 Limited analysis and synthesis of behavior
   2 Reduced verbal fluency/behavioral fluency
   3 Deficient rule creativity
   4 Less goal-directed behavioral creativity and diversity
   5 Less frequent use of behavioral simulations
   6 Immature syntax of behavior

Figure 25.1   *Adapted from Barkley's (1997) hybrid model of executive functions and the cognitive deficits associated with each function*

ADHD, more often than not, is a lifelong condition manifesting itself differently across the developmental stages (Barkley, 1997; Biederman, 1998; Levine, 1998; McGoey et al., 2002; Robin, 1998; Wagner, 2000; Wilens et al., 2002). About 75 percent of individuals with ADHD continue to display symptoms throughout adolescence and adulthood (Wilens et al., 2002). About 2 percent of individuals with ADHD are diagnosed during their preschool years (McGoey et al., 2002). Children identified during preschool typically display behaviors associated with hyperactivity and impulsivity. These children usually are detected early because their behavioral symptoms are so severe that clinic referral is warranted. Frequently, children identified early may also have oppositional behaviors that accompany the attentional difficulties. These children are often described as disorganized, careless, uncontrollable, noncompliant, defiant, and physically/verbally abusive to other children and adults. Intervention during the preschool years is critical for young children with ADHD because of the increasing academic and social demands when they enter school. Medication may be a necessary part of the treatment plan even at this early developmental stage. Recent multi-site studies have found medication to be the most important variable in multimodal treatment programs (Wilens et al., 2002). Additionally, these children are at serious risk for poor outcomes as adolescents or adults, including depression, substance use/abuse, and conduct disorder.

Although one of the diagnostic criteria is the manifestation of symptoms during early development, that is prior to seven years of age, some individuals with ADHD are not identified until early adolescence when they begin to fail in school. These youngsters may be described as predominately inattentive, and their symptoms may have been overlooked or compensated for during elementary school years. However, during middle and senior high school, students are expected to be responsible. Self-control or the ability to self-regulate behavior is associated developmentally with early adolescence. These individuals are characteristically described as inattentive, distractible, disorganized, and inefficient (Robin, 1998). These behaviors generally persist into adulthood and may adversely affect academic, social, and occupational performance. In sum, it is important to understand ADHD from a developmental perspective, as well as to understand the cognitive demands and expectations associated with each developmental stage.

ASSESSMENT AND IDENTIFICATION PROCEDURES

As with all childhood disorders, assessment of ADHD requires a comprehensive and systematic evaluation. Assessment procedures and diagnostic practices for identifying individuals with ADHD have undergone considerable scrutiny by both researchers and clinicians. Historically, the most controversial issue seems to be defining ADHD and reaching agreement on the core symptoms. Operationalizing severity and duration as well as pervasiveness also has been problematic. Furthermore, the social adjustment, cognitive abilities, and educational needs of youngsters with ADHD have been a primary concern, especially for educators (McKinney et al., 1993). More recently, as a result of new developments in the field, researchers have focused on crucial issues such as diagnostic classification and co-morbidity and assessment modality, that is the use of single versus multiple informants in clinical and school settings, and the use of appropriate assessment instruments and how these best fit current diagnostic categories.

Diagnostic classification and co-morbid disorders associated with ADHD

A major purpose of diagnostic classification is to organize a wide range of research and clinical findings into a manageable and coherent set of constructs that will facilitate communication about an individual. As previously indicated, in the text revision of the fourth edition of the DSM-IV-TR (APA, 2000), three subtypes of ADHD were delineated: ADHD-Predominately Inattentive Type; ADHD-Predominately Hyperactive/ Impulsive Type; and ADHD-Combined Type. The DSM-IV-TR specifies the number of symptoms that must be endorsed to establish diagnostic criteria. To reiterate, in order to make a diagnosis of the specific type, a clinician must assess the presence of six out of a possible nine inattention and/or hyperactivity/impulsivity symptoms for at least six months.

This diagnostic practice, although widely used, has been the object of much criticism. One main point of contention is that such an approach assigns all symptoms similar weight and provides clinicians and researchers with no guidance with respect to which symptoms or behaviors are the best indicators and predictors of ADHD. For example, the behavioral indicator 'often fails to give close attention to details or makes careless mistakes in schoolwork, work, or other activities' has the same weight as 'often has difficulties organizing tasks and activities' (APA, 2000). Another point of contention is how to gauge the severity of the symptoms. The DSM-IV-TR fails to address this question directly, leaving severity open to interpretation. Moreover, the symptoms must be present 'for at least 6 months to a degree that is maladaptive and inconsistent with developmental level' (APA, 2000: 83). The diagnostician is left with no assistance as to what degree of maladaptive behavior or to what extent a behavior should be discrepant from normal developmental level in order to meet diagnostic criteria. Power, Costigan et al. (2001) recommended operationalizing the criteria with emphasis on determining the frequency with which a behavior needs to occur in order to qualify as a symptom, the optimal number of endorsed symptoms (for predicting and for ruling out a diagnosis) for each informant, and the ideal approach to combine symptoms from different informants. A diagnostic approach that establishes a set of diagnostic criteria in order to establish the presence or absence of a disorder is commonly considered a categorical approach to assessment. With this approach, the individual either meets the necessary criteria for categorization or does not.

This approach is contrasted with the dimensional approach that provides an assessment of emotional, behavioral, and learning problems along a gamut from average to unusual. There is no clear delimitation of the boundary between normal and atypical behavior. In general, dimensional approaches specify the severity of the child's difficulties on each of several important dimensions of functioning which, in turn, have been operationalized by using such assessment tools as behavior rating scales. Two popular scales are the Child Behavior Checklist (CBCL) (Achenbach, 1991a) and the Behavior Assessment System for Children (BASC) (Reynolds and Kamphaus, 1992). This approach relies on the richness of the information obtained about the extent and type (for example, internalizing and externalizing) of behaviors and allows for more comprehensive treatment planning. In this respect, an increasing number of researchers and clinicians are approaching the assessment and treatment of ADHD in an integrated fashion where functional and diagnostic assessments are integrated to allow for flexible decisions based on student and family strengths and needs.

Another critical aspect of ADHD, in general, and of categorical approaches, in particular, is the issue of co-morbidity with other childhood psychiatric disorders. Prevalence rates vary considerably, but it is well acknowledged that ADHD co-exists with other disorders to a significant degree. For instance, Kaplan et al. (2001) estimated the overlap between ADHD and reading problems to be somewhere in the 35 percent to 50 percent range and to co-exist with language impairments in about 45 percent of the cases. In the same fashion, Sattler (2002) estimated that ADHD overlaps with learning disorders in the 25 percent to 50 percent range, 35 percent with oppositional defiant disorder (ODD), 26 percent with conduct disorder (CD), 18 percent with depressive disorder and 26 percent with anxiety disorder. The validity of the notion of co-morbidity has been questioned, and some have even suggested that in real life the discreet categories proposed by the DSM-IV-TR do not exist. In line with a dimensional approach to assessment, researchers have suggested using the term 'atypical brain development' as an underlying impairment that may manifest with different and often overlapping symptoms (Kaplan et al., 2001). While this position may seem appealing, one should not miss the importance of diagnostic classifications in facilitating a better understanding of an individual's behavior, in facilitating communication about the individual, and in providing a framework for assessment and treatment.

Assessment modality

In addition to inattention, impulsivity and hyperactivity, children with ADHD commonly display a number of associated deficits. Among these are cognitive deficits (for example, information processing, verbal ability, memory), adaptive functioning deficits (for example, social skills, self-monitoring, following rules), language deficits (for example, language development), emotional deficits (for example, appropriate emotional responses) and school performance deficits (for example, achievement, productivity) (Barkley and Murphy, 1998; Weyandt and Willis, 1994). The primary indicators of ADHD (inattention, impulsivity, and hyperactivity) in addition to often co-occurring problems make the assessment and diagnosis of ADHD a major challenge. Depending on the assessment instruments, the informants, and the clinician, different conclusions could be drawn and, in turn, different diagnoses could be made (Vaughn et al., 1997). For example, researchers have reported that individuals with ADHD-Combined Type tend to exhibit more mood disorders, such as anxiety and depression, than do individuals diagnosed with either of the other two subtypes (Faraone et al., 1998). Others have found no significant differences among subtypes on these dimensions (Eiraldi et al., 1997). However, there is substantial concurrence that externalizing behaviors, including oppositional behavior and aggression, tend to be more commonly associated with the combined type than with the other two types (Faraone et al., 1998; Morgan et al., 1996).

One explanation for these discrepancies is associated with the diversity of sources from which the reported data come. For example, while some clinicians base their ADHD diagnoses on information given solely by parents, others may use clinical interviews of children and teachers' ratings. To complicate matters further, data from multiple sources may vary with respect to the degree and severity of described behaviors (Crystal et al., 2001). Yet, for the most part, it is fairly well established that multiple source data generally yield more reliable diagnoses. Despite this knowledge, few research studies collect multiple source data (for example, parent and teacher ratings), and even in studies that do, other methodological problems, that is, small sample size, lead to questionable results (Crystal et al., 2001).

An exception is a large-scale study conducted by Crystal et al. (2001) with children in grades one through four (n = 453) to examine ADHD subtypes as defined by the DSM-IV. They used multiple reporting sources as well as multiple instruments. Parents and teachers completed questionnaires and were also interviewed. One would expect to find similar distribution as the field trials in the DSM-IV across ADHD subtypes. However, the results were quite different. Crystal et al. (2001) found that only 5 percent of the children in their study were classified as ADHD-Hyperactive/Impulsive Type as compared with 18 percent in the DSM field trials, and 52 percent as ADHD-Inattentive Type as compared with only 27 percent in the DSM field trials.

The researchers argued that these discrepancies could have been due to the sample demographics. That is, the study used a school-based sample as opposed to DSM's clinical sample; also, the children were primarily middle-class. Additionally, children under six years of age were not included, in contrast to the DSM-IV trials, which included a significant number of preschoolers (Crystal et al., 2001). This study supports the hypothesis that source (that is, parents, teachers, interviews with children) leads to measurement variance, which can produce significantly different descriptions of DSM-IV ADHD subtypes. Parents perceived the ADHD-Combined group as having significantly more conduct problems and hyperactivity than the ADHD-Inattentive group. Interestingly, teachers did not rate these subtypes differently. Parents also gave significantly higher ratings of inattention to the Combined group on the CBCL than to the Inattentive group, whereas these differences were not reflected on the BASC. Another interesting finding has to do with the differential roles of inattention and hyperactivity in distinguishing between a comparison group and children with ADHD. Previous studies indicated hyperactivity as an informative predictor of ADHD group membership (DuPaul, Anastopoulos et al., 1998). In this study, aggression rather than hyperactivity appeared to be the most salient distinction between the Combined and the Inattention subtypes (Crystal et al., 2001).

The implications of this study are threefold. First, misdiagnosis may continue to occur as long as stringent clinical criteria are used to diagnose non-clinical groups who may present a different range of behaviors. Second, at the very least, these results call attention to the importance and the caveats of using multi-method assessments in researching and classifying children. Finally, the study highlights the diagnostic difficulties in differentiating between different types of disruptive behaviors commonly associated with ADHD. In summary, the use of multiple informants and multiple instruments appears to be a relatively reliable yet not faultless method to assess ADHD. While researchers seem to agree on this, more studies are needed to clarify the equivocal findings and to assist clinicians in making appropriate diagnoses that impact heavily on treatment decisions.

Assessment instruments

The DSM-IV stipulates that in making decisions when diagnosing ADHD it is important to consider the child's functioning in multiple settings, more specifically in the school and home settings; however, the criteria do not specify how to collect this information or how to use the information collected for decision-making purposes. Moreover, a problem with many of the instruments used in the assessment of ADHD is that the factor structure and item content of the subscales are not consistent with the DSM-IV diagnostic criteria (Power, Costigan et al., 2001).

Assessment procedures typically include interviews, behavioral observations, psychological tests and rating scales. Parent, child, and teacher interviews generally provide information about the age of onset of the disorder, the pervasiveness of the child's difficulties, the severity of symptoms across settings, information about factors that interfere with functioning in various settings (that is, home and school), and information about how the child perceives his or her own behavior. Observations are vital since these give the clinician information about antecedents and consequences of disruptive behavior across settings, a requirement for diagnosis according to the DSM-IV criteria. Even though there are no specific tests or test batteries for determining the diagnosis of ADHD, most clinicians include intelligence tests, achievement tests, memory tests and one or more neuropsychological tests typically used to measure attention and/or impulsivity. Intelligence and achievement tests are recommended to assess cognitive strengths and weaknesses as well as areas of academic achievement that may be affected by the disorder. Rating scales are useful in obtaining information from parents, children and teachers. These are easy to administer as well as time efficient and provide the clinician with multiple points of view that may help identify appropriate and inappropriate behaviors, including those associated with ADHD.

In general, there are two groups of scales: broad-band and narrow-band. Broad-band scales, such as the CBCL (Achenbach, 1991b) and the BASC (Reynolds and Kamphaus, 1992), survey a wide spectrum of symptoms and behaviors (for example, externalizing, internalizing). Narrow-band scales, such as the Conner's Rating Scales – Revised (Conners, 1997) and the ADHD Rating Scales (DuPaul, Power et al., 1998), are designed to measure behaviors associated with specific disorders (for example, inattentiveness, depression) (Sattler, 2002).

It should be emphasized that nearly all of these scales have parent and teacher versions, thus allowing for multi-setting assessment. Also, the information provided by the broad-band scales in general tends to be quite similar. For instance, a study of convergent and criterion-related validity of the BASC-Parent Rating Scale (BASC-PRS) as compared to the CBCL 4-18 suggested that both instruments are comparable in predicting membership in diagnostic grouping (for example, no diagnosis, ADHD only, and ADHD with a co-morbid externalizing disorder) (Doyle et al., 1997).

In spite of the predictive validity of these widely used broad-band scales, the quandary surrounding their lack of direct relation with the DSM-IV ADHD diagnostic criteria remains unsettled. The ADHD Rating

Scale-IV (DuPaul, Power et al., 1998) provides a tentative answer to this need, since it has been developed for the specific purpose of providing parent and teacher ratings about ADHD as delineated in the DSM-IV. Power and Eiraldi (2001) investigated strategies for combining inattention and hyperactivity-impulsivity symptoms as best predictors of ADHD diagnosis. The researchers concluded that a categorical approach to diagnosis such as the one recommended in the DSM-IV (that is, use of a fixed cut-off point such as six or more symptoms) does not seem to be the best strategy for making diagnostic decisions. Rather, a better approach could be based on who provides the information (that is, parent, teacher or both) and on whether the purpose of the assessment is to conduct a screening or a full diagnostic evaluation. Also, an optimal approach should aggregate symptoms in the order in which they best predict ADHD as opposed to using any combination of symptoms as suggested in the DSM-IV (Power and Eiraldi, 2001). In short, because the instruments for assessing ADHD are less than perfect and clinical judgment is always involved, caution is essential when assessing for and determining the presence of ADHD in individuals.

TREATMENT/INTERVENTION PRACTICES

Because of the neurobiological nature of ADHD and its impact on individuals across situations and settings, interventions tend to be both nonpharmacological and pharmacological. Nonpharmacological treatment plans typically include a range of strategies, including educational programs and accommodation plans, positive behavior management programs, individual or group counseling, family and parent education, and social skills training. A shift in thinking has occurred over the past few years regarding the design of comprehensive treatment plans for individuals with ADHD. First, professional organizations such as the American Academy of Pediatrics (AAP, 1987) as well as researchers, psychologists, and counselors advocate a multimethod, multi-informant, and multidisciplinary approach to treatment. Second, rather than focus on the individual's deficits, emphasis is placed on identifying the strengths of an individual and building on those strengths. School accommodation plans should be multifaceted with specific strategies for ensuring that teachers and other school staff communicate regularly with parents about their children's program and that a similar reinforcement program is operating at home. Parent involvement is vital to the overall success of a comprehensive treatment program for youngsters with ADHD.

Pharmacological treatments, that is, stimulants, antidepressants, and antihypertensives, are frequently a prime component of a comprehensive intervention program. Over the years, the use of medication, especially with young children, has been highly controversial. However, research consistently supports the beneficial effects of medication with both children and adults with ADHD (Wilens et al., 2002). A recently completed multisite, multi-modal national treatment study conducted with 7- and 9-year-old children suggested that medication is more effective than behavior treatment and as effective as the combination of medication and behavior treatment (The MTA Cooperative Group, 1999a, 1999b). Stimulant medications (for example, Ritalin, Adderall) appear to be the most effective pharmacological treatment with about 80 percent of individuals responding well, followed by tricyclic antidepressants (TCAs) with about 60 percent responding favorably, and bupropion and antihypertensives each with about 55 percent success rate (Wilens et al., 2002). Stimulants include methylphenidate (Ritalin, Concerta, Metadate, and so on), amphetamine (Dexedrine, Adderall), and permoline (Cylert). Until recently, only short-acting medications in which the peaking occurred between one and two hours after administration were available. Extended and sustained release medications are now available and last between six and 12 hours. Stimulants should be introduced with low doses and increased as needed, with close medical and parental supervision. Side effects must be noted and understood by parents, and behavioral monitoring is critical to determine the effects of treatment. Antidepressants (for example, Tofanil, Norpramine, Pamelor) are the second choice if the individual is intolerant of stimulants. Generally, antidepressants require anywhere from two to four weeks for maximum effect to occur. The antihypertensives clonidine and guanfacine have been used to treat hyperactivity and impulsivity symptoms and side effects such as tics, aggression, and sleep disturbances especially in young children. Medication combinations may be effective for individuals who either do not respond to typically prescribed medications or are intolerant. Again, close and ongoing monitoring of the effects of any medication should be the foundation of the medication treatment component of the plan.

As a consequence of numerous studies on the effects of medication, its use has increased at a phenomenal pace. The past decade has seen not only a rapid increase in the identification of individuals with ADHD (Davison, 2001), but also large increases in the use of medication with students, especially those between 15 and 19 and between two and four years old (Zito et al., 2000). At the same time, caveats and recommendations regarding the use of medication have been issued by several professional organizations. For example, the position of the National Association of School Psychologists (NASP, 1995) is that instructional and behavioral interventions should be tried out before medication is introduced into the treatment plan, behavioral monitoring should be systematically designed to include baseline conditions and all medication trials to determine medication effects, and the plan should emphasize communication among all responsible parties including parents and school, medical, and other therapeutic personnel. AAP stressed the importance of having pediatricians work closely with parents and school staff to provide optimal curricular and environmental conditions (AAP, 2000). Collaboration and cooperation among school, home, and community agencies serving individuals with ADHD and their families should be the cornerstone of the intervention program.

CONCLUSION

In conclusion, there remain many unresolved issues and concerns in understanding, assessing, and treating individuals with ADHD. This chapter reviewed several of these issues from an historical and current perspective. With advances in technology, particularly, future research should continue to provide additional insight into the condition and further our understanding of its etiology as well as its assessment, identification, and treatment.

REFERENCES

Achenbach, T.M. (1991a) *Manual for the Child Behavior Checklist/4–18 and 1991 Profile.* Burlington, VT: University of Vermont, Department of Psychiatry.

Achenbach, T.M. (1991b) *Manual for the Youth Self-report and 1991 Profile.* Burlington, VT: University of Vermont, Department of Psychiatry.

American Academy of Pediatrics. (1987) 'Medication for children with an Attention Deficit Disorder', *Pediatrics'*, 80: 758–60.

American Psychiatric Association (1968) *Diagnostic and Statistical Manual of Mental Disorders* (2nd edn, DSM-II). Washington, DC: Author.

American Psychiatric Association (1980) *Diagnostic and Statistical Manual of Mental Disorders* (3rd edn, DSM-III). Washington, DC: Author.

American Psychiatric Association (1987). *Diagnostic and Statistical Manual of Mental Disorders* (3rd edn, rev., DSM-III-R). Washington, DC: Author.

American Psychiatric Association (1994) *Diagnostic and Statistical Manual of Mental Disorders* (4th edn, DSM-IV). Washington, DC: Author.

American Psychiatric Association (2000) *Diagnostic and Statistical Manual of Mental Disorders* (DSM-IV-Text Revision). Washington, DC: Author.

Barkley, R.A. (1997) *ADHD and the Nature of Self-control.* New York: Guilford.

Barkley, R.A. (1998) *Attention-Deficit/Hyperactivity Disorder: A Handbook for diagnosis and Treatment* (2nd edn). New York: Guilford.

Barkley, R.A. and Murphy, K.R. (1998) *Attention-Deficit Hyperactivity Disorder: A Clinical Workbook.* New York: Guilford.

Biederman, J., Faraone, S.V., Taylor, A., Sienna, M., Williamson S. and Fine, C. (1998) 'Diagnostic continuity between child and adolescent ADHD: Findings from a longitudinal clinical sample', *Journal of the American Academy of Child and Adolescent Psychiatry*, 37 (3): 305–13.

Biederman, J., Faraone, S., Milberger, S., Curtis, S., Chen, L., Marrs, A., Quellette, C., Moore, P. and Spencer, T. (1996) 'Predictors of persistence and remission of ADHD into adolescence: Results from a four-year prospective follow-up study', *Journal of the American Academy of Child and Adolescent Psychiatry*, 35: 343–51.

Conners, C.K. (1997) *Manual for the Conner's Rating Scales – Revised*. North Tonawanda, NY: Multi-Health Systems.

Crystal, D.S., Ostrander, R., Chen, R.S. and August, G.J. (2001) 'Multimethod assessment of psychopathology among DSM-IV subtypes of children with attention deficit hyperactivity disorder: Self, parent and teacher reports', *Journal of Abnormal Child Psychology*, 29: 189–202.

Davison, J.C. (2001) 'Attention deficit/hyperactivity disorder: Perspectives of participants in the identification and treatment process', *Journal of Educational Thought*, 35: 227–47.

Doyle, A., Ostrander, R., Skare, S., Crosby, R.D. and August, G.J. (1997) 'Convergent and criterion-related validity of the behavior assessment system for children–parent rating scale', *Journal of Clinical Child Psychology*, 26: 276–84.

DuPaul, G.J., Anastopoulos, A.D., Power, T.J., Reid, R., Ikeda, M.J. and McGoey, K.E. (1998) 'Parent ratings of attention deficit hyperactivity disorder symptoms: Factor structure and normative data', *Journal of Psychopathology and Behavioral Assessment*, 20: 83–102.

DuPaul, G.J., Power, T.J., Anastopoulos, A.D. and Reid, R. (1998) *ADHD Rating Scale-IV: Checklists, Norms and Clinical Interpretation*. New York: Guilford.

Eiraldi, R.B., Power, T.J. and Neru, C.M. (1997) 'Patterns of comorbidity associated with subtypes of attention-deficit hyperactivity among 6- to 12-year old children', *Journal of the American Academy of Child and Adolescent Psychiatry*, 35: 325–33.

Faraone, S.V., Biederman, J., Weber, W. and Russell, R.L. (1998) 'Psychiatric, neuropsychological, and psychosocial features of DSM-IV subtypes of attention deficit hyperactivity disorder: Results from a clinically referred sample', *Journal of the American Academy of Child and Adolescent Psychiatry*, 37: 185–93.

Kaplan, B.J., Dewey, D.M., Crawford, S.G. and Wilson, B.N. (2001) 'The term comorbidity is of questionable value in reference to developmental disorders: Data and theory', *Journal of Learning Disabilities*, 6: 555–65.

Levine, M.D. (1998) *Developmental Variations and Learning Disorders* (2nd edn). Cambridge, MA: Educators Publishing Service.

McGoey, K.E., Eckert, T.L., and DuPaul, G.J. (2002) 'Early intervention for preschool-age children with ADHD: A literature review', *Journal of Emotional and Behavioral Disorders*, 10: 14–28.

McKinney, J.D., Montague, M. and Hocutt, A.M. (1993) 'Educational assessment of students with attention deficit disorder', *Exceptional Children*, 60: 125–31.

Morgan, A., Hynd, G., Riccio, C. and Hall, J. (1996) 'Validity of DSM-IV ADHD predominately inattentive and combined types: Relationship to previous DSM diagnoses/subtypes differences', *Journal of the American Academy of Child and Adolescent Psychiatry*, 35: 333–49.

MTA Cooperative Group (1999a) 'A 14-month randomized clinical trial of treatment strategies for attention deficit/hyperactivity disorder', *Archives of General Psychiatry*, 56: 1073–86.

MTA Cooperative Group (1999b) 'Moderators and mediators of treatment response for children with attention deficit/hyperactivity disorder', *Archives of General Psychiatry*, 56: 1088–96.

National Association of School Psychologists (1995) 'Students with attention deficits', in A. Thomas and J. Grimes (eds), *Best Practices in School Psychology-III*. Washington, DC: Author. pp. 12–18.

Power, T.J., Costigan, T.E., Leff, S.S., Eiraldi, R.B. and Landau, S. (2001) 'Assessing ADHD across settings: Contributions of behavioral assessment to categorical decision making', *Journal of Clinical Child Psychology*, 30: 399–412.

Power, T.J. and Eiraldi, R.B. (2001) 'Educational and psychiatric classification systems', in E.S. Shapiro and T.R. Kratochwill (eds), *Behavioral Assessment in Schools: Theory, Research and Clinical Foundations* (2nd edn). New York: Guilford. pp. 464–88.

Reynolds, C.R. and Kamphaus, R.W. (1992) *BASC: Behavior Assessment System for Children: Manual.* Circle Pines, MN: American Guidance Service.

Robin, A.L. (1998) *ADHD in Adolescents: Diagnosis and Treatment.* New York: Guilford.

Safer, D.J. and Malever, M. (2000) 'Stimulant treatment in Maryland public schools', *Pediatrics*, 106: 533–9.

Sattler, J. (2002) *Assessment of Children: Behavioral and Clinical Applications* (4th edn). San Diego, CA: Sattler.

University of Virginia Health Sciences Center Children's Medical Center (2002a) *Attention Deficit Hyperactivity Disorder.* Accessed 11 December from http://www.med.virginia.edu/medicine/clinical/pediatrics/devbeh/adhdlin/etiology.html

University of Virginia Health Sciences Center Children's Medical Center (2002b) *Attention Deficit Hyperactivity Disorder.* Accessed 11 December from http://www.med.virginia.edu/medicine/clinical/pediatrics/devbeh/adhdlin/neurotra.html

Vaughn, M.L., Riccio, C.A., Hynd, G.W. and Hall, J. (1997) 'Diagnosing ADHD (Predominately inattentive and combined type subtypes): Discriminant validity of the Behavior Assessment System for Children and the Achenbach Parent and Teacher Rating Scales', *Journal of Clinical Child Psychology*, 26: 349–57.

Wagner, B.J. (2000) 'Attention deficit hyperactivity disorder: Current concepts and underlying mechanisms', *Journal of Child and Adolescent Psychiatric Nursing*, 13: 113–24.

Weyandt, L.L. and Willis, W.G. (1994) 'Executive functions in school-aged children: Potential efficacy of tasks in discriminating clinical groups', *Developmental Neuropsychology*, 10: 27–38.

Wilens, T.E., Biederman, J. and Spencer, T.J. (2002) 'Attention deficity/hyperactivity disorder across the lifespan', *Annual Review of Medicine*, 53: 113–31.

Zito, J.M., Safer, D.J., dosReis, S., Gardner, J.F., Boles, M. and Lynch, F. (2000) 'Trends in the prescribing of psychotropic medications to preschoolers', *Journal of the American Medical Association*, 283: 1025–30.

26

Do Teacher Training Courses Prepare Us for the Challenge of Students Experiencing EBD?

CHRISTOPHER BLAKE

A QUESTION OF QUANTITY AND QUALITY

Currently teacher recruitment, preparation and retention in the United States are under acute stress. In terms of the numbers entering and staying within the profession, the situation has become critical across most states and urban centers, with teacher shortages a common phenomenon at the start of each school semester. But demographics alone hide a more complex picture. In certain subjects, such as elementary teaching and social studies, graduates compete for teaching positions in most states. For other subjects the contrary is true, with the label of 'acute shortage' being applied to the availability of teachers of certain subjects by state and federal agencies with increasing frequency. Special education belongs to this category, and across the country's school districts the availability of teaching opportunities in special education grows longer, just as the line of students with individualized educational plans (IEP) does so too. Today, more than 6 million students with disabilities are educated in the United States, comprising 11 percent of the total public school enrollment (Brodsky, 2001). Compounded with this demographic shift is the issue of retention. National data and local experience shows that whilst the numbers entering the profession remain level, the demand for teachers is increasing just at the point where retention of teachers beyond the initial five-year post-certification period is at a crisis level.

That crisis is discernible in terms of the shrinking reality of the professional teaching 'career'. The average classroom life of a special education teacher is now eight years, the lowest duration of the past generation, and the pressure continues downward with attrition from the profession across all subjects, and particularly the shortage areas. Put simply, states are faced with large numbers of early leavers from the profession at an unsustainable rate. This context to the special education is both shared and particular. It is shared because the whole system of teacher training is under scrutiny and change in the United States, with the Bush administration's 'No Child Left Behind' Act of 2001 (USDOE, 2001) providing a federal framework that coheres statewide norms of testing in recent decades with fiscal consequences to educational performance, thus ratcheting the temperature of the accountability climate even higher. It is also particular, because special education faces an unusual tension between the forces of supply and demand, since the demand for special education teachers is heightened through increasing nationwide rates of student IEP identifications at the same time that supply is short.

In this context if might appear odd to focus on issues of training quality when examining the work of teachers of students with serious emotional and behavioral disturbance (EBD) in the United States. It might seem more pertinent to ask whether the quantity rather than the quality of teachers might be the more pressing need. Such reasoning, though, would miss the crux that teacher recruitment and retention is widely connected to the issue of training. There is an emerging consensus from policy-makers, legislators and the profession at large that if the teacher shortage crisis is to be addressed, then questions of training are as much at the heart of any solution as others of working conditions and salaries. Clearly, a nexus of issues lies at the center of the problem, and it would be naïve to consider that employment conditions are not relevant. Indeed, the teacher shortage is creating working environments that directly impact on the quality of learning for students and the conditions of work for those teaching them. Nonetheless, the main professional thrust toward equipping teachers for working with EBD students is to be found in the question of teacher quality and professional development, rather than simply in numbers of trainees getting hired in the field, and this chapter will focus on how teacher preparation might be the clue to both the quantity and quality of special education teachers who work with EBD students. It will do so first in showing how special education has appropriated the same ideology of educational standards that is prevalent in the United States and other Western educational systems. Second, through an examination of ethnographic data obtained in a contemporary research study of special educators, the professional voice of teachers of EBD students in the field will be heard and examined for insights into training needs. Although this data is focused on teachers' voices, it also provides insights into student experiences to which the reform agenda typically turns a deaf ear. From this it will be suggested that an ecological model of professional development is needed before we can come to grips with the changing needs of EBD student learning in modern America as well as the systemic problem of supply and demand of a highly-qualified and competent profession.

RAISING THE STANDARD

The reform agenda in American education, so powerfully epitomized in the Reagan era by the National Commission's *A Nation At Risk* report (1984), and resurrected by the Bush administration in the 'No Child Left Behind' Act (2001), is borne out of a deep distrust of professional autonomy and a conviction of the failing performance of public education (Berliner and Biddle, 1997; Blake, 1999). This ideological force has provided the context for a dominant legislative reform agenda based on twin motifs of standardized control of curriculum management, and entrepreneurial fiscal theory for liberalizing the scope and operations of the market economy within public education. For special educators this feature of modern professional life has been embodied in the organization and influence of the Council for Exceptional Children (CEC), a broad-based professional body that has been accepted as the defining voice and controlling agency for special education at the national level by the federally-mandated accreditation agency for teacher preparation, the National Council for the Accreditation of Teacher Education (NCATE). Together, NCATE and CEC have set the agenda and defined the direction for teacher preparation of special educators.

But aside from bureaucratic and accountability functions, CEC has also maintained a strong sense of professional voice and purpose. By addressing both the problems of special education and a road map to their solution, it has shown itself more willing to identify the real problems facing teachers. A prime example is its *Bright Futures* initiative (2000), which argued that any raising of standards for teacher preparation in special education was meaningless unless the end environment, the classroom, was a place where professionalism could thrive. Significantly, and in contrast to many critics of education, CEC argued that:

... the problem rests not with the special education teachers but with a system that forces them to carry high caseloads and to spend their time completing overwhelming amounts of paperwork among other problems. ... 68% of special education teachers report that they spend less than two hours per week in individualized instruction ... (2000: 1)

The *Bright Futures* report saw the problem both in terms of the conditions of work and the training process that is inadequate for the purpose of attracting quality teachers who might perform well under such conditions. Several key indicators of sub-standard conditions are notable. The growing caseload of students with an IEP, and the inadequate differentiation of individualized needs, headed the CEC list, with the report noting that in resource rooms teachers have a national average of 38 students per class, and in self-contained classrooms an average caseload of 18. The effect is to undermine a key standard of professional practice, collaboration between special and regular educator, and to maintain special education teachers in environments where neither professional collaboration nor administrative and district support is readily experienced at the necessary levels. The net effect is a disqualified or under-qualified teaching force where 30,000 teachers without appropriate licenses are teaching students of special needs. Into this mix, the issue of EBD students is yet another example of the mismatch between supply and demand, with the lack of correlation between EBD-qualified teachers and actual students highlighting the personnel deficiency.

Deficiency is arguably a measured term within the context of data regarding special education and EDB-qualified personnel in the field. According to Billingsley's (2002) report for the US Office of Special Education Programs, the issue of certification is acutely problematic. In special education only 63 percent of beginning teachers are formally qualified for their assignments in schools. Of the remaining 37 percent who lack the appropriate credentials, 5 percent are certified out of field (for example, in another subject or grade level), 20 percent hold emergency certificates, and 4 percent do not hold any teaching certificate. The picture is bleaker still for teachers of EBD students, with over half of beginning teachers of EBD students not fully certified for their positions. This exacerbated credential deficiency for EBD work is reflected in the training routes teachers take to gain their qualifications. Typically, special education has embraced more broadly the variety of routes by which states license teachers for the classroom. Those certification routes have centered variously on Bachelor's degree programs, Master's degree programs, continuing professional development programs, 5th year programs and, more controversially, alternative certification programs of an apprentice-type nature, such as emergency certificate programs and teacher residency programs.

These alternative programs provide a significant route for beginning teachers of EBD students, over and above other special education fields, with 27 percent of beginning EBD students gaining their credentials through alternative routes. The figure is only 10 percent for all special education credentials gained from alternative programs. Of particular noteworthiness is Billingsley's claim that regular preservice approved programs, such as the traditional baccalaureate route, receive extremely high ratings from program completers in terms of teacher satisfaction, with 18 percent regarding their training as *exceptional* and 66 percent rating it as either *good* or *very good*. This approval rating of the conventional means to training suggests a greater level of training satisfaction by non-EDB special education teachers and begs the question of why the approval ratings for the EDB-related alternative routes are lower.

When the *Bright Futures* report examined the work experiences of beginning and early years teachers in the special education field, amongst its mass of findings there emerged consistent and intriguing data to suggest that the most evident and useful support mechanisms for teachers were informal in nature. Nearly all special educators reported that informal help from other colleagues (both regular and special educators) was available, and the kinds of support that were most valued by special education teachers were peer-mediated: 89 percent found such support helpful, with figures dropping by some 18 to 20 percent when other more formal kinds of support, such as in-service and mentoring programs, were considered. This stark illustration of dynamic peer culture as a vital and valued survival mechanism, over and above the institutionalized approaches to support, is an important clue to the problems of retention and attrition from the profession. Building on earlier research findings, the report shows that positive school climate, as created through peer relationships, is critical in retaining special educators, and that attrition from the profession is U-shaped, with the youngest and oldest teachers who are less connected to school culture being the most likely to leave.

Into this complex picture of teacher readiness for special education and EBD students, CEC has advanced a major initiative for standards-based training and performance for teachers. With the endorsement of the main accreditation agency, NCATE, this has ensured that CEC's reform goals have muscle behind them and can be expected to have nationwide impact and significance. Moreover, CEC is steering a cautious and prudent course between two positions that are often set in opposition: one, the simple call for 'raising standards', which for many critics is the euphemistic mantra of teacher-bashing and promulgation of the deficiency model view of education; the other, a teacher union discourse of inadequate funding and inferior working conditions for the profession. CEC has lent its ear and support to both positions, and thus sought to develop a package of professional development proposals that address ways in which teacher competence can meaningfully be achieved with professional vision at its core and in ways that meliorate the negative impact of poor environmental factors. In other words, CEC is looking to raise teacher training and performance through professional collaboration, rather than simply by raising the performance bar. This carrot and stick approach, which is notably more consensual than the Bush administration's policies in 'No Child Left Behind', presents a serious attempt to ground teacher performance in the cultural realities and possibilities of schools, and thus sets the accountability issue within a more broad ecological context. This is apparent on reviewing the kinds of standards for training and performance that CEC set out in its 2000 *Performance-Based Standards*.

In those standards CEC has replicated much of the NCATE approach to accreditation, and this represents a re-valuing of the importance of teacher competence as embodied in systematic program design and evaluation in the training of special education teachers. In short, the idea of special educators being under-qualified for their assignment or professionally developed via an ad hoc piecemeal approach is untenable under the new CEC standards, and the primacy of a coherent and data-driven training process is fundamental to CEC. Programs of training for special education will need to address standards in three areas: field experiences and clinical practices; assessment systems; and special education content standards. Importantly, CEC has avoided detailed performance criteria in preference for the kinds of experiences and competences that underpin the standards. For example, the clinical practice standards do not stipulate hours or weeks required in schools, but instead outline the required experiences, settings and collaborations that all beginning teachers must experience and become proficient within.

Two other aspects of CEC standards are especially noteworthy and herald some promise for EBD training. First, there is flexibility in CEC standards that reflect the diversity of programs and the different knowledge and skill bases within those programs. This means that EBD disorders, amongst others, are individually identified in the CEC knowledge and skill bases, so that programs preparing teachers for specific categories of special education are all brought under the standards umbrella. Second, the new standards are fewer in number and reflect a broader connection to the kinds of quality environments and teaching competences that ideally would feature in special education. The old standards, which were essentially connected to course content and quantification of knowledge, skills and experiences rather than evidence of proficiencies, have been reduced from 15 to 10. As importantly, they reflect an ecological understanding of best practices in special education.

The 10 standards themselves cover a broad range of proficiency areas: foundations; characteristics of learners; individual learning differences; instructional strategies; learning environments and social interactions; language; instructional planning; assessment; professional and ethical practice; and collaboration. Each of these standards is aligned to levels of proficiency at both the beginning and experienced teacher levels, so the standards are described in ways that reflect best practice for experienced teachers, but also the base-line knowledge and skills (both common core and specialty area, such as EBD) within each standard that is expected of the novice. This represents an attempt by CEC to subsume professional *development* within a standards-based approach and suggests a more sophisticated view of standards-based performance than simply a checklist of whether a particular proficiency is practiced or otherwise. It is an approach that is sensitive to the fact that beginning teachers are just that, beginning and not expert, and that there is more than one way of being proficient at a standard. An illustration of this can be seen in this extract from the ninth standard on *Professional and Ethical Practice*, which hitherto has focused on legal requirements and obligations but is now more robust and ecological in its perspective:

> Special educators engage in professional activities and participate in learning communities that benefit individuals with ELN, their families, colleagues, and their professional growth. Special educators view themselves as lifelong learners and regularly reflect on and adjust their practice. (CEC, 2000; Content Standard Nine)

This is a far cry from the kind of bureaucratic, legalistic administration of IEP and other policy implementations that typify many special education practices, and it shows an attempt to harness the professional vision, experience and voice of the classroom special educator. To that professional ethnography, namely the perspective of EBD teachers, the final section of this chapter will turn.

THE PROFESSIONAL VOICE

The *Survey of Beginning and Experienced EBD Teachers* (Blake, 2000) from Mount St. Mary's College, Maryland, has provided baseline and case study data and on the perspectives of 78 special education teachers across the United States who are beginning and advancing their careers with EBD students. This provides an ethnographic picture of the insights gained by practitioners themselves in learning to deal with EBD students and how that learning sheds light on the professional development process that prepares teachers for such work.

Amongst the survey and interview data, several research items have focused upon the training experiences of the teachers. Of the 78 participants to date, 68 percent completed their EBD training through baccalaureate or graduate approved programs, and 32 percent via alternative routes, which reflects closely the national trend described earlier. Within this population, however, a higher rate of teachers were working with the appropriate qualifications for EBD teaching than exists nationally, with 60 percent of the research population being formally credentialed in the EBD specialty field, as opposed to 48 percent nationally.

Of particular importance here is the study's findings regarding the EBD teachers' views of their training and its relationship to their work. Two survey and interview items asked the participants how their training helped them best for their current roles, and what omissions or limitations in their formal training would they rectify for the next generation of EBD teachers. Noteworthy was the consistent reporting by teachers of their valuing and high rating of their formal training, but a clear recognition that much of the practical knowledge needed for EBD work was gained solely through direct classroom experience or in specialty in-service or induction workshops. This ambiguous sense of the both the benefits and limitations of formal training was summed up well by Emily, a veteran EBD teacher of 20 years and now a county supervisor of special education in Oregon:

> Amazingly I had no field placements or internships prior to my first position, and things in that respect are much improved nowadays. For me ignorance was bliss!! Baptism by fire! But … in my current position as supervisor, I feel strongly that the SET program at Lennistown [pseudonym] does an excellent job preparing our interns for teaching SED [aka EBD]. (Blake, 2004)

For John, one of only six male teachers in the study and a beginning teacher in the state of New York, the manner of training was even more pertinent, since he was certified in another field and had come to EBD teaching lately. For him the broader ecological context to student lives was part of his psychology training, and this helped him to make sense of EBD students and their needs:

> As a Psychology major I had an internship with Big Brothers Big Sisters of Albany as a case manager. This position helped me to see many of the problems families go through, such as death, divorce and abuse. Many of the children in my classroom have a rocky family history or have no family at all. … From this I learned that myself and the rest of the staff are the students' 'family' and need to be a positive example because in many cases we are the only ones they have. (Blake, 2004)

John's ability to connect his Major to EBD was vital, but could not prepare him adequately for his assignment. In this context, and typical of the kind of alternative emergency provisions for teachers certified out of field,

John was given eight days of intensive training at Cornell University before starting work, in one area of EBD management known as Therapeutic Crisis Intervention (TCI). His comments reflect the general nature of many EBD beginning teachers, and particularly those who have not received training via a formal approved program dedicated to special education and EBD:

> The week of training was beneficial but I felt that it was an awful lot of information to be thrown at once. I had the feeling that I was in a vacuum and that once I was working with the children I was able to start to learn more from the everyday situations that would occur. I felt that what I learned [in TCI training] was necessary to do my job, I just wish they had waited until we had been working with children and before we had to soak up all this information and that other teachers could have done the training so that we could have used the same approach with the children. (Blake, 2004)

John's comments provide an important clue to the role of in-service education in establishing training partnerships that are vital to the successes of the EBD teacher. But beyond the formal structures that are required, the role of teacher agency is acutely significant in the professional development of EBD teachers. This final excerpt from Lakeesha, a five-year veteran special educator in Maryland, is revealing for its insight into the ways in which EBD teaching depends on the kinds of partnerships that are organic and diverse:

> The kinds of support you need are really varied. My classroom teacher is wonderful in dealing with specific problems, and we meet also as a team with the Reading specialist and the assistant principals weekly to discuss policy. But sometimes you have to try things that are more risky and that means different kinds of collaboration. I decided to open the doors to the grade four next door and to have the two classes intermingle at times. WOW! Parent objection was strong until we had several sessions with the front office and with the parents and convinced them that the children needed peer role models. That school still follows the inclusive model … and parents of 'normal' children were fighting to have them within that inclusion program! It became a status symbol to be a peer role model! Go figure! (Blake, 2004)

These remarks highlight the potency of EBD teaching as a change agent in the school community, forcing teachers, administrators, parents, and students alike to rethink their roles and relationships and to rely on a mix of formal knowledge and practitioner wisdom to make the choices that bring order and learning to the special education environment.

CONCLUSION – BEYOND TRAINING TO GROWTH

In a sense the relationship between the training process and the professional development of teachers has always been an artificial one, both for the regular and special educator. What the EBD environment does is force that artificiality into a starker light: there is little room in that context to mask any shortcomings of knowledge, skills and dispositions that are the hallmarks of a quality pedagogy.

Clearly, the data from the United States shows a mixed picture. On the one hand, there is a lack of human and environment resources in most states and a staffing shortage that approaches crisis proportions: many teachers are simply under-qualified for the task that faces them in dealing with EBD students. On the other hand, teacher innovations and the recognition by the educational establishment of the need for rigorous support of special educators heralds the promise of systematic implementation of ongoing developmental support for both teachers and students. This is most visible in the national standards being implemented, and more organically within other initiatives that CEC has launched concerning mentoring and collaborative partnerships between experienced and beginning teachers. Extensive research and developmental work by CEC in mentoring induction for new teachers is currently underway (White and Mason, 2001), and CEC has set out an improvement agenda, aside from its standards drive, that addresses the structural and environmental shortcomings which face teachers daily in their special education work. This agenda is addressed to legislators, policymakers and administrators, and challenges them to work with teachers in creating new enterprising climates for learning, reducing red tape through administrative support and applied technologies, recruiting and retaining diverse teacher populations who have incentives to remain in the profession, and developing support structures that promote a career development in special education. These are ambitious goals, and time will tell how far they are achievable within the current political and economic climate. Yet they show a broadening of the vision of the professional discourse of special education, and cohere with received wisdom and best practice from those working daily on the chalk-face with EBD students.

In one sense the way in which teachers are prepared for teaching EBD students, and the necessary growth that should accompany the years they spend with such students, is an uncertainty that sits uncomfortably in our managerial, data-driven culture. Education should perhaps retain that sense of exploration and uncertainty that training avoids and seeks to replace with firm knowledge and clear evidence. The old tension between education and training is heightened in the case of EBD teaching, and whilst we can never accept inadequate training, we should be cautious to expect that training alone will ever suffice for dealing with EBD students in particular, and all students in general. There is an essential space for educational exploration that lies beyond the training arena, and this space is inhabited best by those teachers working with the most challenging students and environments. The beginning EBD teacher, however well trained, still stands on the threshold of an experience that will shape them more profoundly and more diversely through the richness of the experience of teaching than any training program can ever achieve. In that sense, William Waller's observations from over seventy years ago ring true for this and the next generation of EBD teachers, no matter how we strive to improve our preparation of those teachers:

> Those who enter the ranks of teachers do not know how to teach, although they may know everything that is in the innumerable books telling them how to teach. [They] are ready to learn to teach, and they are ready, though they know it not, to be formed by teaching. (Blake, 2004)

REFERENCES

Berliner, D.C. and Biddle, B.J. (1997) *The Manufactured Crisis: Myths, Fraud, and the Attack on America's Public Schools*. White Plains, NY: Longman.

Billingsley, B.S. (2002) *Beginning Special Educators: Characteristics, Qualifications, and Experiences. SPeNSE summary sheet — study of personnel needs in special education*. Washington, DC: US Office of Special Education Programs, USDOE.

Blake, C. (1999) 'Deficit ideology and educational reform in the USA', in P. Garner and II. Daniels (eds), *World Handbook of Education*. London: Kogan Page.

Blake, C. (2000) *Survey of Beginning and Experienced EBD Teachers*. Emmitsburg, MD: Mount St. Mary's College.

Blake, C. (2004) Interviews with Special Education Teachers: Research funded by Maryland State Improvement Grant 2002–03. (Baltimore, MD: Maryland State Department of Education). This work is unpublished as a whole.

Brodsky, M. (2001) 'Special education training becomes standard', *NEA Today*, 19 (7): 19–20.

Council for Exceptional Children (2000) *Bright Futures for Exceptional Learners: An Action Agenda to Achieve Quality Conditions for Teaching and Learning*. Reston, VA: CEC.

National Commission (1984) *A Nation at Risk*. Washington, DC: USDOE.

US Department of Education (2001) *Elementary and Secondary Education Act: No Child Left Behind*. Washington, DC: USDOE.

White, M. and Mason, C. (2001) *Mentoring Induction: Principles and Guidelines*. Reston, VA: CEC.

27

How We Prevent the Prevention of Emotional and Behavioral Difficulties in Education[1]

JAMES M. KAUFFMAN

Preventing emotional and behavioral difficulties is a popular idea to which nearly everyone gives lip service. However, people often stymie prevention, even while acknowledging that it makes eminent sense. Public officials may call for prevention, then cut budgets for early intervention. Many educators look with disfavor on pre-emptive treatment in the absence of severe difficulties and reject the treatment of minor problems. No one *says* that only extreme and protracted educational difficulties warrant intervention, yet early intervention is often sidestepped.

Primary prevention keeps difficulties, disorders, or problems ('difficulties' subsequently refers to all such emotional or behavioral troubles) from occurring at all. Once a difficulty is detectable, primary prevention is impossible. The goal of *secondary prevention* is arresting the growth of the difficulty and, if possible, reversing or correcting it. *Tertiary prevention* is designed for difficulties that have reached advanced stages and threaten to produce significant complications. The goal is to keep the difficulty from becoming overwhelming. Prevention of emotional and behavioral difficulties in schools is occasional, not pervasive. Even were primary prevention pervasive, emotional and behavioral difficulties would occur. Even were secondary prevention pervasive, some difficulties would become severe and require tertiary prevention, a response to crisis that often devolves into harsh punishment. Many people become so angry about extreme behavior that physical containment and punishment seem, to them, defensible.

Prevention is not pervasive in part because of public attitudes toward children and their schooling. However, professionals' behavior often precludes prevention and contributes to public antipathy toward prevention.

WHAT RESEARCH SUGGESTS ABOUT PREVENTION

Risk for difficulties is distributed along a continuum from very low to very high. For typical risk, universal preventive interventions are usually effective. For very high risk, only individually designed, intensive, comprehensive, and sustained interventions have any chance of success. At every location on this continuum, 'prevention means early intervention' (Kamps and Tankersley, 1996: 42). Early intervention means supporting adaptive behavior, identifying signs of incipient problems, and resolving problems by intervening early in patterns of recurrent misconduct (Kauffman, Bantz and McCullough, 2002; Kauffman, Mostert et al., 2002; Walker et al., 1995). Problems most clearly signaling elevated risk for difficulties are academic failure, aggression, peer rejection, and social gravitation toward deviant peers. Family, community, and school environments also contribute to risk (Kauffman, 2005). No research supports letting risk-elevating problems become severe before intervening.

Prevention should be based on reward of desirable behavior, nonviolent punishment of inappropriate behavior, effective instruction in academic and social skills, and correction of the environmental conditions that foster deviant behavior (Kauffman, 2005; Kauffman, Mostert et al., 2002; Walker et al., 1995).

For low risk, universal school interventions – effective instruction, clear expectations, close monitoring, standardized consequences – are likely to be sufficient (Nelson et al., 2002). However, for 5 to 10 percent of students in general education, more intrusive, intensive, individualized interventions may be necessary. Secondary or tertiary prevention may require that some students with severe and chronic difficulties be taught in special classes or schools in which teaching is more precise and consistent (Brigham and Kauffman, 1998; Kauffman, Bantz and McCullough, 2002).

All prevention programs yield false positives and false negatives. Nothing always works, and virtually everything *appears* to have worked at least once (Kauffman, 2002). Research consumers may misinterpret findings by exaggerating the meaning of false positives or false negatives.

Prevention research is difficult because large groups of randomly assigned subjects are required to confirm efficacy. Evidence of prevention is strongest for intervention that is *early and sustained*, appropriately *intensive, directive, comprehensive, coordinated*, and *adapted for individual differences* (Strain and Timm, 2001; Walker et al., 1998; Walker et al., 1995).

Prevention is defined by what is avoided – what does *not* happen. Increases in prosocial behavior are desirable, and prosocial behavior may displace some maladaptive behavior, but *success in prevention is defined by the nonoccurrence of maladaptive conduct, not by the occurrence of prosocial behavior*. The most effective and reliable preventives are implemented *earlier rather than later in a child's life* and *earlier rather than later in behavioral sequences leading to more maladaptive conduct*. Special education needs to be more proactive in preventing difficulties and less a reaction to them after they become severe. But being proactive requires taking more services to more children earlier, which appears counterintuitive to many and is contrary to biases against preemptive action.

PREVENTION-PREVENTING BEHAVIOR

The gambits that inhibit prevention are not mutually exclusive but are, in fact, often complementary. Several are typically used together, and:

- *Show greater concern for labeling and stigma than for prevention*
  The most frequent and fervid objection to preventive action is that the child will be labeled and stigmatized (see Kauffman, 1989, 2002, 2003, for discussion). Universal interventions that apply to all, regardless of behavioral characteristics, can be implemented without labels or stigma. No other interventions are possible without labels. Either all students are treated the same, or some are treated differently. Any student who is treated differently is inevitably labeled. Communication about individual differences is impossible without labels, which signify concern (something undesirable) or they are worthless for prevention. Describing difficulties as desirable is a cruel hoax. The social reality of deviance cannot be hidden (Kauffman, 2005).

  Labeling in special education and related fields is ensconced in law in many nations, and personal preferences for words are therefore sometimes obviated. Objections to particular labels may be legitimate or frivolous, but suggesting that labeling per se is dispensable is fantasy, not reality (Kauffman, 1989). Most children with difficulties are already labeled informally by their peers, receiving the *label du jour* for misfits. Formal labeling by adults may help turn away misunderstanding and rejection. Eventually, many of those with difficulties are labeled unequivocally. Their behavior becomes so outrageous that its deviance cannot be denied. They become clients of a variety of social systems, including special education, mental health, and juvenile justice. Their social spoilage is assured by the fact that they did not have early and corrective treatment. Ironically, the horror of labels for comparatively benign problems heightens the stigma of the labels we eventually use and fosters more demeaning labels for severe social deviance.

- *Object to a medical model and to failure-driven services*
  Some critics of special education object to a medical model and call it failure-driven. However, special education is much more aligned with the legal model than the medical model. Furthermore, prevention is inherently failure-driven. To the extent that either law or medicine is preventive, it is driven by failure – actual failure or the risk thereof. Safety laws are designed to prevent failures we call accidents; preventive medicine is designed to prevent failures we call illness and its complications. To complain that special education is badly structured because it is failure-driven is to use a non sequitur. *Prevention is by definition designed to avoid failure.*

- *Choose false negatives over false positives*
  No-fault prevention does not exist in education or any other human service. Every known prevention strategy produces false positives and false negatives – here, children mistakenly identified as having difficulties when they do not (false positives), and children mistakenly assumed not to have difficulties when they actually do (false negatives). Some strategies may produce fewer errors of one or both types, but none is perfect. Primary prevention is weighted toward false positives, as the intervention is assumed to create no significant risk. Primary prevention in medicine and dentistry includes vaccinations, water fluoridation, and personal hygiene routines. Such prevention carries near-zero risk for individuals without health problems, and obvious benefit to those who would otherwise acquire problems. Secondary and tertiary prevention in medicine and dentistry are more controversial and involve weighing personal and economic costs against benefits.
  In medicine, false negatives (overlooking pathology) are the primary concern; false positives (seeing pathology where none exists) are not taken lightly, but the primary concern of physicians is making certain that pathology is not missed. In law, the opposite is true – false conviction is the horror to be most assiduously avoided, not false acquittal.

Special education is like law, not medicine, in preference for false negatives.

High-profile cases of school violence highlight prevention in the minds of the public and many professionals, but these cases are probably not the most important. Less riveting but much more important to prevention are the less highly-visible and more common antisocial acts. These often do not result in public outrage, and often there is no intimation that they are psychopathological. Coercion, bullying, disruption, social isolation, and threatening behavior are examples of conduct that *should* induce preventive action by educators (Sheras, 2002). To be preventive we must intervene at the earliest stages of misconduct, not wait until acceleration has begun (Kauffman, Bantz and McCullough, 2002). Early preventive action requires recognizing the precursors of more serious difficulties. Smith and Churchill (2002) described how functional analysis of precursor behaviors was important in preventing more serious difficulties. The tendency is to await full-blown problems, in part because of greater aversion to false positives than to false negatives. Educators often are unwilling to intervene in precursor behavior (for example, aggressive talk and talk of aggression) because such talk is not *always* or *invariably* followed by aggressive acts. Youngsters themselves or their parents or observers may complain about restriction or repression when teachers take pre-emptive action, further strengthening the tendency to circumvent early intervention.

- *Propose a 'paradigm shift' that blocks prevention*
A popular 'paradigm shift' obviates the need for classification. Its champions suggest that all students can be taught well without distinguishably different instruction or behavior management; because everyone will be treated individually, no one need be considered special. In the 'new paradigm,' prevention will be pervasive but imperceptible. But we cannot prevent what we are unwilling to say is different from the typical or normative, nor can we practice anything other than primary prevention if we are unwilling to categorize interventions as special (Kauffman, 1999b, 2002, 2003; Kauffman, Bantz and McCullough, 2002; Mock and Kauffman, 2004; Sasso, 2001).

A 'paradigm shift' might attack the scientific bases of special education practices, suggesting that alternative, nonpositivist paradigms are morally superior (for example, Danforth and Rhodes, 1997; Gallagher, 1998). This gambit undermines applied behavior analysis research of the past 30 years, leaving a vacuum into which primitive, punitive 'craft knowledge' may be drawn. Most teachers do not have great intuition in dealing productively with difficult students. Great effort is required to induce positive, supportive teaching procedures emanating from decades of scientific research. Neither the fact that the task of teaching these procedures is difficult, nor the fact that their skillful implementation is sometimes ineffective, refutes their value or their scientific base.

Prevention is thwarted by a 'paradigm shift' that either condemns the practice of singling out individuals for special treatment, or rejects the legitimacy of the scientific knowledge base of practices. Such a shift puts prevention in neutral, if not reverse. It is regressive, requiring the denial and distortion of what we know and the adulation of willful ignorance (Sasso, 2001).

- *Call special education ineffective*
  Sometimes special education's ineffectiveness is merely intimated; sometimes the claim that special education has not 'worked' or cannot work as currently structured is made directly and unequivocally (for example, Bolick, 2001; Gartner and Lipsky, 1989). Special education is seen by some as second rate and demeaning of those it serves. If one concludes that on balance special education is ineffective, then preventive intervention is a hoax – except to the extent that children are kept out of contact with special education. Using a medical model, some suggest that special education makes the condition worse. Using a legal model, some are unwilling to deprive students of liberty by identifying them for special education because in exchange they receive no benefit.

  The conclusion that, on balance, special education is a dead end or has been a failure or is flawed in basic structure – or that it is uniformly ineffective or substandard – is not justified by the data (Fuchs and Fuchs, 1995; Kauffman, Bantz and McCullough, 2002; MacMillan and Forness, 1998; Walker et al., 1998). This we cannot escape: To the extent that we believe that special education is predictably ineffective, our preventive efforts are undermined, and we are likely to misunderstand how to keep our interventions minimally intrusive and minimally restrictive.

- *Misconstrue least intrusive, least restrictive intervention*
  Restriction has social costs, as does nonrestriction. Enthusiasm for minimally restrictive environments hides the fact that minimum restriction now may require greater restriction later. A minimally restrictive environment is not necessarily the place in which people without disabilities thrive (Crockett and Kauffman, 1999).

  The least restrictive and intrusive environments can be implemented earliest in a pattern of behavior leading to more serious misconduct (Walker et al., 1995). After misbehavior has accelerated, the *formerly* least intrusive, least restrictive intervention is very unlikely to be effective. Emphasis on minimizing intrusion and restriction without careful attention to the behavior pattern results in a chain of increasingly intrusive and restrictive but decreasingly effective interventions. Minimizing preventive, least intrusive, least restrictive practices *in the long term* thus requires something counterintuitive and typically thought to be unacceptable in a legal model: stepping in earlier to avert maladaptive behavior patterns by anticipating them rather than waiting for misbehavior to occur.

- *Protest percent of students served by special education and uncertainty of identification*
  A commonly heard opinion today is that special education has grown too large, not only in the percentage of time, effort, and money that schools spend on it, but also in the number of students and the percent of the population identified for services. Another frequently encountered opinion is that we are uncertain about just which children should be identified.

  These views are extraordinarily problematic, for far less than half of the youngsters with difficulties have been identified for special education, and they are typically identified only after several years of very serious difficulties (Duncan et al., 1995; Kauffman, 2005). Prevention in an underserved population demands that more individuals be identified, not fewer or the same number. If cases are to be caught earlier, and if many cases are missed (that is, they are for considerable periods of time false negatives), then we must be ready to embrace a considerable increase in the number of students identified – unless we are willing to forego prevention. We cannot prevent what we will not anticipate, but there are other hard truths about prevention as well, including these:

  - measurement produces a distribution of the variable in question;
  - every distribution, no exceptions, has a central tendency that can be described by mean and median (even if the distribution is wildly non-normal or multi-modal);
  - secondary prevention requires catching individuals in the distribution who are closer to or less discrepant from the mean or median;
  - moving the criterion for 'catching' or identifying and intervening closer to the central tendency requires identifying a greater number of individuals; and
  - moving the criterion closer to the central tendency produces larger numbers of false positives and produces uncertainty about a greater number of individuals (Kauffman, 2003).

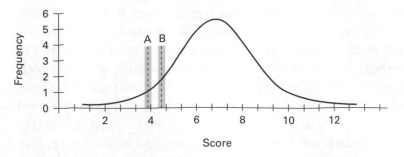

Figure 27.1   *Near-normal statistical distribution of a continuously distributed variable*

An illustration of these truths is shown in Figure 27.1, which depicts a near-normal statistical distribution of a continuously distributed variable. Assume for present discussion that it represents measurement of social behavior, such that deviant or unacceptable social behavior is represented by the left tail of the curve and greater distance from the central tendency represents greater social deviance. As can be seen in Figure 27.1, moving the criterion for identification closer to the central tendency necessarily involves greater numbers of individuals (that is, a larger number of individuals have the score closer to the central tendency; alternatively, we see that a larger percentage of the area under the curve to the left of the criterion is designated when the criterion is moved closer to the central tendency). For example, moving the criterion from the line represented by A to that represented by B shows that an increase in the number of individuals identified is inevitable. The shaded lines paralleling lines A and B represent an estimate of measurement error, which might be interpreted as an index of the uncertainty that an individual actually qualifies or *should* be identified by the criterion. Using the same logic and observation of the mathematical properties of the curve as above, one can see that uncertainty will apply to a greater number of individuals when the criterion is moved toward the central tendency.

Figure 27.2 is an approximation of the assumed relationship between number of individuals and severity of emotional or behavioral difficulties. Let us assume that on this graph a higher score indicates greater social deviance or a more severe difficulty. Regardless of the slope of the line (that is, regardless of whether the slope is to the left or right, straight or curved, steep or gradual), moving the criterion for intervention toward less severe difficulties – moving from left to right in Figure 27.2 – includes a greater number of individuals (a greater proportion

Number-by-severity

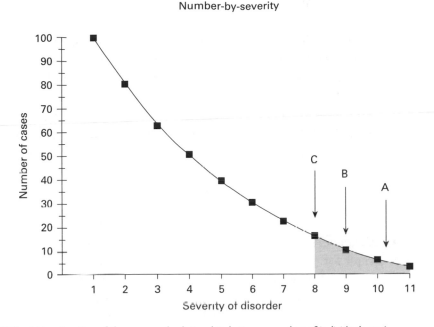

Figure 27.2 *Approximation of the assumed relationship between number of individuals and severity of emotional or behavioral difficulties*

of the population). Were Figure 27.2 to have included chronological age at the onset of a given difficulty rather than problem severity on the horizontal axis, the conclusion would be the same: moving the criterion downward in age inevitably requires serving more individuals. The conclusion that prevention inevitably requires serving more individuals is a logical outcome of the observation that prevention means early intervention.

- *Complain that special education already costs too much*
Prevention costs more money *initially* than nonprevention. It may save money in the long term, but that is not the immediate issue for politicians, school boards, and taxpayers. The inescapable fact is simply this: If we were to initiate preventive action on a large scale, then we would be stuck with a large, immediate financial cost. Education and social service budgets are already tight. Complaints about expenditures for social welfare programs of every description are common. Tax cuts are popular; tax increases are unthinkable to many, if not most. Legislators are typically reluctant to embrace programs that will not produce immediate results and cost savings for which they can take credit. In short, the near-term financial cost of wide-spread preventive programs is a powerful, but usually not articulated argument against their implementation.

- *Maintain developmental optimism or use ineffective early education practices*

    Those who work with young children tend to be overly optimistic about children's development, leading to the assumption that early signs of behavioral difficulty do not predict a stable or increasing pattern of maladaptive behavior. Their assumption seems to be that the child will 'grow out' of it. Preventive action – deliberate correction of patterns of difficulty – is thus delayed until the problem has become severe. Moreover, many individuals who work with young children have an apparent bias toward developmental approaches that do not involve explicit teaching and correction of the first signs of maladaptive behavior.

- *Denounce disproportionality, defend diversity, deny deviance*

    Guilt for past ignorance of or insensitivity toward racial, ethnic, and cultural differences and fear of being accused of such horrors may stop prevention. In the United States, at least, African American children are disproportionately identified as having difficulties, and although this phenomenon is poorly understood, it is frequently suggested that it is a consequence of racism (see, for example, National Research Council, 2002). Moreover, diversity has become a matter of such intense concern that what one professional may see as a difficulty, another will call acceptable cultural diversity. Finally, there are a variety of ways to deny the deviance of behavior. Calling it mere cultural diversity is one denial tactic. Another is saying that deviance and disability are social constructs and therefore somehow not 'real.' Deviance and disability are, indeed, social constructs, but so are childhood, adolescence, citizen, success, social construct, democracy, justice, love, and nearly every other concept that we hold dear or that is necessary to a just and benevolent society. The point is that if we deny deviance, then we are highly unlikely to prevent it.

CONCLUSION

The problem of preventing emotional and behavioral difficulties is not unique. Prevention of many pathologies is an uphill battle. Perhaps the most useful hypotheses about why we do not practice prevention more consistently are based on social learning principles (for example, Bandura, 1986). Specifically, our behavior may be a function of the behavioral and social-cognitive phenomena of delayed negative reinforcement for prevention, immediate positive reinforcement for behavior that averts prevention, social punishment of prevention, and modeling of prevention-preventing behavior, each of which is discussed in a previous publication (Kauffman, 1999a).

The arguments marshaled against prevention must be taken seriously, as they raise important issues that should not be dismissed. Ignoring these legitimate concerns carries high costs, regardless of the fact that they are often used to defeat prevention. Ultimately, however, the cost of failure to practice prevention is even higher.

NOTE

1 This chapter is a revision of material first published by the author in 1999, 'How we prevent the prevention of emotional and behavioral disorders', *Exceptional Children*, 65: 448–68.

REFERENCES

Bandura, A. (1986) *Social Foundations of Thought and Action: A Social Cognitive Theory*. Upper Saddle River, NJ: Prentice-Hall.

Bolick, C. (2001) 'A bad IDEA is disabling public schools', *Education Week*, 21 (1): 56, 63.

Brigham, F. J. and Kauffman, J.M. (1998) 'Creating supportive environments for students with emotional or behavioral disorders', *Effective School Practices*, 17 (2): 25–35.

Crockett, J.B. and Kauffman, J.M. (1999) *The Least Restrictive Environment: Its Origins and Interpretations in Special Education*. Mahwah, NJ: Erlbaum.

Danforth, S. and Rhodes, W.C. (1997) 'Deconstructing disability: A philosophy for inclusion', *Remedial and Special Education*, 18: 357–66.

Duncan, B.B., Forness, S.R. and Hartsough, C. (1995) 'Students identified as seriously emotionally disturbed in day treatment: Cognitive, psychiatric, and special education characteristics', *Behavioral Disorders*, 20: 238–52.

Fuchs, D. and Fuchs, L.S. (1995) 'Special education can work', in J.M. Kauffman, J.W. Lloyd, D.P. Hallahan and T.A. Astuto (eds), *Issues in Educational Placement: Students with Emotional and Behavioral Disorders*. Mahwah, NJ: Erlbaum. pp. 363–77.

Gallagher, D.J. (1998) 'The scientific knowledge base of special education: Do we know what we think we know?', *Exceptional Children*, 64: 493–502.

Gartner, A. and Lipsky, D.K. (1989) *The Yoke of Special Education: How to Break It*. Rochester, NY: National Center on Education and the Economy.

Kamps, D.M. and Tankersley, M. (1996) 'Prevention of behavioral and conduct disorders: Trends and research issues', *Behavioral Disorders*, 22: 41–8.

Kauffman, J.M. (1989) 'The regular education initiative as Reagan-Bush education policy: A trickle-down theory of education of the hard-to-teach', *The Journal of Special Education*, 23: 256–78.

Kauffman, J.M. (1999a) 'How we prevent the prevention of emotional and behavioral disorders', *Exceptional Children*, 65: 448–68.

Kauffman, J.M. (1999b) 'Today's special education and its messages for tomorrow', *Journal of Special Education*, 32: 244–54.

Kauffman, J.M. (2002) *Education Deform: Bright People Sometimes Say Stupid Things About Education*. Lanham, MD: Scarecrow Education.

Kauffman, J.M. (2003) 'Perspectives: Appearances, stigma, and prevention', *Remedial and Special Education*, 24 (4): 195–8.

Kauffman, J.M. (2005) *Characteristics of Emotional and Behavioral Disorders of Children and Youth* (8th edn). Upper Saddle River, NJ: Prentice-Hall.

Kauffman, J.M., Bantz, J. and McCullough, J. (2002) 'Separate and better: A special public school class for students with emotional and behavioral disorders', *Exceptionality*, 10: 149–70.

Kauffman, J.M., Mostert, M.P., Trent, S.C. and Hallahan, D.P. (2002) *Managing Classroom Behavior: A Reflective Case-based Approach* (3rd edn). Boston MA: Allyn and Bacon.

MacMillan, D.L. and Forness, S.R. (1998) 'The role of IQ in special education placement decisions: Primary and determinative or peripheral and inconsequential?', *Remedial and Special Education*, 19: 239–53.

Mock, D.R. and Kauffman, J.M. (2004) 'The delusion of full inclusion', in J.W. Jacobson, J.A. Mulick and R.M. Foxx (eds), *Controversial Therapies for Developmental Disabilities: Fads, Fashion and Science in Professional Practice*. Mahwah, NJ: Erlbaum.

National Research Council (2002) *Minority Students in Special and Gifted Education*. Washington, DC: National Academy Press.

Nelson, J.R., Martella, R.M. and Marchand-Martella, N. (2002) 'Maximizing student learning: The effects of a comprehensive school-based program for preventing problem behavior', *Journal of Emotional and Behavioral Disorders*, 10: 136–48.

Sasso, G.M. (2001) 'The retreat from inquiry and knowledge in special education', *Journal of Special Education*, 34: 178–93.

Sheras, P. (2002) *Your Child: Bully or Victim? Understand and Ending School Yard Tyranny*. New York: Skylight.

Smith, R.G. and Churchill, R.M. (2002) 'Identification of environmental determinants of behavior disorders through functional analysis of precursor behaviors', *Journal of Applied Behavior Analysis*, 35: 125–36.

Strain, P.S. and Timm, M.A. (2001) 'Remediation and prevention of aggression: An evaluation of the Regional Intervention Program over a quarter century', *Behavioral Disorders*, 26: 297–313.

Walker, H.M., Colvin, G. and Ramsey, E. (1995) *Antisocial Behavior in School: Strategies and Best Practices* (2nd edn). Pacific Grove, CA: Brooks/Cole.

Walker, H.M., Forness, S.R., Kauffman, J.M., Epstein, M.H., Gresham, F.M., Nelson, C.M. and Strain, P.S. (1998) 'Macro-social validation: Referencing outcomes in behavioral disorders to societal issues and problems', *Behavioral Disorders*, 24: 7–18.

Index